CW00326672

THE COMPLETE ILLUSTRATED HISTORY OF THE

FIRST & SECOND WORLD WARS

THE COMPLETE ILLUSTRATED HISTORY OF THE

FIRST & SECOND WORLD WARS

WITH MORE THAN 1000 EVOCATIVE PHOTOGRAPHS, MAPS AND BATTLE PLANS

DONALD SOMMERVILLE AND IAN WESTWELL

LORENZ BOOKS

Contents

Introduction 8

WORLD WAR I 12

Timeline 14

ORIGINS OF THE WAR 16

Assassination at Sarajevo 18
July 1914 – The Road to War 20
Allied War Plans 22
Austro-Hungarian and German War Plans 24

1914 – EUROPE GOES TO WAR 26

The German Invasion of Belgium 28
Frontier Fortresses 30
Heavy Artillery 32
The Battles of the Frontiers 34
Reconnaissance Aircraft 36
Mons and Le Cateau 38
Field Artillery 40
The Battle of the Marne 42
Rifles and Bayonets 44
The Race to the Sea 46
The First Battle of Ypres 48
The Invasions of Serbia, 1914–15 50
Russia's Invasion of East Prussia 52
Cavalry 54
The Battle of Tannenberg 56
Operations in Poland and Galicia 58
Operations in China and the Pacific 60
Surface Raiders 62
Germany's African Colonies 64
Naval War in the North Sea 66
Anti-submarine Barriers 68
Coronel and the Falklands 70
Battle-cruisers 72

1915 – TRENCH WARFARE 74

The Second Battle of Ypres 76
Gas Warfare 78
The Second Battle of Artois 80
Trench Systems 82
Battles in Champagne and Artois 84
Early Fighters 86
Winter Offensive against Russia 88
Mortars 90
Germany's Gorlice–Tarnów Offensive 92
Balloons 94
Four Battles along the Isonzo 96
Attacking the Dardanelles 98
Pre-dreadnought Battleships 100
Gallipoli – The Landings 102
Seaplanes and Flying Boats 104
The Caucasus Front 1914–16 106
Palestine, 1914–16 108
The Mesopotamian Campaign, 1914–16 110
The Wider War at Sea 112
Gallipoli – The Withdrawal 114
German Submarines 116
Home Fronts 118
Zeppelins 120
Civilians under Fire, 1914–18 122
Heavy Bombers 124

1916 – THE YEAR OF ATTRITION 126

Verdun – The German Attack 128
The First Day of the Somme 130

Machine-guns 132
Verdun – The French Recovery 134
Trench Warfare Weapons 136
Attrition on the Somme 138
British Tanks 140
Russia Aids Its Allies 142
The Romanian Campaign 144
Camouflage 146
Stalemate on the Italian Front 148
Seaplane Tenders and Aircraft Carriers 150
Operations in Salonika, 1916–17 152
War in East Africa, 1914–18 154
The Battle of Jutland 156
Dreadnoughts 158
The Rise of the U-boats 160
Destroyers 162
Naval War in the Mediterranean, 1914–16 164
Torpedo-boats 166
Allied Submarines 168

1917 – EUROPE'S YEAR OF TRIAL 170

The Battle of Arras 172
Light Bombers 174
The Nivelle Offensive 176
French and German Tanks 178
The Battle of Messines 180
Mine Warfare 182
The Battle of Passchendaele 184
Coastal, Fortress and Railway Artillery 186
The Battle of Cambrai 188
Aces and Fighter Tactics 190
The "February Revolution" 192
The "October Revolution" 194
The Battle of Caporetto 196
Final Battles in the Caucasus, 1917–18 198
The Battle of Beersheba 200
The Mesopotamian Campaign, 1917–18 202
Defeating the U-boats, 1917–18 204
Anti-submarine Weapons 206

1918 – TRIUMPH OF THE ALLIES 208

Operation Michael 210
Later Fighters 212
Anti-aircraft Guns 214
Germany's Final Offensives 216
The Paris Gun 218
Ground-attack Aircraft 220
Equipping the Americans 222
The First American Battles 224
Supply Transport 226
The Meuse–Argonne Offensive 228
Communications 230
Breaking the Hindenburg Line 232
Pistols 234
Armoured Cars 236
Final Battles in Italy 238
Liberating the Balkans 240
The Battle of Megiddo 242
Cruisers 244
Germany's Naval Mutiny 246

THE AFTERMATH OF WAR 248

The Armistice 250
The Peace Treaties 252
The League of Nations 254
War and Remembrance 256

WORLD WAR II 258

Timeline 260

APPROACH TO WAR 262

The Legacy of World War I 264
Failing Economies 266
Fascism and Nazism 268
Aggression – Europe and Asia 270
Troubled Times – USA and USSR 272
Troubled Times – Western Europe 274
Europe on the Brink 276

HITLER'S TRIUMPHS 278

Poland and the Outbreak of War 280
Tanks, 1939–42 282
The Baltic and Scandinavia 284
Heavy Cruisers 286
The Fall of France 288
Light Bombers, Recce and Utility Aircraft 290
The Battle of Britain and the Blitz 292
Fighters, 1939–42 294
Air Combat – Weapons, Tactics and Aces 296
The British Home Front 298
Medium Bombers, 1939–41 300
The Battle of the Atlantic, 1939–41 302
Anti-submarine Escort Ships 304
The Mediterranean Theatre, 1940–1 306
The Balkans and North Africa, 1941–2 308
Torpedo Boats and Midget Submarines 310
The USA and the European War 312
German Rule in Europe 314
Operation Barbarossa 316
Anti-tank Guns, 1939–42 318
Horrors of War – The Eastern Front 320

JAPAN'S PACIFIC CONQUESTS 322

Approach to War in the Pacific 324
Pearl Harbor and Japan's War Plans 326
Battleships and Battle-cruisers 328
The USA at War 330
Japan's First Advances 332
Japan's Continuing Successes 334
Coral Sea and Midway 336
Aircraft Carriers 338
The Turn of the Tide 340
Light Cruisers 342
Japan's Brutal Empire 344

THE GREAT STRUGGLE IN EUROPE 346

To Stalingrad and the Caucasus 348
The Holocaust 350
Field Artillery 352
Stalingrad 354
Infantry Weapons 356
Soviet Winter Victories, 1942–3 358
Assault Guns 360
Propaganda, Art and Popular Culture 362
Alamein and the Advance to Tunisia 364
Light Armoured Vehicles 366
Operation Torch and Victory in Africa 368
Germany Fights Back – Kharkov and Kursk 370
Ground-attack Aircraft 372
Codes and Code Breaking 374
The Defeat of Hitler's Navy, 1942–5 376
Escort Carriers 378
Naval Weapons and Electronics 380
Allied Grand Strategy 382
Medium Tanks, 1942–5 384
Sicily and Italy, 1943–4 386

Infantry Support Weapons 388
Night Bombing of Germany, 1939–44 390
Night Fighters 392
US Strategic Bombing, 1942–3 394
Anti-aircraft Guns 396
Heavy Bombers 398
Clearing the Ukraine 400
Heavy Artillery 402

VICTORY OVER GERMANY 404

D-Day 406
Special Purpose Armoured Vehicles 408
The Battle for Normandy 410
Medium Bombers, 1942–5 412
Resistance 414
Collaboration 416
Crushing Soviet Victories, 1944 418
Heavy Tanks, 1942–5 420
Totalitarian Rule – Germany and the USSR 422
The Defeat of the Luftwaffe 424
Fighters, 1943–5 426
Aircraft Ordnance and Electronics 428
From Normandy to the Rhine 430
Self-propelled Artillery 432
Unarmoured Vehicles 434
The Soviet Invasion of Germany 436
Heavy Mortars and Artillery Rockets 438
V-Weapons 439
Battle of the Bulge 440
Jet Aircraft 442
Anti-tank Guns, 1942–5 444
Victory in the West and Italy 446
Infantry Anti-tank Weapons 448
Mines and Other Defences 449
The Fall of Berlin 450

DESTRUCTION OF THE JAPANESE EMPIRE 452

New Guinea and the Solomons 454
Seaplanes and Naval Support Aircraft 456
The Central Pacific Campaign 458
Landing Craft and Amphibious Vehicles 460
The Marianas Campaign 462
Naval Fighters 464
Submarines and Bombers 466
Submarine Classes 468
Burma, 1943–4 470
The Battle of Leyte Gulf 472
Naval Bombers and Torpedo Aircraft 474
Conquest of the Philippines 476
China's War 478
Victory in Burma, 1944–5 480
Transport Aircraft and Gliders 482
Iwo Jima and Okinawa 484
Destroyers 486
Weapons of Mass Destruction 488
The Japanese Surrender 490

THE LEGACY OF WAR 492

Casualties and Destruction 494
Dealing with the Defeated 496
Europe Divided 498
New Nations 500
The Cold War 502

Picture Credits 504
Index 505
Acknowledgements 512

Introduction

World Wars I and II will forever be a scar across twentieth-century history. This comprehensive volume chronicles these brutal wars and examines the turbulent political and social climates that led to the first truly global conflicts.

World War I was the first truly total worldwide conflict, a titanic struggle between the then leading world powers for not only the domination of Europe but also the large areas of the entire globe that they had colonized in the 19th century. Even with such high stakes, the outbreak of the conflict was greeted with considerable popular enthusiasm in many – if not all – quarters. After years of sabre-rattling and accelerating arms races as well as intensifying economic and geopolitical rivalries, it was thought, not just by militarists, that a short, sharp war would bring a new stability to world affairs.

Like most wars, World War I turned out in ways that the participants did not anticipate at the outset. Almost everyone thought that the war would be brief, a matter of months at the most. Economic and industrial developments were believed to have made it impossible for fighting to continue for long. In fact the reverse was true. Industrialization and mass production meant that armies of previously unequalled size could be supplied and kept fighting – leading to a casualty toll never before seen.

Military leaders struggled to cope with the consequences of the scale of the fighting and the new technologies involved – it was the first major war of aircraft, tanks, submarines, quick-firing artillery, poison gas and much more. It is hardly surprising that generals sometimes failed to make best use of these novel resources; however few were the stupid and unfeeling blunderers of popular belief.

Below: People everywhere welcomed the outbreak of the war. These young Berliners have been called up to serve in the German Army, 1 August 1914.

Right: Belgian infantry manning trenches near Uskub (now usually called Skopje) in 1915. Britain, France and other Allies deployed large forces to the Balkan Front around Salonika from 1915 but they achieved little until the final months of the war.

When the Great War ended after more than four years of bitter combat in which the outcome was in doubt until the final stages of campaigning, few were really able to comprehend the sheer scale of the destructive events they had witnessed. Empires had toppled, new countries had emerged and the United States had been transformed into an international colossus. Despite the heavy loss of life, the victors could at least console themselves with the thought that they had won "the war to end all wars" – the popular rendering of the title of H. G. Wells's overly optimistic 1914 book entitled *The War That Will End War*. Yet the peace they had secured at such immense cost was transitory and was destined to last just two decades.

Within only a few years of its end many people, even those living in the victorious countries, were questioning whether World War I had been a just and necessary war. The same has never been true of World War II, either in the immediate aftermath or in terms of longer historical retrospect. The unmitigated evil that was at the heart of Hitler's Germany and the unrestrained and brutal cruelty of the Japanese regime to its prisoners and subjects were both so plain that, at the time and since, few have argued that it was a war that was not worth fighting. Although the world soon moved into the Cold War,

Below: Troops blinded by poison gas wait for medical attention. Every major army used gas by 1918, though this would have been deemed barbarous a few years before.

an era of potentially even more dangerous confrontation, few have ever suggested that the many Allied lives that were lost in the World War II were lives that were sacrificed in vain.

Far more than any previous major war, World War II saw civilians effectively in the front line. In part this arose from the murderous nature of the totalitarian regimes of both Hitler and Stalin, and the vicious racism of Japan's militarists, but the Anglo-American bombing campaigns meant that those countries' leaders also had far from clean hands.

Unlike World War I – the first war of the combat aircraft, the tank and the submarine – there were no new types of weapon of any importance introduced until almost the very end of World War II. The major military development was the extension of the use of air power to a level far beyond anything previously attempted or contemplated, and many of World War II's battles were fought in the sky. Developments in radio and electronics technology also meant that, both in the air and on the ground, operations could be directed with a new level of sophistication: tank commanders could talk to each other; aircraft could be detected hundreds of miles away; and radar could find the hidden periscope of a submerged enemy submarine at sea.

The war's one new weapon was obviously the atom bomb, which clearly changed the nature of warfare for all time. Its huge destructive power was so great that even when no nuclear retaliation was possible, its owners might hesitate to use it. With such a dire threat to the future of humankind in existence, it was in a sense just as well that people had seen the horrific realities of the flattened cityscapes of Hiroshima and Nagasaki and heard the dreadful evidence of the horrors of the Holocaust. The propagation of the knowledge of just how terrible wars could be, and the realization of the truly awful power that man now had the ability to harness, may have served to make the citizens and governments of the world more likely to resolve their differences peacefully. This is perhaps the lasting benefit brought by World War II – a terrible devastation so complete that its echoes are still reverberating today.

Below: London's St Paul's Cathedral, surrounded by fire during the Blitz, autumn 1940. St Paul's survived with little damage, a symbol of Britain's defiant resistance.

Below: Soviet infantry climb out of their trench to attack nearby German positions during the vicious close-quarter battle for Stalingrad in the late autumn of 1942.

How This Book is Organized

This comprehensive work is split into two equal sized parts, focusing in depth on each of the World Wars. Each has five main chronological chapters, each one looking at a different phase of the war, plus an introductory chapter on the causes of the war and a concluding chapter on the war's aftermath and long-term legacy. Each chapter is split into separate one or two-page sections that cover the war's major battles and campaigns or the developments in the weapons and machinery that were used. In addition there are feature boxes on a variety of subjects including key personalities and points of special interest. Added together, all these elements provide a detailed, highly illustrated history of World Wars I and II that explains every stage of each war's progress, how the wars were fought and the global implications of each.

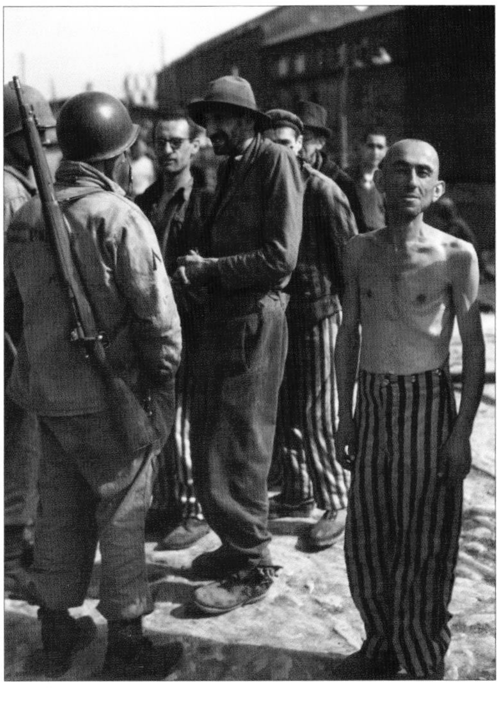

Above: Emaciated survivors of the newly liberated Buchenwald concentration camp talk to some of the American troops who freed the camp, 18 April 1945.

Below: Hitler Youth fighters who have knocked out Soviet tanks are decorated by their leader outside the Berlin bunker where he would commit suicide days later.

WORLD WAR I

1914–1918

Image: British troops listen to a chaplain delivering his Sunday Morning Service from the open cockpit of a World War I aircraft in 1918.

Timeline

Although many accounts of World War I are centred on the war's principal theatre, the Western Front, the actual chronology of events makes it abundantly clear how closely related the developments there were to victories and defeats elsewhere around the world.

1914

INTERNATIONAL EVENTS
Assassination at Sarajevo (28 June); Austria-Hungary declares war on Serbia (28 July); Germany declares war on Russia (1 Aug); Germany declares war on France (3 Aug); Britain declares war on Germany (4 Aug); Austria-Hungary declares war on Russia (5 Aug); Serbia declares war on Germany (6 Aug); France declares war on Austria-Hungary (10 Aug); Britain declares war on Austria-Hungary (12 Aug); Turkey declares war on Allies (1 Nov); Russia and Serbia declare war on Turkey (2 Nov); Britain and France declare war on Turkey (5 Nov)

WESTERN FRONT
Main German invasion of Belgium begins (4 Aug); Battles of the Frontiers (14–25 Aug); Battle of the Marne (5–10 Sept); Race to the Sea (15 Sept–24 Nov); First Battle of Ypres (19 Oct–22 Nov); Battles of Flanders (11 Oct–30 Nov); First Battle of Champagne (20 Dec–30 Mar 1915)

EASTERN FRONT
Russian invasion of East Prussia (15–23 Aug); Battle of Tannenburg (26–30 Aug); First Battle of the Masurian Lakes (7–14 Sept)

BALKAN FRONT First Austro-Hungarian Invasion of Serbia (14–21 Aug); Second invasion of Serbia (6–17 Sept); Third invasion of Serbia (5 Nov–15 Dec)

MESOPOTAMIAN FRONT
British land in Mesopotamia (7 Nov)

WAR AT SEA Battle of Heligoland Bight (28 Aug); Battle of the Falklands (8 Dec)

1915

INTERNATIONAL EVENTS
Italy declares war on Austria-Hungary (23 May); Bulgaria and Serbia declare war on each other (14 Oct)

WESTERN FRONT Second Battle of Ypres (22 April–25 May); Second Battle of Artois (9 May–18 June); Second Battle of Champagne (25 Sept–6 Nov); Battle of Loos (25 Sept–16 Oct)

EASTERN FRONT
Gorlice–Tarnów Offensive (2 May–27 June); Capture of Warsaw (5 Aug)

BALKAN FRONT Austro-German invasion of Serbia (6 Oct)

ITALIAN FRONT First four Battles of the Isonzo (23 June–7 July)

MESOPOTAMIAN FRONT Battle of Nasiriya (24 July); Battle of Ctesiphon (22–26 Nov)

GALLIPOLI CAMPAIGN Allied naval attack on Dardanelles (18 Mar); First Allied landings at Gallipoli (25 April); British evacuate Gallipoli (10 Dec–9 Jan 1916)

1916

INTERNATIONAL EVENTS
Germany declares war on Romania (28 Aug); Italy declares war on Germany (28 Aug)

WESTERN FRONT Battle of Verdun (21 Feb–18 Dec); Battle of the Somme (1 July–18 Nov)

EASTERN FRONT Brusilov Offensive (4 June–20 Sept);

CAUCASUS FRONT Battle of Koprukoy (18 Jan); Battle of Erzerum (13–16 Feb)

ITALIAN FRONT Trentino Offensive (15 May–17 June); Battles of the Isonzo (Fifth 11–29 Mar; Sixth 6–28 Aug; Seventh 14–26 Sept; Eighth 10–12 Oct; Ninth 1–14 Nov)

MESOPOTAMIAN FRONT
Fall of Kut (29 April)

WAR AT SEA Battle of Jutland (31 May–1 June)

1917

INTERNATIONAL EVENTS United States declares war on Germany (6 April); Greece declares war on Central Powers (2 July); China declares war on Austria-Hungary and Germany (14 Aug); Brazil declares war on Germany (26 Oct); United States declares war on Austria-Hungary (7 Dec); Russia agrees to an armistice (15 Dec)
WESTERN FRONT Battle of Arras (9 April–15 May); Nivelle Offensive (16 April–9 May); Battle of Messines (7–14 June); Passchendaele/Third Battle of Ypres (31 July–10 Nov); Battle of Cambrai (20 Nov–7 Dec)
EASTERN FRONT Russian Revolution begins (11 Mar); Russian Kerensky Offensive (1–19 July); German Riga Offensive begins (1 Sept); Bolshevik Revolution begins (7 Nov)
BALKAN FRONT Battle of Lake Prespa/Doiran (11–17 Mar); Battle of the Vardar (5–19 May)
ITALIAN FRONT Tenth Battle of the Isonzo (12 May–8 June); Eleventh Battle of the Isonzo (18 Aug–15 Sept); Battle of Caporetto (24 Oct–12 Nov)
PALESTINE FRONT Battle of Magruntein (8 Jan); First Battle of Gaza (26 Mar); Second Battle of Gaza (17–19 April); Battle of Beersheba (31 Oct); Battle of Junction Station (13–14 Nov); Capture of Jerusalem (9 Dec)
MESOPOTAMIAN FRONT Second Battle of Kut (22–23 Feb); Fall of Baghdad (11 Mar); Battle of Ramadi (27–28 Sept)
CAMPAIGNS IN AFRICA German forces leave German East Africa (25 Nov)
WAR AT SEA Germany announces reintroduction of unrestricted submarine warfare (31 Jan)

1918

INTERNATIONAL EVENTS Russia signs Treaty of Brest-Litovsk (3 Mar); Romania and Central Powers agree peace (8 May); Armistice with Bulgaria (30 Sept); Armistice with Turkey (30 Oct); Armistice with Austria-Hungary (4 Nov); Romania declares war for the second time (10 Nov); Armistice with Germany (11 Nov)
WESTERN FRONT Operation Michael (21 Mar–5 April); Lys Offensive (9–29 April); Aisne Offensive (27 May–17 June); Second Battle of the Marne (15 July–4 Aug); Amiens Offensive (8 Aug–4 Sept); Assault on the Hindenburg Line (26 Aug–12 Oct); Battle of St. Mihiel (12–16 Sept); Meuse–Argonne Offensive (26 Sept–11 Nov); Flanders Offensive (28 Sept–11 Nov); Picardy Offensive (17 Oct–11 Nov)
EASTERN FRONT Germany launches Operation Faustschlag (17 Feb)
BALKAN FRONT Battle of the Vardar (15–25 Sept); Recapture of Belgrade (1 Nov)
CAUCASUS FRONT British enter Baku (24 Aug); Turks recapture Baku (26 Aug–14 Sept)
ITALIAN FRONT Battle of the Piave (15–23 June); Battle of Vittorio Veneto (24 Oct–4 Nov)
PALESTINE FRONT Battle of Megiddo (19–21 Sept); Anglo-Arab capture of Damascus (30 Sept–1 Oct)
MESOPOTAMIAN FRONT Tigris Offensive begins (23 Oct); British enter Mosul (14 Nov)
CAMPAIGNS IN AFRICA German forces from East Africa surrender in Rhodesia (25 Nov)
WAR AT SEA Austro-Hungarian naval mutiny at Cattaro (1 Feb); British raid on Zeebrugge and Ostend (22–23 April); Ostend raid (10 May); German naval mutiny begins (3 Nov); German Navy is interned (21 Nov)

Allied War Plans Volunteers for Britain's "New Army" begin their military drill without uniforms.

July 1914 – The Road to War German troops on the way to take part in the attack on France.

Assassination at Sarajevo Gavrilo Princip is arrested shortly after making his attack.

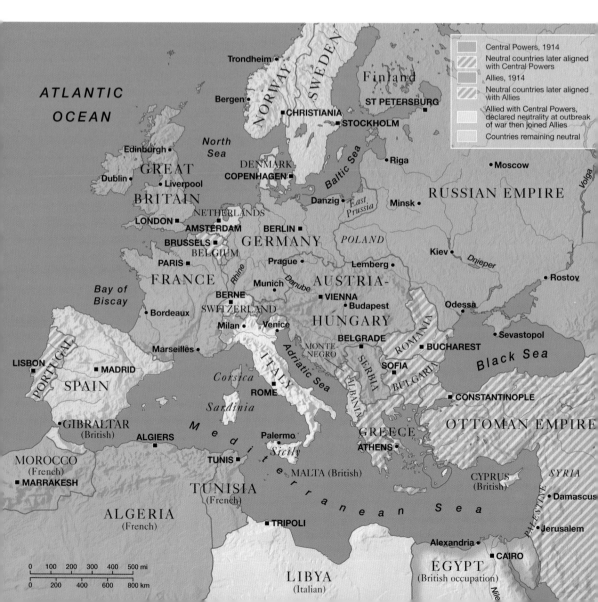

Central Powers, 1914
Neutral countries later aligned with Central Powers
Allies, 1914
Neutral countries later aligned with Allies
Allied with Central Powers, declared neutrality at outbreak of war then joined Allies
Countries remaining neutral

ATLANTIC OCEAN
North Sea
Baltic Sea
Bay of Biscay
Mediterranean Sea
Adriatic Sea
Black Sea
Trondheim
Bergen
NORWAY
SWEDEN
CHRISTIANIA
STOCKHOLM
Finland
ST PETERSBURG
Riga
Moscow
Volga
Edinburgh
GREAT BRITAIN
Dublin
Liverpool
LONDON
DENMARK
COPENHAGEN
Danzig
East Prussia
Minsk
RUSSIAN EMPIRE
NETHERLANDS
AMSTERDAM
BERLIN
BRUSSELS
BELGIUM
GERMANY
POLAND
Kiev
Dnieper
PARIS
Prague
Lemberg
FRANCE
Rhine
Munich
Danube
AUSTRIA-HUNGARY
Rostov
BERNE
VIENNA
Budapest
Odessa
Bordeaux
SWITZERLAND
Milan
Venice
Sevastopol
BELGRADE
ROMANIA
BUCHAREST
Marseilles
MONTENEGRO
SERBIA
SOFIA
BULGARIA
LISBON
PORTUGAL
MADRID
SPAIN
Corsica
ITALY
ROME
ALBANIA
CONSTANTINOPLE
Sardinia
GIBRALTAR (British)
ALGIERS
Palermo
Sicily
GREECE
ATHENS
OTTOMAN EMPIRE
MOROCCO (French)
MARRAKESH
TUNIS
MALTA (British)
CYPRUS (British)
SYRIA
TUNISIA (French)
Damascus
ALGERIA (French)
TRIPOLI
PALESTINE
Jerusalem
Alexandria
CAIRO
EGYPT (British occupation)
LIBYA (Italian)
Nile

0 100 200 300 400 500 mi
0 200 400 600 800 km

ORIGINS OF THE WAR

The assassination of Archduke Franz Ferdinand, heir to the Austro-Hungarian throne, by a Bosnian Serb nationalist on 28 June 1914, caused barely a ripple of public interest across most of Europe when it was first reported. Yet what at first appeared to be no more than the most recent incident in a long-standing but localized squabble over power and influence within the Balkans had much wider repercussions. The assassination on that summer Sunday was not the cause of World War I but it was the catalyst that dragged all of Europe's great powers into a conflict of global proportions in not much more than one month.

World War I was the product of many deep-seated issues dividing the various great European powers – economic, political and territorial, for example – that were exacerbated by the fact that those involved were bound together by secret treaties which placed them in mutually antagonistic camps, commonly referred to as the Central Powers and the Triple Entente. Some key figures also failed, deliberately or otherwise, to do very much to halt the slide to hostilities in July 1914. They were psychologically prepared to go to war to put right their grievances, and it was their sense of the inevitability of war as much as any other factor that made it more than likely that armed conflict would break out sooner or later. Few, however, appreciated that the war would be prolonged, worldwide and destructive on a hitherto unseen scale.

July 1914 – The Road to War Rejoicing crowds in Berlin greet the outbreak of war.

Allied War Plans Men of the 11th Hussars, among the first British troops to fight, crossing to France.

Austro-Hungarian and German War Plans A band plays for soldiers leaving for the war.

Assassination at Sarajevo

The Balkans had been torn apart by international rivalries and local wars before World War I but the assassination of the little-known heir to the throne of the Austro-Hungarian Empire in June 1914 sparked a conflict on a truly global scale.

In the years before the outbreak of World War I, Europe's great powers had divided into two mutually antagonistic political blocs, largely because each country had reason to believe it might be threatened by a neighbour. Austria-Hungary and Russia feared that they might clash over their ongoing rivalries in the Balkans, where Serbia, which had close ties with Russia, was seen as a danger to Austria-Hungary. Germany feared that France would at some stage try to regain the provinces of Alsace and Lorraine that it had been forced to cede to Germany after the Franco-Prussian War (1870–71). Germany tried to maintain good relations with Britain but matters began souring when Kaiser (Emperor) Wilhelm II came to the throne in 1888 and embarked on a vast warship-building programme to challenge Britain's traditional naval supremacy. Britain also grew alarmed at Germany's rapid industrialization and its search for overseas colonies.

KEY FACTS

Date: 28 June 1914

Place: Sarajevo, in the Austro-Hungarian province of Bosnia

Outcome: The assassination of Austria-Hungary's Archduke Franz Ferdinand and his wife sparked a Europe-wide crisis.

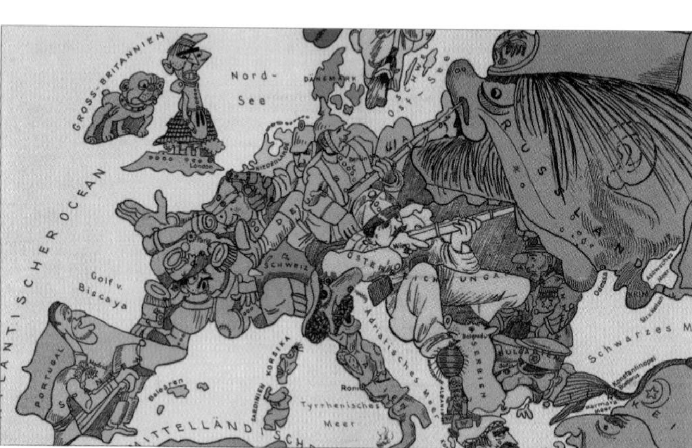

Above: This satirical map indicates how Germany saw itself surrounded by enemies before World War I.

Left: Franz Ferdinand and his wife Sophie are greeted on their arrival at Sarajevo on 28 June 1914.

Competing Alliances

Germany had joined with the Austro-Hungarian Empire to form the Dual Alliance in 1879 and then the Triple Alliance emerged when Italy joined the original pair three years later. Germany and Austria-Hungary agreed to aid Italy if the latter were attacked by France, while Italy agreed to stay neutral if Russia attacked Austria-Hungary. France and Russia entered into an alliance in 1894 and the Anglo-French *Entente Cordiale* was formed in 1904. Kaiser Wilhelm's support for Austria-Hungary in the Balkans angered Russia and this led to an Anglo-Russian alliance, ending long-standing disputes in Central Asia. Britain, France and Russia formed the Triple Entente in 1907.

With such a degree of mutual suspicion in Europe, in an age of rampant nationalism, it was perhaps hardly surprising that militarism took hold, especially in Germany, and that most of the rival nations began to plan for war on the basis that it was better to mobilize first in the

Above: A photograph purportedly showing the arrest of Gavrilo Princip moments after the assassination.

event of a crisis and strike against an enemy before he could take the initiative. Germany faced a potential war on two fronts and perceived a need to attack before France and Russia could bring their numerically superior armies into the field. In the years immediately before World War I, there was even a feeling among generals, and indeed large numbers of ordinary people, that war was probably inevitable, but none expected it to be sparked by the death of a seemingly obscure Austro-Hungarian archduke, Franz Ferdinand, and his wife in the Balkans on 28 June 1914.

Serbia and Bosnia

Ferdinand was heir to the Austro-Hungarian crown and was paying an official visit to Sarajevo, the capital of Bosnia. The former Turkish-controlled province had been incorporated into the Austro-Hungarian Empire in 1906 but the annexation was unpopular both with the Serbian majority living in Bosnia and within neighbouring Serbia itself. A small group of ardent Serbian nationalists led by Gavrilo Princip carried out the assassination and, if the gang had been acting alone, then the matter might have ended with their swift capture. However, it soon emerged that they had planned their mission in Serbia and that certain elements within the Serbian secret service had helped them. Austria-Hungary saw Serbia's complicity in Ferdinand's death as clear evidence of the latter's hostility and as part of its plan to incorporate Bosnia into a greater Serbia. This enlarged and more powerful state would challenge the weakening empire's own position in the Balkans and Serbia was likely to sponsor further unrest among Austria-Hungary's Slavic minority for its own geopolitical ends.

THE BLACK HAND

A Serbian secret society formed in 1911, the Black Hand was officially known as "Unity or Death". Its mission was nothing less than the political integration into Serbia of various Slav minorities in both Austria-Hungary and Turkey. Many of its members were serving Serbian officers, including a colonel by the name of Dragutin Dimitrievic, who helped the assassins involved in the death of Archduke Franz Ferdinand in June 1914. The Black Hand organization was quashed by the exiled Serbian government during 1915–16 and Dimitrievic was executed.

Left: The trial of the Sarajevo assassins. All were found guilty and those of age were sentenced to death. Younger conspirators, including Princip, were imprisoned.

July 1914 – The Road to War

The assassination at Sarajevo initially looked like a localized squabble between Austria-Hungary and Serbia but the crisis soon spread, dragging in all of Europe's great powers in just four weeks.

News of the assassination of Austria-Hungary's Archduke Franz Ferdinand in late June 1914 did not arouse much interest in most of the European press but it did spark a stark diplomatic response from his country's government. Some senior figures, notably the Foreign Minister, Leopold von Berchtold, and the Army's Chief of Staff, Field Marshal Franz Conrad von Hötzendorf, saw the assassination in Sarajevo as a golden opportunity to teach Serbia a lesson, but only if Germany would guarantee to support their actions by preventing Russia from coming to Serbia's aid. Emperor Wilhelm II gave Germany's backing to the Austro-Hungarian ambassador on 5 July, told his ministers of his decision and then left for a cruise.

Above: Theobald von Bethmann-Hollweg, German Chancellor 1909–17, believed that a short, successful war would heal his country's deep political divisions.

Austria Fights Serbia

An ultimatum stating the reparations required because of the assassination was presented to the Serbian government on the evening of the 23rd but the terms were so humiliating that Austria-Hungary did not expect that Serbia would agree to them. Russia now intervened, telling the Serbs to accept the greater part of the ultimatum, but the Russian government also warned Austria-Hungary that it would not allow further action against Serbia. However, Berchtold and Conrad had no intention of accepting Serbia's largely conciliatory reply when it arrived on the 25th – the army had already begun mobilizing the same day – and Berchtold convinced Emperor Franz Joseph to sign a war declaration on the 26th.

Below: German troops expected a quick victory and the graffiti show that Paris was their objective.

Wilhelm II returned from his holiday the same day but was not told of Austria-Hungary's ultimatum until the morning of the 28th, the same time that Berchtold was informing the Serbian ambassador to Vienna that a state of war existed between their two countries. Russia began a partial mobilization of its forces two days later and Wilhelm and his confidants saw the emerging crisis as an opportunity to extend their own country's power and influence. Germany began a general mobilization and on the 31st sent a message to the Russians stating they must cease their now-general mobilization. The Russians refused and Germany declared war that afternoon.

EMPEROR WILHELM II

Wilhelm II (1859–1941) came to the German throne in 1888 as a firm believer in autocracy. He wished to make his realm stronger both economically and militarily and make it a colonial power. He was largely successful in the first two aims but Germany was never more than a second-rate colonizer. Wilhelm, however, was no diplomat and was increasingly seen as an overbearing militarist, one who saw war as a means of uniting his politically polarized country. His character flaws are regarded as being a major factor in bringing about the outbreak of the war.

Above: Emperor Wilhelm II was invariably seen dressed in military costume and was especially fond of his various awards and medals.

Declarations of War

Now the various alliances came into play. France's Prime Minister stated that his country "would act according to its interests", a form of diplomatic speak that Germany took to mean that France would honour its alliance with Russia. Germany declared war against France on 3 August and its troops immediately invaded Belgium and Luxembourg in accordance with a long-standing war plan. Britain was a guarantor of Belgian neutrality and issued a stern warning to Germany on the morning of the 4th. The German Chancellor, Theobald von Bethmann-Hollweg, failed to persuade the British Foreign Secretary, Edward Grey, to renege on his country's treaty obligations and Britain declared war on Germany at midnight. Only Italy stood back from the brink. Its government argued that Austria-Hungary's mobilization against Serbia was outside the defensive provisions of the Triple Alliance accords.

Large crowds appeared in the streets of the combatant nations' capitals in those early days of August. Most were gripped by patriotic war fever and the outbreak of hostilities was greeted with something approaching wild enthusiasm. Most of the people, like the generals and politicians, expected a campaign that would end with the victorious troops being home by Christmas.

Right: Huge crowds gather in the centre of Berlin to celebrate the outbreak of the war in August 1914.

Allied War Plans

The large armies of France and Russia went to war with the intention of attacking their most powerful opponent, Germany, simultaneously from both east and west, while Britain's powerful navy was poised to impose an economic blockade.

France's war-fighting strategy arose out of the loss of the provinces of Alsace and Lorraine in the aftermath of its humiliating defeat during the Franco-Prussian War. Plan XVII was devised by the French Commander-in-Chief, Marshal Joseph Joffre, during 1911–14 and called for the various French armies to muster along a line adjacent to the two provinces, between the Belgian and the Swiss borders, once mobilization had been ordered. They would then drive forward with the utmost aggression into both Alsace and Lorraine. Joffre did realize that his plan left the Franco-Belgian border undefended but he was of the opinion that the Germans would not be able to advance west of the River Meuse without leaving themselves dangerously over-extended.

Below: Britain was gripped by war fever in late summer 1914 and volunteers like these "New Army" recruits flocked to the colours.

Above: Russia's Tsar Nicholas II inspects his troops as they prepare to go to war, August 1914.

Russian Plans

Russia actually had two war plans depending on whether Germany advanced into Russia or France first. In the former case the Russian Army would fight a defensive war, while the French pushed into Alsace and Lorraine. However, it was generally thought that Germany would attack France first and in that case Russia would follow Plan 19. This was originally conceived in 1910 by General Yuri Danilov with the backing of the then Minister for War, General Vladimir Sukhomlinov, and it called for an immediate invasion of the neighbouring German province of East Prussia. Danilov ignored those who thought Austria-Hungary was an equal if not greater threat, those who proposed an advance into central Germany through Silesia, and those who objected to his plan to do away with Russia's frontier fortresses and use their guns elsewhere.

Danilov and Sukhomlinov had powerful rivals, not least the head of the Army, Grand Duke Nicholas, and these gained strength in the years before the war. The idea of making an attack into the Austro-Hungarian province of Galicia became more credible and Plan 19 was modified in May 1912. The attack into East Prussia was kept, although the number of armies earmarked for the operation was reduced from four to two, the frontier fortresses were not downgraded, and three armies were mustered along the border with Austria-Hungary. Another was in reserve to be sent to either East Prussia or Galicia as required.

Above: Mobilization begins in the Russian capital, St Petersburg, as reservists head for their depots.

Belgium and Serbia

Both Belgium's and Serbia's war plans were dictated by geography and the relatively small size of their armed forces. Both intended to defend their frontiers for as long as possible and then fall back into fortified cities, in Belgium's case, or the rugged interior, in Serbia's case. They both hoped that either events elsewhere would see their more powerful opponents divert forces away from them or that their allies, principally France and Russia, would come to their aid.

British Intentions

Britain's war plan was largely dictated by the small size of its army compared with those on the continent and the larger size of its navy in comparison to that of Germany. The small British Expeditionary Force (BEF) was to be transported to France as quickly as possible and fall in on the left flank of the French forces in the north, largely to protect the key Channel ports where the BEF disembarked. The Royal Navy, Britain's greatest military asset, was to blockade Germany. It was to Britain's good fortune that the greater part of its fleet was in home waters for a review during 18–20 July, so that the order for it to disperse was rescinded and its warships were sent to their war stations on the 28th.

Right: Elements of the small British Expeditionary Force sail for France in the first weeks of the war.

Austro-Hungarian and German War Plans

Both Germany and Austria-Hungary had developed intricate war plans before 1914 and these relied on rapid mobilization, using their railway systems, so that they would avoid having to fight on two fronts at the same time.

France and Russia signed what was effectively an anti-German alliance in 1894 and the German Army Chief of Staff, Count Alfred von Schlieffen, recognized that Germany might face an unwinnable war on two fronts at some date in the future. He therefore devised a war-fighting strategy, the Schlieffen Plan, to prevent such an outcome. His aim was to defeat France quickly before Russia could mobilize its huge reserves of manpower.

Above: Count Alfred von Schlieffen was the architect of his country's bold war strategy.

THE SCHLIEFFEN PLAN

Schlieffen realized that any advance from Alsace and Lorraine into eastern France would be slow and costly. This was largely because of the various fortress complexes that the French had built along their mutual frontier since their defeat and the loss of the two provinces in the Franco-Prussian War. A push through the Swiss Alps would also be too ponderous because of the mountainous terrain. Schlieffen therefore decided to send a huge enveloping force through the southern Netherlands and Belgium because their borders were less well defended and the French would be unprepared for such a move.

A holding force would be positioned in Alsace and Lorraine between Metz and the Swiss border and Schlieffen expected that a combination of these troops, the difficult local terrain and Germany's own frontier fortresses would delay the expected French attack there. Schlieffen positioned his main strike force to the north of Metz so that it would swing west and then south to trap the French pushing into Alsace and Lorraine. Once France had been defeated, the bulk of the German Army was to be rapidly transferred east by rail to link up with a small force that had been left to guard East Prussia and then crush Russia with Germany's full strength.

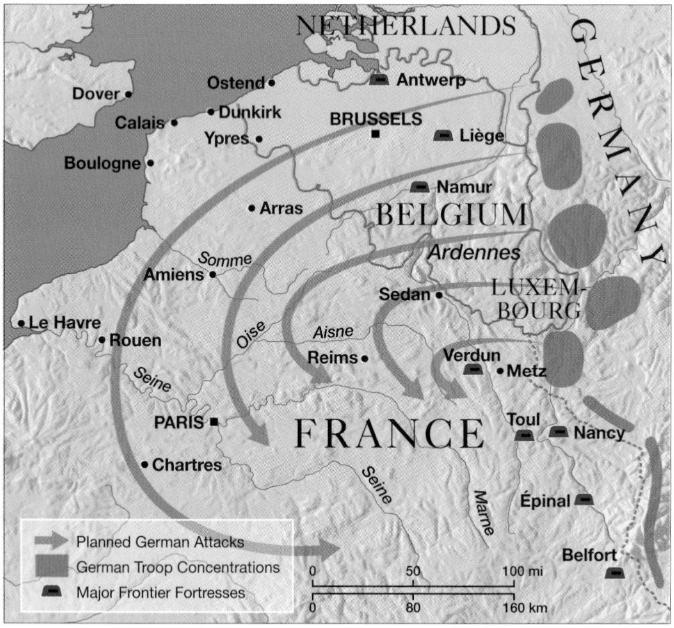

THE SCHLIEFFEN PLAN
The ambitious scope of the original version of the plan.

Above: Germany's efficient rail system was the cornerstone of its plan to defeat France and then turn on Russia. Here, a military brass band serenades the departure of a troop train as loved ones make their goodbyes.

Schlieffen retired in 1906 and was replaced by General Helmuth von Moltke. Moltke felt it necessary to modify the original scheme because Russia was now expected to mobilize faster than his predecessor had envisaged. Nor was he willing to give up any German territory. Thus he strengthened the forces lying between Metz and the Swiss border and those in East Prussia. The former rose from 5 per cent of total mobilized strength to 25 per cent and the latter from 10 to 15 per cent. Thus only 60 rather than 90 per cent of the Germany Army would be committed north of Metz. Moltke also dropped the idea of attacking through the Netherlands in the mistaken belief that Britain might not go to war if only Belgium's neutrality was violated. This modification meant that his forces would have to advance on a narrow front and would face the fortress complex of Liège.

War by Timetable

The Schlieffen Plan relied on timing above all else. No one doubted that Germany's efficient rail system and mobilization programme would be up to the job of getting the troops to the border, but it was an enormous gamble to believe that troops, some marching many miles a day as they moved into enemy territory, would keep to the strict timetable devised by the German General Staff. The plan also made enormous assumptions about how the French and Russians would react once war had broken out.

Austria-Hungary

The Austro-Hungarians had two war plans. One was based on a localized war in the Balkans against Serbia, while the other, more likely, scenario was a war on two fronts against Serbia and its great ally, Russia. In the latter case Austro-Hungarian units would fight alongside German troops and it had been agreed that they would advance into Russian Poland to take the pressure off the German troops in East Prussia.

Above: Field Marshal Helmuth von Moltke was Schlieffen's successor and watered down his war strategy with disastrous consequences.

Field Artillery Russian artillery in action at the start of the war on the Eastern Front.

Frontier Fortresses Storeroom inside Verdun s Fort Douaumont during the great battle in 1916.

Germany's African Colonies British West African troops training in marksmanship.

1914 – EUROPE GOES TO WAR

Even as war was being declared, the clauses in the secret treaties, which bound the Central Powers and Triple Entente together and guaranteed that the various signatories would offer each other military support, came into effect. The mobilization of each country's armed forces mostly went smoothly, largely due to years of planning down to the tiniest detail. Germany and Austria-Hungary mobilized around 6.5 million men in a few days in late July and early August 1914, while the various Allies put about 9 million men into the field. Yet neither side was able to deliver the knock-out blow that the generals and their political masters – and the various general publics – expected.

The fighting in 1914 was concentrated on the Western Front. There were only two major battles in the east and campaigns elsewhere were small. The fighting began with a series of sweeping movements across Belgium and north-east France. However, German plans for a swift victory were thwarted near Paris in early September and, over the next two months, the trench lines began to appear. Just five months of fighting in the west cost the Allies 1.2 million casualties and the Germans at least 680,000. Hopes of swift victory had been dashed but the enthusiasm for war remained largely undimmed.

The Invasions of Serbia 1914–15
Worn out Serbian troops during their retreat from their homeland in 1915.

Coronel and the Falklands
An outgunned British cruiser falls victim to German fire at Coronel.

Operations in Poland and Galicia
Russian besiegers around the Austrian fortress of Przemyśl.

The German Invasion of Belgium

The Schlieffen Plan called for four German armies, consisting of around 940,000 men and 2,900 artillery pieces, to march rapidly through Belgium, a small country defended by fewer than 120,000 troops and 320 guns.

By early August 1914 Germany had two armies positioned in Alsace and Lorraine along its border with France, two more facing Luxembourg and three close to the narrow border with Belgium. The latter five armies were the key components of the Schlieffen Plan and were set to launch a great arcing offensive that would first take them west through Belgium into north-eastern France where they would swing due south. The greatest effort would be made by the northernmost two armies – the First of General Alexander von Kluck and General Karl von Bülow's Second, around 580,000 men and 1,700 guns in all.

KEY FACTS

DATE: 4 – 25 August 1914

PLACE: Belgium

OUTCOME: The advancing Germans pushed rapidly through the country while local and Anglo-French forces were forced to retreat.

FALL OF LIÈGE

As speed was crucial to the success of the Schlieffen Plan, Belgium's frontier fortresses

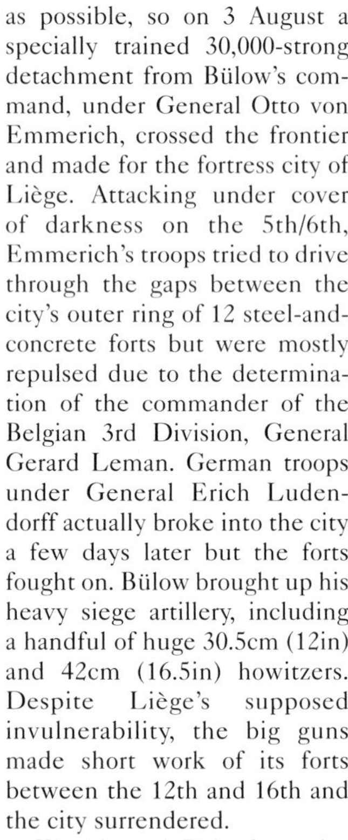

were to be neutralized as soon as possible, so on 3 August a specially trained 30,000-strong detachment from Bülow's command, under General Otto von Emmerich, crossed the frontier and made for the fortress city of Liège. Attacking under cover of darkness on the 5th/6th, Emmerich's troops tried to drive through the gaps between the city's outer ring of 12 steel-and-concrete forts but were mostly repulsed due to the determination of the commander of the Belgian 3rd Division, General Gerard Leman. German troops under General Erich Ludendorff actually broke into the city a few days later but the forts fought on. Bülow brought up his heavy siege artillery, including a handful of huge 30.5cm (12in) and 42cm (16.5in) howitzers. Despite Liège's supposed invulnerability, the big guns made short work of its forts between the 12th and 16th and the city surrendered.

Kluck's and Bülow's armies could now renew their advance through Belgium. Kluck's troops beat off a small Belgian counter-attack near Tirlemont on 18–19 August and occupied Brussels, the capital, the next day, while Bülow advanced along the east–west line of the rivers Meuse and Sambre. King Albert, the Belgian Commander-in-Chief, had by now wisely recognized that his army, which was outnumbered four-to-one and far from well-equipped, had

Below: German mounted troops in the largely deserted streets of a Belgian city in the first weeks of war.

Above: General Alexander von Kluck (fifth from left), commander of the German First Army, poses for a photograph with his staff.

absolutely no means of halting the German steamroller. He therefore sent one of his divisions to garrison Namur, which stood in Bülow's path, while he and the remainder of his force occupied Antwerp. Both cities were protected by rings of fortresses. Kluck detached a corps to blockade Antwerp and prevent any Belgian sorties against his right flank but the bulk of his First Army and Bülow's Second Army still continued westward.

Belgium Conquered

Bülow crossed the Sambre on the 22nd. Namur, which was now behind his lines, had come under attack on the 20th and the siege proper began the next day. The fighting followed the same pattern as at Liège. Heavy howitzers destroyed the outer nine forts in quick succession and the city surrendered on the 25th, although much of the garrison escaped. By the end of the third week of August, virtually all of Belgium had been overrun and, thanks to the heavy howitzers, its fortresses had not unduly upset the Schlieffen Plan's exacting timetable. Nevertheless, both Kluck and Bülow still had a very long way to go to complete their orders and, thanks to a combination of frequent combat and long daily marches under an unusually warm late summer sun, their troops were becoming increasingly fatigued.

Below: Stunned Belgian civilians look on as German troops march through Brussels on 20 August.

THE GERMAN OCCUPATION OF BELGIUM

Virtually the whole of Belgium was occupied by the Germans from 1914 until late 1918 and its citizens suffered greatly. The people lived under strict martial law; any resistance was met by hostage-taking, imprisonment and executions. Some 20,000 Belgians were forcibly transported to Germany for war work in 1916 and 1917. Belgian industry was given over to war production for the Germans and they also stripped the country of rolling stock, food and raw materials.

Right: German troops guard Belgian civilians accused of resisting the occupation.

Frontier Fortresses

Several European countries built elaborate frontier fortresses along their vulnerable borders, supposedly to protect them from invasion, but they proved to be white elephants and many were utterly shattered by heavy artillery.

The idea of building fortresses at vulnerable points along a country's border with a potential enemy was nothing new, though there was something of a mania for constructing or renovating them in the latter part of the 19th century. Many European nations built frontier fortresses but the greatest concentration was to be found along the much-contested border between France and Germany.

Above: The heavily damaged interior of one of Namur's nine main forts gives a good indication as to why the city surrendered after a siege of less than a week (18–23 August 1914).

Fortress Designs

Although there was no set design for frontier fortresses, they did have several features in common. More often than not they were built around a strategically important town or city, often on a river, and the urban area was then ringed by a string of forts that were built roughly equidistant from each other and several miles from the centre. The space between them might be covered by smaller forts or the gap might be plugged by trench lines dug if war seemed likely. Generally, they had only small garrisons – approximately 1,000 men in a bigger fortress – but these could be rapidly reinforced from a central reserve.

One of the most important figures in fortress construction was Belgian Henri Brialmont, who was responsible for the most modern defences of Antwerp, Liège and Namur and whose radical ideas were taken up by other nations. His forts were either triangular or pentagonal in plan according to the terrain. They were based on an underground central section constructed from reinforced concrete, which was topped by armoured cupolas. The concrete was some 2.5m (8ft) thick and overlain with 3m (10ft) of earth. There was a parapet around the central section from where

Below: The centre of the Belgian Fort de Loncin at Liège was smashed by a single German howitzer shell.

infantry could command the interior of the fort and could fire down on any attackers. The central section was further protected by a deep, wide dry ditch with sloping sides, and various other cupolas for artillery and machine-guns were positioned between the parapet and ditch. Barbed-wire entanglements filled the base of the ditch and an "unclimbable" iron fence ran around the outer edge of the fort.

In Brialmont's designs the only visible parts of the fortress were the upper surfaces of the central section and the individual gun cupolas. Some military commentators believed that the cupolas were very vulnerable to artillery fire and came up with designs that could be retracted when the gun was not in action or being reloaded. Two large engineering companies were especially involved in developing such retractable cupolas, France's Saint-Chamond and Germany's Gruson, and their designs were fitted to numerous fortresses across Europe. Among these were Verdun and Belfort in France and Brest-Litovsk in Russia.

Fortresses in Action

The much-vaunted fortresses proved to be of considerably less value during World War I than their most vocal advocates believed. Some, like Liège and Namur, rapidly succumbed to bombardment from heavy artillery; others were simply bypassed and left to "wither on the vine" as the fighting rapidly moved elsewhere, while others were downgraded and had their artillery weapons removed and transferred to field operations. The only prolonged siege of note was that against much-invested Przemyśl, an Austro-Hungarian fortress in Galicia, and this only lasted so long largely because the Russians lacked heavy siege artillery. Even the 1916 Battle of Verdun, the war's longest engagement, was not primarily about capturing the town's various outlying fortresses but rather about the attrition of troops.

Above: The Germans captured this munitions store in Fort Douaumont, Verdun, in February 1916. It was retaken by the French in October.

Right: France's Fort Vaux at Verdun was the scene of an epic five-day underground battle between its garrison and German troops in 1916. It finally fell to the latter on 7 June.

Heavy Artillery

Big guns were very much in short supply in every theatre during the first years of the war but they became the most important weapons in every country's arsenal once the fixed defences of trench warfare had developed.

The general lack of heavy artillery in 1914 partly reflected the recent experiences of the various warring nations. The French were still wedded to the idea of fast-moving warfare in the Napoleonic style of the early 19th century while the British had recently fought the elusive horse-mounted Boer commandos in the Second Anglo-Boer War (1899–1902). Neither saw the need for much more than highly mobile and rapidly deployed horse-drawn field artillery that could keep up with both infantry and cavalry.

Guns and Fortresses

The German and Austro-Hungarian planners had learned some lessons from the Russo-Japanese War (1904–5) in which the Japanese deployed heavy howitzers. Nevertheless, their armies marched to war in 1914 with a preponderance of field guns, though both of their general staffs expected to have to deal with enemy fortresses and knew they needed some heavy artillery. Prussian troops had been involved in sieges during the Franco-Prussian War and had found themselves short of the appropriate firepower. The response of the French to defeat in that war was to build or modernize a series of fortresses that might slow the fast movement of troops that Germany's Schlieffen Plan required. And Belgium, through which German troops would have to pass, had followed France's lead. Austria-Hungary had two potential major enemies – Russia and Italy – and war against either might involve fighting in the natural fortresses of the Carpathian Mountains and the Alps. In both cases shells with a plunging trajectory would be needed.

Below: A British (152mm) 6in gun position on the Western Front in 1917. This weapon fired a 45kg (100lb) shell to 12,500m (13,700yds).

60-POUNDER GUN

This British weapon was introduced in 1905 and was the standard "heavy" gun serving with British divisions at the start of the war. It remained in use throughout the conflict but by the later years had been reclassified as a medium weapon and supplemented by much heavier designs.

Calibre: 127mm (5in)
Gun weight: 4,470kg (4.3 tons)
Gun length: 4.29m (14.06ft)
Shell weight: 27.2kg (60lb)
Muzzle velocity: 634m/sec (2,080ft/sec)
Maximum range: 11,250m (12,300yds)

Above: An Austro-Hungarian Skoda-built 30.5cm (12in) "Schlanke Emma" howitzer in action.

Austria-Hungary led the way with Skoda's "Schlanke Emma" (Skinny Emma) a 30.5cm (12in) howitzer, while Germany's Krupp developed a 42cm (16.5in) weapon nicknamed "Dicke Bertha" (Big Bertha). Their combat debut was against Liège, supposedly the world's strongest fortress complex, on 12 August 1914. To the relief of the Germans and to the shock of their opponents, a dozen or so Emmas and Berthas reduced the city's supposedly impregnable concrete-and-steel fortresses to rubble in a mere four days.

As the trench lines were dug along the Western Front in late 1914, all of the combatants began fully to appreciate the need for heavy artillery to smash barbed wire, crumble trenches and bury deep dugouts in what was a new form of siege warfare, and they set about building such guns in large numbers or redeployed them from the now redundant fortresses. Little more than eight per cent of France's artillery was of the heavy types in 1914, for example, but the figure was close to 50 per cent only four years later.

Increasing Firepower

Vast numbers of different heavy artillery pieces were developed. Some were moved around on wheeled carriages but others were transported in sections and placed on reinforced beds for firing. Some types like the French Army's 220mm (8.7in) Schneider Model 1917 could fling a 90.7kg (200lb) shell out to 22,400m (24,500yds) but most of the heavy howitzer types had shorter ranges. There was a simple trade-off – the heavier the shell, the shorter the range. The overall trend was for heavier, more destructive shells. The shell of the standard German field howitzer in 1914 weighed just 6.8kg (15lb), while that of the 21cm (8.3in) Lange Mörser (Long Mortar) of 1916 was a hefty 113kg (249lb).

KRUPP 21CM MORTAR/HOWITZER

Commonly referred to as the Long 21cm Mortar, this heavy howitzer entered service in 1916. Early versions were fitted with a gun shield but these were dropped for the subsequent variants.

Calibre: 21cm (8.3in)
Weight: 6,680kg (6.57 tons)
Gun length: 2.3m (7.55ft)
Shell weight: 113kg (249lb)
Muzzle velocity: 393m/sec (1,290ft/sec)
Maximum range: 11,100m (12,150yds)

KRUPP 15CM FIELD HOWITZER

This gun made its service debut in 1913 but Krupp produced an updated model, the FH17, during World War I. It actually differed little from its predecessor, except that it was somewhat lighter due to shortages of certain raw materials. The gun remained in German service for training until World War II.

Calibre: 15cm (5.87in)
Weight: 2,200kg (2.17 tons)
Gun length: 2.1m (6.9ft)
Shell weight: 42kg (92.6lb)
Muzzle velocity: 365m/sec (1,197ft/sec)
Maximum range: 8,500m (9,300yds)

The Battles of the Frontiers

This title was the collective name given to a series of huge sprawling battles between Anglo-French and German armies that took place throughout August 1914 on or close to the French border with Germany.

France's war strategy, Plan XVII, provided that, in the event of conflict with Germany, six French armies were to concentrate along the French border from Belgium to Switzerland, roughly from Belfort to Sedan. The French also had an agreement that the British Expeditionary Force (BEF) would take up positions on the extreme left of their line. These plans brought about the Battles of the Frontiers.

Above: French medical orderlies line up with their various dogs, each of which carries vital equipment in pairs of pouches.

French Attacks

General Paul Pau's French Army of Alsace began moving towards Mülhausen (Mulhouse) in Alsace on 8 August. General Auguste Dubail's First Army and General Noël de Castelnau's Second Army pushed into Lorraine. As they advanced on the 14th, two opposing German armies, the Sixth under Crown Prince Rupprecht of Bavaria and General Josias von Heeringen's Seventh, deliberately gave ground. They turned on the 20th and launched a fierce counter-attack. A day later the French retreated – the First Army in good order but the right wing of the Second Army had been destroyed. The battle ended on the 22nd and Moltke allowed Rupprecht and von Heeringen to continue their attack, although the Schlieffen Plan called for no such action.

More French Defeats

Plan XVII also required three armies positioned north of Metz to advance eastward but the commander of the Fifth Army, General Charles Lanrezac, realized that the Germans were in Belgium in strength. He gained permission on 15 August to take

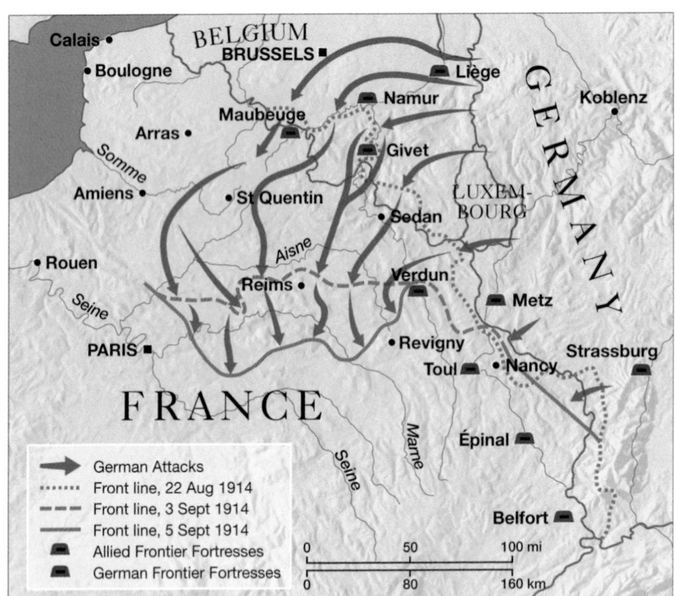

TOWARDS PARIS!
Germany's advance through Belgium and into northern France.

Above: Rows of corpses await burial – a small part of the death toll in the Battles of the Frontiers.

his troops to the west of the River Meuse in southern Belgium and fall in alongside the BEF's right flank. The two remaining armies, General Ferdinand de Langle de Cary's Fourth and General Pierre Ruffey's Third, began moving on the 20th but towards the north-east and into the densely forested Ardennes.

These two French armies were hit by Duke Albrecht of Württemberg's Fourth Army and Crown Prince Wilhelm's Fifth Army on the 22nd. By the 25th the French had been forced into retreat. The Fourth fell back on Verdun while the Third crossed over the Meuse around Sedan and retreated south towards the River Marne. Meanwhile, Lanrezac had placed his Fifth Army between the Sambre and Meuse Rivers by the 20th but it was hit by two German armies, General von Bülow's Second and the Third, under General Max von Hausen, two days later. The Germans came close to enveloping Lanrezac's army during the 22nd, but he was able to withdraw the next day.

The Battles of the Frontiers were all but over and Plan XVII was in ruins. By the end of August France's armies stood on a line that ran east from Paris along the Marne to Verdun and from there south to the Swiss border. France had suffered over 210,000 casualties in four weeks, in part because its generals followed a strategy that claimed that all-out attack was always best. However, the fighting along the frontiers was not quite over as General von Kluck's 320,000-strong First Army crashed into the much smaller BEF on the 23rd.

FRANCE AND THE OFFENSIVE SPIRIT

The French Army went to war in August 1914 dressed in uniforms that would not have looked out of place on a Napoleonic battlefield and used tactics that were equally antiquated. Their troops and generals were wedded to the idea of the "offensive spirit" in which the soldiers' *élan* ("dash" or "bravery") and fixed bayonets would dominate the battlefield. Thus, in the first months of the war, particularly in the Battles of the Frontiers, the French relied on reckless offensive tactics and therefore suffered huge casualties.

Above: The army's brightly coloured uniforms were designed to foster the troops' spirit.

Reconnaissance Aircraft

Aircraft technology was very much in its infancy at the outbreak of World War I but most combatant nations did possess a few reconnaissance aircraft and these types became ever more important once static warfare had begun.

Something like 19 out of every 20 aerial sorties flown throughout World War I were reconnaissance missions. There is no doubt that such aircraft played an increasingly key role in the conflict yet there had been considerable resistance to their introduction before the war – military aviation was still in its infancy in 1914 and many generals doubted its value.

The New Cavalry?

There were also comparatively few aircraft available in 1914; many country's air arms had only recently been founded; and most senior generals had little idea of what to do with them. Traditionally cavalry units were considered an army's eyes but aircraft soon proved their worth in reconnaissance. A German two-seat *Taube* monoplane played an important spotting role during the Battle of Tannenberg on the Eastern Front in late August 1914, for example, and these aircraft soon became indispensable when trench warfare reduced cavalry to immobility all along the Western Front.

Thereafter, reconnaissance aircrafts were deemed so important that fighter aircraft were developed specifically to shoot them down or protect them. They also became more and more sophisticated. Reports delivered in person or written and dropped gave way to immediate radio messages, while bulky hand-held cameras gave way to smaller types fitted within the fuselage. Later versions were stripped of any extra weight, including weapons, to fly higher and faster. They became ubiquitous over every front – more than half of fighter ace Baron Manfred von Richthofen's 80 "kills" were of reconnaissance aircraft.

The first types had only to be stable platforms for observation and did not have to be fast or

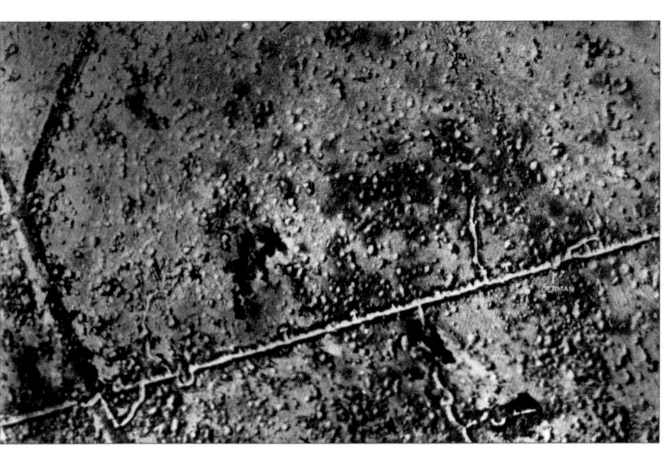

Above: Part of the Western Front photographed from a reconnaissance aircraft. Commanders increasingly relied on photo-mosaics made up of many images like this when planning attacks.

FARMAN MF-11

These French-built "pusher" aircraft were designed by Maurice Farman and were in general service in 1914. They saw action with the British and the French and fought on every front before being withdrawn from combat in 1915.

Type: Reconnaissance/bomber
Engine: 80hp Renault
Crew: 2
Ceiling: 3,000m (9,840ft)
Top speed: 96kph (60mph)
Armament: 1 x 0.303in (7.7mm) machine-gun

NIEUPORT 12

Nieuport built several designs for the French Army during World War I including the Nieuport 10 reconnaissance biplane, which made its debut in 1915. This was soon superseded by the Nieuport 12, enlarged and faster, and fitted with both rear- and forward-firing machine-guns. It was in service until early 1916.

TYPE: Reconnaissance/fighter
ENGINE: 110hp Clerget
CREW: 2
CEILING: 3,400m (11,150ft)
TOP SPEED: 160kph (100mph)
ARMAMENT: 1 or 2 x 0.303in (7.7mm) machine-guns

manoeuvrable as there was little chance of them being downed until fighters appeared. Earlier "pusher" types like the French Farman MF series or the British FE-2a, could manage no more than around 88kph (55mph) and even tractor types, like the German Albatros B-I and B-II, struggled to get above 104kph (65mph). Most of these had no weapons but they began carrying both machine-guns and bombs from late 1914.

LATER DEVELOPMENTS

The newer types that appeared in subsequent years were far more advanced. Albatros, for example, produced a whole range of increasingly advanced armed reconnaissance aircraft, including the C-I to C-III series (1915–16) and the C-V to C-XII types (1916–18). The highly successful C-X carried both bombs and machine-guns and had a top speed of around 196kph (120mph). Germany had other manufacturers, such as Aviatik, who produced the C-1 to C-III series (1915–17), and Halberstadt, who produced the C series (1917–18). Their C-V and Rumpler's C-VII were fitted with radio and cameras, making them the first truly modern photo-reconnaissance aircraft, able to record enemy positions and spot targets for artillery batteries.

Allied designers kept pace with the enemy, producing aircraft like the French Nieuport 10 and 11 (1915–16) with top speeds of around 140kph (85mph) and 155kph (95mph). Some designers opted for multi-purpose aircraft that could perform a number of battlefield functions. The British had the Royal Aircraft Factory's RE-8 (1916–18), a mass-produced multi-purpose biplane that could also undertake bombing and ground-attack missions.

Above: The *Taube* ("Owl") monoplane gained its name because of the bird-like shape of its wings. It was built both in Austria and Germany. Most were withdrawn from service by early 1915.

RUMPLER C-IV

The German company of Rumpler built many types of reconnaissance aircraft starting with the unarmed B-I, available in August 1914. This was replaced by the C-series, from early 1915. Hundreds of these were built, culminating in the C-VIIIR.

TYPE: Reconnaissance/bomber
ENGINE: 260hp Mercedes
CREW: 2
CEILING: 6,350m (20,800ft)
TOP SPEED: 170kph (105mph)
ARMAMENT: 2 x 7.92mm (0.312in) machine-guns + 100kg (220lb) bombs

Mons and Le Cateau

The British Expeditionary Force soon found itself heavily outnumbered when it pushed across the Franco-Belgian border in August 1914 and had to make a fighting withdrawal through north-east France facing repeated German attacks.

The first elements of Field Marshal John French's British Expeditionary Force (BEF) arrived in north-east France on 7 August, just three days after Britain had declared war on Germany, and the cross-Channel movement of around 125,000 men was largely completed by the 16th. The BEF concentrated around Le Cateau in north-east France but moved forward into southern Belgium on 21 August.

The BEF fought its first battle, not much more than a small skirmish between cavalry scouts, during the next day. Forty-eight hours later, however, it was struck by the full might of General Alexander von Kluck's German First Army, the extreme right wing of the Schlieffen Plan, near Mons. Kluck was somewhat caught by surprise as German intelligence had not even reported the arrival of the BEF in France.

KEY FACTS

Date: Mons (23 August 1914); Le Cateau (26 August 1914)

Place: South-west Belgium and north-east France

Outcome: The BEF escaped total destruction to participate in the Battle of the Marne.

Right: A brief respite for men of the British 11th Hussars during the retreat from Mons.

Below: A group of British cavalry photographed during the exhausting withdrawal of August 1914.

Resistance at Mons

Rapid British rifle fire inflicted severe losses on the Germans during the Battle of Mons on the 23rd and French was emboldened enough to contemplate standing his ground the next day. However, he was ordered that night to retreat in order to maintain contact with the French Fifth Army under General Charles Lanrezac that was retreating from Belgium after the Battle of the Sambre. Within a matter of days, therefore, the British were themselves falling back into north-east France down the roads that they had only recently used to move into southern Belgium. French actually wanted to withdraw to the Channel ports but he was overruled by Field Marshal Horatio Kitchener, the Minister for War, who insisted that the BEF must fall back towards the River Marne to keep contact with Lanrezac.

The retreating BEF was pursued closely by Kluck's units and fought frequent rearguard actions in the days after the Battle of Mons but on the 27th its exhausted II Corps under General Horace Smith-Dorrien stood its ground at Le Cateau and became embroiled in the biggest battle the British Army had fought in a hundred years.

THE BATTLE OF NÉRY

This battle took place as the British Expeditionary Force was retreating through north-east France in August–September 1914 and was one of the most remarkable small-scale battles of the entire war. On 1 September the rearguard of the 1st Cavalry Brigade and L Battery of the Royal Horse Artillery turned to face the might of the entire German 4th Cavalry Division. Despite having most of its guns knocked out and with many men killed or wounded, the battery's survivors fought on until all their ammunition was exhausted. Three members of L Battery received the Victoria Cross.

Above: London-born Battery Sergeant-Major George Dorrell won the Victoria Cross for his part in L Battery's heroic stand at Néry on 1 September 1914.

Above: German troops pictured in the centre of Mons after it had been abandoned by the British in August 1914. The Allies, actually Canadians, would not retake the Belgian town until 10 November 1918.

Some 70,000 British troops struggled all day against around 160,000 troops of the First Army as the latter tried to drive around both of their flanks. The battle concluded when darkness fell and the British, who had suffered some 7,800 casualties, then continued their withdrawal. They were aided in this movement by Lanrezac's Fifth Army, which was retiring on a parallel course on their right flank. Marshal Joseph Joffre, the French Commander-in-Chief, ordered Lanrezac to swing through 90 degrees and strike westward against Kluck's exposed left flank.

Kluck's Error

The ensuing Battle of Guise on the 29th did not noticeably slow the German First Army but a subsidiary attack against the German Second Army on its left caused its commander, General Karl von Bülow, considerable problems. He asked for aid from Kluck and the latter agreed, although without seeking permission from his superiors. This was to be a fateful decision as Kluck swung his army to the south-east, a route that would take his units to the east of Paris and not to the west as the Schlieffen Plan had called for. By 2 September his First Army was stretched out along the River Marne between Château-Thierry and Chantilly. Kluck mistakenly believed that there were no significant enemy concentrations on his right flank in the vicinity of Paris. It was a misjudgement that was to have profound consequences for the course of the war.

Field Artillery

Light-weight, quick-firing, field artillery guns drawn by horses were the dominant and most numerous form of artillery at the outset of the war but their importance gradually declined in favour of heavier weapons with bigger shells.

Field artillery consisted of light horse-drawn guns that could keep pace with infantry and cavalry. They were allocated at the divisional level while the distribution of heavier, slower guns was the preserve of higher formation commanders. There were two main types of field artillery – *guns* that fired a high-velocity round on a comparatively flat trajectory, mostly against targets in the open and in the firer's line of sight, and *howitzers* that lobbed a lower-velocity round on an arcing trajectory to strike targets hidden behind cover. Both types could be identified by the diameter of the barrel's bore, the usual system on the European mainland, or alternatively by the approximate weight of the shell they fired, a practice largely confined to Britain. Thus the field gun most widely deployed by the French in 1914 was the Model 1897 75mm (2.95in) while batteries supporting the British infantry relied on the Mark I 18-pounder (3.3in /84mm calibre) and the cavalry supports relied on the lighter 13-pounder (2.95in/75mm).

Rates of Fire

Most guns were quick-firers, capable of firing several rounds a minute. The best of these was the famous French "Soixante-Quinze" ("75"), the field gun that pioneered a recoil system in which only the barrel and not the whole carriage moved when fired. The "75" was phenomenally quick-firing, with a well-trained crew able to get through up to 25 rounds a minute. The crew of the not dissimilar British 18-pounder could manage only eight a minute.

Similar guns were deployed by the other combatant nations. Germany, for example, relied on the 7.7cm (3.03in) field gun, a weapon widely exported to its allies, while Russia deployed the 76.2mm (3in) M1902. Whatever the gun type, field artillery guns usually weighed

Below: British 18-pounder field guns, photographed around the Belgian town of Ypres in late 1914, with their limbers and ammunition caissons close at hand.

roughly 900–1,350kg (2,000–3,000lb). The various field guns and howitzers had a maximum range of 6,500–8,000m (7,100–8,800yds), but under battlefield conditions targets were usually engaged at shorter ranges, often at least a third less than the absolute range. There were variations in the number of guns in individual batteries but most countries deployed four. British cavalry and infantry divisions were the exception with six-gun batteries.

THE FRENCH "75" FIELD GUN

This was a revolutionary weapon when it appeared in 1897. It was light and highly mobile but most important of all it had a novel recoil system which meant that only the barrel and not the whole gun recoiled when fired. It therefore did not need to be re-laid on a target and a well-trained crew could fire an amazing 20-plus rounds in a minute. The 75 was really designed for fast-moving offensives and played a much lesser role in trench warfare.

Calibre: 75mm (2.95in)
Gun weight: 1,160kg (2,560lb)
Gun length: 2.7m (106in)
Shell weight: 7.24kg (15.9lb)
Muzzle velocity: 530m/sec (1,735ft/sec)
Maximum range: 8,500m (9,300yds)

Above: Russian M1902 76.2mm (3in) field guns in action at the start of the war on the Eastern Front.

Shell Types

There were two types of shell in service with field artillery. Shrapnel rounds, a largely anti-personnel weapon, were filled with metal balls and a bursting charge that was detonated by a preset time fuse ideally when in flight just above the enemy. High-explosive rounds had an impact fuse, which detonated when the shell hit the ground or another hard target such as a building. The force of the blast could destroy inanimate objects while both the detonation and splinters from the shell's ruptured casing were lethal to troops. Such rounds might fail to detonate if they struck soft or muddy ground.

Field artillery was essentially a weapon of mobile warfare and as such its importance on the Western Front declined with the advent of trench warfare. Shrapnel was ineffective against troops in cover and the high-explosive rounds fired by field guns were too light to make any impression on deep, strongly constructed dugouts. Despite their lack of firepower, field guns appeared in considerable numbers on the Western Front throughout the war. Improved fuses introduced later in the war meant that field guns could blast barbed-wire defences effectively. The British bombardment that preceded the opening of the Battle of the Somme in 1916 involved some 1,600 artillery pieces of which around 1,200 were either field or slightly larger medium guns. When the Germans launched Operation Michael, the first of their great offensives in 1918, they had 6,473 guns available; 3,965 were 7.7cm (3in) or 10cm (4in) field guns.

The Battle of the Marne

This titanic series of clashes during early September 1914 was masterminded by France's Marshal Joseph Joffre and proved one of the most decisive Allied victories of the war as it saved Paris and confounded Germany's Schlieffen Plan.

The decision by General von Kluck to turn his German First Army to the south, a path that took it to the east rather than the west of Paris as the Schlieffen Plan demanded, did not go unnoticed by the Allies. Aerial reconnaissance spotted the change in direction and Marshal Joseph Joffre, the French Commander-in-Chief, fully intended to exploit the opportunity that had been presented to him. Kluck believed that there were no Anglo-French forces facing his right flank but Joffre had actually been creating a new force near Paris, the Sixth Army under General Michel Maunoury. Joffre intended to use this force against Kluck's over-exposed right flank. Most of the German armies had pushed southward across the River Marne by early September and were lying in a line that began some 48km (30 miles) to the east of Paris when Joffre struck back on the 5th.

KEY FACTS

DATE: 5 – 10 September 1914

PLACE: East of Paris

OUTCOME: The Germans were forced to retreat away from Paris across the River Marne; the Schlieffen Plan had completely failed.

Below: A mass grave for some of the 80,000 French soldiers who died during the Marne fighting.

THE ALLIES ATTACK

The fighting around the Marne was not one but several battles that involved roughly 1 million Anglo-French and some 900,000 German troops. Maunoury was the first to attack, against Kluck's right flank. The Battle of the Ourcq (5–9 September) raged for two days before Kluck realized the danger. He pulled his First Army back across the Marne and then attacked Maunoury. The fighting was fierce but a German breakthrough was prevented once reinforcements arrived from Paris carried in many of the city's taxis.

Kluck's withdrawal left a large hole in the German line between his First and General von Bülow's Second Army. The British Expeditionary Force slowly moved into it, potentially threatening either Kluck's left or Bülow's right flanks, while the French Fifth Army, led by General Louis Franchet d'Espérey, threw itself against Bülow's Second Army along the Petit Morin. Next in line was

MARSHAL JOSEPH JOFFRE

Joffre (1852–1931) became the French Army's Chief of Staff in 1911 and was responsible for formulating the country's war strategy, Plan XVII. He was regarded as calm under pressure and imperturbable: qualities that were needed during the first months of the war. He directed the Allied victory along the Marne in September 1914 and effectively saved France from defeat. Joffre was also inflexible and launched a number of very costly attacks over the following years and, though a national hero, was sacked in late 1916.

Above: Marshal Joffre (second from left) confers with senior British officers.

General Ferdinand Foch's French Ninth Army. This attacked the German Second Army near the St-Gond marshes but quickly found itself fighting part of General Max von Hausen's Third Army as well.

The remainder of the Third Army and the German Fourth Army under Duke Albrecht of Württemberg were attacked by General Langle de Cary's French Fourth Army around Vitry-le-François. Next in line was General Maurice Sarrail's French Third Army which successfully stopped the advance of Crown Prince Wilhelm's Fifth German Army at Revigny in the Argonne. Finally, General Dubail's First and General de Castelnau's Second Armies located around Nancy and along the border with Alsace held off new and ferocious attacks from the reinforced German Sixth and Seventh Armies, commanded by Crown Prince Rupprecht of Bavaria and General Josias von Heeringen.

THE GERMANS RETREAT

By now Field Marshal Helmuth von Moltke, the German Chief of Staff, was receiving only fragmentary and contradictory reports from the Marne so he sent a trusted staff officer, Lieutenant-Colonel Richard Hentsch, to the front. Hentsch had been ordered merely to report on events but he exceeded his authority on the 9th, first by approving Kluck's unauthorized retreat and then permitting Bülow, whose own left flank was coming under more and more pressure, to pull back as well. The other German armies were forced to conform to these movements and withdrew to the line of the River Aisne over the next five days. The Battle of the Marne ended on the 10th and it was an undeniable strategic victory for the Allies though both sides had suffered approximately 25 per cent casualties.

Above: A publication celebrating the arrival of French troops by Paris taxi during the Battle of the Ourcq.

Below: French troops wait to counter-attack the Germans as the invaders begin to cross over the River Marne.

Rifles and Bayonets

The infantryman's rifle with its bayonet was the most ubiquitous weapon of the entire war and both were produced in their millions, but they were not the biggest killers – that "honour" went to machine-guns and, above all, artillery.

The rifle was the most commonly used weapon of World War I and, despite there being a sizeable number of manufacturers across Europe and beyond, all designs in service were largely similar in their mechanism and specifications. All were bolt-action, most of the straight-pull type, and all came with a magazine that allowed several shots to be fired without reloading. Some rifles had removable magazines but most were actually part of the rifle and the firer simply slotted clips of cartridges into them when reloading.

Rifles came in a rather limited variety of calibres. For example, the German Mauser Model 1898 had a calibre of 7.92mm (0.312in), while the Russian Moisin-Nagant was 7.62mm (0.3in) and the Romanian Mannlicher Model 1893 was 6.5mm (0.256in). British rifles were all 0.303in (7.7mm), while US types, like the Model 1903 Springfield, were 0.3in calibre. Most rifles were around 1.25m (50in) long and weighed some 4kg (9lb).

Magazines

Most rifles had a magazine with a five-round capacity but some, especially British and French models, could take somewhat more. The French Lebel Model 1916, for example, had an eight-round magazine, while both the British Lee-Enfield Mark I and the SMLE (Short Magazine Lee-Enfield) Mark III had a detachable ten-round magazine. Both designs reflected the British Army's belief that rapid fire would shatter an attack and its regular infantrymen were able to achieve 15 or 20 aimed shots per minute over short periods. (Most armies considered rapid fire to be 8 or 12 rounds a minute.) The Lee-Enfield's bigger, clip-fed magazine and the rifle's turn-down bolt handle were incorporated into the design to aid quick firing. Hastily trained wartime soldiers could not match the pre-war regulars' standards of speed or marksmanship, however.

Below: British recruits take part in bayonet drill. This was considered an important part of training but bayonets killed very few soldiers.

Right: A good study of a British soldier on campaign. He is armed with an SMLE (Short Magazine Lee-Enfield) rifle, first introduced in 1907.

Effective Ranges

Rifles were generally sighted up to as much as 2,560m (2,800yds) but most armies did not expect individual aimed fire to hit a specific target above 550m (600yds), a distance known as close range. Beyond this lay further zones as defined by the British Army – effective range at 600–1,400 yards (550–1,280m), long range at 1,400–2,000 yards (1,280–1,830m) and distant range at 2,000–2,800 yards (1,830–2,560m). Massed rather than individual targets could be hit at a rifle's effective range but it was not really worthwhile engaging anything at long or distant ranges.

Bayonets

There were three main types of bayonet. The most common were the ones shaped like the blade of a knife, while others were thinner needle types that were prone to snapping, and the comparatively rare knife bayonets with a serrated blade that were mostly used by the Germans. Allied propaganda claimed the serrated edge was deliberately designed to inflict even more horrendous wounds but it was actually for certain pioneering tasks.

Pre-war training manuals stressed the importance of the bayonet charge and most soldiers were inculcated with what the British termed the "spirit of the bayonet". The reality was somewhat different. Charges were extremely rare after 1914 and comparatively few people were killed or wounded by a bayonet thereafter. Bayonets were, of course, still used in trench fighting but an individual soldier faced with one was more likely to flee or surrender than fight it out. Detailed information on the precise number of bayonet wounds inflicted during the war is unavailable but it was undoubtedly extremely low compared with the big killer – artillery. British medical staff included bayonet wounds in their miscellaneous injuries category, which accounted for little more than one per cent of all casualties recorded by the British Army in the war.

GERMAN RIFLES

German infantry had two main types of rifle: the Mauser Gewehr 88 and the Mauser Gewehr 98 – first made in 1888 and 1898. The Gewehr 98 was exceedingly accurate and continued in German use until World War II.

Calibre: 7.92mm (0.312in) (Mauser Gewehr 98)
Magazine: 5 rounds
System: front-locking turn-bolt
Length: 125cm (49.25in)
Weight: 4.3kg (9.5lb)
Muzzle velocity: 870m/sec (2,854ft/sec)

SNIPING

Sniping was a valuable tool throughout the war, more so than in any previous conflict, and became especially important when static trench warfare developed. Snipers often worked as part of a two-man team with the other man being a target spotter equipped with binoculars or, more commonly, a trench periscope that protected him from enemy snipers. Snipers operated from camouflaged hides or behind metal plates with a rifle-sized slit cut into them to avoid being targeted themselves.

Right: A posed photograph of a German sniper, who would normally take up a much less exposed position.

The Race to the Sea

From late September to the end of October, the Anglo-French and German armies moved northward, attempting to swing around each other's exposed flank, but all of these attacks failed and the North Sea ultimately prevented further manoeuvres.

Failure at the Marne in early September led Moltke to order a general German withdrawal north towards the River Aisne, a decision that signalled the collapse of the Schlieffen Plan. This failure doomed Germany to what it had always wanted to avoid – a prolonged war on two fronts – and led to Moltke being replaced as Chief of Staff by General Erich von Falkenhayn on the 14th. After his victory to the east of Paris, Marshal Joffre, Moltke's opposite number, had high hopes of finishing off the German forces and ordered the Anglo-French armies to set off in pursuit. His aim was to swing round the exposed German right flank but the Germans prevented this manoeuvre at the First Battle of the Aisne (15–18 September).

This fighting along the Aisne sparked off a series of attempted flanking movements that became known as the Race to the Sea. Both sides sent forces north towards the North Sea coast with the Allies trying to turn the German right flank and the latter trying to swing around the Anglo-French left. There was fierce fighting in the Picardy region during 22–26 September and then in Artois 27 September – 10 October. Thereafter, the main focus moved farther north still into Flanders where the two sides fought a number of battles but for no tangible strategic reward.

Above: French troops on the march as the fighting moved northward through France during late 1914.

Antwerp Besieged

While the Race to the Sea proceeded, Belgium was fighting for survival. After the fall of Brussels on 20 August, most of the Belgian Army fell back on Antwerp, from where it made two sorties against the German right flank between late August and mid-September. To stymie

Below: A Belgian machine-gun detachment on the move.

Below: German troops in the last phase of open warfare in 1914.

any more threats to their lines of communication, the Germans brought up their heavy howitzers and placed Antwerp under siege on the 28th.

Antwerp's garrison, bolstered by the arrival of a British Naval Division, stood behind strong defences but the port met the same fate as Liège and Namur. The Belgian authorities surrendered on 10 October, though not before most of the garrison had retreated west along the Flanders coast, determined to maintain a toehold on Belgian soil. These Anglo-Belgian troops took up positions along the Yser Canal between Nieuport and Boesinghe. To their south lay the Anglo-French forces that had been involved in the Race to the Sea.

Last German Attacks

Although the lines were solidifying, the Germans made two more attempts to achieve victory. The first, the Battle of the Yser, was fought during 16–31 October but failed after the Belgians took the bold decision to open the sluice gates to the irrigation system that prevented flooding in this low-lying region. By the end of the month a large area stretching southward from Nieuport to Dixmude had been inundated. It was so clearly impassable that the flooded area saw no appreciable action until 1918. The Germans now turned their attention to the south of Dixmude and made their last effort to cut through the Allied lines in 1914 at Ypres.

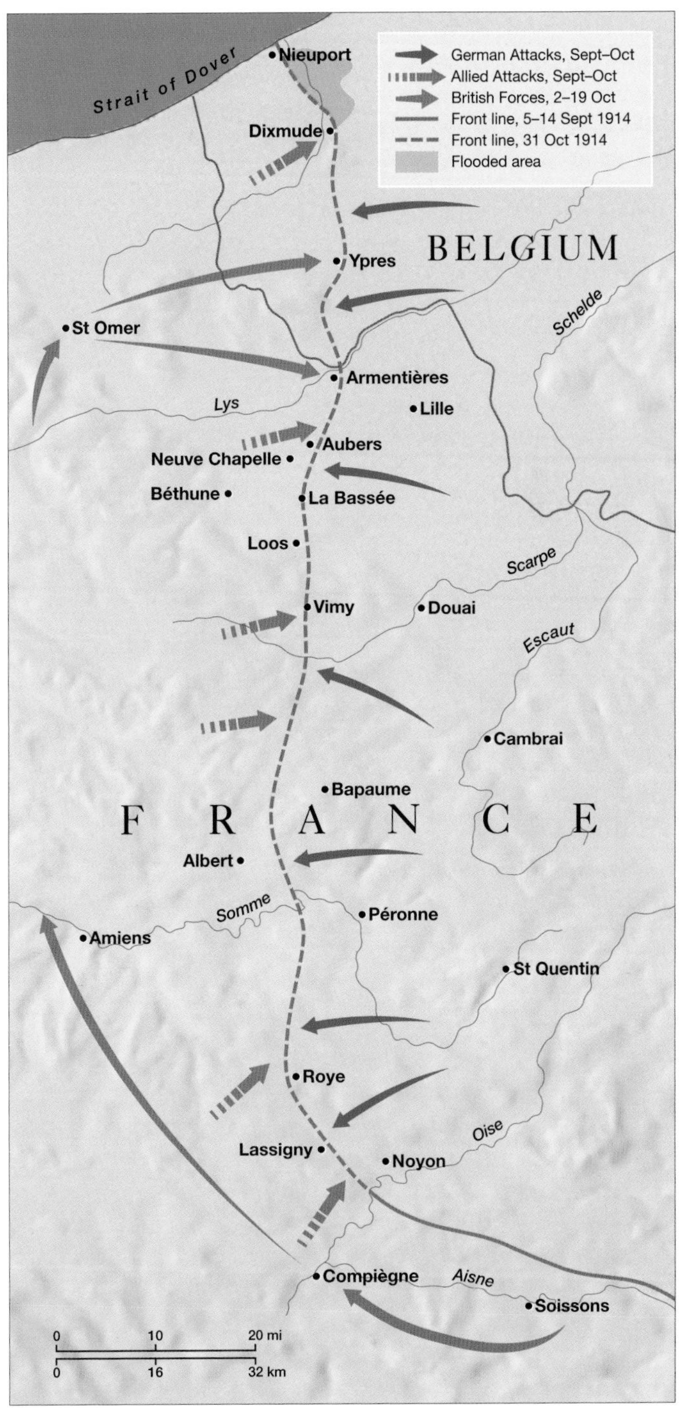

THE RACE TO THE SEA
The succession of outflanking moves in the Race to the Sea.

The First Battle of Ypres

This was the last major offensive by the Germans on the Western Front in 1914. Their attempt to break through to the Channel ports narrowly failed, although the British Expeditionary Force paid a very high price for its narrow victory.

After the Battle of the Aisne had ended in late September, the BEF under Field Marshal French had been switched to the extreme left of the Anglo-French line for the subsequent Race to the Sea. Its chief mission was to protect Boulogne, Calais and Dunkirk, Channel ports vital to the arrival of British reinforcements and supplies, by pushing into Flanders and, if possible, linking up with elements of the Belgian Army. As the Race to the Sea reached its climax in late autumn, part of the now enlarged BEF fought two battles in north-east France at La Bassée and Armentières during mid-October and early November. Some units also pushed into southern Belgium, tipping the Germans out of Ypres on 13 October after a ten-day occupation. It was in this medieval Flemish town that the BEF faced the last major German attack of 1914.

KEY FACTS

DATE: 19 October – 22 November 1914

PLACE: South-west Belgium

OUTCOME: A narrow British victory bought at a high cost that led to the outbreak of static trench warfare.

THE WESTERN FRONT, 1914

The front lines after the war of movement ended in late 1914.

German Aims

The German Chief of Staff, General von Falkenhayn, was fully aware of the importance of the Channel ports to Britain. He had so far failed to take them, and time was running out, but a successful push on Ypres would likely lead to their capture and make Britain's further participation in the war doubtful. The German attacks were led by Duke Albrecht of Württemberg's Fourth Army from the 15th. British rifle fire again cut down the attackers in droves but the British also suffered heavy casualties and units to the north and south of the town were pushed back, forming a salient around the town itself.

The offensive was renewed at the end of the month with the strongest attacks being in the east and south-east. Fourth Army troops took Gheluvelt and crossed the Menin Road on the 31st, although the former was recaptured soon after. Messines Ridge, a key piece of high ground, and the outlying village of Wytschaete were overrun by 1 November, thereby making the salient even smaller. The fall of Ypres seemed imminent, so much so that Emperor Wilhelm II arrived to watch its capture, but the British held on, in part thanks to the arrival of many French reinforcements.

The Germans made two more major efforts to take the town. Matters became so critical that the Allies contemplated abandoning Ypres altogether on the 9th. The plan was rejected but the German pressure intensified, leading to the capture of St Eloi the next day and a ferocious but unsuccessful

Above: German troops man an unusually tidy trench in Belgium after the First Battle of Ypres.

battle to take Gheluvelt for the second time. The last German effort came on the 15th but the battle effectively ended a week later due to mutual exhaustion and increasingly bad weather.

The Casualty Toll

The Allies suffered a total of 75,000 casualties during the First Battle of Ypres – the BEF had been decimated and would need to be entirely rebuilt – while the Germans suffered losses totalling some 135,000 men. The war was a mere five months or so old and the total manpower losses were truly staggering. Belgium recorded around 50,000 men killed, wounded or missing, France 995,000, Germany 677,000 and Britain 75,000.

The French continued to attack as the year ended, launching the First Battle of Champagne on 20 December.

The combatant nations each still believed that a decisive victory was possible but everyone knew that the war would not be over by Christmas, as had originally been hoped. The prospect of further carnage did nothing to raise the spirits of the British and German troops even though some, to the disgust of their generals, crawled out of their newly dug trenches to fraternize on Christmas Day.

THE BRITISH EXPEDITIONARY FORCE

The BEF of 1914 was tiny by European standards, a mere five divisions, but was unusual in being an all-volunteer force with numerous combat-experienced soldiers. It was also well-trained and highly motivated with the men being excellent marksmen. The BEF fought well in the first months of the war but was decimated. Thereafter, it underwent a huge expansion, first through volunteers and then through conscription. By November 1918 it contained some 61 divisions (including units from Canada, Australia, New Zealand and other parts of the British Empire).

Above: British troops prepare to move out.

Right: French troops captured outside the Belgian town of Ypres.

The Invasions of Serbia, 1914–15

Austria-Hungary planned to punish Serbia for its part in the assassination of Archduke Franz Ferdinand but its troops were repulsed and it eventually took a combined attack with both German and Bulgarian support to subdue the country.

Austria-Hungary held Serbia directly responsible for the assassination of Archduke Franz Ferdinand and issued a war declaration on 28 July. Belgrade, the Serbian capital, came under fire from Austro-Hungarian gunboats on the River Danube the next day but troops were not committed until 14 August, when more than 200,000 men under Field Marshal Oskar Potiorek crossed the Sava and Drina Rivers to the north and west of Belgrade. This move began the Battle of the Jadar River. The Austro-Hungarians were caught out when 190,000 Serbian troops led by Marshal Radomir Putnik counter-attacked on the 16th. Although the Serbs were outnumbered and fairly ill-equipped, they forced Potiorek's army back by the 21st.

After a brief interlude, the Serbians pushed into Bosnia, Austro-Hungarian territory, on 6 September but Putnik in turn was forced to withdraw when Potiorek recrossed the Drina to establish footholds on the Serbian side over the following 48 hours. The Serbians threw themselves against the Austro-Hungarian positions but after ten days of bitter fighting they were forced to concede defeat in the Battle of the River Drina. They began falling back to more defensible positions south-west of Belgrade on the 17th.

Above: Field Marshal Oskar Potiorek was sacked for mismanaging Austria-Hungary's invasion of Serbia in 1914.

Austrians Defeated

Now reinforced, the Austro-Hungarians opened another offensive on 5 November and Putnik's troops, who were short of ammunition, were forced to withdraw slowly in the hope of counter-attacking later when the Austro-Hungarians had themselves outrun their supply lines. Belgrade was occupied by the invaders on 2 December but by then Putnik had been

AUSTRO-HUNGARIAN ATROCITIES

Austria-Hungary passed the War Service Law in 1912 and it allowed for the rights of a citizen to be forfeited to the army during a national emergency. The law was first applied to Bosnia and Herzegovina on 25 July 1914 and then Serbia, where all Serbians, whether they were actually pro-Bosnia nationalists or not, became suspect. Austro-Hungarian troops systematically took hostages, burned houses and killed an estimated 4,000 civilians during their invasion of Serbia in 1914. Similar events also took place in Galicia.

Above: Austro-Hungarian troops execute Serbian civilians.

resupplied with ammunition from France and was ready to strike back. The Austro-Hungarians had the flooded River Kolubara to their rear so that when the Serbian forces pushed forward on the 3rd they were trapped. When the Battle of the Kolubara River ended on the 9th, all of the surviving Austro-Hungarian forces were back across the Danube and Sava Rivers. Belgrade was liberated on the 15th and Potiorek, who had lost some 227,000 men, was sacked and replaced by Archduke Eugene.

Above: Exhausted Serbian troops snatch some much-needed rest during their epic retreat through Serbia and Montenegro during 1915–16.

Serbia Finally Beaten

The odds against Serbia surviving a further invasion grew remote in late 1915. Germany needed the railway that ran through Serbia to send aid to Turkey after the only other viable route, through Romania, was closed by the Romanians in June. Bulgaria, Serbia's long-standing rival to the east, joined the Central Powers' cause on 6 September 1915. The German Chief of Staff, General von Falkenhayn, immediately began planning a joint attack on Serbia and command of the invasion was given to an experienced German field marshal, August von Mackensen.

Below: Serbian troops like these lacked much modern equipment but they were hardy fighters and more than a match for the Austro-Hungarian invaders.

On 6 October the Austro-Hungarian Third Army under Field Marshal Hermann Kövess von Kövesshàza and General Max von Gallwitz's German Eleventh Army crossed the Sava and Danube Rivers into Serbian territory. Five days later a pair of Bulgarian armies commanded by General Nikola Zhekov attacked westward into Serbia, making for Nish (Niš) and Uskub (Skopje). Putnik was forced to make an arduous retreat into Montenegro in the depths of winter with his forces suffering some 500,000 casualties. The survivors were all transported to Corfu in Allied warships during January 1916 and would later continue the war from Allied-occupied Salonika. Serbia, Montenegro and much of neighbouring Albania were occupied by the Central Powers until 1918.

Russia's Invasion of East Prussia

The speed of Russia's mobilization caught the German garrison in East Prussia by surprise and the Russian drive over the border caused something akin to panic in the mind of the general ordered to defend Germany's vulnerable province.

The oft-modified Schlieffen Plan was developed to prevent Germany from having to fight a war on two fronts – against France in the west and Russia in the east. It was based on many erroneous assumptions, including the belief that Russia's mobilization would be so slow that most of Germany's forces could be safely deployed against France with only a small force needed in the east. The final version of the plan, which was devised in 1914, did recognize that Russia would be able to go to war faster than had been believed. It therefore allowed for the deployment of more German forces in the east, up from 10 to 15 per cent of the manpower available.

Below: The Battle of Stallupönen, the first clash between German and Russian troops during the war. The Russians repulsed a small attack.

KEY FACTS

Date: 15 – 23 August 1914

Place: German province of East Prussia

Outcome: A tentative Russian push into the province led to a panicked response by the local German commander.

Russian Plans

Despite this reappraisal, the speed with which Russian forces massed against both German East Prussia and along the Austro-Hungarian Empire's Galician border in the first half of August 1914 still came as a shock to both of the Central Powers' high commands. Tsar Nicholas II actually signed the mobilization orders on 30 July; the process itself began on 4 August and the various Russian armies were largely in position by the 15th.

Russia's war-fighting strategy in East Prussia was to attack as quickly as possible to prevent Germany from defeating France and then turning its military might eastward. Two armies were immediately deployed to invade the province. East Prussia jutted into Russian territory but there were actually just two viable invasion routes. To the north and south-west strong fortifications lay around Königsberg (Kaliningrad) and Thorn (Toruń) that could not be bypassed and would take considerable time to overcome. In the centre any invader was confronted by the virtually impassable Masurian Lakes, which the Germans had made even more impenetrable by building yet more fortifications. The Russians therefore had

Above: German troops man a trench somewhere inside East Prussia's eastern border with Russia.

little option but to attack East Prussia simultaneously from the east and south-east. However, the armies would be operating in effect in isolation and, because of the distance between them, would find it difficult to coordinate their actions.

The 150,000-strong Russian First Army under General Paul von Rennenkampf took up positions in the east, while far to the south-east General Alexander Samsonov deployed his larger Second Army below the Masurian Lakes. In total the two generals mustered some 29 divisions and were opposed by just 13 divisions of General Maximilian von Prittwitz's German Eighth Army. Rennenkampf moved first with the intention of drawing Prittwitz towards him so that Samsonov, who was to begin moving two days later, could come up behind the Germans and trap them in a pincer movement. The plan appeared sound but both Rennenkampf and Samsonov were far from optimistic as their forces were under-equipped and relied on a poorly organized supply system.

Early Russian Success

Nevertheless, morale among the First Army was raised shortly after it entered East Prussia when a German raid was beaten off at Stallupönen on the 17th and then a much larger attack at Gumbinnen was defeated three days later. Prittwitz panicked and ordered an unauthorized retreat to the River Vistula, a move that meant abandoning most of the province. His superiors soon countermanded his decision and replaced him with Generals Paul von Hindenburg and Erich Ludendorff on the 23rd. They resolved to strike against first one and then the other of the opposing Russian armies.

Left: Colonel, later General Maximilian Hoffmann, a senior staff officer of the German Eighth Army in East Prussia.

RUSSIAN MOBILIZATION

Germany's war strategy, the Schlieffen Plan, was in part formulated in the belief that Russia's mobilization would be ponderous but this view became less and less tenable in the years before 1914. General Vladimir Sukhomlinov, the Russian Minister for War from 1909, undertook a root-and-branch reform of the country's war machine. He secured greater military spending and began to expand the rail network on which mobilization relied. The expansion was to have been completed by 1916 and this so alarmed the Germans that they were even more willing to contemplate war in 1914.

Above: Russian troops gather around Tsar Nicholas II as they prepare to march off to war.

Cavalry

Most armies had significant numbers of cavalry at the outbreak of the war and, although they were relegated to a secondary role on the Western Front for much of the conflict, they performed well elsewhere, especially in Palestine.

Cavalry units were found in every army, and sometimes in considerable numbers, at the outbreak of World War I. Russia had a staggering 29 divisions, Germany 11, France 10 and Britain just 1, yet they had become virtually irrelevant in most if not all theatres by 1918. At the outset many generals expected that horsemen would play their traditional roles: opposing other cavalry, conducting reconnaissance missions and pursuing a defeated and disorganized enemy. Most cavalrymen continued to carry swords and, to a lesser extent, lances but the vast majority had also been trained to fight on foot with modern firearms.

The Western Front

Cavalry on the Western Front were largely bystanders once trench warfare had begun in late

Above: A German cavalryman – if not his mount – is prepared to deal with a gas attack later in the war.

1914. There were cavalry clashes initially – the British 9th Lancers charged the German 1st Guard Dragoons at Moncel on 6 September, for example, but the omens were not good. Some 70 German cavalrymen charged a dismounted squadron of the 18th Hussars at Faujus a few days later and were hit by a hail of rifle fire. Virtually every attacker was killed or wounded. For the next three years or so the cavalry stood behind the lines waiting to exploit breakthroughs that never came. Mud, machine-guns and barbed wire had effectively denied them use of their greatest asset – mobility.

A measure of open warfare broke out in 1918 but by then cavalry numbers had been greatly reduced. Many units had been disbanded and their men transferred to other duties. The remaining cavalry did occasionally mount up to move to the scene of the action but invariably fought on foot. There were

Below: A column of Indian cavalry on the Western Front in late 1914. Indian mounted units later served with distinction in Palestine.

even British plans to use cavalry in conjunction with Whippet light tanks, but the marriage was an unhappy one. Whippets could not keep up with the cavalry and the cavalry were far too vulnerable to enemy machine-gun fire to press ahead of the bullet-proof tanks.

Above: Belgian lancers move out to protect their homeland from German invasion in August 1914.

Other Theatres

Cavalry units were used more frequently and for longer elsewhere during the conflict. Austria-Hungary, Germany and Russia all deployed them on the Eastern Front largely because warfare there was often more open because of the huge distances involved. It was impossible to build or man trenches that would have had to stretch from the Baltic Sea to the Romanian border. Thus, there was a greater degree of mobility than on the Western Front.

It was in Palestine that cavalry saw the greatest action. The British Empire forces deployed a number of mounted units, particularly ones raised in Australia and New Zealand, and these usually rode into action but fought on foot as the 2nd and 3rd Australian Light Horse did at the Battle of Beersheba in late 1917. Yet, on the same day, two other units, the 4th and 12th Australian Light Horse, actually charged a double line of Turkish trenches some 2,750m (3,000yds) to their front. The Australians had not been issued with swords so instead galloped forward with bayonets drawn and the sight so unnerved the Turkish defenders that most took flight.

By 1918 the Allies had a full corps of cavalry in Palestine with units from Australia, New Zealand, Britain itself, India and France. Britain's Arab allies were almost entirely mounted on horses and camels during their campaign against Turkey in Arabia and into Palestine.

Below: A detachment of Bulgarian cavalry moves through a town somewhere in the Balkans.

The Battle of Tannenberg

The German victory at Tannenberg in late August 1914 relied on the swift movement of troops by rail across East Prussia so that one of two strong but mutually isolated Russian armies could be overwhelmed.

The Russian invasion of East Prussia in August 1914 began to go wrong shortly after General Rennenkampf's First Army's minor victory at Gumbinnen on the 20th. Rennenkampf was meant to continue menacing the German Eighth Army to his front, while the Second Army under General Samsonov advanced from the south-east. Rennenkampf's slowness was noted by the German Eighth Army's chief of operations, General Max Hoffmann, who came up with a bold plan to defeat first one and then the other of the invading armies. His outline was adopted by the new commander of the Eighth Army, General von Hindenburg, and his deputy, General Ludendorff, when they arrived at the front during the 23rd.

Below: German troops advance through a burning town during the Battle of Tannenberg.

KEY FACTS

Date: 26 – 30 August 1914

Place: South-east East Prussia

Outcome: The Germans achieved an overwhelming victory that smashed the Russian Second Army in just a few days.

German Advances

A screen of cavalry was left facing the virtually immobile Rennenkampf, while one of the Eighth Army's four corps was rushed to the south-east by train to take up positions on Samsonov's exposed left flank. Two other German corps marched south from Gumbinnen to take up positions on the Second Army's other flank, while a fourth corps remained where it was near the village of Tannenberg, which now stood directly in Samsonov's path. Samsonov's troops began to push beyond Tannenberg from the 22nd and made some forward progress over the next six days, yet they were becoming over-extended and increasingly short of all kinds of supplies.

Above: A Russian child soldier pictured with his comrades somewhere in East Prussia, 1914.

The German attacks on the Second Army's exposed flanks began developing during the 26th and 27th. It took no more than three days virtually to destroy Samsonov's isolated command – more than half of his 230,000-strong force was either killed, wounded or captured. The defeated general disappeared into a forest and committed suicide on the last day of the month. Hindenburg's

FIELD MARSHAL PAUL VON HINDENBURG

Hindenburg (1847–1934), who had retired in 1911 but returned to service three years later, was the archetypal senior Prussian officer, being both aristocratic and commanding. He had an air of calm authority, some said it was actually vacuity, and was something of a self-publicist. Much of the credit for his efforts should have gone to others, not least General Erich Ludendorff, with whom he effectively ran Germany's war effort from late August 1916. Hindenburg again retired in June 1919 but was President of Germany 1925–34.

Above: Field Marshal Hindenburg adopts a suitably martial pose.

losses totalled no more than 20,000 men and Tannenberg was portrayed as a great victory in Germany, one that made both Hindenburg and Ludendorff into household names. The battle was also seen as a disaster by both Britain and France, but the truth was that the Russian Army could still call on vast reserves of manpower.

NEW ATTACKS

The Germans had fought an essentially defensive battle to overwhelm Samsonov and they now launched an offensive operation to crush Rennenkampf and remove the final threat to East Prussia. To do this, large numbers of troops were transferred from the Western Front at a critical point in early September, a strategic decision that undermined the Schlieffen Plan. The First Battle of the Masurian Lakes opened on the 7th and troops from the German Eighth Army were launched against Rennenkampf's right flank as he belatedly began to push deeper into East Prussia. The attack scythed through the Russian lines south of the lakes but Rennenkampf was just able to retreat before the trap closed.

The battle left Hindenburg a little way inside Russia by the 13th but his army was by now exhausted and suffering from acute supply shortages, while Rennenkampf was safely back across the River Nieman and being reinforced by the Russian Tenth Army. These forces launched a counter-attack, the Battle of the Nieman, on the 25th and after three days of heavy fighting Hindenburg finally called off his advance. Russian casualties reached 125,000, but Germany, too, had suffered, with around 100,000 killed, wounded or missing in East Prussia since August. Yet, for all the bloodshed, the strategic situation along the northern sector of the Eastern Front was largely unchanged.

Below: German troops man a well-camouflaged position in the vicinity of the Masurian Lakes.

Operations in Poland and Galicia

Austria-Hungary launched a largely unsuccessful attack on the Russians at the outbreak of the war and the empire had to call on its German ally for military aid to prevent a near collapse on the Eastern Front.

At the outbreak of war the Austro-Hungarian Chief of Staff, Field Marshal Franz Conrad von Hötzendorf, concentrated three armies in Galicia for a major offensive into the south of Russian Poland, an area that was defended by General Nikolai Ivanov's Southwestern Army Group. Conrad began to advance on a 320km (200 mile) front on 23 August. In the north General Victor Dankl's First Army defeated the Russian Fourth Army at the Battle of Kraśnik during the first two days and General Wenzel von Plehve's Russian Fifth Army was driven back by Field Marshal Moritz Auffenberg's Fourth Army at the Battle of Zamosc-Komarów (26 August – 1 September).

Russian Victories

Matters were very different in the south. Two Russian armies took on the Austro-Hungarian Third Army, which had been slightly reinforced by some units from the Second Army freed from service in Serbia. The Third Army was forced to withdraw towards the fortress of Lemberg (Lvov) after the Battle of Gnila Lipa (26–30 August) and was decisively beaten at the Battle of Rava Russkaya (3–11 September). Lemberg fell and the Austro-Hungarian forces retreated some 160km (100 miles) to the Carpathian Mountains. As more and more Russian troops began arriving in the north, the two Austro-Hungarian armies there also retreated so that the greater part of Galicia was lost by early October. Only the fortress of Przemyśl held out.

The Germans now intervened, largely to prevent a Russian thrust through Russian Poland into Silesia, one of

Above: Although probably posed, this image shows the type of siege lines that the Russians threw around the fortress of Przemyśl during the fighting in Galicia.

Below: The remains of one of Przemyśl's forts after Russian shelling. The town fell in March 1915 but was later recaptured.

Germany's great mineral-producing and industrial areas. The Ninth Army under General Paul von Hindenburg was assembled by rail at great speed around Cracow (Kraków) by late September. Hindenburg launched a spoiling attack into south-west Poland on the 28th but was checked around Ivangorod (Dęblin) by more powerful Russian forces on 12 October. He withdrew but his efforts had inflicted a major delay on Russia's preparations to invade Silesia and Hindenburg's reward came on 1 November. He was promoted to field marshal and made commander-in-chief on the Eastern Front with General Ludendorff named as his deputy.

FIELD MARSHAL FRANZ CONRAD VON HÖTZENDORF

Conrad (1852–1925) was the Austro-Hungarian Army's Chief of Staff from 1906 and had a justified reputation as an arch-militarist, urging attacks on his country's neighbours. When war came in 1914 his plans were bold and optimistic but were far beyond the capabilities of the forces he led. Conrad was increasingly marginalized, especially after the disastrous Trentino Offensive in Italy during 1916, and was sacked in March 1917. He then served in Italy but was dismissed from his post on 15 July 1918.

Above: Conrad had grandiose plans but lacked forces of the quality needed to execute them.

There were no reinforcements available for a follow-up offensive but Ludendorff devised a bold plan that relied on speed of manoeuvre. The Ninth Army, soon to be commanded by General August von Mackensen, was spirited away in a week, again by rail, to the comparatively lightly defended north-west border with Poland. Mackensen struck south-east towards Lódz on 11 November. He drove between General Rennenkampf's First Army and General Schiedmann's Second. Rennenkampf was soon reeling after an attack on his over-extended left wing but an attempted envelopment of the Second Army was checked by the arrival of Plehve's Fifth Army. The battle ended in stalemate on 25 November.

Below: The ruins of a town somewhere in Galicia give a good indication of the fighting's ferocity.

GERMANY IN CONTROL

Lódz can be considered a narrow Russian victory but it was Germany that reaped the strategic rewards. The Russian Commander-in-Chief, Grand Duke Nicholas, called off the invasion of Silesia, not least because he had lost close to 1.8 million men in 1914 and was very short of all manner of war supplies by the year's end. Russia never again threatened an invasion of Germany. The Germans had lost around 275,000 men and their high command was now fully aware that Austria-Hungary, which had suffered close to 1 million casualties, was incapable of independent action. Henceforth, German forces would have to take the lead on the Eastern Front.

Operations in China and the Pacific

Germany's far-flung colonies in the Pacific and Far East were far too isolated and vulnerable to stand alone and they were all captured by various Allied expeditions in the first few months of the conflict.

Germany was never in the same league as either Britain or France when it came to the acquisition of overseas colonies. By 1914 it controlled a handful in Africa, a number of Pacific islands that were used as coaling and radio stations, and part of New Guinea. Its most important possession was Tsingtao (Qingdao), a port on China's Shantung (Shandong) Peninsula. This was acquired during 1898 in compensation for the murder of Lutheran missionaries and was home to the most powerful German naval force outside Europe in 1914. The port had a 4,000-strong garrison but the key element was the East Asiatic Squadron, a flotilla of two armoured cruisers and five light cruisers. Its orders were to attack British shipping and underwater communications cables when war was declared.

Above: Senior Japanese officers and their lone British counterpart stand among the Tsingtao siege lines with a piece of heavy artillery in the background.

Tsingtao Besieged

Yet Germany's Pacific possessions were actually in a hopeless position. They were too far from home to expect any aid and they faced a considerable number of enemies. Britain had a sizeable number of warships stationed at bases such as Hong Kong, while in the south-west Pacific Australia and New Zealand had both declared war. France had bases in Indochina and an even more significant threat came from Britain's ally Japan, a country with ambitions to create a Pacific empire of its own. Recognizing that Germany was unable to defend Tsingtao in any meaningful way, the Japanese government demanded that the port be evacuated on 15 August. Germany refused and Japan declared war eight days later.

By late August a largely Japanese fleet had blockaded Tsingtao and on 2 September the first troops landed on the peninsula to begin the siege

Left: The oil depot at Tsingtao, Germany's only toehold on the Chinese mainland, goes up in flames during the British and Japanese siege that ended with the port's capture on 7 November 1914.

Right: Japanese troops, some of the 24,000 men involved in the siege of Tsingtao, are put ashore on 2 September 1914.

operations. It was an unequal fight as the garrison faced some 23,000 Japanese troops and a smaller 1,300-strong British expeditionary force. The defences took a pounding from Allied warships and artillery, though progress was slow due to bad weather and fierce resistance, but the attackers had reached the garrison's last line of defence by early November. The port finally surrendered on the 7th.

Germany's other Pacific possessions – the Carolines, Marianas, Marshalls, Palaus and Samoa, as well as part of the Solomon Islands and New Guinea – soon fell to the Allies. Australian and New Zealand forces occupied Samoa without firing a shot; British troops faced minimal resistance in the Solomons; while the Japanese finally took the Marshalls in November. Germany had lost virtually all of its Pacific colonies by December 1914 and, after early successes, the East Asiatic Squadron had also been largely destroyed at the Battle of the Falklands.

CHINA AT WAR

China actually declared war on Austria-Hungary and Germany on 14 August 1917 and even offered 300,000 troops for overseas service but the country was so riven by political factionalism that such an effort was beyond its means. It therefore had little direct impact on the Allied combat effort beyond sending a military mission to Europe. China's greatest contribution was the 230,000-plus skilled and unskilled labourers who worked behind the lines in France and elsewhere to keep the machinery of war supply rolling.

Left: Some of the thousands of Chinese who toiled on the Western Front for the Allies are seen here building a light railway.

EMDEN IN ACTION

One of its light cruisers, *Emden*, had separated from the squadron on 8 September and embarked on a brief but spectacular commerce-raiding cruise in the Indian Ocean that saw it sink some 70,000 tons of shipping. It also bombarded oil facilities at Madras on the 22nd and went on to sink an old Russian cruiser, *Zhemchug*, and a French destroyer, *Mousquet*, on 28 October. However, time was running out for *Emden*. Some 14 Allied warships had been detached to hunt it down and its supply ships were being sunk one by one. The end came on 9 November, when it was tracked down by the more powerful Australian cruiser *Sydney*. In a brief battle at Direction Island, part of the Cocos and Keeling group in the southern Indian Ocean, *Emden* was destroyed by long-range gunfire in the first battle ever fought by an Australian warship. Most of the crew were captured but 50 who were ashore when the battle started later made their way back home.

Surface Raiders

The Imperial German Navy intended to launch a variety of surface ships against Britain's maritime trade routes which stretched across the globe but most of the raiders were sunk, lost or interned during the first months of the war.

Crippling an opponent by destroying his maritime trade and merchant fleet was a well-established naval strategy by 1914. As submarines were still an unknown quantity and as those available did not have the range to operate globally, many navies earmarked other vessels to undertake such duties. These were either purpose-built or converted civilian craft and the three main types were generally known as commerce raiders, armed merchant cruisers and auxiliary commerce raiders. They mostly operated far from home and relied on colonies, specially designated freighters or neutral ports for resupply.

Commerce Raiders

Germany had eight commerce raiders. Seven of these were with the East Asiatic Squadron in the Pacific and one, *Karlsruhe*, was in the West Indies. Four of the Pacific raiders were sunk at the Battle of the Falkland Islands in December 1914 while a fifth, *Dresden*, was scuttled in March 1915. The squadron's remaining pair had equally brief careers. *Emden* successfully cruised the south-west Pacific and Indian Ocean between August and early November 1914 but then succumbed to the Australian cruiser *Sydney*.

The squadron's final cruiser, *Königsberg*, headed into the western Indian Ocean intending to sink Allied ships using the Suez Canal. It sank just two ships before the British found its hiding place in the River Rufiji's delta in German East Africa (now in Tanzania). An old ship was scuttled across the river's mouth to prevent any escape and the raider was eventually damaged by fire from two British monitors and then scuttled on 11 July 1915.

The cruiser stationed in the West Indies, *Karlsruhe*, sank three vessels in the mid-Atlantic shortly after the outbreak of war and then sailed into the South Atlantic where it netted some 14 freighters between 31 August and 14 October 1914. *Karlsruhe* then headed into the Caribbean, with the intention of hunting through the Bahamas but succumbed to an unexplained internal explosion while at anchor on 4 November.

Type: Converted sailing ship
Laid down: 1888
Displacement: 1,571 tons
Crew: Not known
Speed: Variable
Main armament: 2 x 10.5cm (4.1in) guns

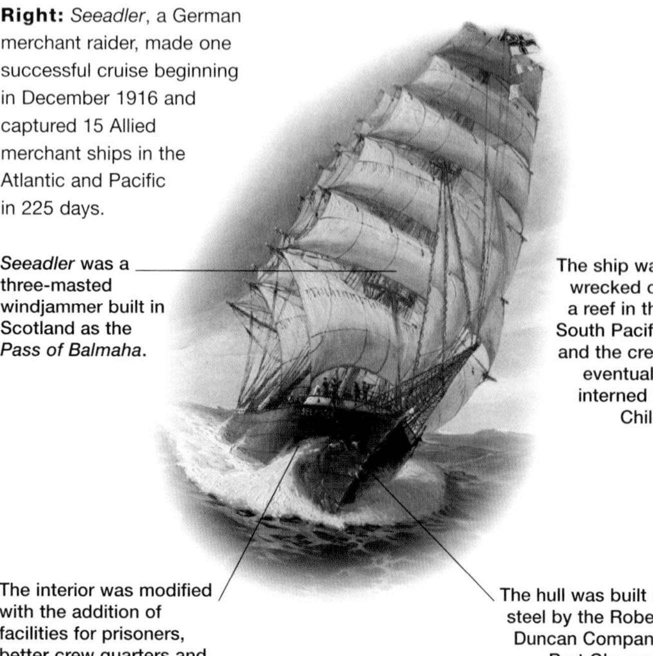

Seeadler was a three-masted windjammer built in Scotland as the *Pass of Balmaha*.
The ship was wrecked on a reef in the South Pacific and the crew eventually interned in Chile.
The interior was modified with the addition of facilities for prisoners, better crew quarters and hidden gun positions.
The hull was built in steel by the Robert Duncan Company, Port Glasgow.

Right: *Seeadler*, a German merchant raider, made one successful cruise beginning in December 1916 and captured 15 Allied merchant ships in the Atlantic and Pacific in 225 days.

Armed Merchant Cruisers

Armed merchant cruisers (AMCs) were usually fast passenger liners converted for military use by being fitted with armaments. They were used by Britain, France and Germany. The British had the greatest number and their 10th Cruiser Squadron consisted of 20 AMCs that protected the sea lanes between Britain and Iceland until 1917. The Allied AMCs proved to be vulnerable both to mines and torpedoes, and losses were unacceptably high – the British lost 12 and the French 13. The survivors were mostly converted to troop transports and hospital ships from 1916.

Germany used its AMCs exclusively in the aggressive role of commerce raiding but they were largely unsuccessful. Some had brief but spectacular careers, like the fast liner *Kaiser Wilhelm der Grosse*, which sank several ships before 26 August 1914 when it was scuttled by its crew after it had been disabled by the British cruiser *Highflyer* off Spanish Morocco. A second, *Cap Trafalgar*, was sunk by a British AMC, *Carmania*, in the South Atlantic on 14 August 1914. Two others, *Prinz Eitel Friedrich* and *Kronprinz Wilhelm*, were interned by the US authorities in March and April 1915, respectively.

Armed Commerce Raiders

Auxiliary commerce raiders were essentially civilian craft fitted with hidden weapons. Germany's were often auxiliary minelayers converted to look like Scandinavian freighters, usually sailing under a neutral flag. Around ten saw service in the war and some were highly successful.

Möwe is considered the most renowned. It sank 34 merchant ships in two sorties and one of its mines sank the British pre-dreadnought battleship *King Edward VII* in January 1916.

Below: HMS *King Edward VII* sinking after hitting *Möwe*'s mine.

SMS *EMDEN*

Emden's career was brief but spectacular. During August – November 1914 it sank 18 British merchant ships, captured 5 and sank a Russian cruiser and a French destroyer. *Emden* is shown below wrecked on Direction Island after being tracked down by Allied ships.

Type: Light cruiser
Laid down: 1908
Displacement: 3,650 tons
Crew: 321
Speed: 24.5 knots
Main armament: 10 x 10.5cm (4.1in) guns

SMS *KÖNIGSBERG*

Königsberg undertook operations off the coast of East Africa, sinking just two ships, including *Pegasus*, an old British cruiser. *Königsberg* took refuge in an East African river delta and was tracked down and sunk in 1915.

Type: Light cruiser
Laid down: 1907
Displacement: 3,400 tons
Crew: 350
Speed: 23.5 knots
Main armament: 10 x 10.5cm (4.1in) guns

Germany's African Colonies

Germany's four colonies in Africa were only lightly defended, could expect little outside help and were largely surrounded by colonies belonging to various of the Allies so it was unsurprising that they mostly soon fell.

Germany's appetite for building a colonial empire came rather late in the 19th century and at a time when the other leading European powers, especially Britain and France, had carved up most of the world between themselves. Thus, by the outbreak of World War I, Germany controlled only a number of island groups in the south-west Pacific, the concession port of Tsingtao in China and, most importantly, four colonies in Africa – Togoland (Togo) and Kamerun in West Africa, German South-West Africa (Namibia) and German East Africa (Burundi, Rwanda and mainland Tanganyika). The African colonies had been acquired in 1884–5 but by 1914 were only lightly garrisoned, despite having some useful port facilities and important radio stations that were capable of intercepting Allied messages and relaying them to Berlin.

Above: A South African train takes on water while carrying troops into German South-West Africa in 1915.

Below: Colonial troops like these spearheaded Britain's war effort against Togoland and Kamerun.

Allied Superiority

The German colonies were largely isolated from their motherland and were ripe for invasion, not least because they were invariably adjacent to Allied colonies that could muster greater forces. The first to come under attack were Togoland, South-West Africa and Kamerun. Togoland was largely surrounded by French-controlled Dahomey (Benin) as well as the Gold Coast (Ghana), a British possession. Togoland was defended by some 300 European troops and 1,200 locally raised *askaris* (native troops) and was the first to fall. The local general abandoned the vulnerable coast and fell back inland to the radio station at Kamina. An attack by Anglo-French troops was beaten off on 22 August 1914 but the station was destroyed on the approach of a large Allied force and the surviving German garrison surrendered four days later.

German South-West Africa was in an equally exposed position as the largely pro-British Union of South Africa lay to the south and the British Bechuanaland Protectorate (Botswana) was to the east. To the north was Angola, a colony of the then neutral but pro-British Portuguese. Although the ports of Swakopmund and Lüderitz with their radio stations were strategically important, they were soon abandoned and the colony's 9,000-strong garrison concentrated around the inland capital, Windhoek.

During 1914 there were Allied landings at Lüderitz on 19 September and Swakopmund on 25 December. South African troops were roundly beaten at Sandfontein on 26 September and it was not until

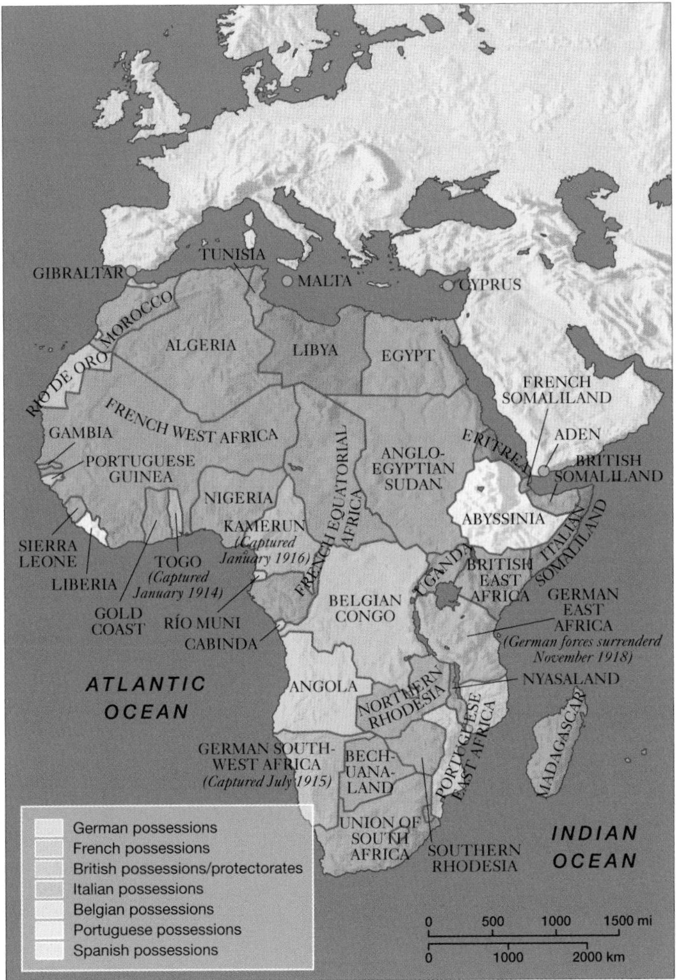

AFRICA IN 1914
The African colonies of the various belligerent powers in 1914.

1915 that the main assault began. The delay was partially due to a pro-German, anti-British revolt in South Africa by a small number of Boer nationalists that was only defeated in February 1915. One column under General Jan Christiaan Smuts pushed east out of Lüderitz and then turned north to inflict a defeat on the Germans at Gibeon on 26 April. The second column, under General Louis Botha, moved out from Swakopmund and took Windhoek on 17 May. The last detachments of the colony's garrison surrendered at Tsumeb on 9 July.

KAMERUN

Despite being surrounded by Allied colonies, the garrison in Kamerun survived the longest. The Allies advanced at several points in August 1914 and took the port of Duala with its radio station in late September. The German commander retreated into the interior and in 1915 three Allied columns were sent to track him down. Progress was slow for much of the year but the fall of the city of Yaoundé on 1 January 1916 signalled the end. Some 800 German troops and 7,000 *askaris* fled into Rio Muni, a Spanish enclave, and the northern town of Mora, the last pocket of resistance, capitulated to Allied forces on 18 February 1916.

Below: German troops are escorted into captivity after the fall of Togoland in August 1914.

Naval War in the North Sea

There were no major clashes between the bulk of the British and German fleets during 1914 but both sides were able to claim some notable propaganda victories from actions at sea in the first months of the naval war.

At the outbreak of war the Royal Navy's main force, the Grand Fleet, took station at various bases in south-east England, eastern Scotland and the Orkneys, while the rival German High Seas Fleet concentrated at Wilhelmshaven and Kiel. Despite public expectations, neither fleet was specially keen to risk a major battle. The British did not want to see their numerical advantage reduced by mines or torpedoes, while the Germans did not want to see the disparity grow. Nevertheless, both sides were willing to undertake sorties if they might yield results out of proportion to the forces deployed.

The first significant battle of the naval war took place on 28 August. British cruisers made a sweep into German home waters in an attempt to draw out some of the Imperial German Navy's warships and lead them towards the guns of Vice-Admiral David Beatty's powerful squadron of battle-cruisers. The Battle of Heligoland Bight did not entirely go to plan as the British light cruisers ran into a more powerful force than expected. Only the arrival of Beatty's battle-cruisers saved the day. Three German light cruisers, *Ariadne*, *Köln* and *Mainz*, and a destroyer were sunk, while the British *Arethusa* was also heavily damaged.

Above: A German U-boat on patrol in the North Sea with the crew keeping watch for Allied warships.

U-boats in Action

In fear of further losses, the freedom of action of Germany's surface warships was curtailed after the battle by Emperor Wilhelm II but his ruling did not apply to the small U-boat fleet. He had authorized submarines and torpedo boats to carry out limited offensive sweeps as early as 6 August but the submariners' performance

Below: The battle-cruiser HMS *New Zealand* fought in three battles – Heligoland Bight, Dogger Bank and Jutland – and survived the war.

Below: British sailors look on as the German light cruiser *Mainz* begins to settle in the water during the Battle of Heligoland Bight in late August 1914.

Above: The British destroyer *Lurcher* (left) approaches *Mainz* to take off survivors. *Mainz* sank just one hour after being put out of action by a torpedo hit.

was not at all good. Three days after receiving permission to commence operations, *U-15* was caught on the surface of the North Sea and rammed by a British warship, *Birmingham*. The U-boats also failed to sink any of the vessels transporting the British Expeditionary Force across the English Channel in the middle two weeks of the same month.

Their performance improved somewhat in September. HMS *Pathfinder*, a cruiser, became the first major warship to fall victim to a torpedo attack in open waters when it was sighted by *U-21* in the Firth of Forth on the 5th.

This victory was soon overshadowed by a much greater feat. British warships, mainly destroyers and cruisers, were patrolling the waters of the southern North Sea as part of the campaign to protect troop transports crossing the English Channel. The patrolling destroyers had to be withdrawn due to bad weather in late September but the cruisers remained on station.

Weddigen's Triumph

On the 22nd, three elderly cruisers, *Aboukir*, *Cressy* and *Hogue*, were spotted by Captain Otto Weddigen's *U-9* as they sailed slowly north along the coast of Holland. *Aboukir* was torpedoed first and sank within 30 minutes. The other cruisers' captains foolishly stood by to rescue survivors and each ship was torpedoed in turn. The loss of three obsolete warships did not significantly upset the naval balance in the North Sea but the sinkings and the death of some 1,400 sailors at the hands of a submarine shocked the British public. It also troubled the admirals of the Royal Navy and they immediately instigated much more stringent anti-submarine procedures.

U-9's success showed sceptics in the German Navy what U-boats were capable of, but there was still much to prove. The boats were not yet the great hunters of merchant ships that they would later become. By year's end 100 Allied or neutral freighters had been sunk but only four by U-boats. Five U-boats had been lost.

CAPTURING GERMANY'S NAVAL CODES

This was one of the most valuable gifts to fall into the hands of British intelligence during the war. The German cruiser *Magdeburg* ran aground in the Gulf of Finland on 26 August 1914. It was shelled by two Russian warships and boarded. The boarders seized codebooks and cipher tables and these reached the British by mid-October. *Magdeburg* was scuttled and the German Navy, believing the books and tables had gone down with it, made no alterations to their codes. They remained unaware of their loss until 1918.

Anti-submarine Barriers

Britain struggled to fight German U-boats in the early days of the war. Barriers of steel-net mesh were moored to the seabed in the hope of entangling the U-boats, while mines and fast warships were used to blow up the boats.

No ship-mounted weapons were capable of sinking submerged submarines when war broke out in August 1914. The British, who had the most to fear from submarines, soon began building maritime net barriers, commonly referred to as barrages. These either forced submarines to the surface, where they could be tackled by naval gunfire or rammed by warships, or left them at the mercy of tethered mines positioned with the nets. Perhaps the most successful barrages were those developed to prevent German U-boats from reaching their hunting grounds in the eastern Atlantic by way of the English Channel or through the North Sea. All U-boats had to pass through these areas on their journeys between their patrol areas and their home bases in occupied Belgium and in Germany itself.

Above: A mine of the type used in the Allied North Sea barrage built during 1918.

Blocking the Channel

The British first built a barrage between Dover and the Belgian coast to prevent attacks on their troopships crossing to France in August 1914. This initial effort was deemed inadequate and a 25km (15.5 mile) barrage stretching between Dover and Ostend was begun the following February. The line comprised indicator nets – lengths of steel mesh up to 100m (110yds) long that were positioned by drifters, set at various depths and moored to the seabed. Any U-boat that became entangled in one would either have to surface or drag the netting and its easily identifiable surface buoys away with it. The drifters were in radio contact with fast warships that could then be directed to the target and tackle the submarine with gunfire or by ramming when it had to surface for air.

Below: A German U-boat at sea. This is the *U-9* which sank three elderly British cruisers off the Dutch coast on 22 September 1914.

Right: A British depth charge explodes during a hunt for a U-boat. Aggressive countermeasures would ultimately prove superior to the passive anti-submarine barriers.

The system, which gradually became more and more extensive and began to incorporate mines, was far from foolproof. The early contact mines were unreliable, while U-boat captains were often able to avoid the nets by travelling on the surface at night. The Dover Barrage did have its successes. U-boats were briefly prohibited from passing through the Channel for 12 months after April 1915, while better mines, more frequent night patrols and searchlights all played their part in improving the barrage. At least 12 submarines were lost in the barrage and the U-boats finally ceased using the Channel route in August 1918.

The route into the North Atlantic by way of the North Sea was not tackled until mid-July 1917. The building of a huge barrage between the Orkneys and the Norwegian coast was largely the brainchild of an American naval officer, Admiral Henry Mayo. He successfully argued that his country's new magnetic mine, which exploded when a submarine entered its magnetic field rather than needing direct contact, was appropriate for the task. The mine-laying took place during June–October 1918 and it was largely undertaken by US crews, who laid more than 80 per cent of the 69,000 mines deployed. Yet for all that effort only three U-boats were confirmed sunk in the minefields.

Otranto Barrage

The third great Allied barrage was built in the Mediterranean as a way of preventing Austro-Hungarian and German surface warships and submarines from entering the sea from their bases in the northern and eastern Adriatic. It stretched across the Strait of Otranto from the heel of Italy to Valona (Vlorë) in Albania. Construction of the barrage began in late 1915 but the 100km (60 miles) of anti-submarine nets patrolled by numbers of warships were never wholly secure and only one U-boat was destroyed.

Right: An aerial photograph of the anti-submarine barrage at Scapa Flow in the Orkneys, the Royal Navy's most important base and home of the bulk of the Grand Fleet.

Coronel and the Falklands

The fortunes of the German and British naval squadrons operating in the South Atlantic and south-east Pacific swung dramatically in 1914 with the British eventually emerging victorious after the Battle of the Falklands.

At the outbreak of war the greater part of the Imperial Germany Navy was based in home waters, but a handful of warships were overseas. Among these were various cruisers, armed merchant cruisers and auxiliary commerce raiders poised to attack Allied shipping and the small Mediterranean Squadron based at Pola (Pula). The largest and most powerful force was Admiral Maximilian von Spee's East Asiatic Squadron based at Tsingtao in China. Spee's squadron comprised two armoured cruisers, *Gneisenau* and *Scharnhorst*, five light cruisers, *Dresden*, *Emden*, *Königsberg*, *Leipzig* and *Nürnberg*, and various support ships. Spee's orders were to cruise the Pacific, attacking British shipping for as long as possible before eventually heading back to Germany.

Commerce Raiding

Spee's light cruisers operated independently during the first two months of the war, making use of Germany's Pacific island colonies for resupply, radio intelligence of possible targets and news of the 30 or so Allied warships hunting them. The *Emden* and *Königsberg* continued their commerce-raiding cruises until sunk in November 1914 and July 1915, respectively, but the remainder of the squadron reunited at Easter Island between 12 and 18 October 1914. They then headed for the west coast of South America. British intelligence identified their general position in the south-east Pacific and the task of destroying Spee was given to the warships of Rear-Admiral Christopher Cradock's South American Squadron based in the Falklands Islands.

Below: The German light cruiser *Leipzig* succumbs to fire from the British armoured cruiser *Cornwall* during the Battle of the Falklands.

Battle of Coronel

Cradock took into action two armoured cruisers, *Good Hope* and *Monmouth*, the light cruiser *Glasgow*, and an armed liner, *Otranto*. With the exception of *Glasgow* his squadron was older, slower and wholly outgunned. The two squadrons finally met off Coronel, a Chilean port, late

Above: The Battle of Coronel on 1 November 1914 saw a weak British squadron outclassed by Germany's East Asiatic Squadron.

Above: Vice-Admiral Frederick Doveton Sturdee (1859–1925) led the victorious British squadron during the Battle of the Falklands.

on 1 November. *Otranto* was ordered away immediately but Cradock tried to bring his other ships into action even though they were outranged. It took just 40 minutes to reduce *Good Hope* and *Monmouth* to blazing wrecks that quickly sank with all hands. *Glasgow* was struck five times but escaped. Spee's ships were undamaged.

Once Cradock's fate became known back in Britain, there was a public outcry and the press demanded that those responsible for the defeat be sacked. First Lord of the Admiralty Winston Churchill, the political head of the Royal Navy, and the military head, Admiral Prince Louis of Battenberg, were targeted. Churchill survived but German-born Battenberg, who had to endure particularly vitriolic attacks because of his background, did not. He was replaced by Admiral John Fisher.

Revenge on Spee

The British sent a powerful task force to the Falklands, including the battle-cruisers *Inflexible* and *Invincible*, two armoured cruisers, three light cruisers, including the *Glasgow*, and an armed merchant cruiser. Spee, unaware of their presence, approached Port Stanley in the Falklands at dawn on 8 December intending to destroy its facilities. The British squadron under Vice-Admiral Sturdee sailed out to meet him. Spee was outgunned and his warships slower so he tried to manoeuvre his way out of trouble but British fire finally told. *Scharnhorst* and *Gneisenau* were sunk first, followed by *Nürnberg* and *Leipzig*. *Dresden* escaped but was scuttled three months later. The East Asiatic Squadron ceased to exist.

ADMIRAL MAXIMILIAN VON SPEE

Spee (1861–1914) was a career admiral in the Imperial German Navy and commanded its powerful East Asiatic Squadron at the outbreak of war. He was widely thought of as one of his country's finest admirals and his command was equally highly regarded, the ships having won several pre-war gunnery contests. Spee was based in China, a long way from home, and was eventually hunted down by the British after his victory at Coronel. He and his two sons were killed at the Battle of the Falklands in December 1914 when most of the ships of his squadron were sunk.

Above: A formal portrait of Admiral Maximilian von Spee.

Battle-cruisers

Inspired by Admiral Fisher, the Royal Navy developed battle-cruisers in what proved to be a rather flawed attempt to create a new class of warship that was armed like a dreadnought battleship but had the greater speed of a cruiser.

Although cruisers were a long-established type of warship by the outbreak of World War I, the larger battle-cruisers were a relatively new concept and had not been tested in action. The idea came from the fertile brain of Britain's Admiral John Fisher, who was also responsible for the powerful dreadnought type of battleship. Fisher wanted a class of warships that could act independently, or form the nucleus of a detached squadron, or work in conjunction with the main battlefleet of dreadnoughts. In this last mission, battle-cruisers were to act in the scouting and reconnaissance role, seeking out the enemy's main fleet and reporting back on its position. Their heavy armament, which was comparable to that of a dreadnought, meant that they could destroy smaller warships, while their high speed meant they could outrun bigger opponents. Battle-cruisers were originally known as fast armoured cruisers but took on their more common name in 1912.

Below: A close-up of one of the turrets of the British battle-cruiser *Tiger* – an early attempt to provide the warship with a means of aerial reconnaissance and firepower.

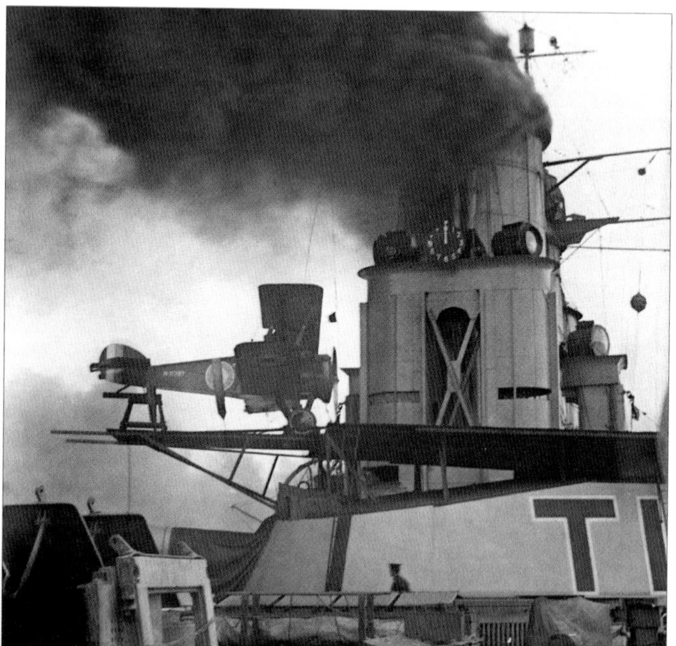

First Battle-cruisers

Britain launched its first three battle-cruisers, HMS *Invincible*, *Indomitable* and *Inflexible*, during 1909. These, and a second group of three, carried eight 12in (305mm) guns (dreadnoughts mostly had ten) and displaced 17,250 tons. Later classes carried larger guns. *Renown* and *Repulse*, launched in 1916, each had six 15in (380mm) guns. The Royal Navy had most battle-cruisers with 12 built in 1908–17. Only Germany and Japan copied the design and had them available in 1914.

Battle-cruisers did have successes. *Invincible* and *Inflexible* sank two less-powerful German armoured cruisers during the Battle of the Falklands in late 1914, while on detached service from the main battlefleet. Germany's own battle-cruisers also enjoyed some successes while acting independently, not least when they severely dented the British public's faith in the Royal Navy by bombarding a number of towns on Britain's east coast. Yet these victories

HMS *TIGER*

Class: Only ship of its type
Laid down: 1912
Displacement: 28,500 tons
Crew: 1,185
Speed: 30 knots
Main armament: 8 x 13.5in (343mm) guns

masked some serious technical and design shortcomings, especially in Britain's battle-cruisers, that were only fully exposed in larger fleet actions.

Part of the problem was that their name was perhaps misinterpreted by some officers and led them to believe mistakenly that battle-cruisers could take their place in the main line of battle. Their armament suggested they could take on similarly armed battle-cruisers or dreadnoughts but their armour, which had been reduced to give them their higher speed, actually meant that they could not stand punishment from the heavy guns carried by either.

SMS *DERFFLINGER*

SMS *Derfflinger* was completed in mid-1914 and took part in raids along the east coast of England and the Battle of the Dogger Bank in early 1915 before being badly damaged during the Battle of Jutland in 1916.

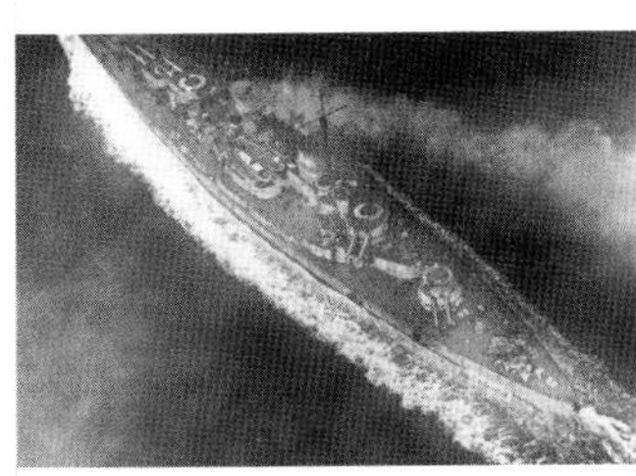

Sister ships: *Hindenburg, Lützow*
Laid down: 1912
Displacement: 28,000 tons
Crew: 1,112
Speed: 28 knots
Main armament: 8 x 30.5cm (12in) guns

SMS *GOEBEN*

Goeben was handed over to the Turkish Navy in August 1914, although still German-crewed. It operated in the Black Sea against Russia and later in the Mediterranean. Damaged by mines in January 1918, it spent the rest of the war in dry dock.

Sister ship: *Moltke*
Laid down: 1909
Displacement: 22,640 tons
Crew: 1,053
Speed: 29 knots
Main armament: 10 x 28cm (11in) guns

Problems in Action

The Battle of Jutland in May 1916 revealed the truth. Three British battle-cruisers, *Invincible*, *Indefatigable* and *Queen Mary*, were sent to the bottom in quick time, blown apart in an instant by single salvoes of shells. The shells easily penetrated their overly thin armour and then exploded causing a fire that detonated ammunition that was being stored incorrectly. Germany's own battle-cruiser squadron did not escape without loss or damage either. The *Lützow* was sunk and all of the other ships were hit repeatedly, not least the *Seydlitz*, yet all reached their home port. Their survival was partly due to luck, but also to good seamanship and design precautions to prevent secondary internal explosions during the heat of battle. Neither Britain nor Germany lost any more battle-cruisers during World War I. Their vulnerability was clear to all but the growth of naval aviation gradually removed the need for them to act in the reconnaissance role for the main battlefleet.

SMS *SEYDLITZ*

Class: Only ship of its type
Laid down: 1911
Displacement: 25,000 tons
Crew: 1,068
Speed: 30 knots
Main armament: 10 x 28cm (11in) guns

The Caucasus Front, 1914–16 Wounded Turkish soldiers taken prisoner by the Russians.

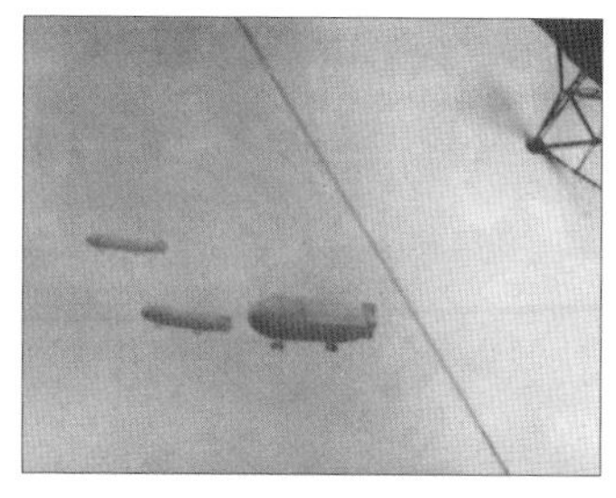

Zeppelins A group of German airships sets out on a bombing mission to England.

Winter Offensive against Russia Troops of the Russian Army march off to the front.

Main Central Powers' attacks
Main Allied attacks
Front line, Jan 1915
Front line, Dec 1915
Front line, Jan 1915
Front line, Dec 1915
Front line, Oct 1915
Front line, Dec 1915
Front line, Jan 1915
Front line, Dec 1915
Front line, May 1915
Front line, Dec 1915

0 100 200 300 400 500 mi
0 200 400 600 800 km

1915 – TRENCH WARFARE

The year opened with both sides confident that victory could still be achieved. The German High Command opted to go on the defensive in the west and strike eastward against Russia, in part because Austria-Hungary was proving a very poor ally. France and Britain would be attacked indirectly at sea by Germany's increasingly important U-boats. The Allies, joined by Italy in May, had a far from clear-cut war plan. The French were wedded to evicting the Germans from their home soil and determined to launch a series of offensives on the Western Front. The British could offer little help as their small army had been virtually destroyed in 1914.

The British were split on where to deploy their meagre resources. Most generals saw the Western Front as the decisive theatre but some politicians, appalled by the blood-letting of 1914, argued for an indirect strategy against the weaker Central Powers. The defeat of Austria-Hungary, Bulgaria or Turkey would, they argued, bring about the collapse of Germany. The Allies opened up a number of subsidiary battlegrounds, chiefly on the Gallipoli Peninsula, in Palestine and in Mesopotamia (Iraq) and forces were also poured into Salonika in the south Balkans to confront the various Central Powers.

Home Fronts British women at work on a farm having taken over jobs done by men now in the army.

Four Battles along the Isonzo Italian Bersaglieri ready for action on the Isonzo front.

Pre-dreadnought Battleships The French ship *Suffren* served in the Dardanelles.

The Second Battle of Ypres

The German Army deployed gas on a large scale for the first time in spring 1915 against the Allied positions around the Belgian town of Ypres in an attempt to eradicate a salient and test the new weapon's capabilities.

Germany's military leaders had decided to concentrate on knocking Russia out of the war during 1915 and were content to remain largely on the defensive on the Western Front. However, the high command's Chief of Staff, General von Falkenhayn, gave permission for a limited spoiling offensive in mid-spring when it was discovered that the British and French were preparing another major attack, even though they had only recently closed down two efforts – the British-led Battle of Neuve Chapelle (10–13 March) and the French Army's Battle of the Woëvre (6–15 April). The German target was Ypres, scene of heavy fighting in late 1914 that had left an Allied-held salient in the German line to the east of the Belgian town. The main German aims were to clear the salient, taking high ground that would give their troops a local advantage, and to test the effectiveness in action of the newly developed but untried chlorine gas.

KEY FACTS

DATE: 22 April – 25 May 1915

PLACE: Ypres, south-west Belgium

OUTCOME: Germany s only major attack on the Western Front in 1915 reduced the Ypres salient by two-thirds.

Below: The badly damaged centre of Ypres pictured in early 1915 after several months of bombardment.

GAS ATTACK

The fighting was left to the German Fourth Army under Duke Albrecht of Württemberg. The action opened on 22 April with a brief artillery barrage. When that ended, the chlorine gas was released from its canisters and drifted over a section of trench north of the town held by French and Algerian troops. Soon many were dying in great pain, unable to breathe. They were completely unprepared for this new threat and fled in terror, leaving a large hole in the defences. The German assault troops were wearing an early form of gas mask and had advanced some 3.2km (2 miles) by the next day but thereafter were halted by counter-attacks from units of General Smith-Dorrien's British Second Army.

NEW ATTACKS

This brought only a temporary respite to the Allies and the Germans attacked again on the 24th, but this time against Canadian troops to the north-east of the city. The fighting quickly spread along most of the east and south-east of the salient as far as Hill 60. Smith-Dorrien believed that further attempts to regain the lost ground would be futile and costly in lives so he requested permission for a general withdrawal to better,

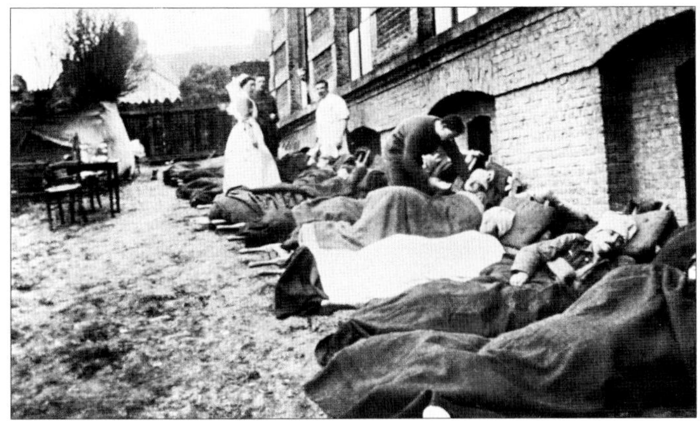

Above: Medical staff tend the wounded, just a few of the 60,000 casualties that the British forces suffered in the battle.

more defensible ground nearer Ypres. This was refused by the BEF's commander, Field Marshal French, and Smith-Dorrien was replaced by General Herbert Plumer. He, too, urged withdrawal and his plan was eventually accepted, but not until a French counter-attack had failed on 29 April. The realignment took place in early May but fighting and gas attacks continued to the 25th.

Duke Albrecht's increasingly exhausted troops did gain some more ground during these final weeks of battle, particularly between 8 and 14 May, and this left them in possession of a line of high ground not much more than 3.2km (2 miles) outside Ypres from where they now looked down on the battered town and would do so until the Battle of Passchendaele in 1917.

In a month or so of fighting the Germans had captured around two-thirds of the salient and inflicted some 60,000 casualties on the British and 10,000 on the French. The German Fourth Army, which had lost some 35,000 men, was exhausted and lacked the manpower to continue offensive operations but its artillery began methodically to raze what remained of Ypres to the ground, making life a misery for the Anglo-French troops left holding the now reduced salient.

Below: A panoramic view of a much fought-over sector of the Ypres battlefield known as Hill 60.

THE DANGER OF SALIENTS

Salients, whether big or small bulges in the front line, were a tricky prospect for both attacking and defending forces. Troops holding a bulge that pushed into an enemy's line could be fired on from the front and both sides of the salient, while attacking troops often found they had punched a salient into the defenders' line and thus came under crossfire. The most infamous salient of the war was that around Ypres, which was formed in late 1914 and not fully eradicated until 1918.

Right: Men of 1st Australian Division in a trench near Gheluvelt, Ypres Salient, 20 September 1917.

Gas Warfare

Gas was deployed in considerable quantities during the war by most of the combatant nations and, although it became lethal and could produce truly horrible injuries, it was never a war-winning weapon.

Gas had been considered as a weapon before the outbreak of war but there was a general consensus that it was wholly "uncivilized". Yet all that changed with trench warfare, a development that sparked a wide-ranging search for technologies that could break the deadlock. Gas became acceptable and the types used changed from mere irritants with only short-term medical impact to ones with almost immediate lethality. Most were not long-lasting on the battlefield but a few were.

First Uses

The Germans were the first to use gas on the battlefield close to Neuve Chapelle on the Western Front in October 1914 and next in January 1915 near Bolimov on the Eastern Front.

Above: British artillerymen pose for a photograph while preparing gas shells for use.

The amount of gas used was small and the results were not promising. At Neuve Chapelle the small quantity of the irritant gas released was not noticed by the targeted French troops while at Bolimov the xylyl bromide, a form of tear gas, froze due to the cold weather and therefore did not disperse. Nevertheless, the Germans persevered and introduced much more dangerous gases and these did have a significant effect.

Chlorine gas, which destroys the respiratory organs in a few seconds, was used to devastating effect during the Second Battle of Ypres in April 1915.

In the war as a whole Germany was the greatest user of gas (68,000 tonnes), while France manufactured 37,000 tonnes and Britain 25,000 tonnes.

Below: German stormtroopers undergo realistic training by advancing through a cloud of gas.

Left: British troops blinded by gas in April 1918 await medical treatment and evacuation to the rear.

Below: Three early respirators, including a German Rahmenmaske (framework mask) and its carrying can (left).

TYPES OF GAS

The most widely used types were the aforementioned chlorine gas and the almost odourless mustard gas, a slow-acting agent that causes internal and external bleeding and vomiting and frequently leads to death. Some proponents of gas warfare concluded that lethality was neither necessary nor desirable. They reasoned that gas casualties who survived with considerable infirmity were a constant drain on medical facilities and detrimental to enemy morale in the long term.

Gas was dispersed in two ways. It was released in vapour form by fixed canisters positioned in or near the front line, a technique that wholly relied on the wind blowing in the right direction and one that meant that gas was effectively a short-range weapon. Artillery shells filled with an agent in liquid form that evaporated after a small explosive charge burst the shell open were widely used from 1916. Gas was also put in high-explosive rounds in small quantities for a "mixed" effect. Artillery shells gave gas greater range and much better accuracy, but some problems still remained insoluble.

Gas was not a truly effective weapon as it needed a long list of ideal conditions. It often failed due to adverse weather, especially the strength and direction of the prevailing wind and the temperature. It was quite common for gas to be blown back into the attackers' faces by contrary winds.

All sides quickly developed gas masks and these became more and more sophisticated. Early ones consisted of thick cotton pads soaked in bicarbonate of soda, to cover the mouth and nose, and separate goggles, but these gave way in all armies to the more familiar combined mask and respirator types. Filters were usually filled with charcoal or chemicals to neutralize the gas.

Below: Both men and animals needed protection against gas attack. The British Army began issuing horse respirators in 1916.

The Second Battle of Artois

The French Commander-in-Chief, Marshal Joffre, launched a major offensive in Artois to drive the Germans from French soil but, despite some early successes, the fighting soon became stalemated and a breakthrough never materialized.

Even as the Second Battle of Ypres was being fought to a conclusion, Marshal Joseph Joffre, the French Commander-in-Chief, launched yet another major offensive with the intention of making a decisive breakthrough. His chosen battlefield was in Artois.

British Attacks

The British First Army under General Douglas Haig was first committed either side of Neuve Chapelle with the aim of pushing Crown Prince Rupprecht's Sixth Army beyond Aubers Ridge and Lille. The attack, the Battle of Aubers Ridge, opened on 9 May and was heralded by a mere 40-minute preliminary bombardment due to a shortage of shells. When the British infantry advanced, they found the German trenches largely undamaged and an alert enemy waiting. Haig called off the attack and the fighting ended next day with the British losing around 11,500 men.

The British tried again on the night of the 15th after Joffre had requested a further effort. This time Haig struck to the south of Neuve Chapelle. This attack, the Battle of Festubert, was preceded by a four-day barrage and did make some initial progress before becoming bogged down. The battle was halted on the 25th by which time the Sixth Army was driven back a mere 730m (800yds) at a cost of some 16,500 casualties. The German losses were around 5,800 men.

Joffre unleashed General Auguste Dubail's Tenth Army on 9 May after a four-day bombardment from more than 1,000 guns had fired 690,000 shells on the German trenches. The main effort took place between Arras and Lens on a 10km (6 mile) front approaching Vimy Ridge, a commanding piece of high ground. A corps in the centre led by General Philippe Pétain broke through and made 5km (3 miles) in the first 90 minutes but that was the high point of the attack. A lack of reserves and the prompt arrival of German reinforcements prevented any further exploitation

KEY FACTS

Date: 9 May – 18 June 1915

Place: Artois region of north-eastern France between Arras and Lille

Outcome: The French-led attack ended in failure and heavy casualties.

Right: The crew of a French heavy mortar pose for a photograph in their artillery emplacement.

Below: The devastation produced by increasing artillery bombardments, near Festubert, March 1915.

Above: A somewhat bizarre remedy to one of the more common problems encountered in trench warfare – a rowing boat used to overcome flooding.

of Pétain's gains. Heavy but inconclusive fighting continued until the 15th and briefly flared again between 15 and 19 June but to no great advantage for either side. The battle officially ended on the 30th by which time French casualties had reached around 100,000 men.

DEFENCE IN DEPTH

This was a battle tactic developed by the Germans but later adopted by the British though not always by the French. Most defenders in the front line would pull back to prepared positions during the opening stages of an enemy offensive and then launch counter-attacks once the latter had pushed beyond their largely static artillery cover and become increasingly immobile. The tactic proved effective against the Allied offensives of 1916 and 1917 but ultimately could not prevent the defenders from suffering losses comparable to those of the attackers.

SHELL SCANDAL

The shortage of ammunition for Haig's artillery had wider political repercussions. The Liberal government of Prime Minister Herbert Asquith had seriously underestimated the volume of war supplies needed by the British Army at a time when it was expanding rapidly and had not undertaken sufficient measures to ensure that the country's economy was up to the job being asked of it. Matters reached a crisis point on 14 May when a report in *The Times* newspaper bluntly stated that the initial failure at Aubers Ridge was due to a serious lack of high-explosive shells.

The article had, in fact, been sanctioned by a powerful anti-Asquith cabal that included the newspaper's influential owner, Lord Northcliffe, various senior politicians and commanders on the Western Front. The "Shell Scandal" seriously damaged the prime minister's position and he was forced to form a coalition government, largely composed of leading Liberals and Conservatives but with one socialist member. Ammunition supply now became the responsibility of the new Ministry of Munitions which was placed under the dynamic Liberal cabinet member David Lloyd George, who had himself been one of the leading anti-Asquith conspirators.

Below: A French infantry detachment takes much-needed water up to the front during a lull in the Artois fighting.

Trench Systems

Trench warfare developed on the Western Front in late 1914 and, although types of trenches varied considerably largely due to the impact of the local terrain, they became progressively deeper, wider and more complex as the war continued.

Trench systems were to some extent a reflection of local conditions, and the continuous lines most associated with the war were by no means their only form. In very mountainous terrain, as on much of the Italian Front or, indeed, in the Vosges region of France, the lines were generally less complete and might consist of a series of mutually supporting mountain-top strong-points. Not all trench systems were below ground but might rather be built up. This could be because the bedrock was near the surface and too difficult to dig through or the water table might be too near the surface so that sunken trenches would be waterlogged. This was true especially on the most northerly part of the Western Front in Belgium, where there was a high water table and the Belgians had deliberately flooded much of the low-lying area near the coast in 1914.

Trenches evolved as the war progressed. They were originally little more than connected scrapes in the ground and not designed for permanent occupation but, once the fronts had become static in late 1914, the defence systems became deeper and more complex. The Germans – probably the most skilled exponents of trench building – began digging second trench lines from late 1915 and a third was added thereafter.

Below: Trench systems everywhere were plagued by rats and hunting them down was a task performed on a regular basis by all sides.

Trench Layouts

The most typical type of system consisted of three lines about 730m (800yds) apart connected by communication trenches. The first line, the one nearest the enemy, was the fire trench, the main line of resistance; the second was the support trench; and the third was the reserve. All trenches usually zigzagged or had angular firebays to minimize the impact of shellfire and prevent an enemy from firing directly down them. Dugouts, either deep underground or just shelters cut into the trench sides, were constructed to give troops even greater shelter and a measure of comfort. Sandbags were added for more protection, wooden shoring placed to prevent the sides from collapsing, and duckboards laid to aid drainage. Repair work to dugouts was needed on an almost constant basis.

Deeper Defences

Although this system held good for much of the war, it did change and the lines became more complex from 1916 onward, when the Germans adopted "defence in depth". The line nearest the enemy consisted of relatively modest defensive outposts – strong-points based on large shell-holes or prefabricated concrete pill-boxes – that were not designed to stop an enemy advance but rather delay him or channel him into more exposed "killing zones". Next, up to 1.5km (1 mile) away, came the front line. Again this was not necessarily continuous but a system

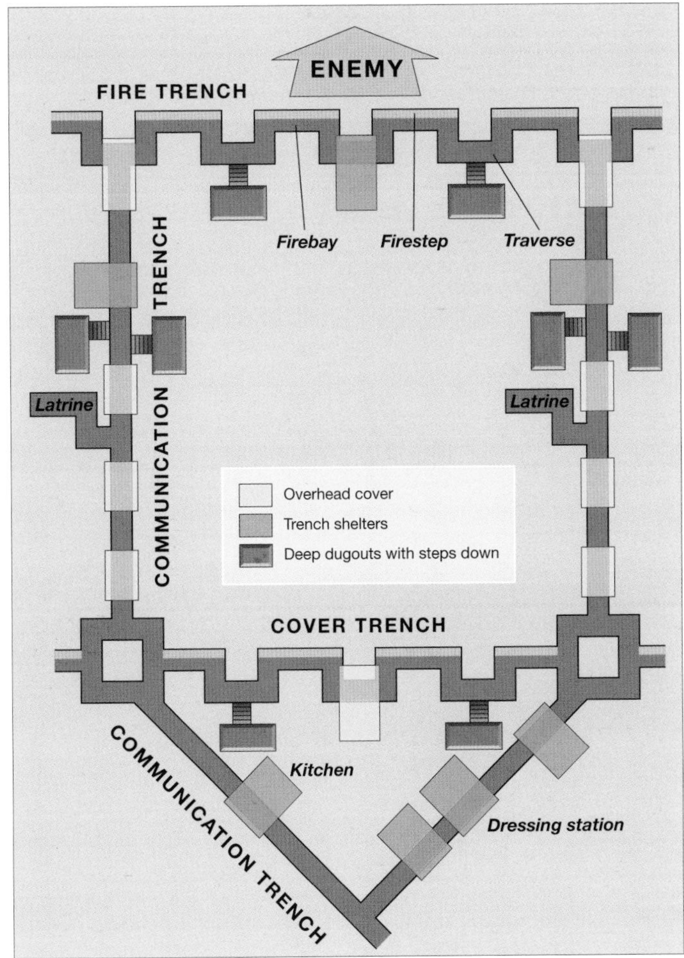

A TYPICAL TRENCH SYSTEM
A standard three-line trench system of the sort used on every war front.

SAPPING

This was a technique used to approach an enemy position without being exposed to fire. Small, narrow trenches, or "saps", were first dug out into No Man's Land and at a certain point the diggers would turn towards each other, thus creating a new trench line. Individual saps were also used as listening posts, particularly by the British who had a philosophy of dominating No Man's Land. Sapping was a tried-and-trusted technique but it was extremely slow and involved much back-breaking work.

The most formidable example of defence in depth was the Hindenburg Line, which ran along the northern and central sector of the Western Front. It was begun in September 1916 and was still under construction in late 1918. It actually comprised a number of large, mutually supporting fortified positions that had a depth of up to 16km (10 miles).

of mutually supporting strong-points that could be fired into from the rear if captured. Next came what was known as the "battle zone", an area perhaps 2km (1.2 miles) wide that consisted of a maze of short trenches and numerous strong-points capable of all-round defence. Behind this was the beginning of the "reserve zone" which might include yet more defensive trench systems and hold prepared emplacements for the artillery.

Below: Some of the dense rows of barbed war that protected the German Hindenburg Line.

Battles in Champagne and Artois

This action by the British Expeditionary Force was part of a joint Anglo-French offensive in late 1915. It made progress at first but was soon halted by a lack of reinforcements and several German counter-attacks.

In autumn 1915 the French Commander-in-Chief, Marshal Joseph Joffre, launched another attempt to crack open the Western Front with both his own expanded forces and Field Marshal French's reinforced BEF. The great effort comprised two simultaneous but geographically separate attacks. The first, known as the Second Battle of Champagne, involved 500,000 French troops attacking on a 16km (10 mile) front in the Argonne area of eastern France. Joffre enjoyed a three-to-one superiority in manpower and the offensive commenced on 25 September after a four-day preliminary bombardment from 2,500 guns. The outnumbered Germans held the high ground and had been forewarned of the offensive. Consequently, the attack made little progress in the first critical days and, despite two attempts to regain the momentum over the following weeks, the battle ended in stalemate on 6 November. The French recorded some 144,000 casualties in the fighting, while the Germans suffered 85,000.

KEY FACTS – LOOS

DATE: 25 September – 16 October 1915

PLACE: Loos, north-eastern France

OUTCOME: Superior German defensive tactics defeated the British offensive.

Above: German prisoners captured by French forces during the Second Battle of Champagne.

The second of Joffre's attacks was a joint Anglo-French affair in the Artois region in the north-east. The French forces engaged in the Third Battle of Artois were largely assigned to capture Vimy Ridge, a piece of crucial high ground that dominated the low-lying plains around Arras. General Dubail's Tenth Army pushed forward on 25 September and soon ran into trouble against the ridge's formidable defensive system which was manned by units from Crown Prince Rupprecht's Sixth Army. Casualties were extremely high. One division did manage to claw its way to the summit on the 29th but this brief success was not matched elsewhere. The attacks continued fitfully due to periods of awful weather but the Third Battle of Artois ended in early November.

BATTLE OF LOOS

The British pincer of this two-pronged effort in the north-east was directed against Loos. Six divisions of General Douglas Haig's First Army advanced on 25 September and made some progress against numerically inferior opponents on the first day, especially on the northern

Left: A typical scene of devastation on the Artois battlefield during 1915.

Above: A contemporary artist's view of Scottish troops charging the German defences at Loos.

FIELD MARSHAL JOHN FRENCH

French (1852–1925) was a cavalry officer who was made Commander of the British Expeditionary Force at the outbreak of war. He was under orders to keep his command intact but was not really up to the task. French's mood swings were notoriously bad; he was often seized by doubt and rarely showed any drive. He was also unable to establish a working relationship with the French High Command and even with some of his own officers. He was dismissed in December 1915 after mismanaging the Battle of Loos.

flank. Despite difficult going and the ongoing shell shortage that had been plaguing the British for months, Loos was captured and troops were on its far outskirts before problems began to arise. Much to Haig's fury, the BEF's increasingly indecisive and demoralized commander withheld much-needed reserves and there were immense difficulties in getting vital supplies to the leading units. The British were forced back by strong German counter-attacks the next day and did not regain any momentum until early October. However, they had suffered heavy losses for precious little gain and thereafter bad weather so blighted the battle that it was finally called off on the 8th.

THE FIGHTING IN 1915

By the end of 1915 the Western Front had hardly moved, despite the series of Anglo-French offensives in Artois and elsewhere. Casualties had been high on all sides. The Artois and Loos fighting between September and November had cost the French around 48,000 casualties and the British some 60,000. German losses were less than half the total Allied figure, a statistic that reflected the undoubted dominance of the defence over attack. Total Western Front casualties for 1915 were enormous – 960,000 French, 295,000 British and approximately 650,000 German soldiers had been killed, wounded or taken prisoner. This scale of loss impacted on the British command structure and Haig replaced French as the BEF's commander-in-chief in December. Joffre was also being criticized for the costly failure of his offensives.

Below: A panoramic view of the Loos battlefield. The various trench lines can be identified by white lines of material dug out to form them.

Early Fighters

The idea of arming aircraft to shoot down other aircraft only truly evolved in the first months of World War I, when it was soon recognized by air power advocates that reconnaissance aircraft were a vital weapon in modern warfare.

There were no purpose-built fighter aircraft in existence in 1914 but they were quickly developed once the trenches had been dug. Their first roles were to protect the increasingly important reconnaissance aircraft that had taken the place of redundant cavalry and to shoot down those of the enemy.

The earliest types, some of them monoplanes but mostly biplanes, were usually conversions of two-seater reconnaissance aircraft that had been fitted with a single machine-gun operated by the observer from the rear of the cockpit. The chief problem was that the machine-gun was easiest to aim when firing forward but most aircraft were of the "tractor" type. The propeller was at the front of the fuselage and there was no means of firing through its arc without shooting the wood to bits.

Pusher Fighters

There was one exception: "pusher" aircraft had the propeller to the rear with the crew positioned at the front, but such aircraft had a much poorer performance. The British Vickers FB-5, which made its appearance in July 1915, was of this type but its top speed of 112kph (70mph) was not especially impressive.

Deflector Gear

A French pilot, Roland Garros, came up with a solution to the tractor problem. In March 1915 he fitted steel plates to the propeller of a Morane-Saulnier L Parasol, a two-seater monoplane, so that bullets would be deflected away without causing damage. France's first dedicated fighter, the Morane-Saulnier N Scout, appeared shortly thereafter. This "deflector gear" gave the Allies an edge in the race to develop better fighters but this advantage was soon lost.

FOKKER E-TYPES

These German Army Air Service aircraft were designed by the Dutchman Antony Fokker and are regarded as the first true fighters. They saw action from mid-1915 and took a terrible toll of Anglo-French machines until spring 1916.

TYPE: E-III monoplane fighter
ENGINE: 100hp Oberursel
CREW: 1
CEILING: 3,650m (12,000ft)
TOP SPEED: 140kph (85mph)
ARMAMENT: 1 or 2 x 8mm (0.315in) machine-gun(s)

MAX IMMELMANN

Immelmann was one of the first *Experten* (or "aces") of the German Army Air Service. He shot down 15 Allied aircraft before his death in June 1916. He invented the Immelmann turn, an aerobatic manoeuvre still used by pilots. This is a combined backward loop and roll that can allow a fighter pilot who is being pursued to turn the tables on his pursuer.

Above: Max Immelmann, the "Eagle of Lille", one of the first fighter aces, who became a popular hero in Germany.

MORANE-SAULNIER TYPE N

This French fighter made its debut in late 1914 and was one of the first true fighters on the Western Front. Early models were fitted with deflector gear but later models carried the more advanced interrupter gear. It also saw service with Britain (as shown) and Russia.

ENGINE: 80/110hp Le Rhône
CREW: 1
CEILING: 4,000m (13,100ft)
TOP SPEED: 160kph (100mph)
ARMAMENT: 1 x 8mm (0.315in) machine-gun

The Germans captured an example of the deflector gear in April 1915 and set about making a better version. Fokker, a Dutch company, came up with interrupter gear, a device that prevented a machine-gun from firing when a propeller blade passed immediately in front of its barrel. It was first tried out on the Fokker E-I monoplane and it had transformed air warfare by late 1915. Some 300 E-types, especially the single-seat E-III with a top speed of around 140kph (85mph), shot down more than a thousand Allied aircraft and took an especially heavy toll of the Vickers FB-5 in what was known as the "Fokker Scourge". The E-types were pre-eminent until the arrival of comparable Allied fighters in the spring of 1916.

VICKERS FB-5

This "pusher" fighter was the first ever British fighter and began arriving on the Western Front in mid-1915. It was soon outclassed by the Fokker E-types and production ended in early 1916 after some 100 aircraft had been built.

ENGINE: 100hp Gnome Monosoupape
CREW: 2
CEILING: 2,700m (8,800ft)
TOP SPEED: 112kph (70mph)
ARMAMENT: 1 x 0.303in (7.7mm) machine-gun

AIR COMBAT TECHNIQUES

As fighters gradually appeared, leading pilots began to develop the tactics of air combat. Complex dogfighting was rare and victory usually went to the pilot who exploited the sun and clouds to sneak up behind his opponent and open fire at close range. Pilots recorded their successes, or "kills", and those who achieved more than five became recognized as "aces". Many were soon killed, however.

Right: Roland Garros (in beret) flew the first Allied aircraft to be fitted with deflector gear.

Winter Offensive against Russia

German forces scored a notable victory over the Russians during the Second Battle of the Masurian Lakes in early 1915 but Austro-Hungarian forces suffered horrendous losses in a botched offensive through the Carpathians.

Germany decided to concentrate on the Eastern Front during 1915, aiming to knock Russia out of the war. The plan was to make two attacks, one in the north and one in the south of the front. The first thrust was to be made from East Prussia by the 100,000 troops of the German Eighth and Tenth Armies. The offensive was preceded by a diversionary attack on 31 January. The German Ninth Army made a feint push towards Warsaw that led to the Battle of Bolimov, noteworthy for one of the first uses of poison gas. The main event in East Prussia began on 7 February, when General Otto von Below's Eighth Army advanced through a blinding snowstorm to hit the left flank of the isolated Russian Tenth Army, thereby initiating the Second Battle of the Masurian Lakes.

Indecisive Attacks

Below's advance, which pushed his opponents back 96km (60 miles) in a week, was joined on the 9th by an attack on the Russian right flank by General Hermann von Eichhorn's Tenth Army. The Russian Tenth Army crumbled, and began a retreat towards Kovno (Kaunas). Three corps were virtually surrounded but one put up a desperate fight in the Augustovo Forest until the 21st that allowed the others to make good their escape. Yet, for all their initial successes, the Germans gained little and they fell back to the East Prussian border in the face of counter-

RUSSIAN DEFEATS, 1915
The Central Powers' advances in Poland and Galicia.

Below: Russian troops moving off to the front.

attacks by the Russian Twelfth Army under General Plehve. In all the Russians lost some 200,000 men during the battle, including 90,000 prisoners.

Carpathian Battles

The second thrust was made by three armies positioned along the Carpathian Mountains. The main force was General Alexander von Linsingen's Austro-German South Army. His mission was to strike northwest through the Carpathians in the direction of Lemberg to relieve the besieged fortress of Przemyśl. The Austro-Hungarian Third Army, commanded by General Svetozar Boroevic von Bojna, was on the South Army's left flank while General Karl von Pflanzer-Baltin's Austro-Hungarian Tenth Army was on the right flank. Both were detailed to act in a supporting role.

Pflanzer-Baltin scored an early success by taking Czernowitz (Cernovcy) with 60,000 prisoners from General Alexei Brusilov's Eighth Army on 17 February but his push was then halted by strong counter-attacks. South Army made little progress, coming to a halt amid the snowbound mountains. The Przemyśl fortress and its garrison surrendered to the Russians on 22 March after a 194-day siege. The Russians launched various local counter-attacks in the following weeks but these ended on 10 April, due to supply difficulties and the arrival of German reinforcements under General Georg von der Marwitz. The Carpathian fighting was a disaster for Austria-Hungary and cost it 800,000 casualties, most due to the appalling weather. The Chief of Staff, Field Marshal Conrad von Hötzendorf, was forced to call on Germany for even more military aid as his demoralized and increasingly ethnically divided army began to disintegrate before his eyes.

Above: Russian supply carts pulled both by horses and slow-moving oxen somewhere in the Carpathians during their spring offensive of 1915.

THE SIEGE OF PRZEMYSL

Przemyśl was a major Austro-Hungarian fortress complex in Galicia. It was briefly besieged by the Russians in September 1914, then relieved for a few weeks in October, and then placed under siege once again. Its salvation became something of a national cause in Austria-Hungary but the failure of the relief operation in early 1915 sealed its fate. The 120,000-strong garrison held out until 22 March but then surrendered. The Russian victory was short-lived as the fortress was retaken by Austrian and German forces on 4 June and never again threatened.

Right: German troops escorting Russian prisoners captured at Przemyśl, June 1915.

Mortars

Trench mortars, a type of specialist artillery that could fire explosive shells in a high trajectory, were not new, having been around for centuries, but the stagnation of trench warfare saw them become one of the most important weapons of the war.

Mortars are short-range infantry-support weapons designed to lob shells in a high arc on to a target. They were originally designed in the 18th century to hit targets sheltering behind either natural features such as hills or constructed defences like fortress walls. Although they had fallen out of fashion somewhat before World War I, several armies soon recognized that they were ideal weapons for hitting enemy troops sheltering in trenches. Germany, France and Britain were the major manufacturers and sold their various designs to their allies.

Below: British armourers prepare a huge number of "toffee apple" rounds for the early type of 2in (51mm) mortar.

9.45IN MORTAR

As the war progressed Britain deployed a wide-range of mortars including the 9.45in type, seen here being loaded with its large projectile, commonly known as the "Flying Pig". Although very effective, these heavier mortars were difficult to manhandle around the battlefield.

Type: Heavy smoothbore mortar
Calibre: 9.45in (240mm)
Weight: 866kg (1,910lb)
Maximum range: 1,600m (1,750yds)
Crew: 9

German Superiority

The Germans had the edge in the quality and provision of mortars for much of the early part of the war, largely because they had recognized that these weapons had played an important part in the siege warfare of the Russo-Japanese War. Consequently, the German

Army had a number of excellent *Minenwerfer* (mine-thrower) types from the outset. Around 150 had been delivered by August 1914. They were bigger, heavier and less portable than later mortars, largely because they had been designed specifically to take on the concrete and steel of France's frontier fortresses. They used a propellant charge to fire a variety of ammunition – explosive, incendiary and gas – that had a range of around 1,000m (1,100yds). Rifling made them quite accurate and their range was increased in later models by lengthening the barrel.

MINENWERFER

The smallest of Germany's late war *Minenwerfer* types is pictured here being pulled by part of its crew. All three calibres had wheeled carriages, which were usually removed before the weapon was used in action.

Type: Light rifled mortar
Calibre: 76mm (3in)
Weight: 100kg (220lb)
Maximum range: 1,000m (1,100yds)
Rate of fire: 20rpm
Crew: 6

They came in a variety of calibres, defined as light, medium and heavy, that fired projectiles weighing 4.08kg, 49.44kg and 95.26kg (9lb, 109lb and 210lb) respectively. The mortars were not really man-portable in the modern sense as most were very heavy. As they could not be broken down into various parts, they were moved about on two-wheeled carriages (the larger types normally horse-drawn) from which they could be fired if required but they were usually found mounted on a steel plate in the trenches. The Germans did attempt to resolve their mobility problem by introducing much smaller *Granatenwerfer* (grenade-thrower) types. These fired a finned grenade out to ranges of 230–275m (250–300yds) and were much lighter.

Allied Designs

France and Britain had no modern mortars in 1914. The French resorted to bringing ancient ones out of retirement while the British experimented with contraptions that would not have looked out of place at a medieval siege. Some looked like miniature siege engines; others were large crossbows, such as the British Leach that could lob a small grenade up to 180m (200yds). One early design of 2in (51mm) calibre fired a bomb that looked like a large toffee apple.

True mortars began to arrive in 1915. The French developed the Batignolles, a series of heavy mortars. Arguably the best and certainly the most modern-looking mortar of the war was the British Stokes design. It was named after its creator, Sir Wilfred Stokes, and began to appear in 1916. These came in a variety of calibres and fired a rocket-shaped grenade. Like all British and French mortars they were smoothbore designs. These were truly man-portable as they broke down into three sections – barrel, baseplate and adjustable bipod.

STOKES MORTAR

The British Stokes mortar could be easily moved by its crew. It was eventually made in 4in (101mm) and 6in (152mm) versions in addition to the most usual 3in calibre.

Type: Light mortar
Calibre: 3in (76.2mm)
Weight: 49kg (108lb)
Max. range: 730m (800yds)
Rate of fire: 22 rounds/min
Crew: 2

Above: An Australian-crewed 3in Stokes Mortar in action in a captured trench near Villers-Bretonneux in July 1918.

Germany's Gorlice–Tarnów Offensive

Germany's major offensive on the Eastern Front in mid-1915 was one of the most successful of the whole war, pushing the Russian Army back hundreds of miles and inflicting more than two million casualties on it in a matter of just five months.

Although Germany had decided to attack Russia in 1915, the first effort during February and March had not delivered a definitive victory. It also revealed that the Austro-Hungarian Army was in poor shape and that German forces would have to shoulder the greater burden of the fighting henceforth. Despite his personal misgivings, the German Chief of Staff, General von Falkenhayn, was persuaded in mid-April to release troops from the Western Front for a second major offensive. Both he and other members of the high command moved eastward to Pless in East Prussia to supervise the operation.

Below: A German soldier gives a wounded Russian soldier a drink on a Galician battlefield, June 1915.

German troops grouped in East Prussia were first used in a diversionary attack north and east into Kurland, the coastal plain bordering the Baltic Sea. The operation began on 26 April with the small German Nieman Army pushing towards Libau (Liepaja), a threat that drew in ever more Russian troops over the following weeks. Due to successes in Galicia during May and June, these operations were extended and led to the fall of the fortress of Kovno (Kaunas) on 17–18 August. A renewal of these operations, the Vilna (Vilnius) Offensive, led to the capture of that city on 26 September but at a high cost.

Capturing Poland

The main, two-pronged attack was against a great salient that included eastern Russian

Above: General August von Mackensen, German commander during the Gorlice–Tarnów Offensive.

Poland and Russian-occupied Galicia, actually part of the Austro-Hungarian Empire. General Max von Gallwitz's German Twelfth Army was poised to strike south-east towards Warsaw itself but the main attack was to be undertaken by some 120,000 men transferred from the Western Front. These formed the German Eleventh Army under General August von Mackensen and the army was located to the south between Gorlice and Tarnów.

The offensive opened on 2 May and Mackensen's troops smashed through the northern flank of the weakened Russian Third Army on a front of nearly

PRELIMINARY BOMBARDMENT

Extensive programmes of shelling before (rather than during) an offensive were the most commonly used type of bombardment. They required an attacker's artillery to fire on the enemy positions in the hope that this deluge would overwhelm the defenders. Such bombardments grew longer and involved more and more heavy guns but it became clear that they could not do what was being asked of them. Worse, they also alerted the defenders to the likelihood of attack and created a devastated landscape in No Man's Land that seriously impeded the progress of the attackers.

Right: A British 60-pounder gun in action during a bombardment near Ypres in April 1918.

48km (30 miles). The Third Army had ceased to exist as a fighting force by the 10th, when it was finally granted permission to withdraw to the River San after losing some 200,000 men, including 140,000 prisoners. The Russian high command, STAVKA, was reluctant to send reinforcements to Galicia because of the developing German attacks in the north.

Despite Russian counter-attacks during 19–25 May, the German-led advance continued – Przemyśl was recaptured on 4 June, the Russians began evacuating most of Galicia from the 22nd and Lemberg was retaken two days later. The offensive in the south wound down in the last days of the month by which time the Germans had taken a staggering 250,000 prisoners and suffered just 90,000 casualties. There was little better news for the Russians in the north of the salient. Gallwitz's Twelfth Army took Warsaw in early August, captured Brest-Litovsk on the 25th and overran Grodno on 2 September.

The New Front Lines

The German-led attacks on the Eastern Front between May and September pushed the Russians back up to 480km (300 miles) and showed that in the east at least mobile warfare was still possible. They also established a front line from north of the Pripet Marshes to the Baltic Sea, which would remain unchanged until late 1917, and to the south, which would remain fixed until June 1916.

The Eastern Front had seen losses on an unparalleled scale in 1915 – Germany suffered around 250,000 casualties, Austria-Hungary over 715,000 and Russia around 2.5 million, including a million prisoners.

Right: A small part of the million or more Russians captured during the Gorlice–Tarnów fighting.

Balloons

Balloons played a number of vital roles in the war, such as protecting vulnerable sites from being attacked by aircraft, but their most important role was that of aerial observation despite the advent of reconnaissance aircraft.

Balloons, lighter-than-air, gas-filled envelopes lacking a metal or wooden frame, were widely used during World War I and were kept aloft by either hot air or a gas. They had two main roles – observation of the enemy on land or at sea, or as components in fixed anti-aircraft defence systems.

Artillery observation balloons were cheap to build and their wicker baskets offered a generally more stable viewing platform than an aircraft. They were tethered to the ground by wire(s) attached to a winch or winches and positioned behind friendly lines so that their crews could look for suitable targets or check the fall of artillery fire and correct it if necessary. They usually operated in groups of two or three to make the triangulation of a target more precise. Communication with the ground was initially by semaphore flags or even by dropping weighted messages before the arrival of portable radio sets. These types of balloon were in service for much of the war, particularly up to 1917, but were increasingly replaced by better reconnaissance aircraft and aerial photography.

Above: The aircraft carrier HMS *Furious* with a Sea Scout Z anti-submarine balloon on its rear flight deck. *Furious* began life as a battle-cruiser but was successively updated for its new role.

Left: British warships in Scapa Flow, the Grand Fleet's main base. A tethered balloon keeps watch for submarines or other hostile activity.

Attacking Balloons

The crews of observation balloons were vulnerable both to ground fire and attacks by fighters, and they were the only British airmen to be issued with parachutes as a matter of course

OBSERVATION BALLOONS

Such balloons were used to watch enemy activity behind the front line or to spot targets and correct the aim of the artillery. Conditions for the spotter were tolerable in good weather but abysmal in other circumstances.

Below: A British balloon is lowered to the ground at the end of a mission on the Western Front.

Above: A row of tethered balloons holding a wire barrage, designed to slice through the wings of any aircraft whose crew failed to spot the wires in time, pictured around north-east London.

as it took such a long time to winch them to the ground in an emergency. Yet pilots detested missions to destroy balloons as they involved flying behind enemy lines into areas usually heavily protected by anti-aircraft batteries and fighters.

Balloons were not easy to shoot down. Before the advent of incendiary or explosive bullets, standard rounds from a fighter's machine-gun would often pass harmlessly through the envelope. There was also a good chance that a fighter, which had to get very close to a balloon to make its machine-guns count, might become fatally entangled in, or have a wing sheared off by, the various steel wires that routinely dangled below the target. Destroying a balloon was such a feat of arms that all of the warring air forces designated it a "kill" in the same way as shooting down an enemy aircraft.

Balloon Barrages

Balloons linked together with chains from which wires dangled to ensnare any attacking aircraft were also deployed to protect vulnerable airspace over valuable targets such as major cities and industrial sites. London was the most prominent case because of the frequent airship and heavy bomber raids it had to endure during the war. These tethered balloons were positioned to the north and east of the capital and were part of a defensive system that included fighter aircraft patrols, anti-aircraft batteries and searchlights.

Aside from their use in land operations, balloons were deployed in anti-submarine warfare, mostly by Britain's Royal Naval Air Service. They largely operated in the English Channel or Irish Sea and had the endurance and speed to act as lookouts for convoys. Several types were developed but the most common were the 70 designated Sea Scout Z (SSZ). These entered service in May 1915 and comprised a balloon from which the fuselage of a BE-2C biplane was suspended. The final development of the Sea Scout was termed the Coastal-class Airship, a design that could stay aloft for up to 24 hours and in which the BE-2C fuselage was replaced by a purpose-built gondola.

Four Battles along the Isonzo

The River Isonzo was effectively the frontier between north-eastern Italy and the Austro-Hungarian Empire and after the Italians sided with the Allies in 1915 it was the site of the first four great – if unsuccessful – Italian offensives of the war.

The Dual Alliance between Germany and Austria-Hungary had been signed in 1879 but it became the Triple Alliance when Italy joined in 1882. While the document was supposed to bind the three powers together, relations between Austria-Hungary and Italy were never good and deteriorated further over the following decades. The alliance was renewed in December 1912 but by then Italy had established close relations with the Entente powers. The chief problem between Austria-Hungary and Italy was territorial. There was a sizeable Italian-speaking population in the Trentino (South Tyrol) region and also around Trieste, but both areas were controlled by Austria-Hungary. Italian irredentism, an ardent nationalist movement dedicated to recovering these lands, was a powerful force in the country's turbulent politics.

KEY FACTS

Date: 23 June – 2 December 1915

Place: Along the River Isonzo, north-eastern Italy

Outcome: The attacking Italians lost more than 180,000 men for little gain.

Right: The Italian Commander-in-Chief July 1914 – November 1917, General Luigi Cadorna.

Below: Italian Bersaglieri, elite light infantry, with their distinctive headgear, on the Isonzo front, 1915.

A New Alliance

Sensing an opportunity, British and French diplomats worked tirelessly to prise Italy away from the Triple Alliance once war had been declared in August 1914. Germany also courted Italy but the Allies won the day. Their promises of significant territorial gains from Austria-Hungary once victory had been achieved led Italy to sign the Treaty of London on 26 April 1915. Italy announced that it was leaving the Triple Alliance on 3 May and then declared war on Austria-Hungary on 23 May; a declaration against Bulgaria followed on 20 October but Italy did not declare war on Germany until 28 August 1916.

Italy's Commander-in-Chief, General Luigi Cadorna, opted to conduct a largely defensive campaign in the South Tyrol and concentrated his efforts against Trieste in the hope of breaking through near there and then driving on to Vienna. His first objective was the town of Gorizia, a little way inside Austro-Hungarian territory on the far side of the River Isonzo. The local terrain, an area of sometimes mountainous

Above: Austro-Hungarian troops refill their water bottles during a lull in the fighting.

ITALIAN IRREDENTISM

Italy's pre-war political life was strongly influenced by irredentism, the fierce nationalist desire to take control of parts of the Austro-Hungarian Empire, especially the Trentino (South Tyrol) and Trieste areas, where sizeable percentages of native Italians lived. The arch-irredentist was the poet Gabriele d'Annunzio (1863–1938), who was also a sparkling orator and became something of a war hero. Dissatisfied with the peace treaties signed in Paris, he led a small force of irredentists to capture Fiume (Rijeka) in 1919 but they were forced to surrender by the Italian Navy in early 1921.

plateaux dissected by river gorges, was difficult in the extreme. The 875,000-strong Italian Army also lacked much modern equipment, especially large stocks of ammunition, artillery and transport.

OPENING OFFENSIVES

The First Battle of the Isonzo in 1915 was spearheaded by 200,000 men and 200 guns, from the Italian Second and Third Armies under General Pietro Frugoni and Emanuele Filiberto, Duke of Aosta. The Austro-Hungarian Army had extended its border defences in the months before war had been declared and the Italians made virtually no impression on them between 23 June and 7 July. Cadorna tried again between 18 July and 3 August. More artillery had been brought up but shells were still in short supply and his troops again failed to make any worthwhile gains. The two battles cost the Austro-Hungarian Army some 45,000 men while the Italians lost around 60,000.

The Third Battle of the Isonzo began on 18 October after Cadorna had rushed much more artillery up to the front. Yet even the firepower from 1,200 guns made little difference and Gorizia still lay out of reach when the fighting ebbed away on 4 November. There was no change during the Fourth Battle fought between 10 November and 2 December. Italian losses in the Third and Fourth battles reached 117,000 and the Austro-Hungarians lost around 72,000 troops. Cadorna would launch further battles along the Isonzo, however.

Right: Italian troops use a military ferry to cross over the River Isonzo in 1915.

Attacking the Dardanelles

The British attempt to force the narrow channel of the Dardanelles was devised to knock Turkey out of the war and create a new supply route to Russia but it ended in abject failure and led to the disastrous Gallipoli land campaign.

Britain and France wanted to send war supplies to Russia's large but ill-equipped armies. The only sea route possible was the difficult North Sea–Arctic passage to ports such as Murmansk and Archangel. The southern route by way of the Mediterranean to the Black Sea was blocked by the narrow Turkish-controlled Dardanelles sea lane.

A pre-war British feasibility study had concluded that it would be possible – if difficult – for warships to bludgeon a safe passage through the Dardanelles and this appeared to be confirmed in November 1914, when a British naval squadron inflicted major damage on the Narrows' outer forts. These were actually undermanned and extremely poorly equipped at the time. However, Turkey responded by strengthening the defences with German aid.

KEY FACTS

DATE: 19 February – 23 March 1915

PLACE: The Dardanelles in the eastern Mediterranean

OUTCOME: Heavy losses were inflicted on Allied warships largely by Turkish mines.

ALLIED STRATEGY

The Dardanelles' issue was raised by Britain's First Lord of the Admiralty, Winston Churchill, in January 1915. He was a strategic "Easterner", one of those who thought that breaking the stalemate on the Western Front would cost too many lives and that Germany might be more easily defeated by crushing its allies first. A naval breakthrough in the Dardanelles might, he believed, deliver a decisive blow against Turkey and thus Germany. Churchill won approval for an Anglo-French operation at the end of the month. The Royal

Above: An illustration from a contemporary French magazine. In reality it was impossible to locate many of the Turkish batteries.

Below: Battleships from the Anglo-French fleet line up across the entrance to the Dardanelles.

Navy provided a task force based around Britain's newest dreadnought, *Queen Elizabeth*, 3 battle-cruisers and 12 older pre-dreadnoughts, under Admiral Sackville Carden, while a smaller French fleet was led by 4 pre-dreadnoughts.

First Naval Attacks

The bombardment of the outer forts began on 19 February 1915 but was ineffective. The ships had to move in closer to complete the attack on the 25th but the Allies still faced problems. Mobile Turkish howitzers were difficult to knock out and these, backed by searchlights, were frustrating night-time attempts by minesweepers to clear the minefields that blocked the Narrows. It was decided that troops would be needed to clear the howitzers, thus leading to the Gallipoli land campaign, but the naval effort was renewed after intelligence reports suggested (correctly) that the Turks were short of ammunition.

Churchill urged Carden to risk all with a charge through the Narrows, but the admiral was ill and collapsed from nervous exhaustion. His deputy, Admiral John de Robeck, oversaw the next attack on 18 March. What followed was an unmitigated disaster. The Allied ships did manage to knock out a few shore batteries but the survivors brought down a heavy fire. Minesweepers were unable to complete their task and several capital ships ran into minefields. The French pre-dreadnoughts *Bouvet* and *Gaulois* were sunk and *Suffren* badly damaged, while the British lost the *Ocean*. No Allied warships remained in the Narrows by dark and the naval attack was abandoned.

The next stage was to assemble land forces to attack the Gallipoli Peninsula and clear the way to Constantinople, but that would prove to be an equally difficult proposition.

WINSTON CHURCHILL

Churchill (1874–1965) was made First Lord of the Admiralty in 1911 and oversaw the continuing reform of the Royal Navy. He was seen as dynamic but prone to impulsive gestures. Churchill's senior appointments upset some naval officers and his interference in operational matters irked others but his reputation was seriously tarnished by the Gallipoli fiasco, which he had promoted. He was sacked in May 1915. Thereafter, he served as a junior minister and as an officer on the Western Front before returning to the heart of government as the Minister of Munitions and then Minister of War.

Above: Winston Churchill, the driving force behind the attempt to force the Dardanelles and the subsequent Gallipoli campaign.

Left: The crew of HMS *Irresistible* passing a tow to HMS *Albion* after the *Albion* ran hard aground during a bombardment off Gaba Tepe in the Dardanelles on 24 May 1915.

Pre-dreadnought Battleships

Although they no longer had the speed and gunpower to lead a battlefleet into a full-scale action, ageing pre-dreadnought types were still able to perform many vital roles to play in the battle for naval supremacy.

When the Royal Navy's HMS *Dreadnought* was launched in 1906, its gunpower made every other battleship in existence obsolete and sparked a worldwide naval arms race. Yet no navy was going to scrap its very costly pre-dreadnought battleships. Consequently many outdated pre-dreadnoughts remained in use when war broke out in 1914.

Numbers in Service

On the Allied side, the Royal Navy had 29 operational pre-dreadnoughts with 20 in mothballs, the French had 17 largely based in the Mediterranean, Italy 8 and Russia 9. Two countries that subsequently joined the Allied cause, Japan and the USA, had 23 and 16 respectively. The fleets of the Central Powers also contained pre-dreadnoughts – Germany had more than 20, Austria-Hungary 12 and Turkey 2.

The pre-dreadnoughts came in a variety of designs and were of varying ages. The Royal Navy and Germany, for example, had such ships that had been built between 1892 and 1908 and, while they differed in detail, they did have some similarities. They typically displaced 10,000–14,000 tons, with the more recent ships being larger. They usually carried four main guns of 28cm (11in) calibre (Germany) and 12in (30.5cm) (Britain) and had secondary armaments of 10–14 lighter guns. Although the pre-dreadnoughts' firepower seemed impressive, they were wholly outclassed by the dreadnoughts, and most naval strategists agreed that the former would take a terrible pounding from the latter in a full-blown fleet action.

At War

The German Navy needed all the large warships it could muster to oppose the British in

Below: The French *Suffren* dated back to 1899 but was torpedoed and sunk by *U-52* off Lisbon in 1916 after service in the Dardanelles.

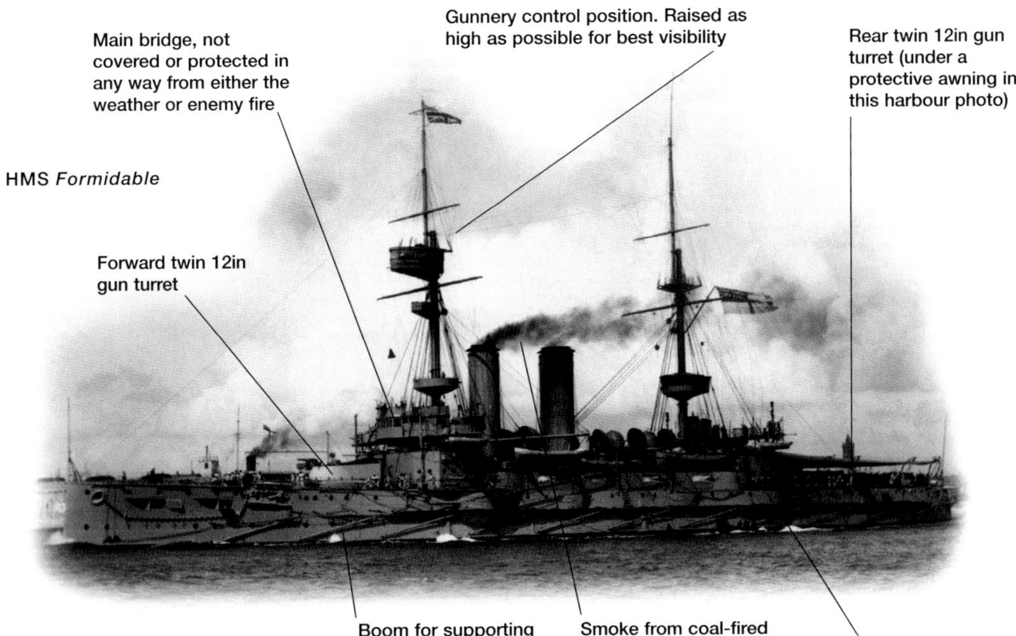

HMS *Formidable*

HMS *FORMIDABLE*

FORMIDABLE CLASS
TYPE: Pre-dreadnought battleship
LAID DOWN: 1898
DISPLACEMENT: 15,000 tons
CREW: 780
SPEED: 18.5 knots
ARMAMENT: 4 x 12in (305mm) + 12 x 6in (152mm) guns

the North Sea so its High Seas Fleet retained some of its pre-dreadnoughts. The gamble paid off, because the fleets only met once and only one German pre-dreadnought was lost to enemy fire – SMS *Pommern* at Jutland in 1916. Other German pre-dreadnoughts did give valuable service in the Baltic but largely in support of ground operations.

The Royal Navy adopted a slightly different plan. Its pre-dreadnoughts were quickly removed from the main Grand Fleet but many were sent on subsidiary missions like shore bombardments, or to theatres where they were unlikely to meet more powerful enemy dreadnoughts. Most ended up in the Mediterranean operating against Turkey.

In all, Britain lost 11 pre-dreadnoughts in the war. France and Russia each lost 4, Italy 2 and Japan 1. The Central Powers also had losses but not on the same scale. Aside from Germany's *Pommern*, the Turkish Navy had two sunk and Austria-Hungary one.

Right: The pre-dreadnought *Pommern* was one of six German pre-dreadnoughts at the Battle of Jutland in 1916. *Pommern* was sunk with all hands by a torpedo from the British destroyer *Faulknor*.

Gallipoli – The Landings

The Gallipoli landings were a British-led effort to put ashore a force that could drive up the peninsula and take the Turkish capital, Constantinople, but they went wrong from the beginning, not least because the campaign was badly managed.

The Gallipoli campaign of 1915–16 grew out of a belief among some leading political figures in Britain that the fighting on the Western Front was stalemated and that Germany might be fatally weakened by adopting an indirect approach, a strategy that knocked out one of its allies. Turkey was chosen largely because its defeat would also open the Dardanelles seaway so that the western Allies would be able to supply Russia's large but under-equipped armies more easily. The campaign was actually the brainchild of the then First Lord of the Admiralty, Winston Churchill, but not all agreed with his views. Senior military figures were very lukewarm and believed that the war could only be won on the Western Front.

KEY FACTS

Date: 25 April 1915

Place: Gallipoli Peninsula, European Turkey

Outcome: British and Commonwealth forces met unexpectedly strong resistance from the Turkish garrison.

Allied Plans

The campaign began as a naval operation but the joint Anglo-French attempt to drive through the Narrows ended in abject failure in March 1915 and it was decided that troops, mostly British but with some French support, would have to be committed. The plan was to land them on the Gallipoli Peninsula and then push rapidly northward to capture the nearby Turkish capital, Constantinople (Istanbul). However, the movement of troops and equipment to the eastern Mediterranean was ponderous and did not go unnoticed by the Turks, who began increasing their garrison on the peninsula.

The Invasion

The landings took place on 25 April at five points on Helles, the southern tip of the peninsula, codenamed S, V, W, X and Y, and at Gaba Tepe, more than 19km (12 miles) farther along Gallipoli's west coast. This last was officially known as Z Beach but was commonly referred to as ANZAC Cove, after the Australian and New Zealand Army Corps troops who landed there. The results were

ANZACS AT WAR

The soldiers of the Australian and New Zealand Army Corps (ANZACs) proved to be some of the best troops to serve with the Allies. They fought with considerable distinction at Gallipoli, in Palestine and on the Western Front. Something like 322,000 Australians served overseas out of a population of 5 million and some 60,000 of them were killed and 220,000 wounded. New Zealand sent some 100,000 men abroad, around 10 per cent of its population, and suffered some 58,000 casualties, including 17,000 killed.

Right: An ingenious rifle mount and a trench periscope used by a two-man Australian sniper team.

mixed. At ANZAC Cove the troops came ashore at the wrong point and had to scale cliffs to advance inland; they did not take Chunuk Bair, a height that dominated the entire peninsula. The landing at Y Beach was unopposed but there was fierce resistance at the other beaches. By nightfall the attackers had seized a foothold on the tip of the peninsula and the ANZAC troops were holding a perimeter that was destined to remain largely unchanged.

The Turkish defenders at Helles withdrew on the morning of the 26th and established positions a little south of the village of Krithia and near to an important piece of high ground known as Achi Baba. The British now attempted to break through this line. The First Battle of Krithia on 28 April cost them 3,000 casualties for no gains and the Second Battle (6–8 May) saw the British push forward a mere 730m (800yds). The Third Battle took place on 6 June and again resulted in very heavy casualties and no real progress.

The Allied campaign was thus in disarray by the end of the first week of June and a form of trench warfare was developing that made a rapid advance on Constantinople unlikely. The greatest problem was that neither Achi Baba nor Chunuk Bair had been taken, meaning that the British and ANZAC positions were overlooked. The Turks had also been able to mount various small counter-attacks, thanks in large part to the energy of a young officer called Mustafa Kemal, that frequently frustrated the attackers. It was also evident that the landings had gone ahead with insufficient troops and a lack of artillery shells. Withdrawal might have been the best option but the opposite course was taken. More troops were sent to Gallipoli and new attacks and landings attempted over the following months.

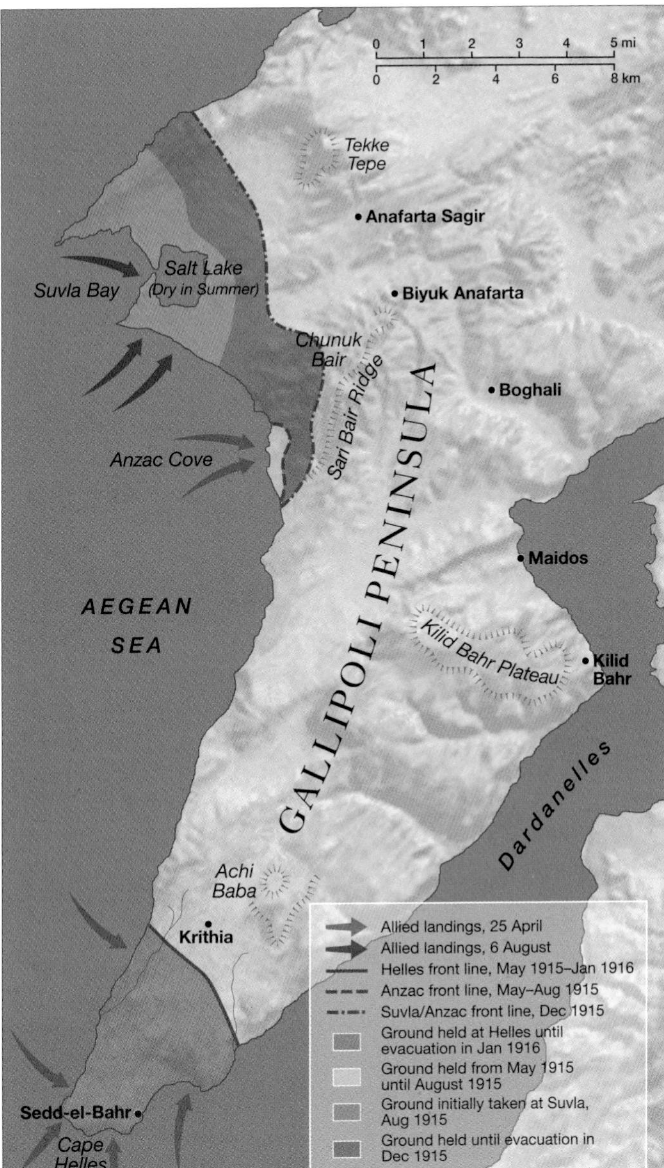

THE GALLIPOLI LANDINGS
The landings and the fighting ashore until the withdrawal in 1916.

Seaplanes and Flying Boats

Amphibious aircraft were an unknown quantity at the outbreak of war but they proved invaluable as they performed several roles including those of reconnaissance and bombing from both coastal bases and warships themselves.

Seaplanes, aircraft fitted with floats so that they can take off and land on water, and flying boats, aircraft with waterproof hulls that can perform similarly, were used by most nations in World War I. Their main role was maritime reconnaissance but they also engaged in air-to-air combat, made anti-shipping sorties and raided coastal installations. Most seaplanes operated from coastal air stations but some, British examples in particular, operated from ships known as seaplane tenders.

However the aircraft were launched and recovered, maritime aviation was still in its infancy and the available aircraft could only be used in calm conditions. Bombs were the main anti-ship weapon. Britain and Germany experimented with torpedoes but found that they were usually too heavy for existing engines to cope with.

In British Service

British seaplanes were operated by the Royal Naval Air Service (RNAS), the largest maritime air force of the conflict, which came into being on 1 January 1914. It eventually had some 50 squadrons that operated from a similar number of coastal stations. The RNAS deployed a variety of seaplanes. The twin-engined Norman Thompson NT-4 and NT-4A equipped several squadrons and carried light bombs for anti-submarine work. One of the most successful later designs was the Felixstowe F-type flying boat, which began operating from 1917. Although slow at 150kph (95mph), these four-man aircraft handled well and could stay aloft for up to 10 hours. An F-type shot down the German airship *L.62* in May 1918 and

Below: A German Friedrichshafen floatplane. The company produced floatplanes during World War I.

Below: A pre-war seaplane built by the German company Albatros. Their main contribution to naval aviation during the conflict was the W-4 single-seat fighter.

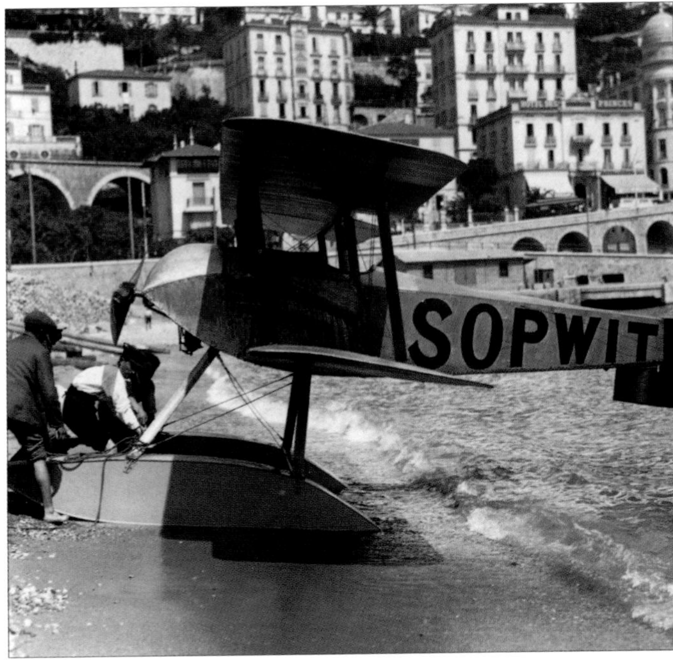

Above: A pre-war version of the British Sopwith Tabloid of the type that, with some modification, served as a naval reconnaissance and light bomber aircraft during the war.

five F-2As with a Curtiss H-12 took part in one of the very few battles between seaplanes. On 4 June 1918, they saw off 14 German aircraft after a dogfight, destroying 6 for the loss of just the Curtiss.

The first successful launch of an aerial torpedo was in July 1914 from a British aircraft and the world's first torpedo-bomber was the two-seat Short 184, which entered service with the RNAS in 1915. A 184 flying off Gallipoli from the seaplane tender *Ben-My-Chree* in August 1915 became the first aircraft to sink a ship with a torpedo. Despite this success, using torpedoes remained dangerous for the dropping aircraft and in the case of the Short 184 and the later 320 their use was discontinued. Other major British seaplanes were Sopwith's Schneider (1915) and Baby (1916).

German Designs

Germany developed its own naval aviation service. It largely relied on a handful of manufacturers, such as Friedrichshafen, which produced the FF-33 series from late 1914. The main reconnaissance model, the FF-33e, was fitted with a two-way radio and carried a load of hand-thrown bombs, while the FF-33l was the seaplane fighter version. These types were superseded by the FF-49 from May 1917, a more robust aircraft that was better suited to the harsh conditions likely to be encountered in the North Sea. Other types included the Albatros W-4 floatplane fighter and the Hansa-Brandenburg series – the CC, KDW, W-12 and W-29.

Both Austria-Hungary and Italy deployed maritime aviation units. The former relied on German types, like the Hansa-Brandenburg CC, but did also produce the two-seat Löhner L flying boat, one of which sank the French submarine *Foucault* on 15 September 1916. The Italians produced several such aircraft including the Macchi M-5 biplane fighter.

SOPWITH SCHNEIDER

The British Schneider, seen here being recovered by HMS *Undaunted*, was based on a pre-war design that had won the 1914 Schneider trophy. The military version appeared in early 1915 and was largely used for anti-submarine and Zeppelin patrols. Some 136 were built before it was replaced in early 1916.

Type: Patrol floatplane
Engine: 100hp Gnome Monosoupape
Crew: 1
Ceiling: 3,000m (9,850ft)
Top speed: 148kph (92mph)
Armament: 1 x 0.303in (7.7mm) machine-gun

The Caucasus Front, 1914–16

The fighting in the remote Caucasus of north-eastern Turkey swung backwards and forwards between 1914 and1916 but by the close of the latter year the Russians held a sizeable portion of Turkish territory in Armenia.

Turkey and Russia held long-standing animosities towards each other, not least over the Balkans, and these soon led to hostilities in World War I. When Turkey went to war against the Allies on 31 October 1914, its navy bombarded Odessa, Sevastopol and Theodosia, ports on Russia's Black Sea coast, the same day. The Russian government then issued its own declaration of war the next day. The main battlefield between the two for the next three years or so would be the mountainous Caucasus.

Right: Germany's Emperor Wilhelm II greets Turkish Minister of War Enver Pasha aboard the battle-cruiser *Goeben*.

Turkey had long craved the Russian Caucasus, a region that lay just over its own north-east border, and Enver Pasha, the country's Minister of War, was set on invading the inhospitable area despite the advice of the head of the German military mission, General Otto Liman von Sanders, who strongly opposed the plan.

Opening Battles

Russia actually struck first, crossing the border into Turkish Armenia at several points, but the advance towards Erzerum was largely halted in late November 1914. Enver took personal command of the Turkish forces in Armenia on 14 December and launched his own major attack a week later, just days after the first heavy snows of winter had fallen. The advance towards Kars was opposed by 100,000 Russian troops, and these inflicted severe casualties on the Turks at the Battle of Sarikamish fought from 26 December 1914 through January 1915. Only 18,000 Turkish troops out of an initial 95,000 survived the battle and the freezing conditions during the retreat to Erzerum. Enver returned to Constantinople.

The Turkish leadership suspected that the Christian Armenians had been covertly

Left: Wounded Turkish soldiers in the Caucasus are treated by their Russian captors.

supporting the Russian invaders and initiated a series of vicious crackdowns that set off a full-blown revolt in April and May. Armenians seized Van on 20 April and held it until Russian forces arrived on 18 May. The Turks struck back in July. General Abdul Kerim crushed a Russian corps at the Battle of Malazgirt (10–26 July) north of Lake Van and retook the town itself on 5 August. His cautious advance was halted in its tracks by a Russian counter-attack a few days later.

YOUNG TURKS

"Young Turks" was the name commonly used to describe members of Turkey's radical and highly nationalistic Union and Progress Party. Turkey was a democracy and a UPP-dominated government was formed in early 1913. The Young Turks, led by War Minister Enver Pasha and Interior Minister Talaat Pasha, effectively held the reigns of power from 1914 onwards. They allied with Germany and oversaw the country's increasingly botched war effort but mostly remained above criticism until mid-1918. The UPP was dissolved on 20 October that year.

Above: Talaat Pasha (centre) on his visit to Austria, when he was prime minister during the war.

RUSSIAN ATTACKS

Grand Duke Nicholas, uncle of Tsar Nicholas II, was appointed to the position of viceroy of Caucasia on 24 September and he laid plans for a major effort in early 1916. This broad-front offensive into Armenia by some 200,000 troops was actually commanded by General Nikolai Yudenich and opened on 11 January 1916. The main thrust was from Kars towards Erzerum. Kerim's Third Army was decisively beaten at Köprukoy a week later and Erzerum itself fell on 16 February after a three-day siege. Yudenich had also made a smaller thrust along the Black Sea coast, which was aided by troops landed from Russian warships, and this culminated in the capture of Trebizond (Trabzon) on 18 April.

In response Enver ordered a two-pronged counter-offensive. The Third Army, now led by Vehip Pasha, pushed along the Black Sea coast but was routed by Yudenich at Erzinjan by 28 July. The second Turkish attack, by Ahmet Izzim Pasha's Second Army, enjoyed some initial success. A corps commanded by Mustafa Kemal of Gallipoli fame captured Mus and Bitlis on 15 August but Yudenich soon retook the two towns, leaving the Russians holding much of Armenia as fighting died down for winter.

Left: Russian troops push forward through a mountain pass during the fighting in the Caucasus. Bitter winters here often led to a seasonal suspension of operations.

Palestine, 1914–16

The Middle East, and Egypt in particular, was crucial to Britain's war effort not least because the Suez Canal, the country's major supply route to India, was highly vulnerable to attack from Turkish troops based in neighbouring Palestine.

Turkey's attacks on the Allies in late October 1914 prompted a swift response from the British government. Britain annexed Cyprus on 5 November, sent cruisers to shell Turkish forts at the entrance to the Dardanelles on the 30th and declared a protectorate over Egypt on 18 December. Egypt's Suez Canal was vital to Britain's interests as the main route to India, cornerstone of the empire. British and Empire troops were soon arriving to defend the canal and General John Maxwell was put in command.

The Turks were aware of the canal's strategic importance and in early 1915 made an attempt to capture it. A 22,000-strong force drawn from the Fourth Army, under Minister of Marine, Djemal Pasha, set out from Beersheba in Palestine on 14 January. That it successfully crossed the waterless Sinai Peninsula was largely due to the organizational skills of Djemal's German Chief of Staff, General Friedrich Kress von Kressenstein. The Turkish force made an attempt to cross the canal on pontoons on 2–3 February but the attack was easily broken up by the defenders' fire and Djemal withdrew back to Beersheba. For the remainder of the year the canal zone remained something of a backwater, not least because both sides were far more concerned with events at Gallipoli and in Mesopotamia.

Above: A lone Turkish cavalryman pictured somewhere in Palestine. Attempts by the Turks to capture the Suez Canal were largely half-hearted and ended with defeat at the Battle of Romani in 1916.

Battles in 1916

The British were preoccupied by two matters in 1916 – a Turkish attack in Sinai and a revolt to their rear. A new commander, General Archibald Murray, had pushed the canal's defences into the Sinai Peninsula and this involved building communications, setting up various forts and developing a satisfactory system for supplying water. For the most part this work went on without the Turks responding in force, although there was some skirmishing against the 3,500-strong Turkish Desert Force led by Kress von Kressenstein.

The Turks finally made a larger effort to disrupt Murray's work in July 1916. This time Kress von Kressenstein commanded some 16,000 troops and was supported by various German machine-gun, artillery and anti-aircraft detachments as well as a dozen aircraft. By mid-July the largely Turkish force was positioned outside Romani, a town some 32km (20 miles)

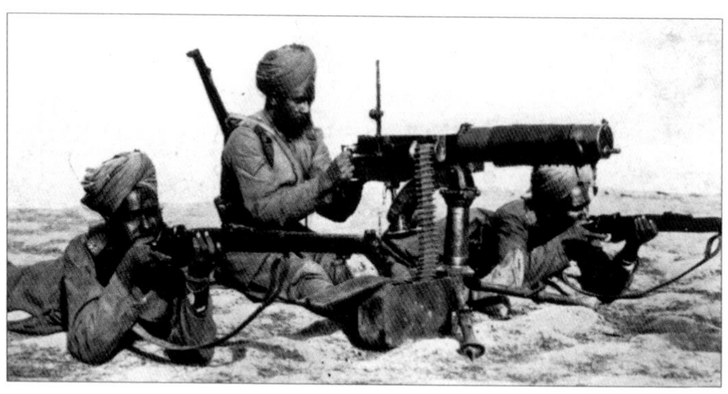

Left: An Indian Vickers machine-gun detachment pictured in Palestine. Such troops made up a sizeable proportion of the British war effort in the region.

Right: Turkish artillerymen manhandle a field gun into position. Such light weapons were better suited to the campaigns in the Middle East, which generally were more fluid than the Western Front.

east of the canal that marked the farthest extent of Murray's advance. The battle began with a surprise attack by the Turks on 4 August that gained some ground but the gains had been lost by the next day. Kress von Kressenstein was then forced to retreat 96km (60 miles) back to El Arish due to growing water shortages. The Battle of Romani cost the Turks roughly 8,000 casualties and the British little more than 1,000. The British victory permanently removed the Turkish threat to the Suez Canal.

Below: A few German troops, like these cavalrymen, fought alongside the Turks in Palestine.

SENUSSI REVOLT

The British did face another problem, however. Germany and Turkey had convinced Sidi Ahmad es Sherif, the leader of the Senussi people of western Egypt and Italian-controlled Tripolitania and Cyrenaica (Libya), to rise against the British in late 1915 and had provided them with various modern weapons by submarine.

The Senussi were opposed by the initially small Anglo-Egyptian Western Frontier Force (WFF) but it was finally able to inflict a decisive defeat on them at Aqqaqia on 26 February 1916. The Senussi resorted to guerrilla warfare that eventually tied down some 60,000 Italian troops and the 35,000-strong WFF. Ahmad was largely beaten by late 1916 to early 1917 but his raids continued into the last year of the war, even though the flow of supplies from Germany and Turkey had long since dried up.

THE CALL OF JIHAD

On 14 November 1914, in a speech given in Constantinople, Sheikh-ul-Islam, a senior Muslim cleric, declared a holy war against the then Allies – Britain, France, Montenegro, Serbia and Russia. He also preached that those Muslims who lived in Allied countries or under their rule and did not heed his call would either burn in hell or suffer unspecified "painful torment". Much of this anti-Allied sentiment stemmed from a well-received visit to the Middle East by Germany's Emperor Wilhelm II in 1898 and the subsequent use of agents to stir up anti-Christian feeling.

The Mesopotamian Campaign, 1914–16

The first part of the prolonged and probably unnecessary British campaign in Turkish-controlled Mesopotamia was characterized by poor planning and bad management and also saw one of Britain's most shocking defeats of the war.

British and Indian troops had been sent to protect some of the Persian Gulf's oil installations shortly after the war in Europe began and responded to Turkey's war declaration in late October 1914 by capturing the port of Basra in Turkish-controlled Mesopotamia (Iraq) on 23 November. The same troops had pushed northward to take Qurna, the point where the Euphrates and Tigris rivers meet, by early December.

British operations in Mesopotamia were originally conceived on a small scale but after two Turkish attacks on Qurna and Ahwaz were easily repulsed in April 1915, Major-General Charles Townshend was ordered to explore the possibility of taking Baghdad. Townshend set off from Basra up the Tigris at the head of a reinforced division and naval flotilla and captured Amara on 3 June. Even better news came when a force under Major-General George Gorringe that was moving along the Euphrates to protect Townshend's western flank inflicted a further defeat on the Turks at Nasiriya on 24 July.

Above: A detachment of Indian troops on anti-aircraft watch with a Lewis machine-gun.

Townshend resumed his own advance in August and made for Kut-el-Amara, a town two-thirds of the way to Baghdad held by 10,000 troops under Nur-ud-Din Pasha. The British units were becoming over-stretched because they had to protect lines of communication that stretched 480km (300 miles) down the Tigris back to Basra. Townshend's 10,000 men won the Battle of Kut on 27–28 September but suffered more than 1,200 irreplaceable casualties in the process.

Reluctant Advance

With Baghdad almost in sight, Townshend was ordered to push on, although he justifiably complained that he lacked both the manpower and supplies needed. He moved forward on 11 November and ran into an extensive line of defences that Nur-ud-Din had built outside Ctesiphon. The Turks could muster some 18,000 troops and 45 guns, while Townshend had scraped together 11,000 troops and 30 guns. The British attacked on the 22nd but Townshend was forced to retreat after four days as Turkish reinforcements had arrived in

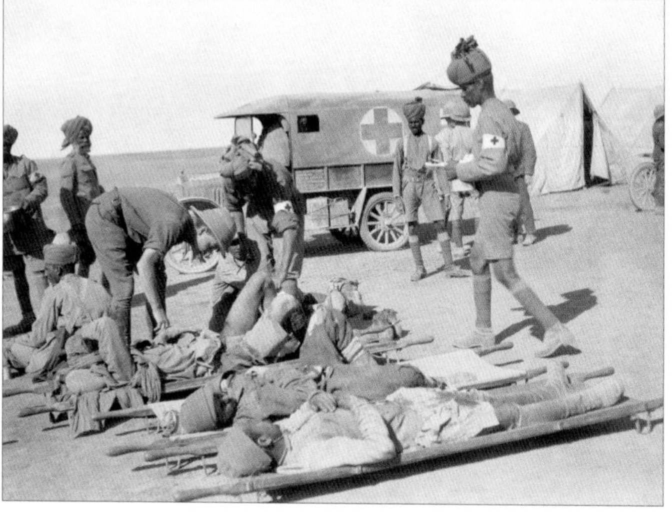

Left: Turkish casualties await evacuation from an Indian Army first-aid station near Tikrit.

strength. The British losses at Ctesiphon totalled 4,600 men, while the Turks lost some 6,200.

SURRENDER AT KUT

The Turks did not pursue the British closely and the retreating force reached Kut on 3 December. However, four days later, the town was placed under siege. Townshend had two months' supplies and awaited relief with some confidence but his faith was misplaced. Two British generals, Fenton Aylmer and Gorringe, led expeditions to break the siege in January and March 1916 but both were repulsed, the latter on 7 March by the Turkish Sixth Army under a German commander, General Kolmar von der Goltz. Townshend and nearly 10,000 troops surrendered on 29 April and went into a captivity that many would not survive. The relief expeditions had suffered some 21,000 casualties.

The British High Command and the War Office now debated the next move. While a new commander, General Frederick Maude, kicked his heels in Basra, some argued for withdrawal, while others backed a renewed advance towards the capital, Baghdad. Finally, on 3 December, Maude led his 166,000-strong Anglo-Indian force back into Mesopotamia along both banks of the Tigris. The campaign was no longer a minor sideshow.

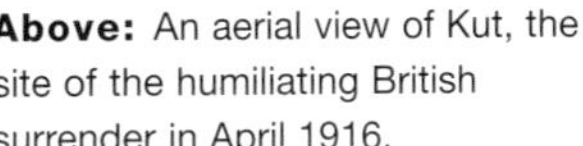

Above: An aerial view of Kut, the site of the humiliating British surrender in April 1916.

WAR IN PERSIA

Oil-rich Persia (Iran) was a relatively undeveloped country in 1914 but it had also been a long-established and highly sensitive strategic buffer zone between the Russian Empire and British-controlled India. It had been split by them into two zones of interest, a British south and Russian north, in 1907, but Germany tried to undermine Anglo-Russian authority once war had been declared. Weapons and money flowed to various dissident Persian nationalist groups and they came close to taking over the country in 1915 but were largely defeated by Russian forces during the following year.

Left: A British 18-pounder (84mm) field gun in action in Mesopotamia.

The Wider War at Sea

The Battle of the Dogger Bank was the sole major clash between surface warships in 1915 but German submarines were becoming a greater menace in the North Atlantic and were also sinking neutral ships in what proved a dangerous strategy.

There was only one major engagement in the North Sea between units of Britain's Grand Fleet and Germany's High Seas Fleet during 1915. The Battle of the Dogger Bank on 24 January came about when British intelligence discovered that Vice-Admiral Franz von Hipper's battle-cruiser squadron intended to raid the English coast and sink fishing trawlers. Hipper was surprised by Admiral David Beatty's battle-cruiser squadron and the German flagship, *Seydlitz*, was badly damaged and *Blücher* sunk in a running fight. Dogger Bank was not a major fleet engagement but it did have considerable consequences. The High Seas Fleet was smaller than the Grand Fleet and the loss of just one major vessel worried the German establishment. The commander of the High Seas Fleet was sacked and Emperor Wilhelm II ordered his fleet to avoid further unnecessary risks.

Above: The killing of civilians during U-boat attacks was used for propaganda purposes by the Allies.

Below: The mortally wounded German battle-cruiser *Blücher* rolls over during the Dogger Bank action.

If the High Seas Fleet could not be risked, the Imperial German Navy would have to use other means to strike back at Britain, chiefly by intensifying the campaign against Britain's trade. The German Navy did not rely entirely on U-boats for this as they were still a relatively untried technology and did not have the endurance of surface ships. Auxiliary commerce raiders and armed merchant cruisers could range much farther and for longer. Some of these were successful but their impact lessened as many were sunk or interned and by spring 1915 U-boats were playing the greater part in the campaign against British shipping. Coastal submarines operated in the North Sea and English Channel, freeing larger boats for service in the Western Approaches.

U-BOAT ATTACKS

A key moment came on 4 February 1915, when Germany announced it would initiate *Handelskrieg* (trade warfare). This allowed its 30 or so submarines to sink Allied merchant ships sailing around Britain and Ireland without warning from the 18th. The decision had not been taken easily and was only reached after bitter argument. The military case was clear-cut but Germany's political leaders knew that unrestricted submarine warfare was a contravention of international law. It would hand the Allies a major propaganda victory as such a strategy would almost certainly lead to

Above: Britain's war effort very much relied on merchant ships like this one, here being manoeuvred into dock, and such vessels were the U-boats' main target.

ADMIRAL DAVID BEATTY

Beatty (1871–1936) was probably Britain's most flamboyant and well-known senior naval officer of the war. He had been made commander of the Grand Fleet's Battle-cruiser Squadron in 1911 and led it in action at Heligoland Bight (1914), Dogger Bank (1915) and Jutland (1916), battles in which his seeming rashness cost his squadron several warships. The losses were not entirely his fault, however, and in late 1916 he was made Commander-in-Chief of the Grand Fleet over the heads of more senior officers. He essentially continued the cautious strategy of his predecessor until the German fleet surrendered in 1918.

the sinking of neutral vessels and the death of citizens from neutral states.

NEUTRAL LOSSES

German U-boats sent roughly one million tons of shipping to the bottom in 1915 and just 17 submarines were lost. Yet, as those opposed to *Handelskrieg* had predicted, these successes had a high political price. The first neutral target of the campaign was the Norwegian tanker *Belridge*, which was damaged on 19 February but a later victim caused wider repercussions. The United States had already issued stern warnings but on 1 May the US tanker *Gulflight* was torpedoed and two crewmen killed. An even more vehement response was required after the British passenger liner *Lusitania* was sunk on 7 May and 128 US citizens died.

Even this did not prevent further loss of US lives – two more civilians died when another British liner, *Arabic*, was lost on 19 August. Germany now decided to back down and on the 30th announced that merchant ships would not be attacked without warning – but the damage had been done and the prohibition on *Handelskrieg* was destined not to last.

Below: The sinking of the *Lusitania* and the death of 128 US nationals led to a suspension of Germany's U-boat campaign.

Gallipoli – The Withdrawal

The British persisted with the stalled Gallipoli campaign throughout the summer of 1915, even making further landings in August, but with the onset of winter it was clear to all that there was no other option than complete withdrawal.

When the British-led amphibious assault on Gallipoli was made on 25 April 1915 the immediate intention was to push along the mountainous peninsula to capture Constantinople and knock Turkey out of the war. Yet these hopes were soon dashed and by early June the campaign had degenerated into the bitterest form of trench warfare. The British had captured Helles, the southern tip of the peninsula, and an even smaller area farther along its west coast held by the Australian and New Zealand Army Corps and christened ANZAC Cove. The Turks held the high ground and could readily call down artillery fire on the beaches.

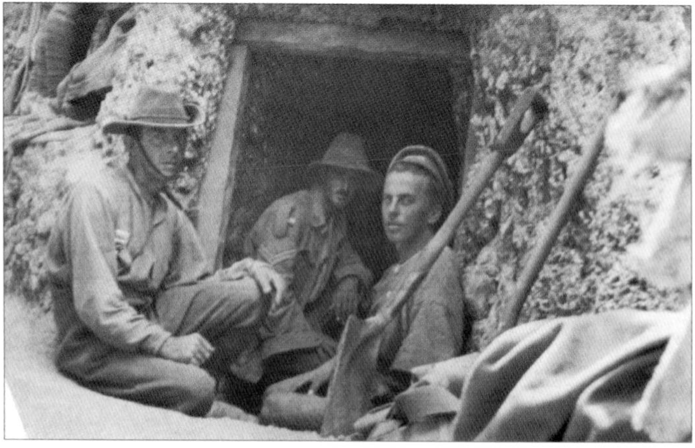

Above: ANZAC troops pictured by one of the many dugouts that were built into the cliff and valley sides that typified the Gallipoli Peninsula.

Below: One of the beaches across which all of the British and ANZAC supplies had to be ferried – often under Turkish gunfire.

Landings at Suvla

General Ian Hamilton, the British commander, tried to break the stalemate by making another landing on the west coast behind the main Turkish lines. While the troops at Helles launched a diversionary attack, the ANZACs were to break out and then swing northward to link up with troops landed at Suvla Bay. The operation took place on 6–10 August and, while the diversionary attack was successful, the ANZACs became bogged down and were unable to cut through the Turkish lines. The force that landed at Suvla, commanded by General F. Stopford, was unopposed but

Above: The British and others made numerous attacks but they were increasingly localized and caused the Turks no great problems.

foolishly failed to push inland at once. The Turks reacted quickly and were soon overlooking the beach in strength.

Suvla was effectively the last throw of the dice for Hamilton and his request for further reinforcements was largely rejected because they were needed elsewhere. The general had also lost the support of his superiors and was relieved of his command on 15 October. His replacement, General Charles Monro, arrived on the 28th, toured the various beaches, and recommended total withdrawal the next day. After various other options were discussed, Monro was finally given permission to evacuate all three of the embattled and claustrophobic beachheads on 3 December.

Secret Withdrawal

In stark contrast to the landings, the two-stage withdrawal was a masterpiece of excellent planning, meticulous staff work and orderly execution. Pessimists in the Allied camp expected a casualty rate of around 50 per cent but they were wholly wrong – just three casualties were reported in all. Suvla Bay and ANZAC Cove were the first to be abandoned. Some 105,000 men, 5,000 animals and 300 guns were removed under cover of darkness between 10 and 20 December. Thanks to a variety of ruses that suggested the trenches were still being manned and first-rate noise discipline, the 100,000 Turkish troops around the two beaches never discovered what was actually taking place. The withdrawal from Helles followed a similar pattern between late December and 9 January 1916, when 35,000 men and 3,700 animals were spirited away.

Below: These barges, known as "Beetles", proved invaluable throughout the fighting for bringing in supplies, not least water, and evacuating the wounded to hospital ships lying offshore.

The multinational campaign had cost the Allies some 276,000 casualties, many of whom were invalided home because they had contracted various sicknesses. Turkish losses are problematical but probably totalled at least 250,000. The Gallipoli fiasco had both political and strategic repercussions in Britain. Its failure led to the resignation of the dynamic First Lord of the Admiralty, Winston Churchill, who had been the driving force behind the campaign. It also meant that there would be no supply route opened to Russia through the Dardanelles to the Black Sea.

The advocates of the strategy to undermine Germany's war effort by knocking out its weaker allies, the so-called "Easterners" like Churchill, were now largely discredited. "Westerners", mostly generals who believed the war could only be won by crushing Germany on the Western Front, were instead in the ascendancy, although the debate would continue.

German Submarines

The Imperial German Navy began the war with very few submarines but they started to grow in importance and eventually became the main weapon in the campaign to bring Britain to its knees by strangling its maritime trade routes.

Germany deployed the most technically advanced and largest fleet of submarines of all during World War I but actually had none in service before 1906. Its navy had around 30 submarines available in August 1914 but by the end of the war a further 350 or so had seen active service. Their operational peak came in June 1917 when 61 were at sea.

The Imperial German Navy actually produced very few different types of boat during the war as its planners rightly believed that concentrating on fewer types made production, maintenance and the training of crews much more straightforward. Larger boats designed for long-range operations were given U- numbers, and there were smaller, short-range UB- and UC-boats that usually operated in shallower coastal waters.

Above: Crewmen watch over the engine room machinery in a U-boat. The image gives a good idea of the cramped working conditions aboard a World War I submarine.

Below: A UB-III class U-boat slices through rough seas off the German island of Heligoland in the south-eastern North Sea.

U-Boat Types

The term U-boat derives from *Unterseeboot* ("submarine boat") and these spearheaded the operations against British maritime commerce. They were built in batches and each differed in some way but overall became larger and more powerful as the war progressed. The

UC-1

UC-1 (illustrated) was Germany's original minelaying submarine, the first of a class of 15, and appeared in 1915. It carried 12 mines which were deployed downwards through hatches in the keel. Surface armament was one machine-gun. It was 55m (180ft) long and had a surface speed of 6.5 knots (5 knots submerged). The *UC-1*'s chief weakness was its endurance, a mere 1,280km (800 miles) at 5 knots. It had a 16-man crew. The boat was lost on 19 July 1917 off Nieuport, Belgium, somewhat ironically probably to a mine.

650-ton *U-21* launched in 1913 had a surface speed of around 15 knots and some 9 knots submerged. It had a crew of 35 and carried four torpedo tubes and an 8.6cm (3.4in) deck gun. *U-140*, launched in late 1917, was much bigger. It displaced 1,930 tons and could cruise on the surface at nearly 16 knots or submerged at close to 8 knots. It had a crew of 64 and its weapons comprised six tubes and two 15cm (5.9in) deck guns. Its range was also more than three times that of *U-21*.

Cargo U-boats

The biggest of the U-boats were the Deutschland class, which appeared in 1916 and started out as unarmed cargo-carrying vessels. *Deutschland* itself caused something of a stir when it sailed as a merchant ship from Kiel to Baltimore in the then-neutral USA, partly to return with war materials but also as a propaganda mission. It arrived at its destination on 9 July and returned home with a cargo of various key metals. The seven vessels, *U-151* to *U-157*, were later converted into fighting submarines. They had two tubes and a 15cm (5.9in) deck gun. Two of them were sunk but *U-155* proved to be very successful, sinking a total of 19 Allied vessels on its first sortie to the Azores area in June–September 1917.

UB-boats became operational from spring 1915. The earliest batches, *UB-1* to *UB-17*, were found to be unsuitable for even the most basic anti-shipping role and were superseded by the larger UB-II class boats, *UB-18* to *UB-47*. These were faster, 9 knots rather than 6, and had a much greater range. The boats were first commissioned in 1915. The next UB-III class (*UB-48* to *UB-136*) did not emerge until the last year of the war. These were larger still, roughly four times the displacement of the first batch, with five torpedo tubes and one deck gun.

UC-boats were similarly conceived for short-range tasks but operated as minelayers. These first appeared in the English Channel in mid-1915 and also served in the Baltic, Black and Mediterranean Seas. Larger UC-II boats, numbers *UC-16* to *UC-79*, began operating in 1916 and they carried 18 rather than 12 mines and had an impressive range. A third batch, the UC-III class, was ordered in 1917 but did not see action.

UB-1

This small submarine was the lead boat in a class of eight. They were all transported in sections to either Belgium or the Adriatic Sea where they operated for the duration. *UB-1* itself was wrecked in the Adriatic Sea and scrapped.

Type: Coastal submarine
Laid down: 1914
Displacement: 127 tons
Crew: 14
Speed: 6.5 knots (surfaced)
Main armament: 2 x 45.7cm (18in) torpedo tubes

Home Fronts

The civilian populations of the various combatant nations largely backed the war when fighting broke out in 1914 but by the conflict's later stages many were suffering from war weariness and many faced very real privations.

Although the various home fronts were different in many ways, they also had some startling similarities. When war broke out in August 1914, for example, it was greeted with widespread enthusiasm in all of the capitals of the major combatant nations, where crowds took to the streets in their thousands. There were exceptions, especially among left-wingers like France's Jean Jaurès, but they were marginalized and faced much public ire. Jaurès was assassinated in a Paris café on 31 July for his anti-war views.

War enthusiasm also meant that people accepted – at least at the outset – tighter state control. This took many forms, not least tight limits on union activity. There were restrictions imposed on enemy aliens or those opposed to the war, especially in the United States where the Espionage Act (1917) and the Sedition Acts led to the imprisonment of 1,600 people. Britain enacted the Defence of the Realm Act in 1914 and restricted access to alcohol, a policy that was also followed in many other countries. Russia took the most extreme measure and banned both the production and consumption of vodka in August 1914. The United States introduced Prohibition in 1918, although it did not begin to operate for another two years.

Food Rationing

Hunger was another common problem. Many Germans suffered because of Britain's naval blockade while the German submarine campaign severely curtailed the movement of foodstuffs to Britain by ship. Bad harvests and poor distribution systems also contributed to the problem. Although it was kept from the public, Britain was just a few weeks from starvation in spring 1917 and nationwide ration books for meat and dairy produce were introduced in July 1918. Britain's allies also suffered. Moscow's supply of food was something like 60 per cent below what was required by January 1917. The French government encouraged "meatless days" at around the same time and then introduced rationing of some foods and fuel in early 1918. German civilians suffered to an even greater degree, particularly during the harsh

Below: German civilians riot – a not uncommon sight as food became increasingly scarce.

Above: British women at work on a farm, replacing men conscripted into the armed forces.

"turnip winter" of 1916–17, and some estimates suggest that 700,000 Germans had died of malnutrition by 1919.

Women at War

The war also brought women into the workplace as never before, despite their facing discrimination and hostility. In Britain there were 175,000 in war production by late 1914; by August 1917 some 750,000 were working in jobs formerly held by men and a further 350,000 were employed in work directly created by the war economy. A further 240,000 women were working in agriculture by 1918.

The picture was similar if patchier in France, Italy and the USA, but Germany lagged behind. Women were not encouraged to enter war-related employment until the introduction of the Hindenburg Programme in late 1916.

Civilians did die through enemy action during the war, but on a small scale compared to World War II. However, the Armistice in 1918 did not halt the suffering as the world was confronting an influenza pandemic. It broke out in spring 1918, lasted for a year or so and cut a swathe through Europe and elsewhere – 229,000 died in Britain, 166,000 in France and 225,000 in Germany. The worldwide figure was an estimated 20 million and 70 per cent of the victims were under 35.

Below: A long but orderly queue of British women and children seeking rationed produce.

PACIFISM

The clamour for war was overwhelming in 1914 but a few figures in many of the combatant nations did oppose the war, often at much risk to themselves. There were two types of pacifism at the outbreak of war. First there was personal pacifism in which an individual opposed violence on moral or religious grounds. Second was political pacifism in which either internationalist or left-wing groups believed war was a capitalist conspiracy against workers or liberal isolationists felt that war was none of their country's business. Pacifism also acquired a third definition referring to those who wanted to bring the ongoing war to an end not through victory but by an immediate peace settlement.

Above: A French magazine celebrates the twin female roles of motherhood and war-factory work.

Zeppelins

German Zeppelins and other airship types carried out dozens of raids against Britain, France and Russia during the war but the British bore the brunt of their attacks, with 53 raids in total between 1914 and 1918.

In World War I rigid-frame airships were used most extensively by the Germany Army Air Service and the Imperial German Navy, in both reconnaissance or night-time bombing roles. Germany built two main types, the well-known Zeppelin and the little known Schütte-Lanz (SL). Both of these were kept aloft by highly pure but potentially explosive hydrogen, though they had different types of rigid frame.

Above: German airships head out on a mission over England. The first attack came in January 1915 but the raids tailed off dramatically from 1917 onward.

AIRSHIP VARIANTS

The more common design was the Zeppelin, which was developed by Graf Zeppelin and was first accepted into German military service in March 1909. Zeppelins had a metal (duralumin) frame and came in a variety of designs. The early *L.3* was around 158.5m (520ft) long, was crewed by 16 men, and had a top speed of 72kph (45mph), while the more advanced R-type measured some 200m (650ft), had a crew of 19 and a top speed of 96kph (60mph).

The smaller Schütte-Lanz type was named after its designers, Professor Schütte and Doctor Lanz. SL airships had the drawback that their plywood frames tended to absorb atmospheric moisture too easily in flight. This made them difficult to control and they became unpopular with their crews.

The German Army put great store in its airships but its faith was shattered in the first weeks of the war. They were deployed

Left: French troops stand watch over the burnt-out remains, mostly twisted metal, of the German airship *L.39* on 6 April 1917.

on daylight reconnaissance missions over heavily defended areas of Belgium and France, and in August 1914 alone four were lost to ground fire and one was destroyed when a British fighter attacked it in its shed. The Army lost interest in airships from late 1916 and then abandoned them altogether in June 1917.

Long-range Raids

The German Navy, which had always led the way in airships, thereafter dominated operations and increasingly turned to night-time bombing. In total the German Naval Airship Division operated 73 airships during the war (59 Zeppelins, 8 Schütte-Lanz and 6 other types, such as the Parseval) and these made 342 bombing and 1,191 reconnaissance flights. Their main bombing targets were in England, especially London and other industrial areas, and Paris, although there were attempted raids on targets in Russia, including Baltic naval bases and the capital Petrograd (St Petersburg). Perhaps the most ambitious Zeppelin operation was that undertaken by *L.59* in late 1917. It was ordered to fly supplies from Bulgaria to German forces in East Africa. The mission (21–25 November) was aborted in mid-flight but *L.59* and its 22-man crew spent some 95 hours in the air and made a round trip of 6,750km (4,200 miles), braving violent storms and mechanical failures.

Zeppelins and SLs were in reality not as menacing as was believed. Their raids over England in particular did cause alarm but little damage and, in truth, they were very vulnerable; 77 out of 115 Zeppelins were destroyed or damaged beyond repair, for example. Many crashed due to adverse weather – high winds and ice were especially dangerous – while others were shot down by ground fire or, increasingly, by high-altitude fighters. Sometimes bombs were dropped on airships from above, while some fighters like the French Nieuport 17 and the British Sopwith Camel were equipped with incendiary rockets, such as the French Le Prieur that appeared in 1916. Rockets were supplanted by incendiary bullets and their use was largely discontinued by 1918.

Accidents were also not uncommon. The worst came in January 1918 when five airships were destroyed in a fire at their base while they were undergoing maintenance.

ZEPPELIN *L.32*

The German naval Zeppelin *L.32* was commissioned on 7 August 1916 but made only 11 flights including two raids on England. It failed to bomb anything significant on 24 August and on 24 September it was first hit by anti-aircraft fire and then downed by a fighter.

Type: "Super Zeppelin"
Engines: 6 x Maybach HSLu
Length: 198m (650ft)
Gas volume: 55,000 cu m (1,950,000 cu ft)
Top speed: 100kph (60mph)
First flight: 4 August 1916

THE LARGEST ZEPPELIN RAID

The biggest German airship raid on England took place on the night of 2 September 1916 and involved 11 Navy and 3 Army airships, most of them Zeppelins. A further two turned back early in the mission. The raiders struck up and down the East Coast, dropping 261 high-explosive and 202 incendiary bombs that did little damage but did kill 4 civilians and injure 12. One airship, *SL.11*, was shot down by a BE-2 fighter over Cuffley in Hertfordshire, just north of London.

Below: The spectacular end of a German airship. It was very rare for crew members to survive the downing of Zeppelins because of their combustibility.

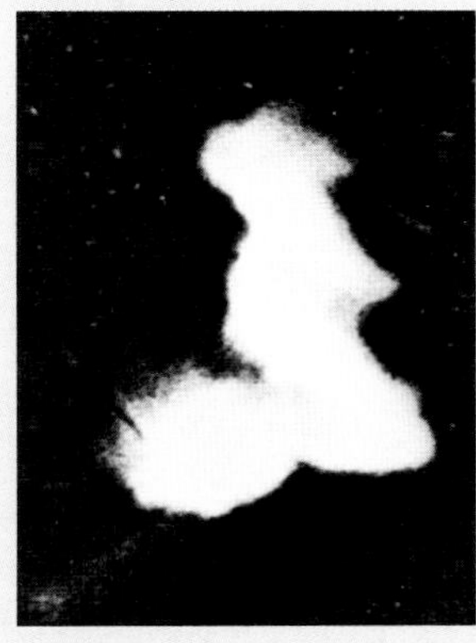

Civilians under Fire, 1914–18

The distinction between civilian and military personnel and property became blurred during World War I. In previous wars civilians might be at risk when the fighting armies were nearby; now cities far from the front were targets.

Although many French and German civilians died due to deliberate enemy action, their British counterparts faced the most sustained onslaught. The first major naval attack on Britain took place on 16 December 1914, when German warships bombarded the ports of Hartlepool, Whitby and Scarborough. Housing and other property were destroyed while casualties amounted to 122 dead and 433 injured. German warships returned to the East Coast in April 1916, hitting Lowestoft and Great Yarmouth. The loss of life was small and the damage minimal but, once again, civilian morale suffered and faith in the Royal Navy weakened. German naval raids left 157 dead and 641 injured in all.

Zeppelin raids on Britain usually involved two or more airships and concentrated on the south-east coast, the industrial North and the Midlands and, above all, London. They began on 19/20 January 1915 and London was hit for the first time on 31 May. There were a further 19 missions that year, 22 in 1916, 7 in 1917 and just 4 in 1918. Most were conducted in darkness and more than 5,750 bombs were dropped. The biggest raid occurred in September 1916 and involved 16 airships. In all some 556 British civilians were killed and 1,350 injured by bombs dropped from Zeppelins during the war.

Above: Bomb damage to a street in London's West End following a visit from a German Zeppelin.

Aircraft Attacks

Although there had been aircraft raids on south-east England since October 1914, true strategic bombing did not begin until early 1917. The main campaign involved heavy bombers, chiefly the Gotha G but also the larger Riesenflugzeug from late October. The first raid against London took place during daylight on 27 May and seven more followed, but in late August heavy losses forced the bombers to turn to night operations. There were a further 19 raids with the final attack coming on 19/20 May 1918. Gothas made 383 sorties and 43 were lost, while Riesenflugzeug types made just 30 sorties with 2 lost. Although the bombers caused little damage, civilian casualties totalled around 850 dead and over 2,000 injured. Morale did suffer until the anti-aircraft defences were improved.

Although British civilians bore the brunt of the German strikes, the French also suffered from such attacks, including 30 air raids on Paris. Parisians also had to endure long-range bombardment by the so-called "Paris Gun" in 1918; almost 900 were killed or injured.

Above: A German airship is manoeuvred out of its shed prior to a mission over England.

Attacking Germany

Germany was also the target of strategic bombing from late 1917 but the raids peaked in the final months of the war. The effort was largely conducted by Britain's Independent Air Force, which was founded in June 1918 under Major-General Hugh Trenchard. It soon began striking targets located in the industrial heartland of western Germany from airfields in eastern France and dropped some 558 tons of bombs out of a total of 665 tons dropped on Germany in 162 raids. Some 450 aircraft in all were lost but the number of German civilian casualties remains unknown.

Below: German bombing raids led to an increased demand for fighters. Here British workers are building their wing sections.

Below: This extensive damage to a building in Paris was caused by a German bombing raid.

Heavy Bombers

Heavy bombers made their debut during World War I. They were mostly deployed to undertake long-range strategic raids against military installation and industrial targets but they were also responsible for the deaths of many civilians.

Russia's Army Air Service had the most reliable heavy bomber at the outbreak of the war. It was based on Igor Sikorsky's civilian "Le Grand" from 1913, the world's first four-engined aircraft, and a military version, the Sikorsky IM (Ilya Mourometz), was ordered by the service in August 1914. It was a biplane design with an enclosed cabin, and a crew of six. It had a top speed of 96kph (60mph), a pair of machine-guns for defence and could carry some 535kg (1,180lb) of bombs. The IMs began operating against targets in eastern Poland in February 1915 and these raids were gradually extended to take in targets in Austria-Hungary and Germany. Some 400 sorties were launched by 73 bombers during 1914–17 and they proved highly successful and largely invulnerable. Only one was shot down, after itself destroying three of a group of attacking fighters, and just two others succumbed to various mechanical problems.

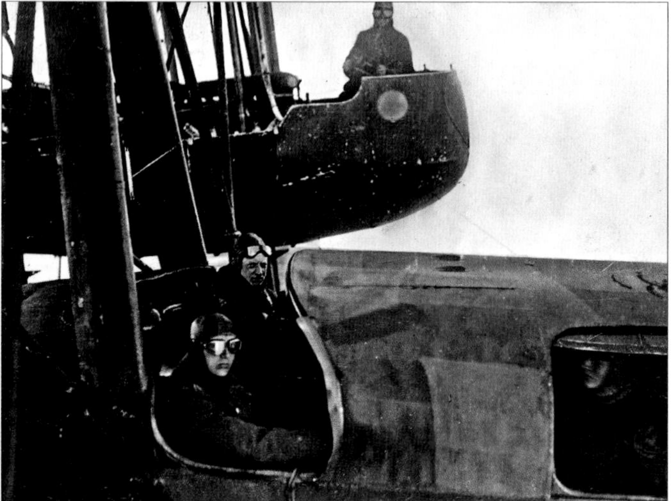

Below: The Russian-built Sikorsky IM (Ilya Mourometz) was one of the world's first successful heavy bombers and had a six-man crew.

Italian Designs

Italy's fledgling air service, the Corpo Aeronautico Militare (CAM), was woefully prepared for war in 1915 but it did have a long-range bomber in the Caproni. CAM had focused on such aircraft because of the local conditions – the likely battlefield was mountainous, making tactical bombing in support of ground operations problematic, but there were tempting long-range targets in both Austria-Hungary and the Balkans. Four types of Capronis (designated Ca2 to Ca5) were developed and around 750 were built in all. They came in several forms: some were biplanes while others were triplanes but they all had three engines. The Ca5 four-man biplane, introduced in

GOTHA G-IV

The Gotha was the mainstay of Germany's heavy-bomber force during the war, and five variants were built in all. The most successful version, with 230 built, was the G-IV, which began operating in early 1917. Gothas were, however, fragile machines and clumsy to fly.

Engine: 3 x 260hp Mercedes DIV
Crew: 3
Ceiling: 6,500m (21,325ft)
Top speed: 140kph (87mph)
Armament: 3 x 7.92mm (0.312in) machine-guns, 500kg (1,100lb) bombs

early 1918, was ultimately the mainstay of the Italian strategic bombing force with a total of 280 being built.

The Gotha Menace

The mainstay of the German Army Air Service's heavy bomber force was the Gotha G-series of twin-engined biplanes (designated G-I to G-V) that first entered service in 1915. These launched the first sustained strategic bombing offensive against London from bases around Ghent from June 1917. The most numerous type was the three-man G-IV which had a speed of around 140kph (87mph) and a range of 480km (300 miles). It was protected by three machine-guns and had a bomb load of some 500kg (1,100lb). The Germans also developed an even larger bomber, the Riesenflugzeug ("giant aircraft"), based on Sikorsky's IM type, that first entered full service in late 1916. Various companies built these advanced biplane bombers and there was no fully standardized design. The best was made by the Zeppelin-Staaken company. Its four-engined RVI first appeared in mid-1917. It had a seven-man crew, four machine-guns for defence, and carried up to 18 bombs.

CAPRONI Ca5

The Caproni range of Italian heavy bombers made their debut during 1911 and launched their first bombing raid of World War I in August 1915. Four variants of the design were built and served with the Italian Army and Navy and the US Army Air Service.

Engine: 3 x 300hp Fiat
Crew: 2–4
Ceiling: 4,550m (14,900ft)
Top speed: 160km/h (100mph)
Armament: 2 x 6.5mm (0.256in) machine-guns, 910kg (2,000lb) bombs

Britain's Reply

Britain's main heavy bombers were the twin-engined Handley Page O/100 (46 built) and O/400 (550 built). The former began operating in November 1916. Heavy O/100 losses during daylight raids led them to adopt night flying. The O/400 was a similar machine and went into full production in late 1917. It was expected to be the mainstay of the Independent Air Force's strategic bombing campaign against Germany in 1919, a role until then carried out by smaller bombers. Britain was also developing other heavy bombers, chiefly the four-engined Handley Page V/1500 and the twin-engined Vickers Vimy, but none saw action.

HANDLEY PAGE O/400

The HP O/400 entered service in the spring of 1918. A number were used in the bombing offensive against Germany. Although they carried a sizeable bomb load, they were also prone to accidents. Some 550 were built in Britain and a further 107 in the United States before the war's end.

Engine: 2 x 275hp Sunbeam or 2 x 375hp Rolls-Royce
Crew: 4
Ceiling: 2,590m (8,500ft)
Top speed: 160kph (100mph)
Armament: 3–5 x 0.303in (7.7mm) machine-guns, 820kg (1,800lb) bombs

The First Day of the Somme Volunteers for Britain s New Army, who fought on the Somme.

Russia Aids Its Allies Poor roads gave Russia many supply difficulties on the Eastern Front.

Battle of Jutland HMS *Queen Mary* blows up after being struck by German shells.

Main Central Powers' attacks
Main Allied attacks
Front line, Jan 1916
Front line, Dec 1916
Front line, Jan 1916
Front line, Dec 1916
Front line, Jan-Dec 1916
Front line, Jan 1916
Front line, Dec 1916
Front line, Jan 1916
Front line, Dec 1916

NORWAY
SWEDEN
North Sea
GREAT BRITAIN
DENMARK
Baltic Sea
MOSCOW
Vilna
RUSSIAN EMPIRE
WARSAW
Lódź
GERMANY
Ypres
Albert
Amiens
Reims
PARIS
Verdun
FRANCE
Lemberg
Czernowitz
AUSTRIA-HUNGARY
BUDAPEST
SWITZERLAND
Asiago
Venice
Gorizia
BELGRADE
BUCHAREST
BOSNIA
SERBIA
ROMANIA
SOFIA
BULGARIA
ITALY
Corsica
Sardinia
Cattaro
MONTENEGRO
Uskub
ALBANIA
Salonika
GREECE
Sicily
Mediterranean Sea
Black Sea
Caspian Sea
Trebizond
Kars
Van
PERSIA
TURKEY
BAGHDAD
Kut
Basra
Damascus
PALESTINE
CAIRO
ALGERIA
TUNISIA
LIBYA
EGYPT

0 100 200 300 400 500 mi
0 200 400 600 800 km

1916 – THE YEAR OF ATTRITION

The Allies focused their main efforts in Europe during 1916 and planned to launch simultaneous offensives on the Western, Eastern and Italian Fronts. These efforts were pre-empted by the Germans, who had opted to hold fast in the east and look for victory in the west. The Germans initiated the longest battle of the war, Verdun, in February and came close to defeating the French in the first few months. The fast-deteriorating situation there led the other Allies to bring forward their own offensives. These helped relieve the pressure on the recovering French but failed to knock Germany out of the war.

All of these attacks fostered great expectations of a decisive breakthrough – yet these hopes soon proved illusory. The German attack at Verdun stalled with fast-growing casualties on all sides by the middle of the year, the British offensive on the Somme suffered a severe setback on its very first day, and the Russian Brusilov Offensive made considerable progress in its first weeks but thereafter degenerated into stalemate. The Italians made no progress against the Austro-Hungarians. Even the war at sea seemed stalemated with neither the British nor German navies able to deliver a knockout blow against each other at Jutland, the largest naval battle of the war.

Stalemate on the Italian Front Austro-Hungarian troops with a captured Italian heavy howitzer.

Machine-guns A French Hotchkiss machine-gun team in position in a reserve trench.

Operations in Salonika, 1916–17 A newly arrived French unit moves up to the front.

Verdun – The German Attack

The German Army Chief of Staff, General Erich von Falkenhayn, made the fateful decision to decimate the French Army at the fortress town of Verdun in 1916 but his plan backfired as his own forces suffered equally horrendous casualties.

Germany's generals had been preoccupied with events on the Eastern Front in 1915 but returned to the attack on the Western Front in 1916. France became the preferred target as General von Falkenhayn knew that the French would hold their ground whatever the cost in lives and were willing to expend more blood in retaking what they had lost. Falkenhayn believed that the French would ultimately sue for peace if their losses became unsustainable. With France defeated Britain would have to seek an end to the war.

KEY FACTS

Date: 21 February – 18 December 1916

Place: Verdun, eastern France

Outcome: Stalemated battle with very heavy French and German casualties.

THE BATTLE OF VERDUN
As with many other of World War I's great battles, the struggle for Verdun took place in a small area, only some 40km (25 miles) across.

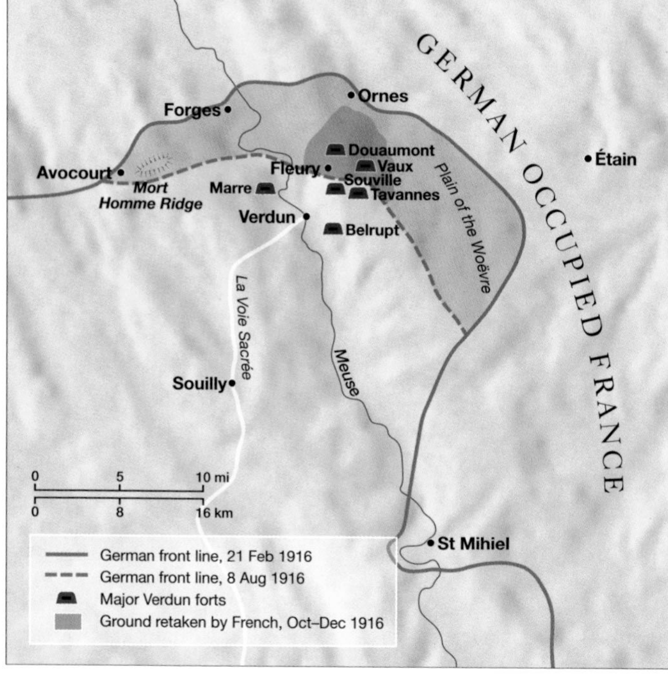

Falkenhayn choose Verdun on the River Meuse for his battle of attrition. The town was surrounded by forts but was close to a German-controlled railhead that would permit a steady flow of men and supplies to the front. Its garrison had been pared to the bone and many of the forts stripped of artillery. The German operation was codenamed Gericht, meaning "judgement" or even "place of execution". The attack was to be made on a narrow front by Crown Prince Wilhelm's Fifth Army, which was supported by some 1,200 artillery pieces and 3 million shells which had been stockpiled in secrecy.

The Killing Begins

Gericht was scheduled to begin on 12 February but snow and rain delayed the preparations and prevented accurate artillery fire. The weather cleared after eight days and the attack began on the 21st. The artillery bombardment created a lunar landscape of almost overlapping shell craters, and set the tone for the remainder of the battle. Some 100,000 shells fell in the first hour alone and 1 million rounds fell on the French before the first German assault units moved out into No Man's Land. Remarkably, some French troops survived the opening inferno and fought back with unexpected stubbornness but the German divisions mostly made steady progress. Fort

Above: French forward artillery observers seek out a suitable target on the skyline.

Douaumont was captured on the 25th, while other units took high ground overlooking the Meuse and inflicted heavy casualties on the numerous French counter-attacks.

Falkenhayn's brutal strategy seemed to be working but there were some ominous developments for the Germans, not least the loss of 25,000 men in just the first week of the battle. The German capture of Fort Douaumont – which might have been seen as a possible breaking point – actually caused a wave of national fervour in France.

Field Marshal Joffre, the French Commander-in-Chief, reacted to the crisis with great calmness. He asked the British on the River Somme to take over the sector of the front held there by the French Tenth Army, thereby freeing up some reinforcements for Verdun. He sent General Noël de Castelnau to Verdun to take temporary charge of the garrison until these reinforcements arrived and a new general, Henri-Philippe Pétain, was in place to direct the defence. He also asked the Russians to bring forward their Lake Naroch offensive to draw German troops eastward.

Continuing Attacks

Pétain arrived on the 27th and ordered his artillery to concentrate more on the German assault troops. German losses rose rapidly. They switched their attack to the north and north-west of the town on 6 March but they were stopped in front of the high ground around La Morte Homme ridge by early April. They now extended their front east as well and, after two months of intense combat, took La Morte Homme on 29 May. Fort Vaux fell on 7 June after a long siege. However, it was clear that both sides were now suffering equally in Falkenhayn's battle of attrition that had been intended to bleed just the French garrison white.

Below: The remains of Fort Vaux. Note the innumerable shell craters and trenches around the position.

SHELLSHOCK

Shellshock in World War I was akin to what is now generally referred to as post-traumatic stress disorder but was then little understood as military psychiatry was still in its infancy. Many senior figures, military, political and civil, simply refused to admit it existed, preferring to believe sufferers were cowards or, in a phrase commonly used, were "lacking moral fibre". Shellshock became manifest in many ways, from comparatively mild if regular panic attacks to the severest forms in which men were reduced to twitching wrecks or ended up in a catatonic state.

The First Day of the Somme

The officers and men of the much-enlarged British Expeditionary Force had high hopes of winning a decisive victory on the Somme but thoughts of triumph were dashed in a few hours on the first day of what was to become a prolonged battle.

When Britain went to war in August 1914 it had a tiny army by European standards and this had been largely destroyed by the year's end. The country was unable to launch any major attacks in 1915 but all that changed the following year. By then the volunteers making up the New Armies were trained and eager to take their place in the line. The aim for the planned offensive was to attack in Picardy north of the River Somme between Amiens and Péronne, break through the German line and then exploit the gap with cavalry. The battle was to be a joint Anglo-French affair but in the event many French troops had to be withdrawn to reinforce Verdun so leaving the British to take over the greater burden.

KEY FACTS

DATE: 1 July 1916

PLACE: Around the River Somme, northern France

OUTCOME: Some British and French successes but no decisive breakthrough and heavy losses.

Above: Evacuating British wounded from No Man's Land while under German artillery fire.

THE BATTLE OF THE SOMME The high hopes of the first day were soon replaced by a grinding attrition.

BRITISH AIMS

General Haig planned a meticulous operation involving some 750,000 men. General Henry Rawlinson's Fourth Army was to make the main effort while the right wing of General Edmund Allenby's First Army to the north would carry out supporting

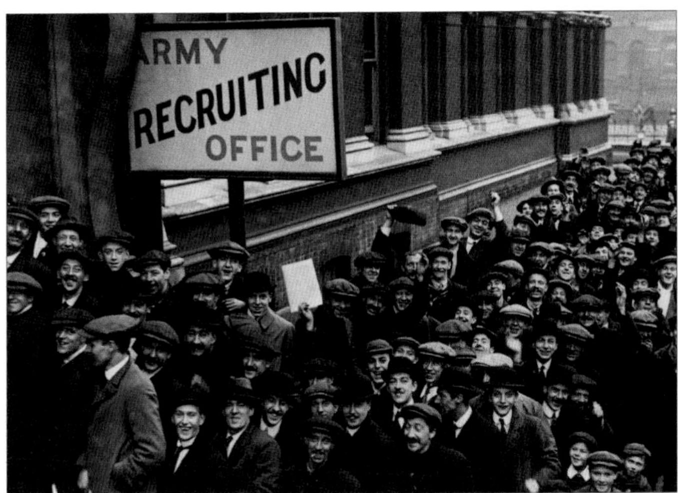

Left: British civilians answer the call for more volunteer recruits for the New Armies.

operations. British confidence was high, particularly among the New Army recruits going into battle for the first time.

The attack began after an eight-day bombardment. The heavily laden British troops moved off across No Man's Land at a steady pace at 07.30 hours on 1 July. Many were very soon hit by machine-gun fire or high-explosive shells as they walked up the gentle chalk slopes leading to the German line. Advances soon stalled in front of intact wire and trenches or broke down before the ruins of heavily defended villages. General Marie Fayolle's French Sixth Army did well in the south but the overall loss of life was appalling. The British recorded 57,470 casualties, including 19,240 dead. German losses are estimated at 4,000 killed or wounded and 2,000 captured.

Reasons for Failure

Why had the battle gone so badly wrong? The bombardment was inadequate; there were too few artillery pieces for the length of front, and most guns were too light to damage the German defences. Most of the shells were of the shrapnel type when high-explosive rounds were needed to cut wire and cave in trenches; many of both types also turned out to be duds. The delay between the barrage ending and the attack starting gave the untouched Germans time to emerge from their deep concrete dugouts and man their positions.

Haig had no alternative plan for 1 July. This was because he did not believe his untested troops were flexible enough to cope with anything other than the step-by-step approach that had been drummed into them before the battle. He knew that the primitive state of communications meant that any intelligence he did receive from the front would be out of date by the time it reached him as would be his new orders when they reached the front.

The first day of the Somme was the worst in the history of the British Army.

FIELD MARSHAL DOUGLAS HAIG

Douglas Haig (1861–1928) commanded the British Expeditionary Force from late 1915 but later became a much-maligned figure, one of the "donkeys" who led "lions". The truth was more complex, however. He was open to new ideas and weaponry, did care for the well-being of his troops and also had to carry on offensives long after the likelihood of a breakthrough had evaporated, largely to help the weakening French. He was undoubtedly in error in continuing to attack during the Battle of Passchendaele in 1917 but this lapse should be balanced by the fact that he went on to preside over the most militarily successful period in the British Army's history between August and November 1918.

Above: A formal portrait of Field Marshal Sir Douglas Haig.

Machine-guns

Machine-guns, which were used both defensively and offensively, were among the most effective weapons of the whole conflict. There were relatively small numbers in use in 1914 but all armies had many thousands by the end of the war.

Modern machine-guns were developed in the second half of the 19th century. They equipped all armies in 1914 and appeared in ever greater numbers as the war progressed. The reason was simple – a heavy machine-gun fired 400–600 rounds a minute and could effectively fulfil the tasks of 80 or more rifle-armed infantry. Heavy machine-guns were mostly associated with defensive roles, in which they would fire on attacking infantry from a fixed position in a trench but they were also used offensively. Gunners were trained to elevate their guns so that the bullets would fly over the heads of advancing infantry and then gravity would bring the rounds down on an enemy target.

The weapon usually came in three parts – a mounting tripod or sledge, the weapon itself and a reservoir of water in a can that fed into the "water jacket" that surrounded the barrel and stopped it overheating. Some guns, like the French 1914 Hotchkiss and the American Colt, were air-cooled but that system was the exception rather than the rule. Bullets were fed into a machine-gun by strips of 30 rounds or, more commonly, longer woven or metal belts.

Cumbersome in Action

Such bulky weapons were as difficult to manhandle as their name suggests. Most weighed 32–40kg (70–90lb), excluding the copious amounts of ammunition needed to keep the weapon firing. A British Vickers heavy machine-gun might have 16 250-round ammunition belts each weighing 10kg (22lb) available for immediate use and many more rounds in reserve.

MASCHINENGEWEHR 08

This weapon, introduced in 1908, was the mainstay of the German Army's heavy machine-gun detachments throughout the war in one form or another and was a very potent weapon indeed. Estimates suggest that it was responsible for around 90 per cent of the 60,000 or so casualties the British suffered on the first day of the Battle of the Somme in July 1916.

Calibre: 7.92mm (0.312in)
Rate of fire: 600rpm
Muzzle velocity: 823m/sec (2,700ft/sec)
Ammunition: 250-round belt
Weight with mount: 56kg (124lb)

Left: A Russian M1910 "Sokolov" Maxim machine-gun and crew. The gunshield protecting the firer was not a common design feature.

VICKERS MARK I

The Vickers was based on the 1884 Maxim, the world's first automatic machine-gun, and entered service with the British Army in 1912. It was lighter than the original Maxim and was known for its reliability.

Calibre: 0.303in (7.7mm)
Rate of fire: 500rpm
Muzzle velocity: 682m/sec (2,240ft/sec)
Ammunition: 250-round belt
Weight with mount: 33kg (73lb)

The average machine-gun needed two or three men to fire it, but most guns were operated by a team of four to six, the rest of whom carried ammunition. Soldiers often lugged heavy machine-guns around in battle but out of action they were broken down and transported by mules or placed on carts.

Light Machine-guns

The war also saw the development of an entirely new type of weapon, the man-portable light machine-gun that could be easily carried so that the user could keep up with attacking infantrymen. They generally weighed 10–14kg (22–30lb), most nearer the former figure than the latter, could fire 250–600 rounds per minute under ideal conditions and were air-cooled. Light machine-guns were either belt- or magazine-fed but magazines proved more practical in battle. Germany produced the Maschinengewehr 08/15, essentially a stripped down version of the Maschinengewehr 08 heavy machine-gun fitted with a pistol butt and bipod, while France had the Chauchat, which remained the French Army's standard light machine-gun throughout the conflict. Something like 250,000 of them were manufactured and they saw service with many Allied forces, including the US Army, which purchased some 34,000 in 1917. Although the Chauchat was very light it was notoriously unreliable due to frequently poor manufacturing standards.

The best light machine-gun of the war was the Lewis, a US design from 1911 which was manufactured in Belgium and Britain. It was quite a heavy weapon and was difficult to lug across a battlefield but it did become the most common infantry support gun in the Belgian and British Armies. It was also highly adaptable and was fitted to aircraft, armoured cars and tanks.

Right: The French Hotchkiss was introduced in 1900 and the first air-cooled version arrived in 1914. The original strip magazine held a mere 30 rounds and was replaced by a 249-round metal belt from 1915.

Verdun – The French Recovery

Although the French suffered horrendous losses in the first months of the battle, they slowly but surely took the initiative away from the Germans and in the final months of the fighting retook many of the most important positions.

The German attack on Verdun in February 1916 was supposed to bleed the French Army white but the plan for this battle of attrition went awry within a month or so of the battle opening. The French had suffered horrendous losses trying to hold their positions as General von Falkenhayn had intended but there was no sign that the lengthening toll of casualties was pushing them towards seeking peace. More worryingly, his own forces had been drawn deeper into the battle of attrition and were suffering losses at a similar rate. The pendulum, if anything, had swung in France's favour by early June.

Above: A French casualty is loaded into a Red Cross ambulance for evacuation from the battle.

Below: French cavalry escort a column of German prisoners captured during the bitter Verdun fighting. Around 17,500 Germans were taken prisoner during several months of combat.

New French Tactics

There were many reasons for this, not least the calibre of the new French commander at Verdun. General Pétain arrived on 26 February to command the Second Army and set about retrieving the situation. Rather than have units stay at the front until they were destroyed, he used a rotation system so that they could recover behind the lines while fresh replacements took their turn in the trenches. The French Army had 330 infantry regiments in 1916 and 259 of them fought in the battle. There was a better supply of artillery, improved food and replacement clothing, and the troops were ordered to hold their ground and avoid major counter-attacks.

Supplying Verdun

Pétain knew that the garrison needed supplies on a vast scale even though the main road and rail links had been severed, leaving a 64km (40 mile) secondary road to Bar-le-Duc as the only means of entering or leaving Verdun. Despite being under almost constant German artillery fire in places, the road, christened *La Voie Sacrée* ("The Sacred Way"), was extended and maintained by thousands of engineers. Trucks working round the clock brought huge quantities of ammunition to the battlefield every week as well as thousands of troops.

Pétain was promoted to army group commander in April and was replaced by General Robert Nivelle, who set about building on his predecessor's groundwork. He was aided in this by the Russians, who began their Brusilov Offensive on 4 June and then by the British, who opened the Battle of the Somme on 1 July. Both diverted German troops away from Verdun – some 15 divisions alone went to the East. The battle had become stalemated by late summer and Falkenhayn paid the price of failure. He was sacked on 29 August and replaced by Field Marshal Paul von Hindenburg and General Erich Ludendorff. They decided to close the battle down.

The initiative had passed to the French by autumn and they began to launch major counter-attacks. General Charles Mangin's Third Army took the lead on 24 October. Fort Douaumont, taken by the Germans on 25 February, was recaptured on the first day of his attack, while Fort Vaux, lost on 7 June, was retaken on 2 November. The battle finally ebbed away in mid-December, leaving the Germans still holding a little of the territory they had captured at the start.

Verdun was the longest battle of the war and both sides suffered roughly equally. The French recorded some 542,000 casualties and the Germans around 434,000. Some 50 per cent of the total were dead.

GENERAL HENRI-PHILIPPE PÉTAIN

Philippe Pétain (1856–1951) was a mere colonel in August 1914 but gained rapid promotion and by July 1915 he was commanding the French Second Army. He was put in charge of the forces at Verdun in February and won popular acclaim for revitalizing its defences. Pétain was then made head of a group of armies in May 1916 and a year later was promoted to Commander-in-Chief of the whole French Army. He dealt with the ongoing mutiny in a firm but fair manner but was subsequently sidelined when Marshal Ferdinand Foch became the Allied supreme commander.

Above: General, later Field Marshal, Philippe Pétain was hailed a French national hero for his part in the battle.

Left: A grim example of the cost of the battle. These are German dead, probably victims of artillery fire, but the French suffered in more or less equal measure.

Trench Warfare Weapons

Trench warfare demanded a whole new range of both fighting skills and specialist weaponry and the latter were often types that could be used at close quarters, not least hand grenades and the very earliest sub-machine-guns.

The need to clear trenches led to the development of specialist equipment. Troops required weapons that were less cumbersome and more lethal at close quarters than rifles and bayonets. Aside from improvised weapons, such as the coshes, clubs, knuckle-dusters and broad-bladed knives used in night-time trench raids, other weapons were developed through official channels.

Grenades were important in trench fighting as they allowed the thrower to attack an enemy without exposing himself to their fire. Yet, with the notable exception of Germany, many nations were slow to introduce them. The British authorities proved especially lax and soldiers at the front improvised grenades out of tin cans, bits of metal for shrapnel, some form of explosive charge and a fuse. There was eventually a plethora of official designs but the most successful mass-produced types were the hand-thrown German Stielhandgranate (stick grenade) and more common "pineapple" design, such as the British Mills bomb, which found favour with both the Allies and Germany. Grenades could also be fired from a rifle with a cup adaptor slipped into its barrel.

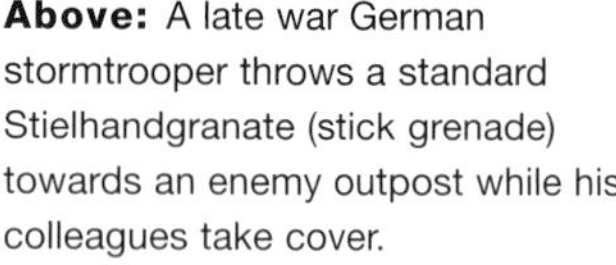

Above: A late war German stormtrooper throws a standard Stielhandgranate (stick grenade) towards an enemy outpost while his colleagues take cover.

Below: Although the Germans were mostly associated with the stick grenade, the early years saw a great deal of improvisation until standard designs entered service.

FLAMETHROWERS

Germany also developed two wholly new weapons. The flamethrower was first tested in

ANTI-TANK TACTICS

When the first British tanks appeared in 1916, they terrified the German troops they attacked, many of whom simply fled. However, the Germans soon developed techniques and weapons to counter the armoured threat. Trenches were made wider, thereby becoming effective anti-tank ditches. In 1918 the Germans also introduced "tank forts", which consisted of two field guns located in a forward position protected by several machine-guns and infantry. These weapons – artillery was the biggest tank killer – could take on tanks at close range as could flamethrowers, as illustrated here. The Germans also developed specialist anti-tank rifles and a special type of bullet that could penetrate a tank's armoured plate.

Germany in 1901 and during World War I it came in both portable and non-portable versions. The latter was effectively static and solely of use defending trenches but the former was more practicable for clearing enemy positions. Both types used an oil and petrol mix projected out of a pipe by a gas such as nitrogen. Fuel and propellant were stored in a cylinder and ignited by a burning taper attached to the pipe's nozzle.

There were two types of German flamethrower. The Kleif (Kleinflammenwerfer – "small flamethrower") was a cumbersome device needing a crew of two, one of whom carried a fuel container the size of a milk churn on his back and the other who aimed and fired the weapon. The more readily manageable Wex was operated by one man who carried the fuel in a lifebelt-like container on his back. The Kleif had a range of some 25m (27yds) and the Wex about 20m (22yds).

The French developed the Schilt, which was named after its creator, a captain in the Paris fire service. It had more fuel than its German counterparts so it could fire up to 10 bursts of flame out to 30m (32yd). The British devised two types of portable flamethrower, the Norris-Menchen and Lawrence, but they were never used in action save for a small version during the raid on Zeebrugge in 1918.

Flamethrowers were actually more of a psychological than a practical weapon and were very vulnerable when used offensively. Because of their short range they had to get very close to their objective, which was no easy feat as their carriers were invariably targeted before they got to close quarters.

Sub-Machine-Guns

The Germans also used the world's first sub-machine-gun – the 9mm (0.345in) Bergmann Maschinenpistole 18/1 – a type of weapon that was ideal for trench fighting. Production began in early 1918 but did not really get into its stride until the middle of the year by which time the Germans were totally incapable of major offensive operations. Nevertheless, it was a basically sound design, light enough to be used in attack, but its 32-round magazine did have teething troubles. It certainly worried the Allies – they put a clause in the Treaty of Versailles prohibiting its manufacture.

Above: British soldiers improvising grenades using tin cans filled with gun cotton, scrap and a basic fuse.

Attrition on the Somme

Although the first day of the attack had dashed many high hopes, the British battled away on the Somme for some 140 days, launching a string of offensives that ground down the opposing German units, which lost many combat veterans.

Despite the appalling losses suffered by the British forces on the Somme during 1 July 1916, there was no question of ending the offensive, not least because of the need to aid the French at Verdun. The fighting lasted until winter but the Battle of the Somme, the name usually given to the whole struggle from early July to late November, was in reality a succession of attacks. The offensive actually began with the Battle of Albert (1–13 July) and ended with the Battle of the Ancre (13–18 November), though the British did not again undertake a mass assault like that of 1 July. Subsequent pushes were smaller and their objectives less ambitious, but nearly every BEF division in France fought on the Somme and many more than once.

Britain's losses mounted as the Battle of Albert gave way to, among others, the battles of Pozières (23 July – 3 September), Thiepval (26–28 September) and the Ancre Heights (1–11 October). Most of these attacks came on either side of the Albert–Bapaume road. They generally nibbled away at the German line but the British did make some progress at the Battle of Flers-Courcelette fought from 15–22 September. That attack marked the debut of the tank. Only a handful took part and most very quickly succumbed to mechanical failure or enemy fire but they so unnerved the German infantry that many troops ran away, allowing British troops to occupy their positions.

Effects of the Battle

By the British Army's reckoning the fighting officially ended on 14 November, some 140 days after the first British troops had gone over the top. The number of men on all sides who were killed, wounded or missing totalled more than 1.3 million, including over 400,000 British casualties. Thus, the battle that had been supposed to win the war for the Allies on that distant July day had become one of attrition in which the BEF's New Army divisions were largely bled white. In five months or so the Anglo-French forces had pushed forward some 10km (6 miles) but the British in the north were still 6.5km (4 miles) short of Bapaume at the end, an objective that was supposed to have fallen on the first day. Yet the effort had not been for nothing as the German Chief of Staff, General Erich

Above left: A Mark I tank with a damaged rear steering wheel. Only a few tanks were deployed at first on the Somme, thereby lessening their impact.

Left: Canadian wounded are ferried away from the fighting around the village of Flers in September 1916.

von Falkenhayn, started to divert troops away from Verdun the day the battle began.

The fighting also had disastrous results for the German Army. It lost around 650,000 men and many generals felt that its fighting edge had been lost. Its veteran non-commissioned officers were the army's backbone and they had suffered greatly. Germany was also facing increasingly acute manpower shortages after the exertions on the Somme and at Verdun and this led its High Command to take an extraordinary step that reflected the growing crisis.

New German Ideas

Falkenhayn was replaced by the Third Supreme Command of Field Marshal Hindenburg and General Ludendorff in August. They decided to build a new defence system some 32km (20 miles) behind the existing lines on the northern and central sections of the Western Front. The aim was simply to shorten their front so that it could be held with fewer men. Work on what the Allies soon called the Hindenburg Line began in September. Its construction signified that Germany was struggling to wage war on two fronts and, as the strategic situation stood, was incapable of making a major offensive effort in the west.

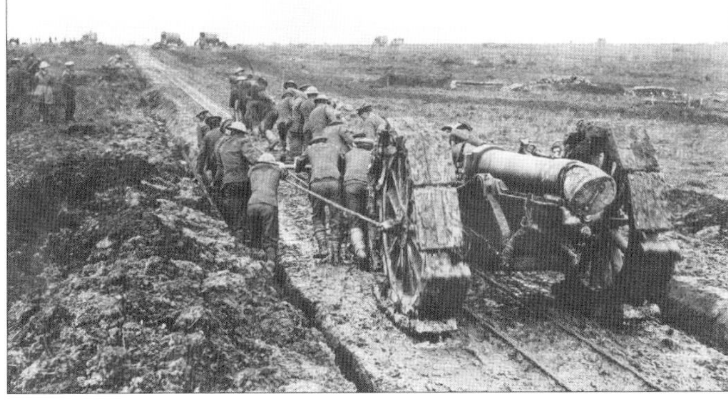

Above: British troops drag a 6in (15cm) howitzer into position on the Somme battlefield. Its wheels have been fitted with "girdles" to spread the load over soft ground and to prevent ruts forming when the gun recoils on firing.

Below: A British soldier gives out water to a group of German prisoners captured near Pozières, the scene of bitter fighting between late July and early September 1916.

PALS BATTALIONS

The outbreak of war in 1914 saw a huge rush to volunteer in Britain. Many recruits from the same towns or working in the same business or industry who joined up together were allowed to serve in the same units, which became known as pals battalions. These new soldiers had excellent morale but suffered badly in their first major offensive, the Battle of the Somme. When a pals battalion took heavy casualties the simultaneous loss of so many men from a particular town often had a devastating impact on local feeling.

British Tanks

The British developed the first truly viable tank at the beginning of 1916 and, while they did score some noteworthy successes, they were generally too underpowered and overly prone to mechanical failure to reach their full potential.

The first tanks, tracked armoured vehicles fitted with some form of armament, were developed in Britain but the concept only emerged slowly and involved many different agencies and individuals. Although the gestation period was prolonged, the design moved swiftly from prototype to production to battle. The prototype, nicknamed Mother, first ran in January 1916 and was rhomboid in shape with two side-mounted "turrets", commonly known as sponsons. Production of the Tank Mark I began in April and they went into action on 15 September during the Battle of the Somme.

Their attack initially went well, literally scaring the Germans out of their trenches, but thereafter their effectiveness diminished rapidly. Due to the appalling conditions inside their armoured cabs, crews were soon left sick and disorientated; many tanks also broke down due to mechanical failure and others simply bogged down in muddy trenches and shell craters. Nevertheless, they had done sufficiently well for more to be ordered.

NAMING THE TANK

It may seem curious but the tank's complex development was partly the responsibility of the Royal Navy, mostly because First Lord of the Admiralty Winston Churchill was a backer of the project. Thus, the first tanks were actually known as His Majesty's Landships. It soon became apparent that the name potentially gave an enemy with a vivid enough imagination the opportunity to guess the nature of the top secret weapon. A less obvious codename was needed and various suggestions were made, each reflecting its shape. Cistern, container and reservoir were all suggested but tank quickly became the preferred option.

Males and Females

Tanks became available with different combinations of weapons. "Males" carried a pair of light artillery guns and four machine-guns and "Females" were armed with six machine-guns. The most widely used tank of the war was the Mark IV. The first of these arrived at the front in April 1917. There were 595 Female Mark IVs and 420

Below: The Mark A Whippet was, as its name suggests, an attempt to create a fast-moving medium tank to exploit any breakthrough but its top speed was still only 13kph (8mph).

Left: Mark V tanks, here fitted with trench-crossing cribs, made their debut in July 1918. They had slightly thicker armour and more powerful engines than earlier types.

Males, but a number of the former were converted into "Hermaphrodites" by replacing the right-hand sponson with a Male sponson with its mix of machine-guns and a light gun.

As the capabilities and limitations of tanks became better understood, they underwent various modifications and improvements. So that they could cross the wider trenches the Germans had dug in part as tank traps, "Tadpole Tails", extensions to the rear of the tank, were tried but proved to be too flimsy so designers much more successfully turned to extending the main body itself. It was, however, more common for tanks to carry fascines on their roofs that could simply be rolled into a trench, thereby making a bridge for them to cross. Early versions were bundles of logs and brushwood held together by chains, but later ones consisted of a steel crib. Tanks were often thwarted by the mud and shell craters of No Man's Land so they were given "ditching gear", essentially a wooden beam that could be drawn under the tracks to give greater purchase, or their tracks' width was extended with plates to spread the load.

Faster Designs

As the value of tanks became clear, the British developed a faster light tank that was supposed to work with cavalry and exploit any breakthrough made by the heavier tanks. The first Medium Mark A, more commonly known as the Whippet, was built in October 1917 and they went into action for the first time on 26 March 1918.

Tanks were neither as good as their exponents believed or as bad as their detractors argued. They made significant advances in the first days of the tank-led Battle of Cambrai in late 1917 but had performed woefully amid the mud of Passchendaele. However, they were never able to make a decisive breakthrough and then keep the momentum of the attack going. This was largely due to their mechanical unreliability.

TANK MARK I

The Mark I was the first tank to go into action. Some 49 were deployed and enjoyed a degree of local success but most were soon knocked out by enemy fire or broke down.

Weight: 28.5 tonnes
Crew: 8
Max. speed: 6.5kph (4mph)
Max. armour: 12mm (0.47in)
Armament: 2 x 6pdr (57mm) and 4 machine-guns (Male)

Russia Aids Its Allies

Like the British on the Somme, the Russians launched their own major offensive to ease the pressure on the French at Verdun during 1916 and the attack, which was masterminded by General Alexei Brusilov, was initially a major success.

The Russians agreed to launch a summer offensive in 1916 to support the Anglo-French effort in the west but Verdun forced the French to ask for an immediate attack. The Russian Chief of Staff, General Mikhail Alexeev, chose to attack north of the Pripet Marshes to the east of Vilna where two of his army groups massed for the Battle of Lake Naroch. The main effort was against Field Marshal von Eichhorn's German Tenth Army and was spearheaded by the Second Army of General Alexei Evert's Western Army Group.

The Second Army advanced on 18 March but the troops were met by a withering fire from the German trenches. By late April, when the fighting ebbed away, the Russians had suffered 100,000 casualties and failed to divert any German troops away from Verdun; Eichhorn lost 20,000 men.

Brusilov's New Plan

The second Russian attack had its origins in Italy where an Austrian onslaught in mid-May led the Italians to request

THE BRUSILOV OFFENSIVE
The first successful large-scale attack by the Russian Army in WWI.

Left: German artillery officers observe the accuracy of their fire. Note how much more temporary the position looks in comparison with those on the Western Front.

Left: A Russian supply column. The generally poor road network on the Eastern Front caused problems for both sides, especially during the spring thaw and heavy autumn rains.

urgent help. The Russian high command were uncertain where to strike. Alexeev favoured another offensive in the north but the idea met with little enthusiasm – and preparations would take two months. Instead, General Alexei Brusilov outlined a radical plan that could be put into action in weeks.

He believed that a breakthrough on a narrow front was unlikely to succeed and suggested a broad-front approach. Brusilov also offered solutions that would regain the element of surprise. He suggested that his armies of the South-west Army Group should take the lead despite the fact they did not outnumber their opponents significantly. These plans were greeted with something close to incredulity by his peers as they believed that an attack on a broad front without huge superiority was bound to fail. The arguments continued into late May until the worsening situation in Italy forced Alexeev's hand and Brusilov was given permission to attack.

The targets of the offensive were five largely Austro-Hungarian armies strung out between the Pripet Marshes and the Romanian border. The attacks opened on 4 June and were almost wholly successful, pushing the Austro-Hungarians back along most of the front. The offensive marked the high point of Russia's involvement in World War I. In just two weeks Brusilov's troops captured some 200,000 prisoners. The greatest victory was in the south, where the Austro-Hungarian Seventh Army was pushed all the way back to the Carpathians.

Casualty Count

The battle ended in autumn. Although the later stages could not match the triumphs of the first days, the offensive had reaped dividends. Brusilov had inflicted 350,000 casualties on the German Army and perhaps 1 million on the Austro-Hungarians. They had to call off their offensive against Italy and the Germans had to transfer troops from the West. Yet Russia had paid a very high price for this victory. Around 1 million of its troops had been killed, wounded or taken prisoner and the morale of the survivors was at a low ebb.

GENERAL ALEXEI BRUSILOV

Brusilov (1853–1926) came from an aristocratic background and is widely thought of as the finest Russian general of the war. He began the conflict as an army commander and was known as an able and meticulous planner. His reputation was such that he took command of an army group in March 1916 and then planned and launched the highly successful Brusilov Offensive. He supported the Provisional Government of March 1917 and was made its Commander-in-Chief. He took part in the short-lived Kerensky Offensive but was replaced on 1 August.

Above: Brusilov studies a map while planning his offensive.

The Romanian Campaign

Romania sided with the Allies in 1916 in the hope of gaining Austro-Hungarian territory but it suffered the wrath of the Central Powers, who invaded the country rapidly and overran much of it in a matter of just a few months.

Pre-war Romania had a mostly unmodernized army of some 550,000 men but a declaration of war in support of either the Allies or Central Powers by Bucharest during 1916 would have given either a significant psychological boost. Romania had been courted by both warring camps, not least Germany as it relied on Romanian grain and oil and used its rail system to maintain contact with Turkey. The Romanian government had swayed first one way and then another depending on the fortunes of war of its various suitors. The royal family itself was divided as King Ferdinand was a cousin of Kaiser Wilhelm, while his wife, Princess Marie, was a granddaughter of Britain's Queen Victoria.

Above: Romanian troops guard one of the several key passes through the Carpathians that led to Austro-Hungarian territory.

Romania Picks Sides

The pendulum finally swung decisively in mid-1916 when Russia's Brusilov Offensive clearly weakened the Austro-Hungarian forces on the Eastern Front and brought the Russians close to the Romanian border. Germany acted immediately, informing the Romanian government that any attack into Austria-Hungary would lead to the commitment of German troops. Turkey and Bulgaria followed suit. Contingency plans to invade Romania by all four were drawn up in secret but no one expected a Romanian war declaration until September after the harvest had been gathered. The Central Powers did not realize just how extensive the Allies' diplomatic charm offensive had been and their promises of new lands once Austria-Hungary had been defeated tipped the balance. Romania signed a military agreement in mid-August and declared war on the 27th.

The announcement sealed Falkenhayn's fate. His failure at Verdun, his mistaken belief that Russia was incapable of serious offensive action in 1916, and a

THE DEFEAT OF ROMANIA
The Central Powers crushed Romania in a campaign that lasted from August 1916 to January 1917.

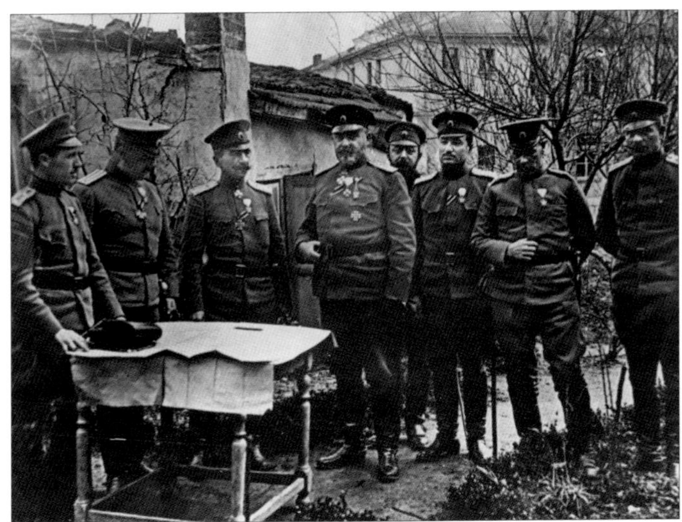

Left: A group of Bulgarian officers pose for the camera. Despite its comparatively small population, the country had a very large army and fielded some 850,000 men by 1918.

prolonged whispering campaign against him by other ambitious generals and senior politicians made his position untenable. He tendered his resignation on 29 August. Henceforth, Germany's war would be directed by the two top officers from the Eastern Front, who had led the anti-Falkenhayn faction, Field Marshal Paul von Hindenburg, who became Chief of Staff, and General Erich Ludendorff, who styled himself First Quartermaster-General. Collectively, they and their staffs were titled the Third Supreme Command.

Hindenburg and Ludendorff moved swiftly to deal with Romania. The Romanian First and Second Armies had made a half-hearted attack northward into Transylvania, Austro-Hungarian territory but home to three million ethnic Romanians. The attackers made sluggish advances through the four main passes across the Transylvanian Alps but were soon facing a battle for survival. Falkenhayn, now in charge of the German Ninth Army, struck and pushed them back through the passes into the province of Wallachia, while Field Marshal August von Mackensen at the head of the Bulgarian–German Danube Army moved up from the Salonika front and invaded the Romanian province of Dobrudja from the south.

Romania Defeated

The decisive clash came in early December 1916 at the four-day Battle of the River Arges during which the Romanians were crushed. Bucharest fell on the 6th and what was left of the Romanian Army headed northward towards the Russians. By the year's end the Romanians were only able to hold on to their province of Moldavia and the government and royal family had settled in the province's capital, Jassy (Iasi). The campaign had cost the Romanians upwards of 300,000 casualties and the invaders around 120,000 men. A British politician, John Norton-Griffiths, who had been sent to Romania to gather intelligence, had the presence of mind to sabotage much of the country's oil-producing facilities and destroy large quantities of stored grain, but there was no disguising the fact that these measures would only hinder Germany temporarily.

Right: Romanian troops cross a makeshift footbridge as they retreat to the north-east of their country.

Camouflage

Because of the real danger of being spotted either by reconnaissance aircraft or tethered balloons and then brought under artillery fire, all sides practised the art of camouflage to protect vital equipment and other military supplies.

Camouflage is essentially a form of visible deception and has always been used in warfare. However, it became even more important during World War I, despite the static nature of the fighting on many fronts. What made camouflage ever more necessary was the advent of reconnaissance aircraft. Previously, observers had been limited to spotting targets that were within their line of sight, so simply positioning troops behind a piece of high ground or beyond normal visual range would be sufficient to hide them from view. Static balloons like those deployed in the American Civil War (1861–65) and the Franco-Prussian War (1870–71) made this a much more difficult proposition but even their observers could reach only as far as their eyes and binoculars could see. Aircraft, however, could range deep behind enemy lines and cover large swathes of territory in a single sortie. These simple truths meant that camouflage became even more essential.

Above: A somewhat half-hearted attempt to camouflage a British tank. They were usually hidden in woods before moving up to attack.

Above: A German artillery observer in a lightly camouflaged position looks through a pair of stereoscopic sights in search of a target.

Concealing Plans

World War I was a war of supply as much as anything else. Rear areas were often filled with huge supply dumps that would grow ever bigger as a major offensive loomed. These were obvious, tempting targets for enemy aircraft and artillery and thus would be hidden in forests or covered in netting. Similarly, the British used to create large marshalling areas for tanks before they were committed to battle and to try to maintain the

Right: A British howitzer crew in action near Ypres. Camouflage netting partially hides their location from enemy counter-battery fire.

element of surprise these were usually hidden away in forests from which the undergrowth was cleared to make movement less difficult when the order to advance was given. It was also not uncommon for flights of aircraft to fly over German lines in a type of aural camouflage to hide the sound of the tanks turning over their engines as they prepared to move out of the rear base and go into action.

Closer to the front, in areas that were under direct enemy observation, vulnerable sections of road were often hidden by lengths of camouflage netting, something akin to washing drying on a line, so that any traffic moving down them would enjoy a measure of invisibility.

Observation Posts

Camouflage was also practised right at the front line and there were several ingenious ruses, mostly developed by the British, to confuse an enemy. Observation of enemy activity was dangerous in daylight and putting a head above a trench parapet foolhardy, so the British in particular developed a series of observation posts that looked like shell-blasted tree stumps so that they blended more easily into the surroundings.

The best camouflage of all was, of course, darkness and much activity took place at night. Men moved off into No Man's Land to dig saps, repair barbed wire cut by artillery fire, launch trench raids and conduct listening operations. If the conditions were wintry and snow lay on the ground, some troops had access to white oversuits. Behind the lines movement could usually be undertaken without being observed but it was always stressed that any supplies and troops moving up to the front needed to be brought forward with as little noise as possible.

DAZZLE CAMOUFLAGE

This form of maritime deception used both extreme colour variations and linear patterns in black, grey and white to obscure features of a ship, such as its waterline, deck or bridge, that a U-boat commander would use to estimate a ship's course, speed and distance. Without accurate information, it was difficult to score a torpedo hit. Dazzle camouflage was applied to over 4,400 Allied merchant and naval vessels but just how effective it was is debatable.

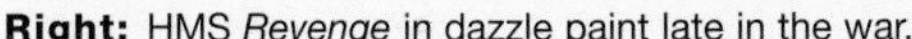

Right: HMS *Revenge* in dazzle paint late in the war.

Stalemate on the Italian Front

The Austro-Hungarians launched their first major offensive on the Italian Front during late spring 1916 but their early gains were soon lost, while the Italians continued to batter away with similarly little success along the River Isonzo.

The Italian Army planned a summer offensive along the River Isonzo once again in 1916, but the fighting at Verdun forced the French to ask them to attack in early spring. The Italian Chief of Staff, General Luigi Cadorna, really lacked the means for a major operation but agreed to aid his ally. The Fifth Battle of the Isonzo opened on 11 March but bad weather intervened and the inconclusive fighting ended on the 29th.

Mountain Battles

Although the Isonzo battles usually dominated the whole Italian campaign, the Austro-Hungarians briefly opened another battle area. This was the mountainous Trentino region of the South Tyrol, an area with a sizeable Italian-speaking population that had been occupied by the Italians during 1915. The main thrust by the Austro-Hungarian forces was directed southward towards the town of Asiago and the aim was to cut off the bulk of the Italian troops along the Isonzo line to the east from the rest of their homeland.

Above: Prisoners march away from the Isonzo fighting. The difficult terrain was typical of the region.

Below: Austro-Hungarian troops push forward as a flamethrower deals with an Italian position.

Despite his request for German aid being rebuffed because of events at Verdun, the Austro-Hungarian Chief of Staff, Field Marshal Conrad von Hötzendorf, felt able to attack in late spring. He had the Third Army under General Kövess von Kövesshàza and General Victor Dankl von Krasnik's Eleventh Army available. They were supported by around 2,000 artillery pieces and outnumbered their opponents, the 100,000-strong Italian First Army under General Roberto Brusati, by a margin of four-to-one. Command for the Asiago Offensive was given to Archduke Eugene but Conrad was the real driving force.

Austrian Progress

The Austro-Hungarians moved forward on a 72km (45 mile) front on 15 May and Conrad's forces made some early progress, pushing the Italians out of Asiago on the 29th before running out of steam. This was due to difficult terrain and the speed with which Cadorna used his homeland's railway system to rush around 400,000 troops to reinforce Brusati. Conrad had

Above: Austro-Hungarian troops surround an Italian heavy howitzer abandoned during the Asiago Offensive.

driven a salient into the Italian line but even this was soon given up as Italian pressure told.

The Eastern Front erupted on 4 June when Russia launched the Brusilov Offensive and Austro-Hungarian units had to be withdrawn from the Trentino a week or so later to shore up their crumbling front in the east. Italian counter-attacks continued and Eugene was finally given permission to withdraw to positions a mere 5km (3 miles) from his starting point. Losses were more or less even, around 150,000 men each, but the Austro-Hungarians had shot their bolt and would never again conduct offensive operations against Italy without German help.

The Asiago Offensive did not prevent Cadorna from renewing his efforts along the Isonzo. He transferred large numbers of troops away from the Trentino and launched them against the depleted Austro-Hungarian forces on 6 August. Although there was no breakthrough, Gorizia was finally taken at a cost of roughly 50,000 casualties. Austro-Hungarian losses had reached 40,000 men by the time the fighting ended on the 17th. A new Italian government felt emboldened enough to declare war on Germany on 28 August, making it likely that the latter would commit troops to the Italian Front.

There were three more Isonzo battles in 1916 – Seventh (14–26 September), Eighth (10–12 October) and Ninth (1–14 November). They made little progress beyond inflicting a further 65,000 or so casualties at a cost of 75,000 Italians killed, wounded or captured.

GENERAL LUIGI CADORNA

Luigi Cadorna (1850–1928) became the Italian Army's Chief of Staff in July 1914. He proved an able organizer but was a strategist of limited originality. Although his efforts were admittedly constrained by mountainous terrain, he conducted a series of highly costly offensives along the River Isonzo between June 1915 and September 1917. His downfall came after his forces largely collapsed in the face of the German-led Caporetto Offensive later in 1917. He lost the support of his own government and the Allied High Command and was sacked in December.

Right: Italian troops move up to the front line in preparation for one of the Isonzo offensives in 1916.

Seaplane Tenders and Aircraft Carriers

Naval aviation was very much in its infancy at the outbreak of the war in 1914 but over the following years the British in particular began to experiment with a variety of warships capable of carrying aircraft into battle.

Attempts to deploy aircraft from warships in World War I were largely advanced by Britain's Royal Naval Air Service. Its first seaplane tender was an old converted cruiser, *Hermes*, sunk by a torpedo in October 1914, but the first true aircraft carrier was *Ark Royal*, an ex-collier that entered service in December 1914. The Royal Navy also transformed several cross-Channel ferries into lightly armed seaplane tenders from 1914 onwards. The ferries' relatively high speed was important because it allowed them to maintain pace with the more conventional warships of the main battlefleet.

First Battles

Three, *Engadine*, *Empress* and *Riviera*, were converted that autumn and, while they could in theory at least fly wheeled aircraft from their decks, they invariably winched seaplanes fitted with floats into and out of the water. Nevertheless, they proved their worth by making the first-ever naval aviation raid when they launched seven aircraft against the Zeppelin sheds near Cuxhaven on 25 December 1914. *Engadine* later served in the North Sea and was present at the Battle of Jutland in 1916.

The three other conversions were the larger *Ben-My-Chree*, *Manxman* and *Videx*. A milestone in naval aviation was achieved by the last in November 1915 when a Bristol Scout C aircraft became the first-ever land-based aircraft to achieve take-off at sea. *Ben-My-Chree* went to the Dardanelles in the summer of 1915 and one of its Short 184 seaplanes made the first successful aerial torpedo attack that August. There was a final group of seaplane tenders that entered service in 1915–17, including the ex-liners *Campania*, *Nairana*

HMS *FURIOUS*

The forward flight deck on the ex-battle-cruiser HMS *Furious* allowed aircraft to take off but they could not land at sea. As first converted, *Furious* could carry 3 Short 184 seaplanes and 5 Sopwith Pup fighters.

Displacement: 22,000 tons
Crew: 737
Speed: 32.5 knots
Main armament: 10 x 4in (101.6mm) guns

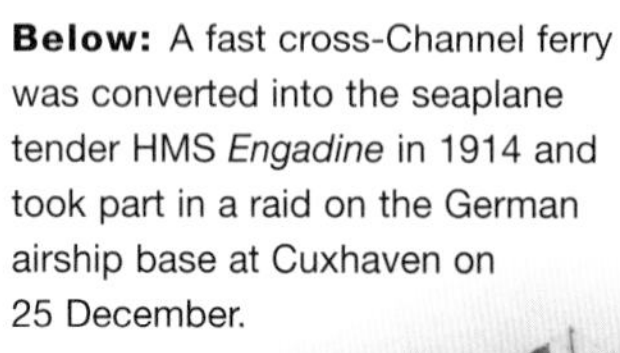

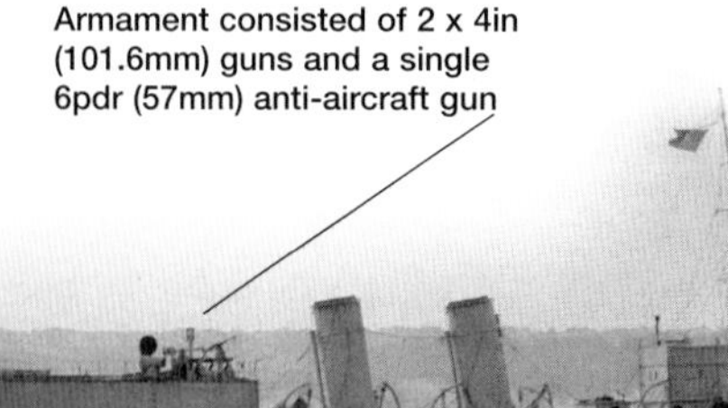

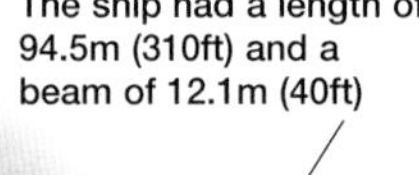

Armament consisted of 2 x 4in (101.6mm) guns and a single 6pdr (57mm) anti-aircraft gun
The ship had a length of 94.5m (310ft) and a beam of 12.1m (40ft)
The hangar could house up to three aircraft
Engadine displaced 1,676 tons

Below: A fast cross-Channel ferry was converted into the seaplane tender HMS *Engadine* in 1914 and took part in a raid on the German airship base at Cuxhaven on 25 December.

Right: HMS *Argus* was the first flush-deck carrier from which aircraft could take off and land but did not enter service until October 1918.

and *Pegasus*, although their performance was generally no better or worse than their predecessors'. *Campania* saw little service before being lost in a storm in late 1918, while *Nairana* and *Pegasus* served in the North Sea before sailing for the Mediterranean during the same year.

France and Russia also developed tenders. The former began by converting a torpedo-boat depot ship, *Foudre*, so that by 1913 it had sufficient hangar space to carry a number of seaplanes. The French built just four more. The ex-passenger liner *Campinas* was converted in 1915 and again served in the eastern Mediterranean. Three cross-Channel ferries were also converted – *Rouen* acted as a convoy escort in the Mediterranean, while *Nord* and *Pas-de-Calais* operated in the Channel. Russia deployed six seaplane tenders with its Black Sea Fleet.

Aircraft Carriers

The use of wheeled aircraft on tenders and carriers was advanced by the arrival in 1916 of more powerful aircraft, notably Sopwith's Strutter and Pup, that could take off from short decks. However, they could not be landed and pilots had to ditch into the sea after a mission. The British tried to resolve this problem by further modifying *Furious*, a former light battle-cruiser, in late 1917. By March 1918 it had two flight decks and extensive hangar space but turbulence from the central superstructure still made landing at sea very hazardous. Conversion work on the first true flush-deck aircraft carrier, the former liner *Argus*, had begun in late 1916 but both it and the first purpose-built carrier, *Hermes*, did not see action before the war's end.

HMS *CAMPANIA*

The ex-liner *Campania* entered service as an aircraft carrier in May 1915. It could carry ten seaplanes but the sloping forward flight deck was too short for aircraft to take off safely.

Laid down: 1893
Displacement: 18,000 tons
Crew: 600
Speed: 22 knots
Main armament: 6 x 4.7in (119mm) guns

THE TONDERN RAID

This British attack against a Zeppelin base on the German–Dutch border on 18 July 1918 was the only occasion in the war when aircraft were launched from an aircraft carrier. Seven Sopwith Camels carrying bombs flew off the deck of *Furious* at dawn; six attacked the target and two airships, *L.54* and *L.60*, were destroyed. Two aircraft made it to neutral Denmark, while three others ditched in the sea. The fate of the sixth aircraft remains unknown but five pilots and one aircraft survived from the attacking force.

Operations in Salonika, 1916–17

The Allies poured vast amounts of men and equipment into the Greek province of Salonika intending to open a new front against the Central Powers but instead they remained largely inactive, suffering greatly from various debilitating diseases.

The build-up of Allied forces in Salonika had begun in late 1915 after Greece became aware of the Central Powers' preparations to invade Serbia and requested urgent military aid. This request was soon withdrawn but the influx of Allied troops continued into 1916, most notably with the arrival of large numbers of Serbians who had been evacuated from their homeland during January. They landed on Corfu and were re-equipped by the Allies before then embarking for mainland Greece. Some 120,000 had arrived by July and they, like the other Allied forces, manned a fortified line that stretched across the neck of the peninsula.

Allied Problems

The Allied effort was plagued by many problems, not least local conditions that produced crippling levels of sickness, chiefly malaria. The mountainous terrain also greatly favoured defensive rather than offensive action. There were also unresolved political issues. The French and British forces did not have a unified command structure and their commanders – General Maurice Sarrail and General Bryan Mahon respectively – often went their own way even though the former was supposedly in charge. Many British and French leaders, both civil and military, felt that Salonika was a sideshow and it was therefore often starved of the necessary military resources.

Above: The build-up of Allied strength in Salonika continues – British troops unload a horse.

Below: Troops march off to the front in Salonika, a small part of one of the most diverse Allied forces in the war.

First Battles

Allied plans for the summer of 1916 centred on a push up the River Vardar in the direction of Uskub (Skopje) in southern Serbia but were pre-empted by a Bulgarian-led advance from south-west Serbia into northern Greece supported by a leavening of German units. These troops inflicted a defeat on the Allies at the Battle of Florina (17–27 August). Sarrail ordered a counter-attack the following month to retake the lost ground. Florina was recaptured on the 18th and, despite bickering between Sarrail and his generals, the advance continued.

The Allies crossed over into Serbia and, after a four-day battle, occupied Monastir (Bitola) on 19 November. The recent fighting had cost around

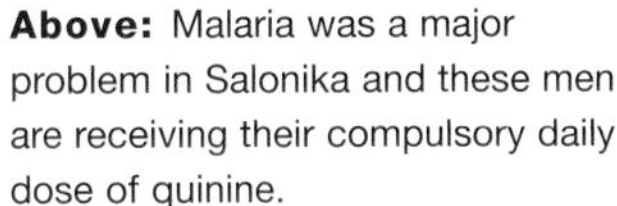

Above: Malaria was a major problem in Salonika and these men are receiving their compulsory daily dose of quinine.

50,000 Allied casualties while the Germans and Bulgarians recorded some 10,000 more. The Balkans saw one final campaign during 1916, although it was largely conducted in isolation. An Italian corps in southern Albania defeated a similarly sized Austro-Hungarian force in November and linked up with Sarrail's command around Lake Ochrida (Ohrid).

The campaigning of 1916 established a front line across northern Greece and a small part of southern Serbia that would remain mostly unchanged until September 1918. Sarrail did try to break the stalemate in 1917 but had just 100,000 men, one-sixth of his command, actually fit for action. Two major battles were fought in the first half of the year, at Lake Prespa (11–17 March) and along the River Vardar (5–19 May), but to little effect. The Allies made no further attacks in 1917. A new French government sacked Sarrail and replaced him with the very able General Adolphe Marie Guillaumat on 10 December.

The Allies had imposed themselves on Greece, an officially neutral state whose political leadership was divided over the war. Greece's King Constantine I, German Emperor Wilhelm II's brother-in-law, leaned towards the Central Powers, while his sometime prime minister, Eleutherios Venizelos, generally favoured the Allies. Matters were settled after the Allies put considerable military and diplomatic pressure on the Greeks over several months. Constantine finally abdicated his throne on 12 June 1917 and the new monarch, Alexander, then re-appointed Venizelos as prime minister on the 26th. Greece issued a war declaration against the Central Powers on 2 July.

Left: Resting British troops look on as a column of freshly arrived French soldiers moves up to the front line.

War in East Africa, 1914–18

The campaign in East Africa was the longest of the war in large part due to the tenacity of the local German commander, General Paul von Lettow-Vorbeck, who only surrendered some days after the signing of the Armistice in November 1918.

There were four German colonies in Africa in August 1914 but three had fallen to the Allies by early 1916. The fourth, German East Africa (Rwanda, Burundi and Tanzania), was a much tougher prospect and its garrison did not finally surrender until two weeks after the Armistice. The campaign was a remarkable feat of arms because East Africa was initially defended by just 3,000 Europeans and 4,600 local troops (*askaris*) and police led by General Paul von Lettow-Vorbeck and was surrounded by British-controlled or neutral colonies. Even more remarkably, Lettow-Vorbeck received virtually no aid from Germany throughout the war, and had to rely on what his troops could capture, scrounge or manufacture locally to maintain the war effort.

PAUL VON LETTOW-VORBECK

Lettow-Vorbeck (1870–1964) was a true career soldier who was appointed commander in German East Africa in February 1914. He never had more than a few thousand, mainly local, troops and received virtually no aid from Germany but tied up many times larger Allied forces throughout the entire war.

Above: Lettow-Vorbeck became a national hero in his homeland.

Early Battles

The British ordered an immediate attack on Lettow-Vorbeck with some 12,000 untried Indian troops but these were roundly defeated during 3–5 November 1914. The major battle was at Tanga, German East Africa's main port. Some 8,000 Indian troops were beaten by Lettow-Vorbeck's 1,000 men and suffered 360 dead and 487 wounded, while he recorded 148 casualties. The British also abandoned 16 machine-guns, several hundred rifles and 600,000 rounds of ammunition. There was no major fighting in 1915 with both sides content to launch cross-border raids. Lettow-Vorbeck was able to build up his strength to 3,000 European and 11,300 local troops during the year and also recovered ten 10.5cm (4.1in) artillery pieces from the light cruiser *Königsberg*, which was destroyed by the British in the River Rufiji's delta on 11 July.

South African General Jan Christiaan Smuts became the new British Commander in February 1916, and he launched a new offensive into northern East Africa between March and September but failed to catch Lettow-Vorbeck and had to withdraw through exhaustion.

Below: A British soldier stands watch over a large artillery piece somewhere in East Africa.

There were two subsidiary expeditions into East Africa – an Anglo-Belgian force halted after taking Tabora in the north-west in September while an advance into the south-west from Northern Rhodesia (Zambia) was halted by the Germans at Iringa in late October. The various expeditions had overrun huge swathes of East Africa but something like 12,000 white troops had been evacuated through sickness and Lettow-Vorbeck's main force was still at large in the south-east.

Above: Trumpeters for a British-officered Nigerian regiment pictured on a troopship bound for East Africa.

Closing In

The British spent much of 1917 repairing damage done by Lettow-Vorbeck's hit-and-run raids, receiving reinforcements and dealing with the so-called Wintgens–Naumann Expedition, an unauthorized campaign by two German officers and just 700 *askaris* that caused havoc in much of occupied northern East Africa. The British did launch attacks against Lettow-Vorbeck in September but these were halted at Mahiwa and he was able to escape into Portuguese East Africa (Mozambique). He now led his remaining 2,200 men on a gruelling 2,000km (1,250 mile) trek that finally brought them back into East Africa on 12 September 1918.

With strong British forces converging on him, Lettow-Vorbeck took his command into Northern Rhodesia and fought a final skirmish at Kamasa on 12 November. He heard of the Armistice the next day and, after negotiations with the British, his small force had been interned in Abercorn by the 25th. His isolated and prolonged campaign had tied down some 160,000 Allied troops as well as many thousands of local labourers. Total British military casualties were around 10,000 but if local porters and labourers are included the figure rises to around 100,000.

THE CURSE OF MALARIA

Malaria, usually a debilitating rather than fatal disease, took a heavy toll of personnel in several theatres of war, notably Salonika and Africa. In the latter case there was something of a myth that locals, many of whom acted as porters, were immune but the figures suggest otherwise. In East Africa, for example, African soldiers fighting for the British suffered 1,377 combat casualties but 2,923 men were admitted to hospital with disease. Malaria was a very real threat to all. Some 50,000 British troops in East Africa were treated for the disease between June and December 1916 alone.

Above: British troops and local porters move through a swamp, an ideal breeding ground for malarial mosquitoes.

The Battle of Jutland

Although the British lost more warships and men in what was by far the largest naval action of the war, they gained an undoubted strategic victory over the German High Seas Fleet, which never left port in such strength again.

The only major fleet action between the German High Seas Fleet and the British Grand Fleet rather came about by accident. Both sides hoped to draw elements of the other into an unequal action in 1916 but the Germans took the initiative and sailed from their home ports during the early afternoon of 30 May. What they did not know was that the British were aware of the plan and their own fleet was already at sea.

Opposing Fleets

The British force comprised the main fleet under Admiral John Jellicoe supported by Admiral David Beatty's battle-cruisers. Opposing them was the High Seas Fleet under Admiral Reinhard Scheer and Admiral Franz von Hipper's battle-cruisers. The British had a total of 151 warships available, led by 28 dreadnoughts and 9 battle-cruisers, while the Germans deployed 16 dreadnoughts, 6 pre-dreadnoughts and 5 battle-cruisers. The rest of the warships on both sides were mostly smaller cruisers and destroyers.

KEY FACTS

Date: 31 May – 1 June 1916

Place: Eastern and south-eastern North Sea

Outcome: The German High Seas Fleet was forced to retreat after sinking several major British warships.

Above: The dreadnought SMS *Ostfriesland* was holed by a mine as it sailed home after Jutland.

Below: The loss of the battle-cruiser HMS *Indefatigable*, a victim of accurate German gunnery, poor design and poorly observed damage-control procedures.

First Blood

Jutland opened at 14.15 hours on the 31st with a clash between smaller cruisers and destroyers, whose radio messages alerted the rival battle-cruisers. The action between these opened some 95 minutes later. Beatty's warships suffered terribly. His own flagship, *Lion*, was badly damaged by shells from *Lützow* but two other British battle-cruisers fared far worse. *Indefatigable* was targeted by *Von der Tann* and was ripped apart by a huge explosion and *Queen Mary* met a similar fate a little later after taking several hits from *Derfflinger*.

Beatty now withdrew and headed towards Jellicoe pursued by Hipper and by Scheer's main fleet. The German admirals did not know of Jellicoe's presence. He manoeuvred his dreadnoughts into an advantageous position in which all their firepower could be directed against the leading German warships as they sailed northward.

The main action began with a new clash between the battle-cruisers and the British lost *Invincible* to another huge explosion while Hipper's flagship, *Lützow*, was badly hit. The rival dreadnoughts finally came in range of each other at around 18.30. Hipper immediately recognized the danger that Scheer was in and used his battle-cruisers to draw the British fire. Scheer managed to turn about and retreat into the gathering darkness. Jellicoe feared torpedo attacks from German destroyers and did not follow closely.

ADMIRAL JOHN JELLICOE

Jellicoe (1859–1935) was Commander of the Grand Fleet, the Royal Navy's main strike force, from 4 August 1914. His main task was to impose a naval blockade on Germany and not be drawn into a major battle in which he might lose his fleet. Jellicoe was criticized for excessive caution even though his strategy was correct, but his performance at Jutland in 1916 was deemed too lukewarm. He was promoted to First Sea Lord the same year but his tenure was deemed mixed – he introduced some better anti-submarine measures but opposed convoys. He was sacked on 24 December 1917.

Above: Admiral Jellicoe was criticized for his caution at Jutland.

Below: The British battle-cruiser *Queen Mary* succumbs to an internal explosion – just eight men survived.

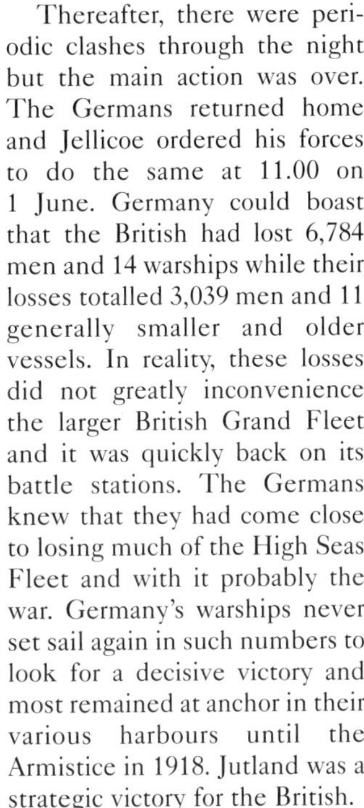

Thereafter, there were periodic clashes through the night but the main action was over. The Germans returned home and Jellicoe ordered his forces to do the same at 11.00 on 1 June. Germany could boast that the British had lost 6,784 men and 14 warships while their losses totalled 3,039 men and 11 generally smaller and older vessels. In reality, these losses did not greatly inconvenience the larger British Grand Fleet and it was quickly back on its battle stations. The Germans knew that they had come close to losing much of the High Seas Fleet and with it probably the war. Germany's warships never set sail again in such numbers to look for a decisive victory and most remained at anchor in their various harbours until the Armistice in 1918. Jutland was a strategic victory for the British.

Dreadnoughts

HMS Dreadnought, *the first modern battleship, was such a revolutionary design when it was launched that it instantly made all previous battleships obsolete and sparked a dangerous naval arms race between Britain and Germany.*

At the outbreak of the war naval commanders believed that the war at sea would be decided by a single titanic clash between surface fleets. This view was especially prevalent among the officers of Britain's Grand Fleet and Germany's High Seas Fleet, two powerful forces of warships that fully expected to clash somewhere in the North Sea. This view was based on key moments in naval history – most recently when the Imperial Japanese Navy had crushed Russia's Baltic Fleet during the Battle of Tsushima in 1905.

Naval engagements had usually been decided by the largest warships of both sides – battleships – taking each other on, and no one believed that World War I naval battles would be any different. Up to the early 1900s all navies had battleships that were generally similar in design but that all changed when HMS *Dreadnought* appeared. This revolutionary British warship was built in a never-matched 14 months and completed in December 1906. The driving force behind the project was the country's First Sea Lord, Admiral John Fisher, arguably the most dynamic and far-sighted naval officer of his generation. *Dreadnought* was a quantum leap in warship design. It quite simply made every other existing battleship outdated at a stroke.

Above: HMS *Dreadnought* is launched in 1906. It served throughout the war, only being decommissioned in 1919.

Below: HMS *Dreadnought*. It sank one warship during the conflict, *U-29* in 1915.

The battleship had a displacement of 17,900 tons and was 160.3m (526ft) long
Its main armament consisted of 10 x 12in (305mm) guns, two of them in this forward turret
Steam turbines gave a top speed of 22 knots

Guns and Turbines

Dreadnought was the first "all big gun" warship and it mounted ten powerful 12in (305mm) guns. By comparison the Royal Navy's latest pre-dreadnought battleships carried just four

Right: Evidence of the growing naval arms race. German Nassau-class dreadnoughts on manoeuvres, September 1911.

12in guns, while Germany's equivalents had four 28cm (11in) guns. Thus, the new design could fire a far greater weight of shells. Fire control was also improved by doing away with the medium guns carried by pre-dreadnoughts.

The extra weight of the big guns, coupled with armour that matched that of existing battleships, made *Dreadnought* much larger than its antecedents, yet its performance was superior. It had a top speed of 22 knots, at least 2 knots better than most pre-dreadnoughts, and a 30 per cent longer range, due to the use, for the first time in a battleship, of steam turbines.

Battleship Building

It was hardly surprising that the appearance of *Dreadnought* soon sparked a naval arms race between Britain and Germany. The Royal Navy launched an additional 23 dreadnoughts between 1909 and 1914 (with a further 11 during the war) while the Germans completed 17 in the same period and a further 2 during the conflict. Other major naval powers undertook similar building programmes – France laid down 7 in 1912–14, Italy 6 in 1912–15 and the United States 12 in 1909–15. Later types were even more powerful than the original and were known as super-dreadnoughts.

Clashes between rival fleets of dreadnoughts were rare with the Battle of Jutland in 1916 being the only example. Sinkings were also few and far between. Germany did not lose any to enemy action. Britain lost two: *Audacious* sank after hitting a German mine in October 1914 and *Vanguard* succumbed to an internal explosion at Scapa Flow in 1917.

Above: The aft 15in (380mm) guns of HMS *Queen Elizabeth*. The Queen Elizabeth class were the most effective British dreadnoughts of the war.

ADMIRAL JOHN FISHER

Fisher (1841–1920) is rightly regarded as one of the towering figures in the history of the Royal Navy. He was made First Sea Lord in 1903 and set in train a vast modernization programme that included such new technologies as aircraft and submarines. His main focus was on surface warships, however. Here Fisher created two entirely new classes – the dreadnought battleship and the battle-cruiser. He did much to prepare the Royal Navy for war with Germany. He retired in 1910, returned as First Sea Lord in 1914 but then resigned the following year after quarrelling with Churchill over the Gallipoli campaign.

The Rise of the U-boats

Germany initially relied on various surface warships to sever Britain's maritime trading links but these were increasingly superseded by the far deadlier U-boats that proved highly elusive and difficult to destroy in the first years of the war.

As most of its surface commerce raiders were swept from the high seas during 1914–15, the Imperial German Navy henceforth had to rely almost entirely on its submarines to attack Britain's maritime trade. U-boats had achieved little in 1914 but they were credited with sinking 396 of the 468 Allied or neutral ships lost the following year. Many senior German officers had been sceptical about their value but such results proved their worth. There were more and more coming off the slipways of Germany's naval yards so their campaign could undoubtedly be intensified in 1916.

Yet the senior figures in Germany's military and political circles were engaged in a struggle over naval strategy, chiefly whether U-boats should be allowed to "sink on sight" any ships they encountered, combatant or not. Some, mainly senior admirals, favoured a return to the strategy of unrestricted submarine warfare, which had been practised for seven months or so in 1915, hoping it would bring Britain to its knees quickly before the British naval blockade did the same to Germany. Others, mostly civilian politicians and diplomats, were more cautious, fearing that a renewal of such a campaign would ultimately bring the United States into the war on the side of the Allies.

U-BOAT ACES

Although underwater warfare was in its infancy in World War I, some U-boat commanders were able to sink a considerable tonnage of Allied ships. Five captains sank more than 210,000 tons of merchant ships and warships but one of them stands head and shoulders above the rest and remains the most successful submarine ace of all time. Lothar von Arnauld de la Perière, captain first of *U-35* and later *U-139*, sank 196 ships of 456,216 tons, almost all of them by gunfire not torpedoes, around a sixth of the total sunk in the war by the whole U-boat force.

Below: A U-boat closes in on one of its victims – a British merchant ship, probably sunk by gunfire.

New Plans

A compromise of sorts was reached. It was decided that only enemy freighters inside the war zone around the British Isles would be sunk without notice and such ships spotted outside the zone would only be sunk without warning if they were armed. Passenger liners would not be touched in either case. The compromise strategy was announced to the wider world on 11 February 1916 and came into operation on the 29th. The controversial decision proved too much for the head of the Imperial Navy, Admiral Alfred von Tirpitz, and he resigned on 29 March.

The new regulations were soon found wanting. *U-29* spotted the British *Sussex* as it was crossing the English Channel on 24 March and, mistaking the passenger steamer for a troopship, sank it. Three US citizens were among the 50 dead and the

United States forcefully demanded that Germany end its "present method of submarine warfare" or face a total break in diplomatic relations. The U-boats were ordered to halt their modified unrestricted campaign on 24 April but the sinkings of other targets continued. They scored a notable success on 5 June when the British armoured cruiser HMS *Hampshire* struck a mine laid by a submarine off the Orkneys. The warship sank within minutes, taking with it the country's Minister of War, Field Marshal Horatio Kitchener, who was setting out on a mission to Russia.

Above: HMS *Hampshire* was sunk by a mine laid by *U-75*. Only 12 of those aboard survived.

Yet More Sinkings

Despite the debate over unrestricted warfare, the U-boats had undoubtedly proved themselves in 1916 and the number of their successes had risen enormously. Some 1,157 Allied and neutral ships, including 396 British vessels, had been sunk and 964 of them were directly attributable to German submarines. Mines, some if not quite all laid by U-boats, accounted for a further 161, while surface warships managed just 32 sinkings. Twenty-two boats had been lost but 108 had been commissioned during the year and there were 149 available for action at the beginning of 1917. The clamour for a full return to unrestricted warfare had also been growing. Field Marshal Paul von Hindenburg and his deputy, General Erich Ludendorff, the senior officers who were effectively running Germany's war effort, had demanded as much on 31 August during a meeting with Emperor Wilhelm II.

LT-CDR LOTHAR VON ARNAULD DE LA PERIÈRE

German U-boat captain de la Perière remains the most successful submarine captain of all time. He led two submarines into action during the war, *U-35* and *U-139*, and in a total of ten cruises in the Mediterranean sank a staggering 194 merchant vessels and 2 warships. *U-35* was also the top-scoring boat of the war with a grand total of 224 sinkings to its credit.

Above: De la Perière's *U-35* (nearer) makes a rendezvous with another German submarine, *U-42*.

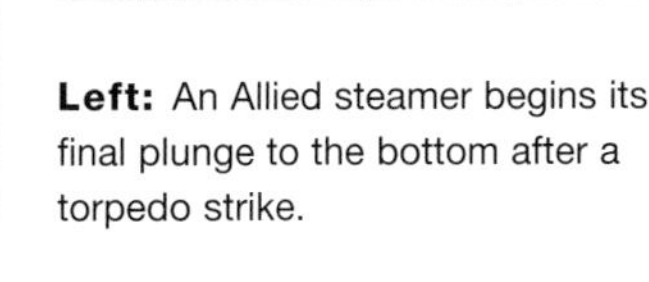

Left: An Allied steamer begins its final plunge to the bottom after a torpedo strike.

Destroyers

Small, fast destroyers were the workhorses of the rival fleets during the war and were arguably the most important surface warships to see service during the war, protecting battlefleets and merchant ships against submarine and surface attacks.

Scores of destroyers were available to all the major navies in 1914, but they were often in short supply once hostilities had begun. Britain had around 300 and Germany 144, but even a lesser navy like that of Austria-Hungary could call on 25. The various navies had major building programmes in the war – Germany managed to construct 107 but this figure was dwarfed by the 329 completed by the British. They served in a variety of roles but had originally been designed to protect larger warships from attacks by torpedo-boats and were therefore often referred to as "torpedo-boat destroyers" in the early days. They continued this task during 1914–18 but anti-submarine operations gradually became their main priority.

GERMAN DESTROYERS

The German Navy, like its rivals, used destroyers for a whole range of missions, not least as the eyes of the main battlefleet. Several classes were built in the pre-war period and rather than being given names they had letter and numerical designations, the letter reflecting the maker. Thus G was the Germania shipyard, S Schichau and V Vulcan, for example.

Type: G40 destroyer
Laid down: 1914
Displacement: 1,050 tons
Crew: 87
Speed: 34.5 knots
Main armament: 3 x 8.5cm (3.3in) guns; 6 x 50.8cm (20in) torpedo tubes

Below: The end of the road for the German destroyer flotillas – interned in Scapa Flow in 1918.

Destroyer Designs

There were two main types of destroyer in service at the outbreak of war. All generally had a top speed of 25–35 knots. A sizeable number were designed for deep-water operations with the main fleets and so sacrificed some speed for endurance. These types largely equipped the British and German navies. Several powers, such as Austria-Hungary and Italy, built smaller destroyers for short-range work in the calmer and more confined waters of the Mediterranean. For example, the Italian Navy's *Astore*, launched in 1907, had a cruising range of 3,335km (1,800 nautical miles) while the British *Gadfly*, commissioned a year earlier and twice as large, had an endurance of 4,075km (2,200 nautical miles).

Whatever the case, destroyers were generally small enough to be built in quantity by the major navies and inexpensive enough to be bought or constructed by second-rank navies. There were many types of destroyer classes in service but most displaced 500–1,200 tons, had crews of between 80 and 150 and carried a mixture of guns and torpedo-launchers.

Roles in Action

They generally operated in groups of between 4 and 10 but some flotillas had as many as 20 destroyers. Those flotillas attached to the main fleet were usually commanded from a

Right: A flotilla of British destroyers sailing in line ahead, part of the Harwich Force that was active in the southern North Sea.

larger warship, such as a light cruiser, and had several roles. They acted as fast scouts, prevented enemy surface ships or submarines from launching torpedo attacks against larger warships, and used their own torpedoes if the opportunity presented itself. Destroyers were indispensable and no main fleet would go to sea without their protective screen. The British committed 73 destroyers to the Battle of Jutland in 1916 while Germany had 61 present.

Destroyers did not just operate with the main fleets and had two main roles when acting independently. First there was coastal defence, stopping raids by rival destroyers against inshore maritime trade routes and ports. Second, and more importantly for the Allies, destroyers were the cornerstone of the anti-submarine warfare campaign against Germany's U-boats. These operations required types with greater range and endurance and later Allied destroyers were something like twice the size of earlier classes. Britain's W class, which appeared in 1917–18, had a displacement of 1,529 tons and an endurance of 6,430km (3,470 nautical miles).

Much of the destroyers' everyday work went unsung but because of their general ubiquity they also suffered considerably. The Allies lost 112 to all causes of which more than 50 per cent were British as the Royal Navy bore the brunt of the anti-submarine campaign. The Central Powers lost 62 destroyers in total of which 53 were German.

Left: HMS *Windsor*, like other British V and W class destroyers, was armed with 4 x 4in (101mm) guns and served on into WWII.

Naval War in the Mediterranean, 1914–16

Controlling the Mediterranean was crucial to the Allies. Thanks to the Suez Canal it was part of the shortest route between Britain and India and, potentially, a means of supplying Russia with military aid.

The Mediterranean was vital to many countries during World War I. Some 75 per cent of Britain's trade passed through the Suez Canal and Straits of Gibraltar, and France and Italy both needed access to their North African colonies. Austria-Hungary's only maritime link with the wider world was through the Adriatic, while Turkey controlled the Dardanelles that led to the Black Sea. The rival naval strategies revolved around maintaining or breaking these links.

Above: The former German battle-cruiser *Goeben* in Turkish service as as *Yavuz Sultan Selim*. *Breslau* became the *Medjilli*.

ESCAPE OF THE *GOEBEN*

The first major incident occurred on 4 August 1914. Two German warships, *Goeben* and *Breslau*, under Vice-Admiral Wilhelm Souchon, shelled Bône (Annaba) and Philippeville (Skikda) in French Algeria and then made for Turkey. Souchon passed two British battle-cruisers but no fire was exchanged as the two countries were not yet at war. Once the midnight deadline had passed, Britain sent a squadron after him. Contact was made to the south-west of Greece but Souchon escaped and reached Turkey on the 10th. Both ships were transferred to the Turkish Navy, helping persuade Turkey to enter the war on Germany's side on 29 October. *Goeben* survived

Below: A British submarine returns to its base after a successful cruise in the eastern Mediterranean.

Above: *Goeben* and *Breslau* were mostly based at Constantinople, as shown here, so they could reach the Black Sea or the Mediterranean.

Above: Japan had an excellent naval tradition and it deployed a destroyer flotilla to the Mediterranean for escort duties.

the war but was badly damaged by mines in early 1918 while *Breslau* was lost.

With the exception of the Anglo-French attempt to force the Dardanelles in early 1915, large fleets saw little action. Britain's remained in northern waters, while the French and Italian Navies were merely kept ready to block any mass breakout by the Austro-Hungarian Navy, but such an event never occurred. Much of the Mediterranean naval campaign was fought by smaller craft.

Submarine Attacks

The British waged a successful submarine campaign in the Dardanelles and the Sea of Marmara between May and September 1915. They sank half of the local Turkish merchant fleet and several of the Turkish Navy's major warships. One submarine, *E-11*, despatched 27 steamers, 58 smaller vessels, 3 cruisers and the battleship *Hairedden Barberosse* in just three missions.

The greatest Central Powers' threat came from the submarines operating from Cattaro (Kotor) in the Adriatic and Constantinople. These laid numerous minefields that proved highly effective at times. The Italian battleship *Regina Margherita* succumbed to a mine off Albania on 11 December 1916, for example. U-boats operating against the main sea routes were even more effective – they sank 900 Allied merchant ships in 1917 alone – and remained so until the latter part of the war. Things began to change in early 1916 when the various navies were allocated specific patrol zones but it was the institution of the convoy system in spring 1918 that dealt the decisive blow.

There were also frequent clashes in the confined waters of the Adriatic. The Allies attempted to seal off the sea by building the Otranto mine barrage between Italy and Albania. It was not wholly effective but it was sufficiently inconvenient for the Austro-Hungarians to attack it in force on the night of 14–15 May 1917 and sink 14 trawlers. Yet the Italian Navy's smallest craft scored the greater successes. Two torpedo-boats sailed into Muggia Bay near Trieste on 9 December 1917 and one sank the battleship *Wien*. Another pair attacked the dreadnought *Szent István* on 10 June 1918 and torpedoes from one sent it to the bottom.

GOEBEN AND *BRESLAU*

Goeben, a battle-cruiser, and *Breslau*, a light cruiser, were German warships handed over to Turkey along with their crews in August 1914. They both opened the war for Turkey by bombarding Russian ports in the Black Sea and mostly remained there until 1917. They transferred to the Mediterranean in January 1918. Both launched a raid on the British base at Mudros but ran into a minefield on the 20th. *Breslau* was sunk and *Goeben* badly damaged, remaining under repair for the remainder of the war.

Torpedo-boats

Torpedoes were deadly weapons that allowed small, fast warships to pack a considerable punch. Torpedo-boats' main targets were meant to be the enemy fleets of old battleships and more modern dreadnoughts.

These light and speedy boats were the first warships to be armed with torpedoes, a weapon that was developed in the late 19th century. Torpedo-boats caused alarm in some naval circles when they first appeared, mainly because they gave the smallest navy a chance to sink the biggest battleships for little financial outlay. As the boats were so relatively cheap to produce, a country with a small defence budget could buy or build dozens of them.

Above: Ships of France's Arquebuse class in port at Toulon.

Most navies had flotillas of torpedo-boats at the outbreak of World War I and they came in two main categories. Some boats were smaller, with only a limited range and were used in coastal waters, while other types were built for longer patrols and more distant operations. The latter were increasingly being superseded by destroyers, bigger and faster warships that also carried torpedoes.

The coastal boats tended to be armed solely with torpedoes, although some were fitted with machine-guns. Speed rather than defensive armament was usually their best chance of survival. If they were sent on longer-range missions, coastal torpedo-boats were usually towed to their target area but some were also deployed from the decks of a class of support vessels generally known as torpedo depot ships.

Below: Sleek German torpedo-boats pictured at anchor in the Kiel Canal in January 1914.

MAS Boats in Action

The Italian Navy operated the most successful coastal torpedo-boats and was the acknowledged world leader in their design at the start of the war. One of the leading producers was the Società Veneziana Automobili Nautiche (SVAN). Their 16-ton MAS (Motobarca Armata SVAN) boats waged a highly effective hit-and-run campaign across the Adriatic Sea during 1915–18. The boats became so successful and renowned for their exploits that the nationalist writer Gabriele d'Annunzio gave them a slogan which translates as "One against a hundred – Attack!"

The MAS boats often operated at night and their most spectacular feat of arms came on 10 June 1918, when a pair of them attacked the Austro-Hungarian dreadnought *Szent István* off Premuda Island in the northern Adriatic at around 03.00 hours and one of them, *MAS 15* captained by Commander Luigi Rizzo, scored a fatal torpedo hit. The dreadnought sank some three hours later and its loss was so psychologically damaging that the main Austro-Hungarian fleet never put to sea again. The attack was Rizzo's second major success of the war as his *MAS 9* had sunk the old Austro-Hungarian battleship *Wien* in Muggia Bay near Trieste on 9 December the previous year.

Baltic Operations

The other major actions involving coastal motor boats (CMBs) actually came some months after the end of the war, when British forces stationed in Russia became embroiled in the ongoing civil war. British torpedo-boats were based on the coast of newly independent Finland and they undertook two highly successful raids against Bolshevik targets. The three-man *CMB4*, commanded by Lieutenant Augustine Agar, sank the cruiser *Oleg* in Kronstadt harbour on 17 June 1919. Their greatest exploit came early on the morning of 19 August, when seven CMBs led by Commander Claude Dobson again broke into the heavily defended harbour at Kronstadt. For the loss of three of his small boats, Dobson's flotilla sank the armoured cruiser *Pamiat Azova* and the dreadnought *Petropavlovsk*, and badly damaged the battleship *Andrei Pervozvanni*.

BRITISH *CMB65A*

Britain developed a number of Coastal Motor Boats, mostly designed by the Thornycroft firm. They came in three types, ranging in length from 12–21m (40–70ft). The torpedoes were fired backwards out of the boat from troughs and the boats had to swerve away quickly to avoid being hit.

Displacement: 10 tons
Length: 16.7m (55ft)
Engine: 350hp Thornycroft Y type
Top speed: 35 knots+
Crew: 3
Armament: 1 or 2 x 18in (457mm) torpedo tubes; 2–4 machine-guns

Right: Destroyers originally evolved to take on smaller torpedo-boats like these French types seen docked at Le Havre in 1913.

Allied Submarines

Although the German U-boat fleet grabbed the headlines during World War I, the Allied navies also deployed their own flotillas of submarines and, even if they were not so spectacularly successful, they played their own part in the final victory.

All the main Allied nations deployed submarines during World War I. In 1914 France had the biggest fleet of all, 123 boats. Italy had 25 mostly short-range types in service and Russia had 41. Few boats were built during the war, just 25 in France, 46 in Italy and 40 in Russia. France's existing types were old and unreliable, Italy's were beset by logistical problems, and Russian submarines were outdated, although they did operate in the Baltic and Black Seas. French, Italian and Russian losses totalled 12, 8 and 20 respectively.

Right: British submarine crewmen stand watch protected from the elements by nothing more than a canvas screen.

Although the British did not have the world's largest fleet of submarines in 1914, they had its largest and most successful one by the Armistice. Some 17 D- and E-class boats were available in August 1914 and these were backed by 40 B- and C-class types that were considered fit only for coastal operations. By the Armistice the numbers had swelled to 137 on active service with a further 78 under construction; 54 were lost during the conflict.

British Actions

The British produced a number of different types but the mainstay were the E-class boats that were active particularly in the Baltic Sea and Dardanelles. Fifty-eight were built from 1913–17 and 22 were lost. The first pair sailed for the Baltic during October 1914, largely to help the Russians as their modern submarines were being crippled by a lack of (German-built) engines. A further four E-class boats reached the Baltic in 1915 and were joined by four C-class types that had been taken apart, carried by ship to Archangel and then transported by rail and barge to the Gulf of Finland where they were then reassembled.

The British submarines sank a number of warships but their greatest contribution to the war effort was to hunt down German freighters transporting Swedish iron ore down the Gulf

BRITISH K-CLASS SUBMARINES

These large submarines (the conning tower and some crew members of *K-6* are shown) were designed to operate with the main surface warships of the Royal Navy but the general concept was flawed, not least because they took an age to submerge as the funnels for their steam turbines had to be made watertight. Collisions with large vessels and even their own kind were not uncommon and 5 of the 17 built before 1919 were lost in accidents.

Displacement: 2,140 tons (surface)
Crew: 50–60
Range: 5,555km (3,000nm)
Armament: 10 x 21in (533mm) torpedo tubes; 3 x 4in (102mm) guns

of Bothnia. This campaign ended with the signing of the Treaty of Brest-Litovsk in March 1918. Under its terms the Germans demanded that the Bolsheviks give up the British submarines. Rather than surrender, the final seven sailed from Helsingfors (Helsinki) on 8 April and their crews scuttled them in deep water.

In the Mediterranean

The Dardanelles campaign in 1915 again involved a number of E-class boats. They crippled the Turkish merchant fleet plying the Sea of Marmara, bombarded various shore installations, and even reached Constantinople. One boat, *E-11* captained by Lieutenant-Commander Martin Nasmith, was particularly successful, sinking 27 steamers and 58 other vessels in three patrols. The campaign netted 2 battleships, 1 destroyer, 5 gunboats, 7 supply ships, 9 troop transports, 35 steamers and 188 other vessels. Four boats were sunk while trying to pass through the Dardanelles; 9 reached the Sea of Marmara and 3 were lost in action there.

The E class was a reliable design but the British also experimented with one of the worst submarines of the war, the steam-driven K class. These were huge boats developed to serve with the Grand Fleet rather than operate as lone hunters. Friendly warships had difficulty in detecting them on the surface in anything but dead calm conditions and the submarines themselves took an age to dive. Collisions and accidents were inevitable, as became clear during an exercise off the Scottish coast on the night of 31 January 1918. *K-4* was sunk by *K-6* and *K-17* was despatched by a British cruiser in the so-called "Battle of May Island".

HMS *E-11*

The British submarine *E-11*, seen here after sailing through the Turkish-controlled Dardanelles, served with great distinction in the Sea of Marmara in 1915, even sinking a Turkish vessel at anchor in Constantinople's Golden Horn on 23 May. In all, 58 E-class boats were built and these also served in the North Sea and Baltic; 22 were lost.

Displacement: 667 tons
Crew: 30
Range: 6,655km (3,600nm)
Armament: 5 x 18in (457mm) torpedo tubes; 1 x 12pdr (76mm) gun

Below: The French submarine *Diane* was lost to an unexplained internal explosion in March 1918.

The Mesopotamian Campaign, 1917–18 Indian labourers at work on a railway line.

The "February Revolution" Disillusioned Russian soldiers surrender en masse to the Germans.

The Battle of Passchendaele British stretcher bearers struggle through the mud with a casualty.

1917 – EUROPE'S YEAR OF TRIAL

1917 was the year in which war-weariness took a firm hold on the peoples of all of the combatant nations. No one now believed the war would be over quickly or that it was in any way glorious; rather it was exacting a fearful butcher's bill. The Allies took the military initiative and focused on the Western Front, launching two huge attacks – the Nivelle Offensive and the Battle of Passchendaele – that led to 1.38 million men killed, wounded or captured and German casualties of around 884,000. However, with the notable exception of the French Army, morale at the front did not collapse and many soldiers appeared psychologically prepared to see the war through to a conclusion.

Both sides could point to successes by the year's end. Germany no longer faced a war on two fronts thanks to the collapse of Russia. However, its unrestricted submarine campaign was failing as the Allies had belatedly introduced the convoy system, and the blockade of Germany was biting ever harder. France and Britain placed their faith in the United States, which declared war on Germany in April, but their relief at having a new ally was tempered with the knowledge that the Americans would not be able to make any worthwhile military contribution to the fight in Europe until well into 1918.

Coastal, Fortress and Railway Artillery A French 155mm rail gun in action.

The Battle of Caporetto Italian troops on the retreat after the German-led attack.

Final Battles in the Caucasus, 1917–18 A field gun in action against the Turks.

The Battle of Arras

The first major attack by the BEF in 1917 began well, especially for the Canadian troops who captured the supposedly impregnable Vimy Ridge, but then it was stopped in its tracks by the formidable defences of the Hindenburg Line.

Marshal Joseph Joffre, the French Commander-in-Chief, had been much criticized for the string of costly offensives he ordered in 1915 and 1916 and was replaced by General Robert Nivelle in December 1916. The ebullient Nivelle devised an Anglo-French strategy to break through the German line in early 1917 but Nivelle's plans were thrown into confusion when the Germans withdrew some 32km (20 miles) to a new and much stronger position, the Hindenburg Line, between Arras and Soissons during late February to early April. They left behind a wasteland of flattened villages, ruined bridges and smashed roads in the area where Nivelle had hoped to attack.

Below: Canadian troops moving supplies by light railway look on as German prisoners are escorted to the rear near Vimy Ridge.

KEY FACTS

DATE: 9 April – 15 May 1917

PLACE: Artois east of Arras

OUTCOME: Early British gains did not lead to a decisive, war-winning victory.

Despite this delay, Nivelle persisted with his plans for the offensive, having convinced his political masters – if not all his fellow generals – that he had found a new method of attack that would win the war. Field Marshal Douglas Haig's BEF launched the opening gambit of Nivelle's offensive in Artois on 9 April. Two British armies were to spearhead the attack – the First under General Henry Horne and General Edmund Allenby's Third. They were arrayed a little to the east of Arras on either side of the River Scarpe and faced the German Sixth Army under General Ludwig von Falkenhausen. Haig was no great believer in Nivelle and also resented the BEF being temporarily placed under the latter's command. Britain's new prime minister, David Lloyd George, had in fact forced the decision upon him.

BLOODY APRIL

The Royal Flying Corps made a major effort to aid the offensive but in "Bloody April" its outclassed machines suffered severe losses to win only temporary air superiority, despite enjoying a large numerical advantage. The preliminary bombardment lasted five days and involved some 2,500 guns but alerted the Germans to the attack. The first day went well, particularly north of Arras, as Allenby's troops pushed forward more than 3km (2 miles) in places and Canadian troops serving under Horne's command stormed the supposedly impregnable Vimy Ridge. The news was less promising south of the Scarpe where troops faced a complete section of the Hindenburg Line and struggled to take the fortified village of Monchy-le-Preux, which eventually fell on the 11th after bitter fighting.

Haig lengthened the line of his attack the same day by unleashing General Hubert

Above: A British gun crew re-lays a field gun on a new target after it has been fired during the Battle of Arras.

Vimy Ridge. The British suffered some 150,000 casualties, a lower rate of attrition among an attacking force than was the norm, while the Germans lost 100,000. With the French Army in total disarray, the BEF would now have to shoulder the greater part of the Anglo-French effort on the Western Front for the rest of the year and into 1918. Haig would have to attack again but this time in Flanders, on ground of his own choosing.

Gough's Fifth Army in the south against another section of the Hindenburg Line. The mismanaged attack stalled almost immediately, especially around the village of Bullecourt, and Gough's Australian troops suffered their worst-ever losses on the Western Front. Haig halted the battle on the 15th to await news of Nivelle's major offensive, which was to open the next day. The French attack was a complete disaster and Haig was therefore forced to renew his battle around Arras on the 23rd to take some of the pressure off his ally. Some ground was gained during the next two days but the impetus was soon lost, although the tired British troops battered away until late May.

Continuing Attacks

Haig was roundly criticized by some politicians for his battle tactics but Arras was seen as a success in military circles, not least because of the capture of

Below: British troops gather round a tank during the Battle of the Scarpe, part of the Arras fighting in April.

CANADA AT WAR

Canada made a major contribution to the Allied war effort. Some 418,000 men fought overseas in the Canadian Expeditionary Force and a further 21,000 served in other capacities, including 13,000 in Britain s air services. Roughly 210,000 men became casualties of whom 56,500 were killed. Canada's war effort went further. It produced large amounts of food for the Allies; its shipyards built 1,000 vessels and by 1917 its factories were producing more than half of Britain's shrapnel as well as huge amounts of heavy shells.

Right: Canadian troops buy oranges from local French civilians outside Arras.

Light Bombers

Largely developed to operate over or immediately beyond the battlefield to attack a wide variety of targets, light bombers later increasingly operated in direct support of attacks to destroy enemy positions that were holding up friendly forces.

Aircraft of this type gradually evolved during World War I as new designs with more powerful engines became available. Unlike the first under-powered aircraft that struggled to get a pilot off the ground, these could carry a practical if modest bomb load and were primarily used against targets in or near the front line. Some also flew longer-range missions but that was the exception rather than the norm. Most light bombers that saw service were two-seater, single-engined biplanes, although there were exceptions like the German AEG G-series that first appeared in 1916, which had three engines and a crew of three or four.

Above: The British Airco DH-4 day bomber was both manoeuvrable and versatile and entered service from March 1917.

Although some countries, notably Britain and France, produced dedicated light bombers, both they and other combatants used fighters or multi-purpose aircraft in the light-bomber role. There was some sense in this as fighters stood a better chance of survival if attacked, although they generally carried smaller bomb loads, while multi-purpose reconnaissance/light-bomber types could easily fulfil two roles. Light bombers often needed fighter escorts anyway as they were slower and less well armed.

The Royal Aircraft Factory's BE-2 of 1912 was one of the first British aircraft to fly bombing

VOISIN 3

France deployed the Voisin 3 pusher biplane, the only aircraft in any air force then to be fitted with a machine-gun as standard, from late 1914. Thanks to its steel airframe, it was a sturdy machine. It proved successful in short-range support missions but was also used as a strategic bomber, notably when 18 attacked two German poison-gas factories on 27 May 1915. Some were also sold to Russia.

ENGINE: 120hp Salmson 9M
CREW: 2
CEILING: 3,350m (11,000ft)
TOP SPEED: 105kph (65mph)
ARMAMENT: 100kg (220lb) bombs; 1 x 8mm (0.315in) machine-gun

missions but its two-man crew could only throw small bombs at a target and had only a rifle or pistol to defend themselves. Its replacement, the RE-7, arrived at the front from late 1915 and was soon found to be under-powered and under-armed, but it was at least given a machine-gun for protection and could carry 155kg (340lb) of bombs. Other British aircraft used in the light-bomber role included Airco's single-engined DH-4, which also saw considerable service with the American forces, and the company's less successful twin-engined DH-9.

French Designs

The development of French light bombers followed a similar pattern. Voisin was perhaps the major manufacturer and its two-seater Voisin 3 was the first aircraft to carry a machine-gun when it began to appear in late 1914. Although its bomb load was limited to just 100kg (220lb), some 800 were built. New models were gradually introduced with better characteristics. The Voisin 8 entered service in late 1916 and could carry some 80 per cent more bombs by weight but sacrificed so much speed and agility that heavy losses relegated it to night-time missions. The Voisin 10 of early 1918 had a better engine and nearly three times the bomb load of the Voisin 3. Other aircraft used in the light-bombing role were the successful multi-purpose Breguet B2 and B4, which saw service in 1915–18, and the Salmson 2, which appeared over the Western Front in early 1918.

BE-2

The BE-2 was designed by Geoffrey de Havilland before the outbreak of the war and continued in service until 1916. One was the first British aircraft to land in France in 1914, while another was flown by the first officer to win a Victoria Cross in aerial warfare.

Engine: 70hp Renault
Crew: 2
Ceiling: 3,000m (10,000ft)
Top speed: 112kph (70mph)
Armament: hand-thrown bombs; sidearms or rifle

German Responses

Germany did not develop many light bombers, although the two-seater LVG C-II was deployed in this role during 1915–17. The German Army Air Service used fighters for light bombing but preferred to develop ground-attack or multi-purpose aircraft to undertake similar operations. LVG's C-V, for example, entered service in mid-1917 and performed reconnaissance, light-bombing and ground-attack missions successfully until the Armistice.

Below: The French Breguet Type XIV B2 light bomber entered service in the summer of 1917.

The Nivelle Offensive

General Robert Nivelle won support for a massive offensive because he convinced the Allied governments that he could achieve a major breakthrough but his attack soon stalled, produced heavy losses and provoked a widespread mutiny.

The major French offensive on the Western Front in April 1917 is sometimes called the Second Battle of the Aisne and a simultaneous subsidiary attack is referred to as the Third Battle of Champagne. However, both are more commonly known as the Nivelle Offensive after their instigator, General Robert Nivelle, French Commander-in-Chief from December 1916. Nivelle was a highly persuasive orator and had convinced his political masters that an offensive along the Chemin des Dames, a road between Soissons and Craonne that ran over a series of wooden ridges, would produce the decisive breakthrough that had eluded the Allies since 1914. Nivelle's boast that he would win the war "in 48 hours" was less well received by both his own generals and those of the British.

Nivelle's plan of attack was not significantly different from what had been tried before but it was on a much bigger scale. The French Reserve Army Group, four armies totalling 1.2 million men and 7,000 guns, was assembled on a 64km (40 mile) front between Soissons and Reims. The two opposing German armies, the Seventh under General Max von Boehn and General Fritz von Below's First, were outnumbered but they had two vital advantages. They were holding strong defences based on the ridges that ran across Nivelle's line of advance and they knew when he was going to attack because they had captured the plans for the battle.

KEY FACTS

Date: 16 April – 9 May 1917

Place: Along the River Aisne

Outcome: Heavy French losses for very little territorial gain were followed by the outbreak of military indiscipline.

Opening Attacks

The much-delayed offensive began on 16 April after a ten-day preliminary bombardment. The main effort along the Chemin des Dames was made by General Olivier Mazel's Fifth Army and General Charles Mangin's Sixth Army but they made little progress at a very high cost. Boehn's troops inflicted some 40,000 casualties on the French on the first day alone and knocked out 150 of their new tanks. The subsidiary attack launched against Below by General François Anthoine's Fourth Army to the east of Reims began the next day and rapidly met a similar fate.

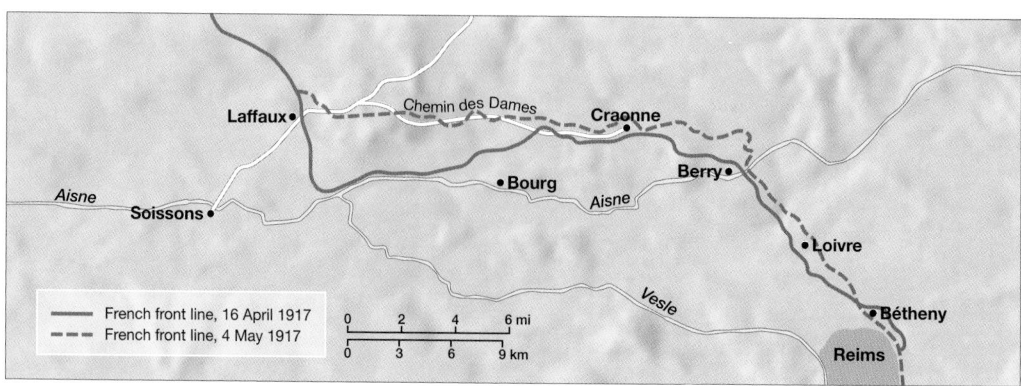

THE NIVELLE OFFENSIVE
The major attacks of the offensive took place from 16–20 April but the battle lasted for another few weeks.

Left: French dead lie scattered in a sunken road, just a small part of the price paid to disprove Nivelle's excessive boasts.

Despite a patent lack of progress, Nivelle continued to grind away until the 20th but the breakthrough he had promised never materialized. The increasingly pointless attacks were soon scaled down and eventually ended on 9 May. The troops did finally manage to capture a small part of the Chemin des Dames ridges by 5 May but this was scant consolation for the loss of 187,000 men. Nivelle was replaced by General Philippe Pétain on the 15th and, in what was to become a decisive move for the Allies' future strategy, General Ferdinand Foch was made the French Army Chief of Staff at the same time.

MUTINY

Nivelle's failure shattered the morale of the long-suffering French Army and it was torn apart by mutiny, brought about not only by the recent heavy losses but also by poor rations, low pay and a lack of leave. The unrest broke out in the last week of April and lasted until mid-June. Many units were involved and there were some executions but the mutineers were mostly persuaded to return to duty. The French Army was not really fit for action until the autumn. The Germans did not capitalize on the unrest as the news blackout was so strict that they did not learn of the mutiny until it was over.

GENERAL ROBERT NIVELLE

Nivelle (1856–1924) was a mere colonel in 1914 but enjoyed rapid promotion, becoming Commander of the French Second Army at Verdun in April 1916. His defence of the embattled fortress town made him a public figure and this, combined with his charisma, ensured that he became French Commander-in-Chief in December. He planned a major attack that would end the war "in 48 hours" but the Nivelle Offensive in April 1917 was a disaster and provoked a widespread mutiny in the French Army. He was sacked from his post in May.

Above: Nivelle's tenure of high command was brief.

Left: A remarkable – but possibly fake – photograph of German troops repelling a French attack at the height of the Nivelle Offensive.

French and German Tanks

Both the French and Germans produced their own armoured fighting vehicles during the war. France put three types of tank into service but Germany built just one model and instead often relied on tanks captured from the British.

The French were the keenest supporters of armoured warfare after the British. There was no one driving force behind their programme and the two Allies' tank plans evolved along largely separate lines. French armoured cars had been of some military worth before the arrival of trench warfare and a few enlightened figures in the Ministry of War believed that vehicles that could operate off-road might break the stalemate on the Western Front. The key figure was a colonel of artillery, Jean-Baptiste Estienne, who proposed a tracked armoured fighting vehicle to the general responsible for weapons procurement in December 1915. Estienne's concept was suitably impressive and an order for 400 *chars d'assaut* (assault vehicles) was issued on 31 January 1916.

Above: A St Chamond tank is camouflaged in the factory before delivery to the French Army in 1917.

First French Designs

Schneider was the first company to be given a procurement order and soon came up with a box-like armoured superstructure mounted on a chassis developed from a US Holt tractor. The vehicle weighed some 13 tonnes and had a top speed of less than 6.5kph (4mph). There were endless delays in production, largely because of shortages of armour plate. The first Schneider reached the army on 8 September 1916 but only seven more had arrived by late November, the date when all 400 should have been built. As Schneider was clearly struggling to fill its order from an early stage, St Chamond, a design company, was asked to fulfil a second order for 400 tanks in April. Its prototype was not dissimilar to the Schneider but was nearly 70 per cent heavier.

Neither tank performed well in action. Their high profile made them vulnerable to

RENAULT FT-17

The French FT-17 was the first tank to have a revolving turret and was designed in 1917. It had an adequate cross-country performance and saw service with both the French and US forces on the Western Front throughout 1918.

Weight: 6.5 tons
Crew: 2
Max. speed: 10kph (6mph)
Max. armour: 16mm (0.63in)
Armament: 1 x 8mm (0.315in) machine-gun or 1 x 37mm (1.46in) gun

artillery fire, their engines were not overly reliable and, worst of all, their trench-crossing abilities were poor. Of the two, the St Chamond was the worse. Its greater weight meant that it was even more likely to sink into soft ground and its superstructure overhung the tracks substantially at the front, making it prone to getting stuck while crossing a trench.

Both types achieved little during their combat debut, the Nivelle Offensive in April 1917. A number remained in service for the rest of the war but they were largely superseded by a light tank, the Renault FT-17, from the end of 1917. This was a much lighter and smaller design used extensively during the later stages of the war by both the French Army and the American Expeditionary Force. The Renault had a good cross-country performance and its turret gave it an all-round field of fire but thin armour made it very vulnerable.

German Scepticism

The German High Command was not overly impressed with tanks, citing their high rate of mechanical failure and their vulnerability to anything from difficult terrain to artillery fire. A German-built type did reach the front from late 1917 onwards but production was limited due to the crippling shortage of raw materials.

The A7V Panzerkampfwagen was by some way the biggest tank of the war. It had a large box-like structure that housed a 16-man crew, while firepower was provided by a single forward-firing 57mm (2.24in) cannon and six heavy machine-guns. The A7V was ponderously slow, prone to mechanical failure and was so top heavy that it was likely to overturn if moved along a slope. Only a few dozen of them were ever built and they were easily outnumbered by the captured and refurbished British tanks that the Germans also used in the later stages of hostilities.

PANZERKAMPFWAGEN A7V

Germany's massive A7V entered service in late 1917 but had a high centre of gravity and inadequate engines that gave it a poor cross-country capability.

Weight: 32 tons
Crew: 16
Max. speed: 13kph (8mph)
Max. armour: 30mm (1.2in)
Armament: 1 x 57mm (2.24in) gun; 6 x 7.92mm (0.312in) machine-guns

Right: The Schneider tank had poor ventilation and thin armour but worst of all its internal petrol tanks lacked adequate protection.

The Battle of Messines

The mining and subsequent attack on Messines Ridge was probably the most rigidly planned and tightly managed operation of the whole war and led to the capture of a supposedly impregnable section of the German front line in a matter of hours.

With the French Army crippled by the Nivelle Offensive and the mutiny that it provoked, Field Marshal Haig's BEF became the principal Allied army on the Western Front from mid-1917 onward. Haig decided to launch a large and long-planned offensive around Ypres in Flanders to break through the German front line. Before he could undertake the main attack it was necessary to eradicate a small German-held salient on an area of high ground around the town of Messines to the immediate south of Ypres. The task of taking Messines Ridge was given to General Herbert Plumer's British Second Army, which also included a sizeable proportion of troops from Australia and New Zealand.

Preparing the Attack

Plumer was in many ways the ideal commander for the job. He had a well-deserved reputation as a thoughtful and meticulous commander and had served in Flanders since 1915 so he knew the area well. He had also been planning an assault on the ridge since mid-1916 and had ordered a number of mines be dug under the German trench lines. The immense efforts to create the shafts began in January 1917 and the dangerous work involved excavating some 8,000m (26,250ft) of tunnels and removing the spoil without alerting the enemy. One shaft was detected by the Germans but the other 21 were never discovered and the tunnellers packed them with hundreds of tons of high explosive.

Plumer also intended to make the best possible use of artillery, tanks and gas to minimize his losses during the opening stages of the attack. Local air superiority ensured that the aircraft of the German Army Air Service would be unable to intervene in the fighting.

The preliminary bombardment by around 2,300 heavy artillery pieces and 300 mortars began on 21 May and increased in intensity seven days later. After another week or so of

KEY FACTS

Date: 7 – 14 June 1917

Place: Messines Ridge, south-west Belgium

Outcome: A clear-cut British victory that led to the eradication of a major German salient.

Above: General Herbert Plumer (with cane), the mastermind behind the attack on Messines Ridge.

Below: A good indication of the devastation wrought on the German positions atop Messines Ridge.

Above: British troops advance towards the top of Messines Ridge – many of its German defenders were too dazed to offer much resistance.

artillery fire, 19 of the surviving mines were detonated at 03.10 hours on 7 June. The simultaneous blasts sent huge columns of debris high into the sky and killed an estimated 10,000 German troops. Nine of the Second Army's divisions then attacked on a 14.5km (9 mile) front behind a creeping barrage in which the artillery dropped shells just a little beyond the advancing infantry so that the Germans kept their heads down in their trenches. The surviving defenders were so dazed that Plumer's units pushed forward against little opposition and captured all of their objectives in the first three hours.

RESULTS OF THE BATTLE

As was by now common practice, German units vigorously counterattacked the following day but they were beaten off everywhere. Their attempts to push the British off the ridge continued but with less ferocity until the 14th by which point the whole of the salient was securely in Plumer's hands.

Plumer's men had suffered around 17,000 casualties during the battle but, unusually for World War I, the defenders had actually recorded greater losses, some 25,000 men in all, including 7,500 prisoners. By the usual standards of the conflict, the Battle of Messines had been an overwhelming success for the BEF but it was only a limited offensive with limited objectives and the main event of Haig's Flanders offensive was yet to come.

Below: Messines Ridge pictured from the British side during the intense preliminary bombardment before the attack.

Mine Warfare

The detonation of huge caches of high-explosive under an enemy's front line was a common aspect of trench warfare and could be highly effective as the explosions not only destroyed defences but also often left any survivors too dazed to fight.

Early versions of modern land mines were developed during World War I but they were rather primitive devices. The Germans, for example, made extensive use of mortar bombs part buried in the ground as an early type of minefield to destroy tanks. Mine warfare usually had a rather different meaning during the conflict and referred to digging shafts under enemy trenches, filling them with high-explosive and then detonating the charges. It was dangerous work due to tunnel collapses, flooding, gas and the danger that the enemy might explode camouflets (counter-charges) to bury the tunnellers in their own shaft. Almost all the mine warfare of World War I took place on the Western Front as the static nature of the fighting gave tunnellers the time they needed to drive their shafts underground.

Above: A lone soldier gives some indication of the size of craters left by a mine detonation.

First Mines

The Germans actually set off the first underground explosion of the war on 20 December 1914, when 10 out of 11 mines were detonated immediately beneath a brigade of Indian troops near Festubert, some 16km (10 miles) south of the Franco-Belgian border. However, the British became the war's greatest exponents of tunnelling but had no specialist units in existence in 1914. They were actually the brainchild of a persistent member of parliament, John Norton Griffiths, who submitted the idea in December 1914. He had a contract to build sewers through the clay soil under a northern town and employed men known as "moles" who "clay kicked"

Below: A vast crater produced by the detonation of just one mine at the beginning of the Battle of the Somme in 1916.

Right: Whoever reached the lip of a crater first after the detonation had the upper hand in the subsequent fghting – in this case the Germans.

or "worked on the cross". They sat in the tunnel with their backs supported on a wooden backrest (cross) with their feet pointed at the tunnel face and used them to work a spade-like implement to dig out the clay, which was then passed back for disposal. Alternative methods using mining machines were rarely tried and not successful.

Formal approval for the creation of specialist mining units was finally issued on 12 February 1915 and the first units were designated 170 to 178 Tunnelling Companies, Royal Engineers. The first recruits were British miners of every sort but companies were later also raised in Australia, Canada and New Zealand.

British Attacks

The first British mines were exploded under Hill 60 near St Eloi on the evening of 17 April and thereafter the operations grew larger and more complex. The biggest mining operation in military history reached fruition in mid-1917 but the idea had first been mooted as far back as 6 January 1916.

The target was Messines, a German-held ridge a little to the south of Ypres. The tunnellers planned 21 explosions in all and the charges were placed in 12 main shafts, some with two or more galleries leading off them, along a 16km (10 mile) stretch of the ridge. The building of the mines was an immense effort – one was over 640m (2,100ft) long. Once completed they were mostly filled with Ammonal, the most powerful explosive then known. One particular mine contained more than 43 tonnes and the tunnellers placed close to 430 tonnes of explosives under the German lines.

Nineteen mines in total were exploded on 7 July 1917 (two failed to go off) and the devastation caused was immense. The largest crater, Lone Tree, was 12m (40ft) deep and 76m (250ft) across. No one knows how many German troops were killed by the simultaneous detonations, which were heard in London and beyond, but some 10,000 men were recorded as missing on the first day of the battle. A further 7,350 were taken prisoner, many in a wholly dazed condition.

Below: German officers prepare to detonate a mine under the enemy trenches in the early part of the war.

The Battle of Passchendaele

Passchendaele, or the Third Battle of Ypres, was planned in the expectation of crashing through the German defences but quickly degenerated into probably the most horrific battle of the war, largely due to the truly awful conditions.

The British victory at the Battle of Messines in June 1917 had captured part of a long ridge to the south and east of the Belgian town of Ypres but the northern section remained in German hands. Field Marshal Haig, commander of the BEF, had intended to launch a major attack in Flanders for some time, partly because he believed – and the success at Messines seemed to confirm – that the German Army was close to collapse. He also saw that a breakthrough at Ypres followed by a drive across Belgium would capture the ports from where German U-boats were decimating Britain's maritime trade.

KEY FACTS

Date: 31 July – 10 November 1917

Place: East of Ypres, south-west Belgium

Outcome: After a terrible struggle, the British captured Passchendaele village.

BATTLE OF PASSCHENDAELE
This map shows the battle's painfully slow progress over several months.

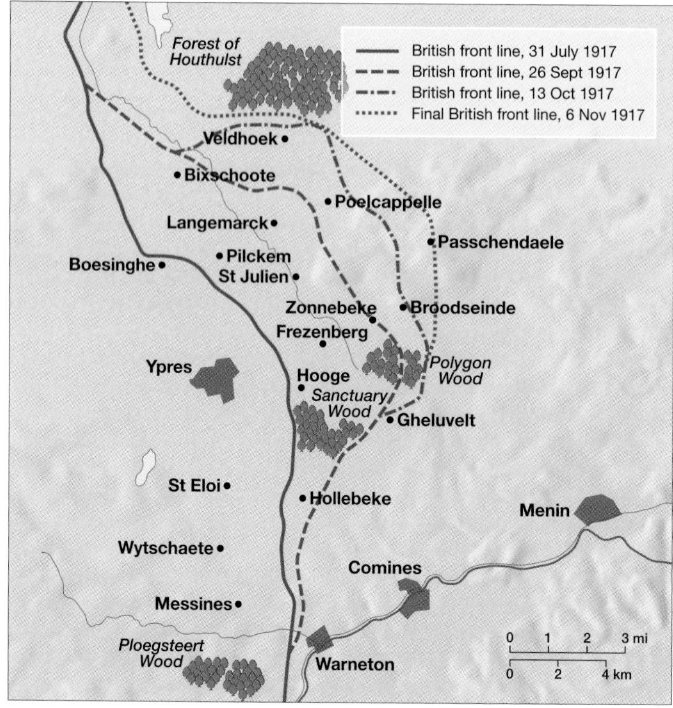

Gough's Attack

The main effort was to be by General Hubert Gough's British Fifth Army with support from the British Second Army under General Herbert Plumer to the south and General François Anthoine's French First Army to the north. There was a 10-day preliminary bombardment from some 3,000 guns before the main attack on an 18km (11 mile) front began at 03.50 hours on 31 July. The barrage had alerted the opposing German Fourth Army under General Sixt von Arnim and he had set about extending the already extensive defence system.

An attack down the Menin Road to the south-east of Ypres was blocked and there were

Below: British casualties, just a small fraction of some 300,000 men listed as killed, wounded, missing or taken prisoner. German losses totalled around 260,000.

Right: A British stretcher party struggles to make any progress through the thick mud that typified the Ypres battlefield.

small gains around Pilckem Ridge to the north-east where the main effort was made. The Battle of Pilckem ended on 2 August with the British having advanced just 2,750m (3,000yds) at a cost of some 32,000 casualties. The battlefield was also being turned into a quagmire due to unseasonable heavy rainfall and the damage inflicted on the land drains by the incessant shelling. Nevertheless, the fighting had to continue. The next major effort was the Battle of Langemarck (16–18 August) but the British attackers again made little progress.

Plumer Takes Over

Haig gave Plumer command of the floundering offensive in late August and the latter devised a new strategy that took into account the awful conditions. Plumer recognized that the idea of a decisive breakthrough was impractical, so he launched a succession of limited offensives that had relatively modest objectives. Rather than punch through the German line, Plumer was going to nibble away at it. What had begun as a war-winning offensive was thus transformed into a battle of attrition. Haig had little choice but to continue as the French were still recovering from the mutiny of May–June that had broken out after the disastrous Nivelle Offensive.

Plumer launched several attacks between 20 September and 10 November, beginning with the Battle of the Menin Road (20–25 September) in the south-east and culminating in the First and Second Battles of Passchendaele (12 October – 10 November) in the north-east. The BEF was finally left holding the greater part of the long ridge that had been mostly in German hands since 1914–15. The British had extended the salient around Ypres by some 8km (5 miles) but the cost had been very high. The British and Empire troops had suffered some 300,000 casualties while the Germans recorded 260,000.

TRENCH FOOT

Trench foot (or, in its more descriptive modern name, immersion foot) is a fungal infection caused by cold, wet and insanitary conditions. If not caught early, the infection can turn gangrenous and require amputation of the limb. The first cases among the British forces became apparent in late 1914 and some 20,000 cases were recorded over that winter. Improved conditions in the trenches, regular foot inspections by officers and changes of socks whenever possible reduced but never stopped the flow of cases. There were potential penalties for those who contracted trench foot, not least because some officers saw it as a type of self-inflicted wound.

Above: Australian troops undergo foot inspection, a necessary routine of trench life especially in cold and wet conditions.

Coastal, Fortress and Railway Artillery

Although most artillery weapons deployed during the war were mounted on wheeled carriages, other artillery pieces were either placed in fixed positions, such as fortresses, or, if especially large, on purpose-built railway mounts.

There was something of a mania across much of Europe for updating existing frontier fortresses or building modern versions of them in the decades before World War I. Austria-Hungary, Germany and Russia all built such fortresses but the greatest exponents were the French and Belgians. Theirs were generally built around strategic towns and cities, like Liège and Namur in Belgium or Verdun and Belfort in France, and comprised a number of outlying forts fitted with heavy artillery pieces and machine-guns. The artillery was positioned inside retractable steel domes in the most modern forts.

Above: The French, like the British and Germans, operated railway artillery. In this case, an improvised 155mm (6.1in) rail gun fires on a distant German position.

BRITISH BL 12-INCH RAIL GUN

The British built just two of these large rail guns initially (the guns themselves were originally designed for naval service). They were in France by late 1915 and two more went into action during 1916.

Weight: 170 tonnes (approx)
Calibre: 12in (305mm)
Weight of shell: 340kg (750lb)
Muzzle velocity: 813m/sec (2,666ft/sec)
Max. range: 30km (18.5 miles)

The frontier fortresses proved to be paper tigers as they could not withstand the newest and heaviest forms of artillery introduced before and during the war. After both supposedly impregnable Liège and Namur had fallen in a matter of a few days in August 1914, the French saw the writing on the wall and began to remove many of their fortress guns, mount them on field carriages or flatbed rail trucks and send them to the field army as it was especially short of heavier forms of artillery no matter how ancient.

Coast Defences

Coastal artillery received a major overhaul in the second half of the 19th century largely due to the development of the armoured warship. Generally, the guns were placed in brick and earth and later concrete emplacements to protect important sections of the coast or key harbours, although lighter types were more mobile and might be placed behind extemporized defences. They were usually supported by various other weapons, such as machine-guns, searchlights and anti-submarine barriers. However, coastal artillery actually saw little action during the war, aside from occasionally replying to long-range fire from distant enemy warships, as amphibious assaults were extremely rare.

The British did keep their coastal artillery largely intact to combat any invasion threat and the Germans also used such types to protect certain bases. The island of Heligoland was heavily defended not least because it protected the seaways leading to the home ports of the High Seas Fleet. The German Navy was also particularly anxious to protect the entrance to the canals at Zeebrugge and Ostend on the coast of occupied Belgium as they led inland to the U-boat base at Bruges. The coastal defences at Zeebrugge and Ostend were both tested by a British attack in April 1918 but they survived mostly unscathed.

Above: An armoured revolving artillery cupola in an Alpine redoubt, of the kind found in many fortresses of the era.

Rail Guns

The heaviest guns deployed in the ground war were usually moved about on rail mounts so that they could be easily transferred from firing position to firing position by locomotives. Such guns were overwhelmingly deployed on the Western Front where there were usually excellent rail links not far behind the static battle lines. The first experiments were carried out by the French, who put redundant coastal or fortress guns on flatbed rolling stock during late 1914. Purpose-built rail guns began to appear later. The chief drawback with these types was that they had limited left–right traverse and thus had often to be moved about on a section of curved track to acquire a new target. Smaller calibre railway guns were commonly mounted in such a way that they could be traversed through 360 degrees.

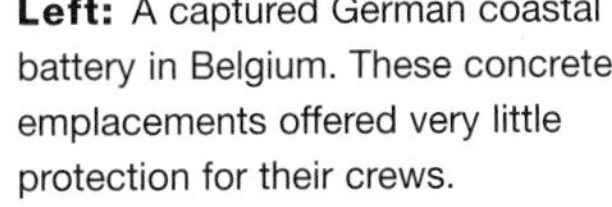

Left: A captured German coastal battery in Belgium. These concrete emplacements offered very little protection for their crews.

The Battle of Cambrai

The British offensive at Cambrai in late 1917 saw the first use of massed tanks in warfare but despite early morale-boosting successes much of the captured ground was soon retaken by the Germans, who were masters of the rapid counter-attack.

The first British tanks went into action in September 1916 during the later stages of the Battle of the Somme, but they had never really been given the chance to prove their true capabilities since their debut. The problem was that they had always been used in small numbers and had frequently been sent into battle across exceptionally difficult terrain, muddy and pitted with shell craters.

An ardent supporter of the tank, Colonel John Fuller, devised a plan to use tanks in a summertime raid against a quiet section of the Hindenburg Line to the south-east of Arras. The terrain there comprised dry ground still relatively undamaged by heavy shellfire.

KEY FACTS

Date: 20 November – 7 December 1917

Place: West of Cambrai, north-east France

Outcome: Early British gains were lost to German counter-attacks.

Planning the Battle

Fuller's plan was approved by General Julian Byng, commander of the British Third Army, but it was rejected by Field Marshal Haig when it was first presented to him. Haig later relented when it became all too apparent that the Battle of Passchendaele was failing badly and he needed a morale-boosting victory to stem the growing tide of criticism being directed against his leadership. Fuller's idea for a raid soon developed into something very much grander – Byng ordered a full-scale breakthrough attack. His subordinate commanders were not overly impressed as the weather in late 1917 was likely to be bad, there were too few reserves to exploit any early gains and the tank crews had been given little time to practise their new battle tactics.

Into Action

Nevertheless, six infantry and two cavalry divisions backed by 1,000 guns were concentrated along a 10km (6 mile) front held by two divisions of General Georg von der Marwitz's German Second Army. The attack opened at around dawn on 20 November 1917 when 475 tanks moved forward without even the slightest preliminary bombardment. The front-line German troops were caught by surprise and in many instances either surrendered or fled.

The tanks and accompanying infantry had made 6km (4 miles) by mid-afternoon, creating a new salient in the line, and the only reverse had been around the village of Flesquières where the local British commander had ordered

Below: Tanks were far from being immune to artillery fire as this comprehensively smashed example at Cambrai clearly shows.

Right: German prisoners help to bring British wounded out of an underground dressing station near Cambrai, 20 November 1917.

his infantry not to work closely with the tanks. Cambrai was in sight by the end of the day but then the Germans threw in local counter-attacks that blocked the way forward.

The tanks had done remarkably well on the first day, taking more ground than in the three-month-plus Third Battle of Ypres, but many were soon either destroyed or more commonly abandoned when they ditched or suffered some form of mechanical failure.

TANK TACTICS

The British developed special trench-clearing techniques for their tanks during the Battle of Cambrai in November 1917. They operated in groups of three. The first tank would turn left at the first trench, firing down into it, while the second would arrive at the trench, drop its fascine into it and cross over. It, too, would then turn left, firing into the trench. The third tank would cross over the trench and push on to the next trench, where it would drop its fascine, cross over and turn left to engage the enemy. The first tank would now cross over the first two trenches, reach the third and drop its own fascine – and so the process would continue.

Above: A pair of British tanks lie abandoned near Cambrai. Many simply suffered mechanical failure rather than falling prey to enemy fire.

Haig ordered the battle to continue but there was no more progress and then the Germans counter-attacked in force on the 30th. The British managed to stop them in the north of the salient but were forced back in the south. When the fighting ended on 7 December the British had abandoned virtually all of the ground the tanks had helped to capture. The British had lost some 45,000 men and the Germans 50,000, including 11,000 prisoners. Only one-third of the tanks deployed on the first day survived the battle – and most of them were in need of a major overhaul.

Cambrai led the British commanders to conclude that an attack did not need a long preliminary bombardment and that the mass use of tanks was a battle winner. The Germans, in contrast, concluded that tanks were too unreliable to be truly useful. These findings would colour both sides' battle tactics in the final year of the war.

Aces and Fighter Tactics

Although the truly great aces were undoubtedly expert pilots and skilled marksmen, they had one particular trait that marked them out from all of their contemporaries – their absolute ruthlessness when in air-to-air combat.

While it is true that the tactics of air combat developed significantly during the war, most aircraft were not shot down after prolonged bouts of air combat, and mass dog-fights between dozens of fighters were virtually unknown until the later years of the conflict. The best way to down an opponent was to get behind and slightly below him at close range, preferably unseen in a faster, more manoeuvrable and better-armed aircraft. This last point cannot be overstressed as the air war in World War I was a technological struggle as much as anything else and the arrival of a better fighter frequently tipped the balance of power – at least until it was superseded by a better enemy aircraft.

Nevertheless, a handful of fighter pilots on all sides proved to be exceptionally skilled and were seen as aces. The French press invented the idea in 1915 to honour a pilot who had shot down five enemy aircraft and then the German Army Air Service required that a pilot score eight (later sixteen) kills before he could receive its highest decoration. The British authorities rather frowned on the idea of this type of personality cult, but set a benchmark in March 1918 announcing that a fighter pilot needed to score eight victories to win the Distinguished Flying Cross.

Above: US ace Edward "Eddie" Rickenbacker trained as a pilot in 1917, then joined and later led the elite 94th "Hat in the Ring" Squadron in 1918.

BILLY BISHOP

Canadian ace William "Billy" Bishop (1894–1956), seen here in front of his French-built Nieuport 17 Scout fighter, was one of the war's top-scoring pilots. He began flying fighters in March 1917 and scored his first victory on the 25th. He received a Victoria Cross in August for attacking a German aerodrome and destroying several enemy aircraft – all in a matter of just 37 minutes on 2 June. After the war, he rose to the rank of air marshal.

Top Aces

As air combat was most intense over the Western Front, it was there where most aces were to be found. Leading the pack was Germany's Baron Manfred von Richthofen with 80 confirmed kills between August 1916 and April 1918. No one else in the German forces came close to his score but the second most successful German ace of the war, Ernst Udet, managed to down 62 aircraft. Three Allied aces came nearer to matching Richthofen – France's René Fonck with a score of 75, English pilot Edward "Mick" Mannock with 73, and Canadian William "Billy" Bishop with 72. Despite their prowess in air combat, aces were far from invulnerable. Mannock was killed by ground fire and it is thought most likely that Richthofen suffered the same fate.

BARON MANFRED VON RICHTHOFEN

Richthofen (1892–1918) was a Prussian cavalry officer but transferred to the German Army Air Service in May 1915. He fought as an air observer on the Eastern Front, flew with bombers in Belgium and then undertook reconnaissance missions over Verdun. He thereafter began flying fighters and by April 1917 had shot down 52 aircraft, becoming a household name in the process. He commanded Jagdgeschwader 1 (Fighter Group 1), the renowned "Flying Circus", from June and his tally grew. He was killed by ground fire on 21 April 1918 with 80 kills to his credit.

Above: As Richthofen's fame grew he became a valuable propaganda tool for Germany but his loss was keenly felt.

ERNST UDET

Ernst Udet (1896–1941), seen here beside his Fokker D-VII fighter, was the highest-scoring German ace to survive the war, amassing 62 victories over the Western Front from the spring of 1918 onward. He was lucky, however, as in an early combat during 1917 he met the outstanding French ace Georges Guynemer. Udet's guns jammed as the fight began but Guynemer saw this and chivalrously flew off without attacking.

Elite Units

Most of the rival air forces also contained fighter squadrons that could boast outstanding combat records and in some cases they also were the focus of intense propaganda campaigns to boost morale on the home front. The most famous of course was Manfred von Richthofen's "Flying Circus", which was a group of four 12-aircraft squadrons formed in late June 1917 that gained its name because of the aircraft's garish colour schemes.

The French also had their fighter elite, the *Cigognes* ("Storks"). This unit originally included just a single squadron but two more were added in 1915 and four more joined at a later date to form Combat Group XII. Most of France's leading aces served with the Storks including both Georges Guynemer (54 kills) and Fonck.

The United States also had an elite squadron but it actually took to the skies before the country entered the war in April 1917. The Lafayette Squadron was founded in 1916, when it was known as the American Squadron, and was staffed by American pilots already serving with the French as volunteers. Its 38 pilots scored 38 confirmed victories before they transferred to the United States Army Air Service in February 1918. The most successful US ace of the war did not actually serve with the squadron but ex-racing driver Eddie Rickenbacker shot down 26 aircraft and balloons in a brief career that began in March 1918.

The "February Revolution"

Even before the war, Russia was a divided nation, largely between the wealthy few and the poor majority, and the strains of war, not least the ever-growing casualty list, brought matters to a head in the spring of 1917.

Ordinary Russians lived in a repressive, undemocratic state and various long-standing and divisive economic, political and social problems became even starker under wartime conditions. Russia had suffered something like 6.6 million men killed, wounded or captured on the Eastern Front by the end of 1916 and Tsar Nicholas II, who had made himself supreme commander in September 1915, had become personally identified with the mismanagement of the war. His domineering German-born wife, Alexandra, had been criticized for her links with the mystic and womanizer Grigori Rasputin, who, she believed, could help her haemophiliac son. While the royal family and nobility continued to live in luxury, the vast majority of people faced hardships that seemingly worsened every day.

The "February Revolution", which actually took place in March by the calendar in use in most of the world (Russia then used the Julian calendar), was spontaneous rather than planned. It was sparked by a series of mass strikes, mostly led by socialist and workers' organizations that began in the capital, Petrograd, on 22 January 1917 when 140,000 workers took to the streets. A further 85,000 struck again on 27 February and the unrest spread rapidly from early March onward. Workers were joined by others protesting about food shortages. Troops in the capital refused to fire on protesters on 11 March and calls for revolution grew shriller.

Tsar Nicholas's cabinet resigned to a man on the 13th and, having lost the backing of the army's senior generals, he abdicated on the 15th. His brother, Grand Duke Michael, then refused the throne, effectively ending the Romanov dynasty. Nicholas and his family hoped to live out their lives in foreign exile but they were eventually sent to the remote town of Ekaterinburg in Siberia later in the year. The royal family remained there under close house arrest until they were murdered by their Bolshevik guards in July 1918.

Below: Signs of the growing opposition to the 1917 Provisional Government – Bolshevik activists under fire in Petrograd.

A New Government

The power vacuum that followed the events of the first two weeks of March 1917 was immediately filled by the creation of the liberal Provisional Government under Prince Lvov on the day of Nicholas II's abdication, yet its authority was challenged from the outset by more radical elements of the political landscape. The most vehement opponents of the new government were the Bolsheviks, a small, rather insignificant group of revolutionary socialists within the broader church of Russian socialism. Their charismatic leader, Vladimir Lenin, was known for his fierce opposition

Above: Forces opposed to the Russian emperor man barricades in the capital, 12 March 1917.

to the war but he was living in exile in Switzerland when the revolution took place. He returned to Russia with German help in April and reached Petrograd on the 16th.

Power to the Soviets

Lenin addressed the Petrograd Soviet (workers' council) the very next day and his speech, the "April Thesis", demanded the transfer of power to the soviets, immediate peace with the Central Powers and the redistribution of wealth. His manifesto attracted some like-minded socialist radicals such as Leon Trotsky, but most moderates proved lukewarm to his agenda. Yet Lenin's April Thesis found support among ordinary Russians. This was in part because of deteriorating conditions on the home front but also because the Provisional Government's Minister of War, Alexander Kerensky, launched another disastrous large-scale offensive with the increasingly demoralized Russian Army in July. The attack broke down in a few days and rates of desertion and insubordination soared.

VLADIMIR ILYICH LENIN

Lenin (1878–1924) was a left-wing revolutionary who came to lead the Bolshevik Party. He fled Russia after the failed 1905 Revolution, first to Austria and then Switzerland but returned home with German help in early 1917. He arrived in Petrograd on 16 April but his attempt to undermine the authority of the Provisional Government failed, and he briefly went into exile in Finland. He returned to co-ordinate the successful October Revolution that brought the Bolsheviks to power. His immediate task was to secure a peace with Germany and then defeat anti-Bolshevik forces.

Above: Lenin was in exile during the first days of the February Revolution but returned home a little later.

Left: The Russian Army collapsed during the Kerensky Offensive, due to poor morale and political agitation for change by Bolshevik activists in the ranks. Here, disgruntled soldiers surrender willingly to the Germans.

The "October Revolution"

In the months after the "February Revolution" the Provisional Government lost its authority as Russia's economy and war effort disintegrated. In November the Bolsheviks felt strong enough to launch their own revolution to seize total power.

Russia descended into even greater chaos following the collapse of the Kerensky Offensive in mid-1917 and the authority of the Provisional Government was increasingly challenged by the Bolsheviks. Evidence of this came when there was an uprising by some troops in Petrograd, the capital, on 16 July that first spread to the naval base at Kronstadt and then to other towns and cities throughout all of Russia. The Bolsheviks joined the unrest, named the "July Days", and gained some kudos among the increasingly anti-war general public for their role but the weak Provisional Government was just able to restore order.

Above: Leon Trotsky, a leading figure in the Bolshevik movement and the main organizer of the "October Revolution".

Matters deteriorated over the following weeks, not least when a recently dismissed senior officer, General Lavrenti Kornilov, marched on Petrograd in September. He was met by local rail workers and forced to surrender on the 14th but the event heightened fears of a tsarist revival and pointed to the weakness of the government. Both factors played into the Bolsheviks' hands and by late October, their leaders, Vladimir Lenin and Leon Trotsky, were demanding that the soviets

Below: The Bolshevik delegation, Leon Trotsky among them, arrive at Brest-Litovsk to discuss peace terms with Germany.

(workers' councils) seize power, arrest members of the government and immediately sue for peace with the Central Powers.

Trotsky, head of the Military Revolutionary Committee (MRC) from 29 October, had effective control of the capital's disgruntled garrison and on 7 November (28 October in the Russian calendar, hence the name "October Revolution") the MRC declared that power had been transferred into the hands of the Petrograd Soviet. The next day saw the creation of a new government, the Soviet of People's Commissars, a wholly Bolshevik body, with Lenin taking office as chairman and Trotsky as foreign minister.

Peace Negotiations

Once in power the Bolsheviks had to consolidate their weak control over greater Russia, which would lead to a prolonged civil war (1917–20), and, more immediately, fulfil their promise to leave the war. Armistice negotiations began at Brest-Litovsk on 3 December and both sides agreed a ceasefire on the 16th. Talks on the substance of any treaty began six days later but the Russians began to prevaricate, largely in the hope that revolutions would break out in Austria-Hungary and Germany and this would obviate the need for any settlement. Germany's patience soon wore thin, not least because it wanted to speed up the transfer of forces to the Western Front for a spring offensive in 1918.

German Harshness

The Germans launched an attack, Operation Faustschlag, on 17 February to bring the Russians back to the table. Their troops advanced around 240km (150 miles) in two days and the Bolsheviks accepted the peace terms 48 hours later. The Treaty of Brest-Litovsk was signed on 3 March and it was exceptionally harsh. Russia lost a huge swathe of territory, including the Baltic States, Finland, Poland and the Ukraine, the last an important grain-producing region whose output eased Germany's acute food shortage.

Left: A posed photograph of Bolshevik troops with an armoured car during the November fighting.

The treaty had an adverse strategic impact on Germany as occupying these lands required keeping 1–1.5 million troops in the East – all at a time when the flow of American troops to France was turning into a flood. Most of the units remained inactive but the Baltic Division under General Rüdiger von der Goltz was sent to newly independent Finland after a civil war had broken out between pro- and anti-Bolshevik forces. Goltz arrived in April and remained until the Armistice.

TSAR NICHOLAS II

Nicholas II (1868–1918) was the last ruler of Russia's Romanov dynasty. Autocratic, rigid and not blessed with great intelligence, he was easily led by courtiers and his domineering wife, Alexandra. He made disastrous wartime decisions, mismanaged the economy and became more repressive as the conflict progressed. By 1916 his own advisers were warning him that revolution was in the air but he refused to make any concessions. He abdicated following the outbreak of the "February Revolution" and he and his family were held in internal exile until executed by the Bolsheviks in July 1918.

Above: Nicholas II photographed in captivity with some of his Bolshevik guards.

The Battle of Caporetto

Italian successes in the Eleventh Battle of the Isonzo prompted the weakening Austro-Hungarian Empire to request urgent German aid and the subsequent Battle of Caporetto almost brought about Italy's military collapse.

The Italian Chief-of-Staff, General Luigi Cadorna, met his French counterpart, General Ferdinand Foch, at Vicenza on 8 April 1917. Cadorna's great worry was that Germany would send troops to the Italian Front to aid the faltering Austro-Hungarian war effort and he wanted to develop a plan for British and French forces to be sent to Italy from the Western Front if the need arose. An agreement was reached and their staffs began to devise a practical scheme. Foch in turn reached an understanding with Cadorna that the Italian Army would launch an offensive to support the major Anglo-French effort on the Western Front that same April.

THE BATTLE OF CAPORETTO
The Italian defeat and the German-led advance to the River Piave.

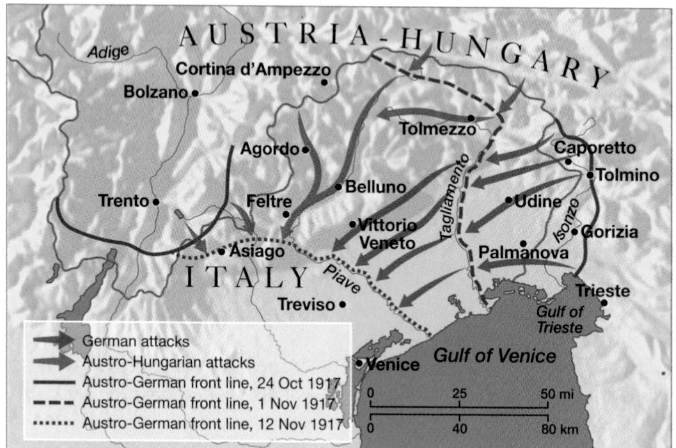

KEY FACTS

DATE: 24 October – 12 November 1917

PLACE: Along the River Isonzo, north-east Italy

OUTCOME: The Italian forces came close to destruction but were in part saved by Allied reinforcements.

Both the French Nivelle Offensive and the British Battle of Arras had largely been concluded before Cadorna finally launched his attack, the Tenth Battle of the Isonzo, on 12 May. The fighting, which took place in difficult mountainous terrain, lasted 17 days but the Italians made little progress and Cadorna called off the fighting on 8 June after his men had suffered 157,000 casualties. The Austro-Hungarians lost 75,000.

Above: An Austro-Hungarian machine-gun detachment in action along the Isonzo.

Cadorna now regrouped and sent reinforcements to north-east Italy in preparation for the Eleventh Battle of the Isonzo. This time he unleashed two armies, the Second under General Luigi Capello and the Duke of Aosta's Third, against the Austro-Hungarians on 18 August. The Duke of Aosta's advance in the south between Gorizia and Trieste was soon halted but Capello's attack in the north made some significant progress by capturing the Bainsizza Plateau. Shortages of supplies forced the Italians to halt the battle on 15 September after they had suffered a further 148,000 casualties.

German Intervention

The Austro-Hungarians had lost some 55,000 men in the Eleventh Battle of the Isonzo

Right: Some of the German troops who helped spearhead the Caporetto offensive in late 1917.

and the surrender of the plateau and a near-collapse in morale now led them to ask for major German assistance. A new Fourteenth Army was created under the command of German General Otto von Below and it included seven well-trained divisions from his homeland. Below was outnumbered in terms of divisions but he concentrated his better-quality forces against the weakest part of the Italian line and attacked on a narrow front around Caporetto and Tolmino in the northern sector of the Isonzo.

The attack on 24 October was heralded by a huge artillery barrage from around 1,500 guns and mortars. The tough German divisions then advanced led by stormtroopers using infiltration tactics to bypass any points of resistance.

Below: Italian troops fall back towards Udine shortly after the beginning of the Battle of Caporetto.

Frantic Retreat

The Italian Second Army collapsed, sparking a wholesale westward retreat of the armies on its flanks. Italian attempts to hold the lines of the Tagliamento and Livenza rivers came to naught but Cadorna was just able to hang on to positions along the lower reaches of the River Piave when the battle ended on 12 November. A total disintegration had been avoided largely because Below's men had outrun their supply lines and the British and French had rushed 11 divisions under General Plumer to Italy in the nick of time. The Italians lost some 40,000 killed or wounded and a staggering 275,000 prisoners – the last a good indicator of a near-total collapse of morale. Austro-Hungarian and German losses reached around 40,000 men. The Battle of Caporetto sealed Cadorna's fate and he was replaced by the more cautious General Armando Diaz on 9 November.

THE RAPALLO CONFERENCE

Rapallo, a port in north-west Italy, was the scene of an emergency conference of the national leaders of Britain, France and Italy in November 1917 when the Italian forces had all but collapsed during the ongoing German-led Battle of Caporetto. Italy was promised economic aid, heavy artillery and reinforcements but the conference's most important decision was to create a committee, later known as the Supreme War Council, to co-ordinate Allied strategy. This would develop into a much-needed unified military command under General Ferdinand Foch.

Final Battles in the Caucasus, 1917–18

The fighting in the Caucasus did not cease with the removal of Russia from the war in 1917 and Turkish, German and British forces struggled for dominance in the region until the very end of the war the following year.

The outbreak of the Russian Revolution in March 1917 effectively ended Russia's war effort against Turkey in the Caucasus and many Turkish troops were freed for operations elsewhere, chiefly Mesopotamia and Palestine. Yet the fighting in the region continued, drawing in not only Turkish and Russian revolutionary troops but also British and German units and local nationalists.

Above: A member of Britain's Dunsterforce pictured with an Armenian soldier near Baku.

Armenian Massacres

Christian Armenians suffered horribly at the hands of the Turkish authorities during the war and an estimated 600,000 died of hunger or lack of water during forced marches, or were simply massacred between mid-1916 and May 1918. Turkey had always denied the Armenians' nationalist aspirations but Russia was more supportive for purely pragmatic reasons as it saw them as a buffer against Turkey. After the February Revolution the Armenians met with representatives of Georgia and Azerbaijan, two neighbouring Russian provinces with similarly frustrated nationalist aspirations, to discuss the formation of a united homeland. The talks began in Tiflis (Tbilisi), Georgia, during August 1917 and, although the

Below: Armenian recruits are put through rifle drill to prepare them for action against the approaching Turkish forces.

three groups were mutually antagonistic, their representatives agreed to establish the Federal Republic of Transcaucasia on 17 September.

New Turkish Invasion

Armenia sought a measure of reconciliation with Turkey in the later part of 1917, but could not prevent Turkey from taking advantage of the Treaty of Brest-Litovsk between Germany and Russia on 3 March 1918. The treaty included a clause that reaffirmed Turkey's right to control the Caucasus provinces. Enver Pasha, the Minister of War, sent some 50,000 troops with a few German units into the Caucasus and northern Persia but general mismanagement of the invasion limited its effects. The Turks and Armenians agreed the Treaty of Batum (Batumi) on 26 May. Transcaucasia was broken up and Armenia proclaimed an independent state but Turkey still had ambitions in the Caucasus. The Turks had occupied Batum on Georgia's Black Sea coast on 15 April and more troops were sent eastward to capture oil-rich Baku on Azerbaijan's Caspian Sea coast.

Baku had been occupied by Russian revolutionary forces in early 1918 and then taken over by Georgian nationalists. They garrisoned the town with some 10,000 ill-equipped men but faced an advancing Turkish force of some 14,000 troops and called on the British for aid. Britain sent a small but highly mobile column, known as "Dunsterforce" after its commander, from Mesopotamia and it had reached Baku by 24 August. The Turks prepared to attack the port and Dunsterforce was withdrawn on the night of 15 September just as Baku fell.

The capture of Baku marked the end of major Turkish operations in the region and most of their forces gradually withdrew from both the Caucasus and northern Persia. An armistice was signed on 31 October 1918 and the British briefly returned to Baku before finally leaving in August 1919. The various parts of Transcaucasia did not remain independent for long – Russian forces occupied Baku in late April 1920, Russian and Turkish troops then took over Armenia the following September, and Georgia was incorporated back into the Russian republic during November 1919.

Above: Baku's oilfields go up in flames to prevent their capture by the Turks in 1918.

Right: Members of an artillery detachment attached to Dunsterforce open fire on Turkish positions aided by Armenian troops.

The Battle of Beersheba

The British effort in Palestine had previously been ponderous and hindered by several setbacks in the first years of the war but in mid-1917 a new commander transformed the fighting and Jerusalem had been captured by December.

General Archibald Murray, British commander in Palestine, began 1917 with the intention of ejecting all the remaining Turkish troops from their positions in the Sinai Peninsula. Murray launched the Battle of Magruntein (or Rafah) on 8 January and within 48 hours his opponents had been routed. The British lost some 500 men but took 1,000 prisoners and a number of artillery pieces. Murray was now authorized to push into Palestine but the manoeuvre was supposed to be limited in scope. The Turks had fallen back to a defensive line stretching inland some 40km (25 miles) from Gaza on the coast to Beersheba that covered the only two practical routes into Palestine.

One of Murray's deputies, General Charles Dobell, attacked on 26 March but the plan fell apart due to weak staff work and poor communications. Some 16,000 British troops were committed to the First Battle of Gaza against a roughly equal number of Turks and Dobell lost 4,000 men before withdrawing later in the day. Murray somehow passed off what was effectively a fiasco as an outright victory and was given permission to march on Jerusalem without further delay.

KEY FACTS

Date: 31 October 1917

Place: Between Gaza and Beersheba, southern Palestine

Outcome: Deception plans helped the British to concentrate against a weak sector of the front and smash through Turkish lines.

Right: The ANZAC cavalrymen seen here spearheaded the main attack on Beersheba.

Failure and Dismissal

Dobell launched the Second Battle of Gaza on 17 April and his troops made a near suicidal frontal attack against the main Turkish line of defence. The British recorded some 6,500 casualties to the Turks' 2,000 by the end of the fighting on the 19th. Dobell was dismissed by Murray who was in turn sacked by the War Office in London. His replacement was an experienced commander, General Edmund Allenby. His orders were to capture Jerusalem by Christmas but he flatly refused to advance until he had received reinforcements to bring his strength up to 200,000 men.

Allenby finally attacked with some 80,000 infantry and 12,000 cavalry on 31 October and was opposed by just 35,000 men of the Turkish Seventh and Eighth Armies. Allenby's imaginative

Left: British troops are moved up to the Beersheba–Gaza line by railway shortly before the battle.

plan called for a diversion against Gaza, which had been under artillery bombardment for six days, while the bulk of his force was flung against Beersheba. This was a risky option as his infantry and cavalry would need to capture the town's wells intact or face acute water shortages. Beersheba fell around dusk in part to a spirited charge into the town by Australian cavalry.

On to Jerusalem

Allenby was delayed for several days as the wells did not yield as much water as possible but the Turks did retreat from the rest of the Beersheba–Gaza line when their commanders mistook a small camel-mounted patrol towards Hebron for a major outflanking attack. The Eighth Army began to retreat along the coast while the Seventh Army fell back towards Jerusalem. The British hit the Eighth Army again on 13–14 November and sent it reeling farther along the coast after the Battle of Junction Station.

Above: General Allenby enters Jerusalem through the city's Jaffa Gate on 11 December 1917, marking the end of several weeks of campaigning.

Allenby now made his bid for Jerusalem but faced a new enemy commander, the former German Chief of Staff, General Erich von Falkenhayn, who established a new defensive line south-west of Jerusalem in the Judean Hills. Turkish reserves were also arriving and it took the British several weeks to overcome the defenders but Allenby entered Jerusalem on foot on 11 December. The campaign had cost Allenby's force 18,000 casualties while the Turks recorded 25,000 losses.

THE ARAB REVOLT

Some Arab nationalists living in the Arabian Peninsula greatly resented living under Turkish rule and, with British aid, rose against their overlords in June 1916. The uprising was led by Feisal ibn Hussein and he was aided by a British officer, T. E. Lawrence, better known as "Lawrence of Arabia". The Arabs conducted a series of wide-ranging guerrilla-style raids, many of which targeted the only railway line that ran through the region. The Arabs eventually took Damascus in early October 1918 but the British reneged on their promise to help the nationalists secure a homeland.

Above: Bedouin chieftains wait to meet Lawrence of Arabia and other Arab leaders.

The Mesopotamian Campaign, 1917–18

The British effort in Mesopotamia had stalled in 1916 but from the next year onward greater military resources and manpower enabled them to push the Turkish garrison farther and farther northward to ensure ultimate victory in 1918.

The British commander in Mesopotamia, General Frederick Maude, had launched a major offensive up both banks of the Tigris towards Baghdad with some 166,000 troops in mid-December 1916. By late February 1917 he was arrayed outside Kut, the site of a major British defeat in April 1916. The Second Battle of Kut was fought on 22–23 February and Maude was able to overwhelm the Turkish defenders after attacking their flanks and forcing them to withdraw northward towards Baghdad. The Turkish troops fought skilful rearguard actions and the British advance briefly faltered at Aziziyeh, some 72km (45 miles) from Baghdad, on the 27th. Maude then brushed aside the Turkish Sixth Army under Khalil Pasha and Baghdad fell on 11 March.

Above: Locals look on as British troops manhandle a 6in (155mm) howitzer gun through the streets of Baghdad.

Maude was now forced to halt all large-scale operations mainly because of the intense heat, but he attacked again during the cool of early autumn. This time he sent his columns in three directions – from Samarrah up the Tigris, from Falluja along the Euphrates and east towards Persia. The main Turkish force in the region was stationed at Tikrit, some 48km (30 miles) north of Samarrah. The portion of Maude's troops advancing up the Euphrates, won the Battle of Ramadi on 27–28 September, while the two other drives also pushed the Turks back and captured Tikrit on 5 November.

Change of Command

Maude succumbed to cholera on 11 November and a new commander, General William Marshall, hoped to complete the campaign. Instead, Marshall was ordered to reduce his forces in early 1918 and was therefore unable to undertake much action, although there was a

Left: Indian troops and labourers were employed extensively during the Mesopotamian campaign. Here, they help build a railway.

brief push along the Euphrates in March. Thereafter, the hot season intervened and the British ceased operations completely. When Marshall was ready to advance again in the autumn, the strategic situation in the Middle East had changed dramatically. This was chiefly because British forces advancing from Palestine into northern Syria had taken Aleppo (Halab) on 26 October, the same day that three Turkish envoys arrived at Mudros (Moudros) on the Aegean island of Limnos to discuss a possible armistice.

TURKISH RETREAT

The capture of Aleppo effectively cut off the Turkish forces in Mesopotamia from their homeland and made their further resistance pointless. Although the isolated Turkish garrison was unlikely to put up much of a fight, Marshall was ordered to undertake one last attack along the Tigris in October mainly to ensure British control of the local oilfields. The demoralized Turkish troops fell back steadily but the British had a stiff fight at the Battle of Sharqat before forcing some 11,000 of them to surrender on the 30th. An armistice was signed on a British warship in Mudros harbour the same day and British–Turkish hostilities ended officially on the 31st. In what was the final act of the offensive, a British flying column took Mosul, some 120km (75 miles) north of Tikrit, on 4 November.

The Mesopotamian campaign had begun as a small-scale affair in October 1914 and for the first two years it had been dogged by incompetence and muddled thinking. Ultimately, it took hundreds of thousands of troops from across the British Empire to win what many considered a sideshow. The British were left in control of the local oilfields as intended but they had suffered some 97,000 casualties, many succumbing to disease, while the number of Turkish casualties is unknown but certainly very much higher.

BRITISH RIVER GUNBOATS

The campaign in Mesopotamia was largely conducted along the banks of the country's two great rivers, the Tigris and Euphrates, which were also the area's most viable lines of communication for moving men and supplies between the front and the rear bases. As most of the fighting took place close to the river, the British opted to supplement their land artillery with a number of shallow-draught gunboats fitted with various types of guns and machine-guns. These provided valuable service in the latter part of the campaign.

Above: The Insect-class gunboat HMS *Ladybird* pictured at Port Said, Egypt, on its way to Mesopotamia, November 1917.

Left: The final week of the war saw the British capture Turkish troops in ever greater numbers.

Defeating the U-boats, 1917–18

No one weapon or tactic sealed the fate of Germany's powerful fleet of U-boats but the tide most definitely turned with the much-delayed introduction of the convoy system in May 1917, shortly after the United States had entered the war.

Germany decided to recommence unrestricted submarine warfare on 9 January 1917 and announced that the new campaign would begin on 1 February. The consensus was that Britain could be brought to its knees in five months or so and that the sinking of neutral vessels and loss of neutral lives was an acceptable risk. The danger was that such a policy would inevitably lead to US entry into the war. President Woodrow Wilson had already broken off diplomatic relations with Germany after *U-53* sank the ship *Housatonic* off the Scilly Isles on 3 January. Nevertheless, Germany's policy-makers convinced themselves that the United States would not be able to intervene to a significant extent either on land or at sea for two or more years after declaring war.

Above: President Woodrow Wilson addresses Congress requesting that those assembled back a declaration of war against Germany. There were few dissenters.

Below: A German U-boat stands off a sinking steamer in 1917.

U-Boats Unleashed

At the beginning of the year the Imperial German Navy had 105 U-boats in service, including 42 under repair, plus 51 on order from the manufacturers. Its submarines sank 180 ships in January and more than a third of these were from neutral nations, but losses soared after 1 February. Some 245 Allied vessels were sunk during that month, 310 in March and a record 373 in April. However, Germany's relations with the United States had noticeably worsened over the same period. The British liner *Laconia* was sunk by a U-boat on 25 February and 4 Americans were among the 12 dead. Further US ships were sunk thereafter leading the US State Department to announce on 12 March that all US merchant ships would be armed. The Department of

THE ZEEBRUGGE RAID

Some German U-boats were based at Bruges, an inland port in Belgium, and could only reach open waters by way of a canal that entered the North Sea at Zeebrugge. The British decided to block the entrance by sinking old warships in the channel and also to destroy various facilities by putting a landing party ashore. The amphibious assault took place on the night of 22 April 1918 and, though the attackers suffered heavy losses, it was portrayed in the media as a great victory. The reality was that the blockships had not been scuttled in the right place and U-boats were again using the canal within a few days.

Right: The cruiser HMS *Vindictive* showing battle damage from the Zeebrugge Raid.

the Navy authorized ships to take action against U-boats the next day.

AMERICA GOES TO WAR

The turning point came on 1 March when the US government made public the Zimmermann Telegram, a note sent to the German ambassador to the USA, Count Bernstorff, by his foreign minister, Alfred Zimmermann, on 17 January. This was decoded and passed on by the British. It suggested that Bernstorff should secretly seek a German alliance with Mexico and that the Mexicans should be allowed to "reconquer the lost territory in Texas, New Mexico and Arizona". US public opinion now turned against Germany and President Woodrow Wilson was able to secure congressional approval for a declaration of war on 6 April. Although the US Army was not ready for war the Navy was and would play its part in the anti-submarine campaign.

In April the British calculated that they would run out of food and other vital materials by June if the U-boats were left unchecked. Attempts to destroy them had so far been largely unsuccessful, with just a handful sunk in the first months of the year. The decision was finally made to adopt the convoy system in which merchant ships sailed together with a protective umbrella of smaller warships and, later, a measure of air cover. The system began on 10 May and did not become fully effective until the last four months of the year – but the results were spectacular.

U-boats had sunk more than 881,000 tons of Allied ships (63 per cent British) in April 1917; by December the total had dropped to under half that and in October 1918, the last full month of the war, the Allies lost just 118,500 tons (50 per cent British) of shipping. U-boat losses had also risen in the final two years of the war. A mere 46 had been sunk between August 1914 and the end of 1916 but a further 132 were lost to all causes during 1917–18.

Below: A convoy escorted by the Royal Navy on its way across the North Atlantic in 1918.

Anti-submarine Weapons

In 1914 no weapons existed that could destroy a submerged submarine but the dangers posed by Germany's U-boats forced the Allies – and especially Britain – to develop a range of passive and aggressive techniques to combat this new menace.

Anti-submarine warfare was very much in its infancy at the outbreak of World War I as most navies had focused their energies on developing offensive surface technologies in previous years. The need to combat submarines became apparent in the first weeks of the conflict and was felt most acutely by the British as their crucial maritime trade and large merchant fleet bore the brunt of Germany's U-boat campaign.

Passive Defences

At first the best defence for vessels, both warships and freighters, was speed and zigzagging as U-boats were very slow both submerged and on the surface and found it difficult to hit targets that were changing course regularly. Ships sailing at night or ones that avoided busy sea lanes also stood a better chance of survival. Next came complex camouflage of the "dazzle" type that covered ships in geometrical patterns of paint to break up their outline. Warships at anchor were often protected by anti-submarine nets that were let down over their sides on booms to stop torpedoes but these were found too cumbersome and of little value. Larger anti-submarine barrages – combinations of nets, minefields and patrolling warships – were also devised to protect narrow stretches of sea and vulnerable routes, such as the English Channel, but they were far from impervious.

Above: One of the first successful depth-charge launchers stands ready for action.

Warships in 1914 could only sink surfaced submarines and then only by ramming or gunfire, while submerged U-boats were effectively invulnerable. For much of the war U-boat captains liked to use gunfire to sink unarmed targets rather than waste torpedoes, so the Allies responded by fitting weapons to merchant vessels. The British also created Q-ships, seemingly unarmed vessels that invited attack on the surface at close range but which actually carried an array of hidden weapons. These were not as successful as hoped and submariners became wary of approaching too close to any likely Q-ship.

The British also developed a system in which a potential target towed a friendly submerged submarine. If a U-boat attacked on the surface, the surface ship could telephone the submerged submarine by a line attached to the tow rope

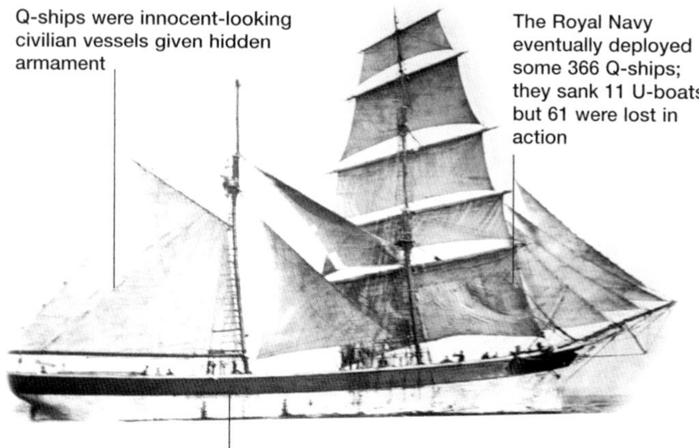

Q-ships were innocent-looking civilian vessels given hidden armament
The Royal Navy eventually deployed some 366 Q-ships; they sank 11 U-boats but 61 were lost in action
Sometimes their holds were filled with wood so that they would stay afloat longer if hit below the waterline

Right: Q-ships like this were a British invention designed to lure U-boats into a surface attack.

and its captain would then slip the rope and manoeuvre into a position to attack the U-boat.

New Weapons

There were other new means of attacking targets. British destroyers towed electronically detonated charges (sweeps) behind them but these needed very close contact to sink a submarine. Depth charges (bombs designed to explode under water) became available in late 1915 but only appeared in quantity from 1917 onward. Hydrophones, directional underwater microphones for listening to U-boat engines, were developed but submariners learned to outfox them by diving deep or by silent running. The first successful attack using both hydrophones and depth charges took place on 16 July 1916. Other means of locating submarines included intercepting their radio messages and using various aircraft and airships to find them on the surface.

Some 178 German U-boats were lost during 1914–18; 38 were sunk in accidents or for some other unknown reason. Of the remaining 140, 50 were sunk by mines, 29 by depth charges, 19 by gunfire, 19 by ramming, 18 by torpedo and 1 in an air attack. The most lethal areas were the waters immediately around the British Isles and the near North Atlantic, where 90 and 44 U-boats were lost, respectively. Most sinkings occurred after convoys were introduced in April 1917.

Above: US troopships head for Europe. The convoy system was so successful that not one troopship carrying the US Army to France was lost to a U-boat attack.

THE SPIDER'S WEB

Mathematical methods were used to develop a pattern of anti-submarine patrols to be conducted by British naval aircraft over the North Sea. A mixture of Curtiss H-12 and Felixstowe flying boats began flying an octagonal pattern of patrol lines from May 1917. and these were calculated to allow just four flying boats to cover some 10,000 sq km (3,860 sq miles) in a mere five hours. The patrols were over routes known to be taken by surfaced U-boats. The British claimed their first success on the 20th and several other kills were recorded. Though these were unconfirmed the web certainly made life more difficult for the U-boats and their crews.

Left: Part of an Allied convoy arrives at an unspecified port. Note the dazzle camouflage pattern.

Final Battles in Italy American troops throwing grenades at Austro-Hungarian positions.

Later Fighters The British Sopwith Camel, probably the leading Allied fighter aircraft of 1917–18.

The Battle of Megiddo Some of the many thousands of Turkish prisoners captured in October 1918.

Main Central Powers' attacks
Main Allied attacks
Dunster force
Front line, Jan 1918
Front line, Nov 1918
Front line, Jan 1918
Front line, Nov 1918
Front line, Jan 1918
Front line, Nov 1918
Front line, Jan 1918
Front line, Nov 1918
Front line, Jan 1918
Front line, Nov 1918

NORWAY
SWEDEN
GREAT BRITAIN
North Sea
DENMARK
Baltic Sea
Riga
MOSCOW
Vilna
RUSSIAN EMPIRE
GERMANY
WARSAW
Lódź
Brest-Litovsk
Ypres
Arras
Amiens
Reims
PARIS
Verdun
FRANCE
Lemberg
AUSTRIA-HUNGARY
Czernowitz
SWITZERLAND
BUDAPEST
Asiago
Venice
Gorizia
BELGRADE
BUCHAREST
BOSNIA
ROMANIA
SERBIA
Black Sea
Caspian Sea
Kars
Trebizond
SOFIA
BULGARIA
Corsica
ITALY
Cattaro
MONTENEGRO
Uskub
ALBANIA
Monastir
Salonika
Sardinia
Van
TURKEY
PERSIA
Mosul
Mediterranean Sea
Sicily
GREECE
Aleppo
BAGHDAD
Ramadi
TUNISIA
ALGERIA
Basra
PALESTINE
Damascus
Gaza
Jerusalem
CAIRO
LIBYA
EGYPT
0 100 200 300 400 500 mi
0 200 400 600 800 km

1918 – TRIUMPH OF THE ALLIES

Both sides began 1918 with a measure of optimism. Germany was shackled to a number of failing allies and could see the United States looming in the near distance but it did have a chance to strike in the West with strength much increased by the end of the war in Russia. The Allies knew that their naval blockade was undermining Germany's war effort and hoped to hang on until sizeable US forces were committed to battle. The key, therefore, was the outcome of Germany's spring offensives – an actual breakthrough or something close to it might force Britain and France to sue for peace but defeat would throw away Germany's last reserves of manpower at a time when hundreds of thousands of US troops were landing in Europe every month.

In the event the Allied line buckled but did not break and Germany did indeed use up its last reserves. The Allies went over to the attack, but simultaneously up and down the Western Front and on a scale that Germany could never match. They did not expect a rapid victory and had begun plans for attacks in 1919, but the Central Powers suddenly collapsed. Armistices were agreed with Austria-Hungary, Bulgaria and Turkey in a matter of five weeks or so. Germany hung on for a few more days but its Armistice with the Allies came into force on 11 November.

Germany's Final Offensives
Indian and Senegalese troops of the British and French forces.

Breaking the Hindenburg Line
A German machine-gunner, unable to halt the Allied advance.

Germany's Naval Mutiny
Armed naval mutineers in the streets of Berlin in November 1918.

Operation Michael

Troops withdrawn from the Eastern Front gave the German High Command a numerical advantage on the Western Front in the spring of 1918 and allowed them to launch an all-or-nothing offensive before the Allies gained a decisive advantage.

During the winter of 1917–18 General Erich Ludendorff, the *de facto* head of the German Army, realized that time was fast running out for his country. The British naval blockade was biting as never before and US troops were arriving in Europe in ever greater numbers. He would have to strike early in 1918 if Germany was to win the war or at least secure a favourable negotiated peace. He placed his faith in troops released from the east after Russia's collapse and a new training regime that produced stormtrooper units, men able to conduct fast-moving operations to bypass points of resistance.

Ludendorff also believed that the French and British had different strategic priorities on the Western Front and that these would make it difficult for them to come to each other's aid if they were hit by a series of large offensives. He felt that the French were preoccupied with the defence of Paris, while the British were more concerned with protecting the Channel ports. He therefore opted to launch his first attack at the point where that part of the Western Front manned by the French gave way to that held by the British.

KEY FACTS

DATE: 21 March – 5 April 1918

PLACE: North-east France between Lens and La Fère

OUTCOME: Despite significant early gains, the German onslaught was eventually contained by the Allies.

Right: A handful of the 72,000 British troops taken prisoner during Operation Michael.

EARLY GAINS

The attack, code-named Operation Michael, was directed against a 96km (60 mile) section of the line between Arras and La Fère held by the British Fifth Army under General Hubert Gough and General Julian Byng's British Third Army. Michael opened on 21 March and was heralded by a five-hour artillery barrage of previously unseen complexity and ferocity. Then the stormtroopers from three German armies advanced under the cover of fog. Gough's army, spread thinly along some 40km (25 miles) of the front, collapsed but Byng's men to the north managed to limit the German gains thanks to their deeper line of defences. Field Marshal Haig committed all his reserves to plug the gap and some French troops were sent to his aid.

Left: German stormtroopers move across a battlefield after the Allied defenders have withdrawn.

Ludendorff ended Michael on 5 April. His troops had advanced up to 64km (40 miles) but there had been no decisive victory, not least because the Allies had reacted swiftly and deployed their formidable air power to help their ground units. The attack had also been hamstrung by three factors – the assault troops had run short of supplies despite capturing some Allied dumps; they had lacked the mobility to exploit their initial gains; and the artillery had been unable to keep up with the leading stormtroopers. The Germans had suffered some 240,000 casualties, roughly the same as the Allies, but whereas the latter's losses could be made good, Ludendorff's could not.

Foch in Command

Michael demonstrated that the Allies had effectively gained air superiority over the Western Front but it also prompted another equally significant event. For the greater part of the conflict the French and British had been waging almost separate wars but matters now changed. The Allied Supreme War Council appointed General Ferdinand Foch as co-ordinator for the Western Front on 26 March and he was made Commander-in-Chief of the Allied forces on 3 April. For political reasons the United States was not technically an ally, but rather an Associated Power; however, the American commander in France, General John Pershing, agreed to accept Foch's authority.

BRUCHMÜLLER'S BARRAGE

Colonel Georg Bruchmüller was a brilliant artillerist who was put in charge of the bombardment for Operation Michael. He brought together 6,500 guns and 3,500 trench mortars and planned to fire 1.6 million shells in just five hours. This whirlwind was broken down precisely into seven distinct phases lasting from two hours down to just five minutes. It proved highly successful and its creator was given a new nickname – *Durchbruch-Müller* ("Breakthrough Müller").

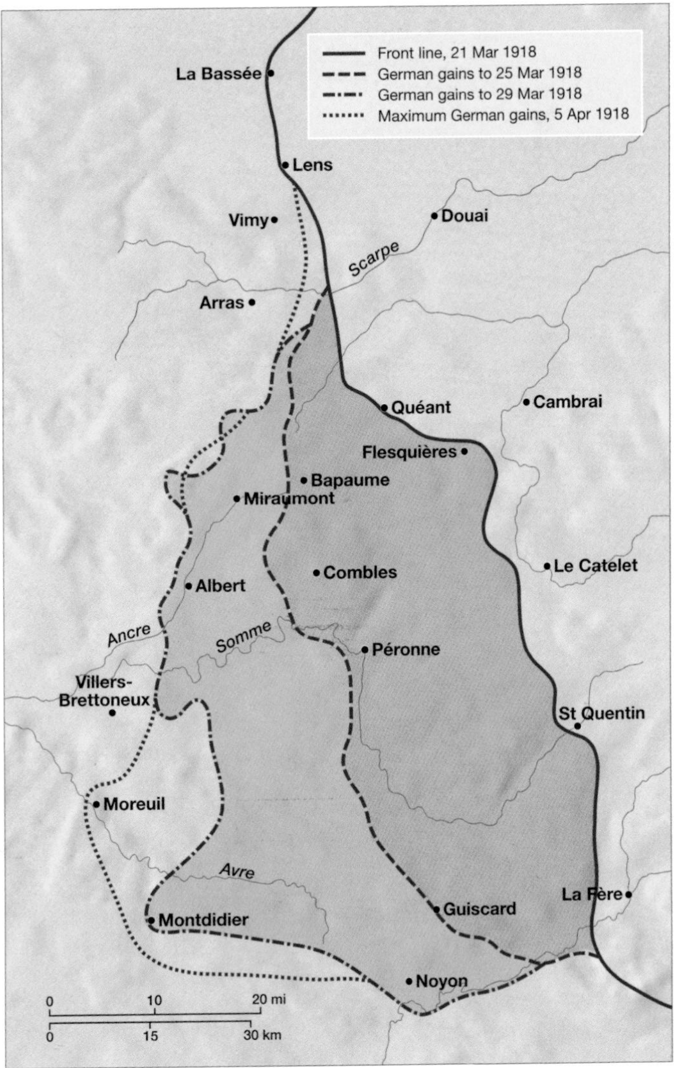

OPERATION MICHAEL
The attack deeply dented the British line but never made a breakthrough.

Later Fighters

The latter part of the war saw the emergence of highly specialized fighters that flew higher and faster than ever before and their emergence meant the battle in the air swayed first one way and then the other in a hard-fought technological struggle.

The fighters of the second half of World War I were far superior to their predecessors. All combatant nations were now able to fit forward-firing machine-guns to their fighters and the later machines were also usually far more streamlined and fitted with more powerful engines. They therefore had a better rate of climb, greater speed, and were much more manoeuvrable. Better fighters appeared on both sides at regular intervals and thus air superiority would switch back and forth between the sides – often in just a few months – as new arrivals outclassed their older opponents.

Above: US ace "Eddie" Rickenbacker pictured in his French-built Spad XIII fighter in June 1918.

Battles in 1917

This was demonstrated in the Battle of Arras in the spring of 1917. The British enjoyed a 3:1 advantage in aircraft over the Germans but were reliant on the Royal Aircraft Factory's two-seater BE-2s and RE-8s. These were no match for the Albatros D-types and, during what became known to the British as "Bloody April", they lost 151 aircraft and 316 crew compared to German figures of 66 and 119. Yet the D-types were soon outclassed by British SE-5s and France's Spad S-VIIs.

The fighters of 1917–18 were mostly biplanes, although there were a few notable three-winged designs, chiefly the British Sopwith Triplane and the famed Fokker Dr-1 as flown for a time by Baron Manfred von Richthofen. The Fokker was introduced in June 1917 but was withdrawn in the autumn after a number of accidents. It briefly re-emerged in 1918 but was obsolescent by the summer.

FOKKER DR-1

This legendary German fighter entered service in the summer of 1917 as a stop-gap design and was not particularly successful – it was not especially fast, though it was very manoeuvrable. Nevertheless, some 329 were built before the war ended.

Engine: 110hp Oberursel or Le Rhône
Crew: 1
Ceiling: 6,100m (20,000ft)
Top speed: 165kph (102mph)
Armament: 2 x 7.92mm (0.312in) machine-guns

SOPWITH F-1 CAMEL

The Sopwith Camel was one of the best fighters of the war and was the first British aircraft to be built with two synchronized machine-guns. It was agile and had a good rate of climb but was difficult to fly. Many less experienced pilots paid the price.

Engine: Various including 130hp Clerget
Crew: 1
Ceiling: 5,500m (18,000ft)
Top speed: 185kph (115mph)
Armament: 2 x 0.303in (7.7mm) machine-guns

The Sopwith Triplane had a similarly short combat history. It made its debut on the Western Front in April 1917 with the Royal Naval Air Service (RNAS) and it simply outflew and outmanoeuvred any of its German rivals, so much so that some units amassed a large number of kills. The Canadian pilots of B Flight of the RNAS's No. 10 Squadron, commonly referred to as the Black Flight as its aircraft had their upper fuselages painted black, were a case in point. The flight consisted of just five Sopwith Triplanes yet these downed 87 German aircraft without loss between May and September 1917. However, their heyday was soon over as the Germans introduced better performing fighters and the last Sopwith Triplane was withdrawn from the Western Front during November.

BIPLANES

Triplanes were the exception and the single-seat biplane fighter fitted with two forward-firing machine-guns was the norm. All sides on the Western Front, where the most extensive air fighting took place, produced some outstanding designs. The French introduced their Spad S-XIII in the late summer of 1917, largely to replace the Spad S-VII, and it became the mainstay of the country's fighter strength as well as equipping Belgian, Italian and US squadrons. The British Sopwith Scout, which was nicknamed "Pup", appeared in numbers in late 1916 and was highly manoeuvrable, if underpowered and lightly armed. The Pup was superseded by the Sopwith F-1 Camel from July 1917 and it became Britain's leading fighter for the remainder of the war, shooting down some 1,300 enemy aircraft. Also in service in large numbers was the effective SE-5.

Germany's last notable biplane fighter was the Fokker D-VII, which was actually built by both Fokker and Albatros. It first saw action in May 1918 but despite its manoeuvrability, especially at high altitudes, the Allies would keep almost total air superiority due to some good aircraft but more importantly thanks to superior numbers.

FOKKER D-VIII

The Fokker D-VIII was one of the last German fighters to enter service on the Western Front and was basically a high-winged monoplane version of the previous D-VII biplane. It won a competition to find a new-generation fighter in April 1918 but it was soon plagued with problems – three of the first six to be delivered suffered catastrophic wing collapses. The problem was traced to some inflexible wing spars and these were replaced. The D-VIII was an extremely fast aircraft but, because of its early design flaws, only 85 ever reached the front.

Left: The Fokker D-VIII had a top speed of 200kph (124mph) and had two forward firing machine-guns but saw limited service.

Below: Australian troops with a captured Albatros D-III fighter, one of the most successful German fighters of the latter part of the war.

Anti-aircraft Guns

There were very few anti-aircraft guns in existence in 1914 but with the rapid development of aerial warfare they soon became an important weapon in the battle for air supremacy and were deployed in their thousands.

No one had given much thought to the threat posed by aircraft in the years before World War I and, therefore, no one had given much thought to developing anti-aircraft guns to knock them out of the sky. Germany was the first country to demonstrate such weapons in 1908–9 and these, which were known as "balloon guns" and built by either Krupp or Rheinmetall, merely consisted of a field gun converted to fire at a high angle from a truck or large automobile. At the time there was a belief that these would actually be able to keep up with the slow-flying aircraft of the day. Other types, usually those positioned to defend targets like major cities, were essentially guns taken from their original carriages and placed on static angled mounts that could be turned through 360 degrees.

As there were so few aircraft around both before and at the outbreak of the fighting in August 1914, there was very little incentive to spend large amounts of money developing dedicated anti-aircraft guns. The British, for example, had no more than a handful of guns on towed mounts, while the French, who were even less prepared, had just two armoured cars based on the De Dion Bouton automobile that each carried a field gun fitted to a special high-angled mount in the rear for anti-aircraft work. Nevertheless, these autocannon were subsequently used extensively by the French and were also sold to Britain to bolster London's air-defence network in 1915–16.

BRITISH 13-POUNDER

This anti-aircraft weapon was a combination of a light field gun used by British horse artillery batteries and a Thornycroft J-type lorry, one of the most ubiquitous petrol-engined vehicles of the war. It first saw service in 1915. A standard gun section was two such weapons accompanied by two other lorries for the crew, range-finding equipment and ammunition.

Shell weight: 5.9kg (13lb)
Gun weight: 975kg (2,150lb)
Elevation: +80 degrees
Vertical range: 4,000m (13,100ft)
Muzzle velocity: 520m/sec (1,700ft/sec)

Left: The crew of a German anti-aircraft machine-gun await the order to open fire. Note the gun s very large ammunition drum.

Mobile Guns

Anti-aircraft guns in the field tended to be a marriage of an existing light or medium field gun placed on a high-angled mount and fitted to a flatbed truck or to a purpose-built carriage that could be towed by another vehicle. Thus, in one case, the British adapted a light field gun, a weapon normally associated with horse artillery batteries that fought alongside cavalry units. It was put on the back of trucks with drop-down sides, chiefly the Peerless Motor Lorry or the Thornycroft J-type. These were usually fitted with stabilizers and screw jacks to prevent the recoil of the gun from overturning them. Guns could typically be elevated between 70 and 90 degrees and their shells generally had a maximum altitude of around 4,000m (13,100ft), although some could reach higher.

FIRE CONTROL

The main problem for the anti-aircraft gunners was trying to hit a target that, although comparatively slow-moving, was effectively able to move in three dimensions. So if a gun was fired directly at the target then by the time the shell arrived at the right altitude, the target would have moved on. The gunners began dealing with the problem by fitting complex sights to their weapons but this was effectively a duplication of effort within a battery and it was found simpler to have what was known as a central post sight. This was positioned in the middle of a group of guns and, once its crew had worked out the necessary data of height, range and speed, the information was given to all of the guns.

In reality, the available anti-aircraft technology was very much in its infancy during the war and, while there are no firm figures of the number of aircraft downed by such batteries, it was overwhelmingly dwarfed by the number of aircraft shot down in combat by other aircraft. However, anti-aircraft fire could be of sufficient nuisance value to disrupt a reconnaissance or put a pilot off when making an attack.

FRENCH 75MM ANTI-AIRCRAFT GUN

The French made extensive use of their famed 75mm (2.95in) gun in the anti-aircraft role, largely because of its high rate of fire. The weapon's wheeled carriage was simply removed and the gun mounted on a De Dion car fitted with several stabilizers, one of which is shown here in front of the rear wheel. Note also the rangefinder on the right.

SHELL WEIGHT: 7.16kg (15.8lb)
GUN WEIGHT: 4,000kg (8,800lb)
ELEVATION: +70 degrees
VERTICAL RANGE: 4,725m (15,500ft)
MUZZLE VELOCITY: 530m/sec (1,740ft/sec)

Right: US troops man a French-built Hotchkiss heavy machine-gun deployed in the anti-aircraft role. This weapon's greatest weakness was the metal strip magazine that can be seen here as it held no more than 30 rounds and thus required frequent changing.

Germany's Final Offensives

Despite the failure of Operation Michael, the German High Command continued to launch major attacks along the Allied line on the Western Front between April and July 1918 but the attacking stormtroopers suffered severe and irreplaceable losses.

Germany's first major offensive in spring 1918 had come so near to breaking the Allied line that General Ludendorff resolved to try again as he knew time was fast running out. His second attack, the Lys Offensive or Operation Georgette, was once more against the British, this time between Ypres and La Bassée. The attack opened on 9 April and the Germans seemed so close to breaking through that Field Marshal Haig issued an order on the 12th that prohibited any more withdrawals. This did the trick. Resistance stiffened and the German advance was halted by the 17th but only after a 16km (10 mile) salient had been punched in the line. The British had suffered around 100,000 casualties but had prevented Ludendorff from reaching the vital Channel ports and had inflicted severe losses on his stormtrooper units.

Above: German stormtroopers push past a British barricade in the town of Bailleul on 15 April 1918.

Striking the French

Ludendorff now turned on the French along the Chemin des Dames. Operation Blücher–Yorck, or the Aisne Offensive, was actually a diversionary attack to mask preparations for another operation against the British forces in Flanders. Two German armies advanced on 27 May and carved out a deep salient some 48km (30 miles) wide and 32km (20 miles) deep. There was no breakthrough but Ludendorff was encouraged to launch another diversionary attack. Operation Gneisenau, the Noyon–Montdidier Offensive, opened on 9 June but the French had been forewarned by deserters and had strengthened their defences. Two German thrusts towards Compiègne, headquarters of the Allied supreme commander, General Foch, were halted by the 13th.

Ludendorff now persisted with targeting the French and launched his final attack, the Marne Offensive, to the west of Reims, on 15 July. His assault troops made no significant gains and he finally conceded defeat, ordering a withdrawal from the great salient his recent attacks

Below: A worrying sight for the Germans – US troops arriving at the front in late May 1918.

Above: Colonial forces, such as these Senegalese and Indian troops, were an important part of both the French and British war efforts.

PEACEFUL PENETRATION

Australian troops devised a new and imaginative offensive tactic and put it into practice for the first time on a large scale at Le Hamel in July 1918. The aim was to seize control of enemy territory not with infantry, who invariably suffered heavy losses in an assault, but by using firepower from aircraft, artillery, machine-guns and tanks to overwhelm a section of the enemy line. Once the enemy defences were subdued, the infantry would advance against minimal opposition, hence the slightly misleading title "peaceful penetration".

had created between Soissons and Reims on the 17th. His forces had suffered some 500,000 casualties in five months and Ludendorff knew that US troops were now arriving at a rate of 300,000 per month, while he had virtually no reserves to call on. He was also aware that his troops' morale was faltering and that cases of indiscipline were rising.

ALLIED ATTACKS

There was to be no respite for the Germans as Foch unleashed a major counter-attack, the Second Battle of the Marne, on the 18th. After a series of hammer blows by the French and eight US divisions, the Soissons–Reims salient was eradicated by 5 August. Ludendorff finally gave up all hope of launching an offensive in Flanders, knowing full well that the initiative on the Western Front had wholly passed to the Allies. Foch, the architect of the Allied victory, was created Marshal of France on 6 August.

Ludendorff suffered yet another blow that August. Anglo-French forces launched the Amiens Offensive on the 8th and the attack, which brilliantly combined infantry, tanks, artillery and aircraft as never before, shattered the German line in hours. Some 15,000 German troops surrendered on the first day alone and many had put up absolutely no resistance. Ludendorff was shocked to the core and called it the "black day of the German Army". The battle ended on 4 September by which time Germany had lost some 100,000 casualties and the Allies just 42,000. The war now entered its final phase.

Below: A battery of US 155mm (6.1in) guns in mid-1918 as mobile warfare returned to the Western Front.

The Paris Gun

German troops pushed to within 160km (100 miles) of Paris in the spring of 1918 and this allowed them to deploy a pair of huge, technologically advanced artillery pieces to bring the French capital and its inhabitants under direct fire.

The Paris Gun was a huge artillery piece designed purely to fire on the French capital to undermine civilian morale at a time when the German Army was launching a series of offensives on the Western Front in March – August 1918. It was officially designated the Lange 21cm Kanone (Long 8.3-in Cannon) but was nicknamed "Wilhelm's Gun" in honour of the German emperor.

Below: Test firing the "Paris Gun". Each shot wore the barrel away significantly so succeeding shells had to be a little larger until, after 60 shots, the barrel had to be changed.

The idea of the gun was first mooted in spring 1916, a time when some sections of the Western Front were "just" 96km (60 miles) east of Paris.

Designing the Gun

The project was masterminded by Krupp and a body known as Artillery Direction, part of the Imperial German Navy. Their work was exceedingly difficult, not least because of the weapon's complex ballistics, and it was made doubly so when German troops withdrew to the Hindenburg Line from autumn 1916, thereby increasing the distance to Paris by a further 20km (12 miles) or so. Nevertheless, they pushed the project forward over the following months and finally conducted successful test firings of the weapon at their Mappen proving ground. The ultimate design could be broken down into sections, transported by rail on specially produced carriages and then reassembled at the required point – but all this was an immense effort

Into Action

The bombardment of Paris was conducted from three positions to the north-east and east of the capital, all near various railway

Left: An interior view of one of the great Krupp armaments factories where the monstrous "Paris Gun" was produced in great secrecy before being deployed to the Western Front in March 1918.

lines running around Laon and Reims and all in the middle of a forest. The work on these positions began in November 1917 and carried on into January and February 1918. Each required much preparation work – new track was laid, emplacements were dug and huge volumes of concrete made to create foundations sound enough to take the weight of the reassembled gun. Great efforts were also made to camouflage the various firing positions. The first of these was located at Crépy-en-Laonnois and was used 23 March – 1 May when 183 rounds were fired; the Bois de Corbie was used on two occasions, 27 May – 11 June (104 rounds) and 5–9 August (66 rounds); while the third position was used only briefly 15–19 July (14 rounds) at the Bois de Bruyères.

Thus, 367 shells fell on or near Paris during the various attacks, killing 256 civilians and wounding a further 620, but there was no set routine. More shells might fall on one day than the next, and several days might pass without any landing at all. This might have been because the gun's barrel needed replacing after just 60 rounds had been fired or because the gun was being moved. One thing did become clear on the second day of the bombardment. The previous day's shells had landed some 20 minutes apart but on the morning of 24 March two struck just three minutes apart, meaning that there were at least two Paris Guns in action.

The Paris Guns proved largely invulnerable and neither was ever destroyed by the Allies. Their bombardment only ended following the successful Allied counter-attacks in August that pushed the German line back so that the French capital was beyond their range. Some of the guns' emplacements were overrun but there was no sign of the weapons themselves. Nor was any trace of them ever found. The most likely explanation is that they were cut up and the high-grade metal put to other uses.

Below: A crowd of curious onlookers examines a little of the damage done by a round from the "Paris Gun".

Ground-attack Aircraft

Close co-operation between ground and air units became a very important part of offensive operations during World War I but few dedicated aircraft were ever built and still fewer entered service before the later stages of the conflict.

Light bombers and fighters were commonly used for close-support missions during World War I infantry offensives but they were not as effective as dedicated ground-attack aircraft. Light bombers tended to drop their ordnance from medium altitude and would often be inaccurate, while fighters could strafe enemy positions with their machine-guns and drop small loads of bombs – but such low-level work was very dangerous and heartily detested by the majority of pilots. Both they and their unprotected aircraft were highly vulnerable to the huge volume of machine-gun and rifle fire that would greet them as they swooped down on a target. True ground-attack aircraft began to appear from 1917 onward and were usually, but not always, fitted with some form of armoured protection to improve the chances of their crews' surviving over the battlefield.

German Designs

Germany's AEG company produced one of the first ground-attack aircraft, the J-type. It was introduced in 1917 and based on the company's C-type, a two-seater reconnaissance aircraft with an armoured engine. The J-type was given a more powerful engine and two downward-firing forward machine-guns. This design was only intended as a stop-gap measure until dedicated ground-attack aircraft appeared but production problems with the latter led the J-type to be used until the end of the war by which time some 600 had been built.

Another of the major German producers was Albatros, who introduced a two-seater, also known as the J-type, on the Western Front from late 1917. It was essentially a replacement for the AEG J-type and was based on the earlier Albatros C-type, which was primarily a two-seater reconnaissance/light bomber series that was also used for ground-support work. The Albatros J-I was by no means fast and had a reputation for being difficult to fly but it had some useful attributes. The designers had added armoured protection for the two-man crew and fitted the aircraft with three machine-guns of which two were positioned to fire down through the fuselage. The J-I's chief weakness in action was that its designers had neglected

Left: A close-up view of the rear gun position of a German AEG C-IV, a multi-purpose aircraft that performed ground-attack missions.

to protect the engine. This oversight was remedied with the J-II, which was introduced in 1918, but few had reached the front before the end of the war.

Two of the leading aeronautical designers of the day, Hugo Junkers and Antony Fokker, developed the Junkers J-1 two-seater biplane as a ground-attack aircraft. It was based on an all-metal prototype but was modified so that its rear fuselage was made of wood. The J-1 first flew in late 1917 and participated in the great German offensives of spring 1918. Its greatest assets were that it was popular with pilots and the crew had a radio so that it could be easily directed to a target by ground units. The biggest drawback was that the J-1 was rather difficult to build and only 227 had entered service by November 1918.

SALMSON 2

This sturdy and agile aircraft entered service with the French in early 1918 and was also purchased by the United States Army Air Force. Despite the crew positions being rather far apart, which made communication difficult, it was a well-liked type and some 3,200 were built in total.

Type: Ground-attack, light bomber, reconnaissance
Engine: 260hp Canton-Unné
Crew: 2
Ceiling: 5,000m (16,400ft)
Top speed: 184kph (114mph)
Range: 500km (310 miles)
Armament: 3 x 0.303in (7.7mm) machine-guns, light bombs

JUNKERS J-1

The Junkers J-1 was an all-metal biplane designed by Hugo Junkers and it first entered service in early 1918. Some 227 were built jointly by the Fokker and Junkers companies before the end of the war. The aircraft was partially armoured and this extra weight necessitated longer take-offs and landings. It was also slow and clumsy in flight and somewhat difficult to handle but it was popular with its crews for its robustness – especially in action at low levels.

Type: Ground-attack, air–ground liaison
Engine: 200hp Benz Bz.IV
Crew: 2
Ceiling: 4,000m (13,120ft)
Top speed: 155kph (96mph)
Armament: 3–5 x 7.92mm (0.312in) machine-guns

Allied Responses

The Allies tended not to build dedicated ground-attack aircraft but relied more on multi-purpose types. The French, for example, introduced their Salmson 2 in early 1918 and it not only undertook ground-attack duties but also flew as a light bomber and conducted reconnaissance sorties.

Britain used its Sopwith F-1 Camel fighter for ground-support work but it suffered heavy losses because it lacked armoured protection and an attempt to produce the TF-1 (Trench Fighting 1) Camel came to nothing. The first true type was the Sopwith TF-2 Salamander, which went into mass production in May 1918 but saw little service.

Equipping the Americans

The United States had to build a mass army of hundreds of thousands from scratch but lacked an industrial base that was geared up for war production to equip its troops so largely relied on Britain and France for its weaponry.

Britain and France had well-developed war industries by mid-1917 but were increasingly short of manpower due to the heavy casualties they had suffered in the preceding years. The United States, in contrast, had huge reserves of untapped manpower but largely lacked the wartime industrial base needed to equip them. Rather than wait for the Americans to clothe and arm their own armed forces, a time-consuming business at a point when speed was of the essence, it was thought better for Britain and France to provide US land and air forces with the means to fight the war. The US Navy, the country's strongest service, was fit to go to war and required no help from either Britain or France.

This decision on supply also meant that the shipboard space that would have been used to carry vast quantities of arms and equipment overseas was left free to ferry greater numbers of US troops to Europe much more quickly. There was no doubt that this plan was a wise one as some two million US troops crossed the North Atlantic during 1917–18.

Above: US troops fighting in the Argonne make use of a French-built 37mm (1.46in) trench gun.

Uniforms and Rifles

US troops did largely go to war in their own uniforms and carrying home-produced small arms but there were exceptions even to this. The infantry mostly wore British steel helmets but troops serving with French formations, generally segregated African-American units, instead wore the French Adrian helmet.

CURTISS JN-4D "JENNY"

The Curtiss JN-4 was the most successful US aircraft of the war period but it was a trainer not a combat type. Nevertheless, this version, the first to be mass-produced, was used in large numbers and some 5,500 had been built by the end of 1918.

Engine: 90hp Curtiss OX-5
Crew: 2
Ceiling: 3,000m (9,850ft)
Top speed: 112kph (70mph)
Armament: none

American troops were equipped with US small arms, including the excellent 1903 Springfield Rifle and the Browning Automatic Rifle but they also used French and British weapons, including the Rifle M1917 (Enfield), derived from a British design, and the wholly French Chauchat light machine-gun. The African-American troops serving with the French were armed with the Lebel and Berthier rifles. The main heavy machine-gun deployed throughout the US Army was the US 1917 Browning.

Artillery

However, when it came to heavy equipment the American Expeditionary Force (AEF) was overwhelmingly dependent on French and British designs. In the case of artillery the AEF relied mainly on the French 75mm (2.95in) field gun and 155mm (6.1in) howitzer. The British also supplied a number of 8in (203mm) howitzers. The AEF's armoured force mainly consisted of French Renault FT-17 light tanks and its few heavier tanks were all British. There were plans to mass produce an "Allied" or "Liberty" tank based on the British Mark VIII design fitted with a US aero-engine at a plant in France but the war ended before it came into service.

The pilots of the United States Army Air Service largely earned their wings on US-built aircraft like the Curtiss JN series but they went into combat flying British and French designs, many of which were built under licence in the United States and fitted with US aero-engines. Others were simply bought from Britain and France; they had delivered 4,881 and 259 aircraft, respectively, by the war's end. The chief fighters flown by US squadrons were the French Nieuport 28 and various Spad S-types, while by later in 1918 the bomber units were mostly equipped with French Breguet 14 and Salmson 2 machines supported by a significant number of American-built DH-4s.

Left: A US communications detachment with a field telephone. Line repair was a constant task.

Below: Most of the American Expeditionary Force was equipped with foreign-built artillery, including the famous French 75mm (2.95in) field gun seen here in action.

The First American Battles

The first US troops arrived in Europe during late May 1917 but they did not appear in combat in any numbers until the first months of 1918 and did not go into action on a significant scale until May to halt a major German offensive.

The United States declared war on Germany on 6 April 1917 but its 200,000-strong army was small by European standards and ill-prepared for battle. Congress agreed the Selective Service Act to introduce conscription on 19 May with the aim of having one million men serving overseas within a year. General John Pershing had been named commander of the American Expeditionary Force on the 10th and he arrived in France on 13 June. The first sizeable body of troops, some 14,000 in all, disembarked on the 28th but months passed before any saw action as they required schooling in the arts of trench warfare. Nevertheless, the first US troops went to the front in October and they suffered their first fatalities on 3 November.

KEY FACTS

Date: May – June 1918

Location: Various points on the Western Front

Outcome: The US forces helped to stem a major German offensive and retook some lost ground.

AMERICA'S BATTLES, 1918
US forces fought several minor actions and the St Mihiel and Meuse–Argonne Offensives in 1918.

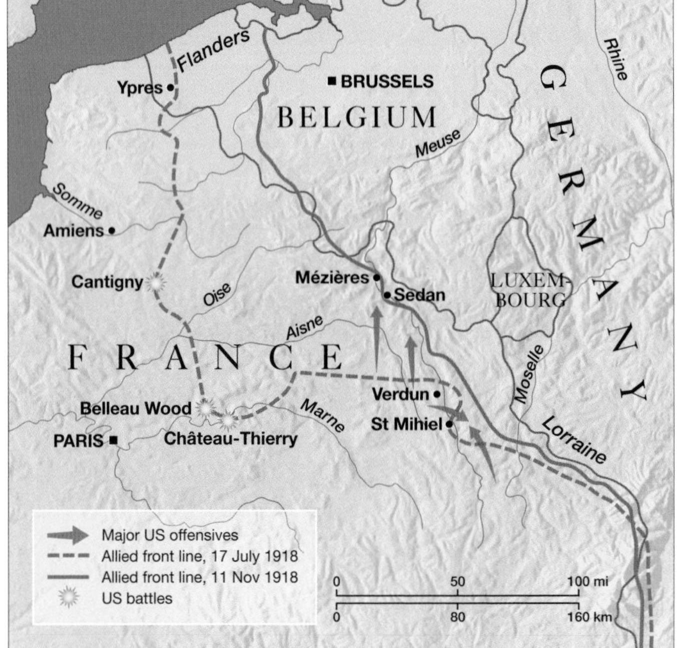

First Engagements

It was not until late May 1918 that AEF units were committed to battle in any strength. The Germans had been hammering away at various parts of the Allied line on the Western Front since late March. On 28 May the US 1st Division under Major General Robert Bullard was ordered to attack Cantigny, which the Germans had captured and turned into a strongly fortified observation post. The village was retaken and then Bullard's men successfully beat off several counter-attacks over the next 48 hours.

Below: A Renault FT-17 tank operated by the AEF lies abandoned after failing to cross a trench.

Above: US troops leave their trench during an attack around Cantigny, 28 May 1918.

BATTLE OF THE MARNE

The Germans opened their Aisne Offensive, between Reims and Montdidier on 27 May. Their forces had reached the River Marne by the next day and the French troops there were on the point of collapse. The US 2nd and 3rd Divisions were deployed to stem the tide from the 30th. The 3rd Division held vital bridges at Château-Thierry, threw back several German assaults and then counter-attacked with French units, driving the Germans back across the river. The 2nd Division was positioned to the west of Château-Thierry, between the villages of Belleau and Vaux, and was also able to stop the German advance. The Aisne Offensive ended on 4 June and the 2nd Division then successfully counter-attacked at several points, most notably Belleau Wood (6–25 June).

Although the AEF's commitment was larger than it might seem because US divisions were twice the size of those of the other Allies, the Battles of Cantigny, Château-Thierry and Belleau Wood were small-scale affairs by the usual standards of the Western Front. The next US attack was of an altogether different magnitude as on 24 July Pershing had finally been able to persuade General Foch, the Allied Commander-in-Chief since March, to assign the AEF a whole sector of the front, one immediately to the south-east of Verdun. The offensive, from 12–16 September, was conducted by the US First Army to nip out a salient around St Mihiel.

Pershing advanced on both the northern and southern flanks of the bulge after a four-hour barrage from some 2,970 guns. The troops made their attack supported by the biggest air armada ever seen. The two pincers had converged at Hattonchâtel by nightfall on the first day and the St Mihiel Offensive was effectively over by the 16th. The Germans had actually evacuated many of their troops before Pershing moved but the operation had been conducted with a great deal of skill, indicating that the AEF was now ready to play a full part in the war. Pershing immediately moved his entire army to the west of Verdun and ten days later launched the largest – and last – US offensive of the war.

GENERAL JOHN PERSHING

Pershing (1860–1948), who commanded the American Expeditionary Force on the Western Front, was a career soldier who had fought against Native Americans and the Spanish and conducted raids into Mexico in early 1917. Much to the chagrin of the British and French, Pershing refused to put his command under their direct control, although he did relent somewhat in times of crisis, but he mostly preferred to conduct his own offensives, notably at St Mihiel and in the Meuse–Argonne. He was promoted to become the first US General of the Armies in 1919.

Above: Pershing with Allied commanders Foch, Haig and Pétain (right to left).

Supply Transport

As befitted a highly industrialized war fought on a vast scale, World War I demanded the production of huge quantities of weapons and equipment and these were transported to the fronts by both long-established and much newer means.

The movement of men and equipment, indeed all types of military necessities up to the front, was a vital if unglamorous part of every country's military effort during World War I. Such items would be transported to the theatre of war by sea and rail, and then be moved by rail to stations usually some way behind the front where they would be unloaded and transported to large supply dumps. From these distribution points they would be sent forward to those who needed the particular supplies. The task of getting such quantities of supplies to the front was immense, virtually ceaseless and the rate of consumption often huge, especially during major battles and offensives.

Above: This shell dump gives a good indication of the huge quantities of all types of war material required to keep the armies fighting.

For example, on 5 September 1914, the first day of the Battle of the Marne, the French had 465,000 rounds of 75mm ammunition stockpiled; five days later they had just 33,000 shells left. The British hit similarly high levels of consumption in 1916 – they fired more rounds in the week before the opening of the Battle of the Somme than they had in the previous 12 months. The Germans stockpiled some 1.16 million shells for their March 1918 offensive and fired virtually all of them in just five hours on the 21st.

Foreign Labour

Several of the combatants scoured the world for workers to keep an existing supply system going or expand it. Both Britain and France used labour drawn from their overseas colonies. Britain alone used more than one million porters from its own

Below: A camel supply column, as used by the British forces during the campaign in Palestine.

and various other African colonies during the war in East Africa but even this was not enough as the average soldier there required three porters. Even in Europe where the war was far less mobile, the supply network required huge numbers of labourers. China was a major contributor and by 1918 some 100,000 Chinese workers, both skilled and unskilled, worked in British labour corps on the Western Front, roughly the same number served with the French and a further 6,000 with the AEF.

Animal Power

World War I was largely powered by the horse. The official establishment of a British infantry division in 1914 included 877 vehicles and close to 5,600 horses, but only 9 motor cars, and matters had not changed much by 1918. The very same division was allocated 822 horse-drawn vehicles and some 8,840 horses but just 11 motor cars, 3 lorries and 21 motor ambulances. The need for horses and other animals, such as mules, camels and even bullocks, was all but insatiable and produced a terrible death toll. Some 542,000 horses died in French service alone during 1914–18, for example, and the British lost close to 485,000 horses and other animals.

Despite these figures, there is little doubt that motor transport did play a growing role in the supply chain. Trucks and a small light railway largely fuelled the French resupply effort during the titanic Battle of Verdun in 1916 and by June some 12,000 vehicles, at times one every 14 seconds, had moved up and down the *Voie Sacrée*, the only available road into the town.

Many of the original motor vehicles were simply civilian types pressed into service. The British, for example, converted around 1,300 buses belonging to the London General Omnibus Corporation into B Type Motor Lorries. Increasingly, however, major vehicle manufacturers, including such companies as Dennis, Leyland and Wolseley, began to supply purpose-built designs. A similar pattern was followed by the French Army, which requisitioned 1,049 civilian buses, 2,500 cars and 6,000 lorries in the final months of 1914, but thereafter Renault, Schneider and others began to supply appropriate vehicles.

LIGHT RAILWAYS

The importance of narrow-gauge railways cannot be overemphasized. Their tracks were usually just 60cm (2ft) apart and this made them much faster to build. The British Army, for example, estimated that a mile of light railway took 1,760–2,400 man-days to build while standard gauge took 4,300. Light railways were used by all sides and were pivotal in supplying the front line with every necessity. Some were also used to bring troops to within easy distance of the trench line.

Left: A British light railway pictured beside the River Scarpe – itself used as a supply artery – during the Battle of Arras in 1917. Water transport was often used to take wounded men to hospital as it gave a smooth ride.

Above: Motor transport, like these French trucks, was little used in 1914 but had become commonplace by later in the war.

The Meuse–Argonne Offensive

The last weeks of the war saw a successful joint US–French effort designed to break through the Western Front in the direction of Sedan but, more importantly, this was the first prolonged major attack made by the American Expeditionary Force.

By late September 1918 Marshal Foch had finalized his plans to deliver a succession of hammer blows on the Western Front. He intended to launch two major offensives against the Germans, realizing that they had used up their strategic reserves during the bitter fighting of March–July and, if attacked simultaneously, there would be no quiet sector of the front from where troops could be sent to reinforce an area facing an attack. Foch aimed to launch French and US forces northward from west of Verdun towards the key rail junction of Mézières, some 48km (30 miles) behind the German line. The British were to attack eastward between Péronne and Lens and seize another key rail centre. He also organized two smaller assaults, one by Belgian, British and French troops stationed in Flanders and one between Péronne and La Fère by French and British units.

KEY FACTS

DATE: 26 September – 11 November 1918

PLACE: Argonne region of eastern France

OUTCOME: Despite stubborn German resistance US forces advanced to the River Meuse.

The Meuse–Argonne attack opened on 26 September and involved some 600,000 Allied troops, 5,000 guns, around 500 tanks and 500 aircraft. The French Fourth Army under General Henri Gouraud was positioned on the left of the line but General Hunter Liggett's US First Army, which was in position between the Rivers Aisne and Meuse, increasingly bore the brunt of the action as it tried to break through four heavily fortified lines that made great use of the difficult terrain found throughout the heavily wooded Argonne area. The US troops made some initial progress but their push on a narrow, congested front ground to a halt in both the Argonne and around the town of Montfaucon as the Germans rushed reinforcements to the area. By late September the US troops had cut through just the first two lines of defences, advancing 16km (10 miles) in all, but had been unable to make headway against the especially formidable third line.

Below: German troops withdrawing from France, abandoning territory captured in 1914.

Renewing the Battle

The US Commander-in-Chief, General Pershing, now paused to regroup and then flung some of his most experienced divisions against the third German line on 4 October. Progress was again costly and painfully slow in the Argonne but the US drive allowed the French Fourth Army to push towards the Aisne. Pershing now split his forces in two, creating the First and Second Armies on 12 October. The First Army continued to batter its way northward and by

Above: US-manned Renault FT-17 tanks move forward for the opening of the Meuse–Argonne Offensive.

the end of the month had at last pushed beyond the Argonne. As this was taking place the Second Army under General Robert Bullard was forming up to the east of Verdun.

The Final Assault

The last stage of the offensive began on 1 November. The First Army cut through the remaining German defences to the north and west of Buzancy. The capture of the town helped the French Fourth Army finally to cross the Aisne, while the First Army drove through open country along the Meuse Valley in the face of disintegrating opposition. The Meuse was reached a little below Sedan on the 6th and US artillery was able to open fire on Mézières. The US Second Army began its drive in the direction of Montmédy on the 10th and had made some progress before hostilities ended with the Armistice at 11.00 hours the next day. The US troops had shown considerable dash during the offensive but their relative inexperience had helped cost them some 117,000 casualties. The Germans lost 100,000 men, including 26,000 prisoners.

MARSHAL FERDINAND FOCH

Foch (1851–1929), a well-established military theorist, took on an active field command when war broke out in 1914 and by 28 August was in charge of the French Ninth Army. He was promoted to army group command in October but was sidelined when General Robert Nivelle became Commander-in-Chief in December 1916. Foch's career recovered in 1917 when he co-ordinated a unified Allied response to the German Caporetto Offensive in Italy and in 1918 he was made the Allied Supreme Commander, a position that required great tact. He was seen as the architect of the Allied victory and was made a marshal on 6 August 1918.

Above: Marshal Ferdinand Foch, effective head of the Allied forces in 1918.

Left: US engineers work to clear away German barbed wire during the final days of the war.

Communications

All generals were dogged by the particularly thorny problem of communicating effectively with their troops at the front and, although various means were tried to overcome the long-standing difficulties, none was wholly satisfactory.

One of the greatest problems faced by any commanding officer in World War I was the difficulty in receiving progress reports and sending orders once a battle had begun. In most previous wars a general had been able simply to roam the comparatively small battlefields at will, seeing for himself what was happening and issuing and revising orders as required, but this was clearly impossible when the 1914–18 battlefields stretched over many miles and might involve much bigger forces. Consequently, commanding officers planned their attacks down to the smallest detail and issued step-by-step timetables for offensives so that every unit knew what it was to do and when. The problem was that battles rarely went to plan and it was difficult to respond to events quickly because of communication problems.

Most belligerents used wireless telegraphy for Morse code transmissions during the hostilities (speech transmission was not yet available) but it suffered two great weaknesses. First it could be intercepted by the enemy and even if the message was in code it might still be read. The Allies were fortunate enough to capture two sets of German naval codes in August 1914 and in one case the Germans did not realize the codebook was in enemy hands until 1918. The second problem was the wireless sets – they were bulky, heavy and fragile. Underpowered early aircraft, for example, could not take off with a wireless on board, while the sets could not long withstand the rigours of front-line service on the ground. Lighter, smaller and more robust models did become available as the war progressed and were commonly found in reconnaissance aircraft and balloons, but other means of communication remained in place on the ground.

Telephone Systems

Once static warfare had developed the preferred method of communicating was either by voice or Morse code via telephone or buzzer but this had one major drawback – its vulnerability. Even though cables were often buried a metre or more below ground, they were repeatedly cut by artillery fire. Repairing such breaks was a difficult and dangerous occupation

Above: A German messenger dog captured in mid-air as it races to the rear to deliver a message.

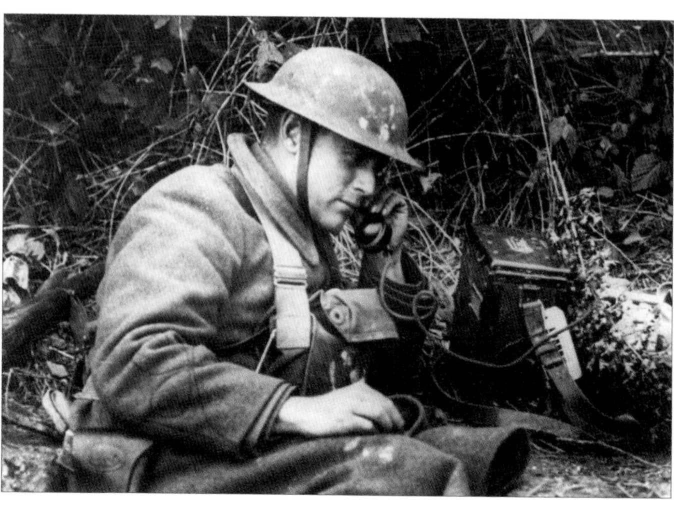

Right: A US soldier mans a field telephone during the fighting in the Argonne in late 1918.

for the signallers whose duty it was to maintain the system. Matters were even worse once a battle had begun. Portable handsets existed but as their cables had to be laid on the surface of No Man's Land, an area undoubtedly under heavy artillery fire and often by both sides, there was a high probability that the cables would be cut.

Live Messengers

More often than not attacking soldiers had to rely on other methods of sending and receiving messages but each had weaknesses. Written or oral messages were often sent by runner. This was arguably the most dangerous occupation on a World War I battlefield with a high probability of death or injury so that the message might never get through. It was also obviously much slower than transmission by telephone, especially if the runner got lost as many did. Carrier pigeons fulfilled a similar role and, although also highly vulnerable, could be effective. One played a pivotal role in the defence of Fort Vaux during 1916's Battle of Verdun and was posthumously awarded France's top award for gallantry.

There were other means of transmitting information but they were generally even more haphazard. Signal rockets were widely used in emergencies, often to call down artillery fire on pre-arranged co-ordinates, and the British even sewed reflective metal triangles on their back packs during the opening stages of the Battle of the Somme in 1916 so that the sun would glint off them and give those in reserve some idea of the troops' progress.

Above: Most of the major combatants deployed carrier pigeon units on the Western Front and the birds were housed in specially built lofts such as this impressive example.

Below: A pigeon is released from the interior of a British tank during the summer of 1916. Some animals were given decorations for their war service.

Breaking the Hindenburg Line

The complex and in-depth defences of the German Hindenburg Line were by any measure exceptionally strong in many places yet the British were able to smash through them in a matter of days from late September 1918.

There were three Allied attacks on the northern Western Front in the final weeks of the war. In the north, between Armentières and the sea, Belgian, British and French divisions were ready by late September, while British, French and US divisions were positioned between La Fère and Épehy in the south. Twenty-seven divisions of the British First and Third Armies lined up in the centre between Épehy and Lens.

Above: British cavalry during the final weeks of the war when mobility returned to the Western Front.

Tough Defences

The main British effort in the central sector opened on 27 September. Field Marshal Haig expected a hard fight as his assault troops were facing the toughest part of the Hindenburg Line. Yet his fears were never fully realized. The whole of the Hindenburg Line had been taken by 9 October and Marshal Foch was able to issue orders for the final advances of the war. The Belgians were to march on Bruges, a key U-boat base, and the BEF was to push towards Maubeuge and Mons, the latter somewhat ironically where it had fought its very first battle of the war back in 1914.

Below: Although German morale was generally poor, some troops, especially machine-gun units as here, fought to the bitter end.

Advances in Belgium

The attack in Flanders had opened on 28 September. The Allied Flanders Group made good progress initially as it pushed east from around Ypres. The high ground was captured by 1 October but thereafter the offensive stalled due to the difficult going and the stubborn resistance offered by the troops of Crown Prince Rupprecht of Bavaria's opposing Army Group North. The key moments came in the middle of the month – Lille was captured by the British and the Belgians took Ostend on the 17th, while Belgian troops occupied Zeebrugge and Bruges two days later, thereby ending the U-boat menace from those ports. All of the Belgian coast up to the Dutch border was in Allied hands by the next day and thereafter the fighting switched to the south.

After breaking the Hindenburg Line, the BEF made for the Rivers Sambre and Scheldt. As a preliminary, the River Selle

FINAL ALLIED ATTACKS

The German Army was decisively defeated by the end of the war.

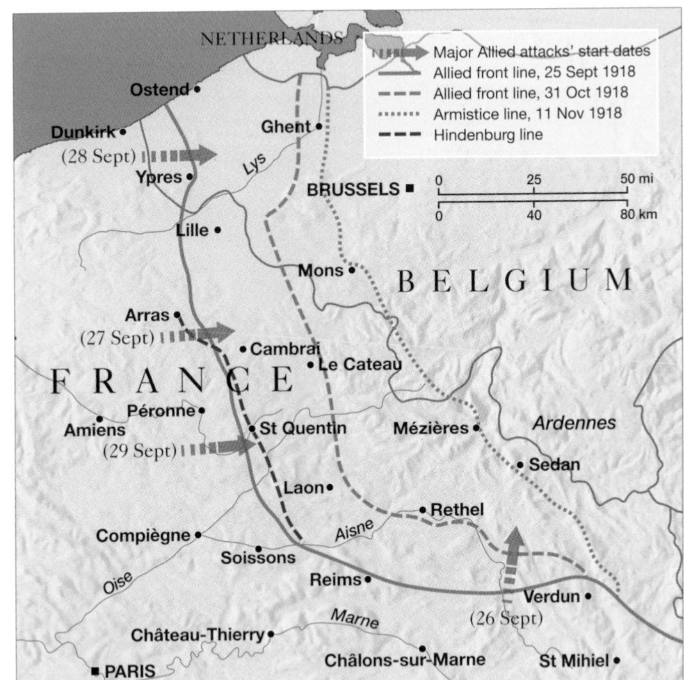

was crossed on 17–20 October. Next came a push into the Franco-Belgian border region on 1 November. The capture of Valenciennes the next day confirmed that German resistance was weakening. The Sambre Offensive was the BEF's last attack of the war. It began on 4 November and, aside from meeting occasional strong pockets of resistance, the troops moved forward with little difficulty. Canadian troops re-entered Mons on the 10th and the British advance was halted when the Armistice came into effect the next day.

The BEF had conducted a stunning series of offensives in the last hundred days, beginning with the victory at Amiens on 8 August, but it had suffered huge casualties. Some 952,000 men were listed as killed, wounded, sick, taken prisoner or missing since January and Britain's allies fared no better. French losses totalled a little over one million, those of the American Expeditionary Force around 280,000, the Belgians some 30,000, the Italians 14,600 and the Portuguese, who had entered the war in 1916, at least 6,000. Germany had suffered equally, recording some 1.5 million casualties – even before the final battles of October and November are included.

THE ST QUENTIN CANAL

This battle, against the most heavily defended part of the Hindenburg Line, was the most important engagement of the last weeks of the war. The attack was spearheaded by an Australian corps and opened on 29 September 1918. The target was a narrow strip of ground, where the canal ran through a tunnel, but the advance soon stalled with heavy casualties. However, other British units crossed the canal at Bellenglise and punched through the line, making the remainder untenable.

Right: Men of the British 46th Division who successfully crossed the St Quentin Canal are congratulated by their commanding officer.

Pistols

Handguns were widely issued to troops during the war but were the main weapon carried by officers, partly as an indication of rank. They were useful weapons in confined spaces, such as trenches and vehicles of various sorts.

Revolvers and automatic pistols were the personal sidearms of officers of every rank, from the youngest second lieutenant to the most senior field marshal, and as such were as much a symbol of authority as a potentially deadly close-quarters weapon. There were other soldiers, some not necessarily of the officer class, who also made use of these weapons and this was in part because they operated in confined areas where it was considered impracticable to wield anything as long as a rifle. The types of troops in this category included airmen, tunnellers and, of course, tank and armoured car crews. The military police were also usually permitted to carry sidearms as they needed their hands free to check paperwork and manhandle troublesome prisoners if necessary.

Pistol Designs

There were three types of pistol available in 1914 – the common revolver that had a rotating chamber holding something like six rounds, and two types of clip-loaded automatics – recoil-operated and "blowback" designs. There tended to be a small number of major pistol manufacturers in each of the main combatant nations and they dominated production. Webley produced a staggering 300,000 of its Mark VI revolver for the British armed forces from 1915, for example, but even with that scale of output pistols were still sometimes in short supply and some less-known types were pressed into service as a stopgap. Britain, for example, made use of US Colt automatics which were largely distributed to the Royal Navy, the Royal Naval Air Service and the Royal Flying Corps.

Other nations also had favoured manufacturers. Luger is synonymous with German pistols but Germany's armed forces also used smaller quantities of designs like the Mauser and Beholla automatics. All of these were also sold to both Bulgaria and Turkey, some 22,000 to the former alone. The armed forces of the other Central Power, Austria-Hungary, also used German designs but they also had their own 1911 Steyr automatic and other types. On the Allied side, the major

MAUSER AUTOMATIC

This weapon, probably the most powerful pistol to see service in the war, went into production in the 1890s and first found favour with the Italian Navy. During World War I it was deployed by the German armed forces but in a modified, re-calibred form from 1916.

First issued: 1894
Calibre: 7.63mm (0.3in)
Magazine: 10 rounds
Overall length: 280mm (11in)
Weight: 1.13kg (40oz)
Muzzle velocity: 440m/sec (1,444ft/sec)

STEYR M1911

The Austrian Steyr "Hahn" M1911 was a successful semi-automatic design and remained in military service until after WWII. It was renowned for its durability and ease of maintenance and was used by several countries.

First issued: 1911
Calibre: 9mm (0.354in)
Magazine: 8 rounds
Overall length: 216mm (8.5in)
Weight: 1.02kg (36oz)
Muzzle velocity: 361m/sec (1,185ft/sec)

sidearms' producers were Lebel in France, Glisenti and Beretta in Italy and Colt and Smith & Wesson in the United States. Belgium, Russia and Serbia either bought in pistols or built them under licence, although Russia did have some home-grown types available.

Combat Use

Pistols did have their uses, despite having a comparatively short range. They were effective in confined spaces and were of some value in trench fighting but more experienced and therefore possibly more wary officers often abandoned them as the war progressed. This was in part because they marked the wearer out as an officer, thus making it easier for the enemy to identify and neutralize him. An officer might prefer to make himself more anonymous by carrying a standard rifle.

However, the revolver or automatic pistol remained a potent signifier of authority throughout the conflict and the vast majority of officers continued to carry them into battle despite the potential risks.

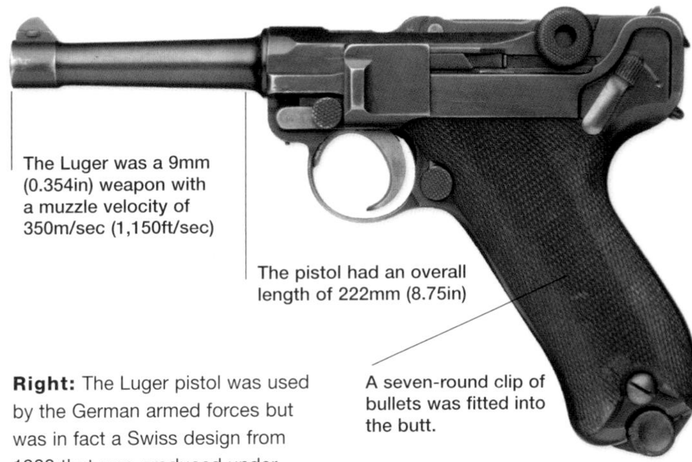
The Luger was a 9mm (0.354in) weapon with a muzzle velocity of 350m/sec (1,150ft/sec)
The pistol had an overall length of 222mm (8.75in)
A seven-round clip of bullets was fitted into the butt.

Right: The Luger pistol was used by the German armed forces but was in fact a Swiss design from 1900 that was produced under licence from 1904 onward.

There is also no doubt that one particular blowback pistol, actually a Belgian-made seven-shot 7.65mm (0.301in) Browning Model 1900, played a key, indeed pivotal, role in World War I – it was the weapon used by 19-year-old Bosnian Serb nationalist Gavrilo Princip to assassinate Archduke Franz Ferdinand and his wife, Sophie, Duchess of Hohenberg, at Sarajevo on 28 June 1914.

WEBLEY MARK V

This weapon in several slightly different marks was arguably the most ubiquitous sidearm of the entire war. It was the standard British service pistol throughout the conflict and hundreds of thousands were produced.

First issued: 1913
Calibre 0.455in (11.4mm)
Magazine: 6 rounds
Overall length 235mm (9.25in)
Weight: 1.0kg (35oz)
Muzzle velocity: 180m/sec (590ft/sec)

D
1465

Left: The Glisenti was a seven-shot 9mm (0.354in) Italian pistol that had an overall length of 216mm (8.5in) and had a muzzle velocity of 275m/sec (900ft/sec).

Armoured Cars

Armoured cars offered scouts a degree of protection and firepower that could not be easily matched by cavalry patrols but they were often fitted with under-powered and unreliable engines and were therefore not really suited to off-road action.

The first viable petrol engine and the first petrol-driven vehicle appeared in 1885 and the first recognizable armoured cars began to emerge in the period after 1902. As is the case with most new technologies, there was generally little standardization at first. Many of the designs were merely experimental or made from what resources were locally available, and only a handful or so ever saw action on the battlefield. Generally, they were built on chassis derived from civilian cars or light trucks and covered in armour plate of various thicknesses that gave them a boxy rather than streamlined shape. They might be fully enclosed or open-topped, and have one or more turrets, while armament ranged from light to heavy machine-guns and up to small-calibre cannon. Most ran on four pneumatic tyres (with two driven wheels) but a small number made in Russia were half-tracked.

Armoured cars were mostly built by the car and truck manufacturers of the day, such as Minerva, Mors and SAVA (Société Anversoise pour Fabrication des Voitures Automobiles) in Belgium; Austin, Lanchester, Talbot, Wolseley and Rolls-Royce in Britain; Peugeot and Renault in France; Büssing, Daimler and Ehrhardt in Germany; and Fiat and Lancia in Italy. Some, especially British and Belgian designs, were produced in one country and exported to other Allied nations but it was not uncommon to find them being captured and used by the enemy. Germany used some British-built Austins taken from Russia, while Austria-Hungary deployed types captured from both Russia and Italy.

Limitations in Action

Armoured cars only truly function during mobile warfare and they are used for reconnaissance and intelligence gathering, launching ambushes, outflanking the enemy, or pursuing a defeated foe. In World War I they served on most fronts, but were more common or saw more active service in some rather than others. This was partly due to the nature of the fighting. On the Western Front, they played an active role in the first stages

ROLLS-ROYCE ADMIRALTY PATTERN

This British-produced armoured car was based on the Silver Ghost civilian car and was used from late 1914 by the Royal Naval Air Service but the various squadrons were taken over by the Army in late 1915.

Engine: 40–50hp Rolls-Royce
Top speed: 80kph (50mph)
Crew: 2–3
Max. armour: 12mm (0.47in)
Armament: 1 x 0.303in (7.7mm) Vickers Maxim

Below: Armoured cars in Russian service – a French-built Peugeot (foreground) and a Belgian Mors.

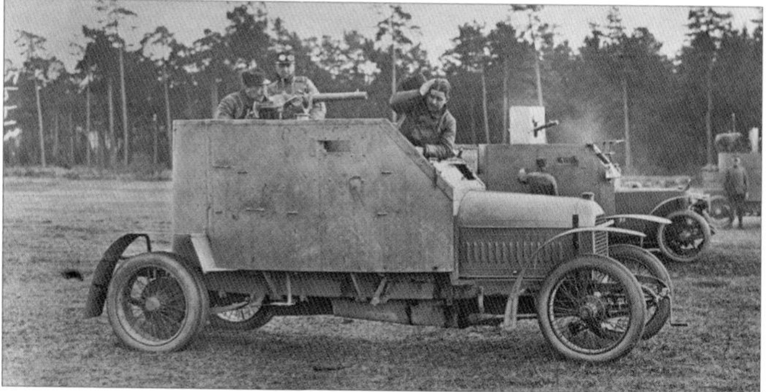

Right: A Belgian Minerva armoured car fitted with a single Hotchkiss machine-gun in action during 1914.

of the fighting in 1914 before the trench lines were dug and in the latter part of 1918 when operations once again became more fluid. Terrain and going also influenced their deployment. Many were heavy, underpowered and lacked traction so they were unsuitable for crossing hills, muddy ground or soft sand. One of the main problems was that the wheels of armoured cars were exposed, thereby making them vulnerable to enemy fire. Equally, the armour plate was effective against small arms fire but only beyond certain distances and was wholly ineffective against any type of artillery fire.

British Designs

Britain led the way in wartime armoured car development in 1914 when a Royal Naval Air Service officer, Commander C. R. Samson, used cars largely sourced from around Dunkirk to rescue downed pilots and report on the movement of enemy troops and airships. Samson began by using poor-quality locally produced armour plate but then started requesting better materials from his superiors who in turn asked a number of British manufacturers to design purpose-built armoured cars. Austin eventually produced the most, many of which were earmarked for Russia, but Rolls-Royce undoubtedly made the best. The first three Rolls-Royce (Admiralty Pattern) types made their debut in December 1914 and both they and later models were sent to the fronts where the fighting was more mobile. They were especially active in the Middle East, serving with considerable success in both Palestine and Mesopotamia (Iraq).

PANZERKRAFTWAGEN EHRHARDT

The Ehrhardt was one of three types of armoured car in service with Germany from 1915 and was arguably the best. An updated version (pictured here), which appeared two years later, was little different except for the addition of armour plate over the headlamps and rear wheels.

Engine: 85hp Ehrhardt
Top speed: 60kph (37mph)
Range: 250km (155 miles)
Crew: 8–9
Maximum armour: 7mm (0.276in)
Armament: 3 x 7.92mm (0.312in) machine-guns

Final Battles in Italy

Italy had come close to disaster in 1917 but in late 1918 its forces, supported by troops from various other Allied nations, inflicted a decisive and crippling defeat on the Austro-Hungarians at the Battle of Vittorio Veneto.

The collapse of Russia in 1917 meant that both Germany and Austria-Hungary could transfer some troops from the Eastern Front, if not quite denude it of forces, and thus bolster their efforts elsewhere. Germany also withdrew its troops from Italy in spring 1918 in preparation for a series of major offensives on the Western Front and urged Austria-Hungary to crush Italy alone. The plan was to launch two simultaneous attacks in the northern Trentino sector of the front and one in the north-east along the River Piave.

Above: Austro-Hungarian troops killed during their army's failed attempt to cross the River Piave in June 1918.

Austrian Aims

Field Marshal Conrad von Hötzendorf, Austria Hungary's Chief of Staff until sacked in November 1917 and now commanding in the Trentino, had targeted Verona as his objective, while recently promoted Field Marshal Svetozar Boroevic von Bojna on the Piave was looking towards Padua. Their efforts would effectively be conducted in isolation because of difficult terrain and a lack of connecting roads. To make matters worse, the reinforcements sent to the Italian Front had been split so that neither was strong enough to carry out his allotted task. The Italian Commander-in-Chief, General Armando Diaz, had also been forewarned of their forthcoming offensives.

Conrad's Eleventh Army attacked on 15 June and made some initial progress against the Italian Sixth and Fourth Armies before it was stopped in its tracks and then thrown back. Boroevic performed only a little better along the lower reaches of the Piave but his advance was halted when heavy rain turned the river into a raging torrent

Below: Two Italian officers pose in front of a medium artillery piece sited in a camouflaged emplacement overlooking the Piave.

and Italian bombers disrupted his supply lines. Diaz then threw in his own reserves and these brought the Battle of the Piave to a halt on the 22nd. The Austro-Hungarians had suffered 190,000 casualties and their army was mostly finished. Demoralized, undermined by mutinies and split by ethnic tensions, the army was able to offer only token resistance by late summer.

Italy's Waiting Game

Diaz did not immediately launch a major counter-attack to finish off the Austro-Hungarian armies, much to the chagrin of his Allies, but spent the next months preparing his troops for action and watching for favourable events on the Western Front that would make his job easier. His offensive finally opened in late October when the Italian Fourth Army pushed forward but it soon met stiff opposition from the Austro-Hungarian Belluno Group and was thrown back at the Battle of Monte Grappo on the 24th.

Left: General Armando Diaz, the Italian Commander-in-Chief from November 1917.

The main attack involved three armies crossing the Piave on the 24th and moving on Vittorio Veneto but the Italian Eighth Army advancing in the centre was stopped almost immediately by the Austro-Hungarian Sixth Army. French units attached to the Italian Twelfth Army, itself led by French General Jean Graziani, did get across the river on the left flank. British troops of the Italian Tenth Army under a British general, the Earl of Cavan, had managed the same feat on the right by the 28th. An ever-growing gap now appeared in the Austro-Hungarian lines and their units simply fell apart, with the Allies eventually taking some 300,000 prisoners in the Battle of Vittorio Veneto. All of northern and north-east Italy had been cleared by Diaz's armies by early November and Trieste, an Italian objective since May 1915, finally fell on the 3rd. Austria-Hungary had asked to discuss armistice terms on 29 September and an agreement was finally signed the day that Trieste was occupied. It came into force at 15.00 hours on 4 November.

Below: US troops, only a few of whom served in Italy, launch grenades against Austro-Hungarian positions in September 1918.

Liberating the Balkans

The many Allied troops in the Balkans had been so inactive that they had become known as the "gardeners of Salonika" but in the last months of the war they achieved significant advances and forced Bulgaria to capitulate.

The Allied effort in the Balkans had largely been moribund since troops had first arrived in Salonika during 1915 but matters changed with the arrival of a new commander, General Marie Guillaumat, on 10 December 1917. Guillaumat was never able to make a major offensive because the Allied high commands were diverting forces and equipment to other more active fronts but the French general, nevertheless, spent his time well. He wholly reorganized and reinvigorated what had been a demoralized command, poured oil on the troubled waters of Anglo-French relations and set about planning a large-scale offensive.

KEY FACTS

DATE: 15 September – 4 November 1918

PLACE: Across the entire Balkans

OUTCOME: The Allies knocked Bulgaria out of the war and advanced to the Danube.

NEW COMMANDER

Guillaumat was transferred back to France in June 1918. His replacement was another able French officer, General Louis Franchet d'Espérey, and he finalized Guillaumat's plan of operations, which involved an offensive all along the line from the Aegean Sea in the east to the Albanian border in the west. German troops had been withdrawn from the Balkans and transferred to the Western Front in early 1918 and the Allies, who had recently been reinforced by various Greek units, faced a roughly equal number of Bulgarians but enjoyed a significant advantage in artillery and air support.

The final Allied offensive began with the Battle of the River Vardar, which opened on

THE BALKANS CAMPAIGN
The Allies struck out north and east from Salonika to clear the Balkans.

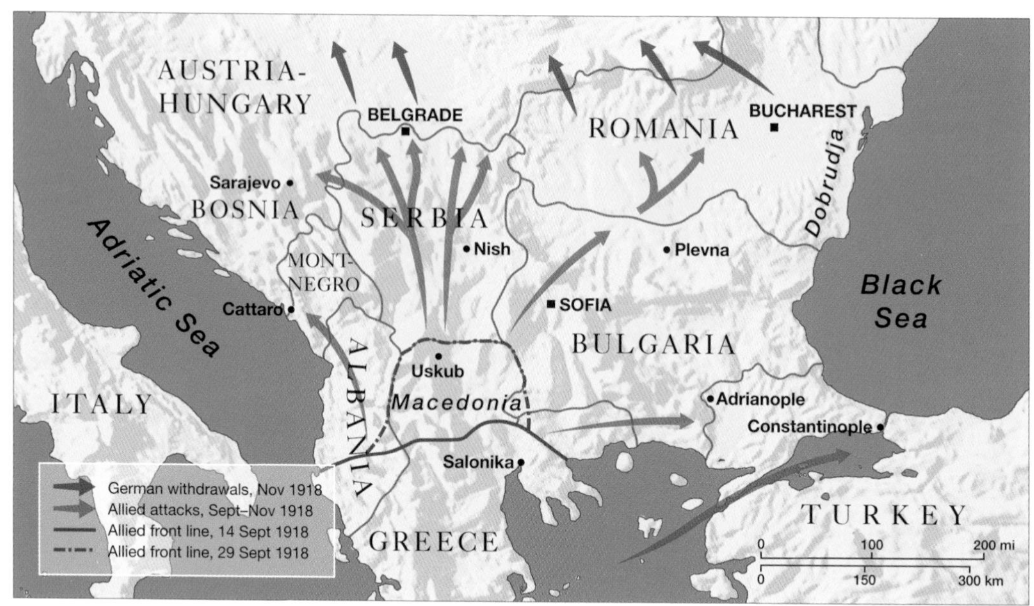

15 September when French and Serbian troops pushed forward on a 24km (15 mile) front. The Bulgarians fell back rapidly and Anglo-Greek forces made similarly good progress when they attacked around Lake Doiran on the 18th. Bulgaria was now so weak that it soon offered a ceasefire but the proposal was rejected by Franchet d'Espérey on the 25th and he ordered his command to press on. British units crossed into Bulgaria the same day, while the French took Uskub (Skopje) in southern Serbia on the 29th.

As pressure mounted elsewhere, especially on the Italian Front, Austria-Hungary began to withdraw its troops from the Balkans, chiefly from Albania, Montenegro and Serbia, and this further isolated Bulgaria. The Bulgarians sought an armistice on 26 September; the talks began in Salonika two days later and Bulgaria officially ceased fighting at 12.00 hours on the 30th.

This did not end the Allied push through the Balkans as Franchet d'Espérey's troops now fanned out in all directions. Serbian units on the western flank liberated their homeland as they advanced while to their right French troops moved into eastern Serbia and overran western Bulgaria. British troops pushed deeper into eastern and coastal Bulgaria and also began driving through European Turkey in the direction of Constantinople. Italian forces stationed in southern Albania joined in the general Allied advance, taking the north of the country from the collapsing Austro-Hungarian Army while Serbian forces liberated neighbouring Montenegro.

Above: Serbian troops on the march. They had the honour of liberating their own capital, Belgrade, on 1 November.

Last Acts

The crowning moment came on 1 November, when the Serbians liberated Belgrade, their capital which had been occupied since late 1915. An armistice with Austria-Hungary came into effect on the 4th at which point the various Allied forces were lined up along the River Danube, the Serb border with Austria-Hungary and Romania. Romania had been largely overrun by the Central Powers in 1917 and had signed the Treaty of Bucharest with Germany in May 1918 but in the last act of the war in the Balkans its government actually declared war on Germany for the second time on 10 November – just one day before the Armistice ended the conflict.

Right: Lightly wounded casualties are evacuated from a British first-aid dressing station by truck somewhere on the Salonika front, late 1918.

The Battle of Megiddo

Many British troops were withdrawn from Palestine in the early part of 1918, but the whole campaign was reinvigorated in September when a short, cleverly planned campaign shattered the opposing Turkish forces.

The British war effort in Palestine was virtually closed down for much of 1918 as their commander, General Edmund Allenby, saw a sizeable part of his forces, some 60,000 men in all, transferred to the Western Front to help deal with Germany's offensives there. Aside from a few minor operations by his own troops, Allenby had to rely on the Arab irregulars under Lawrence of Arabia on his right flank, who were harrying various Turkish positions and the Hejaz railway between Amman and Medina. Allenby was reinforced in late summer, especially by Indian troops, and he laid plans for what would be the final and most spectacular offensive of the campaign.

Three Turkish armies, some 35,000 men and 350 guns under the German General Otto Liman von Sanders, were holding a substantial defensive line running inland from the Mediterranean coast from a point a little north of Jaffa to the valley of the River Jordan. Allenby commanded some 55,000 infantry, 12,000 cavalry and 540 guns and planned to launch the bulk of them, 35,000 infantry and 400 guns, against the Mediterranean flank of the Turkish positions. This was defended by just 8,000 Turkish troops with 130 guns. Once a hole had been punched through the line, Allenby's cavalry would flood through and then the whole of the British line would swing north and east, pivoting on the Jordan Valley.

KEY FACTS

Date: 19–21 September 1918

Place: Palestine between Jericho and Jaffa

Outcome: The Turkish defenders were overwhelmed and forced into a headlong retreat.

Left: Senior British officers are shown around the Mosque of Omar, Jerusalem, in May 1918.

Deception Plans

Allenby used several ruses to mislead the Turks as to his true intentions. British fighters swept the few German aircraft from the skies preventing aerial

Below: A British supply column crossing a river in central Palestine on the eve of the Battle of Megiddo.

Above: Australians of the British-led Imperial Camel Corps in a camp near Jaffa.

GENERAL EDMUND ALLENBY

Allenby (1861–1936) was a cavalryman by training but took over the British Third Army in October 1915. He had frequent clashes with his superior, General, later Field Marshal, Douglas Haig, and was effectively demoted by transfer to Palestine in June 1917. The move transformed Allenby's faltering career and he proved a most imaginative commander, one who used aircraft, artillery, cavalry and infantry in a manner that has been likened to an early form of *Blitzkrieg*. His crowning moment came with the superbly managed Battle of Megiddo in September 1918.

reconnaissance; dummy camps and cavalry lines were built in the east near Jerusalem; a false date for the attack was leaked; and fake plans for horse races on the actual day were publicized. The offensive, known as the Battle of Megiddo, opened on 19 September and was spectacularly successful. The infantry on the coast quickly punched through the Turkish lines and the cavalry poured through, fanning out as they did so. Bombers and ground-attack aircraft struck at communications choke-points and Turkish headquarters all the while, making any cohesive response virtually impossible. The Turks were overwhelmed by the 21st and what began as a retreat soon turned into a wholesale rout.

Into Syria

Allenby drove his forces forward at lightning speed. Damascus was captured by Australian and Arab forces on 1 October and Beirut fell to an Indian division the next day. British mounted units continued to spearhead the advance and took Aleppo on the 26th in what was one of the last major actions of the war in the Middle East. By this stage of the conflict Turkey was crumbling fast and its envoys signed an armistice on the 30th after four days of discussions in Mudros harbour. Hostilities throughout the Middle East ended at noon the next day. Allenby had conducted a brilliant campaign – in 38 days he had advanced around 560km (350 miles) and effectively destroyed three Turkish armies, taking 76,000 prisoners in the process. His own losses were comparatively minor with some 850 men killed, 4,500 wounded and 380 missing.

The campaign in Palestine had effectively lasted from January 1915 to October 1918 and the British Empire forces suffered a total of 51,500 battle casualties, a figure that included some 5,300 ANZACs and 11,000 Indians. In all some 10,000 men were killed. Turkish losses are unknown but probably reached over 135,000, including more than 100,000 prisoners.

Right: Turkish prisoners, just some of the tens of thousands captured in the final weeks of the war.

Cruisers

Cruisers were a key component of all of the world's major navies during World War I and they were capable of operating both independently, often far from home waters, or as part of the main battlefleet in large-scale actions.

Cruisers were originally developed by the British Royal Navy in the latter part of the 19th century. They were smaller than existing battleships but faster and still able to undertake long-range, ocean missions. There were originally two types of cruisers. Armoured cruisers were deployed as scout warships with the main battle-fleet and had large-calibre armaments and significant side armour. Protected cruisers dispensed with the thick side armour but did have some deck armour. These types mainly operated in defence of trade routes or foreign naval stations, or formed the core of the squadrons deployed to defend imperial possessions. All of the combatant nations had cruisers of one type or another by the outbreak of war – for the Allies France had 37 and Russia 15, while for the Central Powers, Germany had 52 and Austria-Hungary 9.

Above: HMS *Warrior* was the lead vessel in a class of four armoured cruisers but was lost at Jutland.

Below: Germany's *Goeben*, a battle-cruiser, leads *Breslau*, one of a class of four light cruisers completed in 1912, out to sea.

Cruiser Roles

Britain had a large force of armoured cruisers in 1914, around 40, but they had in fact been made largely redundant in the scouting role with the main fleet thanks to the development of the dreadnought battle-cruiser, the first of which was launched in 1908. Britain also had some 100 protected cruisers on the eve of war but these increasingly gave way to lighter, faster types. Germany's heavier cruisers were largely relegated to secondary duties by the outbreak of war and its main High Seas Fleet relied mostly on light cruisers. The distinction between armoured and protected cruisers and light cruisers was quite stark. The last were roughly half the displacement, had a high speed and carried guns of much smaller calibre.

Nevertheless, both of the original types continued to see action. The British deployed them to hunt down Germany's surface raiders and sent them overseas where they formed the heart of the local squadrons, often along with older pre-dreadnought battleships. From 1917 onward they were also used nearer home as convoy escorts. Germany, in contrast, used many of its light cruisers to harry Allied shipping lanes and merchant ships in the first few months of the war before they were largely hunted down, although light cruisers also saw action with the country's main battlefleet.

Losses in Combat

Cruisers were therefore present at many major naval battles during the war. There were 13 British and German warships present at the Battle of the Falklands in late 1914, for example, and all but three, all British, were either armoured or light cruisers. Similarly, there were numerous cruisers at the biggest naval engagement of the war, the Battle of Jutland in 1916. The various parts of Britain's Grand Fleet mustered 8 armoured and 26 light cruisers while Germany's High Seas Fleet had 11 light cruisers.

Cruisers were potentially highly vulnerable in battles involving larger warships and this certainly proved to be the case at Jutland. Germany lost four light cruisers, including the *Rostock*, which had to be scuttled after suffering heavy damage from a torpedo fired by a British destroyer, and *Wiesbaden*, which went to the bottom after receiving multiple shell hits. *Elbing* and *Frauenlob* were also sunk by torpedoes. The Grand Fleet lost three of its armoured cruisers, *Black Prince*, *Defence* and *Warrior*, to gunfire from larger warships.

The Allies lost a total of 39 cruisers of all types during the war, while the Central Powers lost 28 to various causes.

LÉON GAMBETTA

The French armoured cruiser *Léon Gambetta* was largely designed for coastal defence and the protection of trade routes and was unfit to serve with the main fleet in large-scale actions, as even by contemporary standards it was slow and poorly armed. The *Léon Gambetta* was sunk in the Gulf of Otranto on the night of 24 April 1915, victim of a torpedo fired by the Austro-Hungarian submarine *U-5* (captained by top Austrian U-boat ace Georg Trapp, later made famous by the musical *The Sound of Music*).

Laid down: 1901
Displacement: 12,250 tons
Crew: 734
Speed: 22 knots
Main armament: 4 x 194mm (7.6in) and 16 x 164.7mm (6.4in) guns

HMS *BLACK PRINCE*

This British armoured cruiser was launched in 1907 and was stationed in the Mediterranean in 1914. It then served with the Grand Fleet's 1st Cruiser Squadron. During the Battle of Jutland in 1916 *Black Prince* was hit by 21 German shells, 15 of them from heavy guns, and sank with all hands.

Laid down: 1903
Displacement: 13,550 tons
Crew: 857
Speed: 23 knots
Main armament: 6 x 9.2in (234mm) and 10 x 6in (152mm) guns

Germany's Naval Mutiny

By late 1918 Germany had effectively lost World War I and both the armed forces and the home front were rocked by political unrest that became manifest in mutinies among the troops and street violence in many towns and cities.

In August 1914, Germany's decision-makers, effectively Emperor Wilhelm II, the men he appointed to his cabinet and the military, promulgated the idea that they were fighting a defensive war to counter French and Russian aggression. This was accepted by the German people and opposition politicians, including the left-leaning Social Democratic Party (SDP). They and their supporters agreed what was termed *Burgfrieden*, a political truce. This lasted until July 1917, when the main centre and left-wing parties united in the Reichstag (German parliament) to force through the "Peace Resolution", a demand for an end to hostilities without annexations or indemnities. It so enraged the military and right-wing parties that its publication effectively ended *Burgfrieden*.

Above: Armed naval mutineers photographed in central Berlin during November 1918.

Strikes and Hunger

Thanks to the ongoing British naval blockade, conditions for ordinary Germans worsened rapidly in 1918 and provoked increased civil unrest. One million workers went on strike in January, leading to a wave of repression and even the temporary arrest of the SDP's leader, Friedrich Ebert.

Matters deteriorated over the following months and in September Field Marshal Paul von Hindenburg and General Erich Ludendorff, who had effectively been running the country's political affairs since the collapse of the *Burgfrieden*, returned power to the Reichstag. They hoped to quell further unrest, preserve their own reputations and shift the blame for Germany's collapse on to the country's politicians. Prince Max of Baden was named as chancellor on 3 October and a coalition government dominated by moderate members of the SDP came to power. Ludendorff was fired on 26 October and Hindenburg retired.

Mutiny and Rebellion

Yet events were spiralling out of control as more radical elements demanded more substantial changes. This was especially so among groups like the Spartacus League, which had been invigorated by the previous year's Bolshevik takeover in Russia. The Imperial German Navy was not immune to such revolutionary zeal and Bolshevik-inspired agitators made use of a rumour that the fleet was to be deployed in a suicide sortie.

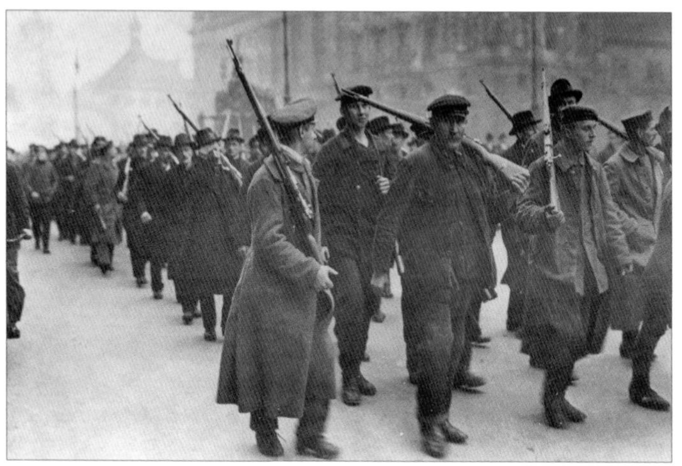

Left: Further signs of the collapse – rebel soldiers join forces with civilians to defy the government.

Above: Socialist activist Rosa Luxemburg was killed by right-wing paramilitaries in 1919.

SCUTTLING THE GERMAN FLEET

The Imperial German Navy was handed over to the Allies, chiefly the British, as part of the Armistice terms of November 1918. The various warships, including nine battleships and five battle-cruisers, sailed from Germany on the 21st and went into internment at the British base at Scapa Flow in the Orkneys the next day. Some of the ships' crews and captains remained on board and these resolved to scuttle their vessels if it looked like they would be handed over to the British as part of the Treaty of Versailles. The order to scuttle was given on 21 June 1919.

Below: The battle-cruiser *Hindenburg* after being scuttled by its crew.

Disgruntled sailors in Kiel, already fed up with poor conditions, mutinied on 3 November, allied themselves with strikers and issued demands for peace and reform. The unrest spread to other naval bases and then broke out in towns and cities across the country.

The government's response was too little, too late. Prince Max resigned on 9 November after announcing – without authority – that Wilhelm II had abdicated. Power was passed to Ebert, although the prince had no legal right to do this, and the Prince's vice-chancellor, Philipp Scheidemann, then announced – without Ebert's agreement – that Germany was to be a republic. Even this was not sufficient to stop the growing unrest. Ebert's provisional government became more and more convinced that the calls for peace and food were being used by the extremists to engineer revolution and the creation of a Bolshevik state.

Ebert turned to the new head of the German Army, the right-wing General Wilhelm Gröner. Gröner and a cabinet member, Gustav Noske, worked on a strategy to put down the unrest. Army units and *ad hoc* groups of ex-soldiers with right-wing sympathies, known as *Freikorps*, used great brutality to quell the revolutionaries. A rising by the Spartacists was dealt with very swiftly in January 1919 and their two leaders, Karl Liebknecht and Rosa Luxemburg, were murdered. The last pockets of resistance had been rooted out by April 1919.

Right: General Wilhelm Gröner, who acted to put down unrest in Germany during 1918–19.

The Peace Treaties British, Italian, French and US leaders at the Paris Peace Conference.

The League of Nations The Assembly of the League during one of its early sessions.

War and Remembrance Germany's grandiose memorial to the victorious Battle of Tannenberg.

0 100 200 300 400 500 mi
0 200 400 600 800 km
FINLAND
NORWAY
SWEDEN
ESTONIA
LATVIA
LITHUANIA
UNITED KINGDOM
North Sea
DENMARK
Baltic Sea
U S S R
Danzig
EAST PRUSSIA
NETHERLANDS
GERMANY
POLAND
BELGIUM
CZECHOSLOVAKIA
FRANCE
SWITZERLAND
AUSTRIA
HUNGARY
ROMANIA
Caspian Sea
YUGOSLAVIA
Black Sea
ITALY
BULGARIA
Corsica
ALBANIA
PERSIA
Sardinia
TURKEY
Mediterranean Sea
Sicily
GREECE
SYRIA (French)
IRAQ (British)
(Italian)
CYPRUS (British)
TUNISIA (French)
PALESTINE (British)
TRANS-JORDAN (British)
ALGERIA (French)
Suez Canal
LIBYA (Italian)
EGYPT (British)

THE AFTERMATH OF WAR

World War I has long been portrayed as an unnecessary war but this view has only a passing relationship with the truth. The various Allies fought for a variety of motives, some not always laudable, and some were to a degree culpable in its outbreak because of their pre-war actions, but they were right to go to war. The popularly accepted misreading of events in part occurred because the "Great War" was soon overshadowed by World War II, a conflict in which the issues were – and are – seen as being absolutely clear-cut. Yet many of the factors that make World War II a just and necessary war were present in 1914–18: the need to oppose dictatorships, naked military aggression, atrocities against civilians, the use of "uncivilized" weapons and genocide, for example, were all unfortunately present in World War I.

World War I was therefore a necessary war but it did not get the peace settlement it deserved. Some of the victors' aims were highly commendable but Britain and France largely wanted a return to a sort of pre-war status quo minus the Central Powers, while Germany was hit by draconian penalties. The treaties were largely if not entirely driven by self-interest and they undoubtedly played their part in the process that would lead to a new world war in just two decades.

The Armistice Joyful Londoners take to the streets to celebrate the end to the fighting in 1918.

The Peace Treaties A French guard of honour greets delegates at the Paris Peace Conference.

War and Remembrance The dedication of France's Tomb of the Unknown Soldier, Paris.

The Armistice

Germany was no longer able to maintain its war effort by October 1918 and in November sought an armistice. There was little in the way of discussion and the terms were wholly dictated by the Allies during a very brief meeting.

The last year of fighting saw Germany's fortunes transformed. In June 1918 its armies controlled more territory than at any other time in the war, yet a few months later the country had been roundly defeated by the Allies and was rent by revolutionary turmoil. There was no one reason why Germany lost the war but its position became untenable for several reasons – not least the British naval blockade, the ongoing arrival of huge numbers of US troops, the failure of its offensives in France between March and July and the succession of Allied attacks from mid-July onwards. The once superb German Army was increasingly undermined by falling morale and political agitation. Morale on the German home front was also collapsing, largely due to shortages of virtually every basic necessity; the political and industrial unrest that this was generating could not be contained.

Above: A joyous victory parade in New York. US troops return home to a thunderous reception.

Below: The other side of the coin. Dispirited German troops return home to little fanfare.

The ultimate cause of Germany's defeat was that the army chiefs who effectively ran the country, Field Marshal Hindenburg and General Ludendorff, finally realized that they had lost the war and, with that realization, they lost their nerve. The two generals effectively relinquished power in late September. They persuaded Emperor Wilhelm II to agree to ask for an armistice and accept that a new government, one not tainted by a close relationship to the crown or military, was needed. Prince Max of Baden became the new chancellor on 3 October and he sent pleas for an armistice to US President Woodrow Wilson on the basis of the latter's Fourteen Points peace proposal of January 1918. There was a flurry of diplomatic notes between the Allies and with Germany before the latter finally agreed to the last of the various Allied pre-conditions, including the abdication of the emperor, on the 20th.

Armistice Talks

Prince Max finally decided to begin substantive talks on 6 November and a delegation was put together, made up of middle-ranking politicians and comparatively junior military officers. Discussions on the details of the

Armistice began at Compiègne, the headquarters of the *de facto* Allied Commander-in-Chief, Marshal Ferdinand Foch, on 8 November. Foch headed a purely Anglo-French delegation and it soon became apparent to the German delegation, headed by Matthias Erzberger, that there was to be no discussion on the basis of Wilson's Fourteen Points but merely a list of draconian demands.

Above: Emperor Wilhelm (third from left) waits at the Dutch–German border as a refugee. He spent the remainder of his life in exile.

Punishing Germany

There were 34 clauses in all and they were essentially designed to cripple Germany militarily and economically. Among other things they required German troops to evacuate all occupied territories in 14 days, including Alsace and Lorraine, and within 28 days Allied troops would take over Germany west of the Rhine and establish bridgeheads to the east up to a depth of some 32km (20 miles). Huge quantities of weapons, 5,000 locomotives, 150,000 pieces of rolling stock, 10,000 trucks, and all submarines and warships were to be given up. All monies taken from foreign banks were to be handed over, there were to be reparations, and the naval blockade was to remain in force.

These clauses stunned the German delegates but, after seeking higher approval, they signed the Armistice at 05.05 hours on the morning of 11 November and it came into force at 11.00 hours. The war was finally over but the peace treaties had yet to be signed.

PRESIDENT WILSON'S FOURTEEN POINTS

US President Woodrow Wilson made several attempts to broker a peace deal culminating in this set of proposals that were put before Congress on 8 January 1918. The first five points covered general principles for a new world, including freedom of the seas, an end to secret treaties and arms limitation. Points 6 to 13 addressed specific territorial issues, such as the Franco-German dispute over Alsace and Lorraine. Point 14 called for the establishment of an international body to settle disputes between member nations.

Right: Londoners celebrate the peace in November 1918, a scene of rejoicing common in towns and cities across Europe.

The Peace Treaties

Although President Wilson wanted to ensure that Germany was not humiliated by Britain and France, he was out-manoeuvred and the Treaty of Versailles imposed harsh reparations on the defeated country that left a legacy of bitterness.

World War I did not end in November 1918, only the fighting stopped. The war was formally concluded by a series of peace treaties, each named after a Paris suburb where the talks were conducted. The discussions, together known as the Paris Peace Conference, lasted from 12 January 1919 until 20 January 1920. The conference was attended by the leaders of 32 Allied countries and Associated Powers and 23 other states that were classified as "powers with special interests", including the Arabs of the Hejaz. Controlling affairs were the major victorious powers – Britain, France, Italy, Japan and the United States – who were collectively known as "powers with general interests". None of the former Central Powers was invited to attend and Russia's Bolshevik government simply refused to travel to Paris.

Above: Allied war leaders meet for the Paris Peace Conference. From left: David Lloyd George, Vittorio Orlando, Georges Clemenceau and Woodrow Wilson.

Below: The signing of the Treaty of Versailles in the Palace's Hall of Mirrors, 28 June 1919.

Aims of the Powers

Two representatives from each power with general interests formed the Council of Ten, a body that was originally established to look into questions of humanitarian aid but soon took on a wider brief and began considering territorial questions. From March 1919 the Council of Four, the leaders of the powers with general interests minus Japan, dominated the ever more fractious discussions.

Left: British troops move into Germany after the Armistice. Allied forces occupied German territory up to the left bank of the River Rhine.

US President Woodrow Wilson looked for conciliation with the Central Powers, especially Germany, while France's Prime Minister Georges Clemenceau wanted to impose severe terms on the defeated. His British counterpart, David Lloyd George, took something of a middle course, while Vittorio Orlando, the Italian Premier, was only concerned with making territorial gains in and around the Mediterranean. He left the conference in April after the other Allies had agreed to give part of the eastern Adriatic to the new state of Yugoslavia.

Treaties Agreed

Five treaties were eventually agreed – Trianon with Hungary (4 June 1919), Versailles with Germany (28 June 1919), St Germain with Austria (10 September 1919), Neuilly with Bulgaria (27 November 1919), and Sèvres with Turkey (10 August 1920). The treaties were in some respects not dissimilar in that they imposed on the Central Powers, especially Germany, various territorial losses, financial reparations and military restrictions. These terms were severe enough to cause lasting resentment among the defeated, particularly in Germany, which was hit hardest and also had to accept a war guilt clause that made it alone wholly responsible for the outbreak of World War I.

Although he secured agreement to establish the League of Nations, a prototype for today's United Nations, Wilson was thwarted in several ambitions, largely due to Britain and France's self-interests. He did manage to create a number of new nation states out of the old Austro-Hungarian Empire but Britain and France stepped in when it came to the Turkish Empire and took over several territories, including Syria, Lebanon and Palestine, as neo-colonial mandates. Japan was permitted to take Chinese territory that had been seized from Germany in 1914, a decision that led China, a power with special interests, to reject the conference's decisions. The Paris Peace Conference actually left many issues unresolved and satisfied few of those who attended. Indeed, the various peace treaties were never fully adopted and the US Congress refused to ratify the Treaty of Versailles when it was put to the vote in November 1919. Wilson's League of Nations project did go ahead but in a much-weakened form.

Right: A French honour guard stands to attention as delegates arrive to discuss the final terms of the Treaty of Trianon with Hungary.

The League of Nations

US President Woodrow Wilson successfully argued for an international body to settle issues between its member states but, although it was a laudable ambition, the League of Nations never really functioned and it faced a succession of major crises.

President Woodrow Wilson went to the Paris Peace Conference of 1919–20 wanting the negotiations to progress along the lines suggested in his Fourteen Points peace proposal of January 1918. This was a document of intent for a safer, more democratic post-war world and one of its key clauses called for the creation of a League of Nations, an international body to arbitrate on differences between states and maintain peace. To some extent his idea captured the mood of the time as many had come to reject the tenets of pre-war diplomacy with its emphasis on maintaining the balance of power and secret treaties.

The League established its headquarters in the city of Geneva in Switzerland, a traditionally neutral country, in 1920 and it had three main bodies. The Secretariat, under a secretary-general, was a permanent body of officials from all of the member states. The Assembly also included representatives of all the member states and each country had one vote. It oversaw the greater part of the League's activities, including its budget, and met annually, although much of its work was undertaken by committees. The Council was originally made up of the five permanent members – Britain, France, Italy, Japan and the United States – and four members elected by the Assembly. The Council met at least every three months, or more often whenever there was an international crisis, and each member had a single vote. The number of permanent members rose to six in 1922 and to nine in 1926.

Above: The League of Nations Assembly in session.

Below: The rise of Italian fascism – Benito Mussolini (in suit) marches on Rome in a successful bid to win dictatorial powers, late 1922.

Above: Troops muster during the Russo-Polish War of 1920. Poland, once part of Russia, was a creation of the peace settlements.

Above: French troops march into the Ruhr in January 1923 after Germany had defaulted on its reparations payments.

Tasks for the League

The League also established a number of other bodies to look at various problems. The Permanent Court of Justice was established at The Hague in the Netherlands in 1921 and consisted of 15 judges of various nationalities who settled legal disputes brought before them. The Mandates Commission oversaw Germany's former colonies and some parts of the former Turkish Empire, while the Disarmament Commission was to control the sale of arms and limit their manufacture. The International Labour Organization was entrusted with improving workers' pay and conditions and monitored trade unions also. The Health Organization coordinated international responses to outbreaks of cholera and typhus in post-war Europe and also had a broader remit to investigate world health.

Success at First

The League of Nations had many laudable aims and it did have some early successes, dealing peacefully with disputes between Finland and Sweden (1921), Germany and Poland (1921), Italy and Greece (1923) and Turkey and Iraq (1924). Yet in truth it was a weak organization that to some seemed too Euro-centric and dominated by the victors of World War I. The United States, which was retreating into isolationism, never actually became a full member; the USSR was a late addition to its membership; and Germany only joined in 1926. The League also lacked financial resources and could only use economic sanctions to enforce its rulings as there were no clear rules for using military force against an erring state.

These weaknesses became clear in the 1930s, when right-wing, militaristic states openly challenged the League. Among these were Benito Mussolini's Fascist Italy and Adolf Hitler's Nazi Germany; Japan simply walked out of the League when its aggression in Manchuria was criticized. The outbreak of World War II in 1939 consigned the League to the dustbin of history but it was not formally dissolved until 18 April 1946.

Right: The Nazi Beer Hall Putsch of November 1923 failed but saw the emergence of Adolf Hitler on to the wider German political scene.

War and Remembrance

There was no single response to the outbreak of peace in November 1918 except relief that the bloodletting was over, and our current attitudes to the conflict have been largely moulded by a series of mythologies rather than hard historical fact.

There is no doubt that many of the world's leading nations paid a high price for taking part in World War I. In broad terms some 65 million men were mobilized between 1914 and 1918 and of these some 42 million served with the various Allies and 22 million with the four Central Powers. The Allies recorded around 4.8 million dead and 12 million wounded, while the Central Powers' figures are roughly 3.1 million and 8.4 million. Civilian deaths, excluding those from influenza, totalled some 6.6 million.

The initial public response to the end of this immense carnage varied considerably. Many people were certainly left grieving or nursing both physical and psychological wounds, while

Above: The memorial at Thiepval on the Somme to 72,000 British troops with no known grave.

Below: The main French cemetery at Verdun, including the vast ossuary housing bones of the unidentified.

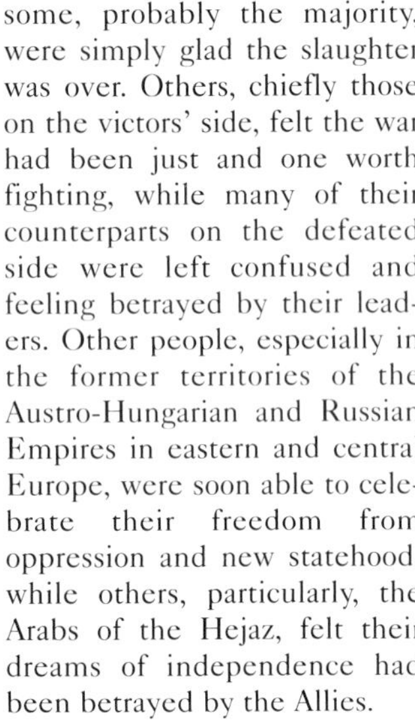

some, probably the majority, were simply glad the slaughter was over. Others, chiefly those on the victors' side, felt the war had been just and one worth fighting, while many of their counterparts on the defeated side were left confused and feeling betrayed by their leaders. Other people, especially in the former territories of the Austro-Hungarian and Russian Empires in eastern and central Europe, were soon able to celebrate their freedom from oppression and new statehood, while others, particularly, the Arabs of the Hejaz, felt their dreams of independence had been betrayed by the Allies.

A Futile War?

World War I has in many ways become mythologized down the decades and no more so than in Britain, where it is largely associated with waste and futility. This is probably in part due to the fact that Britain, almost alone among the combatants, suffered more casualties in World War I than in World War II. But it is also down to bad history. People on the Allied side did believe the war had a just purpose – the British Victory Medal of 1918, for example, carried the words: "The Great War For Civilisation" and the earliest Armistice Days were more about celebrating comradeship than commemorating the dead. Similarly, Germany's biggest memorial to the war was not to its own dead but a massive monument celebrating the victory over the Russians at the Battle of Tannenberg in 1914.

The still widely held view of a pointless war actually began to emerge in the late 1920s, largely due to a plethora of semi-fictionalized personal accounts that highlighted the undoubtedly horrible realities of trench warfare, books like Erich Maria Remarque's *All Quiet on the Western Front* and Robert Graves's *Goodbye to All That*, and the work of poets like Wilfred Owen and Siegfried Sassoon. But these had their counterpoints – Ernst Jünger's *Storm of Steel* positively revels in the war. Yet it was the former that were ultimately more persuasive and helped to engender the myth that the lives of brave men had been wasted by incompetent and unfeeling commanders.

ALL QUIET ON THE WESTERN FRONT

This fictionalized study of German troops on the Western Front, published in 1929 by the pacifist German author Erich Maria Remarque, was one of a slew of mostly anti-war books written in the 1920s and has greatly coloured perception of the conflict. It tells the story of a group of German soldiers, some young, some older, and the somewhat ironic title refers to the "official" German Army communiqué issued on the day that the central character is killed. The book has been filmed on a number of occasions but the US version released in 1930 is widely regarded as the most successful adaptation.

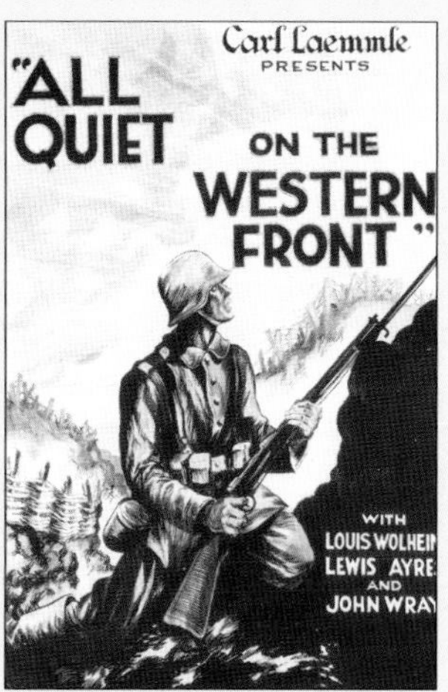

Above: A poster for the first film based on Remarque's book.

JUDGING THE GENERALS

The reality was that most, if not all, generals were both competent and caring and that trench warfare, which was by no means universal, was a product of a temporary technological imbalance that favoured defensive over offensive weapons and tactics. The generals of the time recognized this and tried many ways to overcome the stagnation of trench warfare – different types of artillery barrage, the use of gas and tanks, for example – but the reality was that they were only just able to succeed by 1918. Perhaps the saddest myth concerning World War I was that held by those who had lived through it and, like the author H. G. Wells, believed they had survived "The War to End All Wars".

Below: The dedication ceremony of the grave of France's unknown soldier underneath the Arc de Triomphe in Paris.

Below: Germany's memorial to the Battle of Tannenberg. Hitler ordered the site to be levelled as advancing Soviet forces neared in World War II.

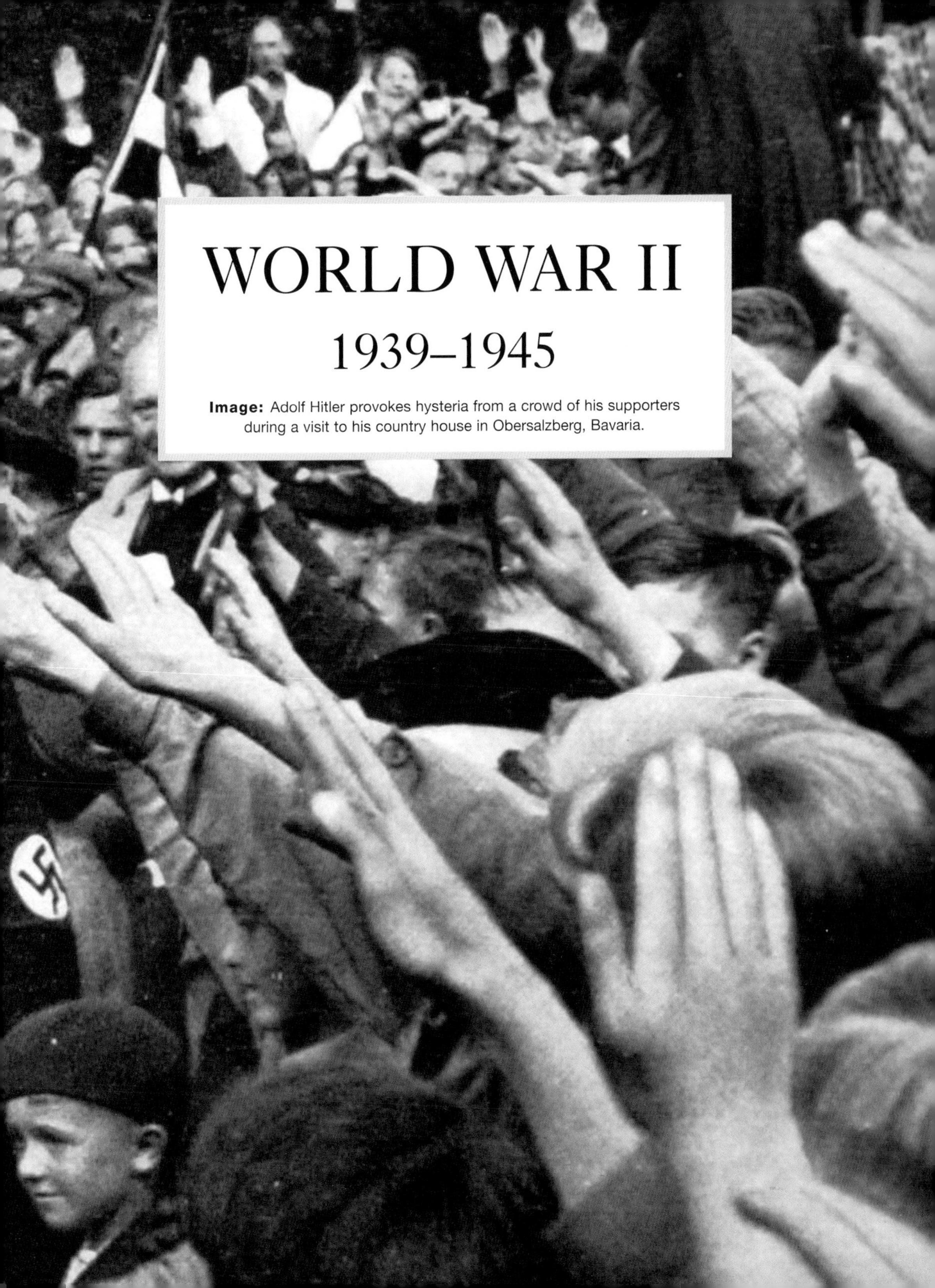

WORLD WAR II

1939–1945

Image: Adolf Hitler provokes hysteria from a crowd of his supporters during a visit to his country house in Obersalzberg, Bavaria.

Timeline

World War II was truly a global conflict, with inter-related campaigns being fought simultaneously on land and in the air across vast areas of Europe, Asia and Africa and in every ocean.

1931–38

INTERNATIONAL EVENTS Japan begins occupation of Manchuria (Sept 1931); Hitler becomes German Chancellor (Jan 1933); Italy invades Abyssinia (Oct 1935); Germany occupies Rhineland (Mar 1936); Italy annexes Abyssinia (May 1936); Japan invades China (July 1937); "Rape of Nanking" (Dec 1937); Germany annexes Austria (Mar 1938); Germany begins occupation of Czechoslovakia (Oct 1938)

1939

INTERNATIONAL EVENTS Britain and France ally with Poland (Mar); Nazi–Soviet Pact agreed (23 Aug); Britain, France, Australia, India and New Zealand declare war on Germany (3 Sept); South Africa declares war on Germany (6 Sept); Canada declares war on Germany (10 Sept); US "Cash and Carry" law starts (Nov)
POLISH CAMPAIGN Germany invades Poland (1 Sept); USSR invades Poland (17 Sept); Warsaw captured (27 Sept); last Polish troops surrender (3 Oct)
RUSSO-FINNISH WAR USSR invades Finland (30 Nov)

1940

INTERNATIONAL EVENTS Italy declares war on France and UK (10 June); Baltic States seized by USSR (July); Italy, Germany and Japan agree Tripartite Pact (Sept); UK–USA "destroyers for bases" deal (Sept)
RUSSO-FINNISH WAR Ends with partial Soviet victory (12 Mar)
NORWAY AND DENMARK Germany invades (9 Apr); Allied resistance ends (9 June)
WESTERN FRONT Germany invades France and Low Countries (10 May); Dunkirk evacuation (26 May–4 June); French surrender (22 June)
BRITAIN Winston Churchill becomes Prime Minister (10 May); Battle of Britain (Aug–Sept); Blitz against British cities (Sept–May 1941)
UNITED STATES Conscription introduced (Sept); President Roosevelt re-elected (Nov)
BALKANS Italy invades Greece from Albania (Oct)
NORTH AFRICA Italy invades Egypt (Sept); British counter-attack begins (9 Dec)

1941

INTERNATIONAL EVENTS Lend-Lease Act becomes law in USA (Mar); Japanese–Soviet neutrality agreement (Apr); Romania and Italy declare war on USSR (22 June); Japan's assets in USA frozen (July); USA and UK agree Atlantic Charter (12 Aug); UK declares war on Finland, Hungary and Romania; UK, USA and many other nations declare war on Japan (8 Dec); Germany and Italy declare war on USA (11 Dec)
BALKANS Germans conquer Yugoslavia (6–17 Apr); Germans conquer mainland Greece (6–30 Apr); Germans invade Crete (20 May–1 June)
NORTH AFRICA German troops arrive (Feb); British Crusader offensive begins (18 Nov)
EASTERN FRONT Germany invades USSR (22 June); Smolensk pocket eliminated (5 Aug); Kiev encirclement complete (19 Sept); German attack on Moscow starts (2 Oct); Moscow counter-offensive begins (5 Dec); Hitler takes over as Commander-in-Chief of German Army (19 Dec)
PACIFIC WAR Japan attacks Pearl Harbor (7 Dec); Japan attacks Malaya and Philippines (8 Dec)

1942

INTERNATIONAL EVENTS United Nations Declaration issued by Allies (1 Jan)

HOLOCAUST Nazi Wannsee Conference plans "Final Solution" (20 Jan)
PACIFIC WAR Japanese capture Manila (2 Jan); Japanese capture Singapore (15 Feb); US troops surrender in Philippines (8 Apr); Battle of Coral Sea (7–9 May); Battle of Midway (4–6 June); US landings on Guadalcanal (7 Aug)
EASTERN FRONT Battle of Kharkov (15–27 May); Battle of Stalingrad begins (mid-Sept); Soviet counter-offensive near Stalingrad (19 Nov)
NORTH AFRICA Rommel attacks Gazala Line (26 May); Battle of El Alamein (23 Oct–4 Nov); Operation Torch begins (8 Nov)

1943

INTERNATIONAL EVENTS Casablanca Conference, Allies announce unconditional surrender policy (14–24 Jan); Italy surrenders to Allies (8 Sept); Italy declares war on Germany (13 Oct); UK, USSR and USA meet in Teheran Conference (Nov–Dec)
PACIFIC WAR Allied landings on New Georgia (20 June); US landings in Gilbert Islands (20 Nov)
EASTERN FRONT German surrender at Stalingrad (2 Feb); Battle of Kursk begins (5 July); Kiev falls to Soviets (6 Nov)
NORTH AFRICA Battle of Kasserine (14–24 Feb); Axis surrender in Tunisia (13 May)
ITALY Invasion of Sicily (10 July); capture of Sicily complete (17 Aug); Salerno landings (9 Sept)

1944

INTERNATIONAL EVENTS Romania agrees armistice with Allies, declares war on Germany (23 & 25 Aug); Bulgaria surrenders (8 Sept); Finland agrees armistice (10 Sept)
EASTERN FRONT End of siege of Leningrad (27 Jan); Soviets capture Minsk (3 July); Warsaw Rising (1 Aug–2 Oct); Partisans liberate Belgrade (20 Oct)
MEDITERRANEAN Allied landings at Anzio (22 Jan); Rome liberated (4 June); British liberate Athens (14 Oct)
WESTERN FRONT D-Day (6 June); Normandy breakout (1 Aug); landings in southern France (15 Aug); Allies capture Antwerp (4 Sept); Operation Market-Garden (17–26 Sept); Battle of Bulge begins (16 Dec)
PACIFIC Battle of Philippine Sea (19–20 June); landings on Leyte (20 Oct); Battle of Leyte Gulf (24–6 Oct)
BURMA Battles of Imphal and Kohima (Mar–July)

1945

INTERNATIONAL EVENTS Roosevelt dies, Truman becomes President of USA (12 Apr); Hitler commits suicide (30 Apr); Germans surrender in: Italy (2 May), north Germany (4 May), sign overall surrender (7 May); VE-Day (8 May); Potsdam Conference (17 July–2 Aug); Attlee becomes UK Prime Minister (26 July); USSR declares war on Japan (8 Aug); Japan agrees surrender (14 Aug); VJ-Day (15 Aug); Japan signs surrender (2 Sept)
WESTERN FRONT Allies cross Rhine at Remagen (7 Mar); US and Soviet troops meet on Elbe (25 Apr)
EASTERN FRONT Soviets take Warsaw (17 Jan); Vienna falls to Soviets (13 Apr); fighting ends in Berlin (2 May); last German troops surrender in Czechoslovakia (13 May)
BURMA British capture Mandalay (20 Mar); British capture Rangoon (3 May)
PACIFIC Landings on Luzon (9 Jan); landings on Iwo Jima (19 Feb); landings on Okinawa (1 Apr); A-bomb attack on Hiroshima (6 Aug); Soviet attack in Manchuria and A-bomb attack on Nagasaki (9 Aug)

Troubled Times – USA and USSR Soviet paratroop training during the 1930s.

Failing Economies A disabled war veteran begging in the streets of Berlin in the 1920s.

Fascism and Nazism Horst Wessel, later lauded as a martyr in the Nazi cause, on parade in 1929.

FINLAND
NORWAY
SWEDEN
ESTONIA
UNITED KINGDOM
North Sea
Baltic Sea
LATVIA
U S S R
DENMARK
LITHUANIA
Danzig
EAST PRUSSIA
NETHER-LANDS
GERMANY
POLAND
BELGIUM
CZECHOSLOVAKIA
FRANCE
Caspian Se
SWITZER-LAND
AUSTRIA
HUNGARY
ROMANIA
YUGOSLAVIA
Black Sea
ITALY
BULGARIA
Corsica
ALBANIA
PERS
Sardinia
TURKEY
Mediterranean Sea
Sicily
GREECE
SYRIA (French)
IRAQ (British)
Dodecanese (Italian)
CYPRUS (British)
TUNISIA (French)
Crete
PALESTINE (British)
TRANS-JORDAN (British)
ALGERIA (French)
Suez Canal
LIBYA (Italian)
EGYPT (British)
0 100 200 300 400 500
0 200 400 600 800

APPROACH TO WAR

World War I – the "war to end all wars" – had been centred in Europe but in fact it solved few of Europe's problems. Indeed, it established other problems that the dictators and militarists of the 1930s would exploit to achieve their ends, or so they hoped – but instead this went on to create a new and more terrible conflict.

WWI had been the most costly conflict in human history, both in terms of loss of life and in physical destruction. Not only the killing but the whole process of war production had been thoroughly mechanized and industrialized. Previous standards of humane conduct in types of weapons used and the involvement of civilians were also quickly disregarded. World War II would take all these trends to new extremes.

Germany's ability to dominate Europe had not been removed by WWI. The public will for this to happen remained a force in German life, not just for Hitler and his fellow fascists. Similarly, Japan's leaders, victorious Allies in WWI, came to feel that they had been denied their just rewards and that their national destiny was being circumscribed by racist Europeans and Americans. In these tough economic times, other nations failed to respond well to such issues. Some chose isolationism, others negotiation – and its feeble cousin appeasement – backed by a half-hearted rearmament. When faced with enemies who were happy to start wars whenever it suited them, these strategies were inadequate.

Troubled Times – Western Europe Nationalist troops in Madrid during the Spanish Civil War.

Fascism and Nazism Mussolini (wearing red sash) seized power in Italy in 1922.

Troubled Times – USA and USSR Josef Stalin's purges gravely weakened the USSR in the 1930s.

The Legacy of World War I

The peace settlement that ended the Great War stored up many problems for the future. The former Anglo-French Commander-in-Chief, Marshal Ferdinand Foch, made the best assessment: "This is not a treaty. It is an armistice for twenty years."

The victorious Allies came to Paris for the negotiation of the treaties to end World War I determined to prevent a repetition of the conflict. However, the steps they took to achieve this proved to be ill-judged. Separate treaties were agreed with each of the former Central Powers (usually referred to as the Treaty of Versailles, however, in fact this was the one concluded with only Germany). The three most powerful victors (the USA, Britain and France) dominated the negotiations, though representatives from many other Allied countries were also present.

However, the leaders of the new USSR and the old Russia were still fighting a destructive and divisive civil war and were not included in talks. Also absent were representatives of the defeated Central Powers; they would be summoned to sign once the text of the treaties had been agreed but had no say in negotiations. These absences were the source of the first great weakness of the Versailles settlement: in Germany, in particular, it would be characterized in years to come as the "Dictate of Versailles" and therefore by definition was rejected as unjust.

Above: The signing of the Treaty of Versailles in the Hall of Mirrors at the palace of Versailles.

A New Europe

The treaties redrew the map of Europe, which again stored up trouble for the future. The Austro-Hungarian Empire was cut apart: Austria and Hungary became separate nations and two new nations, Czechoslovakia and Yugoslavia, were founded. Romania took territory from Hungary and Bulgaria, while the Baltic States became independent, largely being created from the Russian Empire. So, too, was Poland, which also included a former German province and, more controversially, gained access to the sea via the "Polish Corridor" at Danzig. This split the main part of Germany from the province of East Prussia. France regained Alsace and Lorraine, taken by Germany after the Franco-Prussian War

Below: Anti-communist White Russian cavalry in action during the Russian Civil War of 1919–21.

of 1870–1. Belgium and even Denmark also gained former German territory. In all Germany lost 13 per cent of its pre-war area, while its colonies became possessions of one or other of the Allies.

Germany's armed forces were to be reduced to a fraction of their previous size. To add yet more resentment, Germany had to accept a clause stating that the war had been entirely its fault (which was far from true) and that Germany must therefore pay substantial financial reparations for the damage and destruction caused. The size of the bill was to be fixed later.

Above: The German battle-cruiser *Hindenburg* scuttled by its crew in protest over the peace negotiations.

Growing Resentment

There were many problems with all this, not just in the anger stored up in Germany at what were in many ways real injustices. Almost none of the new nations had an ethnically homogeneous population and most were unhappy with where their borders had been set. Although Britain and France were obviously the most powerful European nations, having suffered so much in the war and with problems of their own they were unwilling to take the lead in making the settlement work.

To perform such a role a new international body, the League of Nations, was set up, largely at the urging of the USA's President Woodrow Wilson. However, it remained to be seen how well it would function and, sadly, from the beginning it was limited by the refusal of the US Congress to allow the USA to join.

None of this made World War II inevitable, or anything like it, but anger at the way Germany had been treated did inspire an ex-corporal called Adolf Hitler to join a tiny radical political group named the German Workers' Party in Munich in September 1919.

THE WASHINGTON NAVAL TREATY

Japan, one of the Allied powers in WWI, felt that it had not been adequately rewarded for its efforts because the Versailles Treaty granted it little more than a handful of former German islands in the Pacific. By the early 1920s a naval arms race had developed, with Japan, the USA and Britain all making plans for fleets of new and huge battleships, which in truth no one really wanted or could afford. In February 1922 these three, along with France and Italy, agreed the Washington Treaty to limit their future naval forces. The Japanese, in particular, were reluctant signatories and would come to believe that, yet again, they had been swindled of their just status by a racist conspiracy of Anglo-Saxons. Although the Treaty and later successors would remain in force until the late 1930s, this became another source of trouble for the future.

Below: French troops occupying Essen in the Rhineland in 1919.

Failing Economies

The world economy had been left unbalanced by the debts owed both by the victors and the losers after WWI, and national leaders, with little idea how to manage their domestic economies, were unable to respond effectively to the problems this caused.

The years immediately after WWI saw many hardships and political problems for people all around the world, not just in defeated Germany. Both the Nazi Party and Italian Fascism had their origins in this period. Then, after a period of growing prosperity and seeming progress toward international amity, the collapse of American share prices in 1929 ushered in the Great Depression and an era of political turmoil.

In all the former warring countries, ex-soldiers had to find their way back into civil society but did not always find jobs easy to come by; the many disabled veterans found life particularly difficult.

Poverty was an everyday reality for millions of war widows and orphans. Those higher up the social scale worried that the turmoil of Russia's communist revolution might spread. In Germany right-wingers formed militias to fight socialists and revolutionaries, and in Britain and other countries troops clashed in the streets with strikers and other protesters.

Above: A German housewife uses worthless paper money to light her stove during the 1923 crisis.

Below: Having left Germany when the Versailles Treaty was signed, French troops returned in 1923 when reparations payments were delayed.

With its economic struggles, Germany fell behind in its reparations payments. In retaliation French and Belgian troops occupied the Ruhr in January 1923, an action that triggered a financial crisis and massive inflation in Germany. By late 1923 the mark's foreign exchange value was 130 billion to the dollar. In Germany money was virtually worthless paper and many in the middle classes saw their savings wiped out.

American Loans

In 1924 an Allied committee, which was led by American banker Charles Dawes (shortly to become US Vice-President), set up a new plan for Germany's reparations payments, which brought stability and growth to the German economy (but only on the back of US loans). Other countries were also heavily indebted to the USA for loans raised during WWI; they, too, struggled to repay these because of a decline in international trade, partly caused by the USA's protectionist measures.

For the moment, however, the American economy and stock market were booming, while in international affairs

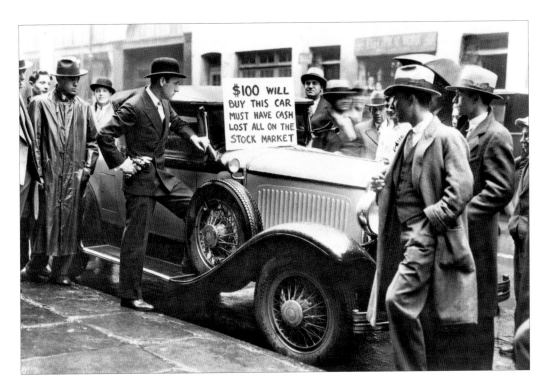

Above: Fooled by steadily rising returns through the 1920s, many Americans speculated on the stock market and had to pay the price.

there seemed to be other promising signs. In 1926 Germany joined the League of Nations and seemed to be reasonably stable in its domestic politics, even though radical parties of both left and right had significant followings.

In 1928 a range of leading nations even signed a treaty – called the Kellogg–Briand Pact (after the US secretary of state and the French foreign minister who led the negotiations) – by which they agreed to renounce the use of aggressive war as an instrument of national policy. Obviously, this agreement did not fulfil its aims, but it has remained important in international law. It would be used after WWII to support a number of the charges made against the leaders of Germany and Japan by the International War Crimes Tribunals.

Below: A street scene in the early 1920s, in fact in Berlin but with equivalents in many places.

In 1929 a plan proposed by Owen Young, another American banker, finally fixed the amount of war reparations Germany still had to pay. Though the terms were milder than those previously in force, many Germans still believed they were overly harsh, even if they allowed this issue finally to be closed.

Economic Collapse

Then, in October 1929, prices collapsed on New York's Stock Exchange and the credit that had financed the USA's own economic growth and kept many foreign economies healthy dried up. Soon there would be millions of unemployed in all industrialized nations and great opportunities for politicians offering radical solutions to these problems.

Fascism and Nazism

In Italy, and then in Germany, radical political movements with dominating leaders took control of the governments and then the whole of national life, remaking these countries in a new, violent, intolerant and ultra-nationalist form.

Both Italy and Germany saw much use of violence to suppress strikes and socialist activities immediately after WWI. In Italy the National Fascist Party, which was led by journalist and war veteran Benito Mussolini, was prominent in these activities. Backed by numerous party thugs (*squadristi*, or Blackshirts), Mussolini took advantage of continuing political instability to have himself appointed Prime Minister in 1922. Then, in 1924–5, a further crisis (caused by the Blackshirt murder of a leading socialist) saw Mussolini discard the pretence of constitutional rule and begin the process of making Italy a fascist state.

Below: A Nazi parade in 1929, led by Horst Wessel, later celebrated as a martyr in the Nazi cause.

Above: Mussolini (wearing sash), during the 1922 "March on Rome" when he seized power in Italy.

Fascist Rule

Mussolini's message was ultranationalist and stated that the good of the nation came before any individual rights or liberties. Elections were first rigged and then abolished, as were political parties and freedom of speech; fascist organizations were set up in every walk of life, starting with one for boys of six and upward. Mussolini himself became *Il Duce* ("the leader") and took unchallenged control of the government, supported by propaganda that claimed, among other things: "Mussolini is always right."

Hitler's rise to power in Germany followed a similar though rather longer route. After building his tiny political party, renamed the National Socialist German Workers' Party, into a significant local force, Hitler mounted an attempted coup in Munich in 1923. This "Beer Hall Putsch" failed and Hitler was jailed for a time. However, he did gain a national reputation from this event – one of his co-conspirators was General Erich Ludendorff, one of Germany's most famous soldiers in WWI.

In jail Hitler wrote his political manifesto *Mein Kampf* (usually translated as "My Struggle"), which set out very clearly the core of his beliefs: a hatred of Jews and communists and an intention to gain new territory for the German race in eastern Europe (*Lebensraum*, or "living space").

Nazis in Power

Hitler and his party remained fairly minor players until the world economic crash began in 1929. Now allied with big business interests and preaching that Germany's ills were caused

ADOLF HITLER

Hitler (1889–1945) alone did not cause WWII, but he did more than anyone else to bring it about. His ideas and plans shaped the war's character, helping make it the most brutal conflict in human history. Hitler, an Austrian by birth, fought as a German soldier in WWI and went into politics shortly after, disgusted by the outcome of the war. His political views were based on anti-communism and anti-semitism, and a sense of his own and Germany's destiny to rule. His regime was chaotic and, as time went by, his orders were increasingly irrational. He was as responsible for Germany's ruinous defeat in 1945 as he had been for the astonishing successes of the early war years.

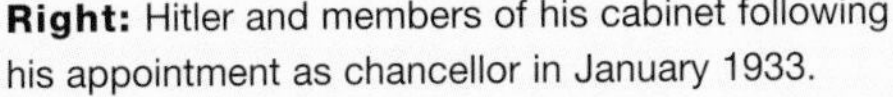

Right: Hitler and members of his cabinet following his appointment as chancellor in January 1933.

from abroad and by the detested Treaty of Versailles, Hitler found substantial new support.

In 1932 the Nazis became the largest party in the Reichstag (Germany's parliament). After further elections and some complicated political manoeuvring, Hitler was then appointed as chancellor at the head of a multi-party government by President Hindenburg in January 1933.

By late 1934, after Hindenburg's death, Hitler had taken complete control and ruled with legally acquired emergency powers. He became the *Führer* ("leader"), combining the offices of president and chancellor; all opposition political parties were banned; concentration camps, the Gestapo secret police and the rest of the apparatus of a police state were established; and the members of Germany's armed forces all swore a loyalty oath to Hitler personally.

In 1934 Hitler also confirmed his own supremacy within the Nazi movement in the "Night of the Long Knives". The party's left-wingers and the leader of the party militia (the SA or Brownshirts) were among those killed. The SS, led by Heinrich Himmler, became more important. Legal persecution of Germany's Jews began in earnest with the Nuremberg Laws of 1935, which withdrew many civil rights. At the same time Jews suffered increasingly from thuggery and intimidation.

Below: Nazi thugs making an example of "criminals" – a Jew and his Christian girlfriend.

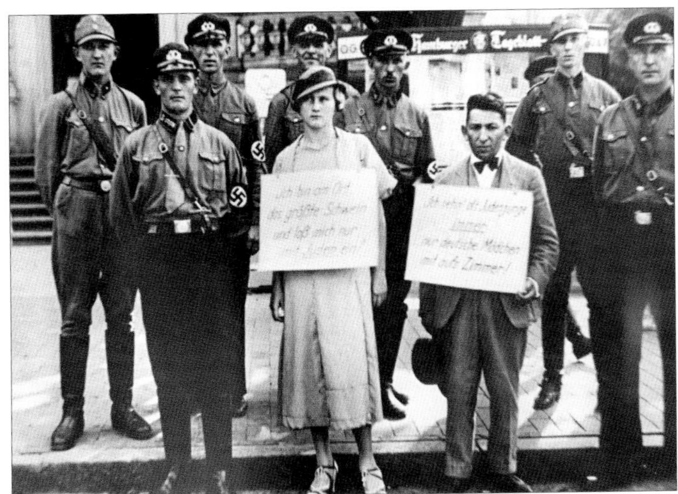

Aggression – Europe and Asia

Throughout the 1930s first Japan, then Italy and finally Germany sought territorial gains by violent means. They backed their aggression with a ruthlessness seldom seen in international affairs and with new and powerful armaments.

World War II began, some would say, in September 1931, when Japan attacked and in effect annexed the Chinese province of Manchuria. The attack was inspired by a conspiracy of middle-ranking Japanese Army officers who faked a sabotage incident on the South Manchurian Railway, owned by the Japanese. The government in Tokyo knew nothing of this but went along with events when a full-scale advance was immediately started. Throughout the approach to war both the Japanese Army and Navy (and factions within them) would in effect be laws unto themselves.

In February 1932 Manchuria was declared independent by the Japanese as Manchukuo, but in reality it was a puppet state economically exploited under Japanese control. In 1933 when a League of Nations investigation finally stated what was obvious (that Japan was the aggressor), Japan simply left the League and increased its military budget.

Above: Japanese troops march into Nanking in December 1937.

The Nazi Threat

Hitler also left the League in 1933 – ostensibly because other countries had refused to disarm to Germany's level, but the reality was different. In 1935 he reintroduced compulsory military service and announced the existence of a German air force, both outright violations of the Treaty of Versailles. Britain, France and, at this stage, Italy condemned these moves but this was a sham. Later the same summer, without prior consultation with France, Britain concluded the Anglo-German Naval Agreement, specifically allowing expansion of the German Navy and the creation of a U-boat force.

Italy was the next to make a move. Aware of the country's modest resources, Mussolini's government had not sought gains abroad in the first decade of fascist rule, though it had brutally consolidated control

Below: German troops crossing the Rhine bridge into Cologne in March 1936, Hitler's first advance.

Below: Puyi, Chinese puppet ruler of Manchukuo, attends a ceremony with his Japanese backers.

over Italy's existing colonies in Africa. However, in October 1935, Italy attacked Abyssinia. By May 1936 it had completed the annexation, despite half-hearted sanctions introduced by the League of Nations.

Encouraged by this, in March 1936 Hitler sent troops into the Rhineland area, demilitarized by the Versailles terms. Again, all Britain and France could muster were brief protests. Hitler made his move despite opposition from his generals. By being proved right, his control over them was made more secure and his belief in his own military judgement confirmed.

In February 1938 he completed his hold over his armed forces by dismissing the two top generals, the war minister and the commander-in-chief, taking over the supreme command himself. In March 1938 the next step was to merge Austria into Germany, sending troops across the border after Austrian Nazis had destabilized the government. Clearly, this was not going to be his last target.

WAR IN CHINA

With the establishment of Manchukuo, there had been various clashes between the Japanese Kwantung Army there and the Chinese across the border in northern China. In July 1937 the Kwantung Army (not under control from Tokyo), used an exchange of shots near the Marco Polo Bridge on the outskirts of Beijing as an excuse for escalation. There was heavy fighting around Shanghai for several months from August, before the Japanese made their move inland to Nanjing (then usually known as Nanking) in December. When they captured the city the Japanese forces went on a rampage of murder, looting and rape for several days. This "rape of Nanking" was reported around the world and widely condemned.

Although stronger than it had previously been, Jiang Jieshi's (Chiang Kai-shek's) Nationalist Chinese government could not prevent the Japanese, with more than a million men deployed, taking control of much of northern and eastern China over the next two years.

CHINA AND MANCHURIA
Japan's annexation of Manchuria and advance into China up to December 1941.

Above: German tanks parade through Vienna in 1938, after Austria's *Anschluss* with Germany.

Troubled Times – USA and USSR

The 1930s were times of social, political and economic upheaval in the USA and USSR. In their very different ways both countries failed to develop effective responses to the new challenges from Germany and Japan.

In the 1930s the USA and the USSR were not the superpowers they became after WWII. As well as being preoccupied with economic difficulties, and political controversy over how to respond, the American people were unsure what their country's role in the world ought to be: should they participate fully or were they better off if they stood apart?

For its part the USSR was rent through the decade by a range of self-inflicted wounds as the economy was completely reworked and the rule of Josef Stalin and the Communist Party became yet more brutal and unchallengeable.

The United States

President Franklin Roosevelt was inaugurated in March 1933 with a quarter of the US workforce unemployed and the gross national product half that of the late 1920s. His New Deal policies encompassed a range of measures: of public works, welfare and poor relief, reform of the banking system and more. For Roosevelt and the American people the priority for the remainder of the decade would always be domestic concerns.

His achievements delighted some Americans while others despised him. Economists remained unsure how effective many of his policies were, but there was no doubt that he greatly enhanced the power and prestige of the presidency in ways that would become important in the following decade.

Most Americans agreed that their nation had blundered unwisely into war in 1917 and felt that their country should avoid future conflicts, especially in Europe. The USA had refused to join the League of Nations in 1919. In 1935, and again in 1937, Congress passed neutrality laws to try to ensure that the USA was not again dragged into war. In any case the USA had comparatively little military muscle. The US Navy was indeed a world force, allowed by treaty to be equal in size with the British Royal Navy. However, only with rearmament measures at the end of the 1930s did it actually build up to its permitted level. In addition, the US Army was so small as to be internationally irrelevant. Nothing in all this was likely to deter aggression.

Above: The Tennessee Valley Authority (TVA) was one of Roosevelt's New Deal initiatives.

The USSR

Throughout the 1930s the USSR was as inward-looking and in an even deeper state

Left: Strikers and police clash at a Michigan car plant in 1937, a common sight in 1930s USA.

of turmoil than the USA. The government's policies of mass industrialization and the collectivization of peasant farms were pushed through. On one hand they created the industrial base that could withstand Hitler's attack in 1941, but on the other the cost was huge, with up to 15 million people dead from murder and famine in the rural areas.

All opposition, whether real or imagined, to the rule of the Communist Party was crushed in the so-called Great Terror, with millions of citizens being shipped off to the brutal labour camps of the Siberian gulag. During this terrifying process the state became governed not by the dictatorship of the proletariat, as provided for in Marxist-Leninist theory, but by the absolute rule of one man: Josef Stalin.

The USSR's huge military potential was clear. Soviet forces had pioneered experiments – in paratroop operations, for example – and later in the decade Marshal Mikhail Tukhachevsky was working to create new tank formations, similar to those that would soon be seen in Germany. In addition, the process of industrialization saw both the quantity and quality of military equipment greatly improve by the late 1930s.

Tukhachevsky, however, and most senior commanders as well as about half the junior officers were all executed during the Terror. Their replacements, Stalin's creatures, like all senior officials, were slow to repair the damage done. Consequently, the USSR was not at all well prepared for the coming war.

JOSEF STALIN

Stalin (1879–1953) was the dictator who ruled the USSR with an increasingly tight grip after the death of Lenin in 1924 and who would extend his control to cover all of eastern Europe by the end of the war. He tolerated no rivals or expressions of dissent. His paranoia was so extreme that millions of loyal Soviet citizens were murdered or sent to the GULag slave-labour camps. His cold and cynical calculations led him astray in 1941 when he refused to prepare properly for Hitler's attack, but otherwise his ruthless energy drove his country forward to victory and the establishment of a new European empire.

Below: Stalin, with Molotov (left), foreign minister throughout WWII, and Marshal Voroshilov, a poor general but a favoured crony of his leader.

Below: Three out of five Soviet marshals were executed in Stalin's Great Terror, including Mikhail Tukhachevsky (shown here).

Below: Soviet paratroop experiments. After the Terror generals reverted to traditional infantry-based tactics.

Troubled Times – Western Europe

Britain and France had played the main part in defeating German aggression in WWI, but their casualties and economic and social problems left them with diminished resources and little will to repeat the process.

In the inter-war years many British people saw WWI as an aberration. They thought that in foreign affairs Britain was an imperial and maritime power and should concentrate on those aspects. Sending a mass conscript army to fight and die in a continental war was not something Britain historically had been accustomed to do and should be reluctant to repeat, especially since it became increasingly clear that the Versailles Treaty had not come close to solving Europe's problems. British resources had been plundered to win WWI and in the economic crisis of the 1930s, British governments could see no way of standing up to Hitler in Europe, if at the same time they had to protect the British Empire against Japan.

Left: Stanley Baldwin, three-times British Prime Minister in the 1920s and '30s, was slow to rearm in the face of Hitler's threats.

There was also a strong feeling in some quarters that the Versailles settlement had indeed been unjust. Some also felt that a Germany restored to a more realistic international status under Hitler's leadership could at least be relied on to help keep the communist menace confined to the USSR.

Overall, Britain avoided co-operating closely with France until 1939. This had the dual effect of preventing another "continental commitment" and also preserving relations with the dominion nations of the Empire, which were reluctant to become involved in Europe's troubles once again. Britain's failure to work with France was shown in 1935, for example. In April that year Britain joined France and Italy in a conference at Stresa to condemn Germany's breaches of the Versailles Treaty – then two months later unilaterally and totally hypocritically negotiated the Anglo-German Naval Agreement, which specifically allowed Germany to make further breaches.

Below: The first meeting, in 1920, of the Council of the League of Nations, the body roughly equivalent to the later UN Security Council.

French Reluctance

The human and physical cost of WWI for France had been vast. Even before the war France's population had been overtaken by that of Germany and the French economy was nowhere near as solid. Continued demographic and economic weakness in the inter-war years went hand in hand with political instability. Successive insecure governments formed and re-formed.

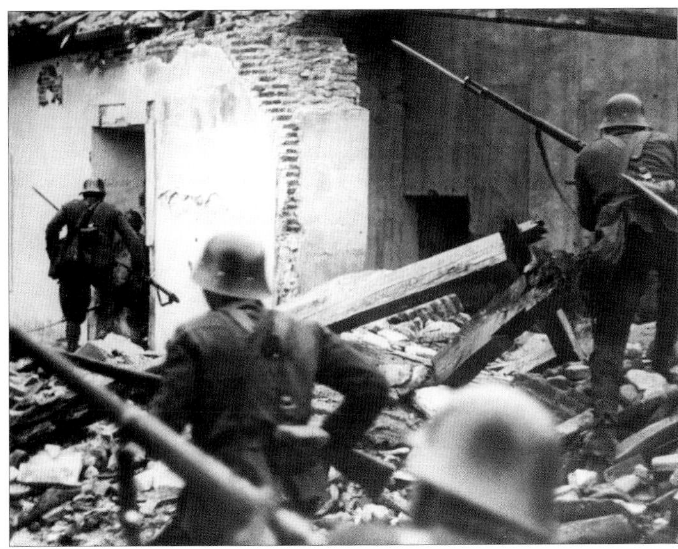

Left: Rebel Spanish Nationalist troops fight their way into Madrid past buildings wrecked by air attacks, a token of much to come.

France had gone to war in 1914 with a wholeheartedly offensive outlook. However, by the 1930s, the situation had changed and any sort of military response in a crisis was out of the question – unless France could muster overwhelming and enthusiastic international support.

THE MAGINOT LINE

Named after André Maginot, the French minister of war who started its construction in 1930, this was a deep and sophisticated system of fortification all along the Franco-German border. Built in line with the overall defensive nature of French strategy, work on it continued through the decade. Blockhouses, anti-tank defences, strong points, major forts and more were all built at a cost of several billion francs. However, the major weakness was that the defences, strong as they were, did not extend to cover the whole of France's northern border.

ABYSSINIA AND SPAIN

Italy's invasion of Abyssinia in 1935 gave the first clear demonstration of how enfeebled Britain and France had become. Already Japan had proved the weakness of the League of Nations by simply walking out and carrying on regardless when the annexation of Manchuria was condemned. British- and French-led League sanctions against Italy for attacking Abyssinia were hardly stringent – oil supplies were not stopped and Italian troopships were still allowed to use the Suez Canal. Sanctions were abandoned in less than a year after the Italians had overrun Abyssinia.

Italy and Germany had been brought closer by the opposition their various measures had met, ineffective though it had been. This process was confirmed, in part, by the next major development: the Spanish Civil War, which began in July 1936.

Both Germany and Italy sent significant help to Spain's right-wing Nationalist rebels. The Soviets sent less valuable help to Spain's Republicans, but France's leftist Popular Front government refused assistance. Britain condemned foreign interference in Spain's affairs but took virtually no action to back their words up.

The war was also important for the lessons major armies drew from it. France and the Soviets concluded that tanks were less effective in battle than some had thought; Germany saw things differently, in particular using Spain as the testing ground for new air-combat and ground-support techniques.

Below: Italian ships pass through the British-controlled Suez Canal, demonstrating the weakness of League of Nations sanctions in 1936.

Europe on the Brink

Prime Minister Chamberlain proclaimed "peace for our time" when he returned from Munich, but the reality was that 1938 and 1939 saw Hitler's relentless expansionism drive Europe into a new and terrible war.

Czechoslovakia had been created by the Versailles Treaty. By 1938 about a third of its population were German speakers who lived principally in the border area known as the Sudetenland. For some time the Sudeten German Party, with Nazi support, had been agitating for union with Germany, and in September 1938 there was a new crisis, provoked by Hitler.

Although the Czechoslovak authorities soon had control of the situation, Britain's Prime Minister Neville Chamberlain decided there needed to be a permanent solution to the problem. It would probably have been wise if Britain and France had stood firm and risked war to help Czechoslovakia: the Czech military and its border defences were very strong and the German armed forces far less prepared for war than was later the case. Instead, although France was resigned to fighting, Chamberlain chose to negotiate.

Above: From left, Chamberlain, Daladier (French premier), Hitler and Mussolini at Munich in 1938.

Below: Joachim von Ribbentrop, Hitler's foreign minister, signs the Nazi–Soviet Pact. Stalin and Molotov smile in the background.

Munich Agreement

Chamberlain flew to Munich to meet Hitler, to negotiate a deal to force Czechoslovakia to cede to Germany areas where the majority of the people were ethnic Germans. Without British support, France had little option but to abandon the Czechs as well. In return Chamberlain had Hitler sign a vague friendship agreement and, on his return, announced that he had secured "peace for our time". He seems to have thought that, fundamentally, Hitler was a reasonable statesman who would keep his word – if that were the case, Czechoslovakia's problems were a local issue not worth provoking another European war over – a war that Britain could not fight without jeopardizing its Empire in the Far East, which was increasingly under threat from the Japanese.

In early October 1938 Germany moved into the Sudetenland and the remainder of Czechoslovakia was split into three autonomous provinces. Then Poland, followed by Hungary, also grabbed disputed areas over the next weeks. In March 1939 Hitler moved in to complete the destruction of Czechoslovakia.

By that point Britain and France were ready to do a little more so they issued a guarantee of support to Poland, which was clearly Hitler's next target. The international status of the city of Danzig (Gdansk), and the Polish Corridor that divided East Prussia from the main part of Germany, had long been seen as an affront to German nationalism. Now Hitler vehemently demanded their return.

Right: Nazis on parade in Danzig (Gdansk) in 1939. Their banner proclaims "Danzig is a German town".

Nazi–Soviet Pact

With Hitler now looking east, the USSR's position became more important. In the summer of 1939 Britain and France half-heartedly began talks in Moscow. However, these made little progress when it became clear that for Stalin any alliance was conditional on having the right to station troops in Poland.

Instead, in mid-August, the world was stunned when the communists and Nazis, formerly implacable enemies, became friends with the signing of the Soviet–German Non-Aggression Pact.

What the rest of the world did not know was that secret parts of this deal provided for Poland to be divided up between Russia and Germany and that the Baltic States and Finland would also lose their independence to Russia.

Earlier that summer Britain and France had finally begun military co-operation planning, and Britain had introduced conscription in May. Even at this last moment Chamberlain was still looking for some compromise concession to Hitler that might avoid war.

When a formal Anglo-Polish alliance treaty was announced on 25 August, Hitler hesitated for a few days, postponing Germany's planned attack on Poland from 26 August to 1 September – but at dawn that morning the invasion began.

Above: The announcement of conscription in Britain in May 1939.

GERMAN EXPANSION, 1936–9

Poland and Hungary also joined in the partition of Czechoslovakia.

Tanks, 1939–42 An early model German Panzer 3 during a river-crossing operation.

Air Combat – Weapons, Tactics and Aces The ball turret of a B-17 Flying Fortress.

Anti-tank Guns, 1939–42 A Soviet 45mm M1937 anti-tank gun coming under artillery fire.

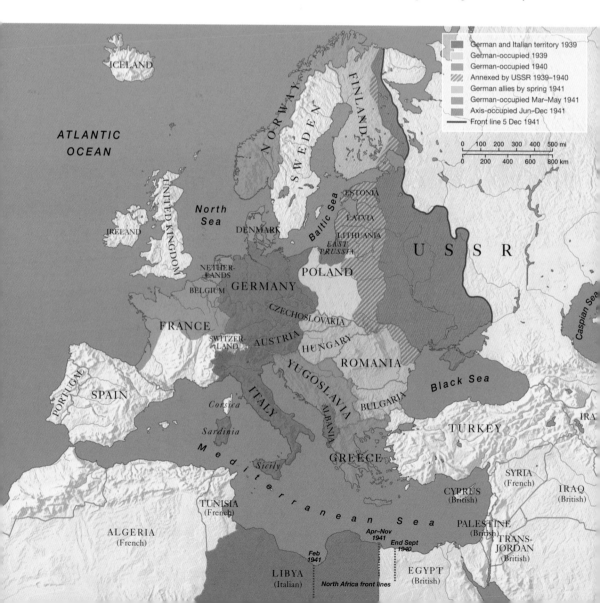

German and Italian territory 1939
German-occupied 1939
German-occupied 1940
Annexed by USSR 1939–1940
German allies by spring 1941
German-occupied Mar–May 1941
Axis-occupied Jun–Dec 1941
Front line 5 Dec 1941

0 100 200 300 400 500 mi
0 200 400 600 800 km

ICELAND
ATLANTIC OCEAN
NORWAY
SWEDEN
FINLAND
ESTONIA
LATVIA
LITHUANIA
EAST PRUSSIA
Baltic Sea
North Sea
UNITED KINGDOM
IRELAND
DENMARK
NETHERLANDS
BELGIUM
GERMANY
POLAND
U S S R
CZECHOSLOVAKIA
FRANCE
SWITZERLAND
AUSTRIA
HUNGARY
ROMANIA
Caspian Sea
Black Sea
YUGOSLAVIA
BULGARIA
ALBANIA
PORTUGAL
SPAIN
Corsica
Sardinia
ITALY
Sicily
GREECE
TURKEY
IRA
Mediterranean Sea
SYRIA (French)
IRAQ (British)
CYPRUS (British)
TUNISIA (French)
ALGERIA (French)
PALESTINE (British)
TRANS-JORDAN (British)
Apr–Nov 1941
End Sept 1940
Feb 1941
LIBYA (Italian)
North Africa front lines
EGYPT (British)

HITLER'S TRIUMPHS

Throughout the period from September 1939 to the autumn of 1941, there was never a moment when an impartial observer would have bet on anyone apart from Germany winning the war. The parade of German military successes seemed endless, with Poland, Denmark and Norway, France and the Low Countries, the Balkans and, finally, most of European Russia coming under German domination. This rapid succession of victories had made Hitler's domestic position unassailable and convinced him of his own military genius, which would prove to be less infallible, however, in the years to come.

Remarkably, Britain was fighting on, with increasing help from the USA, but it was hard to see how anything Britain could do would really hurt Germany – nor did it seem likely that the Red Army could recover from the crushing defeats recently inflicted on it. Also, by late 1941, the brutal nature of the war had been made plain. Both the Nazis and the Soviets had murdered many thousands of Poles, and the Nazis had continued with mass killings of Jews and others on Soviet soil.

Yet the signs of a turning tide were there to be seen. America was rearming fast and inching closer to joining the war even before Japan's surprise attack on Pearl Harbor, while in that same week carefully husbanded Soviet reserves went into action on the Moscow front and threw back the German advance.

The USA and the European War President Roosevelt's "fireside chats" on the radio were famous.

The British Home Front Child evacuees leaving London in 1939 say goodbye to their parents.

The Fall of France A German Ju 87 Stuka bomber, one of the decisive weapons of Blitzkrieg.

Poland and the Outbreak of War

Bolstered by his pact with Stalin, Hitler no longer felt any need to restrain his aggression. Hitler first, and then Stalin, attacked and quickly conquered Poland while Britain and France did nothing other than declare war on Germany.

The first shots of the European half of WWII were fired at a Polish naval base by the old German coast-defence ship *Schleswig-Holstein* early in the morning of 1 September 1939. Already Hitler's Luftwaffe was screaming in to attack Polish air bases and German troops were surging over the borders. Britain and France responded by sending ultimata to Germany demanding an immediate withdrawal. When there was no response they declared war on the 3rd.

KEY FACTS

PLACE: Poland

DATE: 1–28 September 1939

OUTCOME: Poland is attacked and completely overrun by Germany and then the USSR.

THE POLISH CAMPAIGN

Germany deployed 53 divisions for the attack, including all 6 Panzer (or armoured) divisions then in existence. The Army Commander-in-Chief, General Walther von Brauchitsch, controlled the operation with little interference from Hitler. Poland had not begun mobilizing its forces until 30 August, so many reservists were still on their way to their units. The Poles had about 23 divisions deployed, with very few tanks. However, they did have a significant cavalry force, though it is untrue (as sometimes has been suggested) that the cavalry were used to charge German tanks at various points in the fighting.

In the air German superiority was even more marked, with the Luftwaffe using about 1,600 modern aircraft against the Polish force of some 500 mostly obsolescent types.

With their superior strength, equipment and training the Germans soon gained the upper hand. Poland's Commander-in-Chief, Marshal Edward Smigly-Rydz, had decided to defend along the borders and his troops were soon thrown out of the exposed positions this plan committed them to. By the middle of the month the Polish forces had been split into isolated small groups, while the Germans were closing in on Warsaw – which they captured, ending the campaign on the 28th after a vicious artillery and air bombardment.

By then Stalin had taken his share of the spoils. Soviet troops crossed into Poland on the 17th, as agreed with Hitler in the Nazi–Soviet Pact; by the end of the month the Soviets had occupied about half the country. The official Soviet line was that

Below: A Soviet tank passes a line of German troops in Brest-Litovsk, Poland, late September 1939.

Below: German troops in Poland in September 1939. Few German units were motorized like this one.

GLEIWITZ

As a pretext to justify the attack on Poland, an SS unit faked an attack by Polish troops on a German radio station at Gleiwitz (Gliwice) in Silesia near the Polish border. The "attackers" captured the station late on 31 August, made a brief anti-German broadcast, then left after killing a concentration camp prisoner they had brought with them. This unfortunate person was then displayed to foreign pressmen as a civilian victim of Polish brutality.

Above: German troops crossing the San River in southern Poland, watched by their proud *Führer*.

they were intervening to protect the ethnic Belorussians and Ukrainians, but in fact they were annexing this territory. On the 29th the Germans and Soviets announced a friendship treaty that confirmed the partition of Poland.

The Phoney War

As well as Britain and France and their various colonies, who were given no choice in the matter, Britain's so-called "old dominions" declared war on Germany in the first days of September. Each, however, had some reservations.

For example, the Australian government declared war and introduced conscription, but only for home defence. Canada declared war only after this had been debated in parliament and also decided not to have conscription. The United States proclaimed its neutrality – there was no doubt at this stage that most Americans wanted to keep out of the war in Europe.

Although they had gone to war on Poland's behalf, Britain and France did nothing to help the Poles. For the moment Hitler was content not to provoke them further – German forces in the West in September were very weak. British government ministers refused to bomb industries in the Ruhr because the factories were private property, while French troops made only tentative forward moves in a small area of the Saar. This "Phoney War" would continue on the Western Front until Germany's attack in 1940.

Below: British families building Anderson shelters as a precaution against German air raids, during the Phoney War.

Tanks, 1939–42

The successes of Germany's early-war campaigns were based on the power of the much-feared Panzer divisions, giving tanks a prominence in military affairs they had never before attained.

Tanks, as well as anti-tank weapons, were the only types of land-warfare weaponry that saw substantial development during WWII. In 1939 the most powerful tanks mainly had a gun in the 37mm (2pdr) class and were protected by up to 40mm (1.58in) armour. By 1942, 75mm (2.95in) weapons and twice as much armour were typical. These figures increased still further later in the war.

EARLY PANZERS

Nazi Germany's first tank, built during the mid-1930s, was the Panzerkampfwagen (PzKpfw) 1, a light two-man design armed only with machine-guns. This was soon joined by the slightly more powerful PzKpfw 2. Both saw combat into 1941. The best tanks in the Panzer divisions of 1939–41 were the next two in the series. The PzKpfw 3 was available in various marks in the early-war period. Up to April 1940 all carried a 3.7cm (1.46in) main gun but this was replaced by first a 42-calibre 5cm (1.97in) gun and then a more powerful 60-calibre 5cm. The PzKpfw 4 was originally conceived as an infantry-support vehicle and hence began life with a short (24-calibre) 7.5cm (2.95in) gun; by 1942 its 7.5cm gun was a version twice as long. For the first two or three years of the war the Germans also used many Czech-built tanks. The PzKpfw 38(*t*) was a powerful design of similar capabilities to the PzKpfw 3 of the time.

The British and French tanks facing this array in 1940 were a mixed bag; most were additionally

MATILDA 2

The Matilda was the only British tank to see combat throughout the war, remaining in use against the Japanese until 1945. Its main European service was in France and North Africa in 1940–1. (The example shown below is in Egypt, December 1940.) Its thick armour and reasonable anti-tank gun power made it a tough opponent then but it was very slow cross-country. Almost 3,000 were built.

WEIGHT: 26.9 tonnes
LENGTH: 5.6m (18ft 5in)
HEIGHT: 2.5m (8ft 3in)
ARMOUR: 78mm (3.1in)
ROAD SPEED: 25kph (15mph)
ARMAMENT: 1 x 2pdr (40mm) + 1 x machine-gun

Left: M3 Lee tanks and American troops in training in Northern Ireland in 1942. These were some of the first US soldiers to serve in Europe.

hampered by being dispersed in small infantry-support units. Various French designs like the Somua S-35 were well-armed and armoured but were made less efficient in action by their one-man turrets, in which the commander had to make tactical decisions and also load, aim and fire the gun.

Britain had a succession of light, medium and heavy tanks throughout the early-war years. The Light Tank Marks 5 and 6 were armed only with machine-guns – so they were useless for anti-tank combat – but did see extensive service in France and the early North African battles.

The medium (or cruiser) tanks went from the Mark 1, first produced in 1938, to the Mark 6 or Crusader, final versions of which appeared in 1942. All the cruiser tanks had reasonable armour and gun power, but they had appallingly unreliable engines and running gear.

The heavy tanks were better. The Matilda 2 carried the same 2pdr (40mm) gun as most of the cruisers and mounted 78mm (3.1in) armour, which made it very difficult indeed to knock out in its heyday of 1940–1. Its successors, the Valentine and Churchill, were robust and reliable, if under-gunned.

The USA's early-war tanks were the M3 Light Stuart and M3 Medium, known as the Lee in US service and the Grant in the slightly different form used by Britain. The Stuart, with a 37mm (1.46in) gun and 37mm armour, was fast and reliable. Updated as the M5, it was still used extensively in 1944–5. The Lee/Grant was an interim type, a hurried redesign of an earlier model to fit a 75mm (2.95in) gun, but only in a side sponson rather than a turret. Production ended in 1942.

Above: An early-model Panzer 3 with 3.7cm (1.46in) gun during a river-crossing exercise in 1941.

Superior Soviet Types

The most impressive Allied tanks were those of the Red Army. The early-war BT-7 was particularly fast and carried a reasonable 45mm (1.77in) gun, but the next generation of Russian tanks were the finest in service anywhere in their time. The heavy KV-1 came first, making its combat debut in the Russo-Finnish War in 1940. Its 76.2mm (3in) gun and 90mm (3.54in) armour outclassed anything the Germans had available in 1941. Even better was the medium T-34, sometimes described as the tank that won the war for the USSR. Fortunately for the Germans, comparatively few of these two designs were available in 1941.

SOMUA S-35

Designed in 1934–5 the Somua S-35 was intended as a fast "cavalry" tank and fulfilled this brief well. Some 300 saw combat during the 1940 Battle of France, including those shown below. The S-35 was well-armed and armoured but mechanically unreliable.

Weight: 20 tonnes
Length: 5.5m (18ft)
Height: 2.7m (8ft 10in)
Hull armour: 40mm (1.58in)
Road speed: 37kph (23mph)
Armament: 1 x 47mm (1.85in) + 1 x machine-gun

The Baltic and Scandinavia

Northern Europe's smaller nations continued to fall to aggression through 1939 and 1940. The USSR attacked Finland in November 1939 and annexed the Baltic States in 1940, while Norway and Denmark were taken by the Nazis that spring.

Stalin's plans for his Western neighbours were first demonstrated in the Soviet-occupied parts of Poland. By the end of October 1939 mass arrests and deportations of "enemies of socialism" had begun and fraudulent elections had appointed assemblies, which dutifully voted for incorporation into the USSR.

At the same time Lithuania, Latvia and Estonia were forced to conclude "friendship" agreements, giving the Soviets the right to station troops in these countries. In June 1940 Stalin activated these treaties and sent his troops in. The same process as in Poland quickly followed: terror, false elections and annexation by the USSR. In June 1940 the USSR annexed the Northern Bukovina and Bessarabia regions (formerly part of Romania) as well. They, too, had no option but to yield to Stalin's ultimatum.

Above: Finnish troops used their mastery of the winter conditions to defeat the initial Soviet attacks.

Below: A German tank and German infantry on the advance early in the Norwegian campaign.

THE WINTER WAR

These moves were part of a process of extending Soviet power and, at the same time, establishing a buffer zone against a possible German attack. Finland had been assigned to the Soviet sphere of interest by the Nazi–Soviet Pact and, in October 1939, Stalin began moves against the Finns.

He demanded that Finland cede territory in the Karelian Isthmus area in the south and in the far north, in return for land to be ceded to Finland in the central part of their border region. The Finns, fearing that this unusual generosity on Stalin's part was the thin end of a very nasty wedge, refused. On 30 November Stalin sent in the Red Army to attack Finland.

Right: A British anti-aircraft battery in Norway. The Germans had complete air superiority.

The Finns had 9 divisions facing 26 Soviet divisions, which also had massive superiority in air support, artillery, tanks and every other material category. Remarkably, the Finnish troops (well-trained and mobile on their skis) completely outfought the Soviets until early February 1940, when Soviet reinforcements under a new commander, Marshal Semyon Timoshenko, began wearing them down. An armistice came into effect on 13 March – the Finns conceded territory similar to that originally demanded.

The war had several repercussions. It was the final nail in the coffin of the League of Nations – the USSR was expelled but took no notice of this severe punishment. It also made clear the hesitancy of Britain and France, who considered the possibility of sending help to the Finns (even at the risk of war with the USSR) but did nothing until far too late.

Part of the reason for helping Finland was that, in crossing Norway to get there, the Anglo-French forces would also be able to interrupt Germany's iron-ore supplies from northern Sweden. The difficulty was that neither of these neutral countries wanted foreign troops on their territory. Finally, the war also highlighted what seemed to be the low quality of the Red Army – Hitler for one took note.

Denmark and Norway

In the aftermath of the Russo-Finnish War, Hitler became convinced (and correctly) that Britain and France still planned to intervene against his Swedish sources of iron ore by moving through Norway. On 9 April 1940 German forces advanced overland into Denmark and attacked a series of points along the Norwegian coast from the air and sea. Neither country had significant armed forces and the Western Allies were taken completely by surprise. Denmark was conquered within hours. Norway took about two months but the result was never really in doubt from the first days, when Germany established air bases in the country that more than compensated for Britain's superior naval strength.

Small Anglo-French forces arrived to help the Norwegians at various points, but the organization of these expeditions was chaotic. The last ones were withdrawn in early June, in the light of the disasters by then occurring on the Western Front.

Below: The German battle-cruiser *Scharnhorst* firing on the British carrier *Glorious* off Norway in June.

Heavy Cruisers

The heavy cruisers of World War II were the product of an intense arms race during the inter-war period. Japan built particularly large and powerful ships in flagrant violation of treaty limits; other navies strove to keep up.

Since battleship design was very tightly controlled by the Washington Naval Treaty and its successors, much inter-war competition between the leading navies came to be in cruiser construction, whether the heavy cruisers armed with 203mm (8in) guns covered here or lighter 152mm (6in) armed types.

In the inter-war period the "treaty limit" for cruisers was 10,000 tons standard displacement. Japan, Italy and later Germany all flagrantly breached this figure, but other nations generally kept fairly close to it. In fact, the limit of 10,000 tons/8in guns had been arrived at rather arbitrarily. It was actually very difficult to build ships to these figures that also had a reasonable balance of armour protection and engine power.

Left: The pocket battleship *Admiral Graf Spee* in mid-1939. The *Graf Spee* was scuttled in December 1939 after the Battle of the River Plate.

Treaty Cruisers

Japan and Italy were the first to build "treaty" heavy cruisers, in the mid-1920s. Japan's *Furutaka* was a relatively modest design with six single 200mm (7.87in) guns, reasonable side armour and 33-knot speed, on an official displacement of 7,000 tons (actually about 2,000 more).

Italy's *Trento* and *Trieste* were equally fast with 8 x 203mm guns. However, although their true displacement was about 11,500 tons, they were still rather flimsily built. The four later Italian Zara-class ships were much better armoured and several knots slower.

Japan's successor ships to the *Furutaka* also substantially breached the treaty limits. The Myoko and Atago classes were all over 13,000 tons, carried 10 x 203mm guns and a heavy torpedo armament, with armour up to 120mm (4.72in) thick.

In comparison with these, British and American inter-war ships looked rather second-rate.

IJNS *FURUTAKA*

The *Furutaka* had a relatively brief combat career in WWII. After serving in various early battles, *Furutaka* was part of the successful Japanese force in the Battle of Savo Island off Guadalcanal but was sunk in the Cape Esperance engagement in October 1942.

Sister ship: *Kako*
Commissioned: 1926
Displacement: 9,000 tons
Speed: 33 knots
Belt armour: 76mm (3in) max.
Armament: 6 x 200mm (7.87in) + 4 x 119mm (4.7in) guns

Britain built a series of similar ships, collectively known as the County class. They all carried 8 x 8in guns on a displacement very close to 10,000 tons. They had very good range and sea-keeping qualities but had very little armour and a high silhouette, which made them rather vulnerable in action. Britain also built two smaller ships with 8in guns in the early 1930s – the *Exeter* and *York* – but like most

HMS *KENT*

HMS *Kent* was the nameship of the first group of seven County-class cruisers. *Kent* served in the Mediterranean initially but was damaged in 1940. *Kent* is seen below in 1941 after repairs, in service with the Home Fleet, its station for the rest of the war.

SISTER SHIPS: 6, inc. 2 Australian
COMMISSIONED: 1928
DISPLACEMENT: 10,000 tons
SPEED: 32 knots
BELT ARMOUR: 115mm (4.53in)
ARMAMENT: 8 x 8in (203mm)
+ 10 x 4in (102mm) guns

other navies did not build any more 8in heavy cruisers during the war.

Germany operated within a different set of restrictions, having to conform (until Hitler abrogated it) to the Versailles Treaty. In the late 1920s Germany was allowed to begin work on replacements for old coast-defence ships that had previously been permitted under Versailles.

The replacements were three *Panzerschiffe* (armoured ships), soon termed "pocket battleships" by British commentators, but better described as heavy cruisers, as they were eventually officially designated. They carried two triple 280mm (11in) turrets and could reach 26 knots, but significantly exceeded their announced 10,000-ton displacement (cheating that in fact pre-dated Hitler's regime). Supposedly, they had the gunpower to outmatch any cruiser and the speed to escape almost any battleship. However, these ships proved unsatisfactory, with slow-firing armament and unreliable engines. Three later German 203mm-armed cruisers were also built, again large and formidable vessels but troubled by weak engines.

AMERICAN DESIGNS

The US Navy built several classes of "treaty cruisers". First were two Salt Lake City ships with an unusual arrangement of a twin and triple turret fore and aft, with the triples superfiring over the twins; unsurprisingly, they were somewhat top-heavy.

Subsequent American classes changed to three triple 8in turrets, which proved to be a more sensible arrangement. As well as commissioning numerous 6in cruisers, US industrial power also saw the completion of more than a dozen Baltimore-class ships during the war. These kept the same main armament as earlier 8in vessels but increased displacement to 13,600 tons, to fit in the extra equipment that war experience showed to be necessary.

Below: The Astoria-class USS *Vincennes* in July 1942. It was sunk a few weeks later off Guadalcanal.

The Fall of France

The French Army was traditionally one of Europe's strongest, but in 1940 it was utterly defeated in a few weeks of combat. The disaster was caused by poor morale and weak leadership in the face of a ruthless and well-organized enemy.

Although there was no significant fighting on the Western Front before May 1940, many plans were made. Hitler intended to attack, and eventually he approved a radical plan to avoid becoming bogged down in assaults on France's Maginot Line defences. Instead, secondary forces were to advance into Belgium and the Netherlands, defeating these countries but, at the same time, drawing Anglo-French troops forward to help them. Then the main German force, led by most of the Panzer divisions, would advance through the Ardennes region (despite its unpromising terrain) and cut the Allied front in two.

Allied strategy was defensive, aiming to build strength while waiting for Britain's naval blockade of Germany to bite. Their plan, in the event of a German attack, was for the best Allied troops to advance into Belgium and link with both the Belgians and Dutch to present a united front. Unfortunately, in their understandable desperation to remain neutral and do nothing to provoke Hitler, the Belgians and Dutch refused to plan jointly with the Allies, so the whole scheme was never properly worked out.

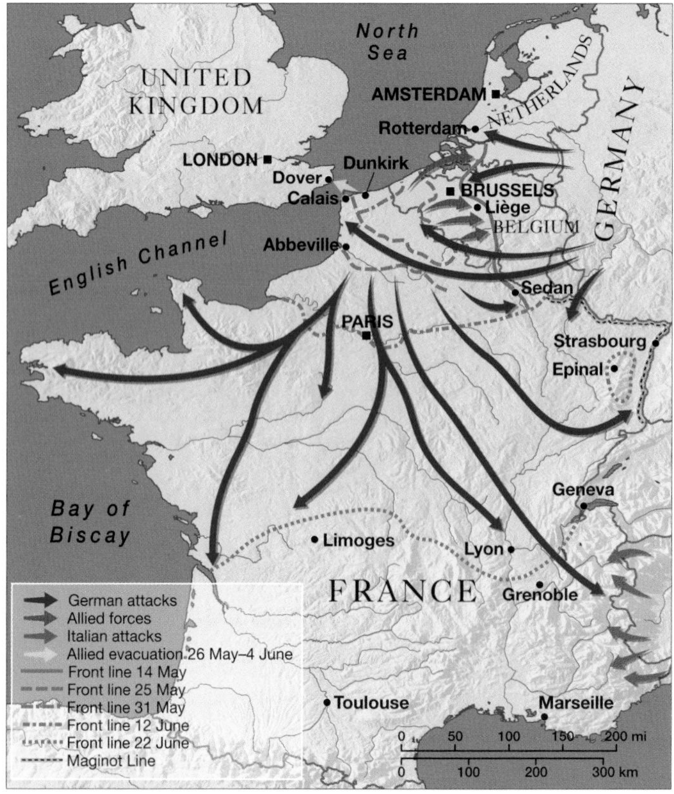

BLITZKRIEG IN THE WEST
France, the Low Countries and the British Expeditionary Force were all defeated in less than six weeks.

Above: A Ju 87 Stuka in its attack dive, a terrifying experience for those targeted on the ground below.

Balance of Forces

Overall, counting the Dutch and Belgians, the two sides' land forces were roughly equal in May 1940, with some 140 divisions and 3,000 tanks each. However, most of the Allied armour was split up into small scattered groups, while Germany's was concentrated in well-trained Panzer divisions. In the air Germany deployed some 3,000 modern combat aircraft; the Allies had about 2,000, many of them older types. This would be a crucial advantage.

The German offensive began on 10 May. As the Germans had intended, attention was concentrated at first in the north. Within days a combination of heavy air attacks, paratroop operations and advances on the ground smashed the Dutch and Belgian forces. On 14 May the Netherlands surrendered. Britain and France played into German hands – the troops advancing into Belgium were reinforced but they were still unable to hold their positions against the German troops directly attacking them.

Crossing the Meuse

In the meantime, the main German force had reached the River Meuse, crossed it on 14–15 May and was soon racing for the Channel. The Germans reached the coast on the 20th, slicing the Allied armies in two, just as they had planned. Unfortunately, the French Commander-in-Chief had kept no reserves to deal with any such emergency.

Over the next two weeks or so the Allied divisions in the north were forced back into an ever-smaller perimeter around the port of Dunkirk. About 340,000 troops were evacuated from there to Britain by 4 June, including some 120,000 French. The British had to leave all their equipment behind and many thousands more French troops were taken prisoner.

By then the Germans had regrouped and were ready to finish the job. On the 5th they attacked south from along the line of the River Somme and were soon advancing speedily, despite some fierce initial resistance from the remaining French forces. They were in Paris on the 14th and, on the 16th, the French government resigned.

France Surrenders

The new government was headed by Marshal Philippe Pétain. Despite being urged to fight on by the British under their recently appointed Prime Minister, Winston Churchill, Pétain and his cabinet decided to ask for an armistice. France duly surrendered on 22 June.

BLITZKRIEG

Germany's many successes in 1939–40 were ascribed to a new form of warfare, Blitzkrieg ("lightning war"), a term which is said to have been coined by Hitler himself. It described the combination of fast-moving tank forces and powerful close air support that overran France in a matter of weeks. Although it seemed to depend mainly on armoured units, the secret of Blitzkrieg was more to do with effective co-operation between all the arms of service. This, and the high levels of initiative shown by commanders at all levels, was the true basis of Germany's victories. The Germany Army would remain superior to all its enemies in these areas for most of the war.

Above: British soldiers crammed aboard a destroyer during the evacuation from Dunkirk.

Below: Panzer 1 light tanks seen during the French campaign. The less capable Panzer 1 and 2 designs were still a significant part of the German force in 1940.

Light Bombers, Recce and Utility Aircraft

Modest armament fits, or even none at all, were the hallmarks of these aircraft types. Paradoxically, perhaps, the least successful of these designs were the light bombers – the unarmed reconnaissance and utility types had a far lower casualty rate.

The light bomber category included a number of designs in service in 1939 but most of these were soon found seriously wanting. They were replaced by either the heavier bombers or by purpose-built ground-attack machines.

Light Bomber Designs

Britain and France both had aircraft of this type in 1939–40. The Fairey Battle had seemed a capable design when it entered service in 1937, but by 1940 its low speed and non-existent armour protection made it, in effect, a deathtrap.

France's Potez 63 series had similar faults and the Breguet 691 was little better, though it did have a more substantial defensive armament. The Bloch 174 was fast (530kph/329mph) and carried a useful 400kg (880lb) bomb load, but only 50 were in service in May 1940. As also to some extent in Britain, the profusion of relatively small French aircraft companies prevented sufficient development

Above: Some 800 examples of the Fw 189 Uhu were used as ground-attack and reconnaissance aircraft.

Below: A Fieseler Storch shows its ability to land (and take off) from unconventional airfields, in this case a Berlin boulevard.

MITSUBISHI Ki-46

The Mitsubishi Ki-46 entered service with the Japanese Army in 1940. It remained in use to 1945, latterly and unsuccessfully as a fighter (shown below), armed with 2 x 20mm (0.79in) cannon in the nose and 1 x 37mm (1.46in) upward-firing gun.

SPEED: 600kph (375mph)
RANGE: 4,000km (2,500 miles)
CREW: 2
ENGINES: 2 x Mitsubishi Ha-102 radials; 1,080hp each
ARMAMENT: 1 x 7.7mm (0.303in) machine-gun

and production effort being given in the pre-war period to the best designs.

Early-war Soviet Sukhoi 2s had similar performance to the above Anglo-French types, with the advantage of reasonable armour protection for the crew. However, many were still shot down by the superior Luftwaffe fighters of 1941.

Although these "modern" designs proved short-lived, some seemingly less capable aircraft (many of them biplanes) fought on in night harassment and similar roles. Aircraft in this category included the Soviet Polikarpov I-153 (originally designed as a fighter) and the German Henschel 123 (built specifically for the attack role). Less capable was the Czech Letov S328, dating back to 1933, still used by some of the Eastern Front's minor air forces in 1944–5.

RECONNAISSANCE

Many well-known aircraft types had variants produced to serve in the reconnaissance role. In the British case specialized versions of both the Spitfire and Mosquito were built for this purpose. Usually, they were unarmed and fitted with uprated engines, along with appropriate cameras for planned high- or low-level missions. The American equivalents included modified Lightning fighters and Havoc bombers. Some designs were given pressurized cabins and other fittings to help them achieve extreme altitudes where they would be very difficult to intercept.

Only one land-based aircraft type was built specifically for the long-range reconnaissance role: Japan's Mitsubishi Ki-46 "Dinah". Over 1,700 of this design were produced and could reach over 600kph (375mph). Range was an impressive 4,000km (2,485 miles).

One of the few aircraft that specialized in the tactical reconnaissance role was Germany's Focke-Wulf 189, which served extensively on the Eastern Front. It was comparatively slow but survived through its toughness and extreme agility.

UTILITY DESIGNS

Most nations had small light transport aircraft, which were also employed for such tasks as artillery spotting and landing agents in enemy territory.

POTEZ 63-11

The Potez 63 family included several bomber, fighter and reconnaissance variants. The 63-11 shown was used mainly in reconnaissance, with about 700 being built, including some for the Vichy air force. Potez 633 bombers served with Romania and Greece.

SPEED: 439kph (273mph)
RANGE: 1,300km (800 miles)
CREW: 3
ENGINES: 2 x Gnome Rhône 14M radials; 700hp each
ARMAMENT: 200kg (440lb) bombs; 3 x machine-guns

These could be found in either army or air force service, according to nationality. General Rommel famously used one such type, a Fieseler Storch, in flights over the North African battlefields, landing from time to time to chivvy on lagging subordinates. Britain's Westland Lysander regularly flew covert missions carrying resistance personnel into France. American equivalents included the Taylorcraft L-2 Grasshopper. The one crucial performance attribute of such aircraft was usually their ability to take off and land in confined and rough areas. None were fast or ever more than lightly armed.

The Battle of Britain and the Blitz

In the summer of 1940 Hitler seemed unbeatable, but his failure to finish Britain off can be seen as the point when the war changed from being a short one, which Germany would win, to a longer one which the Nazis could conceivably lose.

With France beaten and the British Army practically disarmed after the evacuation from Dunkirk, Hitler probably expected Britain to surrender. However, inspired by Churchill, Britain seemed ready to fight on. On 16 July Hitler therefore ordered his armed forces to start preparing for an invasion of England. Already the Luftwaffe had begun attacks on British shipping in the English Channel, in order to draw the Royal Air Force (RAF) into battle. Since Britain's Royal Navy was still very powerful and much of the Germany Navy had been lost during the Norwegian campaign, winning air superiority was an essential prelude to invasion.

Above: Firefighters at work on burning buildings in the City of London during the 1940 Blitz.

Britain's Defences

Fortunately, Britain had made effective preparations. RAF Fighter Command had about 900 Spitfire and Hurricane aircraft, with plenty more being produced to replace the inevitable losses, but trained pilots were in much shorter supply. The defensive organization was excellent, with information from the radar system being fed to a network of control stations and then being used to direct the fighters into combat.

No other nation had such an integrated organization at this time. The Germans did not realize how well this system worked and, accordingly, would not make enough effort to disrupt it by attacks on the radar and control stations.

The Germans had a similar number of single-engined fighters (Messerschmitt Bf 109s) to the RAF, along with over 1,200 twin-engined medium bombers. In addition, they had twin-engined Messerschmitt 110 fighters and Junkers 87 Stuka dive-bombers, about 300 of each; both these types would prove less effective in this campaign than previously.

Whereas Britain was using a defensive system that had been in preparation for many months, Germany had to fight a new sort of battle, very different from their earlier campaigns in support of a land offensive. Their intelligence on RAF strength was very poor, so it was difficult to devise effective plans.

Left: Hawker Hurricane fighters of a squadron with refugee Czech pilots taking off in late 1940.

Right: A formation of Heinkel 111 bombers assembling for a raid during the Battle of Britain.

Above: Air Marshal Hugh Dowding, the successful Commander-in-Chief of RAF Fighter Command during the Battle of Britain.

All-out attacks began in mid-August 1940. There were heavy losses on both sides but the RAF had the advantage initially. Then, for a few days in late August and early September, the Luftwaffe changed its tactics and stepped up strikes against the front-line RAF airfields. This change stretched the RAF to the utmost but the German commanders did not realize that they were winning the battle.

On 7 September Germany switched tactics again and began a series of mass day and night attacks on London, which were heavily defeated on the 15th. On the 17th Hitler postponed his invasion plans. Daylight attacks and air battles continued for several weeks, but the Battle of Britain had been won.

The Blitz

London's ordeal was not over. The German bombers came back almost every night, up to 400 or more strong, until late November. By then they were also attacking a range of major cities that included Coventry, Birmingham and others. From November through to May 1941, when the attacks ended because most of the Luftwaffe was being transferred to eastern Europe, the main targets were various port areas like Merseyside and Clydeside. The British people called these attacks the "Blitz" (from the German word "Blitzkrieg").

At first the British defences were very ineffective. There were few anti-aircraft guns in service and radar-equipped night fighters were only just being developed. Although matters improved as the battle went on, the German loss rate remained low. Some 43,000 British civilians were killed and tens of thousands made homeless in the Blitz, but Britain's war effort was scarcely scratched.

Fighters, 1939–42

In 1940 in the Battle of Britain, the fate of the world depended to a significant degree on the qualities of the two sides' Spitfire, Hurricane and Messerschmitt fighters. Air combat superiority was vital in this and every other campaign.

Like every other kind of military technology, fighters had to have a balance of usually conflicting qualities: speed, rate of climb, manoeuvrability, range, armament, protection and others. Most fighters in service throughout the war were single-piston-engined, pilot-only, low-wing monoplanes. A few biplanes and twin-engined monoplane designs were also produced but generally saw little combat as day fighters.

Biplanes

Some countries with good modern designs still had a number of biplanes in action in 1939: examples being Germany's Heinkel 51 and Britain's Gloster Gladiator. Typically, they were slow and lightly armed – 400kph (250mph) and four rifle-calibre machine-guns for the Gladiator – and came off badly if facing monoplane opponents. Italy, however, had quite significant numbers of Fiat CR 32 and CR 42 biplanes, and some even continued in use until Italy's surrender in 1943.

Monoplanes

The classic designs of the era were the Spitfire, Hurricane and Messerschmitt Bf 109. All first flew in 1935–6 and would continue in combat service, albeit in greatly modified forms, until the end of the war. The Spitfire 1 was slightly faster than the Bf 109E (the main versions in service in 1940) and the Hurricane slower than both the others. Both British fighters were more manoeuvrable than the Bf 109, but their 8 x 0.303in (7.7mm) machine-guns were less effective than the Messerschmitt's 2 x 20mm (0.79in) cannon and 2 x 7.92mm (0.312in) machine-guns. Messerschmitts also had a better rate of climb.

In 1941 the successor 109F was superior to the Spitfire 5, a balance redressed by the later Spitfire 9. Ultimately, though, there was sufficiently little to choose between them that encounters were more often decided by pilot skill and tactics.

Fighters were not a pre-war priority for the US Army Air Force (USAAF) – after all, there was no possibility of air attacks against the American continent.

Below: A USAAF Curtiss P-40. Many of the 13,700 P-40s built served in the war against Japan.

POLIKARPOV I-16

The Polikarpov I-16 (shown below) served successfully in Spain before the war. It had a good rate of climb and manoeuvrability and was, in some variants, the best-armed fighter anywhere. It made up about half of the Soviet fighter strength in 1941.

Speed: 460kph (286mph)
Range: 440km (275 miles)
Engine: Shvetsov M25 radial; 700hp
Armament: 2 x 20mm (0.79in) cannon; 2 x 7.62mm (0.3in) machine-guns

Right: A cannon-armed Spitfire 5b of 303 Squadron, a Polish-crewed unit, in flight in 1942.

The Curtiss P-36 and P-40 had modest capabilities but saw significant service with Britain and France. The P-40 was used extensively by British forces in North Africa in slightly different Kittyhawk and Tomahawk forms, but it could never quite compete with the Bf 109. Later-war USAAF fighters were of much higher quality.

Early Soviet fighters were a mixed bag, made worse by low manufacturing standards and poor pilot training. The mid-1930s' Polikarpov I-16 saw extensive use against Finland and in the early days of Operation Barbarossa. It was reasonably well armed but slow by the standards of 1941. The LaGG-1 and -3 were unusual in being built largely of wood and proved to be rugged but again rather slow in combat service.

The Soviets' MiG design bureau produced the MiG-1 and -3 that were most effective at high altitudes (which must have been an ordeal in the MiG-1's open cockpit), but they were otherwise disappointing. Most important were the various Yak designs. The series reached the Yak-7 variant by 1942 and would see further highly successful development later on in the war.

Japanese Army fighters of the early-war years showed the same characteristics as the better known "Zero" of the Navy (which also served extensively over land). Their excellent manoeuvrability stood them in good stead when faced with the older designs that the Allies deployed to the Pacific in 1941–2. However, their weaknesses of light construction and inadequate protection for pilot and fuel tanks proved more important against upgraded opposition later. Notable types included the Nakajima Ki-43 "Oscar" and Ki-44 "Tojo".

Twin-Engined Types

Perhaps the only twin-engined day fighter to serve successfully was the Lockheed P-38 Lightning, in use from 1941. Its speed and good range meant it performed well in the bomber-escort role. Other types like the Bristol Beaufighter or the Messerschmitt 110 lacked the agility that was needed for day-time air combat but appeared in other roles in due course.

REPORTING NAMES

To avoid confusion resulting from difficulties in pronunciation, American and other Allied forces gave Japanese aircraft "reporting names", which were designed to be short and easily recognizable. Another advantage was that a name could be allocated to a design before its true Japanese designation was known and did not need to be changed thereafter, whatever information later became available. Fighters were given boys' names, while bombers had girls' names.

DEWOITINE D.520

The Dewoitine D.520 was the best French fighter in 1940. Production failures meant that only 100 were available by May. They fought well in the Battle of France and were later briefly used against the Allies by the Vichy forces in Syria. About 900 were built in all.

Speed: 535kph (332mph)
Range: 1,250km (780 miles)
Engine: Hispano-Suiza 12Y45 in-line; 910hp
Armament: 1 x 20mm (0.79in) cannon; 4 x 7.5mm (0.295in) machine-guns

Air Combat – Weapons, Tactics and Aces

Some pre-war theorists thought air combats were a thing of the past because of the increased speed of aircraft. Instead, sudden dogfights and extended air battles took place in every theatre and air aces became as famous as their WWI predecessors.

Aircraft performance was far from being the only determinant of air combat success during WWII. Fighters and bombers both became more heavily armed as the war proceeded and better tactics were developed and practised.

Guns and Gunnery

Most of the air-to-air weapons in use in 1939 were rifle-calibre (approximately 7.7mm/0.303in) machine-guns. Some fighters, like Italy's CR 42, carried as few as two such weapons, and bombers, like Germany's Heinkel 111, might have only three, in hand-held mounts. Experience soon showed that this was inadequate. The speed of air combats and the fleeting moments when an enemy would be in the gunsight made greater firepower essential.

Above: A hand-trained Vickers K machine-gun, the sole defensive weapon fitted to the Fairey Battle.

Below: Loading the nose-mounted 0.79in (20mm) cannon in an RAF Bell P-39 Airacobra in 1941.

Britain had realized that something better would be needed to shoot down German bombers. Initially, the Spitfire and Hurricane were fitted with eight machine-guns but this was also shown to be insufficient because the individual rounds had too little striking power.

Alternatives to the rifle-calibre weapons were heavy machine-guns in the 13mm (0.51in) class and even more powerful but slower-firing 20mm (0.79in) cannon and some still bigger guns. Late-war American fighters generally carried six or eight 0.5in (12.7mm) guns and found this adequate. The Germans, facing numerous Allied heavy bombers, favoured a heavier punch, with weapons fits including 3cm (1.18in) cannon and even 21cm (8.27in) unguided air-to-air rockets.

Late-war bombers like the B-17G Flying Fortress might carry up to 13 x 0.5in (12.7mm) machine-guns in a mix of powered turrets and single mounts, but even that was not enough unless the aircraft also flew in a tight formation with its squadron-mates. The B-29 Superfortress took things a stage further with various of its turrets being remotely controlled, not individually manned.

Combat Tactics

At the start of the war, Britain's Fighter Command instructed its fighter squadrons to use tight formations and planned sequences of manoeuvres to attack enemy bombers. This was soon found to be dangerous and impractical. Shortly, all air forces were using the methods developed by the Germans, in

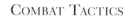

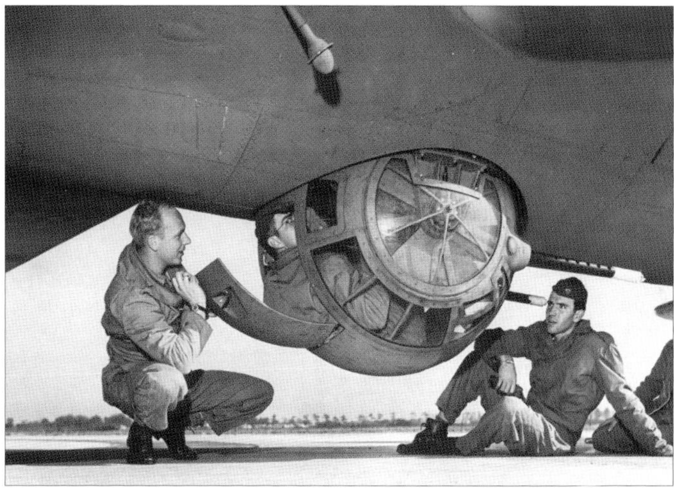

Right: Ball turret gunners on B-17s (twin 0.5in/12.7mm guns) were all small men for obvious reasons.

particular, in their involvement in the Spanish Civil War – the pair and the finger-four.

The basic unit was made up of a leader and his wingman. They kept relatively close together, with the leader responsible for the tactical decisions and most attacks, while the wingman's principal duty was to make sure they were not surprised from the rear. Two such pairs made up what the RAF called the finger-four, so-called because this group would fly in a loose formation shaped like the spread fingertips of the hand.

AIR ACES

As in WWI, pilots in all countries kept count of their "kills" and successful pilots were celebrated as aces, or in the rather more descriptive German term, *Experten*. Different air forces had varying methods of assessing air combat successes and it is certainly true that pilots generally claimed far more enemy aircraft shot down than were ever actually lost. This was probably as much a product of the speed and confusion of air battle as any deliberate attempt to mislead. However, it is also true that detailed examination of some aces' claims has backed up most of their scores.

By far the highest-scoring pilots were various Germans. The highest-scoring of all was Erich Hartmann with 352, while tens of others claimed more than 100. These high totals reflected the fact that the Germans did not rotate top pilots out of combat to other duties as often as other air forces. They were also mostly scored in the earlier years on the Eastern Front where enemy aircraft and pilots were relatively poor. One curiosity of the air fighting on the Eastern Front was that it was one of the few combat functions performed by women, though only on the Soviet side – several women became air aces.

Below: David McCampbell was the top US Navy ace of the war. He was eventually credited with 34 victories.

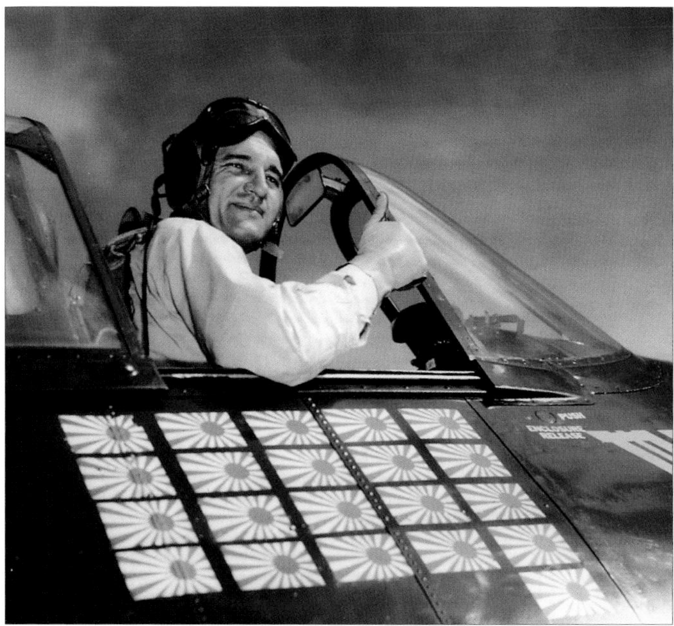

The British Home Front

Although circumstances meant that British troops were never committed to the fight in numbers to match the 1914–18 war, the British people in WWII were more completely mobilized in support of the war effort than in any other country.

Although Britain was and remained a democratic society, governed with the consent of the people, life in Britain during WWII was in many ways as rigorously controlled as in the totalitarian nations. Britain also devoted its national resources more thoroughly to fighting the war than any other country, totalitarian or democratic.

Although in the end Britain was lightly bombed by comparison with the major Axis powers, fears of air attack had important effects from the first. Within weeks of the outbreak of war, over 800,000 unaccompanied children had been evacuated from major cities and billeted with families of strangers in safer areas of the countryside. Many returned home during the Phoney War only to be evacuated again in the Blitz, and repeat the process during the V-weapon attacks of 1944–5. In all some 6 million civilians, adults and children were involved.

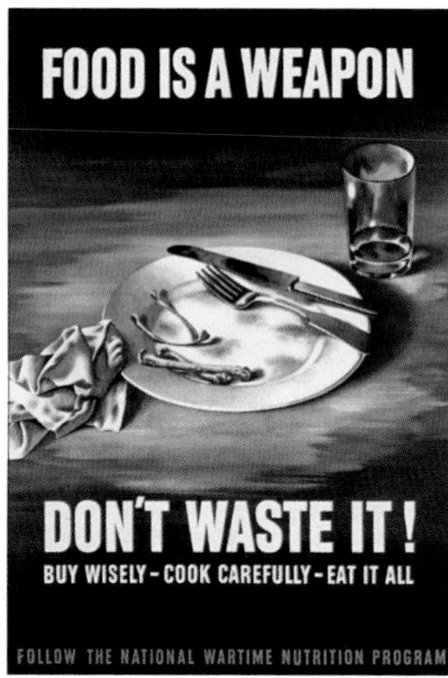

Above: Since much food was imported, reducing waste was vital.

Air Raid Precautions

Various Civil Defence services, including Air Raid Wardens, were organized with hundreds of thousands of members. Public air raid shelters were built or dug in parks; when the sirens sounded Londoners took to the tunnels of the Tube; and 1.5 million householders installed free family refuges called Anderson Shelters. Everyone implemented the blackout at night; it may have done little to misdirect enemy bombers but certainly caused a great increase in road accidents.

Many of the innovations of the war followed from the Emergency Powers Act, which was passed by parliament in May 1940. This act gave the government dictatorial authority over every aspect of life, and it was used extensively. As well as men conscripted into the forces, for example, the government could direct civilian men and women into particular jobs, control their wages in those jobs and forbid them to leave.

Left: Children being evacuated from London in 1939 say their goodbyes to their mothers.

Above: The number of British women working in agriculture more than tripled during the war.

When he took over as Prime Minister in May 1940 and transformed the country's previously lethargic war effort, Churchill formed a coalition government including Labour and Liberal members but principally drawn from his own Conservative Party. Its methods, however, were distinctly socialist in nature, with centralized planning of manpower, food, fuel, the economy and much more. The government was involved in almost every aspect of daily life. The civil service had to double in size to control it all.

Rationing of food, fuel, clothing and other goods was one of the most pervasive effects of the war. Petrol rationing was introduced in the first months of the war, with meat, butter and sugar added in 1940. Staple foods like bread and potatoes were never rationed – and the "Dig for Victory" campaign encouraged people to grow their own food. Factory canteens, relatively unusual until the war, also supplied many decent meals. Naturally, a black market did develop, but generally speaking the system worked well and was seen to be fair. It was also undoubtedly true that the poorest people, often unemployed and undernourished in the pre-war years, were much better fed during wartime.

The Beveridge Report

Planning for a better future was a major theme even when a successful outcome for the war was still uncertain. The Beveridge Report of December 1942 proposed schemes of "social insurance" to combat unemployment and provide health care. These and other developments would be embodied in what came to be described as the welfare state after WWII.

All in all, people in 1945 felt that their country had behaved well. They had stood up to Hitler from the first and had fought in a united and purposeful manner. They had high hopes for the future, not all of which would be fulfilled.

WINSTON CHURCHILL

Churchill (1874–1965) was Britain's Prime Minister from May 1940 until after the end of the war in Europe. He became a government minister in September 1939, after a long period in the political wilderness, because he had been among the first to see the true nature of the menace facing Britain. This and his natural pugnacity won him the premiership the next May. His inspirational leadership would keep Britain fighting over the coming months. At the same time he worked ceaselessly to bring the USA into the war, recognizing far better than anyone else that this alone would bring victory. It is no exaggeration to say that Europe would have entirely fallen to the Nazis without Churchill's courage.

Above: Prime Minister Churchill in a characteristic pose.

Left: Bevin Boys were young men conscripted to work in the coal mines because of the labour shortage later in the war.

Medium Bombers, 1939–41

Whether intended to support ground campaigns or perform longer-range strategic attacks, early-war bombers struggled to achieve a good balance between the conflicting demands of speed, bomb load, range and defensive armament.

There is no exact definition of when an aircraft becomes a bomber rather than a close-support or ground-attack machine, but the "medium bombers" included here are the twin- or three-engined designs used by all air forces of the time for slightly or substantially longer-range missions.

Pre-war air forces almost all believed that formations of bombers each carrying as few as three machine-guns could defend themselves against enemy fighters and go on to bomb their targets accurately by day or by night. Experience would show that these claims were untrue, other than in very exceptional circumstances.

The Blitzkrieg Era

Germany's Luftwaffe seemed to have the most powerful bomber force of the early-war years.

Above: He 111s in the Battle of Britain. Over 7,000 had been built by the time production ended in 1944.

This included three major types. Both the Dornier (Do) 17 and the Heinkel (He) 111 made their combat debuts during the Spanish Civil War, where their speed and the weakness of the opposition made them seem practically invulnerable. This was not confirmed in the Battle of Britain where their weak defensive armament and their modest bomb loads proved more relevant. The third type, the slightly later Junkers 88 (and the upgraded Do 217), were both more capable aircraft.

The contemporary British designs also had their own shortcomings. The Bristol Blenheim Mark 4 had a decent top speed of 428kph (266mph), for example, but only carried 455kg (1,000lb) of bombs. Neither the Blenheim nor its bigger stablemates were well-protected, though some of the larger aircraft included a British innovation of the mid-1930s – the power-operated gun turret. Least satisfactory of all was the Handley Page Hampden, which lost heavily in early daylight

Below: Savoia-Marchetti 79 Sparviero bombers. These were used for torpedo and bomb attacks.

operations and also lacked the range for night strategic bombing. The bigger Armstrong Whitworth Whitley carried a more substantial bomb load (up to 3,175kg/7,000lb) but it was no longer in front-line combat use by late 1943. The Vickers Wellington was much better. Its unusual web-like internal structure gave it enormous strength to go with a reasonable bomb load and speed.

Despite their defeats in 1939–40, various other air forces had aircraft of some potential, though these were seldom available in worthwhile numbers. Poland's PZL P37 was fast and had a good combination of range and bomb load, but the few in service were quickly overwhelmed. France's Farman F223 and Lioré et Olivier 45 both had impressive performance figures and fought well against the odds in 1940.

Various American designs also saw action with British or French forces before December 1941. The most important of these was the Douglas A-20, which was variously known as the Boston and Havoc and was used additionally in significant numbers by the Soviets.

THE MEDITERRANEAN

Italian designs in service in 1940 were essentially the same as those previously used in Abyssinia and Spain. They had been of good quality then, but Italy lacked the resources to develop replacements while also fighting these campaigns. The three-engined Savoia-Marchetti 79 Sparviero and the Fiat BR20 Cicogna were both in this category, though the Cant Z1007 Alcione was better.

DOUGLAS A-20B HAVOC

First used by France in 1940, the Havoc later served with the RAF and USAAF in the attack and night-fighter roles. In all some 9,500 were built up to 1944. The later A-20G variant was very heavily armed.

SPEED: 570kph (355mph)
RANGE: 1,770km (1,100 miles)
CREW: 4
ENGINES: 2 x Wright R-2600 Cyclone radials; 1,600hp each
ARMAMENT: 680kg (1,500lb) bombs; 3 x 0.5in (12.7mm) + 1 x 0.3in (7.62mm) MG

A number of American types also appeared in British service in the Mediterranean, notably the Martin A-22 Maryland and its development, the A-30 Baltimore. Neither saw combat later with the USAAF.

THE FAR EAST

The Japanese Army and Navy both had forces of land-based bombers. Designs that had seen some success in China during the 1930s continued service into the early stages of the Pacific War where they soon proved vulnerable to Allied fighters. These older types included the Mitsubishi Ki-30 "Ann" and the Kawasaki Ki-32 "Mary".

The Mitsubishi Ki-21 "Sally" was a later 1930s' Army design, broadly comparable to Western contemporaries, which included improved defensive armament in later versions. The Navy's Mitsubishi G3M "Nell" and the G4M "Betty" both had long range, but the G4M in particular was poorly protected.

HANDLEY PAGE HAMPDEN

The Hampden came into service in 1938 but was disappointing. Range with maximum bomb load was rather limited and defensive armament was poor. It left the Bomber Command service in 1942. About 700 of the 1,400 built were lost on operations.

SPEED: 410kph (255mph)
RANGE: 1,900km (1,200 miles)
CREW: 4
ENGINES: 2 x Bristol Pegasus XVIII; 980hp each
ARMAMENT: 1,800kg (4,000lb) bombs; 6 x 0.303in (7.7mm) machine-guns

The Battle of the Atlantic, 1939–41

U-boats and Allied anti-submarine forces were in action from the first day of the war to the last. The Battle of the Atlantic was the longest campaign of the war and if Hitler had won it he would almost certainly have won the war, too.

Britain imported roughly half its food, all its oil and many other items essential to the war economy. In addition British forces and the supplies they needed had to be shipped overseas if Britain was to fight its enemies. Since this traffic had to sail to and from British ports, the Atlantic accordingly became a major theatre of war.

THE GERMAN THREAT

Germany's Kriegsmarine was poorly prepared for war in 1939, with few powerful surface ships and a small force of submarines. Only from the spring of 1941 would German U-boat strength increase substantially. For the first year or so of the war about a third of German torpedoes failed to explode, which obviously thwarted many attacks.

Above: Günther Prien, one of the top U-boat commanders of 1940–1. Prien sank HMS *Royal Oak* in 1939.

Drawing on the lessons of WWI, Britain had planned a convoy system to protect its merchantmen, but there were so few escort ships in service initially that this could only be applied to the few hundred kilometres of their journeys nearest the British Isles. Although the escorts did have asdic (later called sonar) for finding a submerged submarine, they did not at first have radar or effective tactics for convoy protection. Britain had few aircraft committed to maritime duties and, until many months into the war, these also did not have radar to find a submarine on the

Above: *U-570* in a British port after surrendering to a British aircraft following damage in an air attack.

MAJOR SURFACE ACTIONS OF THE EUROPEAN WAR

The Royal Navy won most battles against the Germans and Italians.

surface nor weapons likely to damage a U-boat that had dived. However, although the German surface and U-boat forces achieved successes up to June 1940, these were not significant enough to pose a real problem.

"The Happy Time"

The fall of France in 1940 brought a major change. Within hours of the surrender the head of the U-boat force, Admiral Karl Dönitz, had equipment trains rolling to France's Atlantic ports, hundreds of kilometres nearer the convoy routes than previous German bases. What the U-boat crews called the "Happy Time" was about to begin. Until the spring of 1941 a series of U-boat commanders became celebrated as "aces", sinking ship after ship with little loss on the German side.

They used so-called "wolf-pack" tactics whereby the first boat to sight a convoy signalled U-boat headquarters, which then manoeuvred a group into attack positions. Then, at night, the U-boats would sail on the surface right in among the convoy's ships – without radar it was almost impossible to spot a surfaced U-boat. The U-boats would torpedo perhaps several ships and escape into the dark amid the resulting carnage. In this period the Germans also had the upper hand in the code-breaking struggle. Their messages remained secure, but many British ones giving away convoy routes and other movements did not.

Things improved for the Allies in the spring of 1941. Britain began breaking the U-boat codes. Escort ship numbers increased so that convoys could be protected all the way across the Atlantic. The escorts and their few supporting aircraft began to be fitted with effective radar sets. And the USA started taking a more active role, even though still officially neutral.

Above: The German battleship *Bismarck* after sinking HMS *Hood* in May 1941. *Bismarck* is down by the bow because of battle damage.

In April 1941 President Roosevelt extended the Pan-American Neutrality Zone and in July US Marines occupied Iceland. Ships of any nationality travelling between there and the USA were protected by the US Navy. By the autumn the Americans were effectively fighting alongside the British and the much-expanded Royal Canadian Navy. Although Allied shipping losses therefore declined sharply in the second half of 1941, the struggle was clearly by no means over.

SURFACE RAIDERS

The Kriegsmarine also used warships and disguised armed merchant ships in raids on Allied trade routes. Germany's three "pocket battleships" made various generally unsuccessful voyages and one, *Graf Spee*, was sunk in December 1939. The more powerful *Scharnhorst* and *Gneisenau* made a more worthwhile sortie in early 1941. The still bigger *Bismarck* sank HMS *Hood* on 24 May 1941 but was itself hunted down three days later. Seven disguised raiders made a number of voyages during 1940–1 and proved very difficult to track down, operating successfully for extended periods in the Pacific and Indian Oceans as well as the South Atlantic.

Above: A well-ordered convoy is seen from an American patrol aircraft shortly after leaving port.

Anti-submarine Escort Ships

Ships designed for anti-submarine duties did not need to be large or fast or carry numerous guns. Instead the British and US fleets built hundreds of tough and enduring smaller ships, which took a huge toll of enemy submarine forces.

The main anti-submarine vessels in all navies were traditionally destroyers. However, these were expensive to build and their design emphasized speed and anti-ship armament, not endurance and anti-submarine weapons. In World War II, large numbers of smaller and usually slower ships were built, designed and equipped mainly or exclusively for anti-submarine work.

Above: The destroyer escort USS *Huse* and an escort carrier hunting for Atlantic U-boats in 1944.

Japan's Failure

The major operators of ships in this category were the British and Americans (who supplied ships and designs to other Allied navies and also used each other's designs). The other navy with large ocean-going responsibilities, the Japanese, notably failed in anti-submarine operations, especially in defence of merchant ships. There were two reasons for this: first, both before and during the war the Japanese concentrated on offensive operations against enemy warships; and, second, they devoted little effort to developing radar and sonar equipment, crucial in the anti-submarine war. Some Japanese escorts had no underwater sensors as late as 1942, a year in which the Japanese Navy ordered the grand total of eight escort-type ships. By contrast the Royal Navy built around 600 escorts in its principal classes in the course of the war, while the US Navy produced many more.

Important British escort ship classes were: Black Swan sloops, Hunt escort destroyers, Loch and

HMS *LOCH FADA*

Seen here in April 1944 around the time of its commissioning, HMS *Loch Fada* was the first of the 28 Loch-class frigates. The design was a development of the previous River-class frigate, but it had much better anti-submarine weapons and sensors.

Commissioned: 1944
Displacement: 1,400 tons
Crew: 114
Speed: 20 knots
Armament: 1 x 4in (102mm) + various light anti-aircraft guns; 2 x Squid anti-submarine mortars + depth charge rails and throwers

River frigates and Flower and Castle corvettes. The Hunts and Black Swans were built to standard navy specifications and were effectively smaller and slower destroyers. The Hunt class (86 built) were a little over 1,000 tons standard displacement and could make 27 knots with 4 or 6 x 4in (102mm) guns; some carried 3 torpedo tubes. Fewer Black Swan-class ships were built, similar in size and armament but with a lower top speed (20 knots), in exchange for longer endurance.

The other escort ship classes did not have a purely naval heritage but were designed to be suitable for building in yards without naval experience and to use mercantile engines. In addition the Flower class, the most numerous class of all (267 built), had a hull form based on a civilian whale-catcher design.

The Flower class, with only a single 4in (102mm) gun, did have good anti-submarine weapons and sensors. Disadvantages were that they were slow (at only 16 knots a surfaced U-boat could outrun them) and were very uncomfortable for the crew in bad weather, common in the winter North Atlantic. The next most numerous type, the River class, were similar in size and performance to the Black Swans but suitable for building in civilian yards. The US Navy's Tacoma class were very similar.

Above: The USS *England* (in early 1944) had an amazing success rate.

US Navy Types

American production of escort ships was vast. There were six classes of destroyer escorts, over 400 ships built, of similar size and capabilities to the British Hunts. The most numerous of these was the Buckley class, in US Navy service from April 1943. One ship of this type, the USS *England*, achieved the unmatched feat of sinking 6 Japanese submarines within a period of 12 days in May 1944.

Other US escort vessels included a host of smaller types, usually described as submarine chasers. Many of these served with the US Coast Guard and, despite their diminutive size, they too chalked up an impressive record of over 60 submarine kills in the course of the war.

HMS *HONEYSUCKLE*

HMS *Honeysuckle* was a Flower-class corvette built on the Clyde. It is seen here during service with the Arctic convoys in 1945 in the Kola inlet alongside the escort carrier HMS *Trumpeter.* Four Flower-class ships (captured when under construction in France in 1940) were used by the Germans.

Commissioned: 1940
Displacement: 925 tons
Crew: 85
Speed: 16 knots
Armament: 1 x 4in (102mm) + various light anti-aircraft guns; 2 x depth charge rails (as built)

The Mediterranean Theatre, 1940–1

Thrown out of mainland Europe at Dunkirk, Britain concentrated on the Mediterranean and attacks on Germany's ally Italy in the early-war years. Mussolini's declaration of war in June 1940 would soon seem unwise.

As France was crashing to defeat in June 1940, Mussolini declared war on the Allies, determined not to miss out on a share of the spoils. Italy had annexed Albania without a fight in the spring of 1939 (this had been recognized by Britain as part of the then still current appeasement process). Then, in the summer of 1940, Mussolini picked a quarrel with Greece, which had been trying desperately to stay out of the war. On 28 October Italian troops crossed the border from Albania but their advance into Greece was soon halted and turned back by the Greek forces. By March 1941 half of Albania was under Greek control.

Italy also had large armies in its North African colony of Libya, as well as in East Africa in Italian Somaliland and Abyssinia. In August 1940 troops from Abyssinia occupied British and French Somaliland. Then, in September, the Italian Tenth Army crossed from Libya into Egypt but it halted and dug in after a short distance.

Above: Guns and crew of a British A9 cruiser tank in Egypt, May 1940.

In all these campaigns the weakness of the Italian forces was apparent. The troops were generally ill-trained and badly led and had little commitment to the fight. Equipment on land, at sea and in the air had many shortcomings, with flimsy tanks, outmoded biplane aircraft, inaccurate naval guns and more. Results soon made this plain.

Italian Disasters

The most spectacular Italian defeat was in the North African desert. By December 1940 the British force in Egypt was ready to respond to the initial Italian advance. Within two months the Italian Tenth Army had been thrown back to El Agheila (Al-'Uqaylah) and lost 130,000 prisoners at a cost of only 550 British dead. However, the

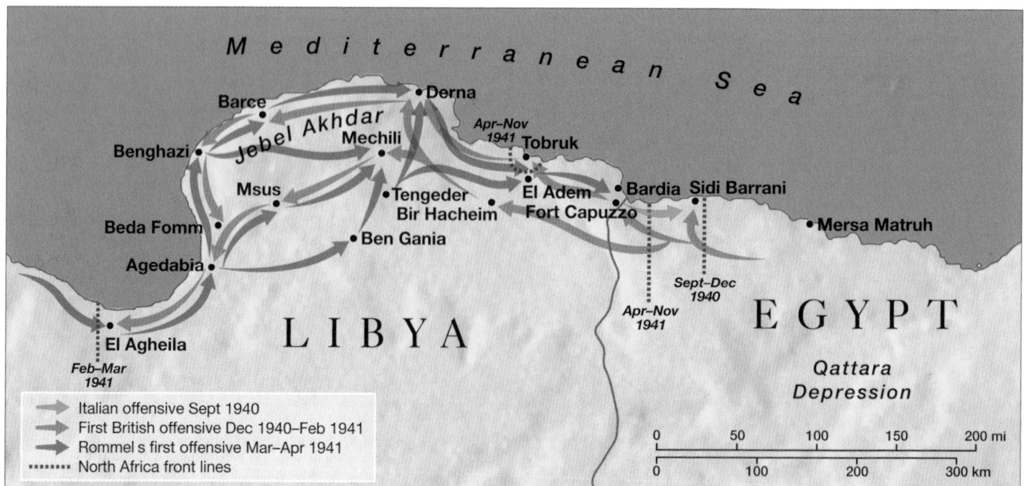

NORTH AFRICA, 1940–2
The Desert War saw a remarkable sequence of changing fortunes, with first one side, then the other on top.

British position was becoming less secure. Troops had already been withdrawn to East Africa; others would soon go to Greece.

Enter Rommel

Embarrassed by his Italian ally's failures, Hitler sent an ambitious young general called Erwin Rommel to Libya in February 1941 with a small force to block any further British advance.

Rommel spotted how weak the British front had become and attacked at the end of March. Within a month the British had been pushed all the way back into Egypt, with their worn-out tanks falling easy victims to the superior German equipment and tactics. Two minor British offensives – at the end of April and again in June – also failed after several further demonstrations of the superior German fighting skills.

Fortunately for the Allied side, one of their campaigns had a much greater success. During January and February 1941 the British, Indian and African troops that had been based in Sudan and Kenya went on the attack into Abyssinia and Italian Somaliland. Most of the Italian troops had been defeated by May though the final surrender did not come until November.

At sea Britain's morale was boosted by substantial gains over the powerful Italian fleet. Early skirmishes went Britain's way. On 11 November 1940, a night air attack by carrier planes on the Italian base at Taranto crippled three battleships. British forces based on Malta were then able to step up their attacks on the supply routes between Italy and North Africa, contributing greatly to the British success in the desert. In turn, when German air forces arrived in Sicily in strength in early 1941, this helped the land battle swing Rommel's way.

In March 1941 the Battle of Matapan confirmed the weakness of the Italian fleet. Three Italian heavy cruisers were caught and sunk while on the retreat from Admiral Andrew Cunningham's Mediterranean Fleet. Even though British naval strength declined substantially in the following months, the Italians would not make a major challenge at sea again.

Above: Damaged ships in Taranto Harbour, here seen in a British photograph taken after the attack.

Right: Some of the tens of thousands of Italian prisoners who were captured by the British in Libya in December 1940.

The Balkans and North Africa, 1941–2

In 1941 Hitler established what looked like a secure grip on the Balkan region, protecting his southern flank for the attack on the USSR. Changing fortunes in North Africa brought the British back to a desperate defence of Egypt in mid-1942.

Hitler's main plan for 1941 was to attack the USSR, but he also wanted to secure German control over south-eastern Europe. In the winter of 1940–1 Hungary, Romania and Bulgaria all in effect allied themselves with Germany. Greece, however, was winning its war with Italy in Albania and was receiving increasing help from Britain. This brought the unwelcome prospect of British aircraft based in Greece within relatively easy striking distance of the Romanian oilfields on which Germany greatly relied.

From late 1940, the Germans therefore prepared an attack on Greece. In late March 1941 when it seemed that the Yugoslavian government, after much pressure, was going to join the German bloc, a military coup reversed the situation and a furious Hitler ordered an immediate German attack.

The Germans deployed overwhelming forces for their offensive both in the air and on the ground. The strike against Yugoslavia started with heavy air raids on Belgrade on 6 April. The main land advance began from Romania on the 8th and was joined in succeeding days by converging attacks from both Hungary and Austria. There was little resistance and the Yugoslavs agreed an armistice on the 17th. German casualties for the campaign were fewer than 200 dead.

Above: German troops in northern Yugoslavia during the rapid and successful invasion of April 1941.

Below: A German transport plane crashes over Suda Bay during the invasion of Crete in May 1941.

By 6 April 1941 three British Empire divisions and supporting forces had been sent to Greece, substantially weakening the British position in North Africa. However, with much of the Greek Army already committed to the Albanian front and the remainder poorly deployed, there was little chance of the combination resisting the Germans for long. By the end of April the whole of mainland Greece had been overrun. The last act of the campaign was the capture of Crete by German airborne forces on 20–31 May.

Desert Battles

After their defeats in the first half of 1941, it took until November for the British forces in North Africa to prepare a new offensive. They started their advance across the border from Egypt into Libya on the 18th.

A bewildering series of manoeuvres and tank battles followed over the next three weeks or so. Much of the Allied superiority in numbers was frittered away by poor command, but eventually the exhausted German forces and their Italian allies had to retreat. As before this meant retiring all the way to El Agheila on the Gulf of Sirte, which Rommel reached at the end of December.

However, the pendulum was set to swing once more. German air strength in the Mediterranean was increased again and British naval power was at a low ebb, while Rommel's supply situation quickly improved. On land much British strength had been dissipated and resources and troops that might have come

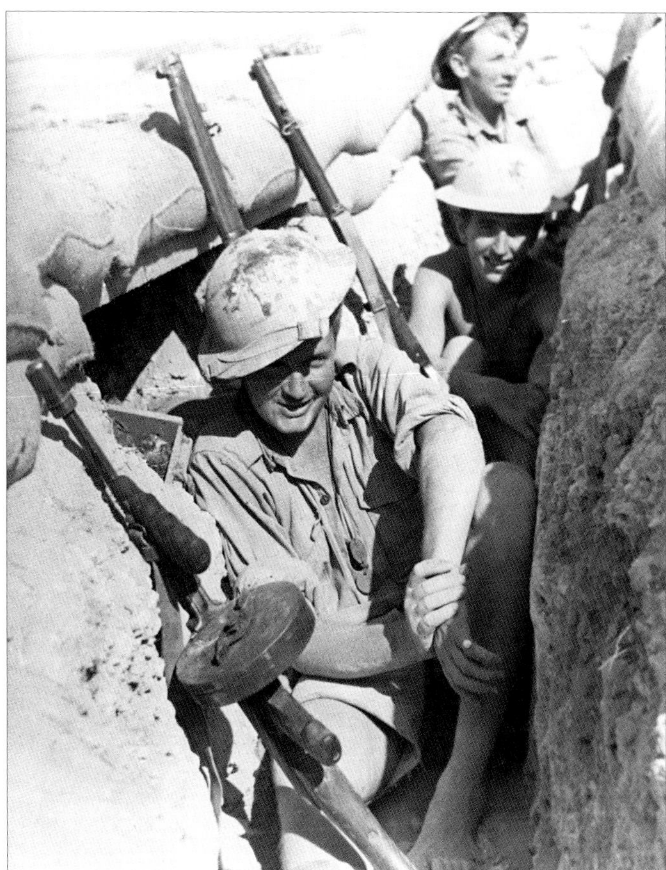

Above: Australian troops like these made up a large part of Tobruk's garrison during the siege in 1941.

to North Africa were instead being sent to face the Japanese advance in the Pacific. Less than a month after ending his retreat, Rommel attacked again.

NEW GERMAN ADVANCE

In the first stage, completed by early February 1942, the British were pushed out of most of the territory they had just captured. Next, in a three-week battle from 26 May, British defences on the so-called Gazala Line were overcome, despite being held by superior forces. Tobruk (Tubruq), which had survived a long siege after Rommel's first advance, was quickly captured this time with a great mass of supplies, which helped support Rommel's *Afrika Korps* for a charge into Egypt. After a disordered and panicky retreat, the British made a stand near an obscure railway halt called El Alamein in the first days of July. Rommel's last desperate attacks were fought to a standstill in the First Battle of El Alamein. Now both sides would settle down to rebuild their worn-out forces.

ERWIN ROMMEL

Field Marshal Rommel (1891–1944) became famous as Germany's commander in North Africa during 1941–2. Rommel took his first steps to fame when he was given command of a Panzer division in 1940. In 1941 he was appointed to lead German troops in Africa, which he did with considerable skill until outmatched by greater Allied resources in the late summer of 1942. In 1944 he commanded the troops opposing the D-Day landings but was wounded in an Allied air attack shortly after. He was forced to commit suicide later in the year because he had been implicated in the Bomb Plot against Hitler.

Above: Rommel (nearest) and Marshal Italo Gariboldi, the commander of the Italian forces in North Africa in 1941.

Torpedo Boats and Midget Submarines

These two varieties of warship were among the fastest and the slowest in service with any navy, but they shared a single quality: they were the smallest vessels capable of sinking an enemy ship of any size.

Victims of midget submarines included several battleships and cruisers in both the Pacific and European wars. Torpedo boats also knocked out a number of cruisers and smaller warships, in addition to having numerous, probably more important, successes against transport vessels of many different kinds in all arenas of war.

Torpedo Boats

Varying in length from roughly 24–34m (80–110ft), the torpedo boats in service during WWII generally carried a pair of torpedo launchers and a selection of 20mm (0.79in) or similar guns and lighter weapons, and might reach top speeds of just over 40 knots. Most navies mainly used petrol engines, but the Germans in particular used diesel. The Germans were also unusual in relying on a rounded hull form, whereas most other torpedo boats followed a flat-bottomed style designed for effective planing at high speed.

German torpedo boats were in fact probably the best in service during the war. They were called *Schnellboote* ("fast boats"), but they were usually referred to on the Allied side as E-boats. Their hull shape proved very effective in poorer weather, often a problem for torpedo boats generally. Their diesel engines were also well silenced by having their exhausts underwater and were in any case less prone to catch fire after combat damage than petrol ones. A variety of types existed, all rather larger than most Allied designs, armed by the late war with a twin 2cm (0.79in) and a single 3.7cm (1.46in) gun, plus machine-guns and the standard pair of torpedoes.

The American equivalents (also extensively used by the British), the PT for "patrol torpedo" boats, came mainly from the Higgins and Elco companies.

Below: British motor torpedo boats on patrol in the Channel during the Normandy invasion.

USS *PT-174*

PT-174, seen here off Rendova in January 1944, served in the Pacific from mid-1943 to the end of the war. *PT-174* was an 80ft Elco type (326 were built). These wooden boats displaced 56 tons, full load, and carried a variety of weapons in service in addition to the typical list below.

Length: 24.4m (80ft)
Speed: 41 knots
Engines: 3 x Packard 4m-2500; 1,500hp each
Armament: 1 x 40mm (1.58in) gun, 4 x 0.5in (12.7mm) MG; 4 x 21in (533mm) torpedoes

The most common of several slightly different Elco boats were 24.4m (80ft) long, carried four torpedo launchers, a 20mm or 40mm (1.58in) gun and numerous machine-guns. The Higgins boats were slightly shorter and a little slower but were probably more seaworthy. Their greatest successes came not in dramatic attacks on major warships, but in numerous minor operations against Japanese supply barges and similar craft in shallow Pacific island waters where bigger Allied vessels could not go.

Midget Submarines

Britain, Germany, Italy and Japan were the main users of midget submarines. Italy and Britain successfully used "human torpedoes" in which frogmen rode on top of a torpedo-like craft and would slowly approach an enemy anchorage to attach explosives to their targets. Britain additionally had X-craft, more like small conventional submarines, carrying massive explosive charges to drop under an anchored enemy ship. The German battleship *Tirpitz* was disabled in one such attack in Altenfjord in 1943.

Other midget submarines relied on firing torpedoes. The smallest were the German *Marder* and *Neger* types, which were in effect manned torpedoes with a second armed one slung underneath. Larger still was the *Seehund* design, a two-man vessel with two underslung torpedoes. These and several other German types appeared in small numbers and achieved scattered successes.

Japan had over 40 midget submarines in 1941, known as the *Type A* or *Ko-hyoteki*. They were approximately 24m (80ft) long and carried two torpedoes. They were used in unsuccessful attacks on Pearl Harbor and on Sydney in Australia. However, they did damage the old British battleship *Ramillies* in a harbour in Madagascar. They were carried close to all these targets by larger "parent" submarines.

Above: A Japanese midget submarine having run aground on a beach in the south-west Pacific.

Suicide Weapons

Japan produced numerous suicide surface and submarine craft. Over 6,000 *Shinyo* motorboats were built for use against various US invasion forces. However, these small craft were ineffective – many were hunted down by PT boats. The only submarine weapon to see action was the *Kaiten*, essentially a "Long Lance" torpedo modified to be controlled by a single crewman and designed to be launched from a larger submarine. Several hundred were built but they achieved little.

SEEHUND TYPE XVIIB

The *Seehund* type was the most successful German midget submarine. Some 138 entered service in 1944–45. They probably sank 9 ships, losing 35 of their number. An advantage of their small size was that when depth-charged, they might be thrown aside rather than being damaged.

Displacement: 17 tons
Crew: 2
Speed: 7 knots
Engines: 60hp diesel; 25hp electric motor
Armament: 2 x 533mm (21in) torpedoes (carried externally)

The USA and the European War

For over two years after Hitler attacked Poland the USA remained neutral, though all the time it sent increasing help to Britain and the other Allies. Even so it took Hitler's declaration of war to confirm that the USA would fight Germany.

Since the end of WWI the United States had returned to its traditional foreign policy of keeping out of overseas conflicts and maintaining only modest armed forces. By September 1939 this "isolationism" had been backed by strict neutrality laws that prevented the US government or private corporations from selling arms or giving loans to countries at war. Most Americans blamed Germany for starting the war and hoped that Britain and France would win it, but they were also very clear that the USA should stay out.

President Roosevelt and his government saw things a little differently. They recognized the evil of the Nazi regime, and of Japan's militarism, and that (as well as being morally repugnant) they presented a real threat to the USA's interests. Roosevelt no more wanted war than did the American people so his policy was to help the European Allies with "all means short of war", while being as tough with the Japanese as possible without provoking them to attack. The details of this changed over time but the general principles held good up to December 1941.

Above: Pioneer aviator Charles Lindbergh, one of the leaders of the isolationist America First movement.

Not Quite Neutral

The first step came in November 1939 when the "cash and carry" law was passed. Countries at war could buy American arms with cash (not on credit), provided they transported them overseas on their own ships. The facts of geography and Britain's large navy meant that this would only benefit the Allies, as was intended.

The hope that this would be enough to ensure an Anglo-French victory fell apart with France's surrender in June 1940. The USA's rearmament was immediately stepped up, in particular by the Two-Ocean Navy

Below: In September 1940 in the "destroyers for bases" deal, Britain was given old US Navy ships like these to fight the U-boat menace.

Below: Roosevelt took leading Republicans into his cabinet, including Frank Knox, here being sworn in as Navy Secretary.

FRANKLIN D. ROOSEVELT

Roosevelt (1882–1945) was President of the USA from 1933 to his death. While Churchill's wartime leadership is almost universally admired, Roosevelt's has always been more controversial. Although he was no warmonger, he saw clearly the threats posed by Germany and Japan and worked steadily to oppose them. Opponents, however, said that he deceived the American people over just how far he was going. He has also been criticized as being naive in his dealings with Stalin and the Chinese Nationalists. On the other hand his generous instincts were shown in his Lend-Lease policy, without which Britain and other Allies could not have continued the fight.

Right: Roosevelt giving one of his famed "fireside chat" radio broadcasts.

Act of July, which provided for a massive increase in American naval forces. This was designed to protect against the German threat but it also worried Japan. It would take a couple of years to build the ships but by then the Japanese would be unable to compete, unless they did something about it first.

Next, in the autumn of 1940, came the Selective Service Act, establishing conscription for the first time in US history when the nation was not at war.

LEND-LEASE

Roosevelt also continued to help Britain, although this carried risks – sending arms to Britain might mean Hitler getting them for free if he won the war. However, there was a new problem – Britain was about to run out of cash and would probably be unable to continue the war at all, never mind pay for more American goods. The answer was the "Lend-Lease" programme, in operation from March 1941. Britain, and later other Allies including the USSR, would be sent vast supplies of arms and other goods, produced initially at American expense, on the basis that they would be paid for or returned after the war.

Roosevelt was well aware that there was no point making arms for Britain only for the Germans to sink them on their way across the Atlantic. Through 1941, therefore, the US Navy played a more active part against Germany's U-boats in the Atlantic, though how far this was going was not made clear to the American people. By autumn US warships in the western Atlantic were doing the same things as the British and Canadians. It was equally clear, though, that Americans still wanted to avoid war. In August 1941 the Selective Service Act was only renewed in Congress by a single vote.

Throughout all this Hitler had been cautious, content to fight only the enemies he already had. Incomprehensibly, four days after Pearl Harbor, he changed his mind and declared war on the USA, a decision that doomed his regime to a defeat as crushing as that awaiting Japan.

Below: Men register for the draft in October 1940, under the terms of the new Selective Service Act.

German Rule in Europe

Life in the countries occupied by the Nazis was exceedingly harsh. Starvation rations, slave labour and other cruelties were everyday realities in all the occupied territories, though Jews and resisters fared worse still.

Racism was the whole basis of Germany's rule in Europe. Everything was to be done and organized for the benefit of both Germany and the *Volk* – the German race, as defined by Hitler and the Nazis. Within this system there were gradations. At the top were those like the Dutch or Norwegians, who were certainly regarded as second-class citizens but still worthy of some respect, and near the bottom were the Slavs, whose lives were valueless even if sometimes their labour was not. Jews were the lowest category of all.

The way in which conquered territories were ruled naturally varied within this hierarchy. In Poland or the Ukraine Nazi cruelty, organized and led by the SS, was open and extreme.

Above: A German officer and a British bobby in the Channel Islands, the only occupied British territory.

Above: *Volksdeutsche* from Bessarabia in Romania, on their way to be resettled in Germany.

Near the other end of the scale were countries like Norway, where local Nazi sympathizers were allowed the appearance of a say in the government. (Norway's Vidkun Quisling has given the English language a word for just this sort of traitor and was executed for his treason after the war.) Finally, there were nations like France where a government at least not hostile to Germany was allowed to control all or part of the country.

The "independence" of Marshal Pétain's Vichy regime was bought at a price, however. More than half of government revenue went straight to Germany to pay for the costs of the occupation forces and almost half of French industrial output was for German benefit. The franc was artificially valued, so that anything the Germans did pay for was acquired on unfair terms.

Food rationing was severe with the official provision set at an inadequate 1,200 calories per day, though many of the poorest did not even manage this – much food was diverted to an expensive black market. The experience of other Western European countries was similar in many of these respects.

Forced Labour

As the war proceeded Germany became increasingly dependent on foreign labour to keep its economy running. This included around 1.5 million prisoners of war and, by 1943–4, some 5 million civilians, most of whom had been forced to work in Germany and many of whom were treated as slaves. Roughly a quarter of the workforce in Germany in the later war years was made up of foreigners.

The process started in 1939–40 when many Poles were brought to Germany as farm labourers. Later, in eastern Europe, men, women and many young children were simply rounded up and sent wherever it suited Germany. In Vichy France men were conscripted to do their national service in the German labour force.

Volksdeutsche

People of German descent (known to the Nazis as *Volksdeutsche*) were living in many

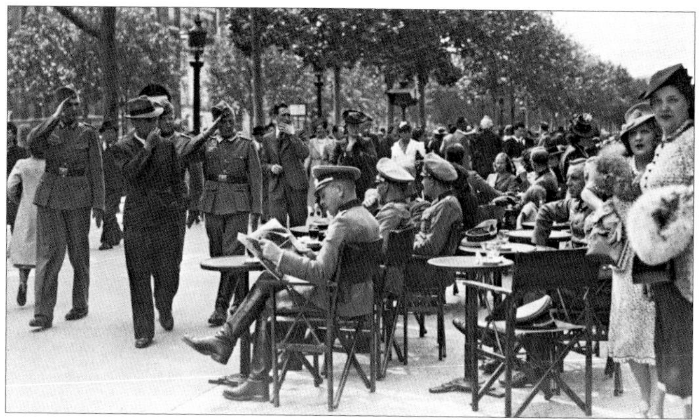

Above: German officers enjoy a Paris café in the gentler early days of the occupation in 1940.

places in eastern Europe; one of the most bizarre aspects of Nazi rule was the plan to reassimilate them with the *Volk*. Hundreds of thousands of people were to be brought back into the Reich. Many were transported from their homes in the Baltic States or western USSR, supposedly to be resettled in captured territories that were to become part of Germany proper. Most ended up among the millions of homeless displaced persons in central Europe after the war.

Perhaps the most heartless aspect of this particular policy was the *Lebensborn* programme. As part of this plan to increase the German race, SS representatives toured occupied territories identifying "racially worthwhile" children and taking them for forced adoption in Germany. Some 300,000 children are believed to have been abducted from their families in this way; 80 per cent of them never returned.

HEINRICH HIMMLER

Himmler (1900–45) was head of the Nazi SS from 1929 to the fall of Hitler's regime. He built the SS up from being a relatively minor Nazi Party organization to a state within the state. He was in charge of Germany's whole police and security apparatus, of the party's murderous "racial policy" and of the German Army's rival, the Waffen-SS. Although he was personally responsible for numerous hideous cruelties, he was also a rather timid personality. He was captured by British forces at the end of the war and poisoned himself when his disguise as a private soldier was exposed.

Above: Reichsführer-SS Heinrich Himmler on parade.

Left: Hitler with his fervent admirer Vidkun Quisling. The Germans never gave Quisling any real power in occupied Norway.

Operation Barbarossa

Germany's invasion of the Soviet Union was the greatest military operation ever seen. Its outcome would decide the result of the war and the campaign would be fought on both sides with a vicious barbarity unequalled elsewhere.

Hitler had first ordered his generals to begin planning an attack on the Soviet Union even before the Battle of Britain was fought. Ultimately, the Nazis intended to occupy the whole of the European USSR, exterminating all Jews and communists and enslaving any surviving "sub-human" Slavs.

Although the Germans deployed a truly massive force of around 3 million men, 3,300 tanks and 2,700 aircraft, the task facing them was huge. They were outnumbered by the Red Army forces in the western USSR, and they greatly underestimated the size of the Soviet reserves in the Far East and elsewhere. They thought little of Soviet weapons or efficiency; indeed, only a quarter of the total 24,000-strong Soviet tank force was in running order – and German intelligence knew little of the superior Soviet weapons like the KV-1 and T-34 tanks, which were coming into service.

Germany's Problems

The huge distances were daunting. The Germans had pressed hundreds of vehicles from every conquered nation into service but still needed over 600,000 horses for their transport needs. Most ordinary soldiers simply had to march. Roads everywhere were unmade or in dreadful condition, and the Soviet rail system ran on a different gauge, so the track would need to be converted before it could be used. The

OPERATION BARBAROSSA
Neither Hitler nor his generals could decide which of their three main advances should have priority.

Below: Soviet troops fought with undoubted bravery in what they soon called the Great Patriotic War.

Above: Muddy roads across the endless steppe, with Panzers at war in the east in 1941.

problems in these areas would escalate the farther the advance went and as the bad weather of autumn and winter set in.

The Germans' greatest asset was that, despite many warnings, Stalin refused to allow proper preparations to be made and no one dared to argue. Why this was is a mystery. He seems to have been so frightened by the chance of a German attack that he tried everything he could to avoid provoking one.

The Battle Begins

The German attack, Operation Barbarossa, began early on the morning of 22 June 1941. Within hours the leading tank forces had penetrated tens of kilometres into the unprepared Soviet defences and over a thousand Soviet aircraft were wrecked on their airfields. Within a week the two Panzer groups leading Army Group Centre's advance had completed a vast encirclement west of Minsk; 300,000 Red Army troops surrendered there by early July. In the meantime the attack had surged on toward Smolensk, another 320km (200 miles) nearer Moscow.

Progress on the other main attack front was also excellent; Army Group North had over-run the Baltic States and was closing in on Leningrad. The less powerful Army Group South, however, was being held up by Soviet resistance just west of Kiev. Neither Hitler nor his generals had been sure about the best strategy for the campaign from the start and now Hitler ordered a change of plan. Guderian's Second Panzer Group was to attack south, to help complete the capture of Kiev and not, as Guderian and other generals urged, immediately continue east to Moscow.

The results seemed to justify the decision. Over half a million Red Army troops were captured east of Kiev by mid-September. The ever wearier German troops redeployed to the Moscow front by the end of the month for what they hoped would be the final decisive attack.

However, the delay had brought the start of bad weather. After yet more fierce fighting, they reached Moscow's outer suburbs in early December but they could go no further. The German units were now a fraction of their former strength and the troops were suffering horribly from the freezing weather. A quick victory had once seemed so certain that no supplies of winter clothing had been prepared. Instead a long, horrible struggle on the Eastern Front was now inevitable.

HEINZ GUDERIAN

General Guderian (1888–1954) was the man most responsible for the creation of the German Army's formidable Panzer arm. His pre-war book *Achtung! Panzer!* explained how tanks might be used in a new fast-moving style of war. He was highly successful in command of a Panzer corps in both Poland and France in 1939–40. These successes were repeated during the early months of Operation Barbarossa, but he was dismissed by Hitler that winter. He served in staff positions later in the war, but by then Hitler was making most of the decisions and Guderian's advice was seldom followed.

Above: General Guderian with his *Panzergruppe* in 1940.

Anti-tank Guns, 1939–42

As tanks were steadily upgraded so, too, were the anti-tank guns used against them by the infantry and artillery. The first anti-tank guns were small, manoeuvrable and easy to conceal, but as they grew in size these qualities came under threat.

When tanks were initially introduced in WWI, the weapons used to counter them were either standard artillery guns or specially powerful rifles. Although anti-tank (AT) rifles were still used by most armies in 1939, it was clear in the 1930s that more powerful specialized AT weapons were needed by the infantry and other forces.

Germany's standard AT gun at the start of the war was a 3.7cm (1.46in) weapon made by the Rheinmetall company from 1936. This gun (formally the Panzerabwehrkanone [PaK] 36) was typical of those in service with other armies, too. It was mounted on a wheeled carriage, giving an overall weight of under half a tonne, and could readily be manhandled in action. It fired a 0.68kg (1.5lb) armour-piercing (AP) shot, capable of defeating 31mm (1.22in) of armour angled at 30 degrees at a distance of 500m (550yd).

Below: A Soviet 45mm (1.77in) M1937 anti-tank gun under fire.

Soviet and US Types

The Soviet Model 1930 37mm gun had originally been developed by Rheinmetall and was very similar to the PaK 36. Japan also had a licence-built version of the PaK 36. The US Army M3A1 37mm, introduced in 1940, was slightly different, though examples of the German gun were studied by the American designers. Over 18,000 of these were produced. Although it was outclassed in Europe by late 1942, this gun saw most service in the Pacific against Japan's weaker tanks.

In 1939 Britain's standard weapon was the 2pdr (40mm), with similar performance, though on a rather heavier and more elaborate carriage. The Soviets also had the 45mm (1.77in) M1937, which was slightly more powerful – and it was later replaced by a longer-barrelled M1942 version.

Heavier Calibres

By 1939 heavier weapons were being developed in the West. Germany stepped up to 5cm (1.97in) in the PaK 38, with more than double the armour penetration of the PaK 36.

3.7cm PaK 36

The 3.7cm PaK 36 anti-tank gun (shown below during a river-crossing operation in the Netherlands in 1940) was the German Army's standard weapon at the start of the war. It was replaced in most units by 1942. A similar weapon was mounted on the Panzer 3 and various other armoured vehicles.

Calibre: 3.7cm (1.46in) L/45
Muzzle velocity: 762m/sec (2,500ft/sec)
Armour penetration: 31mm (1.22in) at 30° at 500m (550yd)
Weight of shot: 0.68kg (1.5lb)

Britain's next type was the 6pdr (57mm), but this was slow to come into service because the switch in production from the 2pdr was delayed by the need to re-equip the army after Dunkirk. The USA's 57mm M1 was essentially a 6pdr manufactured under reverse Lend-Lease. There was also a Soviet 57mm M1943 weapon, produced in relatively limited numbers by Soviet standards. All these nations would make still bigger guns later in the war.

Germany was unusual in the early-war period in having both smaller- and larger-calibre weapons in regular AT use. The larger weapons were 8.8cm (3.46in) guns, originally produced for anti-aircraft (AA) service as the FlaK 18 and 36. As AA guns these already had the high muzzle velocity that was needed for the AT role and, unlike the AA weapons in most other armies, they were supplied with appropriate ammunition and specifically designated for such duty. These were by far the most formidable AT guns of the early-war period.

The smaller-calibre weapon was a so-called "squeeze-bore" design, in which the barrel tapered in size from breech to muzzle with a specially designed round being compressed as it passed down the barrel; the resulting build-up in pressure produced a very high muzzle velocity.

Above: British troops training with a 2pdr (40mm) anti-tank gun in 1942.

The only weapon of this type that saw significant service was Germany's sPzB 41, 2.8cm tapering to 2cm (1.1–0.79in). It had a similar AP performance to the PaK 36 and in the version for airborne troops weighed only 118kg (260lb). Its disadvantage was that it required tungsten-cored ammunition. Tungsten was very scarce in blockaded Germany, so production of these guns was ended in 1943.

This, however, was a pointer to future developments. Most early-war AT rounds were relatively simple solid-shot designs. From around 1942 capped designs and composite construction increasingly took over and would be extensively used in late-war weapons.

8.8cm FLAK 36

Throughout the war Allied tank crews feared the famous "eighty-eight" above all other German weapons. The example shown below is seen in service at El Alamein in 1942. The open spaces of the Desert War favoured the accuracy, armour penetration and range of this powerful gun.

Calibre: 8.8cm (3.46in) L/56
Muzzle velocity: 773m/sec (2,536ft/sec)
Armour penetration: 110mm (4.33in) at 500m (550yd) at 30° (99mm at 1,000m)
Weight of shot: 10.2kg (22.5lb)

Horrors of War – The Eastern Front

The war on the Eastern Front was conducted with a savageness hardly seen elsewhere during WWII. The Nazis saw their enemies as valueless racial inferiors and to the Soviet leaders life was cheap – their own citizens' or anyone else's.

As the German drive on Moscow ground to a halt in temperatures of minus 40 or worse in early December 1941, the pitiless pattern of the war on the Eastern Front was already all too well established. Millions of civilians and prisoners of war (POW) would die near the front and behind the lines as a consequence of the fighting.

Above: A Red Army anti-tank gun crew advancing any way they can during the Battle for Moscow.

Mass Murder

Before Operation Barbarossa began Hitler had ordered that any captured communist officials were to be killed. As it had done during the invasion of Poland, the SS formed *Einsatzgruppen* to follow behind the advancing armies. These murder squads (about 3,000 strong) had orders to eliminate all Jews and communists. By the end of 1941, as their own records attest, these squads had killed over 600,000 Jews in the occupied USSR.

Below: A German soldier gives himself up, winter 1941–2. Many German POWs died of ill treatment.

POW on both sides also faced a grim fate. Over 5 million Red Army soldiers were taken prisoner by the Germans during the war, 3.8 million of them in 1941; only around 35 per cent of these survived their captivity. Prisoners on both sides were given little food. The only medical attention they received was from their own captured medical staff and any supplies they had.

It is likely that some of this maltreatment arose from lack of resources and incompetence, but the racism at the heart of Nazi ideology and the total disregard for human life central to Stalinism played a larger part. And, of course, many more who tried to surrender were simply shot out of hand. The Waffen-SS (a substantial portion of the German forces later in the war) almost never took prisoners on the Eastern Front. The Soviet attitude to POW and potential enemies was clearly shown by their murder at Katyń and elsewhere of some 15,000 Polish Army officers who fell into their hands in 1939.

Around a fifth of the population of the German-occupied territories either fled as refugees or were evacuated by the Soviet authorities. Many were sent to work in the new factories being set up east of the Urals, where living and working conditions were harsh in the extreme. Significant numbers of those who remained behind might well have welcomed the Germans had they been well treated. Instead their lives and property were always at risk –

Right: An exhausted German soldier asleep in his muddy trench on the Eastern Front in early 1942.

whole villages were routinely burnt to the ground in retaliation for partisan activities. On the other hand partisans were often unpopular with civilians; they were tightly controlled by the communist hierarchy and quick to "discipline" those who failed to follow their lead.

Moscow Attack

Some of the most pitiless fighting of the campaign took place in the winter of 1941–2. On 6 December the Soviet forces began a successful counterattack on the Moscow front, using fresh reserve forces assembled from the Far East. Unlike the Germans, the Soviet troops had good winter clothing and equipment fit to withstand the country's extreme cold.

Hitler's response was to order "fanatical resistance" and no retreat. It is possible that his order to stand fast was correct in this case and saved his forces from disintegration, but various of his best generals disagreed and were dismissed. Hitler took over himself as Commander-in-Chief of the Army and would now personally control all major military decisions on the Eastern Front. Although in places they were pushed back some 160km (100 miles), early 1942 saw the Germans solidifying their front line until all operations were halted as usual in the east by the spring thaw.

Below: Mass graves of some of the Polish officers murdered at Katyń.

Below: German soldiers beating a Russian villager as others watch.

Battleships and Battle-cruisers The USS *Indiana* shelling the Japanese coast in 1945.

Coral Sea and Midway Aircraft aboard the carrier USS *Enterprise* during the Battle of Midway.

Japan's Continuing Successes Burmese civilians look on as Japanese invaders pass by.

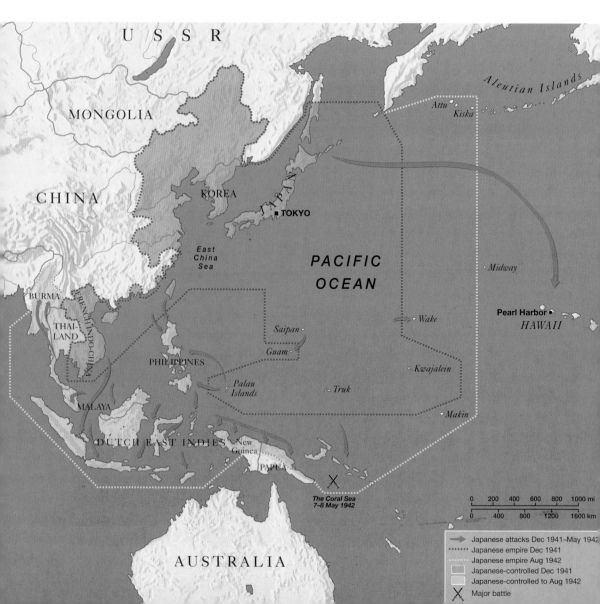

USSR
MONGOLIA
CHINA
KOREA
JAPAN
TOKYO
Aleutian Islands
Attu
Kiska
East China Sea
PACIFIC OCEAN
Midway
Pearl Harbor
HAWAII
Wake
Saipan
Guam
BURMA
THAILAND
FRENCH INDO-CHINA
PHILIPPINES
Kwajalein
Palau Islands
Truk
MALAYA
Makin
DUTCH EAST INDIES
New Guinea
PAPUA
The Coral Sea 7–8 May 1942
AUSTRALIA

0 200 400 600 800 1000 mi
0 400 800 1200 1600 km

Japanese attacks Dec 1941–May 1942
Japanese empire Dec 1941
Japanese empire Aug 1942
Japanese-controlled Dec 1941
Japanese-controlled to Aug 1942
Major battle

JAPAN'S PACIFIC CONQUESTS

Japan's attack on Pearl Harbor began a stunning half year of military triumphs that saw the overrunning of many British, American, French and Dutch colonies – from Burma in the west to a range of Pacific islands in the east and south. As well as the victories on land and the decimation of the US Pacific Fleet, British and other naval forces were practically wiped out throughout the theatre of operations and Allied air power was largely neutralized.

Japanese leaders had hoped that the conquest of these territories would give access to the natural resources their country desperately wanted and create a defensive perimeter that could be defended successfully against the worst their enemies might do. Instead, just as in their earlier and ongoing involvement in China, they were sucked into yet more advances, which confirmed what the most sensible Japanese commanders had long realized: in attacking the USA, as previously in China, they had bitten off far more than they could chew.

Japan also made much of plans for a Greater East Asia Co-Prosperity Sphere, a vague anti-imperialist alliance from which all native Asians might hope to benefit. In fact the expanded Japanese Empire created in 1941–2 turned out to be brutal, racist and exploitative.

The USA at War Making aircraft engines was a new area of work for American women.

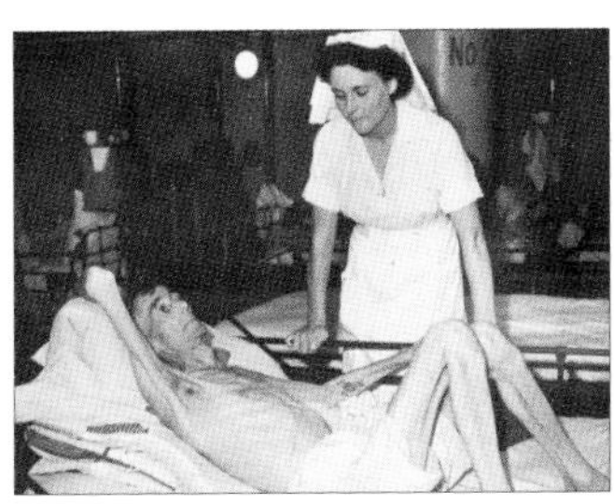

Japan's Brutal Empire A sick British ex-prisoner gets medical treatment after his liberation in 1945.

Japan's First Advances General Percival signs the surrender of Singapore on 15 February 1942.

Approach to War in the Pacific

Throughout 1939–41 tension between Japan and the United States grew. Its armies increasingly bogged down in China, Japan decided to look south for the natural resources and the empire its leaders thought their country needed and deserved.

In early 1939 Japan's leaders were unsure what strategy to adopt to overcome their difficulties in China and their related economic problems. Some wished to attack north against the USSR, others to move south towards the European colonies of South-east Asia, with their substantial natural resources of oil, tin, rubber and much more.

Vital Soviet Victory

Japan had a long-standing enmity with Russia. Through the 1930s there had been frequent battles along the frontier between Japanese-controlled territory in north-east China and the Far Eastern provinces of the USSR. In the summer of 1939 there was particularly fierce fighting in the Khalkhin Gol region on the border between Soviet-backed Mongolia and China – and the Japanese were badly defeated.

Left: US Secretary of State Cordell Hull with Japan's Ambassador Nomura during the final pre-war negotiations in 1941.

These little-known battles were a decisive turning point in history. Both the Japanese Army and the government began looking more urgently at expanding to the south. In April 1941 Japan negotiated a Neutrality Agreement with the Soviets and would stick to this decision, even when tempted to change it by Hitler's attack on the USSR in June 1941.

Tension between Japan and the USA and European colonial powers over events in China had grown in the 1930s. Japan was convinced that supplies reaching China through Burma and French Indo-China were vital in keeping the Chinese fighting. Then, in the summer of 1940, new possibilities opened up. Hitler's victories left the French and Dutch colonies virtually defenceless and British power in Asia gravely weakened while the USA's rearmament still had a long way to go.

In July 1940 the Japanese government formally decided on a twin policy: first, to win their existing war by blocking the supply routes to the Chinese; and second, to gain access to the desired raw materials from Malaysia and the East Indies, if necessary by a new war. This was the moment when war between Japan and the USA became more likely than not. In September Japan took the first step in this plan and moved troops into northern Indo-China, by agreement with

Left: Germany, Japan and Italy sign the Tripartite Pact, September 1940.

the Vichy French. In return the Americans imposed an embargo on some iron and steel exports to Japan. A retaliatory process of escalation had begun.

Diplomatic preparations for new advances came with Japan's signing of the Tripartite Pact with Italy and Germany in September 1940. This was clearly aimed, from Japan's point of view, at limiting the USA's responses in the Pacific by the threat that such responses might involve the USA in a European war.

Into Indo-China

In July 1941 a Japanese government meeting decided to go into southern Indo-China as a first step to further moves south, even if this meant war. However, in the meantime, Japan would continue negotiations with the USA.

American code breakers read reports of the meeting; US leaders concluded that Japan had passed the point of no return, though in fact the Japanese were still uncertain. The Americans decided to step up their economic pressure, cutting off almost all of Japan's oil supplies. This convinced the more militant Japanese that the USA had aggressive intentions, while at the same time they saw their stockpiles of strategic materials gradually diminishing.

Half-hearted negotiations continued into November but by then the new Japanese Prime Minister, General Tojo Hideki, and his government were convinced that their country had dithered for long enough. There seemed no serious possibility of agreement with the Americans without an unthinkable Japanese withdrawal from China. Japan still had a fighting chance, or so they believed, but they must take it immediately. On 29 November they made the decision to go to war.

Left: Soviet troops celebrate their decisive victory over Japan at Khalkhin Gol in 1939.

THE JAPANESE GOVERNMENT

To outsiders, Japan looked to be run in a similar way to countries like Britain, with an elected government and a ceremonial monarch. In fact in Japan the Army and Navy, and even factions within them, largely controlled national policy. The most militant officers were often those with least knowledge of the wider world, but their supposed patriotic motives were widely respected. Men of this kind had provoked the "Manchuria Incident" as far back as 1931, and ten years later their underestimation of US power would lead Japan into another disastrous war.

Above: Prince Konoye and General Tojo, Japan's last premiers before December 1941.

Left: Japanese troops extending their occupation of French Indo-China in August 1941.

Pearl Harbor and Japan's War Plans

Japan seemed to win a stunning victory at Pearl Harbor, but in the longer term the attack on sovereign United States territory, without a declaration of war, could hardly have been less in Japan's interests. The USA would fight on until victory.

On 7 December 1941 planes from six Japanese aircraft carriers made a surprise attack on the main base of the US Pacific Fleet at Pearl Harbor in Hawaii. Japan had not delivered a declaration of war when the attack began; the USA declared war on Japan the next day.

Why Pearl Harbor?

Japan's decision to attack Pearl Harbor came about in a roundabout way. What Japan wanted was control of the natural resources of both the British and Dutch colonies in Malaysia and the East Indies.

KEY FACTS

Place: Oahu Island, Hawaii

Date: 7 December 1941

Outcome: US Pacific Fleet crippled; USA and Japan go to war.

The Philippines, an American commonwealth, stood on the flank of such an advance and therefore would be attacked too, so war with the USA certainly had to be anticipated.

With Britain busy with the European war and the other colonial powers' homelands under German occupation, the main threat to Japan would come from the US Pacific Fleet – the US Navy was formidable though the US Army was not. Hence a strike on Pearl Harbor at the outset would gain time for Japan to grab the territory it sought. Japan would then fortify

Below: Pearl Harbor at peace shortly before the Japanese attack. The Ford Island airstrip (centre) and "Battleship Row" to its left would be prime targets, but the oil storage tanks, further left, would be missed.

Above: Japanese aircrew board their planes, ready to attack Pearl Harbor, 7 December 1941.

a perimeter round its new empire which, Japan's leaders believed, would be so daunting that the feeble and decadent Americans would not dare to attack but instead make peace.

American Precautions

In the weeks before the attack the US government knew from code-breaking information that a Japanese military attack was very likely imminent. They thought that the most likely target would be the Philippines, and that the main danger to Hawaii was sabotage by Japanese agents. However, since the war it has been alleged that President Roosevelt and his government knew of the Japanese plans but did not take proper precautions, so they could mislead the American people into going to war. No real evidence for this claim exists.

From about 07:45 hours that Sunday morning, two waves of Japanese aircraft struck the naval anchorage and various airfields on Oahu for two hours. By the end of the strikes, 2,403 Americans were dead, 6 of the 8 US battleships in port had been sunk, along with other vessels, and 188 American aircraft were destroyed. The Japanese lost 29 aircraft, 5 midget submarines and 1 larger submarine. On the US side a catalogue of errors had made Japan's task easier: radar warnings were ignored; anti-aircraft ammunition boxes were locked; and aircraft were easy targets on the ground because they had been parked together so they could be easily guarded against sabotage.

For the future there was now no doubt that, outraged by what President Roosevelt called "a day of infamy", the American people would fight and would continue their fight until their overwhelming resources had brought a total victory. And they also still had significant means to hand. The Pacific Fleet's aircraft carriers happened to be away from port that Sunday, a chance survival that would help point the way to the methods by which Japan would be defeated.

It was not just the Japanese who acted against their own best interests at Pearl Harbor. On 11 December 1941 Hitler declared war on the Americans. The USA now had to fight in the European war as well.

YAMAMOTO ISOROKU

Admiral Yamamoto (1884–1943) was Japan's principal naval commander of the war until his death in 1943, when his aircraft was intercepted by American fighters acting on code-breaking information. He had played a large part in the development of Japanese naval aviation before the war and was the architect of the Pearl Harbor attack. However, he had opposed going to war with the USA, saying that his fleet would win victories for the first few months, but after that Japan would certainly be crushed. His predictions were absolutely correct.

Above: Admiral Yamamoto working at his chart table.

Above: The Ford Island airfield after the attack as ships in the harbour burn in the background.

Battleships and Battle-cruisers

These "capital ships", with the biggest guns and thickest armour, were traditionally seen as the decisive weapons in naval warfare. WWII saw few battleship versus battleship engagements, but these vessels still played a vital part.

The navies of the major countries fought WWII using a mix of battleships built during WWI and the 1920s and more modern vessels from the late 1930s onward.

In the inter-war period the number of battleships in service and the maximum size of new ships was limited by the Washington Naval Treaty of 1922 and other later agreements. Britain, the USA and Japan were permitted 15, 15 and 10 ships, respectively, with lower numbers for both France and Italy. Germany would also join the naval arms race, which developed as war approached, but no other navy had battleships of any significance.

Below: The USS *North Carolina* off the American coast in 1942, shortly before joining the US Pacific Fleet.

The ships surviving from the WWI era were of two types: battleships (retained by all major navies) and battle-cruisers (Britain and Japan only). Both had similar armaments and were broadly similar in size, but battle-cruisers had thinner armour in a trade-off for higher speed, a combination that had not always proved successful in WWI. Ships commissioned during WWII combined high speed and thick armour, and accordingly increased in size.

The USS *Mississippi* (New Mexico class, completed in 1917) was typical of the "WWI ships" still in service in 1939. On a displacement of 33,000 tons it carried a main armament of 12 x 14in (355mm) guns, could steam at 21 knots and was protected by side armour up to 355mm (14in) thick.

All older capital ships serving in 1939 had been modernized in the inter-war years to some degree. These changes were made principally to improve their anti-aircraft (AA) capabilities. More anti-aircraft guns were fitted, some of them new dual-purpose (DP) designs suitable for use also against surface vessels. For example, HMS *Queen Elizabeth* began the war with 20 x 4.5in (114.3mm) DP

HMS *DUKE OF YORK*

Third of the five King George V-class ships, *Duke of York*'s most notable achievement was the sinking of Germany's *Scharnhorst* in late 1943. The class's unusual main gun set-up of two quadruple turrets and a twin was troublesome at first but eventually efficient.

Commissioned: 1941
Displacement: 37,500 tons
Speed: 30 knots
Belt armour: 15.4in (39cm) max.
Armament: 10 x 14in (355mm) + 16 x 5.24in (133mm) guns

secondary guns, compared to the 2 x 3in (76.2mm) AA guns installed when the ship entered service in 1915. Deck armour was also commonly increased to improve protection against bombs and long-range shellfire. These changes tended to increase displacement (forbidden by treaty), which was partly compensated by fitting lighter but more powerful engines.

Last Treaty Ships

As war approached both Britain and the USA began building modern battleships that reflected these trends. They also attempted to keep within the treaty limitations.

The US Navy's two North Carolina and four South Dakota-class ships carried 9 x 16in (406mm) and 20 x 5in (127mm) DP guns on a displacement (as built) of 37,000 tons; the top speed was 28 knots. Britain's King George V class (the final British class to see war service) was broadly comparable, with slightly less main gun power and slightly thicker armour. America's late-war Iowa class (four ships) displaced a third more than the earlier designs and had a very high speed to escort the aircraft-carrier task forces, which by then formed the heart of the US fleet.

Axis Giants

Germany's *Bismarck* and *Tirpitz*, though begun before the war, made no attempt to keep within the treaty limitations. Both ships were over 42,000 tons and were very well-protected, but had old-fashioned secondary armament featuring separate surface and AA guns.

Japan's most modern battleships were bigger yet. The 65,000-ton *Yamato* and *Musashi* (two sister ships were planned, but not built as battleships) carried 9 x 460mm (18.1in) main guns, a mass of secondary weapons and had 406mm (16in) armour. Ironically, despite their status as the most powerful battleships ever built, these two vessels were among the few WWII battleships actually to succumb to the new menace of air attack while at sea.

TIRPITZ

Like its sister ship *Bismarck*, *Tirpitz* achieved little for Germany. *Tirpitz* never fired its main guns against an enemy ship and was finally sunk by the RAF in 1944.

Commissioned: 1941
Displacement: 42,000 tons
Speed: 30 knots
Belt armour: 32cm (12.6in) max.
Armament: 8 x 38cm (15in) + 12 x 15cm (5.91in) guns

Right: The USS *Indiana* (South Dakota class) shelling the Japanese coast in 1945.

The USA at War

The war was kinder to the United States than to any other warring nation. The country ended the war with the lowest casualty rate of any major combatant and the American people generally prospered in the economic boom the war brought.

In late 1940 President Roosevelt spoke of his wish that the United States would become the "arsenal of democracy". Even before Pearl Harbor this wish was fast becoming a reality and its consequences were transforming the USA and its relationship with the rest of the world. No informed observer in 1939 was in any doubt about the country's potential strength, but when the war in Europe began 15 per cent of the workforce was unemployed, factories were idle and other economic indicators confirmed the gloomy picture.

By 1945 much had changed. In the course of the war the USA manufactured a stunning

Above: Making aircraft engines was one of many new employment areas opened to American women.

total of 300,000 military aircraft, 86,000 tanks and vast amounts of every other conceivable kind of military equipment. The US armed forces were the most lavishly equipped in the world and, over and above their supplies, American production also met an estimated 25 per cent of

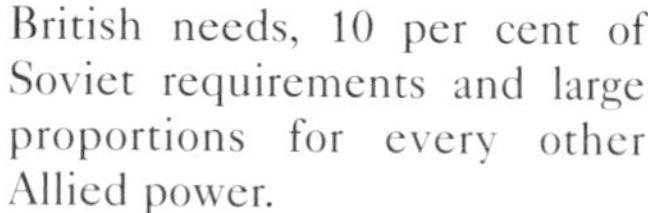

British needs, 10 per cent of Soviet requirements and large proportions for every other Allied power.

Some 15 million men served in the US armed forces during the war along with 350,000 women, a total only surpassed by the Soviets. From 1942 this huge military establishment was controlled from the Pentagon, the world's largest building, which had been newly opened in Washington, DC.

At the heart of the Pentagon was another new body, the Joint Chiefs of Staff, the committee of the armed service chiefs, which co-ordinated American planning and had an effective liaison organization working with its British equivalent. Although there were many disputes, Anglo-American planning was much more effective than the chaotic German or Japanese equivalents, with their capricious leaders and vicious inter-service rivalries. The JCS organization was truly a major factor in the Allied victory.

In December 1941 Congress passed the War Powers Act giving the President more executive authority than he had ever had before. A whole range of government agencies was soon set up to manage various important aspects of the war economy – the War Production Board and Office of War Mobilization being among the most important. Manpower was perhaps the first issue. Conscription

Below: The Chrysler plant in Detroit, producing M3 tanks in 1942.

Above: US rationing in 1941 was so lenient that this driver could fill a spare can as well as his tank.

never dug as deep in the USA as in many other countries – married men were seldom drafted, for example. Men not drafted did not have to take war jobs and women were not compelled to work or serve in any way.

Big business and ordinary people both prospered during the war. Corporate profits soared and so did farm prices. Wages rose 50 per cent in real terms. The number of women working outside the home also expanded by about a third to 22 per cent of the workforce. Previously, women in paid work had generally been young, unmarried or childless, but older women and mothers commonly took jobs during the war.

Although the idea of women doing "man's work" was much publicized, the reality was slightly different. Few women moving into the workforce took over jobs previously done by men; rather they took new jobs, often of types that had not commonly existed previously.

The archetypal character Rosie the Riveter working in a shipyard scarcely existed, if only because shipbuilding was rapidly moving to the more modern welding method of construction. Indeed at the heart of the war production boom were a mass of such productivity improvements: new technologies, better machine tools, greater use of assembly-line methods and more.

Although many women were working and prospering, they were still paid about a third less than men in comparable jobs. A similar situation applied to African-Americans and other racially disadvantaged groups. Their wages rose faster than those of whites during the war, but there was still a large gap and racism remained ubiquitous both in civilian life and in the military. Military units were racially segregated and few non-whites were permitted to serve in combat formations, and fewer still became officers.

JAPANESE-AMERICANS

In 1941 there were about 120,000 Japanese (over 60 per cent of them US citizens) living in the continental USA, and more than a third of the population of Hawaii was of Japanese descent. Though carefully watched, those in Hawaii were allowed to live normally. However, in early 1942, almost all Japanese living along the American West Coast were deported to a number of unpleasant detention camps inland and held there until late 1944. Fears of spying and sabotage were the official reason given, but the true motivation was a racist one. Canada also operated a similar policy for its Japanese population.

Above: Some 110,000 Japanese-Americans were sent to detention camps in 1942. German- and Italian-Americans were not similarly treated.

Japan's First Advances

Japan's initial naval successes were soon matched by triumphs on land. Malaya and Britain's great naval base of Singapore were conquered with ease by mid-February 1942 and the final Allied bastion in the Philippines lasted little longer.

Simultaneously with the attack on Pearl Harbor, Japanese forces began operations against the Philippines and Malaya. The Japanese landings in Malaya began at 01:00 hours on 8 December 1941 (local time). This was actually shortly before the 7 December raid on Pearl Harbor because of the effects of the International Date Line. The first air attacks on Luzon in the Philippines came a few hours later.

As well as these major targets, the Japanese also began a rapid campaign to conquer Hong Kong, while other forces quickly took control of Guam, Wake and other small US-held islands, despite an energetic defence by Allied forces.

Malaya under Attack

The 65,000-strong Twenty-fifth Army, led by General Yamashita Tomoyuki, began its campaign with landings on the South China Sea coast of northern Malaya and southern Siam (now Thailand). They were opposed by almost 90,000 British, Indian and Australian troops under the overall command of Air Marshal Robert Brooke-Popham, with General Arthur Percival as land commander. The Japanese quickly gained command of the air and, after sinking HMS *Prince of Wales* and *Repulse*, had complete control at sea.

Above: Although outdated by European standards, Japanese tanks like this Type 95, in action on Luzon, led their advance in 1942.

Many of the Japanese troops were battle-hardened veterans of the China war but, contrary to popular belief, they had had no special jungle training. They had a few tanks to break up any defensive positions they met and bicycles for mobility. By contrast the Allied troops were mostly badly trained and poorly led at almost every level. The result was that the Allied forces were hustled into retreat, time after time.

Fall of Singapore

By the end of January 1942 the Allied forces had withdrawn to Singapore island, over 950km (590 miles) from the initial Japanese landings. Singapore was supposedly an impregnable fortress, but its defences had been built with a naval attack in

SINKING OF FORCE Z

As relations with Japan deteriorated in late 1941, the British government decided to send naval reinforcements ("Force Z") to Singapore to deter Japanese action. Two battleships, the *Prince of Wales* and *Repulse*, were sent but a planned aircraft carrier did not go. The admiral in charge was one of the least air-minded in the Royal Navy; he made a blundering attempt, without air cover, to intercept Japanese landing forces off Malaya. Instead, on 10 December, the British ships were tracked down and sunk with little difficulty by Japanese land-based aircraft.

Above: *Prince of Wales*, *Repulse* and an escorting destroyer (nearest) seen from a Japanese aircraft.

mind and were not well suited to opposing an advance across the Johor Straits to the north.

On the night of 8–9 February the Japanese surged over and soon pushed the defenders back to the edges of Singapore city itself. General Percival decided to capitulate, though his troops (recently reinforced) greatly outnumbered their attackers.

In the whole Malayan campaign the Japanese lost fewer than 10,000 casualties. The Allies had a similar number of killed and wounded, but in addition some 130,000 went into a brutal Japanese captivity that many would not survive.

Above: American and Filipino soldiers under fire in the defences of the Bataan Peninsula.

The Philippines

Japan's conquest of the Philippines was almost as rapid. General Douglas MacArthur led the defending forces of 110,000 Filipino troops and 30,000 Americans, though inevitably many were dispersed around the Philippine archipelago. Equipment and training were poor but they did have over 200 supporting American aircraft. However, MacArthur's incompetence allowed many of these to be surprised on the ground hours after news of Pearl Harbor arrived. From then on Japan had control in the air. With no prospect of relieving US Navy forces arriving, as pre-Pearl Harbor plans had anticipated, Japan was also dominant at sea.

Troops from General Homma Masaharu's Fourteenth Army landed on the main island of Luzon on 10 December with larger forces following from the 22nd. MacArthur ordered the outmatched Allied troops to withdraw to the Bataan Peninsula area, which they did by early January 1942.

They held out there until 9 April, in part because some of the attacking Japanese troops had been withdrawn to take part in other phases of Japan's offensive. The fortress island of Corregidor offshore did not surrender until 6 May. Again many Allied troops were sent into a cruel captivity.

Meanwhile, MacArthur had been ordered to leave in mid-March to take command of Allied forces in Australia. On his departure MacArthur had promised: "I shall return."

Right: Surrender of Singapore, 15 February 1942. General Yamashita insists that General Percival signs without further delay.

Japan's Continuing Successes

Even before Malaya and the Philippines had fallen, Japanese forces were surging into Burma and landing throughout the Dutch East Indies. Their campaigns there would be just as rapid and successful as those that had gone before.

Japanese troops moved into Burma on 14 December 1941. An attack began in earnest on 20 January 1942 when General Iida Shojiro's Fifteenth Army launched two divisions toward Moulmein from across the border with Thailand. Allied forces fought effectively at first, retreating gradually. On 23 February a vital bridge over the River Sittang was blown up with many Indian troops on the wrong side. After that the retreat turned into a rout.

The Japanese were reinforced with troops from Malaya, now that campaign was over, and Rangoon fell on 8 March. Further Japanese troops then moved in from Thailand, and pushed the remaining British forces northward toward India. Chinese troops, commanded by an American, General Joseph Stilwell, joined in the battle but were also defeated. The last remnants of the Allied force reached India in early May.

Above: Apprehensive Burmese wait by the roadside as Japanese invaders pass by.

Below: Japanese Type 89 tanks on the advance in 1942. Lightly armoured and with a low-powered 57mm (2.24in) gun, the Type 89 was mainly used in China later in the war.

Vital Oilfields

The Dutch East Indies was the greatest prize in Japan's planned advance because of its substantial oilfields, mainly on Sumatra, and the significant production of metal ores and other important commodities. Japan's air and naval superiority was the key to their advance.

There were three main lines of attack, with various units from General Imamura Hitoshi's Sixteenth Army providing the principal ground forces. Sixteenth Army had first moved from Japanese possessions in the Caroline Islands to the southern Philippine island of Mindanao. In early January it struck toward Borneo and the Celebes, using both paratroops and forces landed by sea, before

Left: Japanese infantry capturing the Yenangyaung oilfields in Burma in April 1942. Gaining access to foreign oil was a key Japanese aim.

leap-frogging south to Timor and eastern Java. At the same time other forces landed along Borneo's northern coast and by late February/early March were in Sumatra and western Java. Local Dutch and other Allied forces surrendered on 8 March.

New Naval Victories

There were a number of naval engagements during the campaign, fought on the Allied side by Dutch, British, Australian and US Navy ships, led by the Dutch Admiral Karel Doorman. The Allied force was defeated on 27 February 1942 in the Battle of the Java Sea, and wiped out in follow-up engagements over the next two days.

Australian-ruled territory had also fallen. In January the Japanese captured Rabaul on New Britain (part of Australia's New Guinea mandated territory) and would build up a major base there. On 19 February they further demonstrated their naval superiority in the theatre when four of the aircraft carriers from the Pearl Harbor attack force led a devastating raid on Darwin in Northern Australia. On 8 March Japanese troops landed at Lae and Salamaua in New Guinea proper, as the first stage in a planned advance to Port Moresby on Papua's south coast.

Having supported various of the Japanese landings, the carrier force then moved further west in March to attack Ceylon and British Indian Ocean trade. The main British and Japanese naval forces did not come into action against each other, but two British cruisers and a small aircraft carrier were sunk. The ports of Colombo and Trincomalee were heavily raided, while a subsidiary Japanese force sank numerous merchant ships in the Bay of Bengal.

Japan had achieved a bewildering succession of victories across a vast area, but ambitious generals and admirals planned still more advances. First they planned to attack New Guinea and then (stung by the American pinprick Doolittle Raid on the Japanese Home Islands) they would advance across the central Pacific to Midway.

THE DOOLITTLE RAID

In early 1942 US aircraft carriers began striking back at Japan with minor raids on various Pacific islands. In April a more ambitious plan, an attack on Tokyo, was carried out. On 18 April the carrier *Hornet* launched 16 Army Air Force B-25 bombers, commanded by Colonel James Doolittle, from some 1,000km (625 miles) offshore. Minor damage was caused in the Japanese capital and three other cities. The raid was a major boost to domestic morale in the USA and helped persuade Japan's leaders to carry out what proved to be their disastrous attack on Midway.

Below: A B-25 sets out for Tokyo. Taking off in a B-25 from a carrier was a remarkable feat, but no naval aircraft had the range needed for this mission.

Coral Sea and Midway

These two battles were the first naval engagements in history in which the opposing ships never came into visual contact. They confirmed that aircraft carriers were now the dominant weapons in naval warfare.

As May 1942 began, Japanese commanders planned to extend their conquests by landing at Port Moresby in southern Papua, from where their aircraft might reach targets in Australia. Warned by code-breaking information, Allied naval forces were sent to stop them.

Leading the Allied force were the US carriers *Lexington* and *Yorktown*, supported by American and Australian cruisers and destroyers. Opposing them were three main Japanese forces: the Port Moresby invasion force of troop transports and escorts; a covering force including the small carrier *Shoho* and four cruisers; and a carrier strike force based around the *Zuikaku* and *Shokaku*. Also a small detachment was to land on Tulagi in the Solomon Islands to set up a base there.

KEY FACTS–MIDWAY

PLACE: Central Pacific, near Midway Island

DATE: 4 June 1942

OUTCOME: 4 Japanese aircraft carriers sunk; Japanese naval superiority lost.

THE BATTLE OF MIDWAY
As in other battles in the Pacific, the Japanese plan for Midway was over-complicated and failed to concentrate on the main objective.

CORAL SEA BATTLE

After preliminary skirmishes, the main action began on 7 May. US aircraft sank the *Shoho*; in return the Japanese carriers sank an American tanker and a destroyer. A full-scale carrier battle followed on the 8th. The Japanese came off better, sinking the *Lexington* and damaging

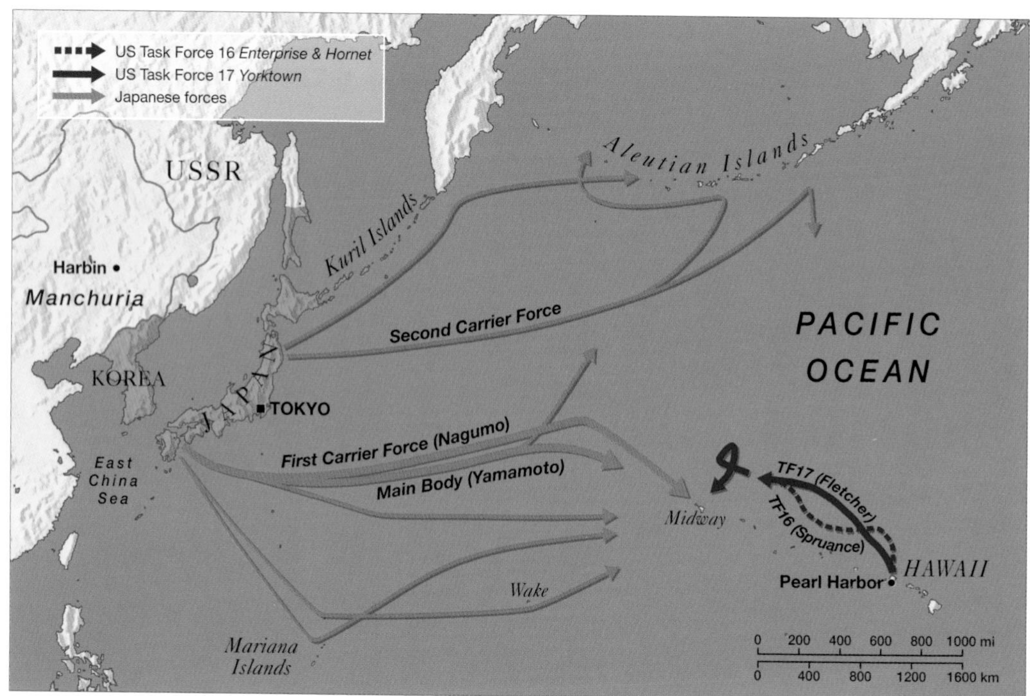

the *Yorktown* badly. However, the *Shokaku* was also heavily hit and many of the *Zuikaku*'s aircraft were destroyed. Neither ship would be able to join the Midway operation, which was scheduled next, and the Port Moresby invasion was called off.

THE MIDWAY PLAN

Admiral Yamamoto, principal Japanese Navy commander, had realized for some time that his victory at Pearl Harbor was incomplete unless he could destroy the US Navy's carrier force. He planned to capture Midway, far across the Central Pacific toward Pearl Harbor, confident that this move would force the Americans into battle.

The Japanese plan was characteristically complicated, with a selection of transport and covering forces closing in on Midway from various directions. Two smaller carriers and other major warships were to carry out a diversion against the Aleutian Islands, while the main forces included four carriers and a battleship and cruiser group.

Unfortunately for the Japanese, their intentions had once again been discovered by the US code-breaking services. The Americans were, therefore, able to ignore the Aleutians force (whose valuable carriers were thus wasted) and concentrate their strongest units near Midway before the Japanese knew they were in the area. The Americans deployed the carriers *Hornet* and *Enterprise* and supporting vessels, which were joined at the last minute by the rapidly repaired *Yorktown* (which the Japanese were convinced would be out of action for much longer).

Above: The Japanese carrier *Shokaku* under attack and on fire during the Coral Sea battle.

Above: A Japanese torpedo strikes home on the *Yorktown* at Midway, despite defensive anti-aircraft fire.

The main action began early on 4 June with Japanese air attacks on Midway Island. Thinking these attacks had not been successful enough and unaware for the moment of the American carriers' presence, Admiral Nagumo Chuichi, commanding the Japanese carriers, then ordered preparations for another attack on Midway.

While this was happening, attack aircraft from Midway Island and then from the American carriers arrived. Most were easily dealt with by the Japanese fighter screen, but a final dive-bomber group from the *Enterprise* inflicted crippling damage on *Akagi*, *Kaga* and *Soryu* (all three would sink later). The fourth Japanese carrier, *Hiryu*, sent a new strike that badly damaged *Yorktown*, but later *Hiryu* was itself fatally hit. Yamamoto abandoned the Midway operation.

Even though *Yorktown* was sunk on 7 June by a Japanese submarine, Midway had been a stunning American success. The backbone of the Japanese fleet was destroyed; not only the lost ships but also the many well-trained aircrew would not be readily replaced.

Below: A Devastator torpedo-bomber squadron ready for take-off on the *Enterprise* at Midway.

Aircraft Carriers

Airpower enthusiasts had been claiming since the 1920s that the aircraft carrier would soon supplant the battleship as the ultimate naval weapon. In the vast spaces of the Pacific Ocean, at least, this certainly proved to be true.

Experiments with aircraft-carrying ships were begun before WWI and the first warship to succumb to air attack was a German vessel sunk by a Japanese aircraft in 1914. But the first two true aircraft carriers with flight decks running from end to end did not enter service with Britain's Royal Navy until shortly after the end of the war.

By the time WWII began, Britain, the USA and Japan had significant aircraft-carrier forces, and built more as the war proceeded. The only other carrier in service in 1939 was France's experimental vessel *Béarn*, which did not ever see combat. Germany was building one and Italy later started two, but none of these was completed.

The three leading navies all developed ideas about carriers in the inter-war period. Both the Japanese and the Americans headed in what proved to be the best direction. They realized that the carrier's best defence – and its best means of attack – were its aircraft and, therefore, the more the better.

Japan and the USA built carriers in which the hangar area under the flight deck was relatively lightly enclosed, with sides that could be opened for ventilation. This allowed the most room for aircraft.

Several of their early ships – Japan's *Akagi* and *Kaga* and the USA's *Lexington* and *Saratoga* – were particularly large, all well over 30,000 tons, and could carry up to 120 aircraft each. And with big air groups they also developed effective techniques for handling them during operations.

IJNS *KAGA*

The largest carriers in service at the start of WWII were, like *Kaga*, conversions of hulls originally planned as battleships or battle-cruisers just after WWI. A reconstruction in 1936 included the installation of an unusual downward-pointing funnel. *Kaga* participated in the Pearl Harbor attack and the raid on Darwin, but it was sunk at Midway.

Commissioned: 1929
Displacement: 38,000 tons
Speed: 28 knots
Aircraft: up to 90
Guns: 10 x 200mm (7.87in) + 16 x 127mm (5in)

Below: The Independence-class light carrier USS *Langley*, with an Essex-class ship behind, at Ulithi atoll in 1944.

British Designs

Britain had led the way in early carrier development but fell far behind in the inter-war years. The main reason for this was that the Royal Air Force – not the Royal Navy – controlled the supply of aircraft and pilots for maritime duties and these were given low priority. The Navy also chose to build carriers with "closed" hangar decks, which reduced aircraft capacity, although it did lead to the development of improved fire-control precautions.

In the late 1930s, aware that their obsolescent aircraft would be unable to protect the carriers completely, especially in the Mediterranean where land-based aircraft would always be within striking range, the British took this process a step further by armouring the flight decks of their new carriers. This reduced capacity even more; HMS *Illustrious*, begun in 1937, initially carried only 36 aircraft, though capacity for *Illustrious* and its 5 similar successors was increased during the war.

HMS *ARK ROYAL*

Probably the most famous British ship of the early war period, HMS *Ark Royal* was wrongly reported as sunk several times by German propaganda. *Ark Royal* mainly served in the Mediterranean (including in the action off Cape Spartivento, seen below) but a Swordfish from *Ark Royal* also made the torpedo hit that crippled *Bismarck*. *Ark Royal* was finally sunk by a U-boat in November 1941.

COMMISSIONED: 1939
DISPLACEMENT: 22,000 tons
SPEED: 30 knots
AIRCRAFT: up to 60
GUNS: 16 x 4.5in (114.3mm)

PACIFIC CARRIERS

Both Japan and the US Navy went to war in 1941 with a number of rather smaller carriers in addition to the largest ships already mentioned. Most were around 18,000 tons and carried 70–80 aircraft. Ships in this category included *Yorktown*, *Enterprise*, *Hiryu* and *Soryu*. Other notable vessels included the 25,000-ton *Shokaku* and *Zuikaku*, and the somewhat smaller *Wasp* and *Ranger*.

Japan introduced a number of smaller carriers in 1941–2, several being conversions of other types of vessel. In all Japan completed 17 carriers (both large and small) during the war. None of these played a substantial part. This was not because they were all inadequate ships but rather that, by the time they came into service, Japan's cadre of trained naval aircrew had been wiped out and could not be quickly replaced.

The US Navy had no such problems. Its 27,000-ton Essex-class ships could carry over a hundred aircraft; 24 saw service from early 1943 onward. In addition the US Navy had the 9 ships of the Independence class of light carriers, some 10,000 tons and carrying around 40 aircraft. With ample numbers of well-trained pilots and excellent aircraft, it was these ships that led the US advance across the Pacific to defeat Japan.

Left: USS *Essex*, lead ship of its class, with about 50 of its large air group parked on deck.

The Turn of the Tide

Desperate struggles in the Solomon Islands and on New Guinea from mid-1942 saw the Japanese advance turned back for the first time. The Allies gained the upper hand in vicious jungle fighting and a series of dramatic naval battles.

Having overrun the East Indies so easily, Japan then planned to capture bases in southern Papua, as a prelude to a possible attack on Australia and others in the Solomon Islands, to threaten communications between Australia and the USA. As well as Australian and American ground and air forces, the resulting battles would draw in the main strength of both the Japanese and US Navies.

New Guinea

After Japan's naval attack was thwarted in the Battle of the Coral Sea, General Horii Tomitaro's South Seas Detachment began an advance in July 1942 from the north coast of Papua over the precipitous Owen Stanley Range on the Kokoda Trail toward Port Moresby. Despite the terrible conditions (for both sides) the Japanese soon pushed back the weak Australian forces, now part of General MacArthur's Allied South-West Pacific Command. Allied air power and some reinforcements halted Horii on the approaches to Port Moresby in September and the Japanese retreated (so short of supplies some resorted to cannibalism).

In the meantime Allied air and naval forces had begun advances round the eastern tip of Papua, beginning at Milne Bay in August. By November Australian troops attacking along the Kokoda Trail and American troops moving along the north coast had closed in on the well-fortified Japanese beachheads at Buna and Gona. The remaining Japanese forces there were wiped out by the end of January 1943.

Guadalcanal Island, the focus of the other flank of the campaign, saw conditions that were just as horrible. Japan had set up a seaplane base at nearby Tulagi in May and a small force was working on an airfield on Guadalcanal itself. The 1st US Marine Division landed on Guadalcanal on 7 August 1942, captured the airfield and put it into Allied service as Henderson Field. At first the Marines were not well supported from the sea; Japanese reinforcements began attacking the Marines' beachhead. During the six-month struggle that followed the Japanese troops fought fiercely, but their attacks were not well co-ordinated and were beaten off after a series of tough battles. Japan evacuated the island in early February 1943.

Naval Battles

Both sides' efforts to supply and reinforce their troops led to six major naval battles and a range of smaller engagements. At first the Japanese had the upper hand. In the early hours of 9 August, in the Battle of Savo Island, night-fighting skills and superior torpedo equipment helped a group of Japanese cruisers and destroyers sink four opponents with little loss.

Above: A wounded Australian near Buna is helped by a Papuan, one of many who assisted the Allied forces.

COAST WATCHERS

The Australian Navy used Coast Watchers, people who provided vital information to Allied forces during the Solomons campaign and other battles. The service had been set up before the war to cover a range of locations across the little-inhabited South-west Pacific. From their lonely and isolated posts, Coast Watchers reported movements by air and sea and also supplied weather reports, which was often just as important. Though they had to defend themselves against Japanese patrols, their role was not to fight. Admiral Halsey said that Guadalcanal would not have been won without their help.

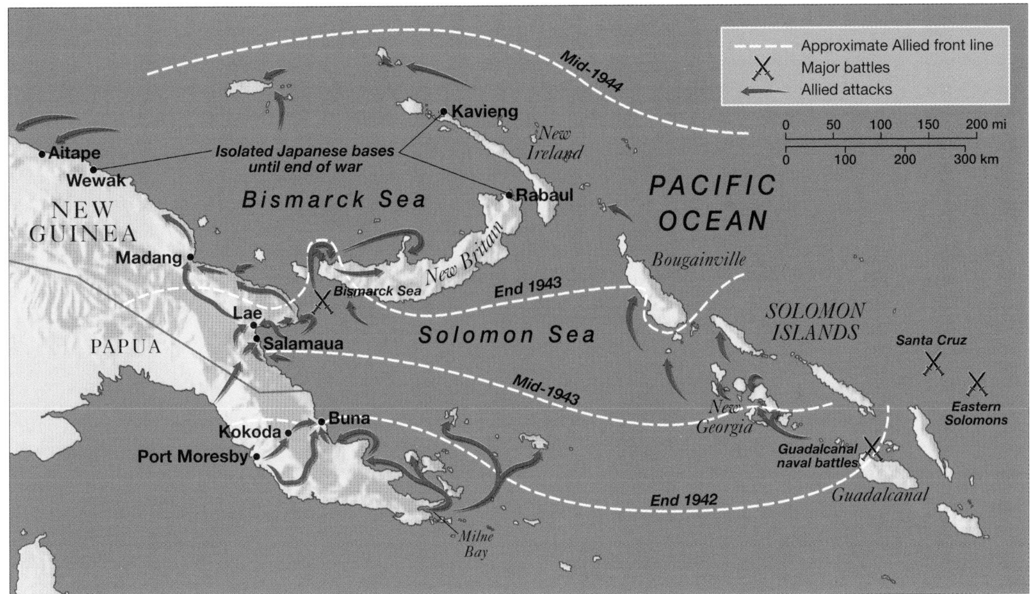

THE SOUTH-WEST PACIFIC
From summer 1942, Allied forces conducted a two-pronged advance along the north coast of New Guinea and up the Solomon Island chain.

On 23–4 August the Battle of the Eastern Solomons between the main carrier forces was a narrow Japanese victory; and in subsequent weeks two US carriers were sunk by submarines. However, by then aircraft from Henderson Field dominated the waters around Guadalcanal by day; but at night Japanese warships under Admiral Tanaka Raizo, known to the Marines as the "Tokyo Express", had the ascendancy.

A second carrier battle on 26 October, the Battle of Santa Cruz, was inconclusive, but the tide turned with the Battle of Guadalcanal taking place on the nights of 12–13 and 14–15 November. By then the American forces were learning to use their superior radar equipment to win night battles. The fighting between the warships was by no means one-sided but several Japanese troop transports were sunk. The Japanese had the better of another night encounter (the Battle of Tassafaronga) in late November. However, by then the attrition of their naval forces had become so severe that in early January the Tokyo Express finally went into reverse – to evacuate rather than supply the island. The Allied counter-offensive in the Pacific was now well under way.

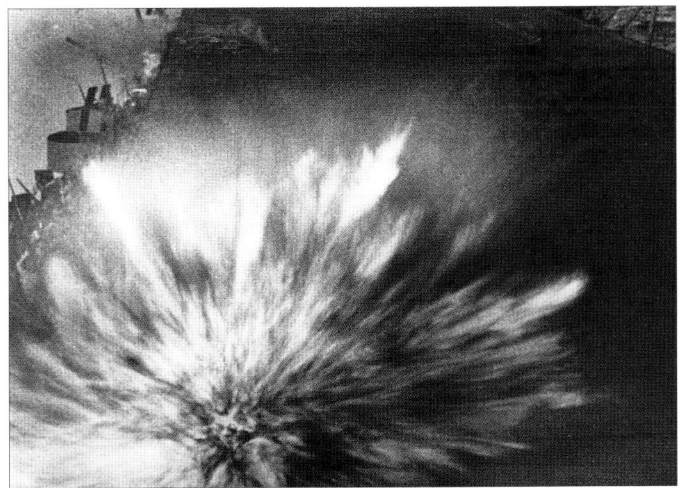

Right: A Japanese bomb explodes aboard the *Enterprise* during the Battle of the Eastern Solomons.

Light Cruisers

Capable of giving a good account of themselves in battle, light cruisers were maids of all work, but they also were used for long-range trade protection missions, shore bombardments and other varied duties.

Cruisers carrying guns of roughly 150mm (5.91in) were probably the most ubiquitous warships of the conflict. They formed a vital part of naval task forces, both large and small, in every campaign.

WWII light cruisers can be divided into three sub-types: larger ships usually displacing at least the Washington Treaty limit of 10,000 tons or more and carrying 12 or 15 main guns, usually in triple turrets; smaller general-purpose ships of 6,000–8,000 tons, armed usually with 8 main guns in twin turrets; and anti-aircraft cruisers of 6,000 tons, armed with 10–12 smaller dual-purpose guns.

Large Light Cruisers

This type developed largely as a result of the pre-war arms race in the Pacific, beginning with Japan's construction of the Mogami class in the 1930s. With an impressive top speed of 35 knots, and 15 x 155mm (6.1in) guns, they supposedly had a relatively modest displacement of 8,500 tons (but, in fact, they were well over 10,000 tons).

The US Navy replied with its Brooklyn class and Britain with the Southampton class. Their wartime successors were the Cleveland (US) and Edinburgh and Fiji (UK) classes, respectively. They were all around 10,000 tons and built with 12 x 6in (152mm) guns in triple turrets (except the Brooklyns, which had 15). During the war some ships had a 6in turret removed and replaced with smaller-calibre AA weapons.

Most of Japan's large cruisers were in the heavy-cruiser category and by Pearl Harbor, the Mogamis had also been rearmed with 203mm (7.99in) guns.

Small Light Cruisers

Although the US and Japanese navies had a number of cruisers of this type dating from the 1920s or earlier, including ten ships of the US Omaha class,

Below: USS *Atlanta* (San Diego class) served in the South Pacific in 1942 but was sunk off Guadalcanal.

most vessels in this category served with European navies. This was the type of cruiser that Britain's Royal Navy most wanted to build in the inter-war period, with a good combination of long range and effective gunpower. The Leander class of the mid-1930s, for example, carried 8 x 6in guns and could make 32 knots on a displacement of some 7,200 tons. France, Germany and Italy all had comparable ships.

However, the most modern German ship, in service from 1935, was the *Nürnberg*, which carried 9 x 15cm (5.91in) guns and was otherwise similar to the ships of the British Royal Navy.

The French and Italian Navies had slightly different priorities. In the 1930s the Italians built very fast ships (and made them seem even faster by falsifying the results of their trials) and the French replied in kind. The Italian Duca d'Aosta class (8,500 tons, 8 x 152mm/5.98in guns), for example, supposedly reached 37 knots.

AA Cruisers

Many of the cruisers described above had relatively limited AA capability because their main gun mountings and control systems were only suitable for use against surface targets. As the war progressed, ships in all navies gained additional light AA guns, but Britain and the USA also saw a need for cruisers with greatly enhanced heavy AA firepower. The US Navy's San Diego and Britain's Dido and Bellona classes all carried large batteries of dual-purpose main guns, 10 x 5.25in (133mm) for the Didos and 12 or even 16 x 5in (127mm) for the San Diegos. All were also fast ships, capable of 33 or 34 knots to keep up with fast aircraft carrier forces.

Above: The *Giuseppe Garibaldi* carried 10 x 152mm (5.98in) guns and could reach a reported 34 knots.

KÖLN

The German Navy built three K-class cruisers in the late 1920s. Unusually, six of the nine main guns were aft. In service *Köln* and its sisters were found to lack stability in heavy weather. In 1940 *Köln* participated in the invasion of Norway but saw little action thereafter before being sunk by air attack in port in 1945.

Commissioned: 1930
Displacement: 6,700 tons
Speed: 32 knots
Aircraft: 2 x Arado 196
Armament: 9 x 15cm (5.9in) + 6 x 8.8cm (3.46in) guns; 12 x 533mm (21in) torpedo tubes

HMS *AJAX*

One of the five British Leander-class light cruisers, *Ajax* had an eventful war career. In 1939 *Ajax* joined two other cruisers, *Exeter* and *Achilles*, in hunting down the *Graf Spee*. In 1944 *Ajax* was one of the ships in the D-Day bombardment force. This record in action proved the usefulness of the relatively small cruisers of this type.

Commissioned: 1935
Displacement: 7,200 tons
Speed: 32 knots
Armour: 102mm (4in) max.
Armament: 8 x 6in (152mm) + 8 x 4in (102mm) guns; 8 x 21in (533mm) torpedo tubes

Japan's Brutal Empire

Japan's military conquests were supported by an authoritarian military government at home and ruthless exploitation of the people and resources of the conquered territories, though this was disguised by anti-imperialist propaganda.

In 1938 Japan's Prime Minister, Prince Konoye Fumimaro, spoke of Japan's aim to create a "New Order" in Asia. In 1940, after a period out of office, Konoye returned as premier and announced Japan's plan to establish a Greater East Asia Co-Prosperity Sphere. These ideas, and their slogan "Asia for the Asiatics" formed part of the backdrop to the creation of Japan's wartime empire. European and American racism and imperialism were to be rejected in favour of a vague commonwealth from which all Asians were to benefit – ideas that were designed to appeal both at home in Japan and throughout Asia.

Above: A Japanese soldier proudly displays the severed head of a Chinese man, Shanghai, 1937.

Below: From 1941 Japanese high-school students had compulsory military training in the curriculum.

MILITARISM AT HOME

From the later 1920s Japan itself became an ever more militaristic and rigorously regimented society. The armed services took effective control of the government. As well as expanding Japan's war in China, factions within the army had no hesitation in assassinating opponents or planning military coups. The economy was increasingly industrialized and militarized, with businesses and trades unions also brought under government control.

The education system emphasized military and nationalistic values: for example, maps in school textbooks showed much of South-east Asia as rightfully forming part of Japan's Empire. And in the background were the Tokko, or Special Higher Police (usually referred to in English as the "Thought Police"), who used torture and other repressive methods to ensure citizens behaved as the government wished.

CRUELTY ABROAD

The reality of Japan's rule overseas belied the intent expressed in Konoye's slogans. Most obvious to the Western Allies was its treatment of prisoners of war. Japanese troops were taught that it was disgraceful to surrender and regarded with contempt any enemy who did so. Many American prisoners, captured in the Philippines in 1942, died of ill-treatment on the so-called Bataan Death March and around 12,000 British and Australians were starved, beaten and worked to death on the

Above: Ho Chi Minh, leader of the anti-Japanese resistance movement in Indo-China, was helped by US special forces later in the war.

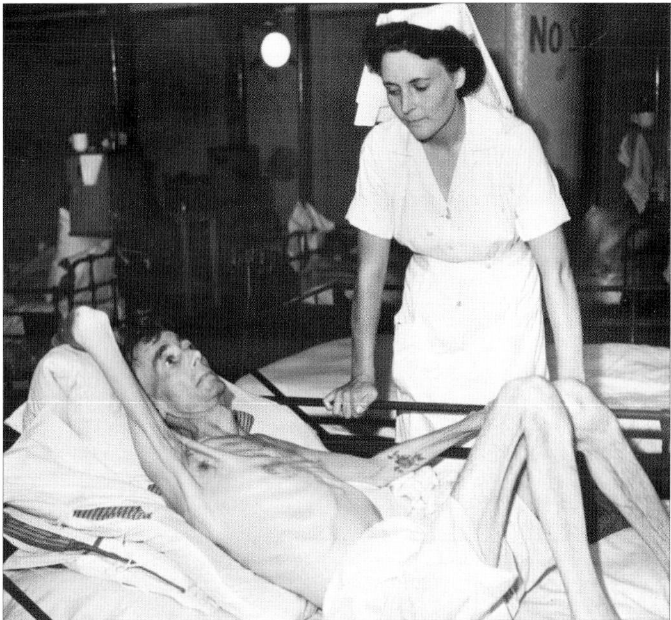

Above: An emaciated British prisoner receives medical treatment after his liberation from Japanese-occupied Hong Kong in 1945.

Siam–Burma railway line, to give only two of numerous notorious examples.

However, if only because relatively few Westerners came into Japanese hands, these brutalities bear little comparison with those inflicted on other Asians – for example, as many as 90,000 Malaysian, Thai and other Asian labourers died on the Burma Railway. Japan's attitude to other Asians was more brutal, racist and exploitative than any of the much-despised colonial powers.

The outside world first became aware of this with the infamous "Rape of Nanking", in December 1937, which was widely reported elsewhere. When Japanese troops captured the town (now usually called Nanjing), they went on an extended rampage of murder, rape, looting and arson, which killed a quarter of a million people (according to some estimates). Throughout the war in China, Japanese tactics made no distinction between civilians and military opponents; the watchwords were the "three alls" – kill all, burn all, loot all.

Other Japanese methods were more insidious. In the puppet state of Manchukuo, for example, the Japanese authorities encouraged and greatly expanded the production of opium. They also pushed users of opium there and in the rest of China to switch to the more dangerous morphine and heroin compounds, as part of a deliberate strategy to keep the indigenous population docile. The revenues from the scheme were used for the benefit of Japan's Kwantung Army.

For all that Japanese rule was far harsher than the colonial regimes that had preceded it, it also discredited such pre-war governments. In the aftermath Asia would soon come to be ruled by Asiatics to an extent unimaginable before.

COMFORT WOMEN

One of the nastiest aspects of Japanese rule was the imposition of forced prostitution on many thousands of mainly non-Japanese women. In part to prevent atrocities like the mass rapes that had occurred at Nanjing, the Japanese Army set up official military brothels in China and elsewhere. Up to 200,000 women worked in these establishments and many of them were teenagers. They were supposed to receive payments, but many were forced into unpaid prostitution. Most of the women were Korean.

The Holocaust Emaciated survivors shortly after the liberation of Buchenwald camp in 1945.

Infantry Weapons An American infantryman training with his M1 Garand semi-automatic rifle.

US Strategic Bombing, 1942–3 A B-24 Liberator falls in flames after being hit by flak.

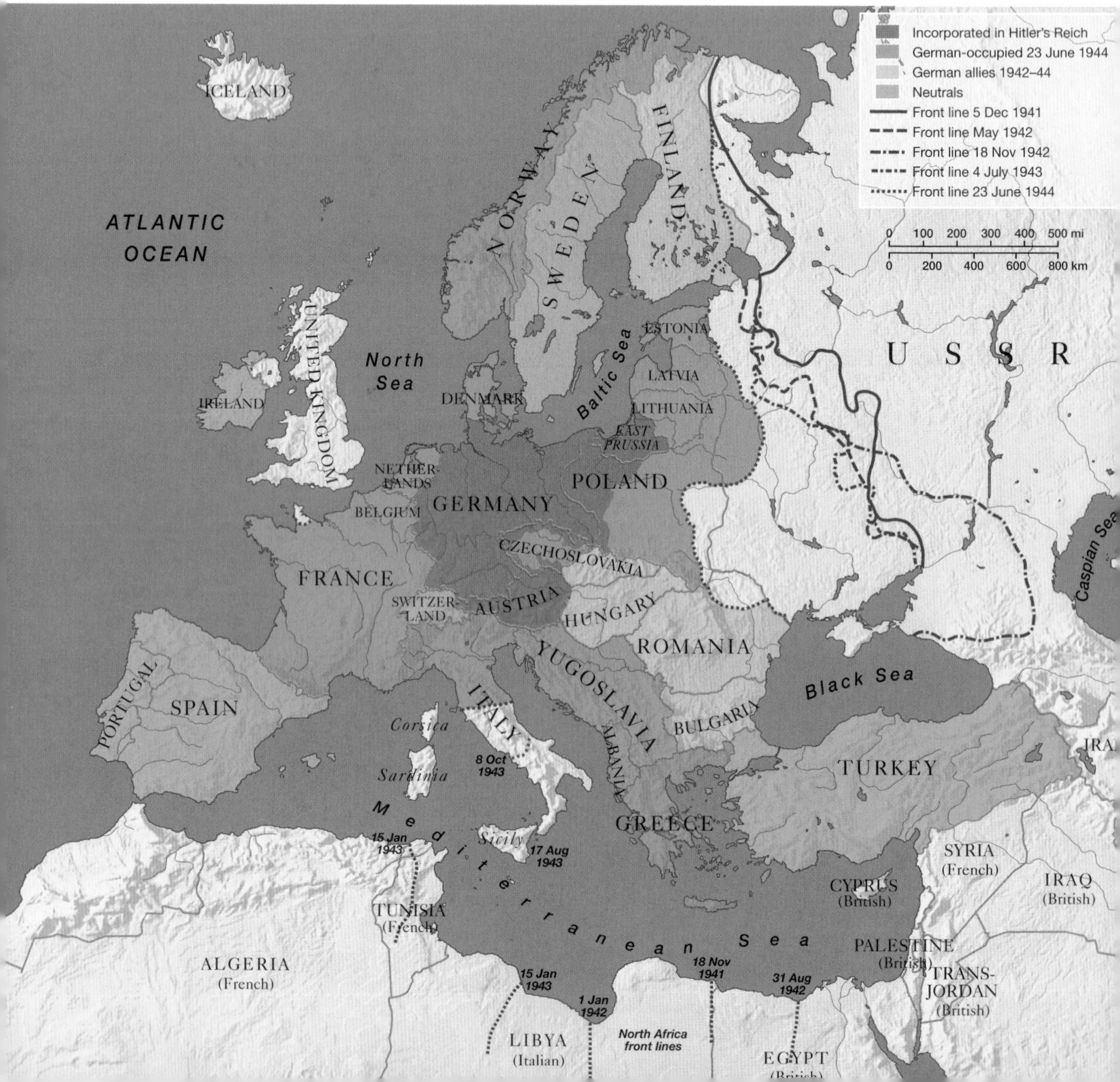

Incorporated in Hitler's Reich
German-occupied 23 June 1944
German allies 1942–44
Neutrals
Front line 5 Dec 1941
Front line May 1942
Front line 18 Nov 1942
Front line 4 July 1943
Front line 23 June 1944

0 100 200 300 400 500 mi
0 200 400 600 800 km

ICELAND
ATLANTIC OCEAN
NORWAY
SWEDEN
FINLAND
U S S R
UNITED KINGDOM
IRELAND
North Sea
DENMARK
Baltic Sea
ESTONIA
LATVIA
LITHUANIA
EAST PRUSSIA
NETHERLANDS
BELGIUM
GERMANY
POLAND
CZECHOSLOVAKIA
FRANCE
SWITZERLAND
AUSTRIA
HUNGARY
ROMANIA
Caspian Sea
Black Sea
YUGOSLAVIA
ITALY
PORTUGAL
SPAIN
Corsica
Sardinia
8 Oct 1943
ALBANIA
BULGARIA
TURKEY
GREECE
Sicily
17 Aug 1943
15 Jan 1943
Mediterranean Sea
SYRIA (French)
IRAQ (British)
CYPRUS (British)
TUNISIA (French)
PALESTINE (British)
TRANS-JORDAN (British)
ALGERIA (French)
15 Jan 1943
1 Jan 1942
18 Nov 1941
31 Aug 1942
LIBYA (Italian)
North Africa front lines
EGYPT (British)

THE GREAT STRUGGLE IN EUROPE

Just as his forces were being pushed back from Moscow in December 1941, Hitler assured his eventual defeat by declaring war on the USA. By the middle of 1944 Axis troops had been thrown out of the USSR and expelled from Africa; Italy had made peace; Anglo-American bombers were pounding Germany from the air; and Allied land forces were poised to return across the Channel in the Normandy invasion. Yet, between these landmarks, there lay many hard-fought campaigns and much dreadful suffering.

This was the period when the Nazi murder campaign against Europe's Jews was at its height. The Eastern Front saw the horrific sieges of Leningrad and Stalingrad and the war's greatest tank battle at Kursk. The Western Allies gradually grew in confidence and strength, initially in their victories in North Africa, then in their burgeoning power at sea and in the air that made first Hitler's Kriegsmarine, and then the Luftwaffe, shadows of the forces they had once been.

In his post-war memoirs Churchill wrote that the Allied victory was inevitable from the moment the USA joined the war. In hindsight this may indeed have been true, but it took the vicious battles of 1942–4 to turn this judgement into a reality.

Assault Guns An American soldier examines a German Jagdpanther knocked out in 1945.

Clearing the Ukraine Red Army troops being welcomed warmly on their recapture of Kiev.

Naval Weapons and Electronics Guns on the foredeck of the battleship USS *Iowa*.

To Stalingrad and the Caucasus

Despite their losses in the first terrible winter of war on the Eastern Front, the Germans were ready to attack again in 1942. Once more they used their superior tactical skills to win early successes, but a final decisive victory remained elusive.

After pushing the Germans back from Moscow with their December 1941 counter-offensive, the Soviets tried to develop a general advance all along the Eastern Front. Although these attacks created large bulges into German-held territory, the major German defensive positions held with relatively little difficulty. By the time the spring thaw brought operations to a halt, it was clear that the Germans would attack again in strength that summer.

Although the German forces had been substantially reinforced by troops from Hungary, Romania, Italy and even Spain, they no longer had the power to attack over the whole Eastern Front. Instead Hitler decided to concentrate in the south. He chose two objectives: a drive into the Caucasus as far as the Caspian coast to gain control of the oilfields there, and an advance to Stalingrad (Volgograd) to establish a protective front along the Don River north to Voronezh.

Above: Romanian troops in action in the Crimea alongside their German allies in June–July 1942.

Below: German infantry advancing during their successful counter-offensive near Kharkov in late May.

Preliminary Attacks

Late spring and early summer saw new German successes. Attacks in the Crimea led by General Erich von Manstein wiped out Soviet forces on the Kerch Peninsula in May and took Sevastopol by early July. To the north a Soviet attack near Kharkov in mid-May was crushed. Together these operations saw a further 450,000 prisoners fall into German hands.

The main German attacks began on 28 June. Voronezh was captured within days as the Soviet front at first fell apart before the German attacks. By late July other German attacks captured Rostov and opened the way south into the Caucasus.

However, Hitler was already changing his mind on priorities and readjusting his forces. In mid-July General Friedrich Paulus's Sixth Army had been told to rush east toward Stalingrad and much of the tank forces of Fourth Panzer Army, which had been meant to lead the drive into the Caucasus, were switched to join the right flank of Sixth Army's advance. To complete the range of contradictory objectives, Hitler also ordered Manstein's victorious troops from the Crimea to

THE GERMAN ADVANCE TO STALINGRAD

German advances in the summer of 1942 greatly lengthened their front line but made no decisive gains.

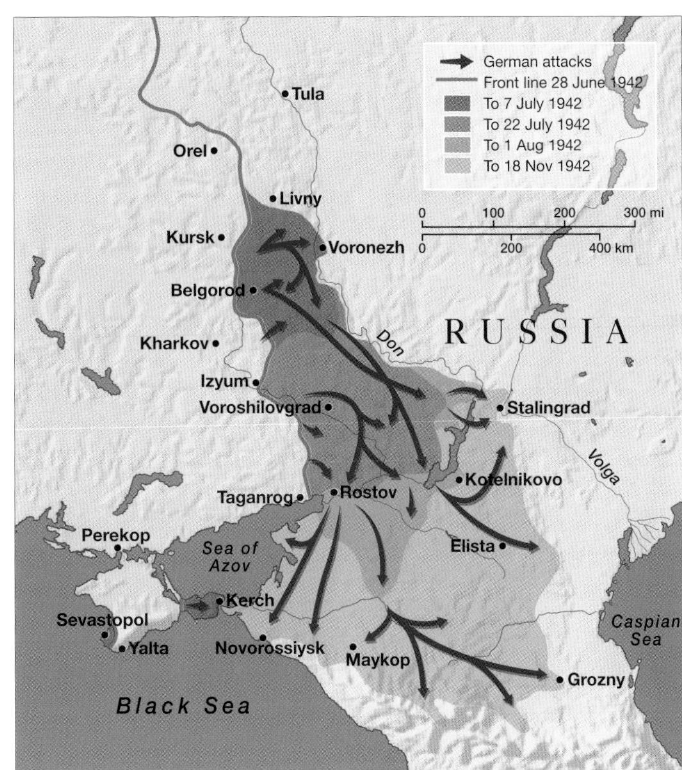

Above: German troops at Maykop in late summer 1942. Retreating Soviets have set the oil wells alight.

move north to Leningrad to finish the destruction of the Soviet resistance there.

Soviet Responses

For his part Stalin had misjudged the direction of the German attacks, fearing an advance toward Moscow from the south and, accordingly, had not deployed his reserves well.

However, the general Soviet organization had greatly improved. New production was being used to create air and tank armies that might provide a proper answer to German power in these respects, while more authority was being given to commanders to control their operations without political interference from their unit commissars. Finally, a group of ruthless and efficient generals was becoming established in senior positions, who would make good use of the ever-stronger Soviet forces.

For the moment the German advance continued. By early August, Sixth Army was destroying the Soviet forces in the Don bend, west of Stalingrad. By the end of the month it had reached the Volga, linked up with Fourth Panzer Army and closed to within a handful of kilometres of the city. Meanwhile, with supplies and air support having been switched to the Stalingrad sector, the advance in the Caucasus had ground to a halt, short of most of its objectives and never to be resumed. For Hitler and for Stalin, capturing or holding Stalingrad was now the only objective that mattered.

Below: A German tank unit halted in the vast and featureless steppe, south of Stalingrad, is overflown by a liaison aircraft.

The Holocaust

In a war of many atrocities one series of actions stands out as particularly horrific – Nazi Germany's attempt, at Hitler's command, to murder all the Jews of Europe solely because of their religion and culture.

There are aspects of the vast history of WWII in which a simple factual account seems inadequate. The list of Jews murdered by the Nazis – at least 2.5 million Poles, 750,000 from the USSR, almost as many each from Hungary and Romania, and tens of thousands more from almost every occupied country in Europe – cannot begin to explain the suffering and vile cruelties involved. At the same time, however, failing to state what happened and how it came to happen can only assist those who would downscale or even deny the nature of these crimes.

Above: Jewish families are taken from the Warsaw ghetto, probably to the Treblinka death camp.

Early Persecutions

Although Jews in pre-war Germany, and in occupied western Europe in 1940–1, were viciously persecuted, there were few killings. Eastern Europe presented, from the Nazi point of view, a different problem. They aimed to make their domains "Jew-free" and here there were many more Jews to deal with. During 1940 most Polish Jews were forced to live in "ghettos" in major towns. These were deliberately made overcrowded and insanitary and a typical food ration was less than 200 calories per day. By the middle of 1941 the half-million Jews in the Warsaw ghetto were dying at the rate of 2,000 daily.

Even this did not satisfy the Nazis. The armies invading the USSR were closely followed by *Einsatzgruppen* – SS murder squads whose mission was to kill Jews and communists. By the end of 1941 at least 600,000 Jews had been rounded up, shot and tumbled into mass graves. This was done quite openly, often watched and photographed by German Army soldiers and other personnel.

Left: An *Einsatzgruppe* killer at work, murdering Jews at Vinnitsa in the Ukraine in 1941–2.

The Final Solution

By this stage leading Nazis were looking for a "final solution to the Jewish problem", by which they meant finding an easy way to murder all of the Jews in Europe. The process began in the autumn of 1941 and was put into high gear by a meeting of top Nazis – known as the Wannsee Conference – in January 1942.

The killing mostly took place in specially established death camps in occupied Poland.

From late 1941 Jews from the Polish ghettos were transported to the camps and gassed, followed later by transports from the rest of German-controlled Europe. Most of the camps killed Jews as soon as they arrived but the largest, Auschwitz-Birkenau, sent only a portion to the gas chambers immediately and worked most of the remainder to death in a range of factories. Survivors from the camps were marched west in 1944, as the Red Army approached, to endure yet more slave labour. A few emaciated victims were liberated in 1945.

Most of the Jews of Germany, Poland and the western USSR died, but elsewhere the picture was less uniform. The Bulgarian government refused to allow any Jews to be sent to the camps, Mussolini's regime largely left them alone, and almost all of Denmark's Jews were smuggled to neutral Sweden, for example.

In all countries many people risked their lives to help Jews, both on a small and larger scale. By contrast some in France's Vichy government willingly assisted in the deportation process, and most countries had collaborators who helped the Nazis in their dirty work. Many Germans later denied knowing anything of what had been done in their name (indeed the Nazis tried to keep secret what was happening in the camps), but the official Nazi explanation that the Jews were taken east for "resettlement" cannot really have fooled many people.

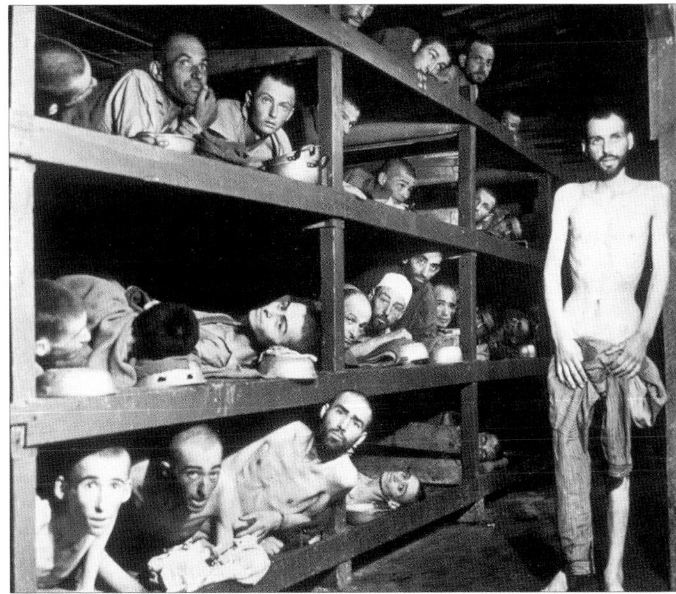

Above: Some of the survivors liberated from Buchenwald in 1945, including the Nobel Laureate Elie Wiesel, in the middle bunk, seventh from the left.

Britain and the USA had a fair idea of what was happening from the middle of 1942 but, other than a few protests, did nothing that might have slowed or halted the murders. Although since blamed on anti-semitism, this failure probably arose because it was so difficult to accept the appalling truth that 6 million Jews were being killed.

Right: Adolf Eichmann, the callous bureaucrat who managed much of the "Final Solution".

EUTHANASIA

Many of the techniques of mass murder used against the Jews had been developed for use in the Nazi euthanasia programmes. During the 1930s over 300,000 carriers of hereditary mental illnesses or disabilities were sterilized. From 1939 onwards, over 100,000 "inferior Germans" were callously murdered, many by the medical staff of the hospitals "caring" for them. Victims included senile patients, the insane and infants with physical handicaps or genetic conditions such as Down's syndrome.

Field Artillery

Despite the more spectacular contributions of tanks and aircraft, World War II was a war dominated by artillery – more than half of all casualties on all battle fronts came from the ever more deadly concentrations of artillery fire.

The backbone of every army's firepower came from the medium-calibre guns of the field artillery units. Divisions invariably included an artillery component dedicated to the support of the division's units, usually on the basis of roughly one artillery battery (of perhaps six guns) for each infantry or tank battalion in the formation. Guns in the field artillery class were usually of 75–105mm (2.95–4.13in) calibre and fired shells, weighing 10–15kg (20–35lb), to a range of 12–15km (7.5–9.5 miles).

Above: A German 10.5cm (4.13in) leFH 18 gun on the advance in the Ardennes in late 1944.

Types of Weapons

A typical weapon of this type was the US Army's standard M2A1 105mm (4.13in) howitzer, a model that had been in service since 1934 and remained in use well into the Vietnam era. In common with most similar weapons, the M2A1 could fire a variety of different types of shell, including high explosive (HE), high explosive anti-tank (HEAT), white phosphorus, smoke, and even a leaflet-carrying type. A variety of propellant charges was also supplied for range adjustments.

Germany's standard weapons, the 10.5cm leFH 18 and slightly modified leFH 18/40, were essentially similar. Britain's main field gun – the 25pdr, with a calibre of 3.45in (87mm) – delivered a slightly smaller shell. However, it lost nothing in range and compensated by being very quick firing. Soviet divisional artillery weapons were a mix of smaller guns still (76.2mm/3in M1936, 1939 or 1942 guns and others) and heavier 122mm (4.8in) types (M1931 guns and M1938 howitzers and others). The 122mm howitzer had a similar range to the field guns discussed above and fired a 21.8kg (48lb) shell.

The other major Axis powers, Italy and Japan, had various 75mm (2.95in) and 105mm weapons, which were comparable in performance to the types noted above. However, neither nation used its artillery very effectively in action.

Organization

Surprisingly, armies generally used fewer artillery weapons in WWII than in WWI. This was mainly because artillery tactics had changed and the techniques used for controlling artillery fire had advanced greatly.

Much of the artillery fire of WWI had been devoted to preparatory bombardments – programmes of shelling in advance of a battle designed to smash enemy positions and disrupt enemy forces. Germany and the Western Allies laid much less emphasis on this type of action in WWII, recognizing that it was of limited effectiveness and could often be counter-productive. Instead they emphasized neutralizing fire while an action was actually

Right: British artillerymen in Burma in action with a 3.7in (94mm) pack howitzer. Dating from WWI but with an improved mounting, the gun could fire a 9kg (20lb) shell.

occurring. The aim was to suppress enemy firepower and ability to manoeuvre.

Although the Red Army deployed a great mass of artillery its use tended to be less sophisticated, especially in the first couple of years of war. Battery commanders might well be the only personnel able to make the calculations needed for more complicated fire plans – their juniors might even be illiterate and have no watches for timing any switches of target.

Communications also played a vital part. Western artillery batteries routinely used forward observation officers (FOO), equipped with radios to direct and adjust their fire, and they had elaborate inter-connections between artillery units. An FOO could call for fire not only from his own battery but also, on occasion, from as many as several hundred other guns within a very short time. This process was assisted by the development of various standard patterns and timetables of fire that could very quickly be put in place by numerous artillery units. The superior British and American artillery organization established by 1943–5 was a significant factor in the Allied victory.

M3 105mm HOWITZER

The M3 105mm howitzer was a lighter version of the standard M2 field gun fitted with a shorter barrel. It was intended for use by airborne forces and was also employed by support companies of infantry units (as shown here in New Guinea in 1943–4). It had roughly two-thirds the range of the parent gun but fired similar ammunition. Some 2,500 were made.

Calibre: 105mm (4.13in)
Weight: 1,135kg (2,500lb)
Length: 3.94m (12ft 11in)
Range: 7,600m (8,300yd)
Shell weight: 15kg (33lb) HE

Stalingrad

The Battle of Stalingrad is rightly regarded as the turning point of WWII. Before then any defeats suffered by Germany were little more than minor setbacks; after the Stalingrad calamity, rant at his generals as he might, Hitler had lost the war.

As the German advance ground toward Stalingrad through the summer of 1942, the war came to the local people in earnest. Stalin at first forbade any evacuation of the civilian population to prevent any suggestion that the city was likely to fall. Work continued in factories that produced the weapons that could be used immediately. T-34s from the former tractor factory would be driven straight into battle, unpainted and often lacking gunsights. Men not already in the army were formed into militia units and sent, untrained, straight into action with predictable horrendous casualties. Women and children toiled to dig trenches and build defences; other women crewed anti-aircraft guns.

KEY FACTS

PLACE: Stalingrad

DATE: 12 September 1942–2 February 1943

OUTCOME: German Sixth Army failed to capture the city and was itself annihilated.

ATTACKING THE CITY

On 12 September the first German troops moved into the city itself. The Germans chose to attack straight into the urban area and soon became embroiled in a vicious house-to-house battle. Soviet tactics were to establish front-line positions as close as possible to the German lines – the safest place from German air and artillery attack.

At the end of August Stalin had sent his top general, Georgi Zhukov, to supervise the whole southern front and now a new commander, Vasili Chuikov, took over 62nd Army in the city itself. While Zhukov prepared for an eventual counter-offensive, Chuikov drove his troops relentlessly into combat. A steady stream of reinforcements was ferried under fire across the Volga into the ruins, just enough arriving (despite repeated crises) to keep at least part of the city in Soviet hands.

Below: German infantry armed with submachine-guns prepare to attack amid the ruins of Stalingrad.

Above: General Vasili Chuikov, the tough commander of 62nd Army in the defence of Stalingrad.

"NOT ONE STEP BACKWARDS"

Underlying the desperate defence of Stalingrad was the brutal and merciless disciplinary system of the Red Army. In August 1941 Stalin had issued an order that anyone trying to surrender should be shot on the spot. On 28 July 1942 his Order 227 (known as "Not One Step Backwards") reinforced this message. Armies were to form a second line of troops behind an attack to shoot anyone who wavered. Officers who "allowed" their men to desert or troops cut off by the Germans but who later returned to Soviet lines were sent to punishment battalions, a virtual death sentence. At least 400,000 died in such units in the course of the war.

Above: Last survivors of the German Stalingrad garrison march off into Soviet captivity.

Soviet losses were huge, but German casualties mounted, too. At the end of September, and again in mid-October, the Germans came close to victory, but the defenders just clung on in a small part of the city's northern factory district.

GERMAN VULNERABILITY

The advance to Stalingrad had brought other consequences for the Axis forces. In the course of the summer Hitler had sacked several of his top generals after quarrels about the strategic plan. Now he himself took many command decisions, both big and small. The advance to Stalingrad had greatly lengthened the German front and, as a consequence, two Romanian armies and an Italian army had been brought into line on the flanks of Sixth Army and Fourth Panzer Army. The Romanian troops were poorly motivated and trained and very badly equipped. They would be the first targets for the planned Soviet counter-offensive.

The Soviets attacked north of Stalingrad on 19 November and to the south the next day. The Romanian fronts were shattered. Within a week the two advancing Red Army forces had joined up and cut Stalingrad off. General Paulus asked for permission to break out – and at that stage could almost certainly have done so – but Hitler refused, promising to supply the trapped troops by air. General Erich von Manstein was brought in to lead a relief attempt that nearly reached the surrounded pocket, but he had to retreat just before Christmas.

In the meantime the air supply effort to Stalingrad's frozen airfields had cost the Luftwaffe hundreds of transport aircraft and delivered only a fraction of the necessary supplies. Short of fuel and ammunition and slowly starving, Sixth Army now faced superior forces on all sides. The end was inevitable. The last German troops in the city surrendered on 2 February 1943.

Above: German Stukas in action over Stalingrad in the early stages of the siege, autumn 1942.

Infantry Weapons

At its most basic level, combat in land warfare depended on the qualities of the infantry soldier's personal weapons. US Marines (like soldiers everywhere) were taught: "My rifle is my best friend. ... Without my rifle I am useless."

The most common personal weapons for soldiers in all armies of World War II were hand grenades, submachine-guns and rifles.

Hand grenades were essential in every close-quarter engagement in all theatres of war and were used in vast numbers. Some grenades had offensive and defensive versions, the former relying solely on blast effects, the latter producing splinters or shrapnel in addition. Special-purpose grenades also included smoke and incendiary types. In outward appearance there were two main kinds: egg-shaped varieties like the British No. 36, based on the WWI Mills bomb, or stick designs like the German Stielhandgranate 24.

Left: A German combat engineer clears a path through some barbed wire during an exercise. He is armed with a Stielhandgranate 24.

Rifles

In 1939, as for decades before, the standard weapon for soldiers in all armies was a magazine-fed single-shot rifle, firing a bullet of roughly 7.7mm (0.3in) calibre. Such a round was lethal, and in theory could be fired accurately, to ranges well over 1,000m (1100yd), but it was an unlucky casualty indeed who was struck by a deliberately aimed shot at even a third of that distance.

The best such weapon was the USA's standard rifle, the 0.3in (7.62mm) M1 Garand, which had the advantage of being a semi-automatic design. Most other major rifles were of the older bolt-action type. The British 0.303in (7.7mm) Lee Enfield No. 4 was perhaps the best of these because its mechanism could be operated most speedily. However, other types like Germany's 7.92mm (0.312in) Mauser 98K, were also sturdy, accurate and reliable.

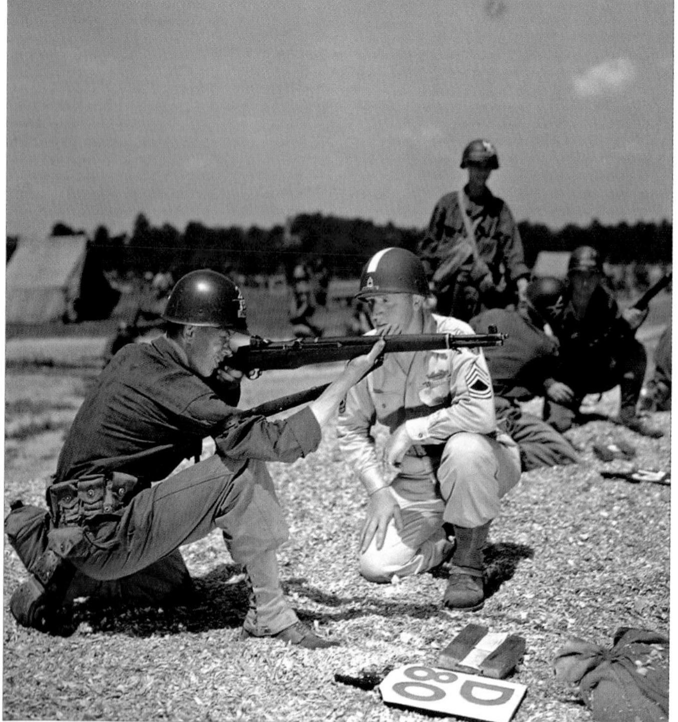

Left: An American recruit is instructed in marksmanship using an M1 Garand 0.3in (7.62mm) rifle.

Above: Soviet infantry attacking. The man nearest the camera has a PPSh-41 submachine-gun. The men on the left have Mosin-Nagant M1891 7.62mm rifles, an old design with only a five-round magazine.

SUBMACHINE-GUNS

Only during the final months of trench combat in WWI were submachine-guns used. They had the advantage over rifles of a far higher rate of fire (ammunition supply permitting), but they were difficult for even a well-trained soldier to fire accurately and also had short ranges because of the low-powered pistol rounds they employed.

The Red Army and the German Army made most widespread use of the submachine-gun. The most common Soviet design (around 6 million made) was the 7.62mm PPSh-41. It was cheap but robust and its drum magazine held a very useful 71 rounds. Germany produced a series of weapons based on the 9mm (0.345in) MP38 and MP40 (which were erroneously referred to as the Schmeisser) that were effective and saw widespread service.

The principal design used by both the British and American armies in the early years of the war was the 0.45in (11.4mm) Thompson, more accurate and reliable than some, but heavy and expensive. Both Britain and the USA also produced utility wartime designs: the 0.45in M3 "Grease Gun" for the USA and the 9mm Sten for Britain. British Stens were particularly inaccurate and of dubious reliability, but they were very cheap and easy to make – an important consideration when equipping a mass army from scratch after Dunkirk. Many were also sent to resistance groups.

ASSAULT RIFLES

In the later years of the war, the Germans introduced a number of self-loading assault rifles that included many of the virtues and avoided some of the vices of both the traditional rifle and the submachine-gun. The most important design was the Sturmgewehr 44, which used a new 7.92mm (0.312in) round that would be employed in the post-war years by early models of the AK-47 Kalashnikov.

STEN GUN

Introduced in 1941, the Sten was cheap and quick to make. Over 4 million were produced in several slightly different marks. As well as being used by the British Army, it was sent to resistance forces who liked its simplicity and that it could use German ammunition.

SPECIFICATION: Sten Mark 2
CALIBRE: 9mm (0.354in)
LENGTH: 762mm (30in)
WEIGHT: 2.96kg (6lb 8oz)
BARREL LENGTH: 196mm (7.75in)
MUZZLE VELOCITY: 381m/sec (1,250ft/sec)
MAGAZINE: 32 rounds

In addition to the above, many combatants and non-combatant personnel in land, sea and air forces of all nations carried pistols (both revolvers and automatics) in a very wide variety of designs and calibres. These were used in action often enough as close-range weapons of last resort. However, they were seldom regarded as first-choice combat weapons.

Soviet Winter Victories, 1942–3

Inspired by their success around Stalingrad, Soviet attacks continued through the winter of 1942–3. Now stronger and better-equipped than ever before, they regained all the territory that had been lost during 1942.

The encirclement of Stalingrad and the eventual destruction of the German Sixth Army was only part of a more general Soviet offensive all along the southern Eastern Front in the winter of 1942–3.

General Manstein's attempt to relieve Stalingrad began on 12 December 1942 and made good progress at first, despite the bitter winter weather. Within days, however, new Soviet attacks on his flanks were posing an additional threat. The Italian Eighth Army to the north was smashed, even as the forces moving toward Stalingrad were being slowed by fierce resistance. By the end of the year Manstein's units were in retreat. To the south the Soviet Stalingrad Front (or Army Group) was striking toward Rostov to cut the German Army Group A off in the Caucasus; the Don Front was tightening the ring around Stalingrad; and the South-West Front was freeing the whole area to the west of the great Don River bend.

Left: General Konstantin Rokossovsky commanded the Don Front around Stalingrad in 1942–3.

New Soviet Attacks

In January the Soviet attacks were extended to the north. Once again troops from one of Germany's satellites were the initial target. Voronezh Front smashed into Hungarian Second Army, as weak and ill-equipped as its Italian and Romanian counterparts. Within days the Hungarian force had been effectively destroyed and German Second Army to its north had also been pushed back.

Off to the south Hitler had delayed giving Army Group A permission to retreat from the Caucasus. The motorized units of First Panzer Army managed

WINTER BATTLES, 1942–3
Despite their brief recovery at Kharkov, the winter battles were disastrous for the German forces.

ROMANIANS ON THE EASTERN FRONT

Romanian troops played a small part in Operation Barbarossa in 1941. The head of government, Marshal Ion Antonescu, saw this as part of a holy crusade against Bolshevism and agreed to increase the Romanian force in 1942. When the Soviets smashed the Axis defences around Stalingrad, over 100,000 Romanians were killed or captured. Even so, strong Romanian forces would continue to fight alongside the Germans until August 1944, when their country changed sides after a coup led by King Michael deposed Antonescu. Substantial Romanian forces then advanced with the Red Army into Hungary and Czechoslovakia.

Above: Romanian prisoners near Stalingrad, late 1942.

to escape through Rostov by the end of January, but the slower-moving infantry of Seventeenth Army were pushed east into a bridgehead in the Taman Peninsula opposite the Crimea.

The Soviet commanders now had new objectives in their sights. On the northern flank they would push forward to both Kursk and Kharkov, and to the south they would cross the Donets and head for the Dniepr to isolate Manstein's forces. These attacks began in the last days of January.

The Soviets also planned to strengthen these attacks by switching the troops that had finally captured Stalingrad to the main battlefront. However, this move took longer than was originally planned.

LAST ADVANCES

Soviet advances did capture Kursk and Rostov in early February and were moving past Kharkov by the middle of the month, but the troops were becoming increasingly worn out. In mid-February Hitler reorganized his forces, putting Manstein, his most able general of all, in charge of what would now be called Army Group South. The great Russian advances had created a number of exposed salients at the same time, because the German retreat had shortened their lines. All this added up to an opportunity for a German riposte, which would begin in mid-February.

Below: Red Army infantry attack. Riflemen advance while a light machine-gun gives covering fire.

Below: Soviet troops often went into action riding on tanks, a practice that risked high casualties.

Assault Guns

Tank turrets were expensive and difficult to build so heavily armoured vehicles, carrying powerful guns in simpler limited-traverse mountings, were also produced in numbers and used very effectively, notably on the Eastern Front.

Weapons in this category were almost exclusively the preserve of the German and Soviet armies. They had at least a reasonable degree of armour protection and carried weapons suitable both for anti-armour use and for direct fire support of assaulting troops and tanks. (Self-propelled guns in Anglo-American service are described in the self-propelled artillery and anti-tank gun categories – along with other Soviet and German designs – which better describe their capabilities and operational uses.)

Even with these limitations the number of vehicles that belong in this category is quite large. Soviet types include the SU-45, -57, -76, -85, -100, -122 and -152, and JSU-122 and -152 designs, too (the figures indicate the calibre of gun fitted). Germany fielded a similar variety. Accordingly, only a few examples on each side can be described.

SU-85

The SU-85 was designed to provide better anti-tank performance than the T-34/76. It was produced during 1943–4 but phased out when the T-34/85 entered service. The example shown is in German service after being captured.

Weight: 29.4 tonnes
Hull length: 5.92m (19ft 5in)
Height: 2.54m (8ft 4in)
Armament: 85mm (3.35in) D-5 M1943
Armour: 54mm (2.13in) max.
Road speed: 55kph (34mph)

Left: A knocked-out Jagdpanther being examined by an American soldier in early 1945.

First Designs

Germany's Sturmgeschütz 3, based on the Panzer 3 chassis, was the first notable weapon of this type. Versions of this design would serve throughout the war from 1940 and, indeed, become Germany's most-produced armoured fighting vehicle (AFV), with over 9,000 made.

Initially the StuG 3 was designed solely for infantry support with a short (L/24 – 24-calibre) 7.5cm (2.95in) gun mounted in the forward superstructure with limited traverse. Later models added first an L/43 7.5cm and then a more powerful L/48 gun to gain an effective anti-tank capability. There was also an essentially similar StuG 4 and a version fitting the 10.5cm (4.13in) howitzer. A further vehicle with comparable capabilities was the Hetzer, a design based on the PzKpfw 38(*t*) chassis and also carrying the L/48 7.5cm gun.

In a different category were various *Jagdpanzer* (usually translated as "tank destroyer") vehicles (confusingly, the Jagdpanzer 4 was really an updated StuG 4, rather than an entirely new type). Three vehicles of this sort should be mentioned.

First was the Elefant, or Ferdinand, based on an alternative design for the Tiger tank. It carried the most formidable

Above: A StuG 3 passes by a knocked-out T-34 during fighting in Poland in 1944.

SU-100

Like the SU-85, the SU-100 was based on the T-34 chassis, but with the more powerful 100mm D-10 gun. Full-scale production started in September 1944 and it saw significant service in 1945.

Weight: 32.5 tonnes
Hull length: 5.92m (19ft 5in)
Height: 2.54m (8ft 4in)
Armament: 100mm (3.94in) D-10 M1944
Armour: 75mm (2.95in) hull front
Road speed: 48kph (30mph)

version of the famous "eighty-eight", the PaK 43 L/71 8.8cm (3.46in) gun, behind very thick armour. Mechanically unreliable and lacking secondary armament to fend off infantry attack, it was not a success.

The Jagdpanther carried the same gun and was well armoured and agile; overall it was probably the most effective tank destroyer of the war. Its larger stablemate, the Jagdtiger, mounted a massive 12.8cm (5.04in) gun, the most powerful anti-tank gun of the war, behind armour up to 250mm (9.84in) thick, but was clumsy and unreliable. Most tellingly, for all their power, the total production of these types was roughly 90 Elefants, 390 Jagdpanthers and 80 Jagdtigers – never enough to stave off Germany's defeat.

Soviet Responses

The first significant Soviet design was the SU-76, which carried the M1942 76.2mm (3in) gun in an open-topped mount on a light-tank chassis. It was designed in response to the German StuG types; over 12,000 were built. Substantially more powerful were the SU-85 introduced in 1943 and SU-100 of late 1944. Neither of these had the same scale of armour as the German tank destroyers, but the SU-100 in particular had the gun power to deal with most German AFVs. By way of comparison at least 1,500 SU-100s were built by mid-1945.

The heaviest Soviet assault-gun types carried 122mm (4.8in) and 152mm (5.98in) guns. These weapons were not primarily designed for anti-tank use, but their heavy shells meant that they had significant anti-tank capabilities nonetheless and were often used in this role.

JAGDTIGER

The Jagdtiger first saw service in late 1944 and a few fought in the Battle of the Bulge. The basic vehicle was a variant of the Tiger 2 chassis, but it was under-powered and hence prone to breakdowns. Only two battalions using Jagdtigers were formed.

Weight: 70 tonnes
Hull length: 7.39m (24ft 3in)
Height: 2.95m (9ft 8in)
Armament: 12.8cm (5.04in) PaK 44 + 1 x machine-gun
Armour: 250mm (9.84in) max.
Road speed: 38kph (24mph)

Propaganda, Art and Popular Culture

Since WWII was indeed a total war, writers, artists, movie-makers, journalists and broadcasters everywhere played their parts in the war effort, either within the dictates of totalitarian rulers or under the gentler controls imposed in the democracies.

In the totalitarian nations, art, entertainment and public information were simply aspects of national life to be managed for the good of the state, whether in war or in peace. The situation was less clear-cut in the democracies, but generally speaking popular and more serious artists and those in the media felt an obligation to make some contribution to their respective war efforts.

Absolute Control

There were many similarities between the situation in the USSR and Germany and even Japan. In all three countries censorship was absolute; nothing was published or broadcast that had not been officially approved, nor was any criticism of the ruling regime tolerated. The Nazis were particularly aware of the power of radio broadcasting. They ensured that cheap radio sets were widely available in Germany but confiscated many radios in occupied countries, banning anyone under their control from listening to Allied broadcasts.

In the visual arts there were also many similarities between the socialist realism style demanded by Soviet authorities and the classicism favoured by Hitler and the Nazis. The stern Aryan soldiers of German war art were little different from the undaunted workers and peasants their opponents depicted.

German and Soviet portrayals of their opponents were nasty in the extreme. The Nazi demonization of communists and Jews needs no elaboration, while on the Soviet side well-known and much-publicized material included poems entitled "Kill Him" and "I Hate".

Depictions of the Axis powers in Britain and the USA were neither as crude nor as vicious, though some well-known wartime films, *The Life and Death of Colonel Blimp* for example, were criticized in some quarters for including characters who were decent Germans. One thing that almost all belligerent nations on both sides had in common was that newspaper circulations increased substantially, though

Below: *Signal* magazine was issued by the Germans in several languages. This French example publicized the Katyń massacre.

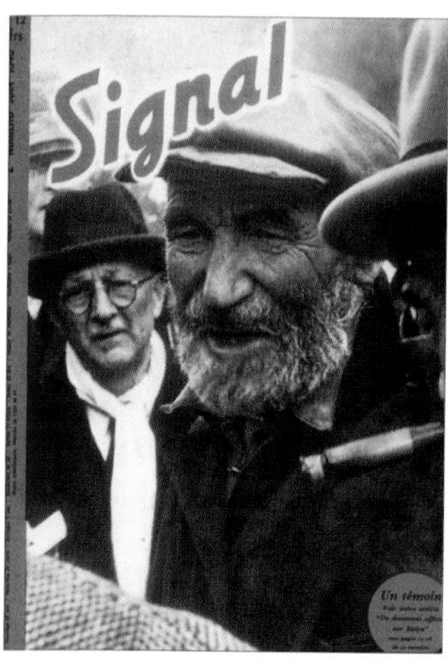

JOSEF GOEBBELS

Goebbels (1897–1945) was the Nazi Propaganda Minister from Hitler's accession to power in 1933 until, after murdering their six children, he and his wife committed suicide in Hitler's bunker in April 1945. He controlled all the media and artistic output in Germany. He used radio broadcasting particularly brilliantly to foster support for the Nazi regime and to create and maintain the image of Hitler as a great leader. He was loyal to Hitler to the end and his efforts played a large part in keeping the German people fighting effectively long after defeat was certain.

Above: Josef Goebbels in full oratorical flow at a Nazi Party rally in 1934.

Above: "Behind the enemy powers: the Jew", a German poster of 1942.

in most countries the number of different publications decreased, while the survivors were reduced by paper rationing to a handful of pages.

Broadcast Media

In Britain and the USA, owners and managers of the press and broadcast media were happy generally to comply with official wishes that they gave no secrets to the enemy and to moderate any criticisms of the government that they might have. But neither government sought to dictate what was printed or broadcast and certainly did not disseminate the sort of outright lies that were a commonplace of Nazi bulletins.

Many in Europe secretly listened to the BBC, in part because they knew that its news was truthful as far as it went, even if it was not always the whole truth. But Germany's English-language broadcasts were mocked in Britain for the stilted style of the principal broadcaster William Joyce (known as "Lord Haw-Haw") and the ludicrous stories he often tried to tell his listeners.

Film was probably the most powerful cultural medium. As well as productions on topical subjects, the output both from Hollywood and the state-run German film industry included much simple escapist entertainment for difficult times. Historical epics featuring past patriots and heroes appeared regularly in Germany and the USSR – *Bismarck* and *Ivan the Terrible* among the titles – and in Britain Laurence Olivier's 1944 version of Shakespeare's *Henry V* had a similar theme.

For many, popular music and song were a source of comfort and pleasure that could transcend boundaries. At the end of the African campaign in 1943 there was an incident in which a formation of British soldiers, marching to their victory parade in Tunis, passed a column from the *Afrika Korps* going into captivity – both groups were singing "Lili Marlene".

l'Humanité

LE COMMUNISME, SEUL ESPOIR DE LA FRANCE

Sous le drapeau de LENINE - STALINE

Above: Underground newspapers, like France's communist *l'Humanité*, provided an alternative source of news in every occupied country.

Right: Laurence Olivier as the king in his 1944 film, *Henry V*.

Alamein and the Advance to Tunisia

Although it could not compare in scale to the massive battles on the Eastern Front, El Alamein is rightly seen as a turning point in Britain's war with Germany. Much hard fighting remained but after Alamein there would be no more big defeats.

Although his charge into Egypt had been halted in the First Battle of El Alamein in July 1942, Rommel was keen to attack again as soon as his forces were strengthened. In the meantime, Prime Minister Churchill had appointed a new command team to the British forces defending Egypt, putting General Bernard Montgomery in charge of Eighth Army.

New British Plans

As soon as he took over, "Monty" began transforming the British force, beginning by rebuilding its morale, which had been shattered by the disasters earlier in the year. He laid down far more clearly than before that there would be no retreat and deployed his forces to make best use of their concentrated firepower, rather than try to compete with the Germans in manoeuvre. Thus, when the Germans attacked late on 30 August, the British units stood firm and by 6 September the Germans had been forced back to where they had started from. This Battle of Alam Halfa was a clear Allied victory.

A significant factor in the German defeat was their shortage of supplies. They were operating many hundreds of kilometres from their nearest port, while the routes between Europe and North Africa were coming under increasingly heavy Allied air and naval attacks. Many of these raids were coming from the island of Malta, very heavily bombarded earlier in the year but by now reinforced after a series of fierce naval convoy battles.

After Alam Halfa, Churchill wanted Montgomery to attack straight away but he refused, insisting that he be allowed to build up his forces substantially first. By the time he did attack

KEY FACTS – EL ALAMEIN

Place: North-west Egypt

Date: 23 October–4 November 1942

Outcome: Italian and German forces defeated and forced to retreat to western Libya.

Above: A Crusader Mark 3 tank during the Battle of El Alamein. Some 4,500 of all versions of the Crusader were built, but all were mechanically unreliable.

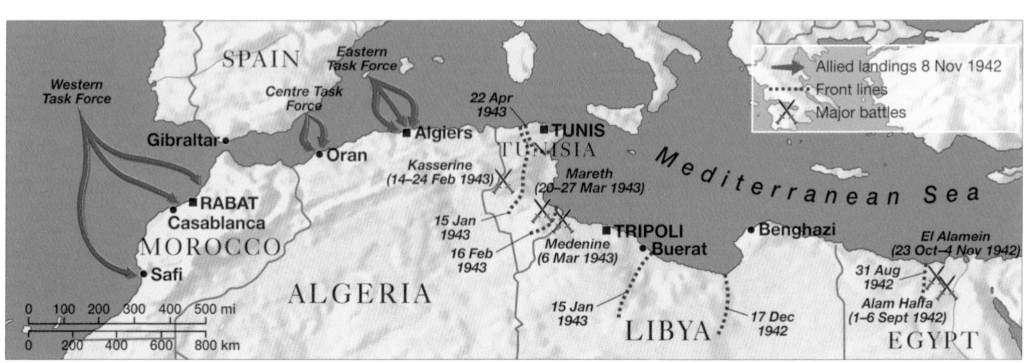

NORTH AFRICA, 1942–3 After victory at El Alamein and the Torch landings, the Allied forces steadily completed their African victory.

Right: A British 5.5in (140mm) gun firing during the heavy bombardment that opened the El Alamein battle.

at El Alamein in October, Eighth Army had about a two to one superiority in men, tanks and guns and a considerable advantage in the air (and much of the Axis force was made up of less effective Italian units).

Rommel had built up a formidable position by using extensive minefields and other defences, but Montgomery had trained his troops meticulously. He made certain that his infantry, tank units and artillery worked together effectively, which had seldom happened in the previous desert battles.

Alamein Victory

Several days of attritional fighting followed the initial Allied advance. Gradually, the German tank units, which provided the backbone of the Axis defences, were worn away. On 2 November Rommel signalled to Hitler that he had to retreat. Hitler responded with his usual unrealistic "no retreat" order, but it made no difference. With only a couple of dozen of the 500 tanks with which he began the battle left in action, Rommel had no alternative. On 4 November he abandoned his whole defensive position.

Partly because Montgomery did not organize an energetic enough pursuit, much of the remaining Axis force got away. A long retreat followed, made even more necessary for Rommel this time because of the Anglo-American Torch landings in north-west Africa from 8 November.

After brief pauses to allow supplies to catch up, Eighth Army captured Tripoli on 23 January 1943, after an advance of some 1,500km (930 miles). Despite German demolitions, the British were able to begin using the port facilities to some extent by the end of the month.

It would be several weeks before the leading troops could be strengthened for further substantial advances, but they did manage to push forward to Medenine, in eastern Tunisia, in early February.

FIELD MARSHAL BERNARD MONTGOMERY

Montgomery (1887–1976) was Britain's most famous general of the war. His careful planning and methodical leadership played a large part in the succession of Allied victories in North Africa, Italy and north-west Europe from autumn 1942 to the end of the war. In particular, it is unlikely that D-Day would have gone so well without his contribution to the planning process. However, some historians believe that he was overcautious and thereby lost opportunities for cheaper and quicker victories.

Above: "Monty" showing off his trademark pair of cap badges.

Below: Italian troops run for cover under Allied air attack in the early stages of the Battle of El Alamein.

Light Armoured Vehicles

With the increasing mechanization of warfare generally, it was natural that the scouting and other support roles were filled by armoured vehicles. Armoured cars and personnel carriers accordingly proliferated in all armies in the European war.

Every army in World War II used armoured vehicles in scouting and support roles. Dozens of types were produced and most of these had numerous substantially different variants, so naturally only a selection can be discussed here.

British and US Types

It is appropriate to begin with the most-produced armoured vehicle ever, the British Army's Bren, or Universal Carrier, of which over 100,000 were made. It could carry a machine-gun or mortar and its ammunition into action, tow a light anti-tank gun or serve in the scouting role, among many other tasks.

Britain was also a substantial user of wheeled armoured cars and their unarmed cousins – the scout cars. The most-produced types were the Daimler Dingo and Humber scout cars. Over 6,000 of the two-man Dingo were made. It had 30mm (1.2in) armour and such refinements as

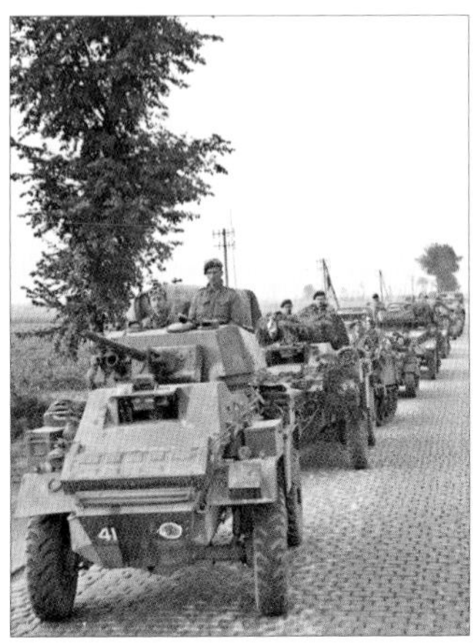

Above: A British Humber armoured car in northern France in 1944.

run-flat tyres and transmission with five forward and reverse gears. Humber and Daimler (in that order) made the most common armoured cars too, both types being in use from 1941. Heavy armoured cars included the indigenous AEC design and the American-built T17 Staghound. Britain also relied on the USA for various (usually half-tracked) personnel carriers and similar vehicles.

Unlike Britain, the USA built and used relatively few armoured car types. By far the most important was the M8, known as the Greyhound in British service. This carried a 37mm (1.46in) gun and had

Left: An American M8 armoured car during training for D-Day "somewhere in England" in 1944.

originally been conceived for the tank-destroyer role. The most important American scout car was the White M3, with over 20,000 built. This could carry up to seven men plus the driver.

The US and German Armies made extensive use of half-tracked vehicles. These had much of the cross-country performance of fully-tracked vehicles but were easier and cheaper to build because of their

SdKfz 251

Initially designed to carry the infantry in armoured divisions, the SdKfz 251 appeared in over 20 variants for other roles, including anti-aircraft, anti-tank and command vehicles. About 13,500 were built in all.

Weight: 7.9 tonnes
Length: 5.8m (19ft)
Height: 1.75m (5ft 9in)
Width: 2.1m (6ft 11in)
Road speed: 53kph (33mph)
Engine: 120bhp Maybach HL42
Armour: 15mm (0.6in) max.

Above: An M3 half track leads a US column in Germany, 1945.

simpler wheeled steering. US models included the smaller M2 and M9, and the larger M3 and M5. The M3 and M5 were 9-tonne vehicles that could carry a full infantry squad. All four were widely used in general front-line transport roles. In addition there were many variants carrying anti-aircraft, anti-tank and close-support weapons. Many US half tracks and scout cars were supplied to the Soviets.

German Designs

The smallest and most unusual vehicle in Germany's half-track class was the SdKfz 2 Kettenkrad, in effect a half-track cargo motorcycle, of which over 8,000 were made. More important were the more conventional 5.9-tonne SdKfz 250 and its derivatives, as well as the larger 7.9-tonne SdKfz 251 and its numerous variants. These types were a little less mobile than the US M2/M3, in part because the front wheels were unpowered, but they served in a similar variety of personnel, transport and weapon-carrying roles. Many were used as command vehicles, being fitted in the early-war years with large and conspicuous "bedstead" aerials for the radios they carried.

Germany also had a variety of 4-, 6- and 8-wheeled armoured cars. The 4-wheel SdKfz 221 was a 4-tonne vehicle with two crew and armed with a single machine-gun. The 6-wheel types were pre-war designs and were mostly withdrawn from service by 1941 or so. They were superseded by the 8 x 8 types from 1937.

The 8-wheel SdKfz 232 carried a 2cm (0.79in) cannon and a machine-gun (confusingly, there was also a 6-wheel SdKfz 232 and other overlapping designations). It was an 8.8-tonne vehicle with a crew of four, including a second driver in the rear of the fighting compartment who could drive the vehicle in reverse. The heaviest variant was the SdKfz 234 Puma, with a 7.5cm (2.95in) anti-tank gun.

BREN GUN CARRIER

The Universal Carrier (as the standardized examples were known from 1940) was the principal British utility vehicle. It often carried light weapons like the Boys anti-tank rifle and Bren Gun, seen here.

Specification: Universal Carrier
Weight: 4.3 tonnes
Length: 3.75m (12ft 4in)
Height: 1.6m (5ft 3in)
Width: 2.1m (6ft 11in)
Road speed: 32kph (20mph)
Engine: 85bhp Ford V8
Armour: 10mm (0.4in) max.

Right: The British AEC Mark 3 heavy armoured car carried a 75mm (2.95in) gun.

Operation Torch and Victory in Africa

American troops made their combat debut in the European theatre in Operation Torch in 1942. After setbacks and much hard fighting, the Allied victory in North Africa was completed in May 1943, as the ring around Germany began to tighten.

From early 1941 US policy in the event of war with Germany and Japan was to give the European theatre priority. From the start US Army leaders were convinced that the way to defeat Hitler was by a cross-Channel attack from England, but it was very soon obvious that this operation could not be mounted for many months. To maintain the "Germany first" policy President Roosevelt ordered that US troops must be sent into battle against Germany during 1942, so it was decided to make landings in Morocco and Algeria to clear North Africa of Axis forces.

Morocco and Algeria were French colonies under the control of Marshal Pétain's Vichy regime. Anglo-French relations remained embittered after the events of 1940 so the Americans took the lead in pre-landing negotiations to try to persuade the leaders of the large Vichy forces in Africa not to resist the Allied advance and, instead, join with the smaller Free French forces already fighting on the Allied side. In the event the French did not resist the landings strongly, but it took months of political wrangling to create a united Free French force.

KEY FACTS – TORCH

PLACE: North-west Africa

DATE: From 8 November 1942

OUTCOME: Allied forces landed successfully in Morocco and Algeria, but German reinforcements poured into Tunisia to slow their advance.

Below: An American M2 105mm (4.13in) howitzer position in southern Tunisia in the spring of 1943.

TORCH LANDINGS

The invasion, known as Operation Torch, began on 8 November 1942, four days after Eighth Army's victory at El Alamein had sent the Italians and Germans reeling out of Egypt. Ideally the attack would have gone as far east as Tunisia, but this was rejected as too risky. Instead landings were made on Morocco's Atlantic coast near Casablanca and around Algiers and Oran in Algeria. The Anglo-American force, First Army, immediately began heading east for Tunis, but too little too late.

Field Marshal Albrecht Kesselring, Germany's very able Commander-in-Chief South, started pouring troops, tanks and aircraft into Tunisia from Sicily on 9 November. These fought the Allied advance to a standstill in the rugged hills of western Tunisia, in a series of bitter battles from late November into early January 1943.

BATTLE FOR TUNISIA

By February 1943 the Axis forces in Tunisia had been joined by Rommel's army, which had successfully completed its retreat from Egypt. Eighth Army was still struggling to bring the port of Tripoli into full use so was not yet ready to push farther into Tunisia in the south. This gave

Above: American troops landing at Oran with a light anti-aircraft gun at the start of Operation Torch.

the Germans an opportunity to strike at First Army, which they took on 14 February.

In the resulting Battle of Kasserine the inexperienced American troops, who were the initial target for the attack, were badly defeated. American and British reinforcements, rushed to the threatened sector, just prevented a decisive breakthrough and then gradually recovered much of the lost ground by late February. General George Patton took over command of the US ground forces in Tunisia and his leadership very quickly improved their combat efficiency.

In early March Eighth Army smashed an attempted German attack and later in the month, in the hard-fought Battle of Mareth, pushed the Axis forces out of their main defence line in southern Tunisia.

Below: US troops examining an abandoned Italian M13/40 tank during the fighting in Tunisia.

In April First and Eighth Armies continued their attacks. They eventually broke out of the hills and advanced to Bizerta and Tunis in early May. The last of around 250,000 Axis troops taken prisoner in these final battles surrendered on 13 May. Africa was now wholly in Allied hands.

GENERAL DWIGHT D. EISENHOWER

Eisenhower (1890–1969) was appointed as Allied supreme commander for Operation Torch and would continue in that role in Sicily and Italy and then finally in north-west Europe in 1944–5. He realized far better than other top Allied commanders the paramount importance of maintaining good relations within the Anglo-American partnership. Although he had numerous problems with egotistical subordinates like Patton and Montgomery, Eisenhower's leadership kept the Allied effort very much on track.

Above: Eisenhower was totally committed to Allied unity.

Germany Fights Back – Kharkov and Kursk

The counter-stroke at Kharkov inspired Hitler to order new attacks at Kursk. For the first time a major German summer offensive in Russia failed to break through, a clear sign that the Soviets were now winning their Great Patriotic War.

The Soviet advances during January and February 1943 had pushed deep into German-held territory to capture the city of Kharkov and threaten Dnepropetrovsk. To the north of this penetration the German Army Group Centre was holding firm around Orel, and to the south General Manstein's Army Group South had good defensive positions along the Mius River. Manstein now had several Panzer divisions available, including strong and well-equipped Waffen-SS units. He was ready to turn the tables on the Soviet attackers in between these bastions.

KEY FACTS - KURSK

Place: Between Orel and Kharkov, Eastern Front

Date: 4–13 July 1943

Outcome: German forces failed to break through in the biggest tank battle of the war.

Below: German troops fighting on the outskirts of Kharkov at the end of February 1943.

Battle of Kharkov

In the second half of February Manstein's tank units struck against the Soviet spearheads near Dnepropetrovsk. By the end of the month four Soviet tank and mechanized corps (each roughly equivalent to a German Panzer division) had been smashed and the survivors pushed back over the Donets.

Taking advantage of the last few days of firm frozen ground before the mud of the spring thaw, Manstein's tanks next headed for Kharkov, taking it by 16 March. Hitler was so heartened by this remarkable comeback that, even before Kharkov fell, he was issuing orders for a new attack against the large Soviet salient centred around Kursk to the north.

Operation Citadel

Although the Germans had lost perhaps half a million casualties over the winter, Hitler still believed he could regain the initiative on the Eastern Front and, at the same time, make provision in western and southern Europe for whatever the Anglo-Americans might attempt during the year. It was clear that the German troops, and especially their tank forces, were still usually more skilled in combat than the Red Army. Hitler also believed that new Tiger and

Panther tanks coming into service would give them a further qualitative edge.

The German plan was for Ninth Army from Field Marshal Günther von Kluge's Army Group Centre to attack the north flank of the salient, while Fourth Panzer Army from Manstein's Army Group South drove into the southern flank. Originally Hitler planned the advance to begin in May, but he repeatedly postponed it until more of the new tanks were ready.

For their part Stalin, Zhukov and Chief of the General Staff Marshal Aleksandr Vasilevsky (in effect the command team who would run the remainder of the Soviet Union's war) decided to stand on the defensive at first, while they also prepared offensives of their own north and south of Kursk. Through spies and other intelligence the Soviets had a reasonable idea of what the Germans planned and accordingly they massively re-inforced their defences in the threatened areas.

The German advances began on 4 July and were fiercely resisted from the start. In the north Ninth Army, with seven Panzer divisions leading its attack, made a little progress at first. The Soviet commanders then committed their tank reserves. On 9 July Kluge told Hitler that he could not break through. On the 12th the Soviets began their offensive north of Orel and Kluge had to retreat.

On the southern front things seemed to go better for the Germans. Fourth Panzer Army advanced about 35km (20 miles) in the first few days, losing heavily but inflicting more casualties than it received. On the 12th there was a giant tank battle near the small town of Prokhorovka. Again, though the Soviets probably came off worse, they had outnumbered the Germans from the start and could afford to do so.

On the 13 July, with no breakthrough in sight and the Anglo-American invasion of Sicily developing, Hitler called off further attacks. With that, the initiative on the Eastern Front finally and permanently passed to the Red Army.

Above: German Panzer 4 tanks advancing across open ground during the Battle of Kursk.

FIELD MARSHAL ERICH VON MANSTEIN

The most talented general of any country during WWII was Germany's Field Marshal von Manstein (1887–1973). He was very largely responsible for the brilliantly successful German plan for attacking France in 1940. Although he failed in the attempt to relieve Stalingrad in late 1942, his leadership over the following months stabilized the Eastern Front and led to the German success at Kharkov. At Kursk his attacks were the most successful part of the German offensive. Thereafter, Manstein fought resourcefully on the retreat until Hitler dismissed him in March 1944.

Right: Field Marshal von Manstein and his staff studying a map to plan their manoeuvres.

Ground-attack Aircraft

Attack operations close to the front line were probably the most effective uses made of air power during the war. The Stuka symbolized Germany's early-war success and the Allied riposte was led by the Shturmovik, Typhoon and Thunderbolt.

In 1939 only the German and Soviet air forces laid any stress on the ground-attack mission. Germany's close integration of land and air power in the Blitzkrieg campaigns of 1939–41 proved that such operations could be very effective indeed. Britain and the USA would develop this capability in the course of the war.

P-47D THUNDERBOLT

The Republic P-47D Thunderbolt was particularly large and heavy for a WWII fighter, but its ample power meant that it could carry a heavy attack load. P-47D pilots claimed the destruction of tens of thousands of German tanks and trucks in Europe in 1944–5.

Crew: 1
Engine: Pratt & Whitney R2800 radial, 2,535hp
Speed: 697kph (433mph)
Armament: 8 x 0.5in (12.7mm) machine-guns + 10 x 5in (127mm) rockets and/or up to 1,130kg (2,500lb) bombs

Germany's Junkers 87 Stuka dive-bomber in effect became the definitive image of Blitzkrieg and was very much feared by opposing forces. In fact it was slow and poorly protected, as was shown when it first faced serious opposition during the Battle of Britain. However, it continued to serve successfully in the early Eastern Front battles – and the Ju-87G model, available from 1943, was fitted with a pair of 3.7cm (1.46in) cannon for the tank-busting role. It served very effectively in this mission, most notably in the hands of Hans-Ulrich Rudel, an ace pilot credited with destroying over 500 Soviet tanks.

Other German ground-attack types included versions of the Focke-Wulf (Fw) 190 fighter and the Fw 189, which was also used for reconnaissance. The Henschel 129 also served in small numbers, with armament including a 7.5cm (2.95in) gun.

The Red Air Force

By 1945 the Soviets had the world's most powerful tactical-support air force, created out of the ruins left by Germany's onslaught in 1941. Although the Soviet leaders had decided to concentrate on tactical aviation shortly before the war, their aircraft designs and training had not caught up with this change when Operation Barbarossa began.

There were various obsolete fighters in service in the attack role, including the biplane

Below: Ground crew bombing up a Typhoon fighter-bomber. It carries the "D-Day stripes" used in 1944–5.

Above: A Ju-87G Stuka armed with 3.7cm (1.46in) anti-tank cannon.

Ilyushin (Il) 153 and the more modern Sukhoi 2. Just entering service was something much better – the Il-2 Bronirovanni Shturmovik (the "Armoured Attacker"), which eventually would become the most-produced military aircraft ever.

The Shturmovik was in effect a flying tank, with substantial armour protection for the crew compartment and other vital parts. It had powerful cannon and machine-gun armament (varying between models), backed by a substantial load of rockets and bombs. Formations of Shturmoviks would often circle round a German position or tank unit, making repeated attacks until their target had been smashed, a tactic called the "Circle of Death". In Soviet eyes it was the most important aircraft of the war.

Secondary, but still produced in substantial numbers (over 11,000), was the Petlyakov 2. This twin-engined design had been conceived as a high-altitude fighter but was converted to the attack role. It was robust and fast and could carry 3 tonnes of bombs.

The Western Allies

In the absence of appropriate aircraft, Anglo-French ground-attack operations in 1940 were disastrous. Subsequently Britain began using versions of the Hurricane and P-40 Kittyhawk fighters in the role. These could carry a useful bomb load and had effective cannon and machine-gun armament – that included a pair of 40mm (1.58in) guns in one Hurricane variant) – but were lacking in performance when so equipped.

Fighter-bomber versions of the Bristol Beaufighter and De Havilland Mosquito were also employed, with some success. Both these large and powerful aircraft could carry formidable weapons loads but accuracy in attack remained uncertain.

From 1943 both British and US attack aircraft began using rockets. Although these lacked the pinpoint accuracy to knock out a tank, they had the ability to swamp a larger or less well-protected target with fire.

Their best-known use was when fitted to aircraft like Britain's Hawker Typhoon and the USA's Republic P-47 Thunderbolt. Both of these were originally pure fighter designs (the Thunderbolt a successful one, the Typhoon less so), which had the power and durability to blossom in the attack role. They played a vital part in the Anglo-American victory in Europe in 1944–5.

IL-2M SHTURMOVIK

The prototype Shturmovik first flew in 1939 and a few were in service in 1941. Initial models were single-seaters but most production was of the two-seat Il-2M and -2M3 versions, which had various other improvements, too. Further changes led to the Il-10, which saw some action in 1945.

Crew: 2
Engine: Mikulin AM-38 in-line, 1,680hp
Speed: 414kph (257mph)
Armament: 2 x 23mm (0.91in) cannon, 1 x 12.7mm (0.5in), 2 x 7.62mm (0.3in) machine-guns + 4 x RS82 or RS132 rockets and/or up to 600kg (1,320lb) bombs

Codes and Code Breaking

The continuous struggle to read enemy messages was an ongoing aspect of every campaign of the war. Signals intelligence contributed to many victories but was probably not the war-winning advantage that is sometimes suggested.

All the major combatants in WWII put considerable effort into reading coded enemy radio messages. Overall, Britain and the USA had the most success and made the best use of the resulting information; the USA and USSR were the most successful in keeping their own messages secure (though even now little is publicly known of Soviet efforts in this field).

Cipher Systems

Encryption methods used in WWII included manual systems (based on printed sets of random numbers) and machines, which were more complex and theoretically more secure. Signals produced on some machines are thought never to have been broken. These included the American Sigaba type and the British Typex. Less secure machines included the German Enigma and Geheimschreiber, the Japanese diplomatic service machine known to the Allies as Purple, and the American M-209 (used for low-grade traffic). Efforts to decode messages led to the development in Britain and the USA of various forms of calculating equipment, including what are now regarded as the first electronic computers.

Britain had various successes, increasingly comprehensive as the war went on, against German and Italian systems. For their part the Axis powers were able to read many Royal Navy messages up to 1943.

Breaking Enigma

The British system built on prewar French and Polish work. The first messages decoded were from the general Luftwaffe Enigma cipher in May 1940 and then other breaks followed. The process was by no means continuous. The main U-boat cipher was broken for much of 1941 but was impenetrable for most of 1942, both times with important

Left: An Enigma machine (bottom left) in use on General Guderian's command vehicle in 1940.

Above: Alan Turing, one of the leading mathematicians in the British code-breaking organization.

effects in the Battle of the Atlantic. One of the strengths of the British set-up was its centralization at the Government Code and Cypher School at Bletchley Park, where the various departments worked together well, enhancing each other's techniques and sharing information.

By contrast Germany, Italy and Japan all had a range of agencies involved in this work and these often competed with each other. And even when information was shared between services or with Axis partners, its recipients did not necessarily trust it – the Italians warned the Germans about Allied code breaking and the Germans warned the Japanese, in both cases with little effect.

The German Navy's B-Dienst had good results with the main Royal Navy operational ciphers at various periods up to 1943 and systems used by Allied merchant ships into 1944. From late 1943 the manual systems were replaced in Royal Navy service by the highly secure Typex machine already used by the other British services.

In the Pacific the American-led Allied effort had great success first with the Japanese diplomatic cipher, then with the Japanese Navy and finally the Army systems. Curiously, among the most valuable results was the insight given into German plans. Japan's diplomats in Berlin and elsewhere sent extensive reports on new German weapons and defences, which were read by the Allies.

The breaking of the Japanese Navy's JN-25 cipher made a major contribution to the US victory at Midway that turned the tide of the Pacific War. Later code-breaking information helped Allied commanders decide which garrisons to attack and which to bypass. However, it is not true (as has sometimes been suggested) that properly interpreted Purple and JN-25 decrypts made by the US, British or Dutch services could have given definite warning of Japan's attack on Pearl Harbor.

Right: General Oshima (left), Japan's ambassador in Berlin, whose messages home were decoded by the Allies.

Below: *U-505* alongside the USS *Pillsbury*. This 1944 capture was based on code-breaking information.

GARDENING

During their normal operations RAF bombers often dropped sea mines near German-controlled ports. This activity was known by the codename "gardening". This was not just done to sink enemy ships, however. Many such operations were meant to be detected by the Germans so that their local HQ would send a warning to its units. Allied cryptographers then used the predictable content of such signals to work out the code-machine settings for the day – and then they would use these settings to read more important messages.

The Defeat of Hitler's Navy, 1942–5

The struggle against Germany's U-boats continued to 1945 but was decisively won in the spring of 1943 by a combination of airpower, scientific research, code-breaking skill, industrial strength – and the bravery of the Allied seamen.

By the end of 1941 the battles between Germany's U-boats and the Allied merchant ships and escorts had already been raging bitterly for many months. Though the threat was serious, Britain was surviving reasonably well. Rationing had reduced consumption substantially and new construction, and the transfer to British control of ships from occupied Allied countries like Norway and Greece, had helped to counteract losses. However, Hitler's declaration of war on the USA in December 1941 brought new opportunities, which his U-boat force soon grabbed.

For the first six months or so of 1942 the U-boats scored many successes off the US East Coast and in the Caribbean. The main reason for this was an astounding failure on the part of American commanders to institute a system of escorted convoys and supporting air units. Convoys linking with those on the trans-Atlantic routes were gradually introduced from April but did not cover the whole area to the Gulf of Mexico until October. Although the situation was thus being brought under control by the summer, the Allied shipping losses of June 1942 were the worst of the war.

Above: A British heavy cruiser in service with an Arctic convoy to Russia in early 1943.

German Advantages

On the German side matters were helped by code changes that shut the British cryptographers out of the main U-boat traffic from February 1942 to the end of the year. The size of the U-boat force was also increasing from some 100 operational boats in January 1942 to

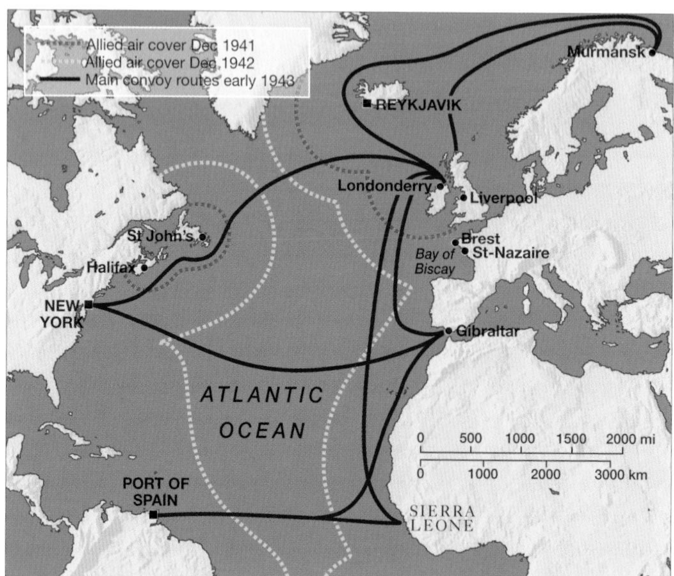

BATTLE OF THE ATLANTIC
Convoy routes and air cover areas at the height of the battle.

over 200 a year later. Ultimately, though, they were fighting a losing battle in the production race. July 1942 was the first month of the war when new ships launched on the Allied side exceeded losses, and the American shipbuilding effort was still expanding rapidly.

Although the point was past when there was any likelihood of Germany winning the Battle of the Atlantic, a further crisis was to come. This was caused by poor allocation of resources on the Allied side. Although shipping losses were delaying the US build-up in Britain, and hence the subsequent invasion of north-west Europe that was supposed to be the principal Allied plan, the forces allocated to the Atlantic battle were relatively weak. This was especially true in the vital category of very long-range aircraft, with hundreds being used by the heavy bomber forces in England and the US Navy in the Pacific but, until well into 1943, only a handful being allocated to the convoy routes.

ADMIRAL KARL DÖNITZ

Dönitz (1891–1980) was the head of the German submarine service from the start of the war and Commander-in-Chief of the German Navy from January 1943. When Hitler committed suicide in 1945, Dönitz briefly became his successor. Dönitz had been a U-boat captain in WWI and commanded the U-boat force very resourcefully throughout WWII. Dönitz thought his U-boats could win the war for Germany, but too few were built to achieve this until far too late.

Above: The merchant ship *Pennsylvania Sun* burning after an attack by *U-571* in July 1942.

Climax of the Battle

In a series of frantic convoy battles in March 1943 the U-boats scored their last significant victories, sinking about a fifth of the ships crossing the Atlantic at that time with very little loss to themselves. Within weeks, however, the situation was transformed. In May, 41 U-boats were sunk, and Admiral Dönitz abandoned his tactic of pack attacks on convoys.

There were many reasons for this sudden change. More Allied aircraft were committed to the battle, both ship-borne in escort carriers and land-based. Allied ship and airborne radars were much improved, as were anti-submarine weapons. Tactics and training of escort ships were much more sophisticated. And, by no means least, the British code breakers were again reliably reading German messages.

The Allies would hold their lead in all these categories until the war's end, despite German efforts to turn the tide with new weapons and tactics. Although numerous U-boats remained in action until May 1945 (and they still achieved a few scattered sinkings), by the final months most new U-boats were being sunk before they finished their first war patrols.

Above: Admiral Ernest King was the highly effective head of the US Navy 1942–5 but was slow to set up the convoy system off the US coast.

Escort Carriers

No escort carriers existed in 1939, but by the end of the war Britain and the USA had well over a hundred ships of this type protecting the vital Atlantic supply routes and supporting amphibious operations in the Pacific.

One of the simplest lessons of WWII was that air power was vital in every area of warfare, by sea as much as by land. The USA, Britain and Japan were the only countries to operate large "fleet carriers" with their main naval forces and were also the only countries to deploy smaller "escort carriers" for what were sometimes seen as more mundane, second-line duties (though Japan's half dozen such completed vessels achieved nothing).

Convoy Air Cover

As the Battle of the Atlantic developed in intensity from the summer of 1940, the British authorities soon decided their Atlantic convoys needed air protection. Since fleet carriers were too scarce and valuable for use in this role, different ships and techniques were devised. At that point the main task envisaged for such ships was to counter the German Focke-Wulf Kondor aircraft, which were attacking convoys and homing-in U-boat packs.

The first expedient, from April 1941, was to fit a single aircraft-launching catapult to a merchant ship to carry a fighter. There were four Royal Navy fighter catapult ships and 35 merchant navy catapult aircraft merchant (CAM) ships. After his mission the pilot either had to make for land or ditch his plane near the convoy and hope to be picked up. Remarkably, this perilous process sometimes worked; six German aircraft are said to have been shot down by CAM-ship aircraft, though a number of the ships were themselves sunk by U-boats.

The first true escort carrier was HMS *Audacity*, operational in June 1941. *Audacity* only sailed with three convoys before being sunk by a U-boat in December 1941, but it had already clearly proved its worth.

By then the US Navy had taken delivery of its first escort carrier and was building more, both for its own use and for the Royal Navy. In all some 130 escort carriers were built, or converted from existing merchant-ship or auxiliary-cruiser hulls.

The Bogue and Casablanca classes were the main types. They usually operated 20–35 aircraft, often a mix of about one-third fighters and two-thirds bomber/reconnaissance

Below: HMS *Audacity*, a converted merchant ship, carried only eight fighters for convoy air defence.

USS *LONG ISLAND*

Commissioned in June 1941, the *Long Island* was the first American escort carrier, and like HMS *Audacity* a converted merchant ship. *Long Island* was mainly used for second-line duties, in aircrew training (as seen here in May 1943) or ferrying aircraft to combat zones. It carried the first aircraft to Guadalcanal in 1942.

Displacement: 13,500 tons
Length: 150m (492ft)
Beam: 21.2m (69.5ft)
Speed: 16.5 knots
Crew: 970
Aircraft: 20 approx.

Right: The CAM-ship *Empire Spray* with a Sea Hurricane fighter on its catapult, seen in October 1941.

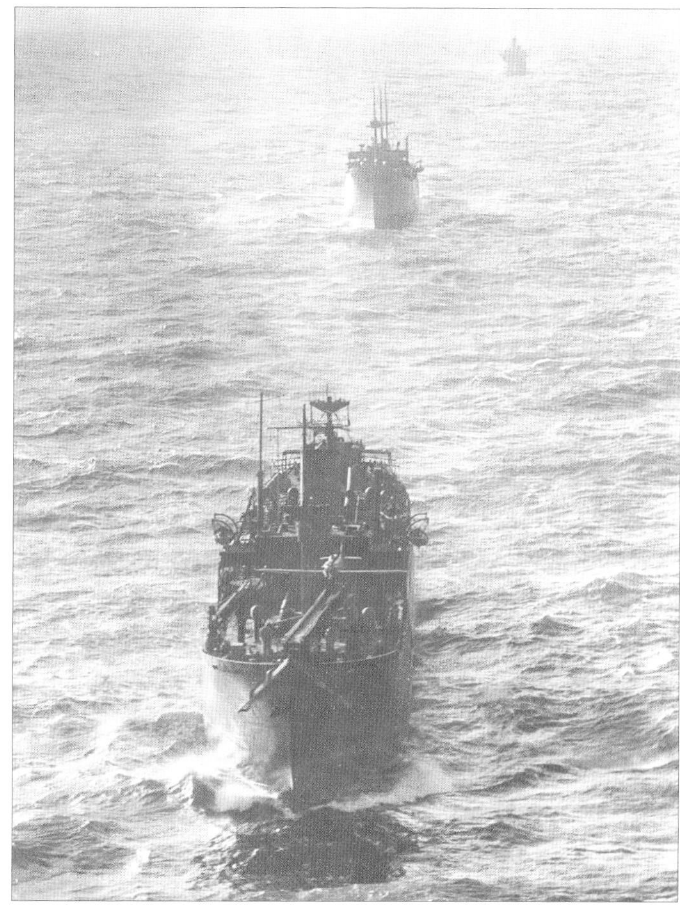

types. They were much slower than fleet carriers and only lightly built, but it was never intended that they should operate in areas where air or surface attack was a significant risk.

For a variety of reasons, few escort carriers came into service on the Atlantic convoy routes until 1943. However, from then until the end of the war, they protected many convoys and hunted down and sank numerous U-boats. In June 1944 the escort carrier USS *Guadalcanal* even assisted in the capture of a German submarine, U-505.

From mid-1943 there were also 19 British merchant aircraft carriers (MAC ships), merchant ships given a very basic flight deck and three or four Swordfish aircraft equipped for the anti-submarine role. These also carried normal cargoes and sailed with convoys; no convoy that included a MAC ship ever lost a vessel to U-boat attack.

Pacific Combats

Some escort carriers were used to train carrier aircrews, but many also saw extensive combat service in the Pacific. As the US counter-offensive developed, escort carrier groups were used to provide close support to the various landing forces, while the main fleet carrier groups wore down Japanese air power and guarded against interventions by the Japanese fleet.

At least that was the theory. At Leyte Gulf, however, it went drastically wrong. In a remarkable action the escort carrier groups successfully fought off an attack by some of the Japanese Navy's most powerful ships. One escort carrier was sunk by gunfire in this action and another by a kamikaze aircraft.

Right: The USS *Makin Island*, a Casablanca-class ship, seen near Leyte in November 1944 early in its combat career.

Naval Weapons and Electronics

No entirely new naval weapons were introduced in the course of WWII, but the existing armoury of guns, torpedoes and depth charges was given new accuracy and striking power by developments in control systems and detection equipment.

Guns in service at sea in WWII ranged from the 460mm (18.1in) monsters fitted to Japan's *Yamato* and its sister ships to the light anti-aircraft weapons of 20mm (0.79in) and upward, which were carried by almost every fighting vessel of all countries' navies.

As well as firing truly formidable projectiles (1,460kg/3,220lb for the *Yamato*), the big guns had a very considerable reach. The longest-range hit ever made by a gun on a moving target – 24km (15 miles) – was by a 15in (380mm) on HMS *Warspite* against the Italian *Giulio Cesare* in July 1940.

Below: The carrier USS *Cowpens* in 1943. SC, SG and SK radar aerials are among the equipment on view, illustrating radar's importance.

Above: Handling 929kg (2,048lb) 16in (406mm) shells in the magazine of the battleship HMS *Nelson*.

Torpedoes

The guns used by all navies were generally comparable in performance (though poorly manufactured Italian shells were notably inaccurate). However, this was less true with the other major anti-ship weapon – the torpedo.

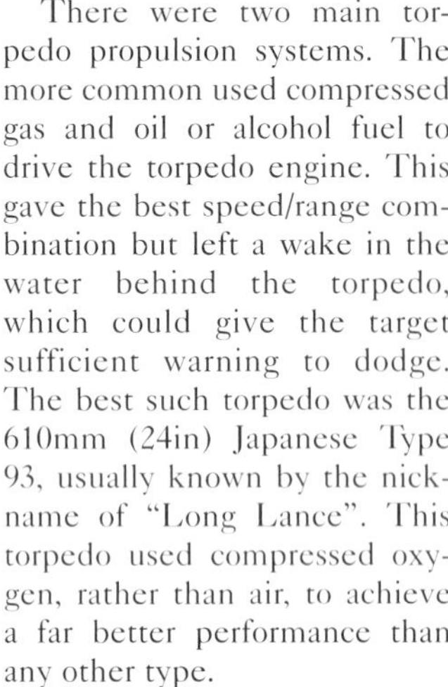

There were two main torpedo propulsion systems. The more common used compressed gas and oil or alcohol fuel to drive the torpedo engine. This gave the best speed/range combination but left a wake in the water behind the torpedo, which could give the target sufficient warning to dodge. The best such torpedo was the 610mm (24in) Japanese Type 93, usually known by the nickname of "Long Lance". This torpedo used compressed oxygen, rather than air, to achieve a far better performance than any other type.

Germany, and later the US Navy, also used battery-powered torpedoes. These had shorter ranges but left no wake.

Early-war torpedoes were designed to run at a fixed depth in a straight line and to detonate either by contact or underneath an enemy ship, by using a magnetic influence device. Both the Germans and Americans had numerous problems with unreliable depth-keeping for many months after they joined the war and all nations found their magnetic influence warheads rather temperamental.

Developments during the war included German torpedoes that could follow a zigzag or looping course to increase the chances of a hit, and acoustic homing torpedoes, produced by both the Germans and the Allies, used against submerged submarines or other targets.

Above: The *Graf Spee* in December 1939, showing signs of damage after the Battle of the River Plate. The ship's Seetakt radar aerial can be seen at the top of the picture.

The main anti-submarine weapons were unguided underwater bombs known as depth charges. These simply sank through the water to explode at a pre-set depth. Typically they had to detonate within 10m (33ft) of a submarine to sink it, so several were usually dropped in a "pattern" with slightly different settings. Depth charges were improved during the war by being filled with increasingly powerful explosive compounds.

Depth charges were supplemented by smaller weapons, either contact or depth fused, which could be thrown ahead of the attacking ship. The most successful were the British Hedgehog and Squid types.

Electronics

The main underwater sensor in use was sonar (officially called asdic in the Royal Navy until 1943). This used sound pulses to find the range and bearing of a target but did not determine the depth of the submarine; it was also blind in the area underneath the ship (hence the utility of forward-firing weapons).

Radar naturally played an important part in the war at sea, detecting enemy ships and aircraft and giving gunnery ranges in bad weather and at night. Germany's Seetakt type, in service in 1939, was a highly effective early-war design. Later-war Allied designs, like the British Type 271 and others, could detect a target as small as a submarine periscope.

Above: A depth charge being deployed from a US escort.

Just as important as target detection and ranging systems was equipment to translate this and other information into firing data. The US Navy in particular developed effective anti-aircraft control systems and the American torpedo data computer fitted in submarines was superior to its equivalents in use in other navies.

Below: A 20mm (0.79in) anti-aircraft gun position on the foredeck of the battleship USS *Iowa* in 1943. Two of the ship's 16in (406mm) main gun turrets can be seen behind.

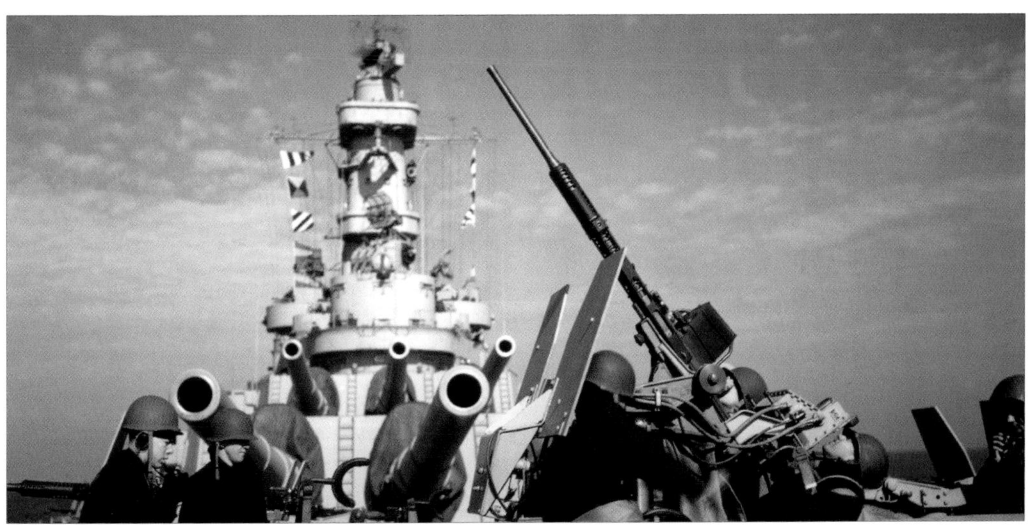

Allied Grand Strategy

Britain and the USA never agreed a formal alliance treaty during WWII but, despite this and their radically different political systems and ways of life, they generally co-operated effectively to defeat Germany.

Throughout the war there were a number of summit meetings between Churchill and Roosevelt and their top advisers. Sometimes these also involved other Allied leaders like the French and Chinese. There were also three summit meetings with Stalin, and Churchill travelled separately to Moscow during 1942.

Military Plans

More important in the very close and generally amicable Anglo-American co-operation that developed was the creation of an integrated military planning system. Britain and the USA both had chiefs of staff committees of their top soldiers, sailors and airmen to oversee their national military operations. However, a new body, the Combined Chiefs of Staff,

Above: Roosevelt and Churchill seen in contemporary coverage of the Casablanca Conference.

Below: Churchill and his Chiefs of Staff in 1945. Front row from left, Air Marshal Portal, General Brooke, Churchill, Admiral Cunningham.

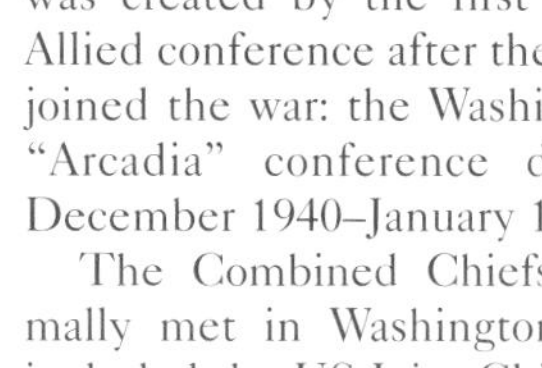

was created by the first inter-Allied conference after the USA joined the war: the Washington "Arcadia" conference during December 1940–January 1941.

The Combined Chiefs normally met in Washington and included the US Joint Chiefs in person and representatives of the British Chiefs permanently assigned to this duty. This body agreed many of the vital details of major military plans and allocated resources accordingly.

At a lower level all major Anglo-American operations in the European theatre, from the D-Day invasion down, were planned and staffed by fully integrated command teams. One of the most notable achievements of General Eisenhower, as Allied Supreme Commander for a number of European operations, was to ensure that disagreements along national lines were avoided as much as possible.

The summits also included meetings of the Combined Chiefs (though in this case the British Chiefs of Staff would be personally present) and here national disagreements were perhaps inevitably more common. There were two Allied conferences at Quebec, a second one at Washington, and one each at Casablanca, Cairo and Malta. Each had complicated discussions and arguments that cannot be outlined in detail here. However, certain important themes can be highlighted.

Cross-Channel Attack

The American leaders consistently believed that the best way to defeat Germany was the most direct: build up forces in Britain, invade across the Channel and head straight to Berlin. From bitter experience the British were all too well aware of the fighting power of the German Army. They were unwilling to risk a major defeat by a premature cross-Channel invasion. They also believed that too single-minded a concentration on this one objective would be to neglect important interests in the Mediterranean and prevent the Allies responding successfully to opportunities that might arise.

Generally speaking the British were more successful in getting their views adopted as policy in 1942–3, when their war effort was still more substantial than the USA's, than in the later period when the USA's strength was still expanding as Britain's declined. In practice this meant that the clearance of North Africa and the subsequent invasion of Sicily and southern Italy in 1942–3 were not originally welcomed by the American Chiefs and that the later removal of many resources from the Italian campaign was bitterly opposed by the British.

The summits with Stalin (in Teheran, Yalta and Potsdam, at the last of which Harry Truman and Clement Attlee replaced Roosevelt and Churchill) were more about how post-war Europe should be organized than about agreeing military plans. Ultimately, one truth became plain: the war would end with the Red Army in control across eastern Europe and Stalin would rule it as he saw fit, whatever wartime promises he might make regarding free elections and similar matters.

Above: Stalin, Roosevelt and Churchill during their first conference at Teheran in 1943.

However, Stalin did keep his promise, made at Teheran in November 1943, to join the war against Japan shortly after the end of the war in Europe.

Right: Managing shipping, like these newly launched American Liberty ships, was a key aspect of Anglo-American co-operation.

Medium Tanks, 1942–5

Although their activities were increasingly constrained by air, artillery and infantry weapons, tanks still played a decisive role in combat, especially the intermediate-sized designs that appeared by the thousand on most European battlefields.

As tanks developed, competition between increased gun power and thicker armour naturally continued, but even more important was sheer quantity.

Mass Production

Although Germany's PzKpfw 5 Panther was the most formidable tank discussed here, only some 6,000 were built compared to over 40,000 Soviet T-34s and 50,000 American Shermans. (There is no exact definition of the difference between a medium and a heavy tank but included here are tanks, regardless of weight, that normally served in the armoured regiments of standard armoured divisions, rather than in separate heavy tank units.)

The T-34 had set the benchmark for future designs during its first significant combats in 1941. It continued to give effective service in only slightly modified forms into 1944. By then its 76.2mm (3in) gun was insufficient to tackle the latest German types. From early 1944 a much better version – the T-34/85, carrying an 85mm (3.35in) gun – was produced. As well as sufficient gun power to destroy a Panther at normal battle ranges, this had a three-man turret. Previously the T-34 commander was also the gunner but now he could concentrate on his main role, which greatly improved combat efficiency.

The principal Anglo-American tank of the later-war years was the American M4 Sherman. When it appeared in 1942 this was broadly comparable with the contemporary T-34/76 or the later versions of the PzKpfw 4 (which would continue in service to the end of the war). Its 75mm (2.95in) main gun then had adequate power and it matched reasonable armour with excellent manoeuvrability and reliability. It was judged to be of sufficient quality that for a time US authorities halted development work on a successor to concentrate on mass production of this design (in many minor variants). Unfortunately this proved to be

COMET A34

The Comet A34 was the final vehicle in the British series of cruiser tanks in service throughout the war. It was a development of the Cromwell, with a much better gun based on the 17pdr and stronger, more reliable suspension.

Weight: 33.2 tonnes
Armament: 1 x 77mm (3in) gun, 2 x machine-guns
Armour: 101mm (4in) max.
Crew: 5
Road speed: 50kph (31mph)

Below: A cast-hull, 75mm-armed model of a Sherman in Italy in 1944.

Above: A Panther in action on the Eastern Front. Far too few Panthers were built to cope with the flood of Allied Shermans and T-34s.

T-34/85

Some 22,500 T-34/85 tanks were built in 1944–5. As well as having a better gun and improved internal arrangements, it retained the wide tracks and good cross-country performance of the earlier T-34/76 models.

Weight: 32 tonnes
Armament: 1 x 85mm (3.35in) ZiS S53 gun, 2 x machine-guns
Armour: 90mm (3.5in)
Crew: 5
Road speed: 50kph (31mph)

an unwise decision as, by 1944–5, its weaknesses had become very plain. The 75mm gun could not penetrate the frontal armour of a Panther or Tiger at all, and when hit itself the Sherman usually quickly burst into flames – a nightmare situation for any tank crewman.

Better Shermans

Improved versions did come into service by 1944–5. Some US Shermans were fitted with a more powerful 76mm (3in) gun and had better ammunition stowage, which reduced the fire problem. But the only model with truly adequate firepower was Britain's Sherman Firefly, with a version of the 17pdr (76mm) anti-tank gun. Even this had drawbacks: rate of fire was slow and Fireflies were often singled out as priority targets by German tanks.

Britain also had indigenous designs, developed from the early-war cruiser tank series. The Cromwell, in widespread use in 1944, was very fast and, unlike its predecessors, fairly reliable. However, it carried the same 75mm gun as the Sherman and had similar armour thickness. It was developed into the Comet, in service from the autumn of 1944, with similar virtues and a version of the 17pdr gun, making it the first wholly British tank of the war with adequate firepower.

By 1944–5 the state of the art was defined by the Panther. Judged by its weight (45 tonnes) this was a heavy tank. It might be more accurately described by the post-war description "main battle tank" for its mix of thick armour, reasonable speed and, above all, substantial gun power. Its gun was an extremely potent 7.5cm KwK 42 and it had very thick and well-sloped armour. Mobility and reliability were its weaknesses, but it was a formidable opponent.

Sherman Firefly

The Firefly was a conversion, not a new-build design. The most important change was the larger turret to fit the more powerful gun, but the hull machine-gun and radio operator were also omitted and the space used for ammunition.

Weight: 32.5 tonnes
Armament: 1 x 17pdr (76mm) gun, 1 x machine-gun
Armour: 76mm (3in)
Crew: 4
Road speed: 39kph (24mph)

Sicily and Italy, 1943–4

The Allied invasion of Sicily in July 1943 was followed by landings in mainland Italy in September. These knocked Italy out of the war, but the German Army's continued stubborn defence meant that there would be no rapid Allied victory.

In their meeting at Casablanca at the start of 1943, the Anglo-American leaders decided to invade Sicily as soon as possible after the campaign in North Africa was over. Accordingly, Operation Husky began on 10 July 1943. The preparations for the operation were bedevilled by many changes of plan in which the overall ground commander, General Harold Alexander, proved unable to direct his principal subordinates: General Montgomery, commanding British Eighth Army, and General Patton, commanding US Seventh Army. As a result, there was never a clear plan for the capture of the island, and opportunities to win the battle quickly and decisively were missed.

Although many of the accompanying airborne troops landed in the sea and drowned because of poor pilot training and bad weather, the initial Allied landings in the south and south-east of Sicily were a success. The large Italian forces put up little resistance and many surrendered readily – however, the German troops were a different matter. They used the rugged terrain expertly in a series of delaying actions, while the Allied commanders quarrelled over how to conduct the campaign. Finally the Germans withdrew across the Straits of Messina in mid-August virtually unmolested by the superior Allied air and naval forces.

After Sicily

With so many troops and resources committed to the Mediterranean by early 1943, and no possibility of organizing a cross-Channel invasion before 1944, the Allied leaders faced a dilemma. Britain wanted to continue Mediterranean operations and, since the alternative was to have the troops stand idle, the Americans agreed in May 1943 that an invasion of mainland Italy would follow the battles

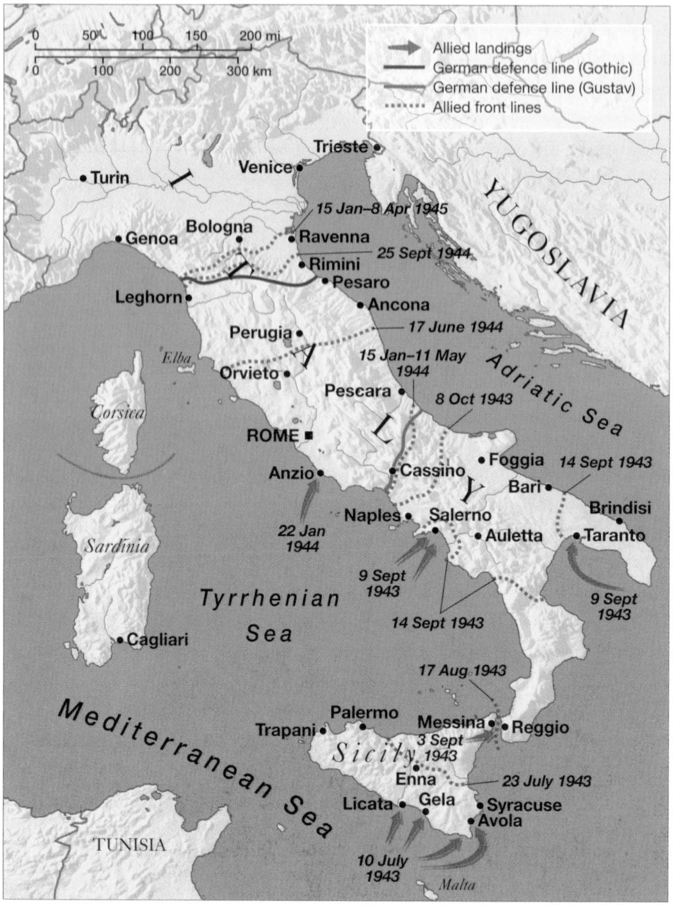

ITALY, 1943–5
Throughout the campaign in Sicily and Italy the Allied forces had to fight hard for every advance.

for Sicily. Once again there were disputes about planning and priorities that would continue to affect the Italian campaign to the end of the war.

Mussolini had been deposed as head of the Italian government in July and the new regime began secret peace talks with the Allies. On 3 September Eighth Army crossed from Sicily to the toe of Italy and on the 8th the Italian surrender was announced. The Germans were ready, however, and had moved reinforcements into the country to take over. On the 9th the main Allied landings, by General Mark Clark's US Fifth Army, went in around Salerno, just south of Naples, and were nearly thrown back into the sea during the first few days.

Slow Retreat

For the rest of the year the Germans fell back slowly from one well-defended river line to the next. Eighth Army pushed up the east side of Italy and Fifth Army to the west. By the turn of the year the Allied advance had reached the Germans' Gustav Line, whose most famous bastion was centred on Monte Cassino, still well to the south of Rome.

In an attempt to break the stalemate the Allied forces made an amphibious landing at Anzio, behind the German lines, on 22 January 1944. The troops there, timidly led, soon found themselves effectively besieged in their beachhead. Repeated attacks on the Gustav Line over the following months also failed.

During May 1944 the Allies at last mounted a properly co-ordinated attack all along the Italian front, and this time they captured Cassino and broke the Gustav Line. By then, however, Montgomery and many veteran troops had left to prepare for D-Day and Italy had slipped down the Allied priority list. Rome fell on 4 June, but by autumn 1944 the Germans were again making a stand, this time on the Gothic Line just north of Florence.

Above: A US cargo ship explodes off a Sicilian beach following a German air attack, July 1943.

Below: German paratroops bring supplies to the Cassino defences.

Below: A British Bofors gun in the ruins below Monte Cassino.

Infantry Support Weapons

Although all infantrymen carried personal weapons, success in battle often came from their heavier equipment. Infantry firepower from the fire-team to battalion level depended above all on machine-guns and mortars.

The principal support weapons employed within infantry units were machine-guns and mortars. Both categories included lighter weapons designed to be manoeuvred quickly between locations, and heavier types for use from longer-established positions in both defence and attack.

Light Machine-guns

Infantry units in all armies worked in squads of roughly ten men with one or more light machine-guns providing the squad's main firepower in both attack and defence. Weapons of this type included the Soviet 7.62mm (0.3in) Degtyarev DP1928, the British 0.303in (7.7mm) Bren and the US 0.3in (7.62mm) Browning Automatic Rifle (BAR), all of them normally bipod-mounted and magazine-fed. The Bren, highly accurate and reliable, and the Degtyarev, with a very useful 47-round magazine, were both more successful designs than the BAR, which was clumsy in action and had a smaller 20-round magazine. Minor weapons also included France's 7.5mm (0.295in) Châtellerault.

Above: A British Bren gunner firing on German positions at Monte Cassino in Italy in early 1944.

Heavy Machine-guns

Most armies had battalion or regimental support companies equipped with machine-guns for use in the sustained-fire role, aiming to deny areas of ground to the enemy in either attack or defence. These weapons were usually tripod-mounted and physically heavier than the squad light machine-guns, but not necessarily in larger calibres.

In fact the German Army used its MG34 and MG42 both as bipod manoeuvre weapons and on tripod mountings in

Left: A German MG34 on a tripod mount for use as a heavy machine-gun on the Eastern Front in 1941.

3-INCH MORTAR

Britain's 3-inch mortar was used throughout the war by the support companies of British infantry battalions. Versions were produced with varying barrel lengths – 130cm (51in) was standard. A lighter 76cm (30in) barrel, designed for jungle warfare, proved to be rather inaccurate.

Calibre: 76.2mm (3in)
Weight: 57.2kg (126lb) – barrel 20kg (44lb), base plate 16.8kg (37lb), bipod 20.4kg (45lb)
Range: 2,560m (2,800yd)
Bomb weight: 4.5kg (10lb)

the sustained-fire role. The US Army filled this latter requirement with the 0.3in Browning M1917 (also used as a light machine-gun); Britain had the 0.303in Vickers; and the Soviets employed the 7.62mm PM1910 and Goryunov SG43. All were belt-fed and thoroughly reliable, though the PM1910 was particularly heavy.

Other nations' designs were often less satisfactory. The Italian Breda 6.5mm (0.256in) Modello 1930 light machine-gun and the heavier Fiat-Revelli Modello 1935 (in the same calibre) were both very prone to jamming.

Various armies also had heavy-calibre machine-guns, often used in a combination of ground and anti-aircraft roles and also commonly fitted to armoured vehicles. Notable types were the Soviet 12.7mm (0.5in) DShK1938 and the American 0.5in Browning M2 HB.

Mortars

Infantry mortars came in two main calibres: roughly 50mm (2in) and 80mm (3in). Japan's 50mm (1.97in) Type 89 was typical of the smaller weapons, firing a 0.8kg (1.76lb) bomb up to 650m (700yd). Allied troops called it the "Knee Mortar", erroneously thinking it could be fired safely while balanced on a soldier's leg.

Another simple design was Britain's 2-inch mortar, which could fire a 1.1kg (2.4lb) bomb some 500m (550yd). In the larger calibres, several countries used versions of a French Brandt design, which included the American 81mm (3.19in) M1, firing a 4.8kg (10.6lb) bomb 2,250m (2,450yd). The Soviet 82mm (3.23in) PM37 and the Japanese 81mm Type 99 had a similar performance. Most mortars in this class came in three man-portable (but still very heavy) parts: barrel, base plate, bipod.

Flamethrowers

Every major army used man-portable flamethrowers for such specialist tasks as bunker-busting. All had similar capabilities and similar drawbacks. All were very heavy (up to 40kg/90lb), and had a limited range (40–50m/yd) and a modest fuel supply (10 seconds or less).

Operating them was hazardous in the extreme, not least because flamethrower men could expect no mercy if they were captured by an enemy. Probably the most prolific use of flamethrowers was by the US Marine Corps in the battles for the Pacific islands.

Below: A German soldier with a Flammenwerfer 35, a particularly heavy early-war flamethrower design.

Night Bombing of Germany, 1939–44

After the French surrender, aerial attack was the only way in which Britain could strike back directly at Germany. RAF leaders welcomed the development of an all-out bombing campaign; they thought that their service could win the war on its own.

Britain's Royal Air Force (RAF) had been created in 1918 specifically to bomb Germany and held to this aim as war approached in the 1930s. A small number of daylight raids during the Phoney War showed that bombers were hopelessly vulnerable to fighter attack and confirmed that, when attacks began in earnest in 1940, they would be made mainly at night.

In the first phase, up to early 1942, very little was achieved, though losses, compared to some later points in the campaign, were also modest. Bombers were sent to attack specific targets – individual factories or rail junctions, for example – but in fact their navigational skills were so poor that they rarely hit them.

Area Bombing

Air Marshal "Bomber" Harris took over at the head of RAF Bomber Command in early 1942 and changed tactics, at that stage with full support from his service and political superiors. Throughout his period in command Harris believed that "area bombing" of the residential districts of enemy cities was the only sensible use of his force and that, correctly applied, it would win the war.

Above: A German poster urging blackout precautions.

The aim was to cripple the German war effort by attacking the morale of the working population, killing some and at least dehousing many others. Little thought was given to whether this was a morally justifiable means of waging war.

The first effective attacks in this vein came in the late spring of 1942, most notably a handful of "thousand-bomber" raids that employed all of Bomber Command's training aircraft, as well as the operational force. These raids coincided with the introduction of Gee, the first significant electronic navigation aid, and the beginning of a process whereby the accuracy of attacks was improved. However, Harris foolishly opposed the creation of a Pathfinder Force to lead attacks and mark targets but he was overruled.

Throughout 1942 the aircraft used by Bomber Command also greatly improved, with the four-engined Halifax and Lancaster types with their large bomb loads predominating by early 1943. Thus, the roughly 5,000 bomber sorties flown in June 1942 dropped 6,950 tonnes of bombs. However, only a year later in June 1943, the 5,800 bomber sorties flown dropped well over 15,500 tonnes.

Left: A classic image of a Lancaster bomber setting off on a mission.

Above: A Lancaster bomber over Hamburg, silhouetted by flares and ground fires in a time-exposure photo taken from another bomber.

In response to these increasingly damaging attacks the Germans built up a formidable night-fighter force and control system. Initially this relied exclusively on ground stations directing twin-engined heavy fighter designs into close enough contact with a target aircraft that their radar systems could complete the interception. Later single-engined day fighters were sent by radio to the skies above the cities being attacked and were able to make visual interceptions.

In response the RAF concentrated its aircraft to swamp particular sectors of the system, as well as jamming radars and using electronic and other deception measures to fool controllers or blind their equipment.

In 1943 Bomber Command devastated many cities across Germany, but the only time it came close to achieving the sort of results Harris expected was in a series of attacks on Hamburg in July. These benefited from a temporary Allied advantage in the electronic warfare struggle and because of this and other special circumstances were never to be repeated.

Battle of Berlin

In the winter of 1943–4 Harris mounted what he called the Battle of Berlin. However, for all the damage inflicted, this series of attacks on the German capital and other cities was ultimately a defeat for Bomber Command. Losses rose to a rate that could not have been sustained for long, while the German economy and civilian morale never came close to collapse. Though Harris complained bitterly and disobeyed his orders as much as possible, it was a respite for Bomber Command to be switched partly to targets in France over the next months, in preparation for D-Day.

AIR MARSHAL ARTHUR HARRIS

Harris (1892–1984) led RAF Bomber Command from February 1942 to the end of the war. Harris fervently believed that, suitably strengthened, his command could win the war on its own by bombing Germany's cities. His leadership undoubtedly transformed the morale and effectiveness of Bomber Command, which were at a very low ebb when he took over. However, his forces lost increasingly heavily in 1943–4 and only their partial diversion to support operations in France saved them from an even greater defeat.

Above: Air Marshal Harris (seated) and senior members of his staff at Bomber Command.

Night Fighters

During WWII radar developments gradually stripped away the cover of darkness from night air operations. Starting with the Blitz in 1940–1, night fighters took an increasing toll of attacking and defending aircraft in a bitter struggle for supremacy.

No night-fighter aircraft existed anywhere at the beginning of WWII; night air defence relied on an inadequate combination of searchlights and anti-aircraft guns. However, by the later stages of the 1940–1 Blitz, Britain had introduced the first effective night fighters, directed by ground radar to a position near the target aircraft and then closing in to attack, using their own airborne radar equipment. Most night fighting would follow this pattern for the remainder of the war, though the radars used grew in range and precision, and counter-measures to defeat them became more sophisticated.

British Designs

The Bristol Beaufighter was the first successful night fighter; like most night fighters of the war, it was a two-seat, twin-engined design. Twin engines left the aircraft nose free for the radar equipment (and usually heavy guns as well) and gave the power necessary to overcome the drag often caused by bulky aerials; the second crewman was the radar operator. The Beaufighter made its operational debut in September 1940 and achieved its first success over the next month.

From 1941 it was joined and eventually replaced by a series of variants of the De Havilland Mosquito. This was fast and long-ranged and very heavily armed – commonly four 20mm (0.79in) cannon and four machine-guns – and equipped with successively improved models of radar. Late-war versions also carried Serrate equipment to home in on German night-fighter radar signals. By then night-intruder operations over enemy territory were the main mission for the Allied night-fighter force.

Since there was little likelihood of night air attack on the USA and the US bomber forces operated by day, American night-fighter development was rather slower. Initially US night-fighter units used the Beaufighter and versions of the A-20 Havoc bomber, but they were converted from mid-1944 to the Northrop P-61 Black

NORTHROP P-61

The P-61 Black Widow first flew in 1942 and was first deployed on operations in June 1944, in both the Pacific and Europe. Some 740 were built in all. Some variants had only the nose-mounted cannon and two crew; others had a fully trainable turret with two or four machine-guns.

Crew: 2 or 3
Engines: 2 x Pratt & Whitney R-2800-65; 2,250hp each
Speed: 589kph (366mph)
Ceiling: 10,100m (33,100ft)
Armament: 4 x 20mm (0.79in) cannon + 4 x 0.5in (12.7mm) machine-guns

HEINKEL 219

Germany's chaotic air procurement system is illustrated by the He 219, only produced after significant private investment by the manufacturer. Speed and altitude performance were generally much better than earlier German types, but it compared poorly with the Mosquito or P-61.

Crew: 2
Engines: 2 x Daimler Benz 603
Speed (A-7): 616kph (383mph)
Range: 1,540km (960 miles)
Ceiling: 9,300m (30,500ft)
Armament: up to 4 x 3cm (1.18in) + 4 x 2cm (0.79in) cannon

Above: A German Ju 88 night fighter fitted with the clumsy aerial array of the Lichtenstein SN-2 radar.

Widow. This was the only purpose-built night fighter to see service with any nation during the war and had virtually identical performance characteristics and armament to the Mosquito.

The US Navy also used a number of Corsair and Hellcat single-seat, single-engined fighters at night, fitted with radar sets in the wings.

Germany's Reply

Since it faced the most sustained night-bombing attacks of the war, Germany naturally responded with significant night-fighter developments, though these were hampered by the poor organization of German aircraft procurement and electronics research.

Early types included versions of the Messerschmitt (Me) Bf 110 fighter and Junkers (Ju) 88 bomber. Both could carry a heavy armament, including the *Schräge Musik* ("Jazz Music") upward-firing cannon used from the blind spot underneath a target aircraft. However, performance suffered because of the drag from the large aerials required by the German Lichtenstein radar sets.

A variety of other models were also used, including the Me 210 and 410, and the Ju 188 and 388. The most capable of all, but produced in limited numbers (fewer than 300), was the Heinkel 219, in service from the summer of 1943.

Germany also made extensive use of unmodified single-engined day fighters in the night-fighter role. Since the British night bombers operated in concentrated streams, a fighter directed to the stream had a reasonable chance of acquiring a target visually, especially close to the bombing target when flares and ground fires gave extra illumination. This *Wilde Sau* ("Wild Boar") tactic was introduced initially when British counter-measures blinded the German radar control system for a time in mid-1943. This was used with success for the remainder of the war.

Japan had a limited night-fighter force, in part because of the lack of effective Japanese radar equipment. The Navy's Nakajima J1N "Irving" had a small number of successes over the Home Islands and elsewhere, and the Army's Kawasaki Ki-102 "Randy" was potentially a capable aircraft but only appeared in modest numbers.

BRISTOL BEAUFIGHTER

Developed from the Beaufort torpedo bomber, the Beaufighter first flew in July 1939. It was used as a radar-equipped night fighter from the autumn of 1940 but was gradually replaced in this role by the Mosquito. Torpedo-bomber and strike variants saw extensive use to the end of the war.

Crew: 2
Engines: 2 x Bristol Hercules III; 1,400hp each
Speed: 540kph (335mph)
Range: 2,400km (1,500 miles)
Ceiling: 8,800m (28,900ft)
Armament: 4 x 20mm (0.79in) cannon

US Strategic Bombing, 1942–3

Formations of American Flying Fortress and Liberator bombers began ranging over Europe in mid-1942. Their leaders hoped to bring the Luftwaffe and the German economy to their knees, but their initial efforts were bloodily defeated.

Like Britain's RAF, the United States Army Air Force (USAAF) entered the war committed to a policy of long-range strategic bombing. Like the RAF in 1939, it believed in making daylight attacks on precise targets, relying on the heavy defensive armament of its bomber aircraft and their tight formations to ward off enemy fighters. Like the RAF it would also discover that bombing accuracy never approached the anticipated results and that bomber formations could not defend themselves adequately against fighter attack.

The principal USAAF heavy-bomber organization throughout the campaign was the Eighth Air Force (AF), based in Britain. The Ninth and Twelfth AF, based in North Africa in 1942–3, also included heavy-bomber units, which were transferred to the Fifteenth AF, operational in southern Italy from the end of October 1943.

Above: B-17 *Memphis Belle* and its crew on their return Stateside after completing their 25-mission tour of duty, one of the first crews to do so.

The first raid over western Europe by a wholly American bomber force was on 17 August 1942 against targets at Rouen in northern France. For the remainder of that year all targets attacked were similarly short-range and the bomber forces were provided with strong fighter escorts, both from the RAF and the American forces. The build-up of the American bomber strength was slow. By the end of the year only some 1,550 sorties had been flown, with 32 aircraft lost.

Attacking Germany

The first raid on a German target was against Wilhelmshaven on 27 January 1943; 91 aircraft attacked, with 3 shot down in return for 6 German fighters. This would prove to be an unusually favourable ratio of losses for the Americans.

For the next several months other German ports were also targeted along with French ports used as U-boat bases. The raids on the French ports, like those conducted by the RAF in the same period, were a fiasco. They flattened the homes of the local French population but barely scratched the thick concrete of the U-boat pens.

Eighth AF first flew over 2,000 sorties in June 1943 and would pass the 6,000 mark monthly in January 1944. The attacks by the British-based

Left: A B-24 Liberator on fire after being hit by flak. Watching comrades die like this was difficult, to say the least, for bomber crews.

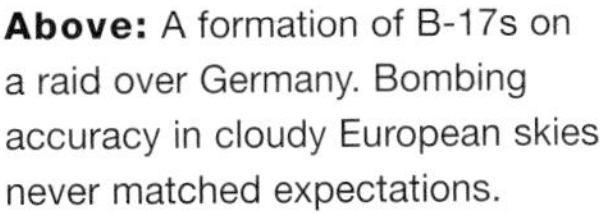

Above: A formation of B-17s on a raid over Germany. Bombing accuracy in cloudy European skies never matched expectations.

Above: Bombs dropping away from a B-17 during a raid on Bremen. Other attacking aircraft leave condensation trails below.

forces were joined, from the early summer of 1943, by raids on targets in Italy and elsewhere from North Africa.

Although the attacks up to mid-1943 had not yet involved concerted attempts to penetrate deep into German airspace, they had brought about a significant strengthening of the German home-defence force, from about 450 to 1,100 day fighters. Despite Anglo-American efforts to bomb aircraft factories, German fighter production increased through 1943 right up to September 1944.

Heavy Losses

The first big tests of the US commanders' belief that their bombers could fight their way to their targets unescorted came in August 1943. On the 1st the Mediterranean force lost very heavily in a raid on the oilfields at Ploesti in Romania. On 17 August some 376 US bombers attacked the Messerschmitt factory at Regensburg and the ball-bearing manufacturing plant at Schweinfurt; 60 bombers were lost and Schweinfurt in particular was little damaged.

Even though part of the bomber escort was made up of P-47 Thunderbolts fitted with longer-range fuel tanks, these could reach only just inside Germany; most of the losses were on the long unescorted leg of the mission between there and the target and back again.

Confirmation of the desperate need for longer-range escort fighters came in October. A series of raids, including one on Schweinfurt on the 14th, cost Eighth AF about half its operational strength. The American commanders abandoned deep-penetration attacks for the moment. The Luftwaffe had won the first round of the battle.

Right: General Ira Eaker, seen in 1942. Eaker commanded Eighth Air Force during its unsuccessful operations in 1943.

Anti-aircraft Guns

Although a single rifle bullet could bring down an aircraft, effective anti-aircraft fire usually depended on a combination of automatic weapons and slower-firing medium guns with greater destructive power and range.

In the course of WWII many thousands of aircraft on all sides were brought down by fire from the ground. High-flying heavy bombers or long-range fighters and low-altitude ground-attack aircraft were all vulnerable, though usually to different weapons. As in most other classes of land-warfare weapons, the types of anti-aircraft (AA) guns in service changed little during 1939–45, though ammunition and control equipment developed substantially.

Light AA Guns

Since lower-flying aircraft appear to be travelling faster to an observer on the ground, weapons to shoot down such planes have to be capable of traversing quickly and firing multiple shots rapidly, since a target might only be in sight for a few moments. In practice this meant weapons of roughly 40mm (1.5in) or less, typically firing a shell weighing less than 1kg (2.2lb) to an effective ceiling of up to 3,500m (11,500ft).

Although soldiers could and did attempt to engage aircraft with firearms of every kind up to and including standard machine-guns on specially adapted mounts, the smallest purpose-built AA system in widespread use with a major army was the American "Quad Fifty". This was a quadruple mounting carrying four 0.5in (12.7mm) M2 Browning heavy machine-guns, which appeared both on a towed trailer and on various self-propelled mounts. However, this was never entirely satisfactory as the individual rounds lacked sufficient striking power to bring down an enemy aircraft reliably.

The Germans had a 2cm (0.79in) weapon (and also developed a four-gun mount) but this had similar shortcomings. Japan, Italy and Britain had similar single-barrel 20mm weapons. Some of the British and Japanese weapons were based on a design originating with the Swiss Oerlikon company.

The next step up for Germany and the USA was to 3.7cm (1.46in), a calibre also used by the Soviets. Britain's main light AA gun was the 40mm (1.58in), built under licence from the Swedish Bofors company, a weapon also used by many other combatant nations. This fired a 0.9kg (2lb) high-explosive shell at a practical rate of 80–100rds/min.

Like most guns in this class the Bofors was usually fitted with simple visual sights, which were often the only ones used. Like other guns it also had various

M3 3-INCH GUN

The M3 3-inch gun was the standard US medium anti-aircraft gun in the early part of the war but was gradually replaced by the M3 90mm. Both guns were also used in ground roles, like this 3-inch shown in New Guinea in 1943.

Calibre: 3in (76.2mm)
Shell weight: 5.6kg (12.3lb)
Rate of fire: 25rds/min
Effective ceiling: 9,100m (30,000ft)
Muzzle velocity: 853m/sec (2,800ft/sec) – HE shell

Right: A German Flakvierling quad 2cm (0.79in) Flak 38, in northern France in 1944.

Above: A British 3.7in (94mm) gun in action at night. Like many other British AA batteries, this one had a mixed male and female complement.

mechanical predictor sights (the type depending on the country), designed to help the gunners allow sufficient "lead" ahead of a fast-moving target.

Heavy AA Guns

Small numbers of guns of around 127mm (5in) were used by various nations, including the German 12.8cm (5.04in) FlaK 40, the US 120mm (4.72in) M1 and Britain's 5.25in (135mm). However, these were at the point where the gain in ceiling and striking power from the larger calibre began to be outweighed by slow rate of fire and clumsiness in action.

More common were lighter weapons similar to Germany's "Eighty-eight", various versions of an 8.8cm (3.46in) gun firing a 9.4kg (20.7lb) shell to over 8,000m (26,200ft). Britain's 3.7in (94mm) and the US 90mm (3.54in) weapons were broadly comparable. Like the Eighty-eight the 90mm on the M2 mount could be used as an anti-tank weapon.

Hitting the Target

In the early-war years all AA guns had to rely, at best, on mechanical predictors calculating where to aim by using human estimates of aircraft height, speed and course.

During the war these were gradually replaced by radar systems which, among other advantages, could be used successfully at night or through cloud. Heavier AA shells initially relied on time or barometric fuses which, when set using radar information, could indeed be extremely accurate.

Better still was an Anglo-American development, the proximity fuse, in effect a radar set that could be fitted in a shell to detonate it when it went close to a target. This was used with great success later in the war against Japanese kamikazes and German V-1 missiles.

Bofors 40mm

The 40mm Bofors gun was designed in the early 1930s and was used by many combatant nations in WWII, both on land and as a ship-borne weapon. A British Army example is illustrated but it was also produced in twin- and quad-barrel versions for naval use.

Calibre: 40mm (1.58in)
Shell weight: 0.9kg (2lb)
Rate of fire: 160rds/min max.
Absolute ceiling: 6,800m (22,300ft)
Muzzle velocity: 880m/sec (2,890ft/sec)

Heavy Bombers

The four-engined heavy bombers of the British and US air forces were among the most potent weapons of the war. They combined high-tech electronic equipment with the brute power to deliver tonnes of bombs deep inside an enemy country.

From the later years of WWI airforce officers in various countries had argued that, if suitably equipped and expanded, their services could win a war by bombing attacks on the industries and people of an enemy homeland. Such attacks were called strategic bombing (as distinct from tactical operations near a land battle front).

In WWII Britain and the USA were the only countries to equip themselves for such operations and try to win the war by carrying them out. At the heart of strategic bombing campaigns were the various four-engined bombers described here.

The first aircraft of this type to enter service was the Boeing B-17 Flying Fortress, first flown in 1935 and in series production from 1939. This had impressive performance but, with only five hand-trained machine-guns and lacking self-sealing fuel tanks and adequate armour protection for the crew, early marks hardly lived up to their name. Significant improvements came with the B-17E version, in use from 1942; the final B-17G carried 13 defensive guns.

Above: A pair of B-24 Liberators escorted by P-40 fighters on a mission in the north Pacific in 1944.

BOEING B-17G FLYING FORTRESS

The B-17G was the definitive version of this aircraft. About two-thirds of the 12,700 B-17s were of this model. Improvements on the original included a lengthened fuselage, larger tail, and chin and tail turrets.

SPEED: 462kph (287mph)
ENGINES: 4 x Wright Cyclone R1820 radials; 1,500hp each
RANGE: 3,200km (2,000 miles)
ARMAMENT: 13 x 0.5in (12.7mm) machine-guns; typically 2,000kg (4,400lb) bombs

At first sight the B-17's near contemporary, the Consolidated B-24 Liberator (first flown in 1939), was superior. It was faster, and had a better range, with the same bomb load and similar defensive armament. However, in action it was found to be less suited to the tight formation flying at high altitude needed for operations over Germany. Like the B-17 it went through various marks before reaching its best defended final version, the B-24J.

DAY BOMBING

Throughout the war in Europe US tactics were to carry out strategic bombing raids by day in the hope of bombing with great accuracy. This dictated the heavy defensive armament fitted to the B-17 and B-24 and

PIAGGIO P.108B

Italy's P.108B was one of the few heavy bombers outside the UK and US forces to see action. The P.108B was a powerful and effective machine with various advanced features, including remotely controlled gun turrets.

Speed: 430kph (267mph)
Engines: 4 x Piaggio PXII RC35 radials; 1,500hp each
Range: 3,540km (2,200 miles)
Armament: 6 x 12.7mm (0.5in) + 2 x 7.7mm (0.303in) machine-guns; 3,500kg (7,700lb) bombs

also resulted in their having relatively modest bomb loads of some 2.5 tonnes. In the event bombing accuracy in cloudy European conditions was much less than in Stateside trials and, until the advent of long-range escort fighters in 1944, bomber losses were extremely heavy.

British Tactics

Britain's RAF began the war equally convinced that its bombers could fight their way to their targets in daylight. However, bitter experience soon proved otherwise and Bomber Command switched to night raids on Germany.

Though twin-engined types featured in these attacks into 1943, four-engined designs to replace these entered service from early 1941. Relying on the cover of darkness, all had weaker defensive armament than the US types but much greater bomb loads. Bombing accuracy was very poor in the early stages of the campaign, but it improved substantially later as electronic aids to navigation were introduced and improved.

The first type, the Short Stirling, only saw front-line use until 1943 – its low service ceiling made it unacceptably vulnerable. The Handley Page Halifax, which came next, was a significant improvement, especially the later Mark 3 type, and served to the end of the war. Undoubtedly the best British heavy bomber of the war, however, was the Avro Lancaster, in squadron service from early 1942. Over 7,000 of this tough and reliable aircraft were built.

Taking the war to Japan demanded a longer-range aircraft than those deployed in Europe, and design work on what became the Boeing B-29 Superfortress began before the war. The prototype first flew in 1942 but, between then and its combat debut in mid-1944, there were many problems and modifications to be addressed. This was largely because, in addition to its great size, it was an extremely complex and technologically advanced aircraft. However, with the development of bases in the Mariana Islands later in 1944, it was able to begin attacks on Japan, culminating in the nuclear missions that finally ended the war.

Below: A flight of Short Stirling bombers during training in 1942. The Stirling was the least effective of the three British four-engined designs.

Clearing the Ukraine

Between mid-summer 1943 and late spring 1944 a series of crushing Soviet attacks drove the Germans out of the Ukraine, pushing them back into pre-war Poland and Romania. In the north the 900-day siege of Leningrad was also lifted.

From the conclusion of the Kursk offensive to the end of the war a little less than two years later, the Red Army would advance relentlessly and almost continuously for victory.

In the first phase of the battles the Soviets pushed forward all along the southern two-thirds of the front, to reach and cross the Dniepr River and recover such major cities as Smolensk, Kiev and Dnepropetrovsk. In the second phase, in the winter and early spring of 1944, there were attacks in the north and south. In the north the bitter siege of Leningrad was finally broken; in the south the rest of the Ukraine was recaptured and the first steps were taken toward the conquest of south-eastern Europe.

Above: German soldiers in the cold and snow of an Eastern Front winter, March 1944.

To the Dniepr

The process began with Soviet attacks on the north of the Kursk salient on 12 July and was extended by a further offensive on the south flank of the salient on 3 August. Although the Germans defended very skilfully against these advances, they had to give up Orel to the northern drive in early August and Kharkov to the southern attack on the 23rd.

By the end of August Soviet forces were advancing everywhere south of Moscow – but especially successfully in a broad area west of Kursk and in another sector in the far south toward Stalino (Donetsk).

Aware of the possible Italian surrender (which became a reality on 8 September), Hitler had already begun to reinforce his troops in Italy. Allied landings on mainland Italy in early September made this still more urgent. He therefore gave permission for the German troops in the eastern Ukraine to retreat

SOVIET VICTORIES, 1943–4
The Red Army's advances cleared the Germans from most of the territory of the pre-war USSR.

Above: Red Army soldiers receive a warm welcome from local people after the recapture of Kiev.

to the Dniepr. As they did so they converged on the various major towns with bridges over the river. The Soviets advanced into the gaps between these and had improvised crossings themselves by the end of the month north of Kiev and west of Dnepropetrovsk. Kiev itself was taken in early November.

On to the Borders

By December, despite the able defensive leadership of Field Marshals Erich von Manstein and Ewald von Kleist, the German front included a number of vulnerable salients, held on Hitler's orders. In attacks beginning on 24 December and extending through March 1944, these were eliminated at the start of new advances. Both field marshals joined the growing list of able German generals dismissed for making withdrawals and arguing too often with their erratic *Führer*.

When this phase of fighting ended in mid-April, the front line ran from the Pripet Marshes via the eastern foothills of the Carpathian Mountains to the Black Sea coast west of Odessa.

SIEGE OF LENINGRAD

In terms of its effect on the outcome of the war, the siege of Leningrad (St Petersburg) was a sideshow at most. However, with probably more than a million civilians dead, most by starvation, disease and cold, it was a human tragedy on a vast scale.

By early September 1941 the Germans' first advances had cut Leningrad off from the rest of the USSR, and Hitler decided to obliterate the city by bombing, shelling and starvation. The Soviet authorities had delayed evacuating the civilian population of 2.5 million: about a third were evacuated in 1942; a third remained in the city, fighting or working in the factories; and a third died in the first dreadful winter.

For more than a year, despite attacks and counterattacks by both sides, a trickle of supplies (but only that) reached the city across Lake Ladoga. The supplies travelled by boat in summer and by truck over the ice in winter, but all the time under German shelling and air attack. New Soviet attacks in January 1943 opened up a narrow land route into the city, easing the worst privations, but got no further. Finally, in January 1944, a new offensive forced a general German retreat. Stalin declared the city liberated on the 27th.

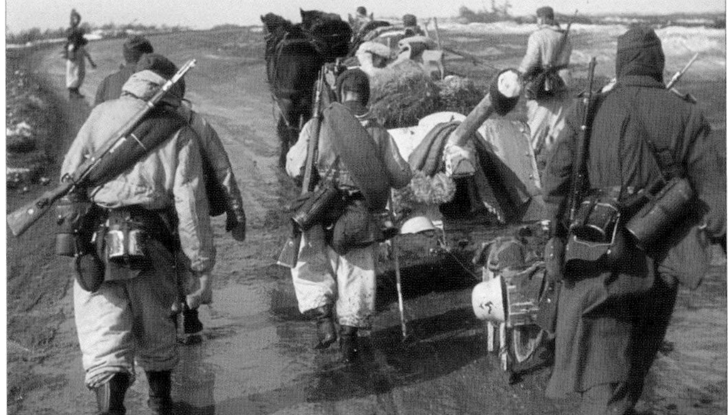

Left: German troops on the retreat with a horse-drawn 5cm (1.97in) PaK 38 anti-tank gun in the Ukraine in the mud of the spring thaw, 1944.

Heavy Artillery

The big guns of the heavy artillery were among the most fearsome land warfare weapons of WWII. They also appeared by the hundred, or more – the Soviets used over 16,000 guns of all calibres in their final attack on Berlin in 1945.

Josef Stalin is said to have described artillery as the "god of war". No soldier on the receiving end of a bombardment from the heavy guns of any major army would have been likely to disagree. Heavy artillery weapons were usually allocated to higher formations (corps and armies or similar) and would be capable of switching their support from unit to unit, both in defence and in attack.

Artillery Tactics

As in other categories of artillery weapon, the Soviets were the most prolific users of heavy guns. Britain and the USA had the most sophisticated organization, able to shoot elaborate suppressive bombardment plans and to respond rapidly to events with stunning concentrations of firepower.

There were numerous weapons of this class in use: Germany had over 200 types of artillery weapon (of all calibres) in service. To give a more particular example, the Soviets had at least five models of 152mm (5.98in) howitzer and two 152mm guns. Accordingly only a representative sample can be discussed here.

Most armies had weapons closely comparable to the Soviet designs just mentioned, firing a shell of roughly 45kg (100lb) to a range of 15km (9.3 miles) for higher-trajectory howitzers or up to 27km (17 miles) for flatter-trajectory guns. Along with their different firing characteristics, the howitzers were also lighter overall and, therefore, usually more mobile and normally cheaper and easier to build, by no means a trivial consideration.

Britain's 5.5in (140mm) gun was typical. It fired a standard 45.4kg (100lb) shell to 14.8km (9.2 miles), or a 37kg (82lb) shell to 16.6km (10.3 miles). A little over 6 tonnes in action, it had a maximum rate of fire of perhaps 3 rounds a minute. The USA's 155mm (6.1in) Gun M1 fired a slightly lighter shell to a range of over 23km (14.3 miles), but the gun and mounting were twice as heavy overall as the 5.5in. Lesser-known but also effective types included Italy's 149mm (5.87in) Cannone da 149/40 M35 and France's 155mm M1932 Schneider.

Super-heavy Weapons

Most nations also included heavier guns and howitzers in their armoury. The US 8in (203mm) Gun M1 came into service mid-war. It could fire a 109kg (240lb) shell 35.5km (22 miles) on long-range-bombardment and counter-battery missions. Bigger still was its contemporary the 240mm (9.45in) Howitzer M1 with a 157kg (346lb) shell and a range of 23km (14.3 miles).

Left: A US 155mm (6.1in) M1 "Long Tom" gun, in action on Leyte during November 1944. The split-trail design gave a very stable firing platform.

5.5-INCH GUN

The British 5.5in (140mm) gun was introduced in 1940 and saw widespread service (the example shown is in Italy in 1943). There was also a slightly longer-ranged 4.5in (114mm) weapon mounted on the same carriage.

Calibre: 5.5in (140mm)
Weight in action: 6.3 tonnes
Shell weight: 45.4kg (100lb) or 37kg (82lb)
Range: 14.8km (16,200yd) – 100lb shell; 16.5km (18,100yd) – 82lb shell
Muzzle velocity: 619m/sec (2,030ft/sec) max.
Crew: 10
Rate of fire: 3rds/min max.

Railway guns were a particular German speciality including the longest-range and heaviest-calibre weapons to see action during the war.

The best-known of these was the 28cm (11in) K5 (E), employed against the Allied beachhead at Anzio among other places. This fired a 255kg (562lb) shell 63km (39 miles) or up to 86.5km (54 miles) with rocket assistance. A 28cm gun was reworked to 31cm (12.2in) calibre for test-firing a fine-stabilized round an even more astonishing 150km (93 miles).

The biggest weapon of all was a massive 80cm (31.5in) calibre. Two such guns were built, but only one is known to have been used (in the German siege of Sevastopol in 1942). The gun weighed some 1,350 tonnes in action, moved on two sets of railway tracks and fired a 7-tonne high-explosive shell up to 47km (29 miles). The design and industrial effort required to produce such a weapon was wholly disproportionate to its highly limited combat worth.

Below: A battery of German 15cm (5.91in) Kanone (E) railway guns in position near the French border in 1940. In fact few of these weapons saw action.

The Soviet Invasion of Germany Fighting in the German town of Küstrin in early 1945.

Totalitarian Rule, Germany and the USSR Inmates of the Sachsenhausen concentration camp.

Resistance Female fighters of the French resistance greet the liberation of Marseille in 1944.

Under German control 7 May 1945
Neutral
Front line 23 June 1944
Front line 26 Aug 1944
Front line 15 Dec 1944
Front line 22 Mar 1945
Front line 7 May 1945

0 100 200 300 400 500 mi
0 200 400 600 800 km

ATLANTIC OCEAN
ICELAND
NORWAY
SWEDEN
FINLAND
North Sea
Baltic Sea
ESTONIA
LATVIA
LITHUANIA
EAST PRUSSIA
U S S R
IRELAND
UNITED KINGDOM
DENMARK
NETHERLANDS
BELGIUM
GERMANY
POLAND
CZECHOSLOVAKIA
FRANCE
SWITZERLAND
AUSTRIA
HUNGARY
ROMANIA
YUGOSLAVIA
Caspian Sea
Black Sea
PORTUGAL
SPAIN
ITALY
Corsica
Sardinia
Sicily
BULGARIA
ALBANIA
GREECE
TURKEY
Declared war on Germany February 1945
IRAN
Mediterranean Sea
SYRIA
CYPRUS (British)
IRAQ (British)
TUNISIA (French)
PALESTINE (British)
TRANS-JORDAN (British)
ALGERIA (French)
LIBYA (Italian)
EGYPT (British)

VICTORY OVER GERMANY

By early 1944 Hitler's Kriegsmarine had been reduced virtually to impotence in the Battle of the Atlantic and that spring the Luftwaffe was decisively defeated in a titanic series of air battles over Germany. Yet, at the start of June, German soldiers stood everywhere on foreign soil and even still maintained a toehold inside the pre-war USSR. By the early autumn the Western Allies had liberated France, Hitler's armies in the east had suffered the devastating defeat known as the destruction of Army Group Centre, and among his erstwhile allies Romania had changed sides and Finland made peace.

Hitler himself, weakened and shaken by his injuries in the Bomb Plot assassination attempt, was increasingly out of touch with reality, while the German economy and its industries were heading into their final collapse. But, despite all that, the German Army remained a formidable and resourceful organization, capable of desperate defence and last-ditch counter-attacks. The true nature of the Nazi regime was finally made plain to all with the liberation of the concentration camps in the spring of 1945, but the European war would not end until almost all of Germany was in Allied hands and Hitler was dead in the ruins of Berlin, capital city of his vaunted "thousand-year *Reich*".

Fighters, 1943–5 A Supermarine Spitfire Mark 14 fighter in flight, the final major production version.

The Battle for Normandy US Army artillerymen in action on the Cotentin Peninsula.

The Fall of Berlin Soviet troops raise their flag over the Reichstag building at the centre of the city.

D-Day

Operation Overlord had been the centrepiece of Anglo-American plans since 1942 and was the largest combined land–sea–air operation in history. The Germans ultimately would have no answer to the Allied firepower and strength.

By the end of 6 June 1944 the Allies had landed some 150,000 men in Normandy. All five landing beaches were secure and everywhere the troops were pushing inland, though not as far as had been hoped and planned. The first day of Operation Overlord had been at least a qualified success.

KEY FACTS

Place: Lower Normandy, France

Date: 6 June 1944

Outcome: Allied air and seaborne landings succeeded despite strong German resistance.

The Plans

Although the Allies had a crushing superiority in the air and at sea, the actual landing forces were not overwhelmingly strong because of limited numbers of landing craft and paratroop aircraft. Several strategies were used to offset this. Months of intensive air attacks had been carried out and would continue against roads, rail lines and bridges all across France, with the aim of making it difficult for the Germans to move reinforcements to Normandy.

At the same time an elaborate deception plan had been set up to convince the Germans that the Allies planned to land farther east in the Pas de Calais region. This continued after the landings to suggest that Normandy was a feint and the real Pas de Calais operation was yet to come. Both phases were extremely successful.

The Allied Supreme Commander, General Dwight D. Eisenhower, led over 3 million men with 13,000 aircraft, 2,500 landing craft, 1,200 warships and a range of new equipment. This included the obstacle-crossing and bunker-busting tanks of the British 79th Armoured Division, used only on the Anglo-Canadian beaches, as well as amphibious tanks used by all attack formations. Follow-up forces would benefit from the Mulberry Harbours and have their fuel needs supplied by PLUTO (Pipe Line Under The Ocean).

Although the Germans were well aware that there would be an invasion, they had no

Right: German troops building beach defences before D-Day run for cover from an Allied aircraft.

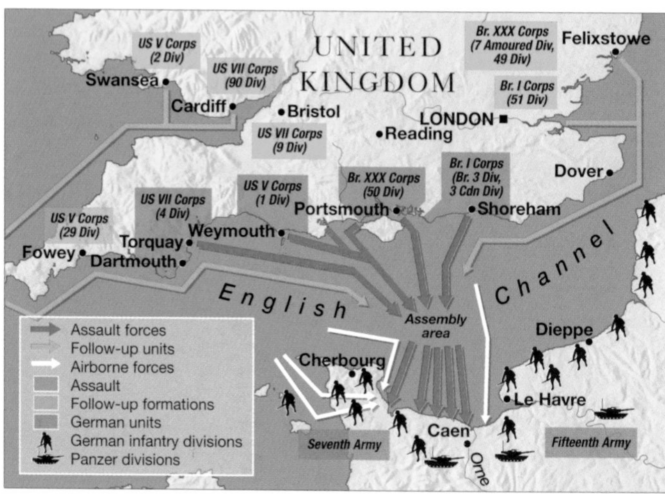

D-DAY PLANS

The Allied attack forces came from bases across the British Isles. German forces were inevitably spread out along the French coast.

Above: A British commando unit on Sword Beach waits for the order to advance inland.

Above: US Army troops landing on the bitterly contested Omaha Beach on the morning of D-Day.

accurate intelligence of its location or strength. Field Marshal Erwin Rommel now commanded the German forces in northern France. He believed that his only chance was to defeat the invasion before it got properly ashore. He wanted to spread his reserves along the coast so that they could immediately attack any landing forces, because he knew the Allied air forces would make it very difficult to redeploy more distant units.

His superior, Commander-in-Chief West Field Marshal Gerd von Rundstedt, wanted a strong central reserve that would only be sent into the attack once it was clear where the main Allied landings were taking place. The Germans ended up with a compromise: some reserves were near the Normandy coast, but they were not allowed to be deployed without permission from Hitler.

The Landings

There were five landing areas – Utah, Omaha, Gold, Juno and Sword, from west to east. The first two involved units of US First Army and the last three British and Canadians of British Second Army. Two US airborne divisions landed by parachute and glider inland from Utah and one British airborne division on the east flank of Sword.

The airborne divisions took most of their objectives and succeeded in disrupting possible enemy counter-attacks. German resistance was fiercest, and Allied casualties heaviest, on Omaha Beach. For a time it looked as if the landing there might fail, but by the end of the day the beach had been cleared. Utah was the easiest of all – with the other three beaches somewhere in between.

Above: One of the vast armament dumps in the UK created by the Allies in preparation for D-Day.

It was important for the Allied troops to grab as much territory as possible at the outset, even if only to make room for the vast follow-up forces. However, the inland advance later in the day came up well short of the D-Day objectives of Caen and Bayeux. Much hard fighting to expand the beachheads clearly lay ahead.

MULBERRY HARBOURS

Since the speed with which supplies and reinforcements could be landed was crucial, and capturing a port would be difficult, the Allied planners decided to solve the problem by taking their own "Mulberry Harbours" with them. Huge breakwaters, causeways and piers were built in Britain, floated across the Channel and then sunk in place off Normandy in the first couple of weeks after D-Day. Two Mulberries were built. One was wrecked in a storm on 19 June, but the other remained in use until late 1944.

Special Purpose Armoured Vehicles

Clearing obstacles and breaching enemy defences were traditionally the tasks of army engineers. Modified tanks and other vehicles designed to carry out these roles were an important factor on D-Day and in other battles.

Battles to overcome elaborate enemy defences as part of an ongoing land campaign, and during waterborne landings at the start of one, were a recurring feature of the Allied counter-offensives in the second half of WWII. Clearing mines, crossing ditches and rivers, as well as destroying enemy strong points were among the tasks required. In line with the mechanization of many aspects of warfare, specialized armoured vehicles to undertake these duties saw significant service – most famously the "Funnies" of the British 79th Armoured Division, which saw action during the D-Day landings and thereafter.

Above: A German Bergepanzer 3 armoured recovery vehicle assists a broken-down Panther battle tank.

Mine Clearing

Two main mine-clearing tank types were developed: flails and rollers. Flails carried a rotating drum fitted with chains on the front that beat the ground as the tank drove forward, exploding mines in its path. These were first used in Matilda Scorpion form at the Battle of El Alamein in October 1942 and, later in the war, appeared in improved Sherman Crab versions. The US Army developed T1 mine rollers that featured an arrangement of steel discs pushed ahead of the tank.

Obstacle Crossing

Ditches and walls were also often encountered. Some tanks were equipped to carry fascines or similar material, which could be dropped into the gap or provide a ramp. Other tanks, notably the Churchill ARK, simply drove into the ditches or up to the walls themselves and then extended ramps in front and behind, so that subsequent vehicles could just drive over the top. The Carpet or Bobbin tanks unrolled a drum of matting over sandy beaches or similar difficult ground – and this provided a roadway for following wheeled vehicles.

All the major armies of the European war also had various forms of bridge-laying equipment. Germany deployed a

Below: DD Sherman tanks during a training exercise. The second tank has not yet lowered its flotation screen, but others have and are immediately ready to fight.

Above: A US T1 Mine Exploder in France in 1944. The 18-tonne rollers could be pushed in front of the Sherman tank at 8kph (5mph).

Above: A Churchill AVRE in late 1944, showing its spigot mortar and obstacle-crossing fascine.

small number of Bruckenleger 4 vehicles, derived from the Panzer 4, in France in 1940, but they were little used. Britain and the USA had Churchill and Sherman bridge-layers.

Perhaps the most important vehicle in this class was the British Churchill Armoured Vehicle Royal Engineers (AVRE). This could carry and position fascines or a short bridge and in addition mounted a spigot mortar to fire demolition charges at pillboxes or other enemy positions. Over 500 AVREs were built; they were extensively used in 1944–5.

Normandy Battles

One adaptation relatively seldom used, other than on D-Day, was also significant. These were the so-called Duplex Drive (DD) tanks – ordinary battle tanks that were made amphibious by being fitted with canvas screens to raise around the hull and a propeller to drive them through the water at some 7kph (4mph). As soon as they reached the landing beach, the tanks would simply drive out of the water, drop the screens and then they would be able to fight entirely normally. The DD concept was originally tested on the Valentine tank from 1941, but by 1944 Shermans were invariably used.

Whether the DD tanks made much difference on D-Day is a debatable issue and relatively few of these were employed. However, a few weeks later a simple improvised modification applied to most of the tanks of US First Army may have made a real difference. This was the Rhino, a set of tusk-like prongs welded to the front of the tank to enable it to cut through hedgerows, rather than being confined by the many high banks that enclosed Normandy's roads.

Right: A Churchill Carpet during training for D-Day. The Carpet's matting could help wheeled vehicles cross barbed-wire obstacles.

The Battle for Normandy

It took two months of bitter combat before the Allied forces were able to break out of their Normandy landing areas. The Allies had overwhelming resources and dominated the air, but German battlefield skill made them fight all the way.

The success or failure of Operation Overlord was not likely to be decided on 6 June 1944. The Allies made vast and elaborate preparations to ensure that D-Day would go well, but in the light of these it was overwhelmingly likely to do so. What mattered, in the days and weeks to come, was building up the Allied force and the area under its control faster than the Germans could assemble their reserves to confine it.

Above: An American field artillery unit in action near the Normandy town of Carentan during the fighting in July 1944.

Montgomery's Plan

All the Allied ground forces, British, American and Canadian, were under the command of General Montgomery's 21st Army Group. Probably more than any other general on the Allied side, he realized that if the Normandy invasion were to succeed, the Allies had to have a clear plan for the advance inland from the beaches. Montgomery developed such a plan and stuck to it so successfully that throughout the battle the Germans largely danced to his tune. His failure was that he never admitted when parts of the plan went astray. Thus, his relationship with other top Allied leaders was poor and his presentation of events to the press was unconvincing.

Montgomery's plan was for British and Canadian attacks on the Allied left to draw in the German reserves, while allowing the American units on the right to advance more rapidly.

Left: British troops on the watch for German snipers amid the rubble of Caen in late July.

Right: American infantrymen move cautiously past a burning Panther tank in a Normandy village.

This, in essence, is exactly what happened. However, it certainly did not all go "according to plan", though Montgomery claimed that it did.

The city and communications centre of Caen on the left (eastern) flank was meant to be captured on D-Day itself, but the advance from the beaches only got about halfway there. Caen did not fall completely until the third week of July, after several full-scale attacks by British Second Army, notably Operation Epsom at the end of June and Goodwood in July.

On the right flank the first task was to link the Utah and Omaha landings with the other beaches, which was achieved on 10 June. Next was an advance west across the Cotentin Peninsula and then north to capture Cherbourg, which was taken on 27 June. The port facilities, however, had been comprehensively wrecked by the Germans before their surrender. It would take many weeks to rebuild the port to full capacity, though it would land some cargoes during July.

German Resistance

All the Allied forces were discovering just how tough the German armed forces were to beat, whether the best Army units like the Panzer Lehr Division or the teenage SS fanatics of the Hitler Youth Division. At all junior and middle-rank levels the standard of German leadership was higher overall, and the German troops fought in the knowledge that their tanks in particular were vastly better than anything the Allies had. However, the Allied generals were playing ever more solidly to their armies' strengths, in particular deploying a weight of artillery and air firepower to which the Germans could have no answer.

Through June into July US First Army was thus slowly and steadily gaining ground, while British Second Army was seemingly bogged down at Caen. Montgomery would have been delighted to have captured Caen sooner and pushed inland from there, but even without that his plan was working. Almost all the German Panzer divisions, the backbone of their force, were fighting on the British sector of the front. This prepared the ground for the decisive Allied breakout against the weaker part of the German line to the west of St-Lô in First Army's Operation Cobra from 25 July.

Below: US troops fighting near Périers during the advance across the Cotentin Peninsula.

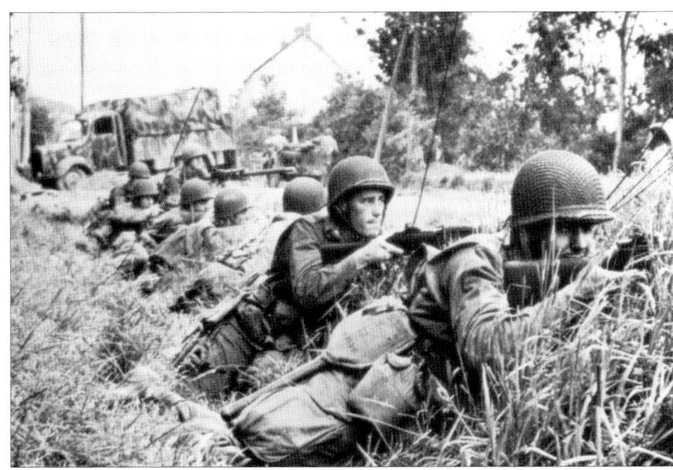

Medium Bombers, 1942–5

By the end of the war the Allied air forces had long since gained total air superiority and this was nowhere better seen than in the operations of the thousands of Anglo-American medium bombers over Europe and in the Pacific.

The British and American medium bombers of 1942–5 include some of the most famous aircraft of the era. However, comparable Axis aircraft of the time remain little known. This is no coincidence. It simply reflects the failure of the Germans and Japanese to respond effectively to the Allied challenge in the air. (The Soviets also had few medium or heavy bombers but this derived from their total concentration on ground-attack aircraft and fighters, not a lack of effective air power.)

The Wooden Wonder

Britain only produced one aircraft in this class, but it was one of the best: the De Havilland Mosquito. Almost 7,000 were built during the war, including photo-reconnaissance, ground-attack and night-fighter variants, as well as bombers.

All were fast and could carry a substantial load of bombs, guns or other equipment – and were made mainly of wood! In service with RAF Bomber Command, Mosquitos supported the main heavy-bomber force by flying diversionary raids and marking targets.

Below: A Mitsubishi Ki-67 *Hiryu* ("Flying Dragon") bomber, known to the Allies as "Peggy". In service from late 1944, the Ki-67 was fast (537kph/334mph) and better armed than previous Japanese bombers.

Main US Types

US medium-bomber aircraft included the Douglas A-20 Havoc/Boston, in service from early in the war, the North American B-25 Mitchell, Martin B-26 Marauder and Douglas A-26 Invader. A-designation aircraft were supposedly optimized for the (ground-) attack role, while the B-types were for the somewhat different medium-bomber mission. In practice

MOSQUITO B MARK 16

Mosquito bombers could carry a 4,000lb bomb (as shown) or a range of flares and target markers. Over 1,200 of the Mark 16 were built, the most numerous bomber version.

Speed: 668kph (415mph)
Range: 2,400km (1,500 miles)
Crew: 2
Engines: 2 x Rolls-Royce Merlin 76/77; 1,710hp each
Armament: 1,800kg (4,000lb) bombs or flares; no guns

Right: A B-25H Mitchell in flight. This was one of the attack variants of the Mitchell, with a solid nose rather than a glazed bombardier's position. It carried eight forward-firing machine-guns and a 75mm cannon.

there was much overlap. The B-25 served throughout US involvement in the war and, like all the American aircraft mentioned above, was supplied in quantity to various Allies under Lend-Lease. Almost 10,000 were produced, in many variants that included several for the attack role, with up to 12 nose-mounted machine-guns and a 75mm (2.95in) cannon. Pure bomber versions could carry up to 2,700kg (6,000lb) of bombs.

There was little to choose between the B-25 and B-26 in performance or service career, though most of the 4,700 B-26s built for the USAAF were sent to Europe. The B-26 eventually had the lowest loss rate of any major USAAF combat aircraft, but when it was first introduced there were numerous accidents, avoided later by aircraft modifications and better pilot training.

Both the B-25 and B-26 saw combat from 1942, but the A-26 did not begin operations until mid-1944; over 1,000 were in use by 1945 and the type continued to serve for many years after the war. It carried similar armament to the Mitchell and Marauder but had only a three-man crew: pilot, navigator/bombardier and air gunner, who operated remotely controlled dorsal and ventral turrets.

Germany and Japan

In the mid-war years German aircraft production planning was virtually non-existent, with a great deal of effort being wasted on minor upgrades of already obsolescent types and the development of numerous prototype designs. When this was set right in 1944–5, far too late, bomber production had to be virtually abandoned in favour of fighters. Thus the Dornier 217K, probably Germany's best bomber of the war, was taken out of production in late 1943.

One notable type that was introduced into service was the Heinkel 177. This unusual design appeared to be twin-engined but actually had a pair of engines in each wing to drive the single propellers. It had reasonable performance figures overall, but early examples in particular were very prone to disastrous engine fires.

Japan's aircraft industry never had the strength to compete with its enemies. Later-war bomber types included the Yokosuka P1Y "Frances", the Nakajima Ki-49 "Helen" and the Mitsubishi Ki-67 "Peggy". Fewer than 1,000 of each bomber were made.

MARTIN B-26 MARAUDER

First flown in 1940, the B-26 saw its first combat in the South Pacific in 1942. Most served in Europe, however. Some 5,300 were built in all and they were used by all the US services and various British Empire air forces.

Speed: 462kph (287mph)
Range: 1,850km (1,150 miles)
Crew: 7
Engines: 2 x Pratt & Whitney R2800; 1,900hp each
Armament: 1,800kg (4,000lb) bombs; 12 x machine-guns

Resistance

Many people in occupied Europe judged that the defeat of Nazi Germany was a cause worth risking their lives for. Their bravery and sacrifice certainly played a large part in ensuring the ultimate Allied victory.

By its nature much resistance was a secret activity with few records kept. Many heroic acts no doubt also went unseen, so it is now impossible to quantify the effects of resistance in any meaningful way.

Resistance was certainly dangerous. Suspected resisters were routinely tortured and, if not executed, sent to concentration camps. Vicious mass reprisals against their communities were common. Unsurprisingly, therefore, more people took an active part in resistance as Germany's defeat became more certain, and those most active at the end were not necessarily those who had the best record throughout.

Resistance took many forms and might not even have had any long-term effect on the war.

Above: Resistance fighters of the Polish Home Army in action during the Warsaw Rising of 1944.

Norwegian history teachers, for example, refused to teach the Nazi-approved syllabus and stood firm to win their point, despite some being deported to concentration camps. Other more significant forms of quiet heroism came from those who hid Jews from the SS, many thousands in Poland and the Netherlands alone.

Some non-violent methods had clear military results. French railway workers deliberately doing their jobs slowly and incompetently may have done more to hinder the movement of German troops and supplies in France in 1944 than the Allied bombers or the active sabotage efforts of their resistance comrades. Similarly, up to 2,000 Anglo-American aircrew who had been shot down were helped to escape from German-occupied territory, an important increment to Allied strength.

Allied Assistance

The Western Allies had various organizations that supported resistance. The USA's Office of Strategic Services (OSS) was involved both in intelligence-gathering (clearly an important function of resistance generally) and the support of military resistance. Britain split these functions between the secret service, MI6, and the wartime Special Operations Executive (SOE). Britain's MI9 and the American MIS-X helped escapees and those who assisted

Left: Resisters in newly liberated Marseille show off their weapons. Resistance was one area in which female combatants played a full part.

them. SOE and OSS trained many operatives for covert service in the occupied countries and had extensive technical sections designing and making special weapons, forging identity documents and carrying out many similar tasks.

Horror in Yugoslavia

Resistance fighting was most intense of all in Yugoslavia. At the end of the war the Partisan movement, led by Josip Broz Tito and by then backed by both the Soviets and the West, effectively liberated the country from the Germans after four years of particularly bloody struggle. The Partisans were the victors after what was really a civil war between them, the Četniks (mainly Serbian nationalists) and the Ustašas (mostly Croatian fascists). Each fought the others and with and against the occupying Germans and Italians at different times. Most of the 1 million plus Yugoslavs who died during the war were killed by other Yugoslavs.

The situation in Western Europe was never as extreme, as the example of France shows. There was certainly tension and distrust between communist and non-communist resistance groups, but almost the whole resistance movement agreed in 1943 to work together under the command of the Free French leaders in exile. In 1944 there were extensive and successful plans to co-ordinate resistance operations with the Normandy invasion. Many resisters were young men who had taken to the hills and forests to avoid compulsory work service in Germany. These Maquis groups played a notably important part in assisting the Allied invasion of southern France. Perhaps 100,000 French people died in resistance activities or in German reprisals against them.

Above: General Charles de Gaulle, leader of the Free French, making a broadcast to his countrymen.

Right: Josip Broz Tito (nearest camera), leader of the Yugoslav Partisan movement, meeting "Draža" Mihailović (dark hair in front row) of the rival Četnik group, which initially received most Allied support.

Collaboration

Collaborators had many motives. Some genuinely supported Nazi ideas; some were merely trying to survive as best they could in impossible circumstances; and some thought of themselves as patriots honestly trying to serve their countries.

Who were collaborators? Government ministers in occupied countries who decided in the early-war period to work with the Germans could be regarded as collaborators – or were they just being realistic in making the best arrangements they could with the country that had effectively won the war? Industrialists might run factories making goods for the Germans and money for themselves, but they were also keeping their workers in decent jobs and preventing them being deported as slave labour to Germany. A village mayor or a policeman had no choice but to obey some German orders, but when did he go beyond that into enthusiastic help? And, at the simplest level of all, was a woman in a relationship with a German soldier a shameful traitor or in fact doing something all too human with a young man scared and far from his home? It was not always easy to decide.

Above: A Waffen-SS poster seeks Norwegian recruits to fight against communism. Norwegians and Danes were eagerly enlisted by the SS.

Almost every country had native fascists and anti-semites who worked willingly with the Nazis, genuinely believing that they were acting patriotically. For example, Anton Mussert's party in the Netherlands had 50,000 members. But he, and his like elsewhere, were given no real power by the Germans.

Poland was probably the country that saw the least collaboration with the Germans, but even there another kind of collaboration was seen. Many pro-communist Poles helped the Soviets consolidate their control from 1944, and would have been seen as collaborators by most of their compatriots.

Joining the SS

Putting on a German uniform and fighting for the Germans was certainly collaboration in most people's eyes. In fact many people born outside Germany enlisted in the Nazi Party's armed elite, the Waffen-SS. They included both ethnic Germans recruited from abroad – *Volksdeutsche* (as the Nazis

Left: Women who had relationships with Germans being forced to parade through the streets of Paris with shaved heads and in their underclothes after the liberation.

Right: Dutch Nazi leader Anton Mussert (in black) meeting SS chief Heinrich Himmler.

called them) – and foreigners from "Germanic" countries like Norway or Denmark. Later in the war the net was cast wider; Ukrainians, Croatian Muslims, Latvians, Estonians and others were all accepted. Eventually, over half of Waffen-SS soldiers were not native Germans.

Substantial numbers of Soviet citizens ended up working for, and sometimes fighting alongside, the German Army. By 1942 many of Germany's units included significant numbers of auxiliaries – *Hilfswillige* (or "Hiwis"). Many of these were former prisoners of war who had made this choice to escape the privations and likely death of captivity. At first they worked mainly in non-combatant support roles, as drivers, cooks and the like, but later they became fighting troops. In Normandy in 1944 German Army regiments regularly included an *Ostbataillon* (or "East Battalion") of such men and some fought effectively.

Russian Nationalists

Other units that were formed by the Germans attempted to use anti-Soviet feeling and even appeal to Russian nationalism. These included various units of non-Slav Soviet citizens – Cossacks, Armenians, Georgians and others – who often fought in anti-partisan operations. Russians as such were also involved. A Russian National Army of Liberation was formed in the Bryansk region. Better known as the Kaminsky Brigade, it gained a brutal reputation, notably during the Warsaw Rising of 1944.

A senior Red Army officer, General Andrei Vlasov, was captured in 1942 and agreed to raise a substantial anti-Stalinist Russian force. Top-level German support was half-hearted and only two divisions were formed, but not used. In the last days of the war one of these turned against the Germans and fought alongside the Czech resistance during the battle for Prague.

The post-war fate of identified collaborators was often harsh. Millions of Soviet citizens were turned over to the Soviet authorities by the Western Allies. Most ended up in the GULag at best; Vlasov and his officers were executed.

Right: Many of the recruits for the Waffen-SS Handschar Division were Bosnian and Croatian Muslims.

Crushing Soviet Victories, 1944

The summer battles of 1944 began with what Soviet historians call the "destruction of Army Group Centre", and by the end of the year Romania and Bulgaria were fighting alongside the Soviets with the front line well into Poland and Hungary.

Misled by the Soviet advance into Romania in the spring of 1944, Hitler and his generals expected the Soviets to continue to concentrate on the southern part of the front for their next big attacks. Accordingly they transferred most of the tanks and many other heavy weapons from German Army Group Centre in Belorussia, just at the time when the Soviets were concentrating over 2 million troops and vast resources to attack it.

Above: A horse-drawn Soviet 45mm (1.77in) anti-tank unit advancing into Poland in 1944.

Advance in Belorussia

The attacks began on 23 June and, partly because of the unimaginative command of Field Marshal Ernst Busch (who was quickly replaced), soon smashed the German front. Three German armies – Third Panzer, Fourth and Ninth – each lost the majority of their strength, around 400,000 men in all. Minsk, the offensive's initial target, was captured on 11 July.

To the north Soviet attacks beginning on 4 July cleared the Germans out of much of Latvia and Lithuania by the end of August. By November virtually all the Baltic States were in Soviet hands, except for the

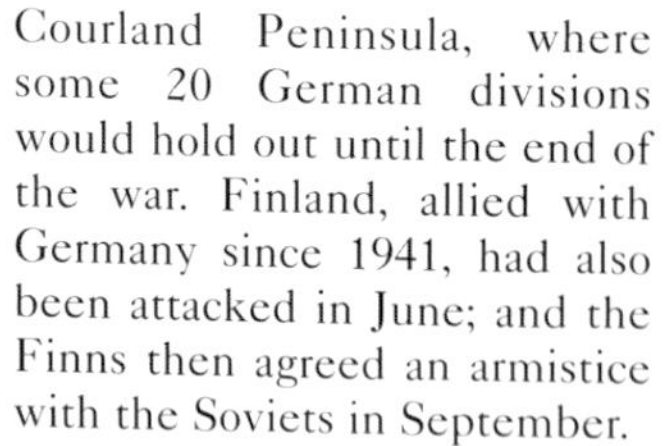

Courland Peninsula, where some 20 German divisions would hold out until the end of the war. Finland, allied with Germany since 1941, had also been attacked in June; and the Finns then agreed an armistice with the Soviets in September.

During July the Soviet Belorussian fronts continued their advances at pace and were joined by new attacks by the Ukrainian fronts to the south. Brest-Litovsk and Lvov were both taken late in the month. By 15 August Soviet troops were on the east bank of the Vistula River opposite Warsaw.

Warsaw Uprising

Resistance fighters of the Polish Home Army had already been helping the Soviet advance and on 1 August they began an all-out uprising in Warsaw. They fought on until early October, by which time over 200,000 Poles had been killed.

The Soviets made no attempt to help them, claiming (not entirely implausibly) that they needed to resupply their front-line forces after the recent advances before they tried to cross the Vistula. However, it also suited Stalin's grim purpose to have the Germans kill off anti-communist Polish patriots for him. Similarly, when Slovaks rose against the Germans in late

Left: Red Army infantry moving up to the front for the Soviet attack on Lvov in July 1944.

Above: Soviet infantry assault pass a burning Panther tank, eastern Poland, summer 1944.

August, the Soviets did little to help. This rising was also largely put down by late October.

INTO THE BALKANS

With its northern forces halting on the Vistula, the Red Army began new attacks in the far south on 20 August. Within days much of German Sixth Army was destroyed near Kishinev. King Michael of Romania mounted a coup on 23 August and his new government brought the country (and its large army) into the war on the Soviet side.

As the German forces continued their fighting retreat through Romania and into Hungary, Bulgaria was next to fall. The last in a sequence of government changes brought a partly communist group to power on 9 September, the day after Soviet troops had crossed into Bulgaria from Romania. The Bulgarians, too, would now join the Allied forces on the Eastern Front, while some Soviet troops remained in their country to ensure communist control.

With these threatening advances to their rear, German troops began pulling out of Greece and Yugoslavia. Yugoslav Partisans liberated Belgrade on 19 October and by the end of the year controlled roughly half of their country. British troops from Italy arrived in Greece to take over there in October too.

By December the Germans had again managed to build a defensive front. The principal fighting was in Hungary, where Budapest was surrounded on 26 December and would endure a bitter siege until mid-February.

GEORGI ZHUKOV

Marshal Zhukov (1896–1974) was the leading Soviet soldier of the war. His first big achievement was the decisive defeat of the Japanese at Khalkhin Gol in 1939. In 1941–2 he was repeatedly switched between staff jobs and front commands by Stalin. He was credited with masterminding the defence of Leningrad, Moscow and Stalingrad, although in each case the timing of his arrival was fortuitous. Zhukov then directed various of the Red Army advances up to and including the capture of Berlin in 1945. As a commander he was ruthless and thorough, one of many such leading generals who made the shambolic Red Army of 1941 into the world's most feared fighting force by 1945.

Above: Marshal Zhukov during the advance to Berlin in 1945.

Left: An SU-76 assault gun in action in a village in south-eastern Europe during the Soviet advance in the late summer of 1944.

Heavy Tanks, 1942–5

Among the most fearsome weapons of the war, heavy tanks were equally formidable in action against enemy strong points and armour. With their great gun power some could pick off opposing tanks at well over a kilometre.

At the start of the war the main users of heavy tanks were Britain and the USSR. The British nomenclature "infantry tanks" well described their function for both nations, which was to accompany and support the infantry assault. The far more formidable machines in service in the second half of the war retained this role in part, but their anti-armour performance generally became more important. The tanks included here normally served in separate heavy tank or infantry support units.

Britain's last infantry tank was the Churchill, in service in a range of variants from 1941. The initial version was rushed into service and, as well as being woefully under-gunned (with a 2pdr/40mm), was extremely unreliable at first. Later marks had the 6pdr (57mm), then a 75mm (2.95in). All versions were well-armoured but slow, though they were very good at climbing slopes and crossing obstacles. Over 6,500 of all marks were built, plus several hundred more for specialized engineer tasks.

Soviet Power

The performance of the Soviet KV-1 heavy tanks in service in 1941 came as a shock to the Germans but gradually improved German guns meant that they lost their invulnerability later, while their own 76.2mm (3in) weapon was inadequate against newer German tank types. Small numbers of a stop-gap KV-85, with an 85mm (3.35in) gun, were produced in the second half of 1943 before production ended. Some 10,000 of all models were built.

Their replacement was the Josef Stalin series. A few examples of this design were built, each with 85mm and 100mm (3.94in) weapons before a final decision on the 122mm (4.8in) D25 gun was made. This had a slightly poorer armour-piercing performance than the 100mm, but this was compensated for in part by its more powerful high-explosive shell for the other aspects of the tank's role. One definite disadvantage, however, was the

JOSEF STALIN 2

The JS-2 was deliberately kept relatively small – it was no heavier than the KV or the German Panther. Even so, it packed a fearsome punch and had well-sloped armour for effective protection.

Weight: 44.7 tonnes
Length: 8.33m (27ft 4in)
Height: 2.72m (8ft 11in)
Width: 3.12m (10ft 3in)
Armour: 120mm (4.7in)
Road speed: 37kph (23mph)
Armament: 1 x 122mm (4.8in) D25T + 4 x machine-guns

Below: Tiger tanks preparing for an attack on the Eastern Front.

TIGER 2/KÖNIGSTIGER

For all their great fighting power, only 454 Tiger 2s were built, serving in only a handful of heavy-tank battalions. The group shown were photographed for a propaganda film in France in summer 1944.

Weight: 69.4 tonnes
Length: 7.23m (23ft 9in)
Height: 3.07m (10ft 1in)
Width: 3.73m (12ft 3in)
Armour: 180mm (7.1in)
Road speed: 35kph (22mph)
Armament: 1 x 8.8cm (3.46in) KwK 42 + 2 x machine-guns

Above: M26 Pershings of the US 2nd Armored Division in the streets of Magdeburg on the Elbe in 1945.

slow rate of fire of the 122mm and the fact that only 28 rounds could be carried. Probably about 4,000 of the JS-1 and JS-2 variants saw service; a JS-3 version was in production by 1945 but did not see combat.

Tigers in Action

The first of the German designs that outmatched the KV-1 was the famous PzKpfw 6 Tiger, introduced in September 1942 on the Eastern Front. Design work on the Tiger had begun before Operation Barbarossa revealed the strength of the Soviet armour but was then greatly speeded up. When introduced, the Tiger mounted the then most powerful tank gun in the world (the 8.8cm/3.46in KwK 36) behind very thick armour; it quickly gained a fearsome reputation for its gun power and defensive strength. Mobility and reliability were never strong points, but it was still a tough opponent when the last of 1,355 came off the production line in August 1944.

Its replacement was the Tiger 2 (also know as the Königstiger; 454 built by 1945). It first saw service in Normandy in July 1944. At some 70 tonnes it was massively armoured and its 8.8cm KwK 42 was substantially more powerful than the Tiger 1's gun. Predictably its weak point was its mobility, but in the defensive battles then being mainly fought by the German Army this was not necessarily a great disadvantage.

After delays in the mid-war period, the modest capabilities of the M4 Sherman, in comparison to the German Tigers and Panthers, finally spurred production of something better for the US Army from later in 1944. The M26 Pershing first saw combat in February 1945 and a few hundred were shipped to Europe by VE-Day. It carried an effective 90mm (3.54in) M3 gun and had a good balance of protection and engine power.

Totalitarian Rule – Germany and the USSR

For all that the two countries were the bitterest enemies, there were many close comparisons in the methods of government in Nazi Germany and the USSR, starting with the cruel and murderous nature of the regimes.

It is hardly surprising that there were a great many similarities between Nazi Germany and the Communist USSR in the WWII period. Both countries were dominated by a single political party whose organs and whose secret police featured in every corner of national life. And at their head was a single ruler with the power of life and death and absolute control over every aspect of state policy.

Police and Security

Both countries' regimes had a unified apparatus for security, policing and public discipline matters. In Germany the Reich Main Security Office (RSHA), a major division of Heinrich Himmler's SS, was the controlling body. Its main chiefs were first Reinhard Heydrich and later Ernst Kaltenbrunner; its subordinate departments included the SS security service and the Gestapo secret police. The RSHA was surprisingly small, only some 50,000 people in all in 1944, but it also maintained an extensive network of informers all too ready to denounce "defeatists" or "asocials".

Above: Lavrenti Beria controlled the USSR's security apparatus from 1938–53, murdering at Stalin's command and for his own pleasure.

Below: One of the 1944 Bomb Plotters faces the ranting Nazi judge Roland Freisler at his show trial before his inevitable execution.

In the USSR the organization varied at different times in the war but included both the NKVD and NKGB. However, both came under the control of Lavrenti Beria, the Commissar for State Security. Unlike the rather squeamish Himmler, who disliked personal involvement in the atrocities he ordered, Beria was himself a vicious and enthusiastic torturer and killer.

The principal instruments of coercion in both countries were the prison camps. No one knows how many unfortunates suffered in the Soviet camps, the gulag, but it is clear that to be sent to the camps was virtually a death sentence. Estimates suggest that during the war 1 million prisoners a year died of overwork, starvation and every other kind of cruelty. The process of selection was haphazard; many prisoners had done nothing to offend the regime.

Most of those in Germany's concentration camps were in some way obnoxious to the Nazis: habitual criminals, left-wingers and many more. At first prisoners were at least meant to be kept alive to work (the death camps where Jews were sent had a different mission). Camp prisoners slaved in vile conditions in quarries, mines and factories – many run as highly profitable businesses by the SS. Half a million is a common estimate of the number who died in the concentration camps.

Discipline in the armed forces was also stunningly harsh. The German Army executed at least 10,000 of its men (and probably many more) for military crimes like cowardice and desertion. (The US Army executed one.) The Red Army had numerous punishment units to which several hundred thousand men were sent for astonishingly trivial reasons. These units were used on repeated near-suicidal missions, which few of their soldiers survived.

The Home Fronts

Generally speaking civilian life was relatively comfortable for Germans until 1943 at least. Rations were reasonable; consumer goods were available; women were not required to do war work; and many prosperous families even had servants.

None of this was true in the USSR. Only workers in important industries got rations much above starvation levels. Millions of people were moved to the new industrial and mining areas out of the Germans' reach. Employees in the new factories built in 1941–2 often started work before the roof was even on and slept among the machines because they had no houses. Remarkably they did so very willingly on the whole, a level of commitment that was central to the USSR's victory in what its leaders taught the people to call the Great Patriotic War.

Indeed despite all the cruelties of the ruling regimes, the German and Soviet peoples fought hard for their countries throughout the war.

Right: A German poster appealing for donations of old clothes and woollens for the war effort.

ASSASSINATING HITLER

There were several attempts to assassinate Hitler. The most nearly successful was on 20 July 1944, when he was injured by a bomb placed in his conference room. The group of officers responsible planned a military coup, but this fell apart when it became clear Hitler had survived. About 5,000 people were executed in the aftermath. Hitler became even more mentally unstable than before and trusted his generals even less.

Below: Prisoners at the Nazi Sachsenhausen concentration camp in 1938. About 100,000 died there.

The Defeat of the Luftwaffe

American air victories over Germany in early 1944 set both the British and American bomber forces free to smash Germany's war effort. Heavily outnumbered and practically out of fuel, the Luftwaffe could do little to resist.

Two vital command decisions ensured the crushing defeat of the Luftwaffe in early 1944. Although the leaders of the American bomber force had not fully appreciated the importance of fighter escorts for their attacks, in late October 1943 General "Hap" Arnold, Chief of Staff of the USAAF, ordered that all P-51 Mustang production for the next three months was to go to Eighth AF for bomber support. The second decision came in January 1944 when General James Doolittle, new commander of Eighth AF, ordered his fighters not to be tied to the close-escort mission but to seek out and destroy their German counterparts. Together these set the scene for a series of massive air battles in which the USAAF would win air superiority over Germany.

Early 1944 saw RAF Bomber Command continuing to lose heavily in the Battle of Berlin. This culminated in a disastrous attack on Nuremberg on the night of 30–31 March, in which 96 out of 795 bombers were lost. Although Air Marshal Harris bitterly opposed the decision and made as many "area bombing" attacks on German targets as he could get away with, it was fortunate for his men that they were mainly sent against targets in France, over the next several months, in support of the coming D-Day landings.

"Big Week"

The first real chance for the American forces to put the new policy into effect came in mid-February, in a series of attacks on the German aircraft industry known as "Big Week". Contrary to what the Allies believed at the time, these barely dented German aircraft production, which continued to increase until September 1944 because of improved organization. Nor was there a clear-cut victory for either side in the air – the American forces lost some 250 bombers in return for 355

Left: A reconnaissance photo of bomb craters around the Dortmund–Ems Canal. Once used to transport U-boat parts, the canal was emptied by RAF attacks in late 1944.

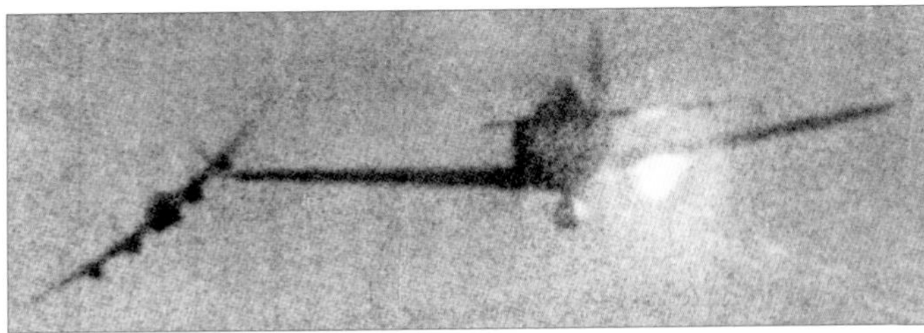

Above: A camera-gun picture from a British fighter shooting down an Fw 190 trying to attack a Lancaster bomber over Germany in late 1944.

German fighters downed. However, over 100 irreplaceable German pilots were killed. Fighter-pilot training and experience levels on the American side were on the increase; other than for a diminishing band of top aces, the reverse was now true for the Germans.

The process continued relentlessly, notably with missions to Berlin itself in March. Even though the US heavy bombers, like RAF Bomber Command, came under General Eisenhower's control on 1 April in preparation for D-Day, they continued to make some telling attacks on targets in Germany and Central Europe.

Oil Attacks

From May both the USAAF and RAF Bomber Command made an increasing number of strikes on Germany's synthetic oil production sites. Although Harris had been right to deride previous attempts to pick off key German target systems as ineffective "panaceas", this proved to be something different. By September 1944 German aviation fuel production was around 7 per cent of the already inadequate level achieved in May. This hampered operations and made training of the new pilots now in urgent demand virtually impossible. Those who did leave the training system were increasingly easy meat for the better prepared Allied fighters.

In August, in perhaps the clearest token of how things had changed, RAF Bomber Command returned to daylight operations over Germany. From then until attacks were wound down in the final weeks of the war, both British and American heavy bombers ranged almost at will over Germany, flattening cities and devastating industries with a weight of destructive power and levels of accuracy out of all proportion to anything ever before achieved.

Below: A damaged B-17 Flying Fortress drops its bombs on Berlin during a raid in August 1944.

DRESDEN

Since the war, and to some degree during it, some people have questioned the morality of heavy-bomber attacks on enemy populations and have doubted whether they were an efficient use of resources. The bombing by the RAF of the city of Dresden on 13–14 February 1945 has been particularly controversial. There were no military targets of importance in the city and it was packed with refugees, yet it was smashed by over 700 bombers and as many as 70,000 or perhaps more people were killed.

Above: Bodies litter the streets of Dresden after the attacks.

Fighters, 1943–5

By late 1944, thanks to the British, American and Soviet fighter forces and their range of superb aircraft, Allied heavy bombers ranged freely over Germany and Japan and ground-attack aircraft dominated the Axis land forces on all fronts.

From mid-1943 Allied air superiority over every battlefront was clear, and during 1944 was extended to cover both the German and the Japanese homelands by day and by night. It was the Allied fighters that made this happen. Although Germany and Japan both continued to field highly effective piston-engined fighters, overall the Allies had a qualitative advantage (other than over Germany's jets) to add to their enormous numerical superiority.

Allied Designs

The USAAF was the world's strongest air force in 1944–5 and had the fighters to match. The main types were the North American P-51 Mustang and the Republic P-47 Thunderbolt, both dating from 1940–1, although the earlier P-38 Lightning also remained in use.

The P-47 seemed the more promising design initially. It was based around a particularly large and powerful radial engine, which gave it an impressive rate of climb and dive despite its imposing size and weight. The P-47D version was the most built subtype of any fighter ever, with over 12,000 made.

After an unpromising start the P-51 Mustang developed into the aircraft that did more than any other to win the air war over western Europe. Fitted with the initial Allison engine, the Mustang had disappointing flight performance, especially at altitude; but in 1942 a version with a Rolls-Royce Merlin engine was tested and the Mustang was transformed. Fitted with drop tanks for additional fuel, the new aircraft had the range to escort bombers from England to Berlin and beyond and was superior to almost all Luftwaffe fighters when it got there, a combination of range and performance previously thought to be impossible.

In the final stages of the war many British fighter units continued to use the Spitfire Mark 9, introduced in 1942. This was joined by variants, notably the Mark 14, in which the Merlin engine was replaced by a more powerful Rolls-Royce Griffon. These gave nothing away to contemporaries in speed and manoeuvrability but, like earlier Spitfires, lacked range.

Completing the formidable Allied line-up was a range of impressive Soviet designs, the best of which came from the Yakovlev and Lavochkin design bureaux. The Yak-9, introduced in 1942, was an effective upgrade of the earlier Yak-7, with a more powerful engine and better armament fit. Its upgrade to the 9U version in 1944 was even more impressive. The ultimate Yak fighter of the war, also introduced in 1944, was the confusingly designated Yak-3.

Left: Late-war P-47 Thunderbolts were fitted with a "bubble" cockpit canopy to improve pilot visibility.

P-51D MUSTANG

The P-51D is regarded as the definitive wartime version of the Mustang. Like its B and C model predecessors, it was fitted with an American-built Packard Merlin engine but had two extra machine-guns and a "bubble" cockpit canopy for improved pilot visibility. Over 8,000 P-51Ds and some 16,000 of all P-51 marks were built.

Speed: 703kph (437mph)
Range: 2,655km (1,650 miles), with drop tanks
Crew: 1
Engine: Packard Merlin V-1650; 1,695hp
Armament: 6 x 0.5in (12.7mm) machine-guns

Above: A formation of Yak-9D escort fighters in flight. Over 16,500 Yak-9 fighters were built.

This was an extremely fast and manoeuvrable design, probably the best fighter of the war on the Eastern Front. The La-5 and La-7, developed from the previous LaGG designs, were both also very effective if not quite the equals of the Yak types.

Axis Replies

Germany's Focke-Wulf 190 had outclassed the RAF's Spitfires when introduced in 1941. Versions of this design and later marks of the Messerschmitt Bf 109 remained the principal German fighters until the end of the war. By 1944 the Bf 109 and the radial-engined versions of the Fw 190 struggled to compete with the best Allied aircraft. The Fw 190D, fitted with an in-line engine and available from late 1944, was faster and more formidable.

In the Pacific War Japan's aircraft industry also failed to keep up with new designs. As a token of this, the Kawasaki Ki-61 "Tony" (one of the most significant later-war Japanese fighters) was only one of several Japanese aircraft relying on licence-built versions of German engines. The best Japanese Army fighter of the war was the Nakajima Ki-84 "Frank", in service from April 1944.

Below: A Griffon-engined Spitfire Mark 14 in flight. The Mark 14 had a top speed of 721kph (448mph).

FOCKE-WULF 190

Over 20,000 Fw 190s were built in numerous variants, including the radically different D model and successors with an in-line rather than a radial engine. The Fw 190 served as a fighter, including some with heavy armour and armament for the bomber-attack role, and as a fighter-bomber.

Specification: Fw 190A-3
Speed: 640kph (398mph)
Range: 800km (500 miles)
Crew: 1
Engine: BMW 801 D-2; 1,730hp
Armament: 2 x 20mm (0.79in) cannon + 2 x 7.92mm (0.312in) machine-guns

Aircraft Ordnance and Electronics

Air attacks were meaningless without effective weapons and systems to guide aircraft to their targets. Bombs, rockets, radar, navigation aids and equipment to jam or home in on enemy transmissions all saw substantial development during the war.

It is well known that WWII saw much behind-the-scenes innovation in radar and other aspects of aircraft electronics, but developments in seemingly mundane fields like bomb design were also significant.

Bombs and Rockets

Many different bombs were used, from 1.8kg (4lb) incendiaries, dropped by the millions, to the RAF's 9,980kg (22,000lb) Grand Slam of which 41 were used in 1945. By the later stages of the war a typical British heavy-bomber load for an attack on a German city would include a single "cookie" (a large, high-capacity, high-explosive bomb) to blast buildings open, as well as a range of incendiaries to set them on fire. In the 1945 US attacks on Japanese cities incendiary bombs were the principal types used. By 1945 ground-attack and anti-shipping aircraft in US, British and Soviet service were also using unguided air-to-ground rockets as a major part of their armoury.

Although most bombs were "dumb" free-fall weapons, various guided and powered bombs were developed. German types included the rocket-powered Hs 293 and the free-fall Fritz-X; the American Azon type was similar to the Fritz-X. All were radio-controlled from the dropping aircraft, which had to keep the bomb and the target in sight throughout, always tricky and often dangerous. The American Bat type was potentially more capable because it included its own radar set, which it used to home in on its target. German successes included the sinking of the Italian battleship *Roma* by a Fritz-X in September 1943.

Above: A *Mistel* composite aircraft. The pair would be flown to the target by the fighter pilot who would then release the crewless but explosive-filled bomber to complete the attack. *Mistel* aircraft achieved little success.

Electronic Warfare

All major nations had some degree of radar capability in 1939, but Britain, the USA and Germany were the only ones to make substantial developments in this field. The accuracy of radar sets increased substantially during the war, as did the variety of methods to fool them and in turn the devices made to overcome these.

The most used anti-radar device was strips of metal foil dropped from an aircraft to give a mass of false radar returns on enemy screens – provided the strips were cut to the correct size according to the radar wavelength. This was first used by

Left: A Messerschmitt 110 night fighter fitted with Lichtenstein radar.

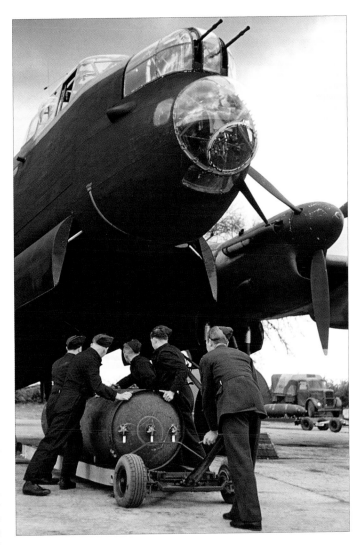

Right: Ground crewmen loading a 4,000lb (1,815kg) High Capacity bomb into a Lancaster.

British forces in July 1943 and in updated forms provided significant protection to British and American aircraft over Germany and Japan to the end of the war.

The Luftwaffe was the only air force in 1939 to appreciate the difficulty of finding bombing targets by night or in bad weather and had various radio-beam systems (Knickebein, X-Gerät and Y-Gerät) in service to achieve this. These were used with some success during the Blitz in 1940–1, but once British scientists had worked out how they operated, the systems were relatively easy to jam.

The British Gee, introduced in 1942, worked on a similar triangulation principle and was also jammed after a few months' use. The later Oboe used radar to measure the range between the aircraft and various ground stations. A disadvantage of all these was that their range was limited by the curvature of the Earth to about 450km (280 miles).

Slightly later still was the H2S system (used by American forces as H2X and in an improved APS-20 form), a ground-mapping radar operated by the aircraft independently of any ground station. This worked best when the ground below had distinctive features like a river or coastline. With devices like these, the RAF heavy-bomber force of 1944–5 was able to attack at least as accurately at night as the American bomber groups by day.

All such devices brought a disadvantage, however. The enemy could use any radio or radar transmitter in an aircraft to home in on it. Late-war British Mosquito night fighters, for example, had effective equipment called Perfectos and Serrate to do just this to their German counterparts.

Right: An Avro Lancaster in flight with the distinctive bulge of its H2S ground-mapping radar clearly visible under the rear fuselage.

From Normandy to the Rhine

At the end of July 1944 the continued Allied pressure in Normandy finally cracked the German front. Within a month the Allied troops had liberated most of France and Belgium but hopes of winning the war in 1944 would soon be abandoned.

On 25 July US First Army was able to begin Operation Cobra to break out from the Normandy bridgehead. Over the next few days the attack made good progress south past Avranches. By 1 August the German front in the area had crumbled away and a new Allied formation, US Third Army led by General George Patton, burst out into the open. Part of Third Army cleared Brittany to the west, eventually taking the ports of St-Malo and Brest, but other units headed south-east for Le Mans and the interior of France.

Hitler now intervened. Although all the other Allied forces were also pushing foward and his generals were sensibly beginning to think about a retreat, he ordered an attack through Mortain to Avranches to cut off the Third Army advance where it began. This attack was fought to a standstill on 7–8 August and by then the whole German force in Normandy was in deep trouble.

The Falaise Pocket

Around 20 divisions were caught in a pocket between British and Canadians in the north and Americans in the south. They had no option but to retreat frantically to the east past Falaise, while trying to fend off Allied attacks all the way. Although many of the German troops in the so-called Falaise Pocket did manage to escape before its neck was closed, they no longer formed effective military formations. And, to complete the Allied victory in Normandy, Allied troops were already across the River Seine west of Paris.

There was yet more bad news for the Germans. On 15 August French and American troops landed on the Mediterranean coast between Cannes and Toulon. The German forces in southern France were too weak to provide real opposition and were also being seriously harassed by French resistance fighters. By the end of August the invasion force was advancing steadily up the Rhône Valley

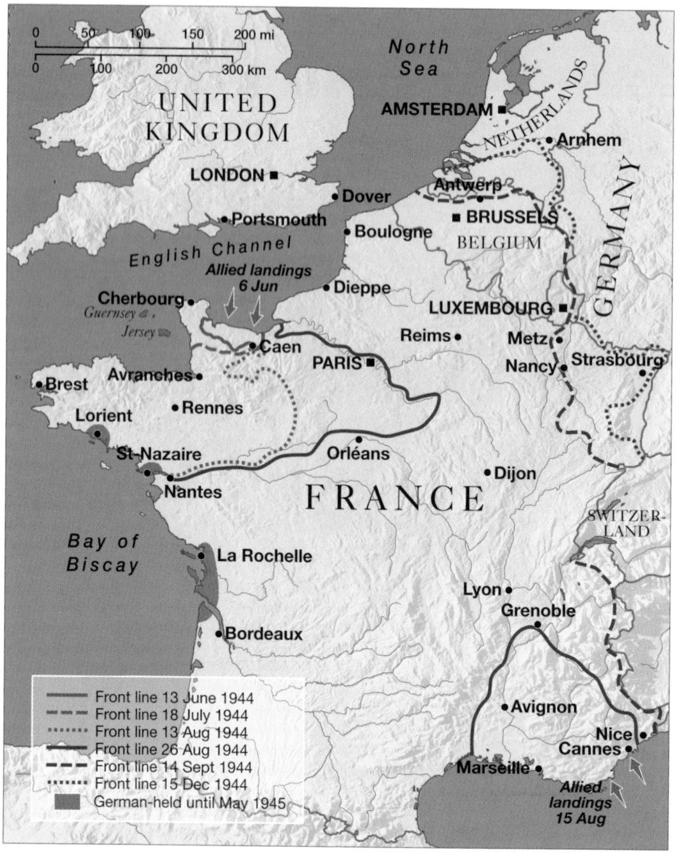

LIBERATION OF FRANCE

After a long and bitter struggle in Normandy, Allied forces liberated the rest of France in only a few weeks.

Above: Many German troops and vehicles were hit by Allied air attacks in the Falaise Pocket.

Above: Allied Sherman tanks crossing the Nijmegen Bridge on their way to Arnhem.

and would link up with troops advancing from Normandy on 12 September.

After the slow slog through Normandy the campaign was transformed. Paris was liberated on 25 August. By the end of the month most of France was free and most of Belgium followed in the next few days. By now, the Allied forces were out-running their supply resources and the top generals were arguing over what to do next. The port of Antwerp, which had the capacity to land all the supplies the armies were likely to need, had fallen on 4 September, but its estuary was still in German hands. The best plan would probably have been to have immediately mounted a campaign to clear the estuary and solve the supply problems, but this was not done until October and the first cargoes were not landed until late November.

A Bridge Too Far

Instead Montgomery persuaded Eisenhower, the Supreme Commander, that the best plan was to cross the series of river barriers blocking the route into Germany in a joint airborne and ground-forces attack. Operation Market Garden seized several major bridges but the last, over the Rhine at Arnhem, could not be taken. The Allied advance ground to a halt all along the front by the end of September.

While the British and Canadian forces were finally clearing the Scheldt estuary, the American armies were fighting hard for small gains around Aachen and in the Saar and Moselle regions to the south. It was an autumn and early winter of bitter disappointment after the high hopes of only weeks before. And the Germans were recovering fast from their Normandy disaster and assembling reserves for a new attack.

GENERAL GEORGE PATTON

Patton (1885–1945) was probably the most able American general of the war, though his talents were marred by showmanship and a love of publicity. He successfully commanded US troops in North Africa and Sicily but was then sidelined for a time after striking two hospitalized soldiers he wrongly accused of malingering. He commanded US Third Army in 1944–5, leading it particularly brilliantly during the advance in August 1944 and in the Battle of the Bulge in December.

Right: General Patton, photographed shortly before the Sicilian campaign during which he quarrelled fiercely with General Montgomery.

Self-propelled Artillery

In a fast-moving war, armoured units needed their artillery to be as mobile as their tanks and a variety of self-propelled guns was developed to fill this role. Most were based on standard field gun weapons but some were in the heavy artillery class.

Weapons in this category are those self-propelled (SP) guns whose armament was designed principally or even exclusively for use with high-explosive or similar ammunition – and which normally lacked the armour protection to allow their regular use within direct-fire range of the enemy.

Designs in this class in both British and American service were regarded as pure artillery weapons, serving in the American case in "armored field artillery regiments" and operating like towed field artillery units with additional mobility. For the Soviet and German Armies the distinction between weapons of this type and those described as assault guns is not always clear-cut.

The Western Allies

The earliest Anglo-American types made their debuts in the Desert War in 1942. The first British design was the Bishop, a 25pdr (87mm) gun mounted in a high box-like superstructure on a Valentine tank chassis. This was not a success – among other faults the mounting greatly limited the gun's elevation, halving its normal range.

The most-produced US design first fought at Alamein in 1942 in British hands. This was the M7 105mm HMC (or Priest in British service). It carried a standard 105mm (4.13in) M2 Howitzer (with restricted elevation, though not as badly as the Bishop) on a chassis based on the M3 Lee tank. It continued in use through 1945. British forces used a similar vehicle, fitted with a full-elevation 25pdr and known as the Sexton.

Other American designs included two light types, mounting 75mm (2.95in) guns. The M3 GMC was mounted on a converted M3 half track and the M8 HMC on a modified M5 Stuart tank chassis. Neither was a great success.

A small number of M12 155mm GMCs, carrying a WWI-era 155mm (6.1in) gun, were used in north-west Europe in 1944–5. Other designs using rather more modern 155mm guns and howitzers were developed but not produced in time to see action.

Below: A German Wespe 10.5cm battery with vehicles whitewashed for winter camouflage.

BISHOP

The need to produce artillery weapons that could keep up with fast-moving tank battles in the Desert War led to the rushed development of the Bishop. About 100 saw action in North Africa, like this one, shown in Tunisia in 1943.

Weight: 17.4 tonnes
Length: 5.53m (18ft 2in)
Height: 2.76m (9ft 1in)
Width: 2.61m (8ft 7in)
Armour: 60mm (2.4in) max.
Road speed: 24kph (15mph)
Armament: 1 x 25pdr (87mm) Gun Mark 2; 32 rounds carried

Right: M7 105mm guns in front of Notre Dame during the French 2nd Armoured Division's triumphant liberation of Paris in August 1944.

The Eastern Front

Soviet designs covered here include several mounting versions of the 152mm (5.98in) gun. The early-war KV-1 heavy tank was accompanied by a 152mm-armed KV-2. This was well-armoured, but its high, boxy shape made it clumsy and vulnerable. The next type, the SU-152, also used the KV chassis but was much more effective, in service from the Battle of Kursk in 1943. Around 700 were built. It was replaced in production in 1944 by the JSU-152, carrying the same weapon but based on the JS-series of heavy tanks. All of these weapons also had a significant anti-tank capability.

German designs were more varied. The Wespe was roughly equivalent to the American M7. It carried the standard 10.5cm leFh 18 howitzer on a Panzer 2 chassis and was allocated to the artillery units of Panzer divisions. Some 700 were built and served from 1943. Its heavier partner in the Panzer force was the Hummel, fitted with the 15cm (5.91in) sFH 18.

In addition a small number of vehicles on a variety of chassis were built to carry the sIG 33 15cm gun. A further design (over 300 made) was the Sturmpanzer 4, sometimes known as the Brummbär, a well-armoured type carrying a 15cm StuH 43.

At the other extreme was the Karl Gerät, a 60cm (23.6in) siege mortar mounted on tracks. Six were made and they were provided with alternative 54cm (21.3in) barrels for longer range. The 60cm shell weighed 2,170kg (4,784lb) and could reach 6,580m (7,200yd).

STURMPANZER 4 BRUMMBÄR

The Brummbär ("Grizzly Bear") was an infantry support gun carried on a Panzer 4 chassis. Its 15cm howitzer fired a heavier (38kg/84lb) shell than the earlier StuG 3. It served successfully from 1943 and about 300 were built or converted.

Weight: 28.6 tonnes
Length: 5.93m (19ft 5in)
Height: 2.52m (8ft 3in)
Width: 2.88m (9ft 5in)
Armour: 100mm (3.9in) max.
Road speed: 40kph (25mph)
Armament: 1 x 15cm (5.91in) StuH 43; 38 rounds carried

Unarmoured Vehicles

Fighting armies consumed vast quantities of fuel and ammunition and fighting soldiers naturally needed to be fed. Transport vehicles to achieve these tasks were thus, if anything, more important than fighting equipment.

By the end of June 1944 the Allied forces had landed 150,000 vehicles in Normandy to support the 850,000 men by then deployed. Many of these were armoured fighting vehicles, but many more were soft-skin transport lorries, artillery tractors, repair trucks and other varieties. Another telling statistic is that during the invasion of the USSR in 1941 the Germans employed 2,000 different types of vehicle – and their army was only partly mechanized and still also had hundreds of thousands of draught animals. The importance of motor vehicles is thus obvious, as is the impossibility of detailing more than a sample of those used.

Probably the most famous transport vehicle of the war was the Jeep, originally designed by the Willys company and built mainly by Ford. To the US Army it was the "Truck ¼-ton, 4 x 4". Over 600,000 were made and many supplied to almost every Allied nation, in addition to their use with US forces. And as well as these there were vast numbers of ½-ton and ¾-ton vehicles from Ford, Dodge, Chevrolet and others in the light-truck class.

Other countries had equivalent equipment. The Soviets built GAZ-67 copies of the Jeep to supplement their Lend-Lease supplies. The Germans had the Kübelwagen, based on the original pre-war Volkswagen design. Even the Italians had a Fiat 508 type, which was used effectively in North Africa.

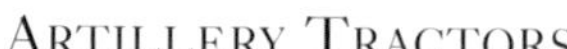

Artillery Tractors

Jeeps were often used to tow anti-tank guns but all nations had specialized designs for the artillery-tractor role. British 25pdr guns were often towed by Morris C8 "Quad" tractors and heavier weapons by AEC Matadors. US heavy artillery units used several models of fully-tracked vehicle in the same role, which were surprisingly fast and had good cross-country capabilities. Many of these were made by the Allis-Chalmers company, previously known for its farm tractors.

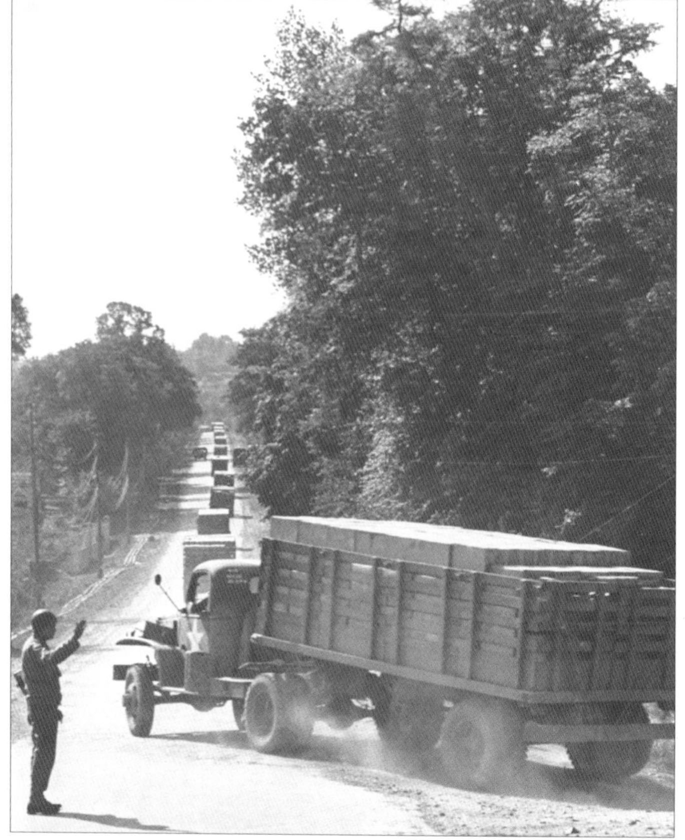

Left: An American truck convoy on the Red Ball Express route in France in 1944.

Above: Tractors pull Soviet heavy artillery guns during the advance to Berlin in early 1945.

Above: A Scammel tank transporter leads a British column in the advance after El Alamein in 1942.

Soviet heavy artillery units also employed tracked vehicles produced by the tractor industry. German heavy towing vehicles included SdKfz 8 and 9 half tracks, which could also be used for tank-recovery duties.

Moving tanks to and from the battle area and recovering damaged ones in the field was a highly important support role. American tank-transporter types, also used by the British, included vehicles by Diamond T and Mack, while native British types included examples from Albion and Scammel.

Cargo Vehicles

For simple cargo-carrying duties the USA's 2½-ton ("deuce and a half") design stands out. A truly massive 800,000 were built, mostly by General Motors, and they were supplied to all the Allies. By the end of the war the Soviets had more American trucks in use on the Eastern Front than indigenous ones.

Most countries had equivalent designs of roughly 3-tonne capacity, made by their own famous motor manufacturers, and usually a smaller number of larger vehicles up to the 10-tonne or 12-tonne class. Examples included Britain's 10-tonne Leyland Hippo or the Soviet YAG-10, an 8-tonne design.

The best-known use of transport lorries in the war was in the so-called Red Ball Express, set up by the Allied forces in France during 1944 in a desperate attempt to keep their advancing forces supplied. This used several thousand trucks running on a loop of one-way roads between St-Lô and Chartres. However, even this vast effort could not keep the armies going by mid-September 1944, when they were upward of 700km (435 miles) from the Normandy beaches, where their supplies were being landed.

TRANSPORT ANIMALS

The degree to which armies were mechanized varied considerably. Britain and the USA used motor transport whenever possible but in 1941, for example, the German Army had over 600,000 horses participating in Operation Barbarossa. In the course of the war the USSR probably lost 14 million horses, though many of these would not have been working with the Red Army. Even the British and Americans made significant use of transport animals, mainly mules, in particularly difficult terrain in Sicily, Italy and Burma. And over 1,000 elephants were used by the Allied forces in Burma.

Above: German transport crossing a river in Russia.

The Soviet Invasion of Germany

As millions of refugees fled in terror before the Soviet advance, the Red Army ground its way remorselessly from Warsaw to the Oder in the first months of 1945 and from March began attacks to conquer Czechoslovakia and Austria.

By January 1945 the Soviets were ready to resume their main attacks into Germany. Some 4 million men and masses of tanks, guns and aircraft were set to advance all along the front, from southern Poland to the Baltic coast of Lithuania.

Stalin had made it clear that he alone was in overall charge. Marshal Zhukov had been posted away from his position on the central staff to the front line, albeit to lead 1st Belorussian Front in the advance on Berlin; and Marshal Vasilevsky, the Chief of Staff, would also be given an operational command in February and replaced by a more junior officer.

The Soviet offensive began on 12 January with the strongest attacks coming from the bridgeheads west of the Vistula that had been held for some months by 1st Belorussian Front and Marshal Ivan Konev's 1st Ukrainian Front to the south. Within a week these troops had advanced well into Silesia, and Warsaw itself fell on the 17th.

Above: Soviet gunners fighting on the outskirts of Breslau (Wroclaw). The city was surrounded in February 1945 but held out, on Hitler's orders, not surrendering until May.

The advance accelerated as the German front collapsed. For a time a panicked Hitler even put SS chief Heinrich Himmler, a man with no military training and less aptitude for generalship, in charge of Army Group Vistula, a new command that was meant to halt the rot. Instead, by early February, Zhukov's tanks had reached the Oder only 65km (40 miles) from Berlin.

Taking East Prussia

By then Germany's province of East Prussia had been largely overrun. The 2nd and 3rd Belorussian Fronts had attacked from the south and north-east at the same time as the Vistula offensive began. The southern attacks reached the Baltic near Elbing (Elblag) in early February, cutting East Prussia off from the rest of Germany. Almost all the rest of the province was taken by early April, when the capital Königsberg (Kaliningrad) surrendered.

Throughout this period there was a mass naval evacuation, with many casualties, of German troops and civilians from all

Left: Soviet engineers use a flamethrower in their attack on Küstrin (Kostrzyn) on the Elbe in early 1945.

Above: The Soviet advance was preceded by a tide of German refugees, rightly fearful of atrocities.

around the Bay of Danzig to ports like Kiel safely to the west. A few pockets on the coast remained in German hands until the surrender in May.

Pause on the Elbe

By February the Soviet spearheads seemed poised to drive on to Berlin, and probably could have done so relatively easily. However, for reasons that have never been clear, Stalin chose not to do this. Instead the Soviet forces spent several weeks taking control of Pomerania and southern Silesia. The best explanation seems to be that Stalin did not want the war to end before he had direct control of as much Polish and German territory as possible. And at this stage, with the Western Allies still fighting their way slowly to the Rhine, there seemed little prospect of them getting to Berlin first.

The Soviet forces south of Poland did little attacking in the first months of 1945 but did finish off the siege of Budapest in February. Bizarrely there now followed Germany's last significant offensive of the war. After the failure of the Battle of the Bulge, Hitler switched the elite Sixth SS Panzer Army to the Hungarian front and its attacks made limited gains in the Lake Balaton area in the first couple of weeks of March. These were retaken immediately the Soviet offensives resumed on 16 March. In April the Soviets conquered much of Austria and by early May had moved well into Czechoslovakia.

The successful Anglo-American Rhine crossings in March had by then brought a new urgency to the operations on the main fronts. At the end of March Stalin finally gave orders for the decisive attack on Berlin.

Right: Members of the *Volkssturm*, or Home Guard, parade before Nazi chiefs in Posen (Poznań).

Heavy Mortars and Artillery Rockets

Germany's Nebelwerfer and the Soviet Katyusha were among the most-feared land weapons of WWII. Heavy mortars, too, generated awesome firepower concentrations and caused many casualties.

Heavy mortars and ground-to-ground rockets produced some of the most devastating sudden bombardments of the war. Rockets and mortars in fact had advantages over traditional artillery guns. They could bring down a heavy volume of fire quickly and fairly accurately on a target; and the more nearly vertical trajectory of their shells ensured that their fragmentation pattern was highly effective. More than half of the British casualties in north-west Europe in 1944–5 were inflicted by these weapons, for example.

In addition to the mortars used for infantry support, most armies also had heavier types, but the Germans and Soviets made most use of these. The Soviet 120mm (4.72in) HM38 (based on a French Brandt design) fired a 16kg (35lb) bomb up to 6,000m (6,500yd). Other Soviet weapons were 160mm (6.3in) and 240mm (9.45in) designs. The German 12cm (4.72in) design was a copy of the Soviet HM38. The USA and Britain both used 4.2in (107mm) weapons. The American type was unusual in having a rifled barrel; most other mortars were smoothbore weapons.

Rocket Artillery

The Soviets and the Germans made more extensive use than other armies of rocket artillery. The German Nebelwerfer types included 6-tube 15cm (5.91in) and 5-tube 21cm (8.27in) designs as well as larger calibres. The Soviet Katyushas were often truck mounted and included the M8 firing 32 x 82mm (3.23in) rockets and the M13 firing 16 x 132mm (5.2in) rockets. These latter had an 18kg (40lb) warhead and could reach a range of 8,500m (9,300yd).

Rocket weapons often had a distinctive noise when fired: Anglo-American troops knew the Nebelwerfer types as "Moaning Minnies"; Red Army troops called their Katyushas "Stalin's Organs".

Below: A Soviet 120mm (4.72in) mortar battery in action in the streets of Berlin at the end of the war.

SdKfz 4/1 Maultier

The SdKfz 4 was a half-track version of Germany's standard 3-tonne trucks. It was designed to cope with difficult ground on the Eastern Front. About 300 were built to carry Panzerwerfer 42 rocket launchers.

Weight: 7.1 tonnes
Length: 6m (19ft 8in)
Height: 2.5m (8ft 2in)
Armour: 8mm (0.3in)
Road speed: 40kph (25mph)
Armament: 10 x 15cm (5.91in) Panzerwerfer 42 rockets

V-Weapons

Hitler thought that these "Retaliation Weapons" would win the war for Germany, but despite their sinister reputation their effectiveness was more limited. Producing them also cost the lives of thousands of slave labourers.

Cruise missiles and ballistic missiles are part of the everyday military vocabulary of the 21st century; their ultimate ancestors were the German Fi-103 and A-4, which saw much use in WWII. Both types had a variety of codenames and designations: most are commonly known by the V designation (V for *Vergeltungswaffe*, or "retaliation weapon"), first coined by German propaganda and then officially endorsed by Hitler.

FIESELER 103/V-1

Fuselage length: 6.65m (21ft 10in)
Wingspan: 5.33m (17ft 6in)
Engine: Argus 109-014 pulse jet; 310kg (680lb) max. thrust
Max. speed: 670kph (415mph)
Max. range: 200km (125 miles)
Warhead: 850kg (1,870lb)

V-1 Flying Bomb

The Fieseler 103, or V-1 flying bomb, was a small pilotless aircraft powered by a pulse-jet engine, fitted with an auto-pilot to guide it to its target. Tested from 1942, it was put into action in June 1944, a few days after the D-Day landings.

In the early stages most of the missiles fired were targeted on London. Of the roughly 8,600 launched before the French bases were overrun by the Allied armies, about a quarter reached their targets. Later in the war Antwerp and other Belgian cities were targeted, again with modest accuracy; about half of the missiles launched landed within a dozen kilometres of their targets.

Although the V-1 was cheap to make (around 5,000 marks each, 2.5 per cent of the price of a V-2), the 30,000 made took up more than half of German explosives production in 1944–5 and inflicted fewer than 7,000 fatalities on the British people.

V-2 Rocket

The A-4/V-2 ballistic missile was an altogether more high-tech weapon. Its liquid-fuel rocket carried it 80km (50 miles) into the stratosphere before it fell at supersonic speed onto its target. Unlike the V-1 it could not be intercepted by fighter aircraft or anti-aircraft gunfire.

About 3,500 were fired at London and other cities from September 1944, carrying in all less explosive power than a single large Allied bombing raid on Germany in the same period. More slave labourers died in the Nazi factories making the V-2 than were killed by the missile attacks. With a more powerful warhead, the story might have been different. However, in this vein, it has also been calculated that the development cost of the V-2 was about the same as the American expenditure in making the atom bomb.

A-4C/V-2

Length: 14m (45ft 11in)
Fuselage diameter: 1.64m (5ft 5in)
Engine: Liquid-fuel rocket
Flight time: 330 seconds
Max. range: 314km (195 miles)
Warhead: 730–975kg (1,600–2,150lb)

Battle of the Bulge

Hitler aimed to repeat the triumph of 1940 in an attack through the Ardennes region to cut the Allied armies in two. Instead Germany's last reserves were defeated in a series of desperate winter battles.

By the late autumn of 1944 the German Army had recovered some of its strength after the disasters of both the summer in Normandy and the Eastern Front. However, the American armies were pushing forward slowly in eastern France and Belgium, while the British had finally succeeded in clearing the Scheldt estuary, so that the great port facilities of Antwerp could at long last begin to alleviate the Allied supply problems.

Hitler decided to use the assembling German reserve force in the west, where he was convinced a major success would bring quarrels between Britain and the USA, persuade them to make peace and perhaps even join him in fighting the Soviets. The plan was to advance through the Ardennes region, just as in May 1940, and then drive in a north-easterly direction to Antwerp, cutting the Allied front in two. All this was fantasy but Hitler insisted the attack would go ahead, despite protests from the commanders who would actually have to carry it out.

Below: Draped with machine-gun ammunition and much other equipment, an SS trooper prepares to attack during the Ardennes battle.

Above: An M36 tank destroyer in the Ardennes. The M36's 90mm (3.54in) gun was the best US anti-tank weapon in 1944–5.

Allied intelligence was aware of the assembly of German reserves but believed they were intended as a counter-attack force against any future Allied advances. The Ardennes region was indeed one of the weakest parts of the Allied line, held by an unfortunate mix of resting veterans and inexperienced newcomers. The Allied commitment to advances to the north and south of the region also meant that there were few reserves available to use elsewhere. Altogether the Germans assembled ten Panzer divisions, equipped with many of the newest heavy tanks, and a number of newly raised *Volksgrenadier* infantry units. Three armies were deployed; together they formed Field Marshal Walther Model's Army Group B.

Initial German Gains

The Germans attacked on 16 December and achieved complete surprise. They quickly broke through the Allied line all along the attack front, while small groups of special forces penetrated deeper into Allied territory, spreading confusion and panic. A few Allied reinforcements were quickly sent to the area and they, and the survivors of the original front-line force, established themselves especially around the towns of St-Vith and Bastogne. They were both important road junctions, particularly vital for movement in an area of steep and densely wooded hillsides.

By the 19th the top Allied commanders were taking the situation in hand. All Allied attacks elsewhere were halted and new arrangements to deal with the threat established. Field Marshal Montgomery was put in charge of the Anglo-American forces north of the German advance, and General Omar Bradley of the US forces to the south. Part of Patton's US Third Army changed front with

Above: Men of US 75th Division advancing toward St-Vith during the Allied counter-attack in January 1945.

BODENPLATTE

The Luftwaffe planned a knock-out blow – Operation Bodenplatte – against Allied air bases in Belgium to accompany the Ardennes offensive. It was finally delivered on 1 January 1945 with something approaching 900 German aircraft taking part, many flown by novice pilots. They surprised a number of Allied airfields and destroyed about 150 aircraft, mostly on the ground, but about 300 of the German planes and many of the most experienced pilots were shot down. It was yet another serious defeat for the Luftwaffe.

astonishing speed and began attacking north to relieve Bastogne and reduce the bulge the Germans had now driven into the Allied line.

Up to this point bad weather had kept Allied air support to a minimum, but on the 22nd it cleared. The German supply system was already stretched; now both it and the front-line forces came under continuous attack. A few German troops almost reached the River Meuse by late on the 24th and would go no further. Their generals were already begging Hitler's permission to call off the attack (and being refused).

THE ALLIED RESPONSE

After an epic defence, Bastogne was relieved by Patton's advance on 26 December. Major attacks from the north of the Bulge began on 3 January, and it had largely been recovered by the middle of the month. The Germans lost about 100,000 men and most of the tanks used in the operation. Allied losses were similar in number but theirs could be replaced. Germany's could not.

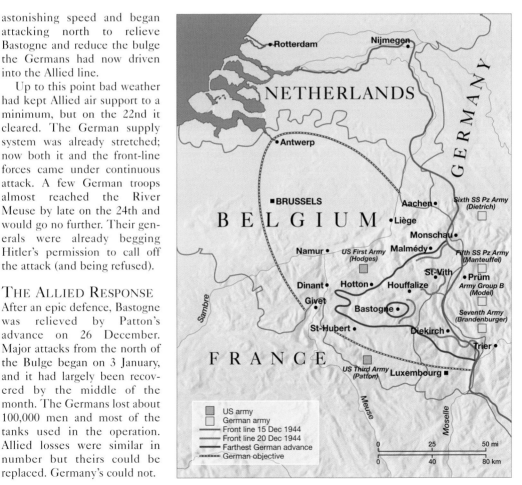

BATTLE OF THE BULGE

The German plan for the Ardennes offensive was to split the Allied armies apart and capture their principal supply port, Antwerp.

Jet Aircraft

Although the piston-engined aircraft in service in 1944–5 were vastly superior to those used at the start of the war, they were clearly outclassed by the new turbojet types, even though all of these had reliability issues and other problems.

Although the power of aircraft piston engines was improved very substantially during the course of WWII, it was also clear that there was more potential for the future in rocket and turbojet propulsion. All the major combatants were working on such designs by 1945, but only Germany and Britain used jet aircraft in combat before the end of the war; the USA had jets in service but not yet deployed on operations.

First Jets

The first workable jet engines were made in 1937 in separate research programmes in Britain and Germany. At that stage the British design by Frank Whittle was more advanced, but Heinz von Ohain's engine was the first to fly, in the Heinkel (He) 178 in 1939. Whittle's Gloster E.28/39 first flew in 1941. Neither of these was intended as a combat aircraft, but two designs which were took to the air in 1941–2: the Messerschmitt (Me) 163 and Me 262.

The Me 163 came from a completely different line of development. With an entirely unconventional arrowhead shape and powered by a Walther rocket engine, it could reach an incredible 960kph (596mph). Disadvantages were that it only carried fuel for about ten minutes of flight; that the fuel itself was dangerously prone to explosion; and that after its brief flight the aircraft had to glide back to base and land using skids, not a proper undercarriage. It began operations in mid-1944 and achieved a few successes against Allied bombers, but accidents and other problems were common.

The turbojet and Me 262 offered better prospects, though it took two years from the type's first flight in July 1942 for it to reach combat. This was mainly caused by engine and other faults, but Hitler's order that it was to be adapted as a fast bomber certainly did not help.

Although perhaps 1,400 were built, far fewer reached the squadrons and they suffered fuel shortages and other problems. They could outfly any Allied aircraft and were well-armed for bomber interception, but many were shot down while

GLOSTER METEOR F 1

The Gloster Meteor was the first operational Allied jet. The illustrated example, an F 1, is in flight over Kent in August 1944, days after the type's combat debut. The later F 3 had better Derwent engines and improved aerodynamics.

Speed: 670kph (417mph)
Range: 880km (550 miles)
Crew: 1
Engines: 2 x Rolls-Royce W2B Welland turbojets
Armament: 4 x 20mm (0.79in) cannon

Left: The Me 163 rocket fighter was stunningly fast but probably shot down fewer than 20 Allied aircraft.

Left: By 1945 Allied air superiority had forced many factories underground. Here He 162 fighters are being built in a salt mine.

landing or taking off from their bases when they were slow-moving and vulnerable.

Two more German jets were built and made operational but saw little combat. Over 200 Arado 234 bombers were produced in 1944–5 but saw only scattered action, notably against the Rhine Bridge at Remagen.

Some 50 of a simplified fighter type, the He 162 Volksjäger (or "People's Fighter") were built in the final months of the war. This design was meant to be suitable for operation by inexperienced pilots, but by the time it was available there was little fuel to be found. It probably flew a handful of combat missions in April 1945.

Allied Types

On the Allied side the American Bell P-59 Airacomet first flew in October 1942 but met repeated problems and was never taken into operational service. Two more US designs, the Lockheed P-80 and the Ryan FR-1 (this type having both a piston and a jet engine fitted), were being deployed when Japan surrendered but did not see combat.

Britain's Gloster Meteor flew in 1943 and came into operational use in July 1944. Initially F 1 models were employed in the home-defence role, operating against V-1 flying bombs, but a few much improved F 3s were deployed to bases on the Continent in 1945. Like the other early jets, it suffered from many teething problems and successive production batches showed numerous minor improvements to address these.

ARADO 234

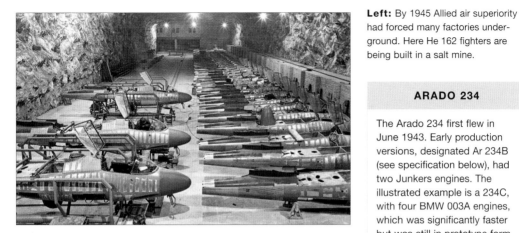

The Arado 234 first flew in June 1943. Early production versions, designated Ar 234B (see specification below), had two Junkers engines. The illustrated example is a 234C, with four BMW 003A engines, which was significantly faster but was still in prototype form when the war ended.

Speed: 742kph (461mph)
Range: 1,100km (680 miles) with bomb load
Crew: 1
Engines: 2 x Junkers Jumo 004B-1 turbojets
Armament: 1,500kg (3,300lb) bombs; usually no guns

Right: A bomb-armed Me 262. Hitler insisted that the type should be developed as a fast bomber.

Anti-tank Guns, 1942–5

Higher muzzle velocities and new types of ammunition ensured that anti-tank guns still posed a formidable threat to even the monster heavy tanks produced for the final battles of the war.

The increase in power seen in anti-tank guns of the early-war years continued during the second half of the war, though with the improvements being derived more from new types of ammunition rather than large increases in calibre. Armies also found that towed anti-tank guns in the larger calibres could be clumsy in action and more difficult to conceal; accordingly they turned increasingly to self-propelled (SP) weapons in the anti-tank role.

New Ammunition

In ammunition, simple solid-shot armour-piercing (AP) designs were found to be prone to shattering on impact, because of the higher velocities being used. They were also more likely to glance off the sloped armour that more and more tanks included. This led to the introduction of capped rounds (APC) to achieve better impacts and ballistic caps on top of these (APCBC) to restore ideal shapes.

Composite rounds with a dense penetrating core encased in a lighter carrier (armour-piercing composite rigid – APCR; or high velocity armour-piercing in the US designation – HVAP) were also introduced, as well as a better version of these in which the light carrier fell away on leaving the barrel (armour-piercing discarding sabot – APDS). These had an ideal combination of lightness to accelerate quickly in the gun barrel but with a hard and dense munition with good carrying power, penetration and accuracy. Various guns had a different range of ammunition developed at different times during the

NASHORN

The Nashorn ("Rhinoceros"; also known as the Hornisse, or "Hornet") was a very effective tank destroyer armed with the long-barrel 8.8cm gun. The basic vehicle was a modified Panzer 4 chassis. It was first used at Kursk in 1943.

Weight: 24 tonnes
Length: 7.17m (23ft 6in)
Height: 2.65m (8ft 8in)
Width: 2.8m (9ft 2in)
Armour: 30mm (1.2in) max.
Road speed: 42kph (26mph)
Armament: 1 x 8.8cm (3.46in) PaK 43; 25 rounds carried

Below: A 17pdr (76mm) anti-tank gun of the 2nd New Zealand Division in action at Monte Cassino in Italy in early 1944.

Right: American infantry pass a pair of knocked-out Hetzer tank destroyers. The Hetzer was built on the old PzKpfw 38(t) chassis.

war; APDS was a British speciality introduced for the 6pdr (57mm) in the spring of 1944, for example.

Earlier weapons like the 6pdr remained in use to the end of the war, in part thanks to improved ammunition, but also because they could still be effective against most opponents at shorter ranges. In British service, however, the 6pdr was supplemented from 1942 by the 17pdr (76mm). The essentially identical US 57mm was supplemented by the 3in (76mm) M5 and the dual-purpose version of the 90mm (3.54in), originally made as an anti-aircraft gun.

Self-propelled Guns

All of these weapons featured on SP mounts. Indeed the towed and SP guns served together in the American tank-destroyer units. The most notable of these were the M10 (with the 3in gun) and the M36 (90mm), as well as a lighter, faster design, the M18 Hellcat, which mounted the same 76mm weapon as later US Sherman tanks. For Britain, the 17pdr gun was mounted in an M10 variant – the Achilles – and in a vehicle derived from the Valentine tank – the Archer.

Soviet anti-tank weapons included the ZiS-3 76.2mm (3in) field gun, which had a respectable AP performance. This gun was made by the tens of thousands, along with the very formidable 100mm (3.94in) BS-3 introduced in 1944. Most Soviet SP guns with a significant anti-tank capability were more heavily armoured SU-series assault guns.

As well as its assault guns, Germany also had various *Panzerjäger* (or "tank-hunter") types, as well as towed weapons of course. The 7.5cm (2.95in) PaK 40 towed gun was introduced in late 1941 and served to the end of the war. There was also an improved version of the "Eighty-eight" – the 71-calibre 8.8cm (3.46in) PaK 43.

The *Panzerjäger* vehicles included several types known as the Marder. These were based on a variety of chassis and armed with either the German PaK 40 gun or captured Soviet 76.2mm weapons. They were introduced in 1942–3. The later Hetzer was the most numerous *Panzerjäger*, with some 2,500 produced, and also carried a 7.5cm gun. The Nashorn was more formidable, carrying the long-barrelled PaK 43, but only some 500 were made.

M36 GMC

The M36 Gun Motor Carriage entered service in 1944. Several variants existed, built with different engines and hulls. All carried the anti-tank version of the 90mm anti-aircraft gun and could defeat Panther or Tiger tanks.

Weight: 28.1 tonnes
Length: 6.15m (20ft 2in)
Height: 2.72m (8ft 11in)
Width: 3.04m (10ft)
Armour: 50mm (2in) max.
Road speed: 48kph (30mph)
Armament: 1 x 90mm (3.54in) M3; 47 rounds carried

Victory in the West and Italy

Allied commanders anticipated a hard struggle to conquer Germany. Instead, after they crossed the Rhine, German resistance collapsed within weeks. However, the great prize of Berlin was left for the Soviets to take.

After the disappointments of the autumn of 1944 and the hard fighting of the Battle of the Bulge at the turn of the year, the Allied commanders did not expect to finish the campaign against Germany easily. In particular they thought that crossing the Rhine against tough German opposition would be difficult, but events proved them wrong.

British and Canadian troops opened the Allied offensive at the north end of the line in early February, fighting a vicious battle through the Reichswald forest to close up to the Rhine. US Ninth Army on their southern flank was meant to join the attack shortly after but was delayed by extensive flooding, deliberately caused by the Germans. By early March, however, Ninth Army was on the move and had been joined by US First and Third Armies farther to the south still.

Above: Men of British Eighth Army near Ferrara during the final Allied attacks in Italy in April 1945.

Within days the Allied troops had reached the Rhine everywhere north of Cologne, and on 7 March US First Army reached Remagen some 45km (28 miles) to the south.

Better still, the Americans captured the railway bridge over the river there before it could be destroyed by the retreating Germans, and immediately started rushing troops across. Finally, the last Allied armies, US Seventh and French First, overran almost all the remaining German-held territory west of the river by mid-month.

Montgomery's British forces made their long-planned assault crossing of the Rhine from late on the 23rd around Wesel, with much less difficulty than anticipated. Originally this had been conceived as the main Allied advance but the crossing at Remagen had been joined on the 22nd by another – by Third Army south of Mainz. Patton was determined to steal Monty's glory. A few days earlier General Eisenhower had already decided to modify Allied plans by strengthening these attacks south of the Ruhr.

Encircling the Ruhr

Hitler was still issuing his usual orders that there should be no retreat and fanatical resistance. However, the reality was that increasing numbers of German troops were now only too glad to surrender to the Western Allies

Left: American troops at the bridge at Remagen, the first crossing point over the Rhine captured by the Allies.

in order to keep themselves safe from the Russians. New Allied advances at the end of March encircled the whole Ruhr area and the troops there – over 300,000 strong – surrendered in mid-April.

By this stage Soviet troops were on the Oder, only 65km (40 miles) from Berlin and seemed well-placed to capture it. In mid-March Eisenhower therefore decided that his forces would not try to reach Berlin but would concentrate their advances farther south against a feared (though actually non-existent) National Redoubt that fanatical Nazis were supposedly building for a last stand in southern Germany.

In fact the Anglo-American armies were now advancing at speed all along the front, while the Soviets were not yet ready for their final drive to Berlin. US troops reached the Elbe west of the German capital in mid-April and halted there, with first contact with the Soviets coming a little to the south-west on the 25th at Torgau.

Last Battles in Italy

After the capture of Rome in June 1944, Allied troops had been taken from Italy for the invasion of southern France. The remaining Allied units continued a slow advance into early 1945. In April they renewed their attacks, now with more success. German forces in Italy surrendered on 2 May, and on 4 May the advancing Allied troops linked up at the Brenner Pass with US Seventh Army coming down through Bavaria.

By early May most of what would become West Germany was in Anglo-American hands and the formal surrenders began here, too. German forces in the north capitulated to Montgomery on the 4th, followed by a complete German surrender that was signed at Eisenhower's headquarters on the 7th.

Above: Tanks and troops of US Third Army crossing the Rhine near Koblenz on a pontoon bridge.

Below: An Allied M3 half track on the advance through the ruins of a German town in early 1945.

Infantry Anti-tank Weapons

By 1945 infantrymen in the best-equipped armies had man-portable weapons that could destroy even the heaviest tank – if they were brave enough to get desperately close to the metal monsters.

Specially powerful rifles had been used as anti-tank weapons almost from the moment tanks were introduced in WWI. Versions of these were still in service when WWII broke out but were soon made obsolete by improvements in tank armour.

From 1942–3, Britain, the USA and Germany introduced weapons using the hollow-charge principle to focus explosive power. These gave the infantry weapons that could kill a tank, or smash open a pillbox or other fortification.

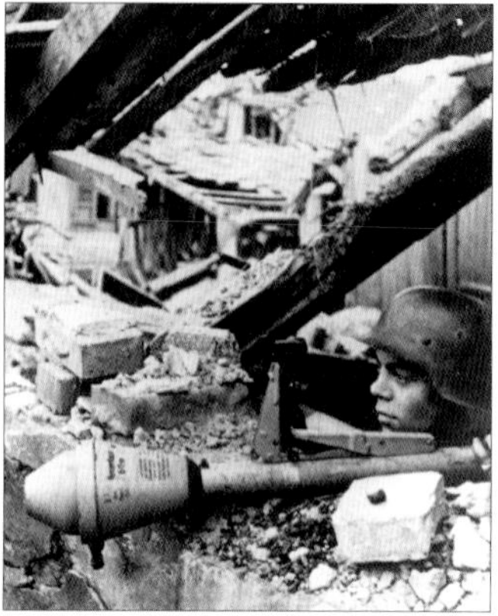

Above: A young German soldier waits in a ruined house with his Panzerfaust at the ready.

Anti-tank Rifles

In the early-war years anti-tank rifles in service included the British Boys type, in 0.55in (14mm) calibre, and two Soviet designs – the PTRD 1941 and PTRS 1941 – both in 14.55mm (0.57in) calibre. These all had similar performance, being capable of penetrating some 25mm (1in) of armour at 400m (440yd). Smaller-calibre types included the Polish Maroszek Wz 35 (also used in significant numbers by the Italians) and the German Panzerbüsche 38 and 39, all in 7.92mm (0.312in).

Rocket Launchers

The US Army had no anti-tank rifle when it entered the war but soon acquired something better – the 2.36in (60mm) M1 Rocket Launcher (called the Bazooka). This could destroy most contemporary Axis tanks and had a range of up to 400m (440yd), though accuracy at this distance was far from certain. Later versions had the calibre increased to 3in (76.2mm) with improved armour-piercing performance.

Germany's 8.8cm (3.46in) Panzerschreck (or "Tank Terror") was essentially a copy of the Bazooka. Britain's Projector Infantry Anti-Tank (PIAT) looked clumsy and primitive, but it was able to fire a useful 1.4kg (3.1lb) bomb.

Germany also used the even more innovative Panzerfaust (or "Tank Fist"), a light and simple single-shot weapon with the firing tube designed to be discarded after use. The longest-range Panzerfaust variant could only reach 100m (110yd), but its power and ease of use made it a formidable threat to any tank, especially in close country or a built-up area.

No other army developed such weapons during WWII.

Left: Later in the war the Soviets often used anti-tank rifles, as here, against enemy positions, not tanks.

Mines and Other Defences

Mines, and their close relatives booby traps, are sometimes called silent soldiers, lying patiently in wait for an enemy. They were a threat on every battlefield of the war, capable of killing in battle and long after fighting had moved elsewhere.

There were two main categories of mine that were in use during WWII – anti-personnel and anti-tank – the former usually being smaller and requiring a lighter force to set them off, the latter larger and heavier. Minefields could be set in any open area and contain one, or more often both, types; and individual or small numbers of mines could be used for point defence or as booby traps virtually anywhere.

Troops hated enemy mines, with some justification. Anti-personnel mines were often designed more to maim than to kill, since a wounded soldier often got assistance, taking perhaps several combatants out of the firing line.

The design of mines also often inspired fear. Both Germany and the USA used mines that had two charges – one to throw the mine into the air when it was disturbed; and a second main charge to detonate it there. Germany's Schrapnellmine, for example, blasted out some 350 shrapnel balls from a position roughly 1.5m (5ft) above ground, with devastating effect.

Anti-tank mines could be both bar- and discus-shaped. The Italian forces were the first to use them, in the Western Desert in 1940. Common designs included the Soviet TM/39 which carried a 3kg (6.6lb) charge or the slightly heavier British Mark V.

Above: A Canadian engineer preparing to clear an enemy anti-tank mine in Italy.

Germany and the USSR were the most prolific users of mines. As well as the most often encountered Tellermine anti-tank designs, Germany also had a variety of anti-tank and anti-personnel types in glass, plastic and wooden cases, all designed to make detection harder. Many mines of all nations were also fitted with anti-lifting devices to make their removal more difficult and dangerous.

Right: Soviet engineers laying mines to block a German advance on the Eastern Front in 1942.

The Fall of Berlin

In the last weeks of the war the ruin that Hitler had brought to Europe was visited in a yet more terrible form on Berlin, as the Soviet armies rampaged through the city above his bunker and across much of Germany.

From the start, WWII had been a total war, prosecuted with the utmost violence and cruelty, and its final great battle saw this trend continue to the last. At the end of March 1945 General Eisenhower had told the Soviets that his forces would stop short of Berlin and make no attempt to capture the city. Stalin did not believe him and hurried forward the Red Army's preparations to get there first.

KEY FACTS

PLACE: Berlin

DATE: 16 April–2 May 1945

OUTCOME: Soviet troops advanced from the River Oder to conquer Berlin; Hitler committed suicide.

ODER BREAKTHROUGH

The Soviet attack began on 16 April with some 2.5 million men and a truly astonishing 16,000 artillery weapons deployed. The Germans had perhaps one million men, but many of them were over-age or very young. They had nothing like the scale of equipment of their enemies, and even when they did have tanks they had scarcely any fuel for them. Even so, the initial Soviet attacks, by Zhukov's 1st Belorussian Front, against the Seelow Heights west of Küstrin failed to break through, in part because Army Group Vistula was now led by an acknowledged defensive expert, General Gotthard Heinrici.

However, by 20 April the German resistance had inevitably fallen apart. Zhukov's surge toward Berlin and round its north side had also been joined by a major drive by Konev's 2nd Belorussian Front over the Neisse a little to the south.

To ensure the fastest progress Stalin gave both his marshals permission to take Berlin, according to which got there first. Zhukov's troops reached the edges of the city on the 21st and the two fronts met to complete the encirclement west of Potsdam on the 25th. On the same day Konev's men made contact with US troops at Torgau on the Elbe to the south.

Over the next few days the Soviets fought their way from street to street and house to house. On 30 April they stormed the Reichstag building, only 400m (440yd) from Hitler's command bunker. On the 29th Hitler had named Admiral Dönitz as his successor and then killed himself. The fighting went on a little longer, but on 2 May the Soviet fronts linked up from north and south and the last of the garrison surrendered.

In the meantime the remaining troops of the German Ninth Army, part of the defence force on the Oder a couple of weeks before, were attacking desperately to the west to escape the Soviets and surrender to the Americans. They knew only too well the fate that probably would await them in Soviet captivity. Since the Soviets had

Left: Raising the Red Flag over Germany's parliament, the Reichstag.

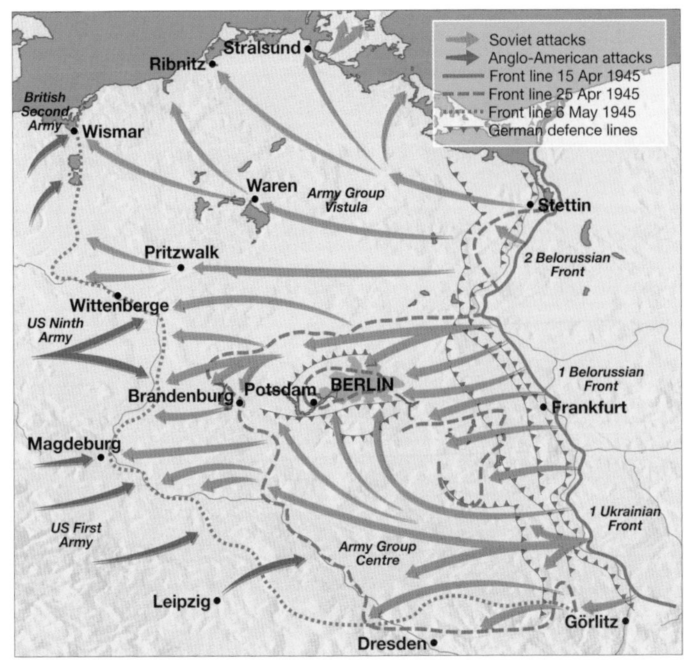

MARSHAL IVAN KONEV

Konev (1897–1973) was a tough and competent Soviet commander who held senior posts throughout the war. He played a notable part as a front commander in the defence of Moscow in late 1941 but then, and later in his career, he was somewhat overshadowed by Zhukov, with whom he had a great rivalry. Konev's public reputation grew with his part in the Ukraine and Polish battles of 1943–4. In 1945 he shared in the conquest of Berlin, inevitably with Zhukov, but Konev finished the war off on his own by leading the capture of Prague.

BATTLE OF BERLIN
The Soviet advance from the Oder took only about three weeks to overwhelm Berlin.

entered Germany, their advance had been marked by a rampage of murder, rape and drunken looting, which now reached a terrible climax in and around the enemy capital.

GERMANY SURRENDERS

With Hitler dead, the end was certain. German troops in Italy surrendered on 2 May, in north Germany on 4 May and in south Germany on 5 May. On 7 May Dönitz's representatives signed the overall surrender at Eisenhower's HQ at Reims. Stalin suspiciously insisted that the signing be repeated late on the 8th in Berlin. The Western Allies, however, celebrated VE-Day (Victory in Europe) on the 8th, the Soviets on the 9th.

Even then the killing was not over. Some of the last German units holding out by late April were in Czechoslovakia. On 5 May the people of Prague rose against the Germans, who fought back fiercely. Over the next week Soviet units closed in from the east and north, and the final German force surrendered on the 13th. The war in Europe was finally over.

Right: Soviet Josef Stalin tanks in front of the captured Reichstag.

The Battle of Leyte Gulf Japanese kamikaze pilots at a pre-mission ceremony.

Landing Craft and Amphibious Vehicles A wrecked Japanese landing barge on Saipan.

Submarines and Bombers Admiral Lockwood aboard the submarine USS *Balao*.

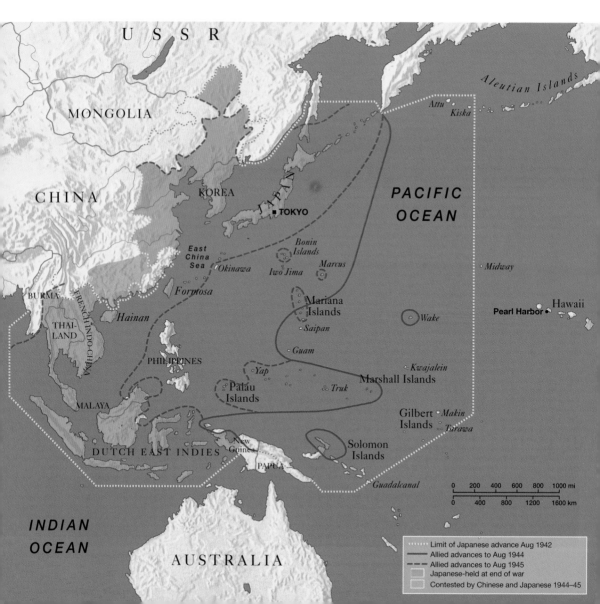

U S S R
MONGOLIA
CHINA
KOREA
JAPAN
TOKYO
PACIFIC OCEAN
Aleutian Islands
Attu
Kiska
East China Sea
Okinawa
Bonin Islands
Iwo Jima
Marcus
Formosa
Hainan
BURMA
FRENCH INDO-CHINA
THAI-LAND
PHILIPPINES
Mariana Islands
Saipan
Guam
Yap
Palau Islands
Truk
Marshall Islands
Kwajalein
Wake
Midway
Pearl Harbor
Hawaii
Gilbert Islands
Makin
Tarawa
Solomon Islands
Guadalcanal
MALAYA
DUTCH EAST INDIES
New Guinea
PAPUA
INDIAN OCEAN
AUSTRALIA

0 200 400 600 800 1000 mi
0 400 800 1200 1600 km

Limit of Japanese advance Aug 1942
Allied advances to Aug 1944
Allied advances to Aug 1945
Japanese-held at end of war
Contested by Chinese and Japanese 1944–45

DESTRUCTION OF THE JAPANESE EMPIRE

By 1943 the vast expansion of America's military strength was taking effect. Despite large increases in its own war production Japan could not begin to compete. From relatively small beginnings in New Guinea and the Solomons, the Allied counter-offensive soon developed in pace and strength. The US Navy and Marines began their island-hopping advance across the Central Pacific and MacArthur's Allied South-west Pacific Command surged toward the Philippines. By mid-1944 a relentless submarine campaign was making Japan's vaunted empire practically useless to the homeland, which was itself coming under heavy bombing attack. On the Asian mainland Japan could still advance against weak Chinese forces, but plans to invade India from Burma had been smashed by the British–Indian Fourteenth Army.

The second half of 1944 and early 1945 saw the ring around Japan tighten with the fall of the Philippines, Iwo Jima and Okinawa. The desperate expedient of suicidal kamikaze attacks did little to slow the American advance. Allied plans for an invasion of Japan were well in hand by August 1945, when everything changed with the atom bomb attacks on Hiroshima and Nagasaki and the crushing Soviet offensive on mainland Asia. Japan's surrender followed within days.

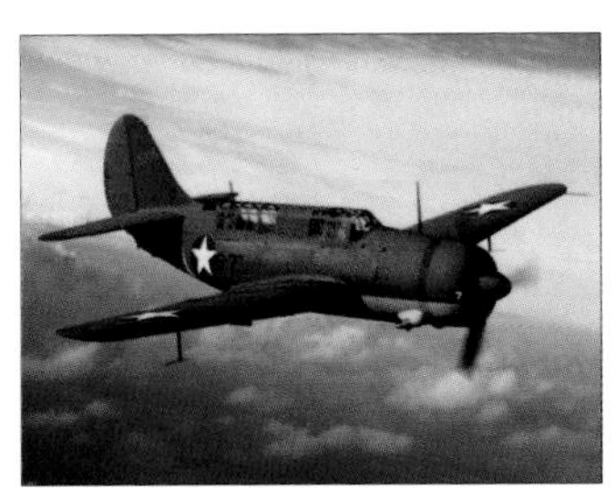

Naval Bombers and Torpedo Aircraft A US Navy Curtiss SB2C Helldiver in flight.

Conquest of the Philippines US Navy landing ships unloading troops and supplies on Leyte.

The Japanese Surrender The mushroom cloud of an atomic explosion rises above Nagasaki.

New Guinea and the Solomons

Japan's troops began paying the price for their reckless early-war conquests. Garrisons were isolated and then either picked off or left to starve as the Allied forces pushed past in their counter-offensive toward the Philippines.

After the triumph at Midway, American strategists knew that they could move to the attack in the Pacific, but there was fierce debate on how to develop the counter-offensive. General MacArthur, now established in Australia at the head of the Allied South-west Pacific Command, argued forcibly for an advance through the Solomons and along the north coast of New Guinea toward eventual fulfilment of his promise to return to the Philippines.

Admiral Chester Nimitz, commanding the Pacific Ocean Areas from his base in Hawaii, wanted to advance via the island groups of the Central Pacific. Like MacArthur's, this was a strategy that favoured his own command and his own service, the US Navy, but in truth it was also likely to be more direct and economical in casualties and material. However, American resources were becoming so ample that both plans could be pursued. Indeed it would have been very difficult politically for the President and his advisers, with whom the decision ultimately rested, to have chosen one strategy exclusively.

Above: Stuart tanks leading a search for Japanese positions, New Georgia Island, August 1943.

Air Superiority

All the Allied advances were based on air power, an area in which they were clearly superior by the end of 1942. This was well demonstrated in the Battle of the Bismarck Sea in the first days of March 1943. A Japanese convoy had sailed from Rabaul to reinforce their forward positions on New Guinea around Lae but was attacked en route. A dozen ships were sunk and around 4,000 soldiers drowned.

The attacks were made possible by code-breaking information, which would play a vital part throughout the remainder of the campaign. Time and again the Allied forces would attack weakly defended locations and quickly build air bases to ensure dominance over any stronger Japanese forces nearby.

Major Japanese positions were neutralized by air attacks and then in effect ignored, left to "wither on the vine" while the Allied advance moved on elsewhere. This technique was even applied to the principal Japanese strongholds of Rabaul and Kavieng, which eventually were left isolated and impotent (though early plans had provided for their capture).

New Guinea

In the first phase of the advance the Japanese were drawn forward, by air landings and naval attacks by Australian and American forces, toward Wau and Salamaua – and then kept off balance by other forces leap-

Left: B-25 bombers of US Fifth Air Force attacking a Japanese airfield on New Guinea, February 1943.

frogging on to the Markham Valley and Huon Peninsula areas. In the second phase, in April–May 1944, landings at Aitape and Hollandia isolated tens of thousands of Japanese troops around Wewak. The final landings on western New Guinea and nearby islands established bases to support the Marianas and Philippines operations, which were to follow.

The Solomons

Again the same techniques were followed in the Solomons campaign. This was most clearly seen in the landings on Bougainville, which began on 1 November 1943. The island had a garrison of some 60,000 Japanese troops concentrated in the south around Buin. Instead of attacking directly, US Marines landed 120km (75 miles) away on the east coast at Empress Augusta Bay. By the time the Japanese had crossed the jungle to the Allied beachhead it was easily strong enough to repel their attacks.

Although fighting on Bougainville continued to the end of the war, by then being conducted on the Allied side mainly by Australian forces, the starving Japanese garrison, like others in the region, was contributing nothing of value to Japan's war effort.

Above: Australian troops in a landing craft shortly before the attack on Lae, September 1943.

Above: US Army troops advance cautiously through dense jungle on Vella Lavella Island in the New Georgia group, September 1943.

GENERAL DOUGLAS MACARTHUR

MacArthur (1880–1964) was the top US Army general in the Pacific throughout the war. He commanded the American and local forces in the Philippines in 1941 but was quickly defeated by the first Japanese attacks. MacArthur was ordered to leave and take over a new Allied South-west Pacific Command, which he led successfully in the New Guinea campaign until the return to the Philippines in 1944–5. Like many top commanders, he was a great egotist and self-publicist, but he was nonetheless also a talented and effective general.

Below: General MacArthur in the Philippines in early 1945 after his promotion to General of the Army.

Seaplanes and Naval Support Aircraft

Distant patrols far out across stormy oceans, perhaps ending in a sudden attack on an enemy submarine, were the stock-in-trade of maritime aircraft. As in many other military duties there might be hours of boredom, then moments of desperate fear.

Maritime patrol aircraft included large long-range seaplanes, smaller floatplanes (often launched from a catapult aboard a ship other than an aircraft carrier) and, especially later on in the war as radar equipment was developed, land-based types used for long-range anti-submarine work. The leading maritime powers (the UK, USA and Japan) made most use of such aircraft, but all nations with a navy of any size employed them to some extent.

Floatplanes

There were numerous designs of this type in service. France, the USA and Germany each had more than ten types, so only a few can be highlighted here. The most numerous American design was the Vought OS2U Kingfisher (over 1,500 built). It had a range of some 1,300km (800 miles) and flew from catapults aboard many US Navy battleships and cruisers.

The two notable Japanese machines were the biplane Mitsubishi F1M "Pete", which had a surprisingly good performance, and the more capable Aichi E13A "Jake" with a 2,100km (1,300 miles) range.

Germany's best aircraft in this class was the Heinkel 115, but the Arado 196 also saw significant use.

Below: Vought OS2U Kingfisher floatplanes on their catapults aboard the heavy cruiser USS *Quincy*, 1944.

Britain's most common small floatplane was the Supermarine Walrus, an obsolescent pusher biplane, which saw widespread and effective service even so.

Many seaplanes were altogether more modern and impressive than the floatplanes, however. Britain and the USA

ARADO 196

The Arado 196 was designed to be used as a catapult-launched reconnaissance aircraft but also saw service operating from land bases. Over 500 were made and the first entered service a few weeks before the start of the war. Among other successes Arado 196s participated in the capture of the British submarine *Seal* in 1940.

Speed: 311kph (193mph)
Range: 1,080km (670 miles)
Engine: 830hp Bramo 323
Crew: 2
Armament: 100kg (220lb) bombs, 2 x 20mm (0.79in) cannon + 2 machine-guns

converted the long-range civilian flying boats of Imperial Airways and Pan Am to military duties but in addition had purpose-built machines. Britain's was the Short Sunderland, with a patrol endurance of up to 16 hours and a weapons fit of depth charges, bombs or mines and many defensive machine-guns.

Other Designs

The USA had two highly successful twin-engined designs: the Martin PBM Mariner and the Consolidated PBY Catalina (the Catalina in particular also served with numerous Allied countries). The Mariner was a slightly more capable design than the Catalina, with a longer range (5,600km/3,500 miles) and larger bomb capacity. However, the Catalina was produced in slightly larger numbers and was better known. The USA's four-engined type (the Consolidated PB2Y Coronado) was not as successful as its smaller stablemates.

By contrast Japan's main four-engined type was probably the best seaplane in use in WWII. The extended-range versions of the Kawanishi H8K "Mavis" could cover over 7,000km (4,350 miles) and were so heavily armed that they were very difficult to shoot down.

Even bigger was Germany's six-engined Blohm und Voss 222 Wiking, with an astonishing endurance of up to 28 hours; however, it was mainly used for transport duties.

Land-based Support

Various nations employed smaller utility types for maritime patrol duties, including (in the early-war years) Britain's Avro Anson. It was very slow but highly reliable – engine failures far out to sea were never very popular with crews.

Effective longer-range patrol and anti-submarine operations came into their own with Anglo-American developments in air-to-surface radar. Variants of a number of large bombers were used for this role, most notably versions of the Consolidated B-24 Liberator. In addition there was the PB4Y-2 Privateer, a new type based on the Liberator and specifically designed for maritime strike and reconnaissance. It was larger than the B-24 and had a single not a twin tail. Several hundred saw service in 1944–5.

Small numbers of Germany's Focke-Wulf 200 Kondor, a converted airliner, played a significant role in the early stages of the Battle of the Atlantic. However, the Luftwaffe generally neglected maritime tasks – much to Germany's detriment.

Above: A US PBY-5 Catalina on patrol off the Aleutian Islands in the North Pacific, early 1944.

SHORT SUNDERLAND

The Short Sunderland entered RAF service in 1938 and 749 were built before production ended in 1946. Several marks were produced with increased defensive armament and improved radar and other systems. As well as sinking U-boats, several Sunderlands fought off attacks by up to eight German aircraft.

Speed: 336kph (210mph)
Range: 2,850km (1,770 miles)
Engines: 4 x 1,065hp Bristol Pegasus XVIII (in Mk 2)
Crew: 8–11
Armament: 900kg (2,000lb) bombs, 8 x 0.303in (7.7mm) machine-guns

The Central Pacific Campaign

From late 1943, the US Navy and Marines fought a new kind of war across the Central Pacific, characterized by the description "island-hopping", which relied as much on novel methods of logistical support as the efforts of the combat forces.

In 1943 the US Navy took 15 fleet or light aircraft carriers into service, but the Japanese commissioned only 1. The USA also out-produced Japan by 4 to 1 in submarines, roughly 10 to 1 in destroyers and by similar wide margins in every other class of munitions.

Nor was Japan husbanding its resources well. The already diminished cadre of trained carrier aircrews was further decimated in the early part of the year by being deployed on land in the Solomons and New Guinea. Training and improved equipment (notably better aircraft and radar) were also offsetting Japan's previous qualitative advantage in some areas, in air combat and naval night fighting, for example.

KEY FACTS

PLACE: Tarawa Atoll, Gilbert Islands

DATE: 20–3 November 1943

OUTCOME: Japanese garrison wiped out despite heavy American casualties.

Right: The carrier USS *Lexington* refuelling at sea during the Tarawa operation, November 1943.

Below: US Marines lie dead amid the devastation and debris on the beach at Tarawa.

Even with potential combat superiority, the US forces still had the problem of distance to overcome: the US Pacific Fleet's base at Pearl Harbor was 3,200km (2,000 miles) from the West Coast; the Solomon Islands 14,500km (9,000 miles) from California; Australia still farther. To keep troops, ships and aircraft fed, fuelled and armed over such vast distances required a huge logistic effort.

The solution was a new type of naval organization, the fleet train, including tankers and other kinds of supply ship, so that combat vessels could be replenished at sea during assault operations far from any base. Then a range of new bases was improvised by rapidly building shore installations and installing floating docks in various previously tranquil Pacific lagoons – like Ulithi in the Caroline Islands (an important base from September 1944).

THE GILBERT ISLANDS

The first step was to make landings from 20 November 1943 on the Tarawa and Makin Atolls in the Gilbert Islands. The Makin landings, mainly on Butaritari Island, were fiercely contested, but the US Army troops wiped out all resistance by the 23rd.

Above: US Marines ready to move inland from their landing beach, Eniwetok, February 1944.

However, Betio Island, the main target in the Tarawa Atoll, was a different matter.

Only 3km (2 miles) long and nowhere wider than 800m (880yd), none of Betio is more than 3m (9ft) above sea level. By November 1943 the 4,800-strong Japanese garrison had built a formidable network of bunkers and gun positions that largely survived the preliminary bombardments. The landing force, principally the 2nd US Marine Division, also lacked information on the depth of water in the lagoon and over the coral reef. For these reasons some 1,500 of the initial 5,000-man assault force became casualties on the first day, but the survivors held on. By the 23rd the only living Japanese were a handful of wounded, plus a few captured Korean labourers. US Marine casualties were over 1,000 dead and 2,000 wounded.

The Marshall Islands

The next stage was to seize control of the Marshall Islands. These were not as strongly fortified as was feared, although there were significant air forces deployed across a number of islands. These were gradually worn down from late 1943 by carrier attacks and land-based aircraft from the Gilberts.

On 31 January 1944 US troops began landings on Kwajalein, Roi-Namur and Majuro. The fiercest fighting was on Kwajalein, but by 4 February the 8,700-strong garrison had fought virtually to the last man, inflicting 370 dead on the attackers. Later in February Eniwetok was also captured. At the same time Japan's greatest overseas base, at Truk in the Caroline Islands, was heavily hit by the US carrier forces. The USA's relentless progress would continue without respite for the Japanese.

SEABEES

The Seabees were in effect combat engineers of the US Navy, working and, when necessary, fighting on land. They were first organized from late 1941 and their popular name derives from the initials "CB" for Construction Battalions, which was their official designation. At first all the men were volunteer civilian craftsmen or engineers, though draftees joined later. They served in all theatres but mainly in the Pacific. Typically they would land very shortly after the initial assault force and immediately begin work on airstrips and other base facilities. Without their efforts the island-hopping strategy would have been impossible.

Above: Seabees setting up communications facilities on one of the Gilbert Islands.

Landing Craft and Amphibious Vehicles

Amphibious vehicles and the many kinds of larger landing craft were vital to the Anglo-American war effort. Without them the whole counter-offensive in the Pacific and the defeat of Germany in western Europe would have been impossible.

Although amphibious operations had a long history, as late as a 1938 exercise (led by a certain Brigadier Montgomery) British troops were mainly using rowing boats to get ashore.

By then, however, the Japanese had a purpose-built 8,000-ton landing ship in service – the *Shinshu Maru* – which could deploy new Daihatsu landing craft from the stern. Japan subsequently introduced a small number of additional landing ships and landing craft, employing them successfully in its early offensive campaigns. In addition there were a few Toyota SUKI amphibious trucks in service, too.

US Marine Ideas

The other pioneer in landing operations was the US Marine Corps. In the inter-war period the Marines developed many of the ideas on amphibious warfare that would be put into action in WWII. In 1938 they began tests on so-called Higgins boats (in part copied from Daihatsu types seen in action in China). The wooden Higgins boats would be developed into more robust metal Landing Craft, Vehicle, personnel (LCVP), used by the thousand in many WWII campaigns. In 1941 the Marines also ordered the first of the important Landing Vehicle Tracked (LVT) series of amphibians. Later LVTs could carry 3 tonnes of cargo and be armed with weapons as large as a 75mm (2.95in) howitzer. Over 18,000 were built.

Below: US Army troops aboard an LCVP heading for Omaha Beach on D-Day. An LCVP typically carried 36 troops and 3 crew.

LCT MARK V

Several designs of Landing Craft Tank were built in Britain and the US from November 1940. The Mark V was a US design. This example is shown during operations on Rendova Island in the New Georgia group during 1943.

Length: 35m (114ft 2in)
Beam: 10m (32ft 8in)
Displacement: 120 tonnes
Load: 127 tonnes cargo or 5 M4 Sherman tanks
Speed: 7 knots
Armament: 2 x 20mm (0.79in) AA guns
Crew: 13

Even more prolifically produced was the DUKW amphibious truck. A final American amphibian was the smaller Studebaker M29 Weasel cargo carrier. All these amphibians were also used by the British.

British Types

By 1940 Britain had a small number of Landing Craft Assault (LCA) and Landing Craft Mechanized (LCM) in service – capable of carrying an infantry platoon or a tank, respectively – and soon added a number of other types. There was more than one variety of Landing Ship Infantry (LSI), converted either from ferries or small liners, and purpose-built Landing Ships Dock (LSD).

Rough American equivalents were Auxiliary Personnel Attack (APA) ships and Attack Cargo (AKA) ships. These various "ships" were not designed to reach all the way to landing beaches themselves but carried smaller "craft" into which they would load troops and supplies for the assault landings.

Also designed in Britain from 1940 – and subsequently made in large numbers in the USA – were various marks of Landing Craft Tank (LCT). The largest were around 56m (185ft) long and could carry nine Sherman tanks, landing them from a ramp at the bow.

These landing craft were among the smallest of a variety of types made for so-called shore-to-shore operations. They would be loaded in friendly territory and then sail under their own power to the landing area. Such vessels included Landing Ships Tank (LST) and Landing Craft Infantry, Large (LCI/L); around a thousand of each were built. An LST could carry some 20 tanks and an LCI/L 180–210 infantrymen.

Above: In the later stages of the Pacific war many Japanese landing craft, like this one on Saipan, were destroyed while trying to support island garrisons under attack.

Other Uses

Many landing vessels of all sizes were converted to specialized uses. Some became command or hospital vessels and others gave covering anti-aircraft fire. The most spectacular were the rocket-armed versions, which could fire a devastating barrage of up to 1,000 rockets into a landing area. By 1945 the variety and sophistication of landing craft and their tactics, and the weight of fire support available, meant that an assault landing could be made successfully against almost any opposition – hence the Japanese decision on Okinawa not to oppose the American landings at all.

DUKW

The DUKW amphibian was a 6 x 6 on land, based on a 2.5-tonne General Motors truck. It was used by the thousand in all theatres to unload transport ships and carry their cargoes inland to the troops. The examples shown are in British service preparing for D-Day.

Length: 9.45m (31ft)
Width: 2.49m (8ft 2in)
Weight: 6.7 tonnes + 2.3 tonnes cargo
Engine: 91.5hp GMC
Speed: 80kph (50mph) land; 10kph (6.2mph) water

The Marianas Campaign

The capture of the Marianas and Japan's crushing defeat in the naval Battle of the Philippine Sea ruptured the perimeter of its empire. The southern areas were being cut off as the war approached ever nearer to the Home Islands.

Although by mid-1944 the outer reaches of the Japanese Empire were increasingly helpless in the face of American advances, Japan's leaders still dreamed of setting all right by victory in a decisive naval battle. Their plan, code-named A-Go, was to mount a series of attacks by carrier and land-based aircraft to defeat the main American forces.

Unfortunately, not only did the American fleet have twice as many carrier aircraft (950:470) but – in addition to the by now usual American advantages in code breaking and intelligence generally – the A-Go plan had been passed to them after being taken from a Japanese officer's crashed aircraft by guerrillas in the Philippines.

Above: Admiral Ozawa commanded Japanese naval forces in the Battle of the Philippine Sea and the carrier decoy force at Leyte Gulf.

Below: US troops in action on Saipan. The landings were made by the 2nd and 4th Marine Divisions and the 27th (Army) Infantry Division.

Saipan, Tinian, Guam

On 15 June two US Marine divisions landed on Saipan to set the land fighting in motion. Saipan had the strongest Japanese garrison in the area, some 27,000 men, but by 9 July the last effective resistance was destroyed. The landings on nearby Tinian began on 24 July; here the 6,200-strong garrison had been wiped out by 1 August. Guam was also captured from its 19,000-man garrison after fierce fighting, with the landings beginning on 21 July; organized Japanese resistance ceased by 10 August.

The Japanese garrisons all fought virtually to the last man. The American forces, mainly US Marines, lost some 5,000 dead. By then, however, the A-Go battle had long since been fought.

Battle of the Philippine Sea

When the preliminary American air attacks on the islands started, Admiral Toyoda Soemu, Commander of the Japanese Combined Fleet, gave the order for A-Go to begin. Almost immediately things went wrong

Above: The carrier *Zuikaku* and several destroyers trying to dodge US air attacks, 20 July 1944. *Zuikaku* was hit but not sunk.

for the Japanese. As the fleet approached it was spotted by US submarines. At the same time American air attacks destroyed most of the Japanese aircraft force on the Mariana Islands themselves, as well as those on Iwo Jima and other islands that were meant to be sent to the Marianas. Crucially, the local commander on the Marianas hid the bad news from the fleet's tactical commander, Admiral Ozawa Jisaburo, who believed that the American forces were being worn down as he approached.

The one remaining Japanese advantage was in the range of both their combat and reconnaissance aircraft. It enabled them to find the American carriers and send off their strikes first, in the morning of 19 June. In all Ozawa sent off 4 strikes involving some 370 aircraft in the course of the day; about two-thirds were shot down while other Japanese planes were destroyed over Guam. Only one American ship was hit by a bomb and only 29 American aircraft lost.

Japanese aircraft and their hastily trained crews could no longer compete with the American pilots and anti-aircraft gunners, who called the day's events the "Great Marianas Turkey Shoot". Even worse for the Japanese, two of their largest carriers – the *Taiho* and *Shokaku* – were torpedoed and sunk by American submarines.

Despite all this, Ozawa tried to continue the battle, believing the optimistic reports that were still reaching him. On 20 June American reconnaissance did not fix the Japanese position until well into the afternoon when some 130 bombers and 85 fighters were sent to attack, even though the American commanders knew that their pilots would have to return to the carriers after dark. Another Japanese carrier was sunk and 3 more damaged for the loss of 20 American aircraft. Over 70 craft were lost while returning to their carriers, but most of the crews were picked up.

By contrast hardly any crew members of the more than 400 Japanese aircraft lost in the battle were saved. Thus, the biggest ever carrier battle also marked the effective demise of the Japanese carrier force. They still had ships but hardly any trained crews to fly from them.

ADMIRAL CHESTER NIMITZ

Nimitz (1885–1966) commanded the US Pacific Fleet from a few days after Pearl Harbor until the end of the war. His leadership, more than that of any other commander, was responsible for the series of crushing defeats inflicted on Japan and the transformation of the US Navy from the low ebb of December 1941 to absolute dominance in 1944–5. His leadership was probably best seen in the difficult times of 1942, when his able use of intelligence led directly to the first great success at Midway.

Above: Fleet Admiral Chester Nimitz pictured in 1945.

Naval Fighters

Like their land-based counterparts, fighters designed for operations from aircraft carriers had to be fast, manoeuvrable and well armed, but long range and robust construction for operations in difficult maritime conditions were equally valuable.

Since only Britain, the USA and Japan operated aircraft carriers, these were the only nations that had aircraft in this class, though on occasion the aircraft concerned also operated from land bases.

British Designs

Britain's early-war naval fighters were particularly poor. In 1939 Britain's Fleet Air Arm still employed the biplane Sea Gladiator type and also had the turret-armed Blackburn Roc, which (though a monoplane) was even slower than the Gladiator. These were replaced from 1940 by the Fairey Fulmar, which fought reasonably effectively against Italian aircraft in the Mediterranean but did not compare well with other nations' designs. The later Fairey Firefly, also a relatively large two-seat aircraft, had performance of a more modern standard, with a top speed of 508kph (316mph), and could also carry a useful bomb load.

The best home-made pure fighters employed afloat by the Royal Navy were conversions of the Spitfire, known in naval service as the Seafire. Various marks of Seafire were used and, like the parent design, were fast, manoeuvrable and well armed – but lacking in range. In the later-war years most naval fighters in British service were the US types described below.

The Japanese Navy

The best-known Japanese naval fighters came from the Mitsubishi company. The A5M

Below: Grumman Hellcats leading an air group preparing to take off from the carrier *Lexington* in 1944.

Above: A formation of US Navy Grumman F4F Wildcats in flight.

Above: Like other two-seat fighters, the Fairey Fulmar did not fare well in combat with modern single-seat designs, despite its heavy armament.

"Claude" served in China in the late 1930s and to some extent in the early part of the Pacific War. With a top speed of some 435kph (270mph), it was surprisingly fast for a fixed-undercarriage design and highly manoeuvrable.

The next Mitsubishi fighter – the A6M Type 0 "Zeke" (or "Zero") – was truly remarkable. In service from 1940, it had unequalled combat manoeuvrability at that time, was well armed with 2 x 20mm (0.79in) cannon and 2 machine-guns and had an astonishing 950km (600 mile) radius of action. It outclassed all Allied opponents until at least late 1942. The more powerful late-war A6M5 variant was the most-produced Zero. However, by then the Allies had well-trained pilots in abundance and aircraft with the heavy armament and performance to exploit the Zero's weaknesses of light construction and lack of armour for the pilot.

Other notable Japanese Navy fighters were various models of the Mitsubishi J2M Raiden "Jack" and the Kawanishi N1K Shiden "George". These mostly served in land-based roles, latterly in defence of the Home Islands against American B-29 bombing raids.

American Types

The US Navy also began the war with a soon-to-be-phased-out pre-war design, the Brewster F2A Buffalo, the US Navy's first monoplane fighter. This served at Midway and with the British RAF in Malaya in 1941–2 but was clearly no match for the Zero.

Already replacing it by then was the Grumman F4F Wildcat (also known as the Martlet in British service). Updated variants of the Wildcat remained in service until 1945. By then it had been supplemented by a larger and more powerful Grumman design – the F6F Hellcat – which some commentators describe as the best carrier fighter of the war. It was highly manoeuvrable and extremely robust, an advantage not just in combat but also in the common occurrence of heavy carrier landings. With a top speed of 620kph (385mph), it had more than adequate performance.

Challenging the Hellcat was the US Navy's other main late-war fighter – the Chance Vought F4U Corsair (in service from October 1942). Significantly faster than the Hellcat – over 700kph (435mph) in late-war variants – the F4U was also used effectively as a fighter-bomber.

MITSUBISHI A6M2 ZERO

In 1941–2 the Zero fighter seemed invincible, with better performance than any Allied aircraft. However, it was very lightly built with at first no cockpit armour or self-sealing fuel tanks. These were introduced in later models in use until 1945.

Crew: 1
Speed: 533kph (331mph)
Range: 3,100km (1,930 miles) with drop tank
Engine: 940hp Nakajima NK1C Sakae radial
Armament: 2 x 20mm (0.79in) cannon + 2 x 7.7mm (0.303in) machine-guns

Submarines and Bombers

For months before its surrender Japan's empire had been made useless to the mother country by American submarine attacks, while virtually every major city in the Home Islands was flattened in the American bombing campaign of 1944–5.

Japan's plans to expand its empire and gain access to the natural resources that the Home Islands lacked had been maturing for years before the war. But remarkably little thought had been given to protecting Japan's links with the empire or to moving the empire's products safely. If not perhaps a cause of Japan's defeat, this glaring oversight was certainly a large part of the reason why the USA won the war so quickly.

After Pearl Harbor the only part of the US Pacific Fleet that could immediately attack was the submarine force but, like the Germans in 1939–40, their torpedoes were very poor, often failing to explode or going off course. The problems were not fully solved until mid-1943. From then until the end of the war American submarines took an ever greater toll of Japan's shipping. Although Japan depended on imports to keep its economy operating and needed to send troops, supplies and arms to all its outposts, the Japanese Navy had neglected anti-submarine operations. For example, few ships had underwater sensors even as late as 1942, nor were there plans for a convoy system.

Above: General Curtis LeMay commanded the US bomber forces in the Marianas from January 1945.

The US code-breaking and intelligence service often guided submarines to the right places; once there, they benefitted from radar to find their targets and warn of air attacks.

Crippling Losses

By the end of the war, almost 5 million tonnes of shipping, along with numerous warships, had been sunk directly by submarines and over 2 million tons more by mines, both air- and

Below: Emperor Hirohito (centre) inspects the scenes of devastation in Tokyo, March 1945. About a quarter of the city was destroyed.

Below: As well as attacking enemy forces US submarines often rescued downed airmen, like these aboard the USS *Tang* in 1944.

Below: A sinking Japanese merchant ship seen through the periscope of the USS *Wahoo*, 1943.

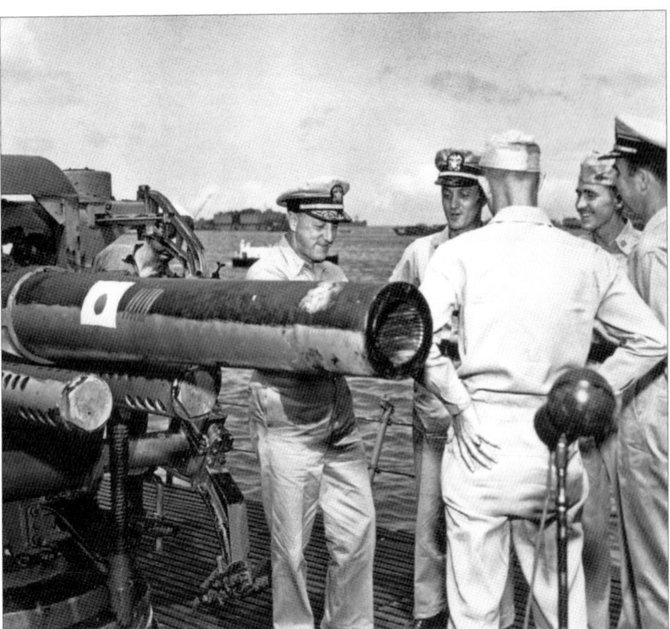

Right: Admiral Charles Lockwood (left), the very able commander of US Pacific Fleet submarines, aboard the USS *Balao* in 1945.

submarine-laid. By the summer of 1945 American submarines were even operating in the land-locked Sea of Japan, cutting the links between Japan and its large armies on the Asian mainland. Japan was in effect now totally blockaded.

RUIN FROM THE AIR

Unlike the submarine attacks, the bombing of Japan could only start when the long-range Boeing B-29 Superfortress aircraft became available. The campaign began on 15 June 1944 when 50 B-29s based in India flew via airfields in China to attack targets on Kyushu, the southernmost of the main Japanese islands. A further 50 or so attacks were flown using the Chinese bases before Japanese Army advances overran them in early 1945, but only a handful struck targets in Japan itself.

By November 1944 new bases in the Marianas had been opened from which virtually the whole of Japan could be hit. At first, US tactics were to make high-altitude daylight raids, attempting precision bombing of aircraft factories and similar targets. These met determined Japanese air defences and achieved disappointing results.

Early in 1945 experiments with a new technique were begun – low-level incendiary bombing of cities by night. This had several potential advantages: if attacking civilians directly was acceptable, then Japan's cities, with buildings predominately made of wood and paper, were vulnerable; Japan had little night-fighting capability so losses would be lower; and bombers could carry heavier loads and yet suffer fewer mechanical problems because of the lower altitudes.

After a number of trial operations, the new tactic was put into action in earnest on the night of 9–10 March 1945, when some 280 B-29s attacked Tokyo. The incendiaries raised a huge firestorm that left perhaps 120,000 Japanese civilians dead, making it the most devastating air raid of the war (not excluding the atomic attacks yet to come). In succeeding weeks city after city suffered a similar fate, with the attacks being supported from late April by escort fighters flying from airfields on newly captured Iwo Jima.

By late July the bombers were running out of large towns to target, Japan's economy was in ruins, at least 800,000 were dead and up to 10 million homeless. Perhaps most important of all, the Emperor and some of Japan's civilian leaders were becoming convinced that the war would have to be ended.

Submarine Classes

WWII submarines had limited capabilities, but no one doubted that they were potentially war-winning weapons. Germany's 1,000 U-boats failed in the Battle of the Atlantic, but the US Navy's submarines fatally weakened Japan.

Germany's U-boat force depended for most of the war on two main designs: the smaller (750 tons surfaced) Type VII and larger (1,000 tons) Type IX. These designs, clearly derived from WWI U-boats, were both well-engineered and robustly built for deep diving.

U-boat Developments

Ten Type XIV supply U-boats were also built. These played an important role in extending the operational range, especially of the Type VIIs, but all the Type XIVs were hunted down as a priority by the Allied forces using code-breaking information. By the mid-war years the U-boats were outmatched by Allied anti-submarine forces, so work on new technologies to overcome this was stepped up. First introduced was a breathing tube, or *Schnorchel* (a pre-war Dutch invention), designed to enable the submarine to run its main engines while submerged and difficult to detect. This worked up to a point but had various disadvantages when in use. More promising was work to streamline submarine hulls and step up battery capacity. A few Type XXI and XXIII U-boats using this technology came into service shortly before the end of the war – their high underwater speed made them very difficult to counter. More might have been built if Germany had not wasted much

Above: The Gato-class USS *Barb*, seen in San Francisco Bay in May 1945, returning to action after a refit.

Below: The Italian Tritone-class boat *Marea* off Bermuda in 1944. *Marea* was then being used by the Allies for anti-submarine training.

effort on the abortive development of the Walther system, which used hydrogen peroxide to provide oxygen so that the main engines could run when the boat was submerged.

European Classes

Britain had three main classes of submarine during the war: U, S and T (in ascending order of size). The 550-ton U-class boats were designed for training duties but, in the event, were used effectively in action in the confined Mediterranean waters. All the British boats had the merit of being fast-diving and carrying a heavy armament of bow torpedo tubes – eight in the T class compared to six or even four in other nations' boats.

Submarines built for Pacific service (including the British T class) tended to be larger than those designed for European waters. In 1939 the largest submarine in service was France's *Surcouf* – 3,250 tons, armed with a twin 203mm (7.99in) turret and carrying a floatplane.

Japanese Submarines

Japan's wartime I-400 class (three built) were even bigger, at 5,200 tons, and could carry three aircraft, intended to attack the locks on the Panama Canal. Other nations experimented with monster submarines before WWII, but these were the only examples to see any service.

Japan's standard submarines were unremarkable: relatively slow-diving and unable to dive very deep. Their advantage was using a 533mm (21in) version of the famous "Long Lance" torpedo, by far the best submarine torpedo of the war. Japanese tactics also emphasized attacks on enemy warships and disregarded attacks on supply ships. Though Japanese submarines sank the carriers *Wasp* and *Yorktown* among other successes, their contribution was limited. The largest-sized class was the 2,200-ton I-15 type.

US Navy Types

American fleet submarines were all of high quality. The similar Gato, Balao and Tench classes saw much service. They were all roughly 1,500 tons and well designed, both in terms of radar and sonar equipment, as well as incidentals like air conditioning that helped make long Pacific patrols more comfortable for the crews. Unfortunately, for more than a year after Pearl Harbor, their torpedoes were very poor. When this fault was rectified US submarines practically wiped out the Japanese merchant fleet and sank many of the naval vessels sent to hunt them down.

HMS *TUDOR*

The British T-class submarine *Tudor* was commissioned in 1944 and served against Japan to the end of the war, sinking ten ships. In all, 53 boats of the T class were completed, several of them serving with the Dutch Navy.

Displacement: 1,290 tons surfaced; 1,560 tons submerged
Length: 84.3m (276.5ft)
Surface speed: 15.5 knots
Submerged speed: 9 knots
Armament: 11 x 21in (533mm) torpedo tubes + 1 x 4in (102mm) gun

Below: A U-boat after its surrender in 1945. Note the heavy anti-aircraft armament carried by most U-boats by this time.

Burma, 1943–4

The retreat in Burma in 1942 was the longest in British history, but by mid-1944 the British–Indian Fourteenth Army had inflicted what was then Japan's worst-ever defeat on land in the Battles of Imphal and Kohima.

Japan's aim in attacking Burma in 1942 was to cut the vital Burma Road supply route to China and, in due course, to advance onward to India. British intentions were to defend India and in time recover Burma and later Malaya, while US leaders were less interested in victory in Burma for its own sake than as a means of reopening a supply route to China and the development there of powerful attacks on Japan. In the end, though Japan's advance on India was thrown back in 1944, Burma's position far down the Allied priority list helped ensure neither British nor American plans would come fully to fruition.

Burma's monsoon season made large-scale military operations impossible each year from late May to early November. By later in 1942 Allied forces had been rebuilt sufficiently after the debacle earlier in the year to attempt a modest offensive in the coastal Arakan region. After several months of fighting, the Japanese recaptured most of the ground briefly gained – an outcome which confirmed that they still held the upper hand tactically and psychologically in jungle battle.

Above: Orde Wingate led the Chindits in 1943, but died in 1944 during a second Chindit operation.

Below: A British 25pdr (88mm) gun position in the Burmese jungle.

The Chindits

The only other offensive move possible in that period was an entirely novel "long-range penetration" operation by a force called the Chindits, led by the charismatic (and barely sane) Brigadier Orde Wingate. Supplied from the air, they operated well behind Japanese lines, cutting communications and attacking bases for some weeks before being ordered to return to India. Wingate was lionized by Churchill; he and his men were celebrated in the press as having shown that the Japanese were not invincible in the jungle. Reality was different: a third of the force was lost, hardly any of the survivors were fit for future operations and their attacks achieved nothing.

The real way forward was shown by another series of Arakan battles in late 1943–early 1944. The British advance there was intended as part of a general Allied offensive, while the Japanese planned their own attack as a preliminary to a drive into India in the Imphal area, far inland to the north-east. In the event part of the British force was surrounded for a time, a circumstance that had often led to

Right: Japanese and Indian National Army men during the Imphal campaign.

defeat in the past. Now better-trained, the troops stood their ground (with the benefit of air supply) and simply out-fought the Japanese. Much of this success was down to General Bill Slim, in command of the British forces in Burma, Fourteenth Army, since October 1943.

Imphal and Kohima

A similar pattern emerged on the main inland battle front, after much hard fighting. Under the codename U-Go, the Japanese planned to advance into India with attacks led by General Mutaguchi Renya's Fifteenth Army. Slim and other British commanders expected a Japanese attack but were caught by surprise by the speed of their advance. As a result a small force was surrounded at Kohima and a larger one at Imphal on 4–5 April. Once again the plan was to hold firm with air support until relief troops fought their way through from the north.

The siege of Kohima was broken by late April after a vicious close-quarter battle in and around the town. It took until well into June for the advance to link up with the Imphal garrison and another month before the Japanese finally retreated. While Slim's men had been receiving thousands of tons of supplies and substantial reinforcements by air throughout the battle, the Japanese had been operating on a logistical shoestring; many were now starving. They lost about 60,000 casualties, more than half of them dead, compared to some 17,000 British and Indian killed and wounded.

Below: British troops serving with the 19th Indian Division in action with 3in (76.2mm) mortars near Imphal.

THE INDIAN NATIONAL ARMY

This force, recruited mainly from Indian Army prisoners of war captured in Malaya in 1942, was formed to support the cause of Indian independence by fighting with the Japanese against the British. It had various changes of leaders and organization but from mid-1943 was led by Subhas Chandra Bose and had a maximum strength of about 20,000. It was never fully trusted by the Japanese and was mainly used in small detachments. INA troops fought (but usually not very effectively) in various battles in Burma from early 1944 to the end of the war.

The Battle of Leyte Gulf

The three separate engagements comprising the Battle of Leyte Gulf together make up the largest naval battle in history. Despite their huge superiority, the US forces only just escaped terrible losses to the Leyte invasion fleet.

As the US advance gathered pace in mid-1944, commanders argued about how to attack Japan. General MacArthur felt the Philippines should be recaptured, but US Navy leaders favoured Formosa (now Taiwan) as the next target. In the end, landings on Leyte were planned for 20 October, with the main Philippine island of Luzon to be attacked at the end of the year.

The Japanese Plan

Japan still had many big-gun ships, including the *Yamato* and *Musashi*, the largest battleships ever built. Japan's admirals also wanted an all-out battle in which these ships might turn the tide of the war. The Japanese naval air arm was no longer powerful: it had aircraft carriers but few trained crews or planes. Admiral Toyoda's Sho-Go plan (Operation Victory) called for carriers to divert the main American strength to the north, with most of the heavy ships attacking the vulnerable US landing fleet from the west through various channels between the Philippine Islands.

The US landings on Leyte began on 20 October. The main Japanese force, Force A, sailed from Borneo on the 22nd. US submarines sank two cruisers and reported Force A's move the next day. On 24 October the American carrier *Princeton* was sunk by land-based aircraft.

KEY FACTS

Place: Three separate battles among and near the Philippine Islands

Date: 24–5 October 1944

Outcome: Americans narrowly avoided a disaster to win a major victory.

THE BATTLE OF LEYTE GULF
The Japanese approach and the three Leyte Gulf battles, within the Philippine Islands complex.

Cape Engaño
Carrier Decoy Force
Cape Engaño
PACIFIC OCEAN
Task Force 38
Second Striking Force
9 Jan 1945
Luzon
Mindoro
PHILIPPINE ISLANDS
15 Dec 1944
Masbate
Samar
20 Oct 1944
Samar
US Seventh Fleet
Panay
Leyte
Cebu
Surigao Strait
Negros
Bohol
Force A
28 Feb 1945
Palawan
Force C
Mindanao
Sulu Sea
10 Mar 1945
US naval forces
Japanese forces
Major US landings
Japanese-held at end of war
Major battles
0 100 200 300 mi
0 200 400 km

Above: Admiral Thomas Kinkaid (left) and General Walter Krueger, commander of Sixth Army on Leyte.

Above: The carrier USS *Princeton* on fire and sinking, 24 October.

Force A was attacked by US carrier aircraft in the Sibuyan Sea; the *Musashi* was sunk by bombs and torpedoes. Admiral Kurita Takeo ordered a brief turn away because of these attacks.

Halsey's Mistake

The two main US naval forces were Admiral William Halsey's Third Fleet, including the main carrier force, Task Force 38; and Admiral Thomas Kinkaid's Seventh Fleet of transport and support vessels. Halsey now assumed (incorrectly) that Force A had retreated for good and (correctly) that Kinkaid's shore-bombardment ships could cope with the Japanese southern force. He therefore felt free to take his main force north against the Japanese carriers.

Thus, in the early hours of the 25th, the old battleships of the Seventh Fleet triumphed in a night gun and torpedo battle in the Surigao Strait; two Japanese battleships were among the vessels sunk. Now, after earlier abortive strikes, the Japanese carriers in the north had barely a couple of dozen aircraft left between them to face the ten full-strength carriers of TF 38. Three Japanese carriers and several other ships were sunk during the 25th in the Battle of Cape Engaño.

More would have been sent down but part of the US attack had to be called off by emergency messages from the fleet off Leyte, suddenly facing Force A. This should easily have had the gun-power to brush aside the weak escort carriers and destroyers that stood between it and the virtually defenceless invasion transports.

Instead resolute American defence and a developing fuel shortage persuaded Kurita to turn away feebly after an inconclusive combat, known as the Battle of Samar. The various Japanese forces suffered further losses during their retreats. When all were counted, what might have been an American disaster thus turned into another catastrophe for Japan's fleet.

Below: The destroyer *Akizuki*, sunk during the Battle of Cape Engaño.

KAMIKAZE ATTACKS

By 1944 numerous Japanese garrisons had made desperate suicidal attacks as a last resort but suicide kamikaze attacks, from October 1944, became a deliberate first-choice tactic. The first organized kamikaze attack was on 21 October off Leyte; the cruiser HMAS *Australia* was badly damaged. The first kamikazes used standard fighters, but aircraft fitted with heavy bombs were later employed along with various purpose-built craft, including piloted flying bombs, explosive motor boats, manned torpedoes and midget submarines. Around 500 kamikaze air attacks were made during the Philippine campaign and perhaps 2,000 during the fighting on Okinawa in 1945.

Above: Kamikaze pilots are given their ceremonial headbands.

Naval Bombers and Torpedo Aircraft

An effective air strike by a naval force usually employed a mixture of dive-bombers and torpedo-carrying aircraft. Aircraft in both these roles could be desperately vulnerable to fighters and anti-aircraft fire; casualties were often heavy.

As in other categories of maritime aircraft, the only countries with designs of these types were Britain, Japan and the USA. In 1939 the British aircraft in service were already outdated and later designs were little better. However, for the Japanese, aircraft types that were effective at first – especially when backed by a superior naval fighter – were not adequately replaced when faced with ever stronger and more sophisticated American forces.

The Royal Navy

Britain's main torpedo-bomber in 1939 was the ancient-looking Fairey Swordfish biplane, slow and with a range of only 880km (550 miles) on a full load. Remarkably, fitted with radar and carrying depth charges and rockets, Swordfish were still in use in the anti-submarine role in 1945. By this time the Swordfish's replacement, the biplane Fairey Albacore, had already been retired. The early-war dive-bomber, the monoplane Blackburn Skua, was also poor: slow and with a bomb load of only 226kg (500lb). From 1943 a further Fairey design – the Barracuda (this time finally a monoplane) – entered service. It was more often used as a bomber, though it had been designed as a torpedo aircraft.

Below: Nakajima B5N "Kate" torpedo-bombers in flight over a Japanese fleet base before the war.

American Designs

The US Navy's early-war aircraft were both from the Douglas company. The SBD Dauntless was the dive-bomber. Its crews claimed that its designation stood for "Slow But Deadly". In battles like Midway it was indeed very successful. It was used by some units until 1945. Its early-war companion was the TBD Devastator, which was not so well regarded: slow and under-powered and obviously very vulnerable.

The Dauntless was replaced in front-line carrier service from late 1943 by the Curtiss SB2C Helldiver. This had good performance figures, but also

CURTISS SB2C HELLDIVER

First flown in 1940, the Curtiss Helldiver made its operational debut in an attack on Rabaul in November 1943. In all 7,140 examples were built. It served with several Allied countries through 1945.

Speed: 473kph (294mph)
Range: 1,900km (1,200 miles)
Crew: 2
Engine: 1,900hp Wright R-2600 Cyclone radial
Armament: 900kg (2,000lb) bombs, half in internal bomb bay; 2 x 0.79in (20mm) cannon + 2 x 0.3in (7.62mm) machine-guns

Above: A Douglas Dauntless over New Guinea in 1944. Almost 6,000 of the type were built.

had reliability problems; it was not well liked by its crews. The replacement for the Devastator was more successful.

Designed and originally produced as the TBF by Grumman – and later made by Eastern Aircraft as the TBM – the Avenger was a robust and capable aircraft. Conceived only in 1940, and rushed into action in mid-1942, it served successfully for the remainder of the war. It more often carried bombs or even air-to-ground rockets than the torpedo for which it had been designed.

Japan's Reply

The attack on Pearl Harbor by Japan was carried out by aircraft that became known to the Allies as the "Val" and "Kate". The Aichi D3A "Val" dive-bomber could carry only the relatively modest bomb load of 360kg (800lb) but was surprisingly fast, at 397kph (247mph), for an aircraft with a fixed undercarriage and was credited with particular accuracy when dive-bombing.

It was replaced by the Yokosuka D4Y "Judy", which was produced in a number of sub-types, but none of them was satisfactory. A further Aichi design, the B7A "Grace", was potentially better but it only entered service in 1944.

With the "Val" in 1941 was the Nakajima B5N "Kate". Again it performed well in the early months of war but it, too, dated back to the later 1930s and was due for replacement. The new type, the Nakajima B6N "Jill", arrived only in June 1944. It would have been an effective aircraft, with good range and ordnance-carrying capabilities, but unfortunately the Japanese Navy no longer had any trained pilots and aircraft carriers for it to fly from.

FAIREY SWORDFISH MARK 1

Although it had first flown in 1934, the "Stringbag" was still in widespread use in 1945. It played a vital role in many successful battles, including Taranto and the sinking of the *Bismarck*. In all 2,392 were built.

Speed: 222kph (138mph)
Range: 880km (550 miles)
Crew: 3
Engine: 690hp Bristol Pegasus III radial
Armament: 1 x 18in (457mm) torpedo or 680kg (1,500lb) bombs; 2 x 0.303in (7.7mm) machine-guns

Conquest of the Philippines

When General MacArthur had left the Philippines in 1942, he had pledged: "I shall return." He landed on Leyte to fulfil that pledge in October 1944, but Japanese forces were still holding out on Luzon when the war ended almost a year later.

The planned Allied landings on Leyte in the south-west of the Philippine archipelago were hurriedly brought forward when aircraft carrier attacks suggested that the island might be relatively lightly defended. This proved to be a false hope, but in the end the established pattern of Pacific engagements was repeated, with the American forces gradually wearing down a tough and determined defending force.

The Battle for Leyte

General Walter Krueger's Sixth Army landed some 130,000 troops on the east coast of Leyte on 20 October 1944, the first day of the operation. General MacArthur was also present, dramatically wading ashore from a landing craft (and then typically repeating the process for the benefit of the assembled press cameramen). The initial Japanese force on Leyte was some 20,000 strong but General Yamashita, recently appointed as Japan's top commander in the Philippines, sent some 50,000 reinforcements to the island, though these took significant casualties and lost much equipment in transit.

Above: General MacArthur (in sunglasses) wades ashore on Leyte on his return to the Philippines.

Below: The material strength Japan could never approach. Massed US LSTs land supplies on Leyte.

Although the Japanese Navy was in the end decisively defeated in its attempts to intervene in the Battle of Leyte Gulf, the fighting on land was bitterly contested. Ultimately the Japanese had no answer to the American land and air firepower and organized resistance came to an end by late December. Casualties were as disproportionate as ever – over 60,000 Japanese dead compared to 3,600 Americans.

By then the US Eighth Army, commanded by General Robert Eichelberger, was also involved in the fight, having begun landings on the lightly defended Mindoro Island on the 15th of that month. As usual, they quickly built airfields to support future operations.

Liberating Luzon

General Yamashita had about a quarter of a million men left on Luzon by the end of the year, but inevitably they were greatly dispersed across the island's substantial area and were not well armed or equipped. Therefore, Yamashita decided not to

Above: A US M10 Tank Destroyer in action in the infantry-support role on Leyte in late 1944.

Above: An American casualty is taken for treatment amid the wreckage of Manila, February 1945.

contest in any great strength whatever landing beaches the Americans selected, but rather to retire gradually into the mountainous interior and hold out there for as long as possible.

On 9 January 1945 General MacArthur sent Sixth Army ashore in Lingayen Gulf. Kamikaze and conventional air attacks caused some damage to the landing fleet en route, but soon the few surviving Japanese aircraft were flown out to Formosa (Taiwan) and elsewhere.

Toward Manila

As the Japanese invaders had in 1942, the US forces soon pushed south toward Manila, the capital. Here, in an exception to Yamashita's overall plan, the Japanese forces chose to stand and fight. The battle for Manila lasted for a month, from early February to 3 March. Although MacArthur forbade air attacks, what the artillery bombardments and ground combat did not destroy, the Japanese blew up or set on fire. The city was flattened and about 1,000 Americans and 16,000 Japanese died in the battle along with probably 100,000 local civilians.

Operations on Luzon and elsewhere in the Philippines continued for the rest of the war, with organized Japanese forces gradually being confined in ever smaller and more remote areas. Filipino guerrillas, who had been active to some extent during the Japanese occupation, played an increasingly important role alongside the Americans in these operations. However, Yamashita still had 50,000 men under his command when he surrendered in August.

Right: A battery of 105mm (4.13in) howitzers shelling the Intramuros area of Manila in February 1945.

China's War

China lost more casualties in the war than any other nation apart from the Soviet Union, and the war between China and Japan was the longest of the series of conflicts that made up WWII.

The war in China was not a simple contest between two sides, as it was in most other areas of the conflict. By the late 1930s even as the Chinese Nationalist government of Jiang Jieshi (or Chiang Kai-shek in the then usual English spelling) was being pushed out of large areas of northern and coastal China, it was also coming into conflict with the growing power of the Chinese Communists, who were led by Mao Zedong (Mao Tse-tung).

Internal Struggles

In addition to these forces, and the million and a half Japanese troops in China and Manchuria by late 1941, were the significant armies of the puppet regimes set up by the Japanese and various local groupings of shifting loyalty. After Japan's attack in 1937, there was an official truce between the Nationalists and Communists, but in fact there was continued fighting between their forces at a local level. In the period up to December 1941 China's Communists were also successful in greatly expanding their organization in supposedly Japanese-controlled areas.

Above: Chinese Nationalist troops like these fought in Burma in 1944–5 to open the Ledo Road supply route.

Below: Mao Zedong inspecting men of the Communist Eighth Route Army in Shensi province in 1944.

After Pearl Harbor, the Western Allies hoped, and the USA's leaders believed, that large and efficient Chinese Nationalist armies could be created and would play a major role in defeating Japan. However, for their parts Jiang and Mao were aware of two things: that there would one day be a showdown between them, and that Japan would be defeated by the USA without their aid and forced to leave China. This knowledge governed their conduct throughout the war.

The Communists would be more active in opposing the Japanese: in part for the credit they knew would increase their popularity among the Chinese people; and in part by default because the areas where they were building up their strength were also the areas where the Japanese were most active.

Jiang's position at the head of the Nationalist movement depended on his personal control over the army. Removing corruption and professionalizing it (as his American advisers, led by General Joseph Stilwell, wanted) would have jeopardized this control, so it was not done. Instead of being employed against the Japanese, American supplies were largely used, or held for later use, against the Communists.

By 1941 Japan's advances in China had mostly come to a halt. From then until 1944 the Japanese made few significant forward moves. Although Japan had forces deployed across large swathes of China, they did not actually hold much more than the major cities and the links between them. They fought repeated "anti-bandit" campaigns in the countryside, plundering and destroying as they went. During the war years the Japanese-controlled areas came under increasing Communist influence – most of the "bandits" were in fact Communist guerrillas.

Above: A US C-46 flying supplies on the difficult "Over the Hump" route from India to China.

Japanese Offensives

There was one significant Japanese offensive in 1942 after some of the Doolittle raiders had flown on to China following their attack on Tokyo. Various Chinese and American air bases were captured and in all perhaps a quarter of a million Chinese were killed, a significant proportion of them by biological weapons.

By 1944 the USA had built up its Fourteenth Air Force in China. Its attacks within China (and the first raids on Japan itself that followed) provoked a major Japanese attack, notably in south China – the Ichi-Go Offensive from April that year. The Nationalist forces facing this advance collapsed and the American air bases were easily overrun. The Chinese did regain some ground in the far south in 1945, but by then no one believed that China had much part to play in finally defeating Japan.

Below: Chongqing, the Chinese Nationalists' wartime capital, after a Japanese air attack in May 1939.

Victory in Burma, 1944–5

Fourteenth Army's series of brilliant victories continued from late 1944 to the end of the war. The successes at Meiktila and Mandalay ensured that Burma would be almost completely liberated by May 1945.

Although any Japanese thoughts of invading India had been crushed at Imphal in the first half of 1944, the Allied aims of opening a road to China and recovering Burma were still to be fulfilled. British, Indian and other British Empire troops of Fourteenth Army would make the main advance into central Burma, as well as a secondary move along the coast. At the same time a combination of Chinese, American and British troops fought farther north and inland to create the land supply route to China.

The Ledo Road

US leaders, including General Joseph Stilwell (the USA's top soldier in China until October 1944) believed that the Chinese Nationalists could play a major role in defeating Japan, if only they could be adequately equipped by the Allies. Although great efforts had been made to fly supplies "Over the Hump" of the mountain ranges between India and China, truly significant quantities could only be delivered by land.

The route chosen started at Ledo, the north-eastern end of India's rail system, and then ran southward into Japanese-held territory to link with the old Burma Road, which had supplied China before Pearl Harbor. Construction began in late 1942, accompanied by advances to clear the Japanese out of the way. The road was finally opened in January 1945.

Below: British infantrymen watch Indian Army Sherman tanks approaching Meiktila, March 1945.

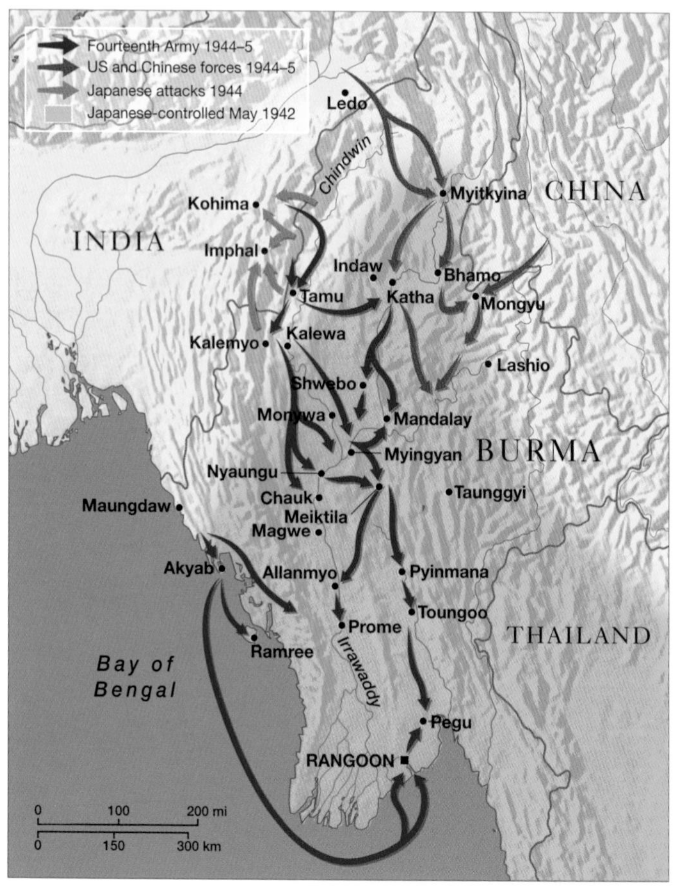

BURMA CAMPAIGN, 1943–5

Japan's defeats at Imphal and Kohima and the Allied offensive to liberate Burma.

Above: British troops crossing the River Chindwin at the start of their advance in late 1944.

The main battles in this sector were fought from late 1943 to August 1944, with the fighting being especially fierce around the town of Myitkyina. The Allied forces involved included the so-called Chinese Army in India, an American formation known as Merrill's Marauders and a second Chindit expedition that was much larger than the first.

Slim's Masterpiece

British leaders had a far more jaundiced (and as it turned out more realistic) view of what the Chinese Nationalists might contribute to the Allied war effort, preferring instead to advance in central Burma and plan seaborne operations farther south later.

Although the Japanese had substantially rebuilt their forces in Burma after the Imphal disaster, they were now clearly outmatched. The men of Fourteenth Army described themselves as the "forgotten army" because of their position far from home and well down the Allied priority list. However, they were in no doubt that the quality of their training, tactics and weaponry made them more than the equal of the Japanese in combat. They also had lavish air support and, above all, in General Slim, a resourceful and totally trusted commander.

When the advance began in late 1944, a deception scheme helped convince the Japanese that Mandalay (the traditional capital of Burma) was the Allied target. Instead General Slim's main plan was to capture the vital communications centre of Meiktila to the south, which was taken in early March. The force at Meiktila was isolated for several weeks by Japanese counter-attacks, but by late March these had been defeated – and the relentless pressure from other parts of Fourteenth Army had also taken Mandalay.

The Japanese were now in all-out retreat, though still capable of fighting tough rear-guard actions on occasion. With the monsoon season fast approaching, a seaborne attack on Rangoon was sent in. This took the city (which had been evacuated by the Japanese) shortly before Fourteenth Army arrived from the north.

The Japanese troops defending the coastal region were now cut off and trying to escape to the east. In the last fighting of the campaign before Japan finally surrendered, thousands of these men were killed at the cost of little more than a handful of Allied casualties.

GENERAL WILLIAM SLIM

Slim (1891–1970) was the principal British general in Burma for most of the war. After holding junior commands in East Africa and Syria in 1940–1, Slim came to Burma in April 1942 when the great retreat was already well under way. He took over the newly formed Fourteenth Army in October 1943 and led it with great skill until the end of the war. Unusually for a top commander, he was a modest man. He was greatly liked and respected by those he led, who called him "Uncle Bill".

Above: General Slim in characteristic resolute pose.

Transport Aircraft and Gliders

Air supply operations on an entirely new scale were possible in WWII, in Burma and China and many other places. Mass airborne operations also began, using aircraft and gliders to bring thousands of troops suddenly into action.

World War II was the first conflict in which air transport played a significant role. It was also the first in which airborne warfare, using parachute and glider-borne troops, was employed in major battles.

Transport Aircraft

The best-known transport aircraft of the early-war years was Germany's Junkers 52. Dating back to the early 1930s and with an unusual three-engined configuration, the Ju 52 had modest flight performance and could carry 18 fully armed troops. It dropped paratroops and towed gliders in Germany's early campaigns, but was less successful as a cargo carrier ferrying supplies to the surrounded Sixth Army at Stalingrad.

Above: A flight of Horsa gliders being towed aloft (by converted Whitley bombers) in training in 1943.

Germany also had the huge six-engined Messerschmitt 323, converted from a glider. It could carry an unequalled 21 tonnes of cargo but was very slow and vulnerable to fighter attack.

Britain depended mainly on American designs for its transport aircraft but did employ some converted heavy bombers in the role. Whitleys, Stirlings and Halifaxes all towed gliders and dropped paratroops; Avro York conversions of the Lancaster could carry 10 tonnes of cargo. The Armstrong Whitworth Albemarle, originally intended as a bomber, saw most service as a glider tug.

The USA made far more use of transport aircraft than any other nation, as well as supplying

Below: A Ju 52 on a Russian airfield, 1941–2. Ju 52s supplied many surrounded troops that winter but failed to repeat the feat in 1942–3.

many of these to all the Allies. The oldest design, based on the Douglas DC-3 airliner of the mid-1930s, served as the C-47 Skytrain (or Dakota in British service). Over 10,000 were made and served in all transport roles in all theatres (when configured to carry paratroops they were officially known as C-53 Skytroopers).

Serving mainly against Japan was a second twin-engined design, the Curtiss C-46 Commando. Though it was faster and could carry much more cargo than the C-47, only about 3,300 were made. Most served on the notoriously demanding "Over the Hump" supply route to China. Finally, the US had the four-engined C-54 Skymaster, based on the pre-war Douglas DC-4 airliner. This could carry up to 50 personnel or an equivalent cargo and mainly operated to and from bases in the USA.

Above: US paratroops embark in a C-53 Skytrooper. A typical load was 15–18 troops and their equipment.

C-54 SKYMASTER

The C-54 was developed from the pre-war Douglas DC-4 airliner, first flown in 1938. The first C-54 entered service in 1942 and in all 1,170 were built. It also served with the US Navy as the R5D and with various Allied countries. A number of C-54s were used for VIP transport, including one by President Roosevelt.

Engines: 4 x 1,450hp Pratt & Whitney R-2000 Cyclone radials
Cruising speed: 310kph (190mph)
Range: 6,400km (4,000 miles)
Crew: 4
Capacity: 50 passengers or equivalent cargo

Gliders

Even if at first glance they might seem dangerously unsuited to military uses, gliders had valuable attributes that helped them see much effective war service. They could carry significant numbers of troops into action and land each planeload in a concentrated group (paratroops might be scattered far and wide); they flew silently and could land very accurately beside, or even on top of, an objective (as was done by the Germans at Eben Emael in 1940 and by various British units on D-Day); and the troops they carried did not need to be carefully selected or given specialized parachute training. Countries using significant numbers of gliders were Britain, Germany and the USA.

Germany's main glider was the DFS 230. It could carry ten men, including the pilot. (Glider pilots in all nations were usually expected to get out and fight after landing.) Larger types included the Gotha 242 and the Me 321 Gigant, parent design of the Me 323 described above. The Gigant needed three Me 110s or a specially adapted Heinkel 111 to tow it aloft, so it was not a success.

British gliders included the Airspeed Horsa, which could carry 30 men or an anti-tank gun or similar cargo, and the much larger General Aircraft Hamilcar, which could lift a light tank. The main American glider (over 12,000 built) was the CG-4A Waco, which could carry 15 men or an equivalent cargo. British and American gliders played a vital part in the invasions of Sicily and Normandy and other major airborne operations.

Iwo Jima and Okinawa

The landings on these two islands were the last major operations planned before the invasion of the main parts of the Japanese homeland. Despite their disparity in size and terrain, both saw ferocious battles before the American forces gained control.

By 1945 American planners were clear that winning the war depended on taking bases from which the invasion of Japan could be mounted and supported. Iwo Jima offered airfields within fighter range of Tokyo; Okinawa had base and harbour areas suitable for supporting the vast force needed for the final invasion operations.

Iwo Jima

No more than a dot on the map of the Pacific, closer up Iwo Jima island is pear-shaped, 8km (5 miles) long and a maximum of 3km (2 miles) wide. In 1945 it had three airstrips but was mostly barren volcanic rock, with a 150m (500ft) extinct volcano, Mount Suribachi, at the southern end. In 1945 it was also perhaps the most heavily fortified area in the history of warfare, with a garrison of 21,000 men under General Kuribayashi Tadamichi, prepared to defend it to the last.

Kuribayashi's defences survived the extensive preliminary air and sea bombardment – he planned to let the attackers land before opening fire and revealing his positions. The landings began on 19 February with some 30,000 US Marines of V Amphibious Corps going ashore on the first day. Soon the Marines were being hit from all directions from the complex of trenches, tunnels and other strong points, which riddled the island. The result of the fighting was never in doubt, but the battle was vicious and bloody.

KEY FACTS - OKINAWA

Place: Okinawa, Ryukyu Islands

Date: 1 April–21 June 1945

Outcome: US forces captured a final base for the invasion of Japan after very heavy casualties on both sides.

THE CAPTURE OF OKINAWA
The Japanese forces chose to defend only the south of the island in strength.

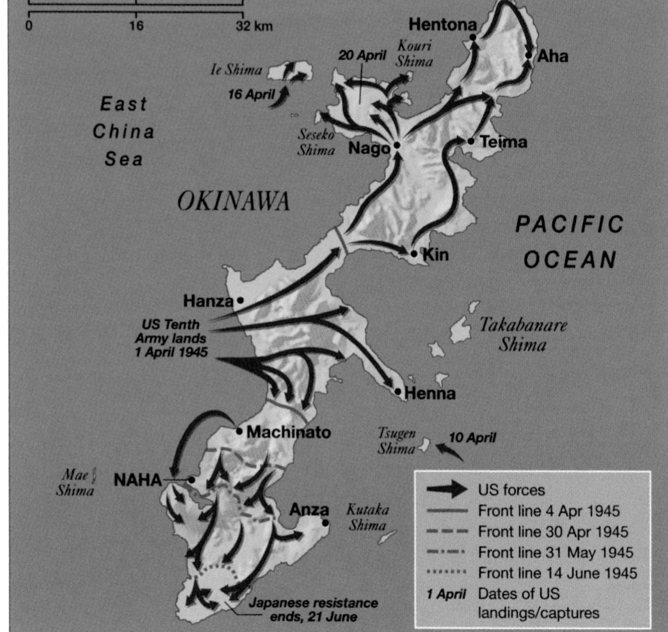

Above: A rocket-armed landing ship – LSM(R) – bombarding the Okinawa beaches, 1 April 1945.

Right: Smoke rises above Iwo Jima as US Marine amphibians approach the shore.

It took until 26 March to wipe out the defenders and cost the Marines almost 6,000 dead and over 17,000 wounded. By then, however, P-51 Mustang fighters were already operating from the island and its airfields were also providing emergency landing grounds for the B-29 force flying from the Marianas.

Okinawa

The next target was a different and much bigger proposition. Although Okinawa is 560km (350 miles) from the nearest of the main Japanese Home Islands, it is part of "mainland" Japan (as is Iwo Jima). It would therefore be fiercely defended.

The Thirty-second Army defending the island, under the command of General Ushijima Mitsuru, was 120,000 strong. He had no intention of fighting on the beaches, for he had too much respect for American firepower. Instead he concentrated his troops in a relatively small but heavily fortified area of the south of the island, where the broken terrain would aid the defence in every way.

In all some half a million US troops and over 1,200 warships (including a significant British contingent) took part in the attack on Okinawa and various smaller islands nearby.

The naval forces suffered a blizzard of kamikaze attacks that sunk or damaged over 400 ships but never seriously disrupted Allied plans. The giant battleship *Yamato* was used as a suicide vessel, sailing from Japan with only enough fuel to reach Okinawa – it was sent to the bottom by air attacks on 7 April before it even came close.

The American landings had begun on 1 April and overran the northern three-quarters of the island by the middle of the month with relative ease. By then much harder fighting had started on the so-called Shuri Line to the south. It took two more months of vicious close-quarter battle before Japanese resistance ceased.

Below: A kamikaze about to strike (and lightly damage) the battleship *Missouri* off Okinawa, 17 April 1945.

The US forces lost 12,500 dead on land and at sea and 35,000 wounded – frightening totals, considering the much bigger task of invading Japan itself that was in prospect.

However, the cost on the Japanese side was immense. Almost all the garrison troops were killed, as well as numerous civilians. Many more civilians committed suicide. As a final horror, among these were hundreds of children killed by their parents, who did not want them to suffer the brutalities that they had been told the Americans would commit.

Above: American troops riding up to the battlefront aboard a Sherman tank, Okinawa, 5 May 1945.

Destroyers

Destroyers were multi-purpose warships, fast and deadly hunters of surface ships and submarines with their torpedo and depth-charge armament. They served in their hundreds and saw combat after combat in every theatre of war.

Destroyers were invented to protect battlefleets from torpedo attack, and to carry out such attacks themselves. These essentially remained their main functions in WWII, though by then of course torpedo attack could come from submarines as well as surface craft.

Destroyers of WWII were generally 1,500–2,000 tons displacement and typically carried 4–6 main guns of 127mm (5in) or similar calibre and 8–10 torpedo tubes (TT), and had a top speed of about 35 knots. All also carried depth-charge equipment and a number of lighter anti-aircraft guns. More of both these types of weapon generally were added as the war progressed, along with new and improved varieties of radar and sonar equipment. Britain, the USA and Japan each began the war with over 100 destroyers in service, built many more in the course of the conflict – and each lost more than 100 in combat.

European Designs

Among European navies Britain built relatively small destroyers in the inter-war years. Known as the A to I classes (a class of nine or so was built yearly during the 1930s), these 1,400-ton ships carried 4 x 4.7in (119mm) guns and 8 or 10 TT. However, the 4.7in gun could not be used for AA defence, so these ships were poorly equipped to withstand air attack. Britain also had the larger Tribal class with 8 x 4.7in guns and a reduced torpedo armament. Both France and Italy built some extremely large destroyers, including the Fantasque and Navigatori classes; these were large and very fast ships but paid a price in seaworthiness and reliability.

HMAS *NESTOR*

Built in Britain and commissioned in 1941, the *Nestor* served in the *Bismarck* chase and was sunk during a Malta convoy operation in June 1942. *Nestor* was one of 24 similar J, K and N class ships built for the British and Allied navies, 1937–42. Although an Australian Navy ship, *Nestor* never visited Australia.

Displacement: 1,770 tons standard, 2,300 tons full load
Crew: 180
Speed: 36 knots
Range: 5,500nm (10,200km) at 15 knots (27.8kph)
Length: 111.4m (356.5ft)
Beam: 10.9m (35.75ft)
Armament: 6 x 4.7in (119mm) guns + 5 x 21in (533 mm) TT; 1 x 4in (102mm) AA gun + numerous light AA weapons

Left: The Kagero-class *Yukikaze*, pictured in January 1940. *Yukikaze* was the only one of the 19 ships in the class to survive the war.

Above: USS *Fletcher* in July 1942. The 177-ship Fletcher class was the most numerous destroyer type ever.

Above: The German destroyer *Z14* or *Friedrich Ihn* pictured in 1942, one of 12 ships of the 1934A class.

Germany's pre-war and wartime ships were a mix of larger vessels classed as "destroyers" and smaller "torpedo boats". Destroyer or *Zerstörer* types were typically 2,400 tons, with 5 x 12.7cm (5in) guns. British wartime destroyers, in lettered classes up to W, were generally slightly larger than their predecessors, with better AA capability. Some had 4in (102mm) AA guns as main armament instead of the 4.7in weapons.

Pacific Navies

Japan and the USA favoured slightly larger ships than the British for their pre-war classes and had the advantage of having suitable dual-purpose (DP) surface/AA gun mounts with which to arm them. Japan also had the 610mm (24in) "Long Lance" torpedo, far superior to anything in Allied service. In addition the Japanese fitted their ships with torpedo reloading equipment that could be used in action, allowing multiple attacks to be carried out.

Japan's Fubuki class (24 completed by 1932) were the most powerful destroyers in the world when built (1,800 tons, 6 x 127mm, 9 TT); they proved too flimsy so were extensively rebuilt early in their service. Another notable class was the 2,000-ton Kagero type with similar armament to the Fubukis.

The US Navy had the best DP main gun: the 5in/38-calibre Mark 12, fitted in most US destroyers from the Farragut class (1934, 1,400 tons, 5 x 5in, 8 TT) onward. The Porter class of 1936–7 was larger (1,850 tons, 8 x 5in), in an attempt to match the big Japanese designs, but these destroyers had stability and seaworthiness problems.

However, US Navy classes built during the war years were the best destroyers of the time. The Fletcher class (2,100 tons, 5 x 5in, 10 TT, 35 knots) had an excellent balance of firepower, stability and speed, and the capacity to fit additional AA guns and other equipment shown to be necessary by wartime experience. The later Allen M. Sumner and Gearing classes were slightly bigger but generally similar, with the exception that the Fletchers' five single 5in mounts were replaced by three twin turrets.

Right: The USS *Wilson*, one of ten Benham-class destroyers of the US Navy, seen in January 1941.

Weapons of Mass Destruction

Although thousands had died from the effects of poison gas in WWI and cities were razed to the ground by conventional bombing attacks in WWII, the atomic, chemical and biological weapons developed by 1945 were a new and more terrible threat.

By the late 1930s scientists were familiar with the idea that chain reactions might be created in certain elements to give off vast amounts of energy that could conceivably be used in some type of bomb.

Scientists in Japan and the USSR were among those who realized this possibility, but neither of those countries pursued the idea at that stage – and American research was not then extensive.

Britain, however, took things further. Rudolph Peierls and Otto Frisch, Jewish refugees from the Nazis, made the breakthrough; they calculated that a relatively small quantity of the rare uranium 235 isotope would be needed for a bomb. (Ironically, the two were only working in this field because they were not yet fully trusted to join native British scientists in "more vital" electronics and radar research.) Other scientists, in Britain and the USA, also worked out a second method of "bomb-making". This involved the creation of a new element – plutonium – from the common uranium 238 isotope.

Above: General Leslie Groves (right) and J. R. Oppenheimer, respectively military head and chief scientist of the Manhattan Project.

The First A-Bombs

British developments were shared with the Americans, who began more serious work in late 1941. This soon developed into the huge Manhattan Project, to which the British scientists were transferred. By early 1945 both U235 and plutonium were being produced in sufficient quantities and two designs of bomb were being finalized.

On 16 July 1945 a plutonium device was exploded in a test at Alamogordo, New Mexico. Its yield was calculated as equivalent to at least 15,000 tonnes of TNT; the explosion was visible and audible up to 275km (170 miles) away. The bomb dropped on Nagasaki, known as "Fat Man", was a second plutonium weapon. The Hiroshima device, "Little Boy", was based on the U235 isotope.

Although the greatest motivation in starting the research was to forestall German development of similar weapons, US leaders soon realized that the unprecedented power of atomic weapons could transform international affairs. Ideas that Japan be given a demonstration of the bomb's power before it was used were never taken seriously. With Allied lives at stake, there was never any question that the bomb would be used in action as soon as possible.

Gases and Poisons

WWII also saw developments in chemical and biological warfare. Fortunately such weapons were little used, mainly from fear that any use would bring equivalent retaliation and therefore gain nothing. However, it was a great relief to Allied

Below: The two atomic bombs used against Japan in 1945. "Little Boy" dropped on Hiroshima (right), and "Fat Man", the Nagasaki weapon (left).

Above: "Be prepared to ward off chemical weapons" – a Soviet poster from WWII.

HEAVY WATER

One method of making plutonium used so-called "heavy water" (a compound featuring the hydrogen isotope deuterium), for which the best source under German control was a hydroelectric plant at Rjukan in Norway. British and Norwegian special forces sabotaged the plant in 1943 and in 1944 prevented its production reaching Germany. By then, unknown to the Allies, Germany's atomic research had been effectively abandoned because the amount of U235 needed for a bomb had been miscalculated.

leaders that Germany's V-weapons had only conventional explosive warheads.

All nations took precautions against the use of poison gas, as they had in WWI. Gas masks were issued to troops and civilians; generally stocks of WWI gases like mustard gas and phosgene were ready for retaliatory use. Italy employed mustard gas in its conquest of Abyssinia, but such weapons were not used otherwise in WWII. Germany alone developed nerve gases – tabun and sarin – but did not deploy them. This research fell into Soviet hands in 1945.

Several countries experimented with biological agents and produced weapons to use them, though Hitler forbade such research in Germany. Both Britain and the USA had anthrax and botulin weapons ready by the end of the war, but only Japan used weapons of this type. The Japanese researchers (known as Unit 731 and commanded by General Ishii Shiro) killed many hundreds of Chinese prisoners of war in experiments in this field. They made successful attempts to spread diseases like cholera, typhoid and plague against the Chinese forces, notably in 1942 in Kiangsi province.

Above: Governments took the threat of chemical attack seriously as this 1943 British exercise shows.

Ishii and his team were captured by the Americans in 1945 and given immunity from prosecution in return for information about their research.

The Japanese Surrender

Japan had already suffered greatly by August 1945, but then came a succession of hammer blows: the atomic attacks on Hiroshima and Nagasaki and the Soviet declaration of war and subsequent crushing land offensive in Manchuria.

Ever since the Casablanca Conference in January 1943 the official Anglo-American policy was to seek the unconditional surrender of Japan. At that mid-war period, facing the prospect of a longer struggle to close in on Japan than in fact transpired, both the USA and Britain were keen to persuade the Soviets to join the war in the Far East. With offers of territorial and other concessions, Stalin duly promised at the Teheran Conference in late 1943 to declare war on Japan shortly after the war in Europe had been won.

When the Allied leaders met again at Potsdam in July 1945 much had changed: Hitler was dead in the ruins of nearby Berlin; Japan was far nearer to defeat in a shorter time than had once seemed possible; and on the day before the conference started, the world's first nuclear bomb was tested in New Mexico. News of its power was rushed to the new US President Harry Truman and the British leaders at Potsdam.

Above: The distinctive atomic mushroom cloud forms above the devastated city of Nagasaki.

Below: The centre of Hiroshima. Only a few stoutly constructed buildings still stand after the attack.

The Japanese government had already begun making peace feelers through its embassy in Moscow but it was clear from these that they wanted guarantees that Emperor Hirohito's position would not be at risk. The Allies could not accept this, feeling that to do so might be taken as a sign of weakness, which would encourage prolonged resistance.

Instead they issued the "Potsdam Declaration", which mentioned nothing about the Emperor but merely repeated the demand for unconditional surrender, threatening unspecfied "utter destruction" if the demand was not met. In the meantime Stalin was officially told (though he already knew through his spies) that the USA had a new and powerful weapon ready for use against Japan and confirmed that he would soon be ready to attack Japan.

When the Japanese Prime Minister, Admiral Suzuki Kantaro, replied publicly to the declaration he said he would not comment on it for the moment; but he was misunderstood as saying that Japan would ignore it. With that Truman gave the order for the bomb to be used.

Atomic Attacks

The first atomic bomb was dropped on Hiroshima on the morning of 6 August 1945 by a B-29 bomber flown from the island of Tinian. The bomb killed about 80,000 people more or less instantly; an estimated 50,000 more died from its short- and long-term radiation effects.

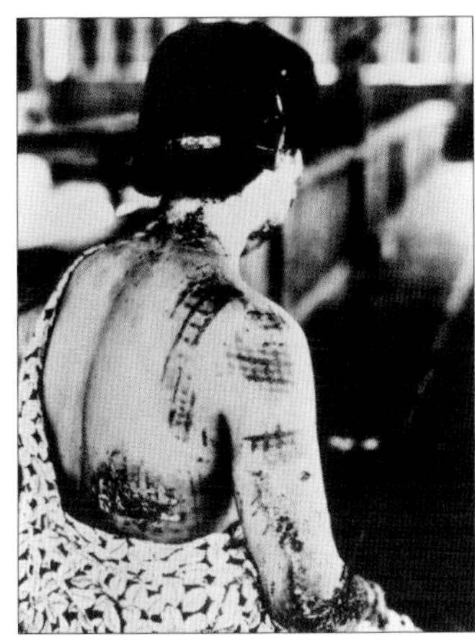

Above: Many of the survivors, like this woman from Hiroshima, suffered terrible burns in the atomic attacks.

Nagasaki suffered a similar fate, but with slightly fewer casualties, on 9 August.

There is no doubt that Truman's decision to use the bomb was made in large part in the hope that it would spare lives by making Japan surrender. However, the historical record is also clear that part of the motive was to intimidate the Soviets and lay down a marker for the post-war world.

The Soviets issued their promised declaration of war on the 8th and their forces crashed across the border into Japanese-held Manchuria the next day. Japan's supposedly elite Kwantung Army, outnumbered and outmatched in every category of weaponry, simply fell apart. Manchuria and northern Korea were overrun within days.

The Surrender

Emperor Hirohito now intervened to tell the diehard militarists in his government that the war must be ended. To the last there was the same dithering and failure to face facts at the heart of Japan's government as had helped get Japan into the mess in the first place. This was epitomized in Hirohito's broadcast to his people in which he blandly stated that "the war situation has developed not necessarily to Japan's advantage".

Even so that same day, 15 August, was celebrated by the Allies as VJ-Day. Japan's formal surrender was signed on the US battleship *Missouri* in Tokyo Bay on 2 September.

Below: General MacArthur, backed by a row of Allied representatives, at the surrender ceremony.

INVASION OF JAPAN

The planned Allied invasion of Japan would have been the largest landing operation in history. Two phases were intended: Operation Olympic against the island of Kyushu in November 1945, and, using bases gained there, Operation Coronet, the final decisive attack on the Kanto Plain on Honshu, near Tokyo, scheduled for March 1946. Casualty estimates varied widely, but typical figures were 400,000 Allied dead (including significant British Empire forces, not just Americans) and more than ten times that number of Japanese.

New Nations Refugees at Amritsar in the last days of pre-independence India.

Dealing with the Defeated Leading Nazis in the dock during the Nuremberg trials.

The Cold War American transport aircraft unloading supplies in Berlin during the Airlift in 1948.

THE LEGACY OF WAR

No one claimed in 1945 that World War II would become the "war to end all wars", but it did establish that any future war would have different causes. The expansionist militarism that had characterized both Germany and Japan since the early years of the 20th century was discredited for good in the eyes of most German and Japanese people, as was the murderous racism that accompanied it.

For a time after 1945 it also seemed that the US atomic monopoly (in the event lasting only until 1949) would deter attacks on the USA and its friends. However, the mutual suspicions between the USSR and the Western Allies (some of them justified, some not) brought the increasing tension and competition of the Cold War. Although the Cold War itself did not outlast the century, its legacy remains important in the new millennium.

Many of the more controversial methods employed in modern conflicts can trace their history directly to WWII. The resistance movements and similar organizations of the war used tactics familiar 60 years on to freedom fighters and terrorists and, for all their precision weapons, 21st-century air forces still bomb civilians as regularly and with as little scruple as their forebears did.

Dealing with the Defeated Temporary housing being built amid the devastation of Hiroshima.

The Cold War President Truman signs the NATO treaty, committing the USA to the defence of Europe.

Europe Divided German civilians trying desperately to gather coal for fuel on a mine spoil heap.

Casualties and Destruction

World War II was the most brutal conflict in human history, with a death toll several times that of any previous war. Death came to civilians far from the front line, as it did to soldiers, with a dreadful thoroughness never before contemplated.

The human cost of WWII was truly enormous but is still impossible to measure exactly. Even in the early 21st century, when most records have been opened to historical study and most of the bitterness associated with the war has long subsided, no one has been able to calculate exact figures, nor ever will be. The lowest figure that is at all plausible is some 40 million dead, but other estimates go as high as 55 million. Also on top of that huge figure were probably three times as many wounded, of whom many would have to live with pain and disability for the remainder of their lives. And as well as these were the many more still, who were emotionally scarred by their experiences or the loss of loved ones. The weight of suffering was immense.

Harrowing Toll

There is no question that the losses of the Soviet Union were the greatest of all and that the Eastern Front was the theatre in which the fighting was the largest in scale and the least restrained by moral limitations. The Soviet armed forces lost at least 10 million killed, including a large proportion who died of ill-treatment as prisoners in German hands and many who, once liberated from German captivity or returned to Soviet control by the Western Allies, were sent straight to the gulag. Soviet civilian deaths amounted to 10 million or more, the largest proportion of these being murdered by Stalin's regime.

Above: A memorial to the children of the Czech village of Lidice, destroyed by the Nazis in 1942.

Dominating the list of European civilian casualties are the 6 million Jews murdered by the Nazis, who came all too close to their objective of making Europe Jew-free – only around 300,000 Jews from areas that had been Nazi-controlled survived the war.

The country second on the list after the USSR is China, another for which any exact reckoning is impossible. Common estimates are in the range of 10–15 million, of whom 2–3 million were fighters in one or other of the armies.

The major Axis powers both fared badly, though in each case military casualties predominated over civilian. Perhaps 4.5 million German soldiers died and another 2 million civilians. Japan's total casualties were about 2 million. Poland and Yugoslavia both suffered particularly severely. Poland lost some 4–4.5 million, more than half of them Jews, and Yugoslavia over 1.5 million in the country's vicious resistance and civil-war struggle.

Of the major Allied powers, Britain lost some 350,000 dead, considerably fewer than in WWI, and the countries of the British Empire an additional 120,000. In proportion to its population the losses of the USA were by far the lowest of any

Left: A memorial at the former Dachau concentration camp near Munich, one of the first to be set up.

major combatant: approximately 275,000, of whom all but a handful were military personnel.

In addition to the millions killed or injured were the millions more who ended the war as refugees. Even if they did have homes to return to, many had no wish to do this because wartime events or subsequent political changes meant they would be in danger or unwelcome. There may have been as many as 30 million "displaced persons" (as they were known) in Europe at the end of the war and millions more in China.

Physical Destruction

As well as the human cost of the war the scale of physical damage was stunning. Even in Britain, which was comparatively lightly bombed and saw no land fighting, hundreds of thousands of homes suffered war damage. In Germany and Japan whole cities were virtually demolished by Allied bombing. In the western USSR roughly two-thirds of the homes, factories and other resources were destroyed in the fighting or by the scorched-earth policies applied in retreat, first by the Soviets themselves and later by the Germans.

Above: The British War Graves Commission cemetery at El Alamein, seen shortly after the war.

Left: A British soldier returns to his family, in their new "prefab" home, after a four-year absence.

Right: Displaced persons crowding a train in Berlin in June 1945.

Dealing with the Defeated

Unlike in WWI, when the Allies only occupied part of Germany, in 1945 both Germany and Japan were occupied and administered by the Allied powers. International tribunals also tried and punished war criminals in both countries.

At the Casablanca Conference in January 1943 President Roosevelt had declared (and Prime Minister Churchill agreed) that the Allies would seek the unconditional surrender of Germany and Japan. Later in 1943 Britain, the USA and the USSR established the European Advisory Commission to draw up surrender terms for Germany and to work out occupation arrangements for Germany (and Austria, which the Allies decided should be separated from Germany again) and the minor Axis powers. These plans were eventually agreed by the heads of government at the Yalta and Potsdam conferences in 1945.

Allied Control Commissions were set up to run the occupied Axis countries. In the case of Germany this meant that the country was to be divided into four occupation zones – one each for the USA, UK, USSR and France – and Berlin would also be similarly divided.

Above: July 1945, a typical Berlin street scene. Locals trudge past the rubble with their few belongings.

Various plans for Japan were considered, including versions with the country divided into Allied zones. Instead, when the time came, General MacArthur was appointed Allied Supreme Commander for the occupation. All of Japan's main islands came under American control, with MacArthur acting almost as a ruling monarch. The Soviets occupied (and would retain as Soviet territory) the Kurile Islands and the southern half of Sakhalin, while the occupation forces of the main Japanese islands included a British Empire contingent.

Punishing the Guilty

In 1943 the Allies had also announced their intention to punish Nazi war criminals. In the Potsdam declaration in 1945 the process was extended to include Japanese leaders. This resulted in two sets of major international war crimes trials, at Nuremberg and Tokyo, in which some of the most senior figures were tried. In the end 22 Germans and 25 Japanese were tried (indictments in both trials named others who died, were judged unfit to plead or committed suicide). There were also numerous trials conducted by the individual Allied powers of those accused of crimes affecting only one Allied nation.

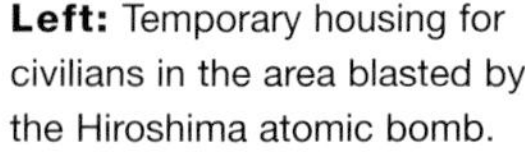

Left: Temporary housing for civilians in the area blasted by the Hiroshima atomic bomb.

The charges at the major trials included two new concepts in international law, crimes against peace and crimes against humanity, as well as the better-established concept of war crimes in breach of previous internationally agreed standards regarding such things as treatment of prisoners of war. There were three outright acquittals at Nuremberg but none at Tokyo, though some defendants were found not guilty on some of the charges brought against them. Punishments included 19 death sentences and various long terms of imprisonment.

VICTORS' JUSTICE?

Some aspects of the trials were unsatisfactory. Certainly there was an element of victors' justice – for example, Stalin was just as guilty for his invasion of Poland in 1939 and the subsequent murders of thousands of Poles as any of the Nazis. And a truly impartial court might well have considered the Anglo-American strategic bombing campaigns as war crimes.

Above: General Tojo, Japan's Prime Minister for most of the war, was executed after the Tokyo trials.

In the Japanese case the defendants were selected and the prosecution evidence slanted so that Emperor Hirohito and his family were left untainted, because this suited the Allied occupation policies.

Although there has been much discussion since about the legality and fairness of the proceedings, they definitely established the principle that national leaders can be brought to account before the international community and that soldiers everywhere have a duty to disobey unlawful orders. And the evidence at Nuremberg proved beyond all doubt that the Nazis did murder some 6 million Jews among much else, however much some have since tried to deny this. Whatever flaws there may have been, these were valuable precedents.

Below: Top Nazis in the dock at the Nuremberg trials. Hermann Göring (front left) was the most senior figure to stand trial.

Europe Divided

In a famous speech in 1946 Winston Churchill described how Europe had been divided by an Iron Curtain. The suspicions that had hindered the wartime alliance between Britain, the USA and USSR were hardening into something more serious.

Although the war ended in 1945 with Western and Soviet troops in control of respective halves of Europe, very few would have expected this to be a long-lasting state of affairs. Indeed the leading Allied powers, including the Soviets, had issued the so-called Declaration on Liberated Europe at the Yalta Conference in early 1945. This stated that they intended to see democratic governments and free elections in countries they had liberated from German control.

Western Europe

There was never any question that these pledges would be fulfilled in Western Europe. The Allied powers had backed governments-in-exile of all these countries during the war. The removal of the Germans in 1944–5 was followed shortly after by elections. Local communist parties, which had been prominent in the resistance movements to the German occupation, participated fully in these elections and, notably in France and Italy, won a significant number of votes.

It was clear that conditions in Eastern Europe would be different. Even as the Yalta Conference was taking place, the Soviets were already working to ensure that communists would take control in Bulgaria and in March 1945 they set up a communist government in Romania.

Above: Germans searching through the spoil from a coal mine in a desperate hunt for scarce fuel.

Below: Czech politician Jan Masaryk died in suspicious circumstances after the communist takeover in 1948.

THE UNITED NATIONS

The history of the United Nations (UN) dates to the Four Power Declaration (by the USA, UK, USSR and China) in October 1943 that they intended to establish an international organization after the war to maintain "international peace and security". After further discussions the UN was established by the San Francisco Conference in 1945, attended by delegates from 50 countries. Even at that early stage there were problems. Poland was not represented because the USA and USSR did not agree about the composition of a legitimate Polish government.

Right: A US atomic test at Bikini Atoll, 1946. Old warships are placed nearby to assess the blast's power.

Britain (and later the USA) had supported a Polish government-in-exile in London from the early stages of the war but, as the Red Army advanced in 1944, the Soviets put forward an alternative communist group, which they recognized at the end of the year as the provisional government. Some of the "London Poles" did return home in 1945, but they had been removed from government and all opposition silenced by early 1947. During 1947–8 there were further communist takeovers in Hungary and Czechoslovakia.

Opposing Communism

Concerns over these developments and disagreements about how to deal with Germany soon provoked changes on the Anglo-American side. At the start of 1946 President Truman spoke about the need to "get tough with Russia" and other senior figures urged that the USA adopt a policy of "firm and vigilant containment of Russian expansionist tendencies". Winston Churchill's "Iron Curtain" speech followed shortly after and, though he was by then an ex-prime minister, the British government agreed with him.

Since the end of WWII Britain had been helping the Greek government to combat a communist-led civil war, but in early 1947 Britain, in dire economic trouble, told the USA that it could no longer afford to do so.

Stalin had kept his wartime promise not to interfere in Greece and such external aid as the Greek communists were receiving came from Yugoslavia, which was not at all the same thing as saying it came from Moscow. But this was not clearly understood then in the West.

Instead the USA agreed to take over Britain's role in Greece and also to help Turkey. This policy was summed up in March 1947 by President Truman's promise to "support free peoples" resisting subversion. This was the start of what became known as the Truman Doctrine.

Europe's economies as a whole were still suffering from the destruction of the war years and the particularly severe winter of 1946–7 had not helped. In 1946 Britain and the USA had agreed to stop taking reparations from Germany. By early 1947 they were beginning to consider supporting a German economic recovery as part of a concerted strategy to revive European prosperity. This would also be beneficial to the Americans because of the markets it would create.

Western and Soviet policies were rapidly moving farther apart than ever.

Right: President Truman addressing the first meeting of the United Nations in June 1945.

New Nations

Japanese rule in Asia had been brutal and racist but it made a restoration of the European colonies impossible. In the Middle East substantial Jewish immigration after the war also meant that new conditions prevailed.

The wartime slogan of Japan's Greater East Asia Co-Prosperity Sphere had been "Asia for the Asiatics" and, for all the brutality of their subsequent rule, the Japanese triumphs of 1941–2 had largely discredited the former colonial masters. The Anglo-American Atlantic Charter of 1941 had, at American insistence, openly supported the right of people everywhere to choose their own governments – and American policy throughout the war was avowedly anti-colonial. Both of these factors assisted the developing forces of nationalism.

Above: A French soldier in Indo-China in 1951 during the fruitless attempt to maintain French rule.

Below: Refugees in Amritsar, among the millions forced to move because of their religion when India and Pakistan became independent.

Colonial Struggles

In French Indo-China (now Laos, Cambodia and Vietnam), for example, the American Office of Strategic Services supported a Vietnamese nationalist coalition led by the communist Ho Chi Minh during the war. Ho's Viet Minh forces fought against the Japanese and, at the end of the war, proclaimed the existence of a Democratic Republic of Vietnam. France subsequently tried (unsuccessfully) to reimpose colonial rule. Thus began the long conflict, which would only end with the North Vietnamese victory over South Vietnam in 1975.

In the Dutch East Indies the pre-war colonial power also tried and failed to reimpose its control after the war. Here the Japanese had worked with the nationalist leader Achmad Sukarno during the war and in 1944 had promised to grant independence. With help from the Japanese, Sukarno went on to proclaim Indonesia as an independent country in August 1945. This was finally recognized by the Dutch in 1949 after a bitter, armed struggle.

Unlike the Dutch and the French, Britain had substantial forces available to re-occupy Malaya and the other territories that remained under Japanese control in August 1945. However, whether they had been Japanese-occupied at any stage or not, almost all British colonies in Asia quickly gained their independence. In 1939, despite the well-established system of partial self-government, Britain's viceroy in India had declared the country to be

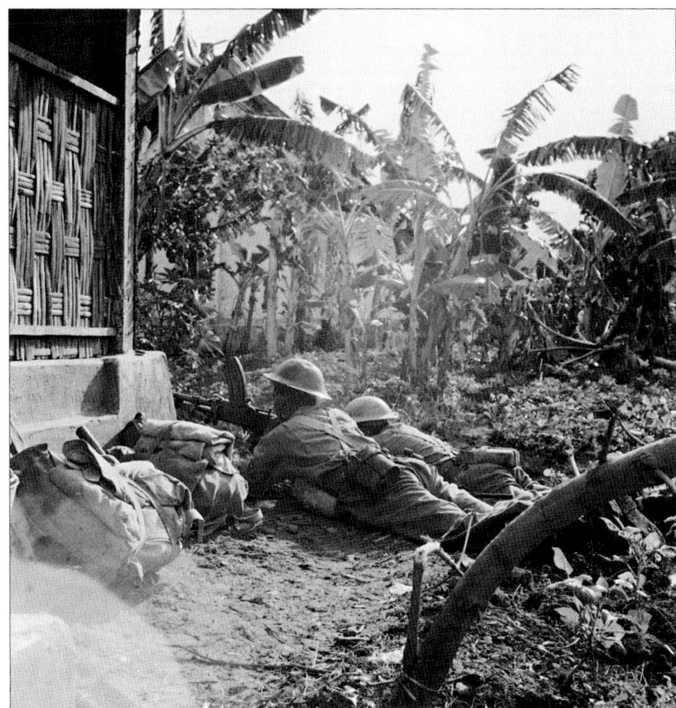

Right: British Indian Army troops fighting in Java in late 1945 against Indonesian nationalists. British forces initially took control in Indonesia after Japan's surrender.

at war with Germany without consulting a single Indian. By 1945 there was no doubt that those days were past, and in August 1947 India and Pakistan became independent.

Israel and the Arabs

European rule had also had its day in the Middle East. The pre-war French mandate in Syria was never restored and the country became independent in effect in 1944. Britain's pre-war mandate in Palestine had been troubled by violence between Jews and Arabs and the British authorities; various plans had been proposed for separate and joint Jewish and Arab states.

British control continued as a United Nations' mandate after the war amid growing violence. Jewish immigration and the experience of the Holocaust lent more force to Zionism than previously, while UN attempts to broker a deal between Arabs and Jews came to nothing. In 1948, when the British mandate expired, the state of Israel was proclaimed; Israel had been successfully established by 1949. Perhaps around 700,000 Palestinian Arabs were displaced from their homes, creating a legacy of bitterness that persists into the 21st century.

Communist China

The biggest of the post-war changes was in China. For all the Allied aid that had been sent to the Nationalists, the Communists had done better out of the war. Their armed forces were better organized and in 1945 they already had an effective presence in most of the supposedly Japanese-controlled areas of the country.

Over the following years, the communists gradually gained the upper hand throughout the country and in 1949 proclaimed the People's Republic of China; the defeated Nationalists withdrew to Taiwan. In the West this looked like an important victory for world communism, as directed from Moscow. In reality the Chinese communists were masters in their own house, but for the moment their success only contributed to the development of Cold War tensions.

Right: David Ben-Gurion, first Prime Minister of Israel.

The Cold War

By 1949 the focus of international affairs was no longer on dealing with the effects of WWII. Instead the USA, USSR and many other nations were preoccupied by a new and, in an era of nuclear weapons, possibly more dangerous conflict, the Cold War.

By the middle of 1947 the relationship between the USA and USSR was already at a low ebb. The two had never entirely trusted each other as wartime allies and things had since got much worse. For the moment the USA still had a monopoly of atomic weapons and could be fairly sure that it and its friends were immune from any direct military attack.

However, Europe's economies were still failing to make any substantial recovery from the disastrous conditions of 1945. In this atmosphere, American leaders feared that communist ideas might make headway. A central part of the problem was that Allied policies had in fact prevented the reconstruction of Germany. Instead, led by the Soviets, the Allies had stripped German industry of much plant and other resources.

Above: Konrad Adenauer, first Chancellor of the new nation of West Germany, is congratulated by a supporter after his election victory in August 1949.

The Marshall Plan

This all changed with the announcement of the Marshall Plan. By its terms, American aid was to be offered to all the nations of Europe, including the USSR. President Truman and his advisers attached conditions to the aid – among other things countries receiving it would have to submit to American inspections of how the money was being spent – which they correctly calculated would make it unacceptable to the Soviets. They duly rejected it and ensured that their satellites in eastern Europe did so too.

Marshall Plan aid began to flow in 1948 and over $12 billion would be provided to a range of countries until 1951. During these years the European economies grew substantially and levels of prosperity surpassed those of the late 1930s. International trade also revived, to the benefit not just of the Europeans but also of the American economy. And finally, because they had been forced to work together to decide how the aid should be split up, the European nations began the process of economic co-operation that would lead to the establishment in 1957 of the European Economic Community and in time to the present-day European Union.

New Germanies

In March 1948 the USA, Britain and France agreed to merge their occupation zones of Germany into a single entity. In June they introduced a new

Left: Unloading transport aircraft at Tempelhof airfield, June 1948, during the Berlin Blockade.

Left: Watched by Allied diplomats, President Truman signs the North Atlantic Treaty establishing the NATO alliance in 1949.

currency for the whole area to replace the Hitler-era Reichsmarks that were still in use.

Since the main aim of Soviet policy in Europe after the war was to ensure that Germany could never again dominate the continent, any measures that presaged a German economic revival were seen as threatening. The Soviet response to the Allied currency reforms and other measures was to close all road and rail routes to the Allied sectors in Berlin. This Berlin Blockade is commonly seen as the first clear confrontation of the Cold War.

The Soviets presumably hoped that the Allies would back down over their plans for Germany. They had not reckoned on the ability of the Allies to supply the city by air. Hundreds of American and British aircraft made daily transport flights into the city carrying everything that the Berliners needed. Thus supplied, the city held out until the Soviets relented in 1949.

By then the Cold War had truly begun. In 1949 West and East Germany were established as new countries, with the first elections in the West in August. In April, 12 countries, including Britain, the USA and Canada, signed the North Atlantic Treaty, agreeing that an attack on any one would be regarded as an attack on all. This NATO alliance was an open commitment by the USA not to return to the policies of isolationism that had prevailed before WWII. On the other side there was a new threat. In August 1949 the Soviets tested their first atomic weapon and would establish their own military alliance of Soviet-bloc countries, the Warsaw Pact, in the 1950s.

The Cold War competition between NATO and the Warsaw Pact and the accompanying nuclear balance of terror would dominate international affairs for the next forty years. The great issues that had brought about WWII were now relegated to history.

GEORGE MARSHALL

General Marshall (1880–1959) was Chief of Staff of the US Army from 1939 to the end of the war. He is regarded as the main organizer of the US victory in WWII. First, in 1939–41, he substantially expanded and updated his service and laid the ground for the greater expansion that followed. Throughout the war he worked hard to maintain the principles of "Germany first" and that Germany should be defeated by a direct cross-Channel invasion. After the war he served as Secretary of State, helping devise and implement the Foreign Assistance Act, which came to be known as the Marshall Plan.

Above: General George Marshall in US Army uniform late in the war.

akg-images 16l and m, 17l and r, 18t, 20b, 21b, 22b, 25t, 27m, 33r, 42, 43t, 44l, 45t, 52, 53b, 56b, 57t, 60b, 62, 63bl and br, 68b, 71tl, 71b, 73t, ml and br, 74tm, 78b, 84b, 86r, 87b, 92t, 96t, 97t, 98t, 109b, 113b, 118, 119bl, 121l, 126tr, 127tm, 130, 131b, 132l, 136b, 157b, 188, 191t, 193br, 194t, 195b, 223t, 247b, 248tr, 249m, 250b, 251t, 253b, 254b, 255tl, 255b, 257br, 260r, 261tl, 262tm, 264t, 265t, 267b, 271b, 276b, 278tl, 279l, m and r, 283t, 285t, 288t, 290b, 293r, 298b, 309b, 313t, 314t, 317t, 321bl, 323l, 330t, 348t and b, 349tl and b, 354r, 357t, 358t, 359bl, 362bl, 363tl, 371b, 375tr, 388b, 390t and b, 404tl, 416t, 417t, 418b, 419t, 423t, 425b, 433b, 434t and b, 436l, 478b, 491tl, 493r, 502b; Bildarkiv Pisarek 249r, 257bl; Erich Lessing 204b; Jean Pierre Verney 43b, 49t; RIA Novosti 107t; ullstein bild 23t, 37b, 41b, 45b, 49b, 50t, 57b, 77m, 79t, 80b, 108t, 109t, 117t, 120t, 124bl, 126tm, 129b, 135l, 142, 143t, 174b, 179t, 189b, 209bl, 212bl, 217t and b, 225r, 231b, 237b, 239t, 267t, 283b, 284t, 289t, 297b, 300t, 318r, 319b, 323r, 329t, 333b, 346tm, 347bl, 352, 355b, 356b, 360b, 361t, 371t, 384br, 385t, 387bl and br, 393tl, 403b, 408t, 417b, 426b, 428b, 431tl, 436r, 441b, 446t, 456r, 471t, **Aviation Images** 213t, 294r, 373tl, 474b; H.Cowin 291l and r, 301t, 392r, 393r, 399t, 442b, 443m; Mark Wagner 373tr; P. Jarret 221b, 295b, 300b, 301b, 412b, 413b, 427tl; R. Winslade 405l, 427b; Royal Aeronautical Society 412t; TRHP 427tr; **Corbis** 20t, 33bm, 50b, 59t, 66t, 116b, 148, 154l, 177bl, 190l, 201t, 204t, 206t, 208tl, 209bm, 215b, 224r, 228, 229t, 231t, 232t and b, 233t, 239b, 248tl, 252t, 261bml, 276t, 280r, 294l, 326, 327b, 341b, 343bl, 344t, 353b, 375b, 381tr, 404tm, 408b, 411b, 422b, 423b, 434, 439l, 441t, 452tm, 453m, 458t and b, 459t, 461t, 463t, 465tr, 467l, 468b, 472r, 476b, 483b, 485br, 493m, 499b, 503t; Alinari Archives 238b; Bettmann 9b, 16r, 18b, 19t, 21t, 22t, 24t, 25b, 29t, 53mr, 55t, 61t, 66br, 75bm, 93b, 96b, 99t, 101b, 112b, 113t, 114t and b, 120b, 125t, 127tr, 129t, 134t, 135r, 141t, 170tm, 186t, 193bl, 200b, 208tm, 212t and br, 230r, 246b, 252b, 260mr, 261tmr, 261bl, 264b, 266t, 270t, 272t, 272b, 273bl, 277t, 282l, 308t, 309t, 311b, 312t and bl, 315t, 322tm and tr, 325br, 331t, 334t and b, 337b, 342, 343br, 346tr, 347m, 362r, 369t, 382b, 383b, 394t and b, 401t, 404tr, 406t, 407tr, 410b, 414b, 419br, 431b, 437b, 443t, 446b, 453l, 455br, 462b, 466t and bl, 469b, 470t, 474t, 476t, 477b, 490b, 492tl and tm, 497t and b, 500t and b, 501b, 503b; Christel Gerstenberg 389b; The Dmitri Baltermants Collection 359t, 435tl; DPA 351b, 354bl, 492tr, 498t; EPA 491tl; Godong/ Franois Galland 494b; Hulton-Deutsch Collection 26r, 27l, 32r, 35t, 39t, 51t and b, 53t, 64t and b, 75bl, 82, 84t, 86l, 92b, 97b, 98b, 115t, 116t, 119t, 126tl, 131t, 134t, 141b, 144t, 145t, 151t, 152b, 171bl and bm, 183t, 194b, 196, 197b, 210t, 229bl and br, 233b, 236b, 242t, 248tm, 254t, 269t, 270bl, 274t and b, 345tl, 350t, 369bl, 405r, 429t, 449t and b, 450, 461b, 479b, 499t, 502t; LLC 298t; Minnesota Historical Society 313b; Museum of Flight 222b, 454b; National Aviation Museum 37tr, 104t and b, 105t; Richard Klune 256t; Robert Harding World Imagery/Richard Nebesky 261br, 494t; Scheufler Collection 30, 262tl, 273br; Sean Sexton Collection 61b; Underwood & Underwood 29b, 344b; **Getty-Images** 152t; AFP 414t; Hulton Archive 18b, 26l, 27r, 28, 29m, 41t, 54t, 55b, 56t, 58t, 60t, 65b, 68t, 69t, 74tl, 76, 87mr, 95r, 106b, 108b, 132r, 133, 134b, 136t, 137b, 140, 145b, 146b, 148b, 149t & b, 153b, 154r, 155b, 157t, 158b, 160, 161m and b, 164t, 165l and r, 166b, 168t and b, 169b, 170tr, 173b, 175t, 177t and br, 178b, 183b, 185t, 191b, 199t, 200t, 201b, 207t and b, 208tr, 209br, 210b, 213b, 214b, 215t, 216t and b, 220, 222t, 223b, 225l, 227b, 237t, 238t, 241t, 243b, 246t, 247t, 249l, 250t, 251b, 253t, 255tr, 257t, 260ml, 261tml, 262tr, 263l, 265b, 266b, 268b, 269b, 270br, 275t and b, 277bl, 279m, 280l, 281t and b, 284b, 292t and b, 293l, 295t, 296b, 299t, bl and br, 302t and br, 303b, 308b, 312br, 315br, 316br, 317b, 320t and b, 321t and bl, 324b, 325t and bl, 327tl and tr, 332t, 333t, 346tl, 349tl, 351t, 355t, 359br, 365bl, 366bl, 367tr, 370, 372bl, 372br, 382t, 383t, 391r, 392l, 395tr, 398b, 400t, 405m, 410t, 411t, 415t and b, 416b, 418t, 422t, 425m, 426b, 428t, 437t, 444r, 446t, 447t, 448b, 451b, 453r, 457b, 460b, 465tl, 475b, 477tl, 481t, 482t, 483t, 484r, 488t, 488br, 489b, 490t, 495t and bl, 496t; Roger Viollet 36r, 37l, 54b, 127bl, 166t, 167b, 245r, 256b, 263r, 273t, 363tr; Silver Screen Collection/Hulton Archive 363b; Time & Life Pictures 42ml, 70, 184, AFP 192, 193t, 195t, 11b, 261tr, 278tm and tr, 297t, 318bl, 324t, 330b, 331b, 335b, 337tl and tr, 340t, 368, 369br, 375tl, 387t, 391t, 395b, 398t, 402, 413t, 440b, 452tl, 454t, 455bl, 457t, 459b, 460t, 462t, 464, 470b, 473b, 475t, 477tr, 478t, 479t, 485bl, 487b, 493l, 495br, 496b, 498b; **Photographs reproduced by permission of the Trustees of The Imperial War Museum, London** 17m Q 51128, 23b Q 51128, 32l Q 5004, 34t Q 53509, 36l Q 58653, 38b Q 60706, 39b Q 79792, 44r COL 224, 46bl Q 48445, 49mr Q 6157, 63t SP 438, 66bl Q 64301, 69b SP 1053, 71tr Q 18062, 72 SP 374, 77t Q 114867 and b E AVS 862, 78t PD CRO 30, 79tr Toucan Books, 79b Q 34105, 83b CO 3392, 85b Q 29001, 87t Q 65882, 90l Q 1375 and r Q 4092, 91l Q 23816 and r E(AUS) 2677, 94t Q 20640 and b SP 365, 95l Q 61156, 99b Q 13806, 101t Q 38891, 102 Q 13427, 105b SP 1141, 106t Q 23732, 110t Q 24781 and b Q 24440, 111t Q 107237, 112t Q 79823, 115b Q 13667, 117b Q 20220, 119m Q 56276, 121r Q 68200, 122 LC 32, 123t Q 58470, bl Q 110343 and br HO 128 A, 125b Q 12033, 137t Q 43463, 138t CO 991 and b CO 811, 139t Q1490 and b Q 4057, 143b Q 54534, 146t Q 9248, 147t E(AUS) 694 and b SP 1892, 150t Q 20627 and b SP 413, 151b SP 114, 153t Q 32159, 155t Q 15597, 156t Q 20794 and b Q 64302, 158b Q 38705 and b Q 13239, 161t Q 39007, 162 SP 748, 163t SP 1501 and b SP 2501, 164b SP 771, 167t Q 20636, 170tl Q 24739, 171br Q 24869, 166 CO 1178, 173t Q 5171 and m Q 6434, 174t Q 80861, 175b Q 67910, 182b Q 3999, 185b E(AUS) 939, 186b Q 1371, 187b Q 7134, 189t Q 6282, 190r CO 1751, 197t Q 86175, 192l Q 24891 and b Q 24926, 199b Q 24869, 196l Q 24191 and b Q 24739, 203t SP 560 and b Q 24294, 205t Q 18887 and b Q 19954, 206b SP 2270, 214t E(AUS) 757, 221t Q 67228, 226t Q 3245 and b Q 50845, 227t Q 5829, 230l Q 50649, 241b Q 31801, 242b Q 12971, 243t HU 75737, 244t Q 21940, 245l Q 38292, 247m SP 1635, 282r E 1416, 287l A 6165, 296t C 1653, 304b FL 14721, 305b A 28203, 306t E 100, 307t CM164, 307b E 1376, 310b A 24047, 314b HU 1761, 319t H 23836, 323m A 30523, 328br A 30080, 332b HU 2762, 339t A 2298, 345tr A 30523, 353t SE 358, 357r B 15007, 365t E 14775, 366t BU 823, 367b H 36806, 122 MH 29100, 378bl FL 1204, 379t C 4050, 380t A 2003, 384l BU 2756, 385tr B 15229, 388t TR 1800, 389t H 25860, 395tl HU 4052, 397tl TR 450, 397tr H 34424, 399b TR 37, 403t TR 1402, 407tl B 5090, 409br H 37859, 424 CL 1756, 425t C 4919, 429b E (MOS) 1403, 431tr EA 44531, 433t BU 127, 435tr E 19296, 442t CL 2946, 469t A 21447, 471b IND 4723, 480r SE 3073, 482b COL 353, 486t A 9060, 488bl MH 6810, 501t SE 5661; **Mirrorpix** 481b; **Photo12.com** 81t and b; Keystone Pressedienst 315bl; **RIA-Novosti** 419bl; **Royal Armouries Museum, Leeds** 234l and r, 235t, bl and br, **Royal Navy Submarine Museum** 169; **Popperfoto.com** 8, 46br, **The Tank Museum** (www.tankmuseum.org.uk) 360t, 361tr, 361b, 366br, 367tl, 385b, 409t and bl, 420l and r, 421l and r, 432l and r, 433b, 440t, 444l, 445t and b, 447b; **TopFoto** 9t, 33t, 38t, 58b, 59b, 67t, 74tr, 75br, 88br, 89t and b, 93t, 100b, 107b, 111b, 124r, 159b, 180 t and b, 181b, 182t, 187t, 335t, 364, 365br, 376t, 407b, 487tr; Alinari 46t, 343t; Artmedia/HIP 356t; Feltz 290t; Heritage-Images 35b, 80t, 85t, 181t, 236t; Keystone 439r; Roger-Viollet 26m, 30b, 31t and b, 40, 178t, 179b, 396r; Ullstein Bild 244b, 289b, 401b; **US Army Signal Corps** (www.history.army.mil) 396l, 455t, **US Naval Historical Center** 261bmr, 285b, 286l and r, 287r, 303t, 304t, 305t, 310t, 311t, 322tl, 328l, 329b, 338t, 338b, 339b, 347r, 377t and b, 378r, 379b, 380b, 381tl and b, 452tr, 456l, 463b, 465b, 466br, 467r, 468t, 473t and m, 485t, 486b, 487tl, 491r.

A

Abyssinia, annexation of 271, 275, 489
Adenauer, Konrad 502
Africa 64–5, 154–5
air aces 36, 86, 87, 190–1, 212
air combat 296–7, 372, 482–3
aircraft: aircraft ordnance 428–9; bombers 124–5, 174–5, 290–1, 300–1, 398–9, 412–13, 466–7, 474–5; fighter-bombers 373; fighters 86–7, 212–13, 294–5, 373, 392–3, 426–7, 464–5; flying boats 104–5; gliders 483; ground-attack aircraft 220–1, 372–3; jet aircraft 442–3; naval-support aircraft 456–7; reconnaissance aircraft 36–7, 146, 291; seaplanes 104–5, 150–1, 456–7; torpedo aircraft 474–5; trainer aircraft 222; transport aircraft 482–3; utility aircraft 291
Aisne: Aisne Offensive 225; Battles of the 46, 48, 176
Alam Halfa, Battle of 364
Albania, annexation of 306
Albert, Battle of 138
Albert, King of Belgium 28, 232
Albrecht of Württemberg, Duke 35, 43, 48, 76–7
Alexeev, Mikhail 142–3
Algeria 364, 368
Allenby, Edmund 130, 172, 200–1, 242–3
Allies 16, 26, 74, 126, 170, 208, 264, 265, 306, 346, 432; aerial warfare 340, 376, 386, 412–13, 426–7, 443, 454; the Ardennes 440–1; Armistice 250–1; Balkans 240–1; Burma 470–1, 480–1; East Africa 154–5; Eastern Front 127; final attacks 233; Gallipoli 103, 114–15; Germany 446–7, 495, 496–7; Grand Strategy of 382–3; Italian Front 127; Italy 386–7, 400, 447; Japan 496; mobilization 27; naval warfare 98–9, 168–9, 206–7, 244, 302–4, 335, 336, 340, 376–7, 380–1, 386; Normandy 406–7, 410–11, 430–1; North Africa 307, 308, 364–5, 368–9; in the Pacific 332, 333, 336, 340–1, 452, 476–7; the Philippines 476–7; Romania 144; Salonika 152–3; Sicily 386–7; Solomon Islands 340–1; South-east Asia 334–5, 470–1; US support for 303, 312, 313; victory 250–1; war plans 22–3, 75; Western Front 47, 127, 130, 210–11, 224–5, 233, 288, 406–7, 410–11, 430–1, 440–1 *see also* Australia; Belgium; Britain; Canada; France; India; New Zealand; USA; USSR
Amiens Offensive 217
amphibious vehicles 409, 460–1
Ancre, Battle of the 138
Ancre Heights, Battle of the 138
Anglo-American forces: in Europe 373, 406–7, 437, 450–1; in North Africa 365, 368–9 *see also* Britain; United States
Anglo-French forces 285, 373 *see also* Britain; France
Anglo-German Naval Agreement (1935) 270, 274
Anglo-Polish alliance (1939) 277
Anthoine, François 176, 184
anti-aircraft guns 214–15
Antonescu, Marshal Ion 359
ANZACs: Gallipoli 102–3, 114–15; Palestine 243
Anzio 386, 387, 402
Arabs, Palestinian 501
Ardennes 352, 440–1
Arges, Battle of the River 145
Armenia 106–7
armistices 119, 154, 155, 209, 239, 241, 247, 250–1; German Armistice 233, 250–1
armoured vehicles 236–7, 360–1, 366–7, 408–9
Arras, Battle of 172–3, 212
artillery 30, 32–3, 40–1, 186–7, 223; anti-aircraft guns 396–7; anti-tank guns 318–9, 444–5; field artillery 352–3; heavy artillery 402–3; rockets 438, 439, 448; self-propelled 432–3 *see also* guns
Artois 172–3; Battles of 80–1, 84–5
Asia 334–5, 452; the 1930s 270–1
Asiago Offensive 148–9
Atlantic, Battle of the 302–3, 375–8, 457, 468
atomic bombs 488, 490–1, 499, 503
Attlee, Clement 383
Aubers Ridge, Battle of 80, 81
Auschwitz-Birkenau 351
Australia 77; Gallipoli 102–3, 114–15; naval warfare 486; New Guinea 340, 454–5; Palestine 55, 243
Austria 264, 436, 437; annexation of 271

Austria-Hungary: armistice 209, 239, 241; atrocities by 50; declaration of war 21; declaration of war by China 61; Eastern Front 58–9, 88, 142, 144; Italian Front 96–7, 196; mobilization 24, 27; naval warfare 162, 165, 167, 244; Serbia 18–19, 50–1; war plans 24–5; withdrawal from Balkans 241

B

Baldwin, Stanley 274
Balkans 18–19, 308; liberation of 240–1
balloons 94–5, 146
Baltic States 264, 277, 284–5, 317, 418
Batum, Treaty of 199
Beatty, David 66, 112–13, 156
Beersheba, Battle of 55, 200–1
Belgium 265, 266, 288, 441; Allied advances (1918) 232–3; colonies 65; German invasion 28–9, 289; liberation of 431; siege of Antwerp 46–7; war plans 23; Western Front 24, 34, 48–9, 184, 224, 233
Belleau Wood, Battle of 225
Belorussia 418
Below, Otto von 88, 176, 197
Ben-Gurion, David 501
Berchtold, Leopold von 20–1
Berlin: Battle of 391, 424; Berlin Blockade 502, 503; fall of 450–1; post-war division of 496
Bethmann-Hollweg, Theobald von 20, 21
Beveridge Report 299
biological weapons 488–9
Bishop, William "Billy" 190
Bismarck 302, 303, 329, 475
Bismarck Sea, Battle of the 341, 454

HMS *Black Prince* 245
Bletchley Park 375
Blitzkrieg 288, 289, 300, 372
Bolimov, Battle of 88
Bolsheviks 192–5
Boroevic von Bojna, Svetozar 89, 238
Bose, Subhas Chandra 471
Bosnia 18–19
Breslau 164, 165
Brest-Litovsk, Treaty of 169, 195, 199
Brialmont, Henri 30, 31
Britain: 264, 265, 280, 298; the 1930s 274, 275; aerial warfare 86–7, 104–5, 120–1, 125, 150–1, 174–5, 190–1, 212–13, 221, 290, 292–3, 296–7, 300–1, 307, 372, 373, 390–3, 398–9, 412–13, 424–6, 428–9, 442–3, 456–7, 464; air raids over 120–3; Battle of Britain 292–4, 372; the Blitz 292–3, 298, 392; British Expeditionary Force (BEF) 23, 48–9, 84, 130–1, 288; British intelligence 67; Bulgaria 241; Burma 470–1, 480–1; Caucasus Front 198–9; colonies 65, 226; conscription 277; Dardanelles 98–9, 165, 168–9; declaration of war 21; East Africa 154–5, 227; Gallipoli 98, 99, 102–3, 114–15; Germany 390–1, 399, 424–5, 496; home front 118–19, 298–9; Java 501; London 292–3, 298, 439; Mediterranean 164–5; Mesopotamia 110–11, 202–3; mine warfare 182–3; naval warfare 62–3, 66–73, 94–5, 98–101, 112–13, 147, 150–1, 156–65, 167–9, 203–7, 244–5, 286–7, 302–4, 307, 311, 313, 328–9, 338–9, 342–3, 376, 378–9, 381, 469, 474, 486–7; "New Army" recruits 22; Normandy 410, 430–1; North Africa 306–8, 364–5, 495; Palestine 108–9, 200–1, 242–3; pals battalions 139; and Poland 277, 280, 281; post-war 498–9; Royal Naval Air Service 95, 104, 150, 213; tank warfare 140–1, 282–3, 385, 420; Tondern Raid 151; Turkey 241; war plans 23, 75; Western Front 47, 48–9, 130, 184, 430–1 *see also* Allies; Anglo-American forces; Anglo-French forces
Bruchmüller, Georg 211
Brusilov, Alexei 89, 142, 143
Brusilov Offensive 142–4, 149
Buchenwald 351
Bulgaria 152–3, 209, 240–1, 264, 418, 419, 498
Bulge, Battle of the 361, 431, 437, 440–1, 446
Bullard, Robert 224, 229
Bülow, Karl von 28, 29, 35, 39, 42–3
Burma 322, 334, 335, 345, 353; Japanese defeat in 470–1, 480–1
Byng, Julian 188, 210

C

Cadorna, Luigi 96, 148, 149, 196–7
Cambrai, Battle of 141, 188–9
camouflage 146–7
HMS *Campania* 151
Canada 76; aerial warfare 190, 213; Canadian Expeditionary Force 173; naval warfare 303, 313; Normandy 410, 430–1; Western Front 430–1 *see also* Allies
Cantigny, Battle of 225
Cape Engaño, Battle of 473
Caporetto, Battle of 149, 196–7, 229
Carpathian Mountains 88–9
casualty figures 293, 494–5
Caucasus 106–7, 198–9, 348–9, 358
cavalry 38, 54–5
Central Powers 16, 17, 26, 27, 74–5, 126, 170, 208–9; Eastern Front 88; Greece 152–3; naval warfare 101, 163, 244–5; Romania 144–5; Russia 193–4; Treaty of Brest-Litovsk 195; Western Front 224–5 *see also* Austria-Hungary; Bulgaria; Germany; Turkey
Ceylon, Japanese attacks on 335
Chamberlain, Neville 276, 277
Champagne, Battles of 49, 84–5, 176

Château-Thierry, Battle of 225
chemical warfare 488–9
China 60–1, 253, 452, 494; Burma 480; declaration of war 61; internal struggles in 478–9; Japanese occupation of 271, 344–5, 478–9; post-war 501
Chindits 470, 481
Chuikov, General Vasili 354
Churchill, Winston 71, 140, 289, 299, 313, 382, 383, 496, 498, 499; Dardanelles 98–9; Gallipoli 102
civilian casualties 113, 122–3, 160, 204
Clemenceau, Georges 252, 253
codes and codebreaking 374–5
Cold War 502–3
collaboration 416–7
communications (in the field) 230–1
concentration camps 350–1, 422, 423, 494; liberation of 351, 405
Conrad von Hötzendorf, Franz 20, 58, 59, 89, 148, 238
Constantinople 102, 103
convoys 303, 376–9
Coral Sea: Battle of 322, 336–7, 340
Coronel, Battle of 70–1
Cunningham, Admiral Andrew 307, 382
Czechoslovakia 264, 359, 437, 438, 451, 498; partition of 276, 277

D

D-Day 406–11, 460
Dachau 494
Dardanelles 98–9, 164–5, 168–9
de Cary, Langle 35, 43
de Castelnau, Noël 34, 43, 129
de Gaulle, General Charles 415
de la Perière, Lothar 160–1
Denmark 265; fall of 284–5
depth charges 206, 207
SMS *Derfflinger* 73
d'Espérey, Louis Franchet 42, 240–1
Diaz, Armando 197, 238, 239
Dogger Bank, Battle of 66, 112, 113
Dönitz, Admiral Karl 303, 377, 450
Doolittle, Colonel James 335, 424
Dorrell, George 39
Dowding, Air Marshal Hugh 293
HMS *Dreadnought* 100, 158–9
Dresden 425
Dubail, Auguste 34, 43, 80, 84
Dunkirk 289
Dutch East Indies 322, 452; fall of 334–5; post-war 500

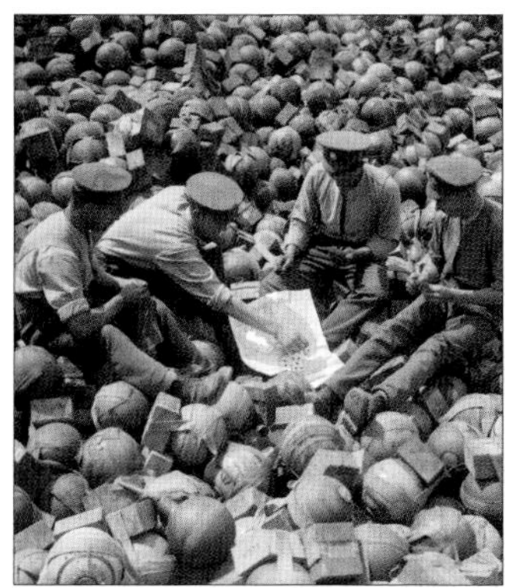

E

Eaker, General Ira 395
East Africa 154–5
East Germany 503
East Prussia 52–3, 56–7, 264, 276, 436
Eastern Front 26, 58–9, 74, 88, 92–3, 126–7, 142, 144, 170, 208, 240, 278, 316–17, 320–1, 346–9, 354–5, 358–9, 370–2, 404, 418–19, 433, 436–7
Eastern Solomons, Battle of the 341
Ebert, Friedrich 246, 247
Egypt 306–7, 364
Eichhorn, Hermann von 88, 142
Eichmann, Adolf 351
Eisenhower, General Dwight D. 369, 382, 406, 431, 446, 447, 450
El Alamein, Battles of 309, 364–5, 368, 495
Enigma cipher 374–5
SMS *Emden* 61, 63
Enver Pasha 106, 107, 199
Estonia 284
Eugene, Archduke 47, 148
Europe 278, 346, 404, 492, 494; the 1930s 270–1, 274–7; collaboration in 416–17; post-war 494–9, 502–3; resistance in 414–5; victory in 373, 451

F

Falkenhayn, Erich von 46, 48, 51, 76, 92, 128–9, 134–5, 139, 144–5, 201
Falklands, Battle of the 61, 63, 70–1, 245
"February Revolution" 192–3, 195
Ferdinand, Archduke Franz 18; assassination of 17–20, 50, 235
Festubert, Battle of 80
Final Solution 350–1, 422
Finland 277; armistice with USSR 418; invasion of 284, 285
Fisher, John 71–2, 158–9
Flers-Courcelette, Battle of 138
Florina, Battle of 152
Foch, Ferdinand 43, 135, 177, 196, 211, 216–17, 225, 228–9, 232, 251, 264
Fokker aircraft 86–7, 212–13
food rationing 118–19
HMS *Formidable* 101
fortresses, frontier 30–1, 34, 88, 128, 186
France 34, 264–6, 280, 281, 288, 404, 430; the 1930s 274–7; aerial warfare 36–7, 86–7, 120–1, 174–5, 190–1, 213, 221, 290, 301; air raids over 122–3; army mutiny 177; Balkans 241; colonies 65, 226; Dardanelles 165; fall of 288–9, 312; Indo-China 500; liberation of 430–1; Meuse-Argonne Offensive 228–9; naval warfare 151, 165–7, 244–5, 343, 495; Nivelle Offensive 176–7, 179–80, 185; Paris 42, 218–19; and Poland 277, 280, 281; post-war 496; resistance in 414–15; tank warfare 282–3; Vichy regime 314, 325, 351; Verdun 128, 134–5; Western Front 24, 34, 47, 48–9, 127–8, 130, 176, 210–11, 224, 228–9, 233
Franco-Prussian War (1870–71) 18, 22, 24, 32, 146, 264
French, John 38, 48, 77, 85
front lines 26, 34, 47–8, 74, 88, 103, 126, 128, 130, 142, 170, 176, 184, 196, 208, 211, 224, 233, 240; Berlin (1945) 451; Eastern Front 278, 316, 346, 349, 358, 400, 404; France (1944) 404, 430; in Italy 386, 404; North Africa 306, 364; in the Pacific 341, 484; Western Front 288, 404, 430, 441
Frontiers, Battles of the 34–5
HMS *Furious* 94, 150

G

Galicia 58–9
Gallipoli 98, 99, 102–3, 114–15; front lines (1916) 103
Gallwitz, Max von 51, 92–3
Gariboldi, Marshal Italo 309
Garros, Roland 86–7
gas warfare 76, 78–9, 488–9
Gaza, Battles of 200
Germany: 264, 265, 288, 441, 494; the 1920s 266; the 1930s 274, 275; aerial warfare 36–7, 86–7, 104–5, 120–1, 124–5, 174–5, 190–1, 212–13, 220–1, 280, 288–9, 291–4, 296–7, 300, 372, 378, 387, 393, 413, 424–5, 427, 428, 442–3, 456–7; air raids over 122–3; Allied victories in 446–7; the Ardennes 352, 440–1; Armistice 119, 154, 155, 209, 233, 241, 247, 250–1; Austria 271; Balkans 240–1, 308; Baltic States 418; Belgium 288, 289; Berlin 391, 424, 450–1, 496, 502, 503; bombing of 390–1, 394–5, 399, 424–5, 495; capture of Poland 92–3; Caucasus Front 198–9; China 61; colonies 60–1, 64–5, 154–5; declaration of war 21; Denmark 284–5; East Africa 154–5; Eastern Front 88, 92–3, 142, 144, 316–17, 320–1, 346, 348–9, 354–5, 358–9, 370–1, 400–1, 404, 418–19, 436–7; Eastern Front final offensives (1918) 216–17, 224–15; European rule 314–15; expansion of (1919–39) 277; France 288–9, 406–7, 410–11, 430–1; Gorlice-Tarnów Offensive 92–3; Greece 308; home front 118–19; invasion of Belgium 28–9; invasion of France 34–5; Italian Front 196; Italy 386–7; and Jews 269, 314, 316, 320, 350–1, 422, 494, 497; Luftwaffe, defeat of 424–5; Mediterranean 164–5; mine warfare 182–3; mobilization 24, 27; naval blockade of 22, 171, 246, 250; naval mutiny 246–7; naval warfare 62–3, 66–73, 100–1, 112–13, 116–17, 147, 156–66, 204–207, 244–47, 287, 302–3, 310–11, 313, 328–9, 343, 376–81, 468–9, 487; navy, defeat of 376–7; Nazi Germany 255; the Netherlands 288, 289; Normandy 406–7, 410–11, 430–1; North Africa 307, 308–9, 364–5, 368–9; Norway 284–5; Poland 277, 280–1, 312, 350–1; post-war 494–7, 502–3; Operation Faustschlag 195; the Rhineland 270, 271; Salonika 152–3; scuttling of fleet (1919) 247; Sicily 386–7; sinking of neutral ships 112–13; Soviet forces in

436–7, 450–1; the Sudetanland 276; surrender of 451, 496; surrender of fleet 113; tank warfare 282–3, 360–1, 384, 421; totalitarian rule in 422–3; the Ukraine 400–1; USA 313, 327; USSR 316–17, 348–9, 354–5, 358–9, 370–1, 400–1, 436–7, 450–1; war plans 24–5, 75; Western Front 24, 34, 47, 48–9, 54–5, 127, 128, 130, 210–11, 224–5, 288–9, 404, 406–7, 410–11, 430–1, 440–1
Gilbert Islands 458–9
Gnila Lipa, Battle of 58
Goebbels, Josef 362
SMS *Goeben* 73, 164–5, 244
Göring, Hermann 497
Gorlice-Tarnów Offensive 92–3
Gorringe, George 110–11
Gough, Hubert 173, 184, 210
Graf Spee 286, 303, 381
Greece 152–3, 308, 419, 499; declaration of war 153
Gröner, Wilhelm 247
Guadalcanal 287, 340, 378; Battle of 341
Guam 462
Guderian, General Heinz 317, 374
Guillaumat, Marie 153, 240
Guise, Battle of 39
gunboats 203
guns 357, 367; machine-guns 388–9; rifles 356, 357, 448; submachine-guns 357 *see also* artillery

HI

Haig, Douglas 80–1, 84, 85, 130, 131, 172, 180, 184–5, 188, 210, 216, 225, 232, 243
Halsey, Admiral William 340, 473
Hamilton, Ian 114–15
Harris, Air Marshal Arthur "Bomber" 390, 391, 424, 425
Hausen, Max von 35, 43
Heligoland Bight, Battle of 66, 113
Hentsch, Richard 43
Heydrich, Reinhard 422
Himmler, Heinrich 269, 417, 422, 436
Hindenburg Line 83, 139, 172–3, 188, 218; breaking the 232–3
Hindenburg, Paul von 53, 56–7, 59, 135, 139, 145, 246, 250
Hipper, Franz von 112, 156, 157
Hirohito, Emperor 466, 490, 491, 497
Hiroshima 488, 490–1, 496
Hitler, Adolf 265, 268, 269, 276, 277, 280, 281, 285, 288, 292, 293, 308, 313, 315, 316, 321, 327, 348, 349, 355, 359, 370, 371, 400, 401, 418, 430, 436, 440, 442, 443, 489; assassination attempts on 423; declaration of war on USA 313, 327; suicide of 377, 450
Ho Chi Minh 345, 500
Hoffmann, Max 53, 56
Holocaust 350–1
home fronts 118–19
Home Islands 466
Hong Kong, occupation of 345
Hood 302, 303
howitzers 33
Hull, Cordell 324
Hungary 264, 359, 418, 419; and Czechoslovakia 276, 277
Hurricanes 292, 294, 296, 373
Hussein, Feisal ibn 201
Ichi-Go Offensive 479
Iida Shojiro 334
Immelmann, Max 86
Imphal, Battle of 470–1, 480
India: 500, 501; Burma 470–1, 480–1; East Africa 154; Mesopotamia 110–11, 202; Palestine 242, 243
Indo-China: occupation of 325, 345; post-war 500
Indonesia 500
International War Crimes Tribunals 266, 496–7
infantry 318–19, 356–7, 359, 388–9
Iron Curtain 498–9
Isonzo, Battles of the 96–7, 148, 196
Israel 501

Italian Front 127
Italy 233, 386–7; Abyssinia 271, 275, 489; aerial warfare 124–5, 301, 399; Albania 306; Allies in 306, 386–7, 400, 447; Austro-Hungarian armistice 239; colonies 65; declaration of war 96; fascism 254, 255; final battles in 238–9; irredentism 96, 97; Italian Front 96–7, 127, 148–9, 196; naval warfare 162, 165, 166–7, 286, 307, 311, 328, 343, 486; North Africa 306, 307, 309, 365, 368–9; Western Front 288
Iwo Jima 463, 484–5

J

Jadar River, Battle of the 50
Japan 266, 452, 494; the 1930s 274, 275; aerial warfare 291, 295, 301, 326–7, 332, 379, 393, 413, 427, 456–7, 463, 464–5, 473, 485; biological weapons 489; bombing of 394–5, 466, 467, 488, 490–1, 495, 496; brutality of 344–5; Burma 322, 334, 470–1, 480–1; Ceylon 335; China, occupation of 271, 344–5, 478–9; Dutch East Indies 322, 334–5; Gilbert Islands 458–9; Guadalcanal 341; Hiroshima 488, 490–1, 496; Hong Kong 345; Indo-China 325, 345; Iwo Jima 484–5; Malaya 322, 332; Manchuria 270, 271, 275, 478, 491; the Marianas 462–3; Marshall Islands 459; Nagasaki 488, 490–1; naval warfare 158, 165, 286, 304, 305, 311, 328–9, 336–42, 378–80, 463, 469, 472, 474–5, 486–7; New Guinea 322, 340, 341, 454–5; Okinawa 484–5; in the Pacific 322, 326–7, 332–3, 336–7, 340–1, 452, 454–5, 458–9, 462–3, 472–3, 476–7, 484–5; Pearl Harbor 322, 323, 326–7, 475; the Philippines 322, 332–3, 476–7; post-war 494–7; prisoners of war, treatment of 344–5; shipping losses 466–7; Singapore 332–3; Solomon Islands 340–1, 455; surrender of 490–1, 496; Tokyo 466, 467, 496, 497; US landings 461, 484–5; USSR 324, 490–1
Java 501; Battle of the Java Sea 335
Jellicoe, John 156, 157
Jerusalem 201

Jews: and Arabs 501; in Israel 501; mass killings of 316, 320, 350–1, 422, 494, 497; persecution of 269, 314
Jiang Jieshi 271, 478
Joffre, Joseph 22, 39, 42–3, 46, 80, 84, 129, 172
Junction Station, Battle of 201
Jutland, Battle of 66, 73, 113, 150, 156–7, 163, 244, 245

K

Kamerun 65
kamikaze attacks 473, 485
Kasserine, Battle of 364, 369
Katyn 320, 321
Kesselring, Field Marshal Albrecht 368
Kharkov, Battle of 370, 371
King, Admiral Ernest 377
Kinkaid, Admiral Thomas 472
Kitchener, Horatio 38
Kluck, Alexander von 28, 29, 35, 38, 39, 42, 43
Kohima, Battle of 470–1, 480
Kolubara River, Battle of the 51
Konev, Marshal Ivan 436, 450, 451
SMS *Königsberg* 63
Kövess von Kövesshâza, Hermann 51, 148
Krasnik, Battle of 60
Kress von Kressenstein, Friedrich 108–9
Krithia, Battles of 103
Krueger, General Walter 472, 476
Kursk, Battle of 370–1, 433
Kut, Battles of 110, 202

L

landing craft 460–1
Langemarck, Battle of 185
Lanrezac, Charles 34, 38, 39
Latvia 284, 418
Lawrence of Arabia 201, 242
Le Cateau 38–9
League of Nations 253, 254–5, 265–7, 270–2, 274, 275, 285
Lenin, Vladimir Ilyich 192–4
Leningrad 317, 349, 419; Siege of 400, 401
Léon Gambetta 245
Lettow-Vorbek, Paul von 154–5
Leyte Gulf, Battle of 472–3, 476
Lloyd George, David 81, 172, 252–3

Libya 306–8, 364
Lithuania 284, 418
London, raids on 292–3, 298, 439
Loos, Battle of 84–5
Lord Haw-Haw 363
Ludendorff, Erich 28, 53, 56–7, 59, 135, 139, 145, 210–11, 216–17, 246, 250
Luftwaffe, defeat of 424–5
Lusitania 113
Luxemburg, Rosa 247
Luzon, liberation of 476–7
Lys Offensive 216

M

MacArthur, General Douglas 333, 340, 454, 455, 472, 476, 477, 491, 496
machine-guns 132–3, 137
Mackensen, August von 51, 59, 92, 145
Maginot Line 275, 288
Magruntein, Battle of 200
malaria 153, 155
Malaya 322; fall of 332; re-occupation of 500
Malazgirt, Battle of 107
Manchuria: Japanese defeat in 491; Japanese occupation of 270, 271, 275, 478
Mangin, Charles 135, 176
Manhattan Project 488
Manila 477
Manstein, General Erich von 348, 355, 358, 359, 370, 371, 401
Mao Zedong 478
Marianas 452, 462–3
Marne, Battles of the 38, 42–3, 217, 225, 226
Marne Offensive 216
Marshall, General George 503
Marshall Islands 452, 459
Marshall Plan 502–3
Marshall, William 202, 203
Marwitz, Georg von der 89, 188
Masaryk, Jan 498
Masurian Lakes, Battles of 57, 88
Matapan, Battle of 307
Maude, Frederick 111, 202
Max of Baden, Prince 246, 247, 250
May Island, Battle of 169
McCampbell, David 297
Mediterranean 164–5, 169, 306–7
Megiddo, Battle of 242–3
Menin Road, Battle of the 185
Mesopotamian Campaigns 110–11, 202–3
Messerschmitts 292, 294, 393, 427
Messines, Battle of 180–1, 184
Messines Ridge 48, 180–1, 183
Meuse-Argonne Offensive 224, 225, 228–9
Michael of Romania, King 359, 419
Middle East, post-war 500–1
Midway, Battle of 336–7, 454, 463
mine warfare 182–3, 408–9, 449
mobilization 23, 24, 27, 53
Moltke, Helmuth von 25, 34, 43, 46
Mons, Battle of 38–9
Monte Cassino 387
Monte Grappo, Battle of 239
Montgomery, Field Marshal Bernard 364, 365, 369, 386, 387, 410, 411, 431, 400, 447
Morocco 364, 368
mortars 90–1, 389, 438
Moscow 419; Battle for 320, 321
Mosquitoes 291, 373, 393, 412
Mulberry Harbours 406, 407
Munich Agreement 276
Murray, Archibald 108, 200
Mussert, Anton 416, 417
Mussolini, Benito 268, 270, 276, 306, 351, 387
mutinies 178, 246–7

N

Nagasaki 488, 490–1
Nanking, Rape of 345
NATO alliance 492, 503
naval weapons 380–1
Nazi-Soviet Pact 277, 280, 284
Nazism 266, 268–9, 314–16, 350, 416, 417, 494, 496, 497
Néry, Battle of 39
Netherlands 288; surrender of the 289

Neuilly, Treaty of 253
Neuve Chapelle, Battle of 76
New Guinea 322, 340, 341, 353, 454–5
New Zealand: Gallipoli 102–3, 114–15; Palestine 55
Nicholas, Grand Duke 22, 59, 107
Nicholas II, Tsar 22, 52, 53, 192, 195
Nieman, Battle of the 57
Nimitz, Admiral Chester 454, 463
Nivelle Offensive 176–7, 179, 180, 185
Nivelle, Robert 134, 172, 173, 176, 177, 229
Normandy 410–11, 421, 430–1, 434; Normandy landings 406–7, 410–11
North Africa 306, 298–9, 364–5, 431, 432; Allied victory in 368–9
North Atlantic 112–13
North Sea 46–7, 66–7, 156–7
Norton-Griffiths, John 145, 182
Norway, fall of 284–5
Nuremberg trials 496, 497

O

"October Revolution" 194–5
Okinawa 461, 484–5
Omaha Beach 407, 411, 460
Operation Barbarossa 295, 316–17, 320, 359, 372, 421, 435
Operation Bodenplatte 441
Operation Faustschlag 195, 216
Operation Gneisenau 216
Operation Husky 386
Operation Michael 210–5
Operation Overlord 406–7, 410
Operation Torch 365, 368–9
Oppenheimer, J.R. 488
Orlando, Vittorio 252–3
Ourcq, Battle of the 42–3
Ozawa Jisaburo, Admiral 462, 463

PQ

Pacific, war in the 60–1, 322, 324–7, 334–41, 452, 454–5, 458–9, 462–3, 466–7, 472–3, 476–7, 484–5
pacifism 119
Palestine 108–9, 200–1, 242–3, 501; aerial warfare 243; Senussi revolt 109
Paris 42; bombardment of 218–19; liberation of 431
Paris Peace Conference 252, 254–5
Passchendaele, Battle of 77, 131, 141, 184–5, 188
Patton, General George 369, 430, 431, 440, 441
Paulus, General Friedrich 348, 355
peace treaties 137, 169, 195, 199, 247, 249, 252–3
Pearl Harbor 313, 322, 323, 326–7, 332, 333, 337, 338, 375, 475
Percival, General Arthur 332, 333
Pershing, John 211, 224–5, 228
Persia 110–11
Pétain, Henri Philippe 80, 129, 134–5, 177, 225, 289, 314
Philippines 322, 332–3, 452, 455, 472–3; Battle of the Philippine Sea 462; conquest of the 476–7; fall of the 333
Phoney War 281, 298
Piave, Battle of the 239
Pilckem, Battle of 185
pistols 234–5
Plehve, Wenzel von 58, 89
Plumer, Herbert 77, 180, 184–5, 197
Poland 58–9, 316, 320, 321, 494; and Czechoslovakia 276, 277; capture of 92–3; Eastern Front 88; fall of 280–1; ghettos 350, 351; Gleiwitz 281; occupied Poland 277, 280–1, 312, 350–1, 497; Polish Corridor 264, 276; post-war 499; resistance in 414, 418; Warsaw uprising 418
Portugal 233; colonies 65
Potiorek, Oskar 50
Potsdam Conference 490, 496
Pozières, Battle of 138
Prien, Günther 302
prisoners of war 314, 320, 344–5, 359, 489
Princip, Gavrilo 19, 235
propaganda 362–3
Przemyśl 89, 93
Quisling, Vidkun 314, 315

R

Race to the Sea 46–7
radar 380, 381
railways 227; rail guns 186, 187
Ramadi, Battle of 202
Rapallo Conference 197
rationing 299, 314, 376
Rava Ruska, Battle of 58
Rennenkampf, Paul von 53, 56–7, 59
resistance movements 414–15, 418
Rhine, the 430–1, 437, 446
Rhineland, German occupation of 270, 271
Ribbentrop, Joachim von 276
Richthofen, Manfred von (Baron) 36, 191, 212
Rickenbacker, Edward "Eddie" 190–1, 212
River Plate, Battle of the 286, 381
rifles 44–5, 222
River Drina, Battle of the 50
Romani, Battle of 108, 109
Romania 240–1, 264, 359, 418, 419, 498; declarations of war 144, 241; defeat by Central Powers 144–5; Eastern Front 144
Rommel, General Erwin 291, 306–7, 364, 365, 368, 407
Roosevelt, Franklin D. 272, 303, 312, 313, 327, 368, 382, 383, 496
Ruhr 266, 466–7
Rupprecht, Crown Prince 34, 43, 80, 84, 232
Russia 98, 264, 277, 316; aerial warfare 120–1, 124; Austro-Hungarian attack on 58; Caucasus Front 106–7; collapse of 171, 238; Eastern Front 58–9, 88, 92–3, 142, 144; German offensive against 88–9; invasion of East Prussia 52–3; Kerensky Offensive 193, 194; mobilization 23, 53; naval warfare 151, 158, 244; occupation of Armenia 106; revolutions 192–5, 198; Treaty of Brest-Litovsk 195; war plans 22 *see also* USSR
Russo-Polish War (1920) 255

S

Sachsenhausen 423
St Germain, Treaty of 253
St Mihiel Offensive 224, 225
St Quentin Canal 233
Saipan 462
Salonika 152–3
Samar, Battle of 473
Sambre, Battle of the 38
Sambre Offensive 232
Samsonov, Alexander 53, 56, 57
Sanders, Otto Liman von 106, 242
Santa Cruz, Battle of 341
Sarajevo, assassination at 18–19, 235
Sarikamish, Battle of 106
Sarrail, Maurice 43, 152, 153
Savo Island, Battle of 340
Scandinavia 284–5
Scapa Flow 94, 247
Scheer, Reinhard 156, 157

Schlieffen, Count Alfred von 24, 25
Schlieffen Plan 24, 42, 46, 52, 53, 57
seaplanes 104–5, 150–1
SMS *Seeadler* 62
Serbia 19, 20–1, 23, 240–1; the Black Hand 19; defeat of 51; invasions of 50–1; liberation of Belgrade 241; war plans 23
Sèvres, Treaty of 253
SMS *Seydlitz* 73
Sharqat, Battle of 203
shellshock 129
ships: aircraft carriers 94, 150–1, 338–7, 464; anti-submarine escort ships 304–5; battle-cruisers 72–3, 328–9; battleships 100–1, 158–9, 304–5; cruisers 244–5, 286–7, 342–3; destroyers 162–3, 304–5, 486–7; escort carriers 378–9; gunboats 203; Q-ships 206; seaplane tenders 150–1; submarines 68–9, 116–17, 164–5, 168–9, 310–11, 466–9; surface raiders 62–3; torpedo-boats 166–7, 310–11; troopships 207; U-boats 66–9, 112–13, 116–17, 160–1, 165, 204–207, 270, 302–3, 313, 376–7, 468–9
Sicily 386–7
Siegfried Line 441
Singapore: fall of 332–3
Slim, General William 471, 481
Smith-Dorrien, Horace 38, 76–7
Smuts, Jan Christiaan 65, 154
Solomon Islands 340–1, 452, 455
Somme, Battle of the 130–2, 135, 138–9, 188, 226, 227
Sopwith aircraft 105, 212
Spanish Civil War 275, 297
Spitfires 291, 292, 294–6, 426, 427
Spee, Maximilian von 70–1
Stalin, Josef 272, 273, 277, 280, 313, 317, 349, 382, 383, 401, 402, 418, 436, 437, 450, 490, 497, 499
Stalingrad 348–9, 358, 359, 371, 419; Battle of 354–5
Stallupönen, Battle of 52
Stilwell, General Joseph 334, 478, 480
submarines 68–9, 116–17, 164, 165, 168–9, 206–7, 310–11, 466–9 *see also* U-boats
Suez Canal 108–9, 275
Sukarno, Ahmed 500
Sukhomlinov, Vladimir 22, 53
Sulva, landings at 114–15
supply transport 226–7
Sweden 351
Syria 203, 243

T

Talaat Pasha 107
Tanga, Battle of 154
tanks 137, 140–1, 178–9, 188–9, 282–3, 360–1, 384–5, 409, 420–1; anti-tank tactics 137, 318–19, 444–5, 448
Tannenberg, Battle of 36, 56–7, 257
Tassafaronga, Battle of 341
telephones 230–1
Thiepval, Battle of 138
HMS *Tiger* 72
Tinian 462
Tirpitz (battleship) 302, 328
Tirpitz, Alfred von 160
Tito, Josip Broz 415
Tobruk 309
Tojo Hideki, General 325, 497
torpedo-boats 166–7
torpedoes 380, 474–5
Tokyo: bombing of 466, 467; Tokyo trials 496, 497
Townshend, Charles 110, 111
Toyoda Soemu, Admiral 462, 472
treaties *see* peace treaties
Treblinka 350
trench warfare 32–3, 136–7; sapping 83; trench foot 185; trench mortars 90–1; trench systems 82–3
Trianon, Treaty of 253
Tripartite Pact 324, 325
Triple Entente 17–18, 27
Tripoli 364, 365, 368
Trotsky, Leon 193–5
Truman, Harry 383, 490, 491, 499, 502, 503
Tsingtao, siege of 60–1
Tsushima, Battle of 158
Tunisia 364, 365, 368, 369
Turing, Alan 375
Turkey 106–11, 499; armistice 209; Caucasus Front 106–7, 198–9; Dardanelles 98–9; Gallipoli 102–3, 114–15; Mesopotamian Campaigns 110–11, 202–3; Palestine 108–9, 200–1, 242–3; Treaty of Sèvres 253; Young Turks 107

U

U-boats 66–9, 112–13, 116–17, 160–1, 165, 204–207, 270, 302–3, 313, 376–7, 468–9
Udet, Ernst 191
Ukraine, German retreat from 400–1
unarmoured vehicles 434–5
United States: 264, 330–1, 494–5; the 1920s 266–7; the 1930s 272–3; aerial warfare 190–1, 212, 221–2, 291, 296–7, 336, 372–3, 378, 392–5, 398–9, 412–13, 424–6, 428–9, 456–7, 463–7, 479; Allies, early support for 303, 312, 313; American Expeditionary Force 179; Burma 480; China 479; civilians lost at sea 113, 160, 204; and the Cold War 502–3; declaration of war (1917) 171, 205, 224; equipping of 222–3; and the European War 312–13, 327, 394–5, 424–5, 496; Germany, bombing of 394–5, 424–5; Gilbert Islands 458–9; Iwo Jima 484–5; Japan, bombing of 394–5; Japanese-Americans 331; Lafayette Squadron 191; Lend-Lease 313, 319; the Marianas 462–3; Marshall Islands 459; Meuse-Argonne Offensive 228–9; naval warfare 207, 287, 304, 305, 310, 313, 328–9, 336–9, 341, 342–3, 378–81, 463, 466–9, 472–5, 486–7; neutrality of 281, 312–13; Normandy 430–1; North Africa 431; Okinawa 461, 484–5; in the Pacific 324–7, 336–7, 340–1, 455, 458–9, 462–3, 466–7, 472–3, 476–7, 484–5; Pearl Harbor 326–7; the Philippines 476–7; post-war 498–9, 502–3; Solomon Islands 455; tank warfare 283, 384–5, 421; Western Front 224–5, 228–9, 441 *see also* Allies; Anglo-American forces
USSR 264, 494; the 1930s 272–4; aerial warfare 291, 295, 372, 373, 426–8; Baltic States 418; Berlin

450–1; and the Cold War 502–3; Communist Party 272, 273; Finland 284, 285, 418; Germany 316–17, 320–1, 346, 348–9, 354–5, 358–9, 370–1, 400–1, 436–7, 450–1, 496; Japan 324, 490–1; Manchuria, victory in 491; Poland 280–1, 418; post-war 498–9, 502–3; Soviet victories 354–5, 358–9, 400–1, 418–19, 491; tank warfare 283, 360–1, 420; totalitarian rule in 422–3; Ukraine 400–1 *see also* Russia
Utah landings 407, 411

VW

V-weapons 439, 489
Vardar, Battle of the River 240
Vasilevsky, Marshal Aleksandr 371, 436
VE-Day 451
Verdun, Battle of 31, 128–9, 134–5, 138–9, 148, 177, 227, 231
Versailles, Treaty of (1919) 137, 247, 252–3, 264, 265, 274, 276, 287; violations of 270
Vickers aircraft 86–7

Vimy Ridge 84, 172–3
VJ-Day 491
von Heeringen, Josias 34, 43
Waffen-SS 314, 416, 417
Wannsee Conference 350
war crimes 496–7
Warsaw: capture of 280; Warsaw ghetto 350
Warsaw Pact 492, 503
Washington Naval Treaty 265, 286, 328, 342
West Africa 64–5
West Germany 502, 503
Western Front 24, 26, 34, 47, 48–9, 54–5, 74, 82–3, 126–8, 130, 170, 176, 184, 208, 210–11, 224–5, 233, 257, 288–9, 404, 406–7, 410–11, 430–1, 440–1
Wilhelm, Crown Prince 36, 43, 128
Wilhelm II, Emperor 18, 20–1, 48, 66, 106, 109, 112, 144, 153, 246, 247, 250–1
Wilson, President Woodrow 204, 250–4, 265
Wingate, Orde 470
Woëvre, Battle of the 76
women at war 119
World War I, legacy of 264–7
World War II, legacy of 492–503

YZ

Yalta Conference 496, 498
Yamamoto Isoroku, Admiral 327, 337
Yamashita Tomoyuki, General 332, 333, 476, 477
Ypres, Battles of 48–9, 76–7, 80, 147, 184–5, 189
Yser, Battle of the 47
Yugoslavia 264, 494, 299; resistance in 415
Zeebrugge Raid 205
Zeppelins 120–22, 151
Zhukov, Marshal Georgi 354, 371, 419, 436, 450, 451

This edition is published by Lorenz Books, an imprint of Anness Publishing Ltd, Blaby Road, Wigston, Leicestershire LE18 4SE; info@anness.com

www.lorenzbooks.com; www.annesspublishing.com

Anness Publishing has a new picture agency outlet for images for publishing, promotions or advertising. Please visit our website www.practicalpictures.com for more information.

Anness Publishing Limited
Publisher: Joanna Lorenz
Editorial Director: Helen Sudell
Project Editor: Dan Hurst
Proofreading Manager: Lindsay Zamponi
Production Controller: Don Campaniello

Produced for Lorenz Books by Toucan Books

Toucan Books:
Managing Director: Ellen Dupont
Editor: Donald Sommerville
Project Manager: Hannah Bowen
Designer: Elizabeth Healey
Picture Researcher: Debra Weatherley
Maps: Julian Baker
Proofreader: Marion Dent
Indexer: Michael Dent

A CIP catalogue record for this book is available from the British Library.

Previously published in two separate volumes, *The Complete Illustrated History of World War I and The Complete Illustrated History of World War II*